Salut!

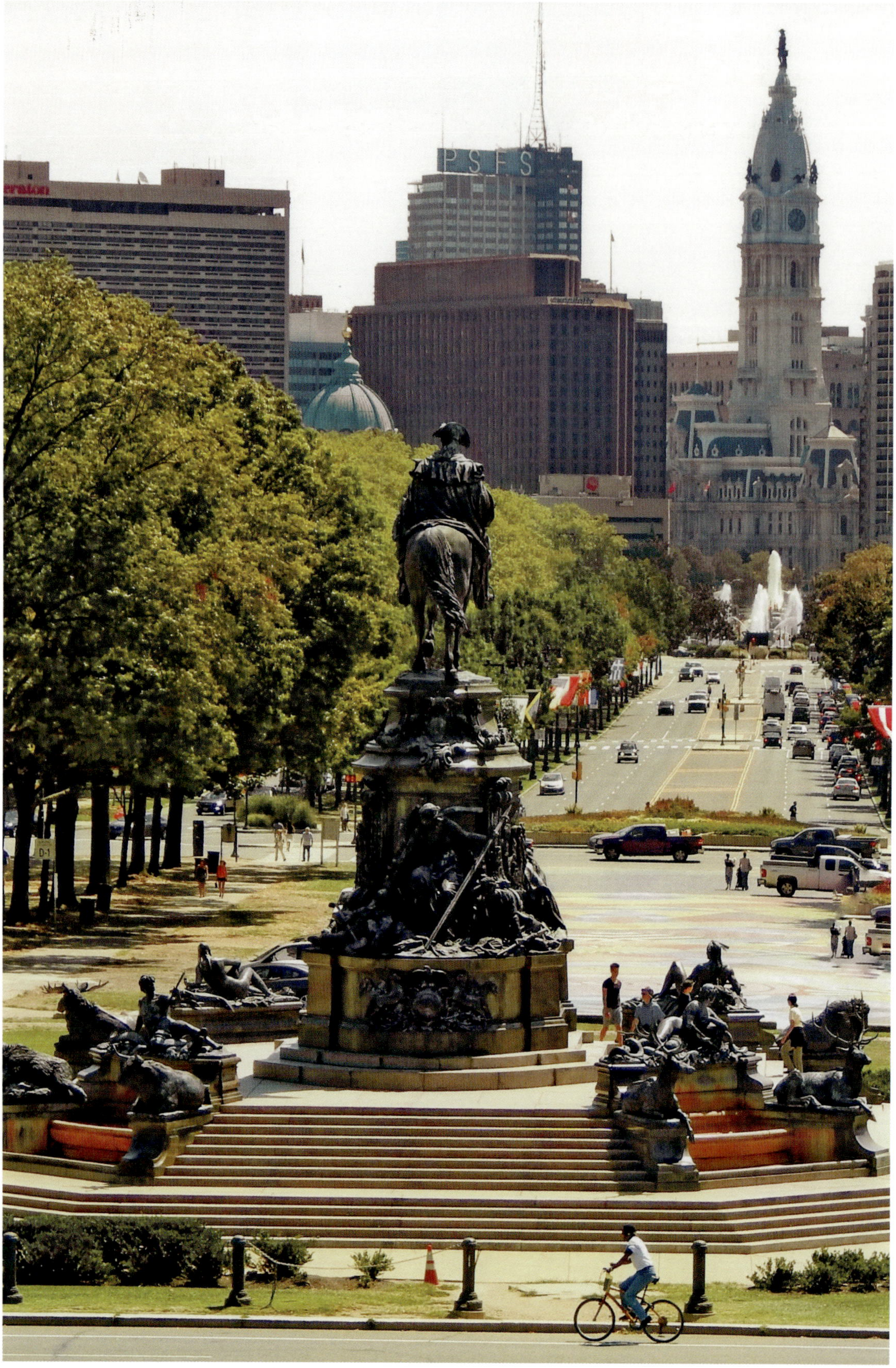
PSFS

Lynn Miller and Therese Dolan

Salut!

FRANCE MEETS PHILADELPHIA

The French presence in Philadelphia's history, culture, and art

TEMPLE UNIVERSITY PRESS
Philadelphia | Rome | Tokyo

TEMPLE UNIVERSITY PRESS
Philadelphia, Pennsylvania 19122
tupress.temple.edu

Published 2021

All photographs not otherwise attributed are by Lynn Miller.

Design by Kate Nichols

Library of Congress Cataloging-in-Publication Data

Names: Miller, Lynn H., author. | Dolan, Therese, 1946– author.
Title: Salut! : France meets Philadelphia : the French presence in Philadelphia's history, culture, and art / Lynn Miller and Therese Dolan.
Description: Philadelphia : Temple University Press, 2021. | Includes bibliographical references and index. | Summary: "Provides a thorough account of the impact on Philadelphia and its surrounding area of the French people and the Francophone community over the course of the city's more than 300-year history"—Provided by publisher.
Identifiers: LCCN 2019058000 | ISBN 9781439917121 (cloth)
Subjects: LCSH: French Americans—Pennsylvania—Philadelphia—History. | Art—Pennsylvania—Philadelphia—History. | Philadelphia (Pa.)—Civilization—French influence. | Philadelphia (Pa.)—Intellectual life—History.
Classification: LCC F158.9.F8 M56 2021 | DDC 974.8/11—dc23
LC record available at https://lccn.loc.gov/2019058000

∞ The paper used in this publication meets the requirements of the American National Standard for Information Sciences—Permanence of Paper for Printed Library Materials, ANSI Z39.48-1992

Printed in the United States of America

9 8 7 6 5 4 3 2 1

To the Alliance Française de Philadelphie,

for faithfully pursuing its mission,

from the time of its founding in 1903,

to promote the French language and culture in

the Philadelphia region

[Contents]

[Illustrations]

[Acknowledgments]

As Francophiles and Philadelphians throughout most of their lives, each of the authors has learned from, and been influenced by, far more of what is relevant to this joint effort of ours than we can possibly acknowledge here. But we extend our thanks first to those who assisted in the financial support of our book, making it possible for Temple University Press to produce a volume of the highest quality. These are the following: Carolyn Adams, the Alliance Française de Philadelphie, the Apgar-Black Foundation, Peter Benoliel and Willo Carey, Barbara Donnelly Bentivoglio, Donald and Caroline Brooks, Elizabeth Browne, Martine Chauvet, Hailung Dai, Dieter and Sara Forster, Nancy J. Gabel and George Broder, Robert Hansen and Gary Westerfer, W. Cecil Jones, Delphine Lawrence, Jim McClelland, Lawrence F. Meehan Jr. and Susan Tomita, Michael E. Scullin, and Carole Shanis. This project was also funded in part by a Tyler School of Art and Architecture Dean's Grant and by an Internationalization Grant, both from Temple University.

Others contributed their time and talents in myriad and invaluable ways as readers, commentators, and sources of essential information. They are Ruth A. Bohan, professor emerita of American Art and Material Culture, University of Missouri, Saint Louis; Susan Branson, professor of History, Syracuse University; Susan Cahan, dean, Tyler School of Art and Architecture; Christopher Campbell, artist and photographer; Bill Craig, principal, Mershon Design LLC; Rebecca Cypess, Mason Gross School of the Arts, Rutgers University; Karie Diethorn, chief curator at Independence National Historical Park; Barry Eiswerth, AIA, NA, H2L2 Architects; Kathleen A. Foster, Robert L. McNeil Jr., senior curator of American Art and director of the Center for American Art at the Philadelphia Museum of Art; Laura Turner Igoe, curator of American Art at the Michener Art Museum; David Knapp, senior associate, H2L2

Architects; Bruce Laverty, Gladys Brooks curator of Architecture, Athenaeum of Philadelphia; Nancy Locke, professor of Art History, Penn State; Pierre Ravacon, French Benevolent Society, Philadelphia; Zabeth Teelucksingh, executive director, Global Philadelphia Association; Jennifer Thompson, Gloria and Jack Drosdick curator of European Painting and Sculpture and curator of the John G. Johnson Collection at the Philadelphia Museum of Art; Peter Tucci, past president, French-American Chamber of Commerce; Judith Ujobai, executive director, French-American Chamber of Commerce.

Our heartfelt thanks to all of these individuals and organizations.

[Introduction]

How the French Have Helped Shape Philadelphia

How have France and the French influenced Philadelphia? Not at all in the city's origins, we may suppose, since Philadelphia began as the direct product of English, not French, history. The founding of Pennsylvania, and therefore Philadelphia, was made possible by an enormous land grant from King Charles II for a debt owed by the crown to a naval officer who had been one of its chief defenders. Following that man's death, when the actual grant went to his son on March 4, 1681, William Penn used it to give life to one of the most radical experiments undertaken by a group of Christian dissenters to come out of England. Thus, a royal grant from an English monarch to the young leader of an English-born religious group made the new town on North America's Delaware River a thoroughly English project from the start.

Except that there were French connections from the outset. As an eighteen-year-old, William Penn had been sent to France by his father, the admiral, who was desperate to cure the boy of his inclination toward the radical, pacifist teachings of the Quakers. But once in France, the son met the theologian and humanist Moise Amyraut, known for how he had moderated some of the teachings of John Calvin, the French giant of the Protestant Reformation.[1] Soon, young Penn moved into the religiously tolerant home of Amyraut in Saumur, where he was mentored for a year and encouraged to seek his own spiritual path. After he returned to England, that path soon led him to a lifelong commitment to the Society of Friends. Decades after Penn's own lifetime, the examples he set for religious toleration, fair dealing, and contract-based government drew the admiration of the age's leading philosophe, Voltaire.[2] By the time Penn's Philadelphia held center stage in the creation of a new nation, it had been crucially shaped by the Enlightenment ideas sprung from both English and French minds.

Through its first century, from the 1680s into the 1780s, Philadelphia remained an essentially British colony in North America. While it grew as an urban center, its reputation as a place of religious toleration attracted nonconformists. In addition to English Quakers and Puritans, German Pietists and French Huguenots soon were drawn to this increasingly cosmopolitan community. With the coming of the American Revolution, its leaders turned to France, Great Britain's historical enemy, for assistance in their drive for independence. The alliance with France brought a multitude of leading Frenchmen, including some who commanded armies, to Philadelphia. By the time it served as the capital of the new nation, between 1790 and 1800, the revolutions in France and then in Saint-Domingue in the Caribbean brought many more displaced French speakers to this city; in that decade, an estimated 10 percent of Philadelphia's population settled there from France and its empire.

The new nation required the invention of visual symbols to proclaim military victories, record the likenesses of its leaders and heroes, and create a distinctive image of its independence from Great Britain. The Puritan shunning of images that marked the early colonial days in Boston yielded to a burgeoning market for visual symbols in Philadelphia as the city became the focal point of revolutionary sentiment. The diplomatic missions of Benjamin Franklin and Thomas Jefferson in Paris not only deepened their exposure to French Enlightenment ideas that would continue to shape the country's ideals but also familiarized them with prominent artists and aesthetic traditions that would significantly impact late eighteenth-century American art. Jean-Antoine Houdon's sculpted images of George Washington and Benjamin Franklin have remained fixed in the American mind as iconic representations of our founding fathers. His likeness of Thomas Jefferson remains on the American nickel to this day.

Charles Willson Peale's numerous portraits of the leading figures who shaped America included eminent French supporters of the cause, such as the Marquis de Lafayette, Conrad Alexandre Gérard, the first French minister to the United States, and portrait busts of key French figures whose service to the nation helped secure American victory. These portraits eventually resided in Peale's American museum alongside his collection of botanical, biological, and archaeological specimens. The Peale family helped establish the Pennsylvania Academy of the Fine Arts in Philadelphia, the first and oldest art museum and art school in the United States.

The French presence faded somewhat in the nineteenth century, although a number of individuals of French heritage—Stephen Girard, Pierre Duponceau, Michel Bouvier, and Napoleon LeBrun, among others—contributed greatly to the intellectual and physical landscape of the city. Add the work of the Du Pont family in neighboring Delaware, and the French legacy was continued, most often by members of the social and political elite. That legacy also included the influence of France and its culture on Americans. Several of Peale's sons became noted painters. Rembrandt Peale's stay in Paris in the early years of the nineteenth century had significant impact on his style and technique. The establishment in 1812 of his own picture gallery, which he named the Apollodorian Gallery, signaled his embrace of the French post-revolutionary neoclassicism as an appropriate style for the new nation.

The Marquis de Lafayette's triumphal return visit in 1824 stimulated a whirlwind of portraiture of him around the country, with Thomas Sully receiving an important commission to paint the Frenchman while he was being feted in Philadelphia. Gilbert Stuart arrived in Philadelphia in 1795 and painted two of the most iconic images of George Washington while in the city. He based his Athenaeum portrait of 1796 on Houdon's likeness and used Pierre-Imbert Drevet's engraving of a portrait of Jacques-Bénigne Bossuet by Hyacinthe Rigaud for many elements of the pose and details in the painting. Stuart's Lansdowne portrait relied heavily on a French engraving of a seventeenth-century French bishop and another of Louis XIV.[3]

The established Parisian ateliers of Jean-Léon Gérôme, William Bouguereau, and the Académie Julian drew many American artists of the mid- to late nineteenth century to France to train in the academic style. Thomas Eakins studied in Paris between 1866 and 1870, bringing many of the teaching methods he learned in the studio of Jean-Léon Gérôme back to the Pennsylvania Academy of Fine Arts when he returned to Philadelphia. Mary Stevenson Cassatt and Henry Ossawa Tanner, as gender and racial minorities among artists, found France more hospitable to the advancement of their talents and careers. Despite living the majority of their professional careers abroad, both kept close ties with Philadelphia, exhibiting their work frequently at the Pennsylvania Academy. Edward Redfield, Walter Elmer Schofield, and Daniel Garber capitalized on their stays in France. Along with Mary Cassatt, they were highly influential in bringing impressionism to America and, more specifically, to the Philadelphia region.[4] Robert Henri and William Glackens, both of whom spent substantial time in France, became prominent members of The Eight, also known as the Ashcan School. They distinguished their realist urban art from the landscape scenes that dominated American impressionist works, mounting significant exhibitions in New York that eventually led to the 1913 Armory Show, also known as the International Exhibition of Modern Art, that challenged the authority of the National Academy of Design, which had based many of its precepts on the French Académie.

The long effort that brought the Benjamin Franklin Parkway into being early in the twentieth century produced a Parisian-style boulevard from the hands of two distinguished French architects, Paul Philippe Cret and Jacques Gréber. Its midpoint at Logan Square is Philadelphia's version of the Place de la Concorde, while it terminates at the magnificent French Renaissance Revival landmark, City Hall.

The museum district of the parkway also houses two of the largest collections of French art outside of France, one at the Philadelphia Museum of Art, the second at the Barnes Foundation. Between them sits the Rodin Museum's largest collection of that artist's work outside France. Two prominent Philadelphia collectors, Albert C. Barnes and Jules Mastbaum, amassed vast amounts of French painting and sculpture. The Barnes Foundation boasts of more works by Auguste Renoir and Paul Cézanne than are owned by France, while Mastbaum's donation of his collection of the sculptures of Auguste Rodin to the city comprises one of the largest collections of the master's work, where examples of every phase of his creative career can be experienced, outside of Paris.

Philadelphia also became a repository of sculpture with the work of French-born Joseph Alexis Bailly, whose image of George Washington greets visitors to Independence Hall (see Figure I.1), while nearby in the Public Ledger Building his enormous bronze image of Benjamin Franklin, said to be the best likeness of the Philadelphian, contemplates his lightning rod. Emmanuel Frémiet's sculpture of Joan of Arc facing the north side of the Philadelphia Museum of Art duplicates the original work located at the Place des Pyramides in Paris, near where Joan of Arc was wounded during her failed attempt to take Paris. Antoine-Louis Barye's bronze *Lion Crushing a Serpent* became the first sculpture installed in Rittenhouse Square.

During the past half century, the French legacy in this city has grown to include an array of French restaurants and distinguished chefs. Georges Perrier, one of the first, became nationally renowned and attracted both gastronomes and other restaurateurs. Perrier is perhaps more responsible than any other individual for changing Philadelphia in the last decades of the twentieth century from a culinary semidesert into a gastronomic destination. During the same period, French hotels became prominent in the city's burgeoning hospitality industry, France-based enterprises flourished within the regional economy, and individuals of French heritage continued to add their own contributions to the city's social, cultural, and political life. (See Figure I.2.)

As this brief sketch suggests, French influence on Philadelphia has existed from the beginning. Sometimes its impact has been clear and obvious, sometimes oblique or hidden beneath the surface. It has been diverse when it comes to those aspects of the city's life where it has made itself felt, sometimes having tangible, sometimes much more intangible results. French connections have been multifarious, produced by both major social upheavals and the singular acts of individuals. Over more than three centuries, the impact France and the French have made on Philadelphia has waxed and waned, as has the friendship between Philadelphians and the people of France. In this respect, the Franco-Philadelphia story is something of a microcosm of that between France and the United States as a whole. Yet, even though Philadelphia's relations with France and the French have generally mirrored those of the nation, occasionally—as in the creation of the Benjamin Franklin Parkway a century ago—the enduring visual impact of a French legacy has perhaps been greater in this city than anywhere else in America.

Our goals in this study are to explore the connections between Philadelphia and France throughout the city's history and to show the ways in which they have helped make Philadelphia the distinctive urban center that it is today. Obviously, Philadelphia is not a "French" city in the way that, say, New Orleans or Montreal clearly are. Nor do we claim that the influence of French culture or social history are in any way the dominant ones, either today or—with likely brief exceptions—at any time in the past. We have not engaged in a comprehensive survey of the cross-cultural influences from the colonial period to the present. Still, there is an important reason for undertaking this project. It is simply to pull to the surface the strand, or strands, of French influence on this metropolitan area as a way of acknowledging and understanding its importance. If it has always been a distinctive characteristic of American cities that

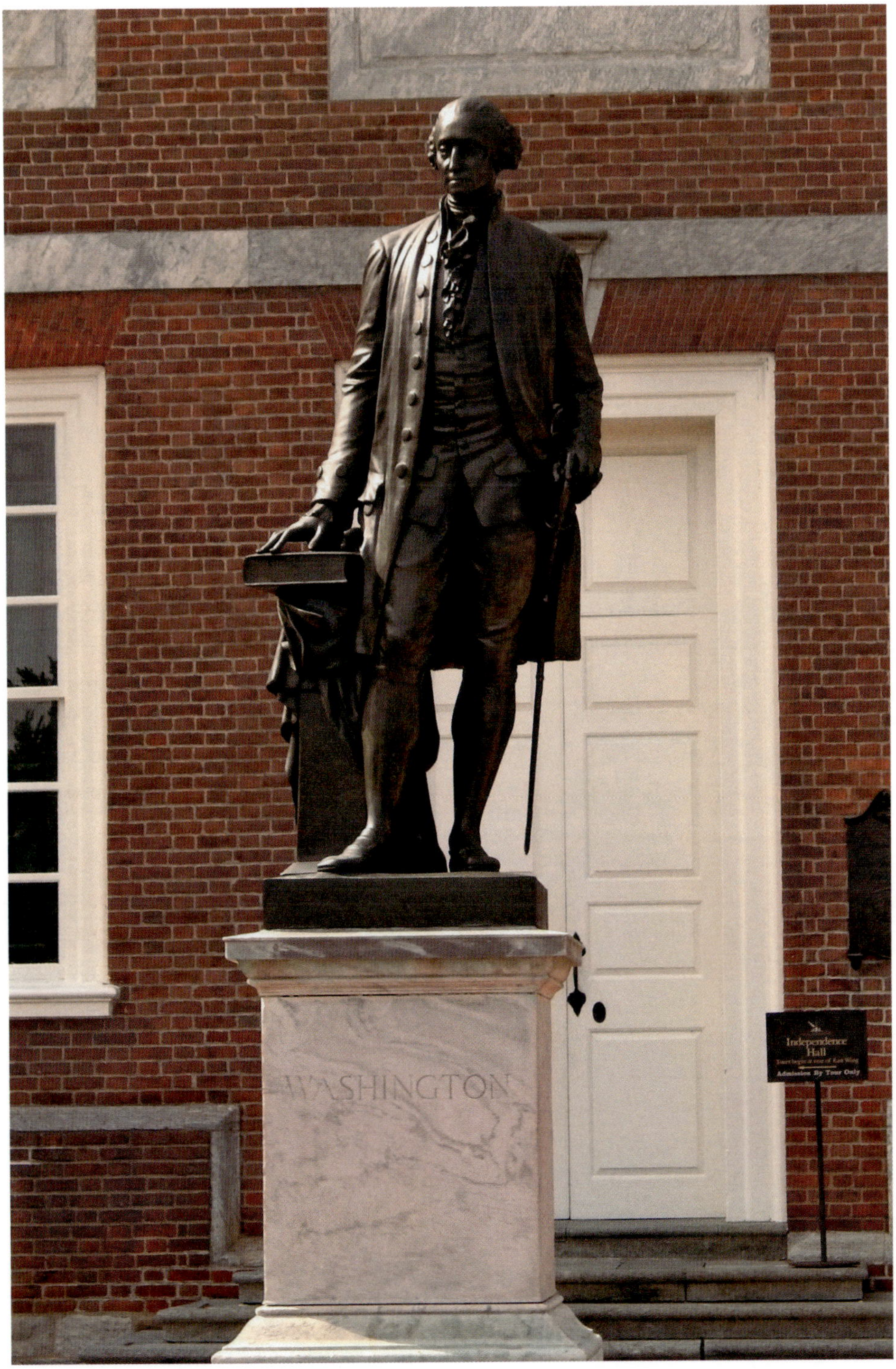

FIGURE I.1 Joseph Alexis Bailly, *George Washington*. Bronze. Marble original 1869, bronze replica 1908. 260 × 79 × 79 cm (102 × 31 × 31 in.). This bronze casting of the marble sculpture of George Washington by the French immigrant artist Bailly was placed in front of Independence Hall when the marble original was moved for display inside City Hall.

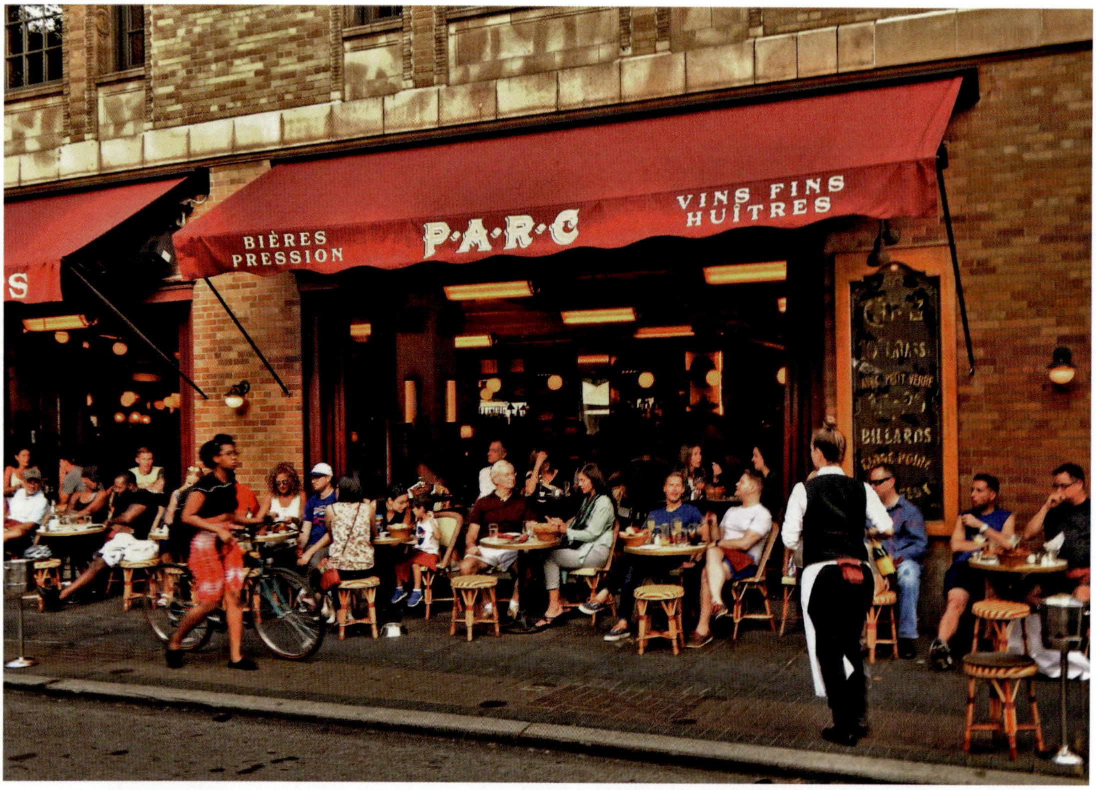

FIGURE I.2 This popular bistro facing Rittenhouse Square is one of several French-themed restaurants in the neighborhood, now designated Philadelphia's "French Quarter."

they are melting pots, then it should be instructive to examine some of the ingredients that have gone into that mix in one of those cities. In our examination of one piece of what has made Philadelphia a cosmopolitan city today—one designated in 2014 as the first World Heritage City in the United States—we find much to celebrate, even though there have been moments when Franco-American relations have brought discord. That may be the perennial description of the impact of cultural exchange on societies. But, given the ever-greater diversity of modern cities around the globe, it may not be presumptuous to think that the influence of one nation and its culture on one American city may both resonate with and guide the experiences of others.

For some three hundred years, one feature of the French presence in Philadelphia has made it historically unique. It is this: the contributions of comparatively few individuals have very much outweighed the rather small numbers of French and francophone people who have immigrated to the Philadelphia region. Perhaps some of this may have been foreordained by the influence of French intellectuals from the Enlightenment who so powerfully informed the nation's founders, contributing the fundamental ideas that have shaped the United States, including, of course, Philadelphia, from its birth down to the present day. But that disproportionate influence of the few upon the many has recurred several times since Penn created his "greene Countrie Towne" in the 1680s. It is evident in the way French immigrants became part of the region's business and professional elite from late in the eighteenth century. It accounts for the Parisian cast to Philadelphia's most iconic boulevard and for the Beaux-Arts style of many of its important buildings and public spaces. It is evident in how Philadelphia came to house some of the world's most impressive collections of French art. It also helps explain the late twentieth-century development of Philadelphia as a culinary destination, with French restaurants and restaurateurs leading the way.

Because this influence of a comparative few is that of a cultural and social elite, it means that the contributions have generally been made to the city's high, rather than to its mass, culture. We see French influence in the prominence of its fine arts holdings, impressive public structures, elegant boulevard, and fine restaurants rather than in what is peculiar to its popular music, public celebrations, or sports.[5] All in all, the presence of the French and the heritage of France have contributed greatly to Philadelphia's character as a cultural, educational, and commercial center. They have thereby left their special marks on one of America's greatest and most distinctive cities.

[1]

The French in Colonial Pennsylvania

In 1681, the year before William Penn arrived in his newly granted colony to lay out the city of Philadelphia, only about five hundred white settlers, mostly Swedes, lived in or near the site of Penn's future city. In all of Pennsylvania, populations of Native Americans had been so decimated by illness, largely by diseases carried to the New World from Europe, that their numbers had been reduced to no more than a few hundred. All at once, the number of Europeans rose dramatically when seventy-two hundred settlers recruited by Penn arrived in 1685. That began a continuing influx of Europeans. Five years later, nearly three times as many people were living in and around Philadelphia, which by then was on its way to becoming the largest city in the British colonies of North America.[1]

Competition was already well underway between the governments of France and Great Britain for empire building on the North American continent. Small numbers of French settlers were established in Quebec and Acadia in eastern Canada, and France claimed the Mississippi Valley and much of the Ohio Valley to the west. At almost exactly the time that Penn's settlers first arrived in Philadelphia, Louis XIV of France proclaimed the Edict of Fontainebleau (1685), ending the toleration of Protestants that had been the official policy of the kingdom for nearly a century. Not only were Huguenots in France forbidden to hold Protestant services; they were prohibited from emigrating—a decree that immediately prompted hundreds of thousands of Huguenots to flee the country. They went in large numbers to the Netherlands and Flanders, as well as England. Some four thousand sought their fortunes in the British colonies of North America, settling mostly in New York and Virginia.[2]

A much smaller number arrived in Pennsylvania, most of whom then moved on into the interior where, for the most part, they began to assimilate with other Protestant settlers. Their religion should have raised no qualms in Quaker Philadelphia, which was welcoming all manner of Protestants. But their nationality no doubt caused them to be viewed with suspicion by the English-speakers in this new but rapidly growing city. Philadelphians were fully aware of their two nations' ongoing enmity and competition for territory in the New World.[3] (Ironically, in spite of Penn's vaunted policy of religious toleration, Catholicism may have been a bridge too far in the early days. It would be several decades before Catholics of any nationality would be able to establish themselves in Philadelphia; even then, in 1733, their first church, Saint Joseph's, was hidden away in a courtyard as a sign of the questionable welcome its parishioners felt in their city. Nonetheless, Philadelphia was remarkably progressive for its time. Until the American Revolution, Saint Joseph's was the only place in the British Empire where the Catholic mass could legally be offered in public.) (See Figure 1.1.)

The imperial contest between France and Britain brought them into nearly constant conflict over their North American claims throughout the seventeenth and into the eighteenth centuries. The front line was often in the territory to the northeast of New England, named Acadia by the French and Nova Scotia by the English. It passed back and forth between French and British rule until the War of Spanish Succession ended with the Treaty of Utrecht in 1713. That made the territory definitively a part of the British Empire. Still, it did not produce agreement on the borders of the two colonial empires. The British demanded an unconditional oath of loyalty from the French Acadians, who had been farming the marshy coastal lands for generations; the Acadians, in return, agreed only to an oath of neutrality. Soon, the British increased the pressure by bringing many English settlers into the colony. Between 1750 and 1760, some seven thousand British and twenty-four hundred Germans were settled in Nova Scotia.

In the summer of 1755, the English general commanding His Majesty's forces in North America, Edward Braddock, met a disastrous defeat in western Pennsylvania when he tried to capture the French bastion at Fort Duquesne, the site of present-day Pittsburgh. Braddock was killed in the battle, along with nearly a thousand of his force of 1,459 men.[4] An aide-de-camp, the twenty-three-year-old George Washington, helped carry the mortally wounded general off the field. This defeat was one of several reversals for the English early in the Seven Years' War (known in America as the French and Indian War), making officials in Nova Scotia grow more alarmed about the possible enmity of the French-speaking Acadians in their midst. Urged on also by their counterparts in New England, who feared French predations from the north, they ordered the forcible deportation of these French-speakers to various English colonies along the Atlantic seaboard.

Over the next several years, more than six thousand Acadians were forced out of their homes, their property confiscated. They then were split up into groups to form distinct quotas forced to depart for different destinations.[5] Between November 18 and November 20, 1755, three ships carrying 454 Acadians landed in Philadelphia. The colonial government immediately placed them under armed guard until the legislature could decide what to do with them.[6] Such repressive measures evidently seemed called

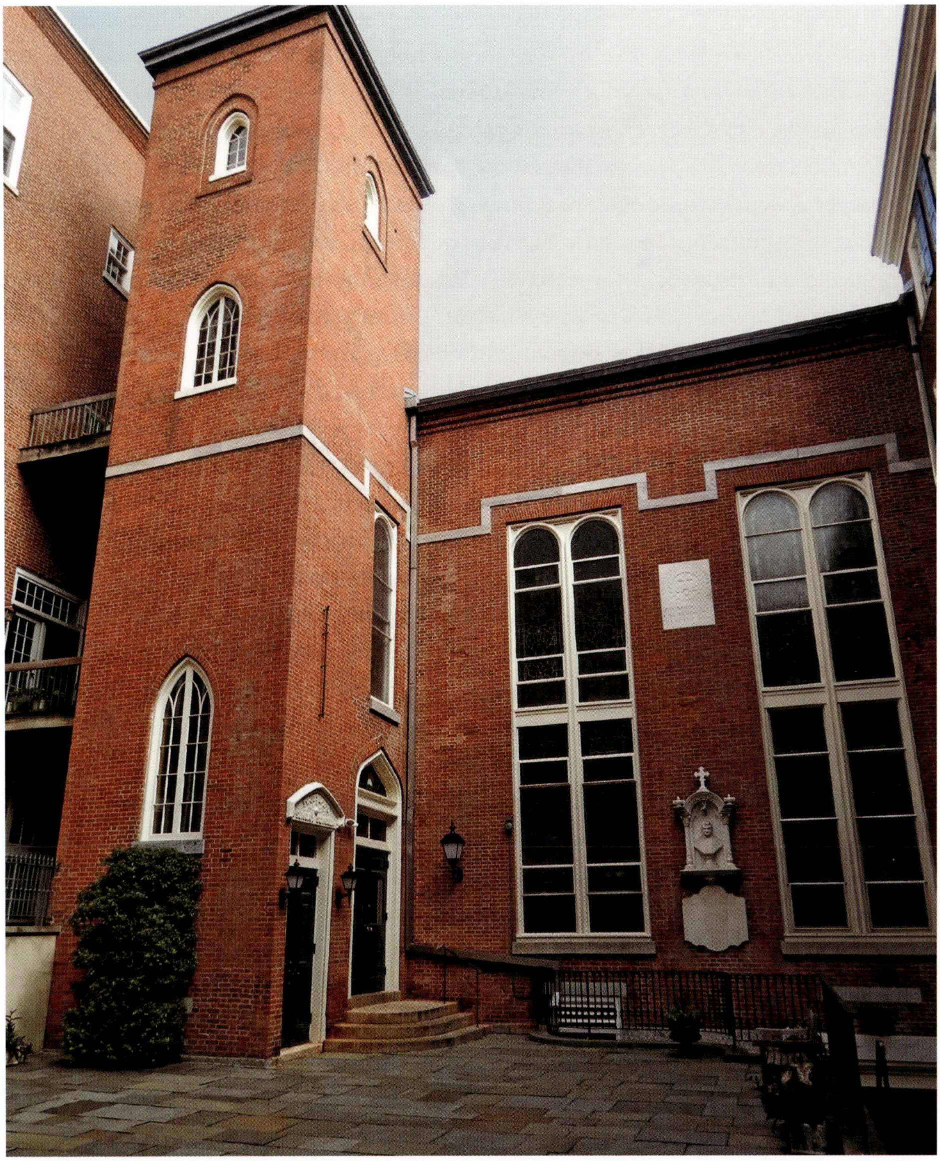

Figure 1.1 Saint Joseph's Roman Catholic Church was established in 1733 and became a place of worship for many French immigrants to Philadelphia.

for at a time when one unidentified Pennsylvanian wrote, "May God be pleased to give us success against all our copper-colored cannibals and French savages, equally cruel and perfidious in their nature."[7]

With disease spreading rapidly through the ships moored in the Delaware, officials soon ordered them to be off-loaded onto Province Island several miles south of the city.[8] Provisions were made to supply them with rations: a half pound of meat and a pound of bread per person per day. They were largely attended to by a French-born Philadelphia Quaker, Anthony (Antoine) Benezet (1713–1784), who had emigrated with his family in 1731. The family had been well-to-do Huguenots but converted to the Society of Friends after immigrating to England. Young Anthony was fourteen at the time. Four years later, in Philadelphia, Benezet became a leading progressive educator and social reformer, in keeping with Quaker commitments established from the time the city was founded.[9] By the time the Acadians landed in the Delaware, he had taught at what would later be known as the William Penn Charter School and organized a public school for girls, the first such institution in America. He would go on to create the first school for enslaved Africans and the first antislavery society in the colony.[10]

This French-born Quaker was in many respects the spiritual descendent of William Penn himself, extending the founder's great social experiment farther than Penn had done, to the education of Africans and the effort to abolish slavery. To his fellow Quakers, Benezet argued that slaveholding was inconsistent with Christian doctrine. By the time displaced Acadians came under his care, he was publishing pamphlets in the effort to persuade British authorities that their ban on slavery should be extended to their North American colonies. Even before American independence was won, his advocacy helped lead to the 1780 act of the Pennsylvania legislature that gradually abolished slavery within the Commonwealth, the first such enactment in America. After his death, Benezet's Society for the Relief of Free Negroes Unlawfully Held in Bondage was reconstituted by Benjamin Franklin and Benjamin Rush as the Pennsylvania Society for the Abolition of Slavery.[11]

In the 1750s, however, the Acadians sent to Pennsylvania continued to languish on Province Island. In March 1756, a bill was passed by the legislature that divided them into groups and assigned them to the counties of Philadelphia, Bucks, Chester, and Lancaster. It stipulated that no more than one family should be assigned to any one township. The Acadians protested at being split up, while many of the townships did not want to receive them. As a result, little changed in the lives of the displaced. Some were moved, and many simply waited. Increasingly, they succumbed to smallpox. Those who were able found odd jobs, while others pilfered what they could to sustain themselves and their families. In January 1757, the governor approved a bill that provided for Acadian boys and girls to be bound out as apprentices, and that they should be taught to read and write the English language. The Acadians then submitted a petition to the assembly praying that they not be separated from their children. "Be pleased to tell us," they pleaded, "whether we are Subjects, Prisoners, Slaves or Freemen?" They asked permission to leave the province, saying that they were willing to sell the remains of their household goods to regain their liberty. "Be merciful," they implored, to a people "plunged into an Abyss of Bitterness and Sorrow."[12]

The provincial government refused to act on their petition. Rather, it continued to provide meager aid year after year. For more than twenty years, from the time of their arrival until 1776, some ten thousand pounds was paid out of the provincial treasury for the relief of Philadelphia's Acadians. Meanwhile, Anthony Benezet led an effort, assisted by several Huguenots, to raise the funds needed to build a number of one-story wooden houses on the north side of Pine Street between Fifth and Sixth Streets, where many of them were housed. Benezet also taught some of their children and fought to enroll others in public schools. Gradually, those that remained in Philadelphia and were able-bodied entered the workforce. The records of marriages and births among the parishioners of Saint Joseph's Church include some of these exiles, those numbers dwindling after the mid-1760s. Smallpox victims—and there were many—were buried, along with other indigent Philadelphians, in Southeast (Washington) Square.[13]

Some eventually made their way to Saint-Domingue. But when, years later, that richest of the French colonies in the Caribbean erupted in a slave insurrection, virtually all the survivors of the Acadian exile made their way to Louisiana. There they created the distinctive, and distinctively American, culture known as "Cajun," a corruption of the name "Acadian" with which they had begun. In 1847, an epic poem by Henry Wadsworth Longfellow, *Evangeline*, swept the nation. It told the story of a fictional Acadian girl separated from her betrothed, Gabriel, by the Great Upheaval of 1755 and her lifelong effort to find him as she searched across America. Ending her days as a Sister of Mercy in Philadelphia, she is finally reunited with the dying Gabriel. Longfellow's lines describe the burial place for his fictional couple. Although it may have been at Saint Joseph's Church, the description more nearly fits the churchyard of Holy Trinity, at Sixth and Spruce Streets. (See Figure 1.2.) The latter was built in 1789 for the city's German Catholic community. But it quickly became the parish church of French people living in the city, including the remaining Acadians:[14]

Still stands the forest primeval; but far away from its shadow,
Side by side, in their nameless grave, the lovers are sleeping.
Under the humble walls of the little Catholic churchyard,
In the heart of the city, they lie, unknown and unnoticed.

Longfellow's poem helped create a legend about the travails of the Acadians more than a century earlier—that passage of time no doubt essential before romance could be made of tragic history. Their story became part of the larger one still taking shape about the nature of this distinctive nation.

By the time America was on the cusp of organizing as a nation, visual artists sought to create an imagery appropriate to the achievements of the republic, one that would express the character of the country to a group of colonials who had emigrated from many countries. That made their goals quite different from those of earlier artists in North America. The Puritans who came over on the Mayflower repudiated the opulence and corruption of European courts and forbade any religious depiction of spiritual beings, their culture being primarily literary rather than pictorial. Portraiture flourished in New England as there was little danger of idolatry in recording the likenesses of public figures. Colonial period portraiture primarily imitated British examples, with Americans drawing upon their known cultural heritage while they

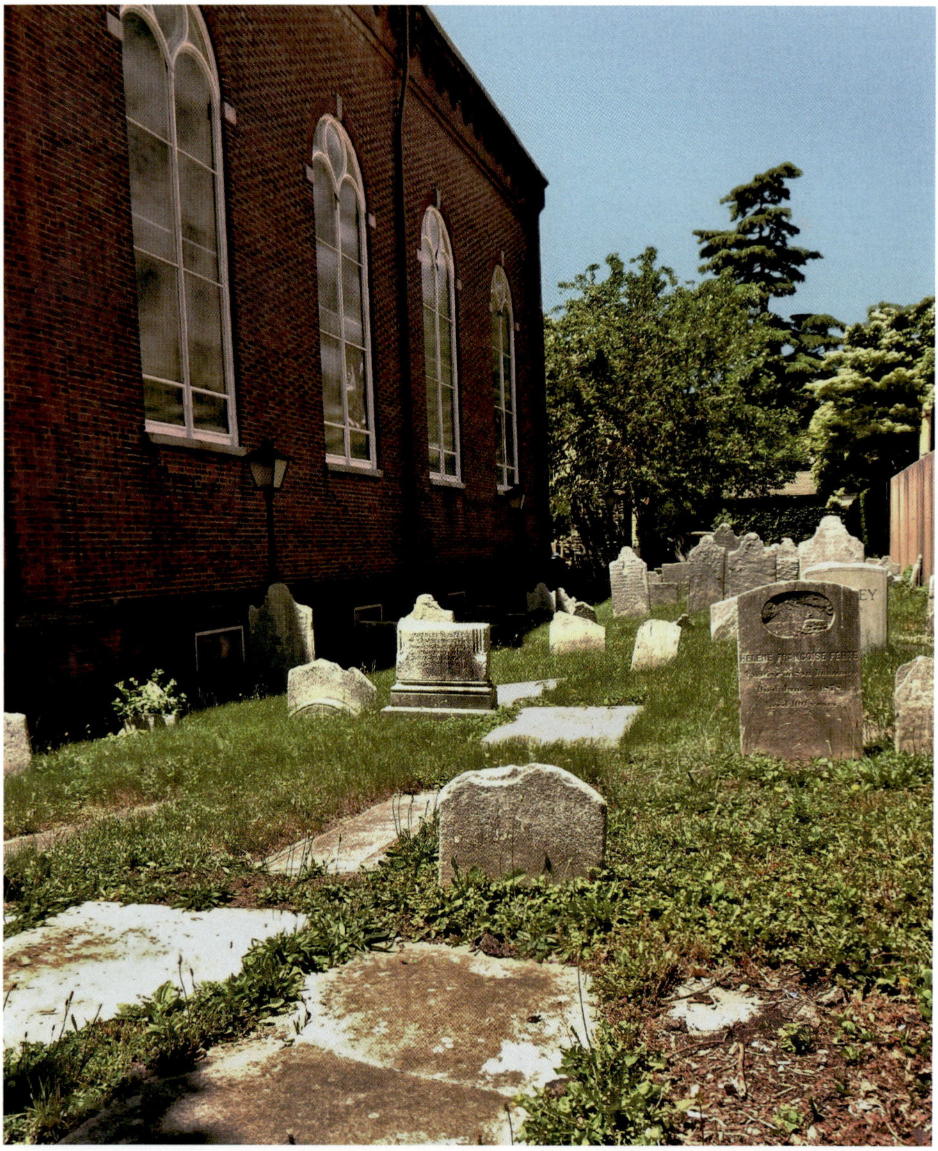

FIGURE 1.2 The parish church, Holy Trinity, was home to many French Roman Catholics in the eighteenth and early nineteenth centuries. Its graveyard is the imagined burial ground for Longfellow's fictional couple, Evangeline and Gabriel.

gradually invented new forms to express their distinctive identity. Quaker Philadelphia saw little in the way of painting since the precepts of the religion officially forbade it as a practice and profession; any tendency to a lavish lifestyle was prohibited and needlessly distracted from practical endeavors. One sees this with William Penn who sat for his portrait at the age of twenty-two in a handsome armored breastplate. Once he converted to Quakerism, he refused to have his likeness depicted. Yet the compulsion to copy the human face saw its way in the craft of making cut out silhouettes

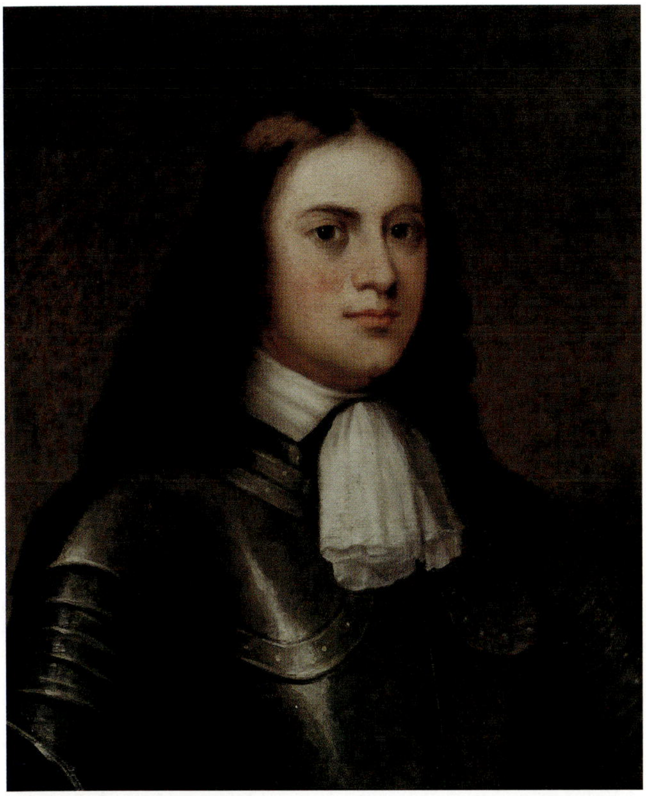

Figure 1.3 Portrait of William Penn in armor. Copy of a lost original from 1666 known as the "Armor Portrait." Oil on canvas, 33 × 38 in. (Courtesy of the State Museum of Pennsylvania, Pennsylvania Historical and Museum Commission)

from dark paper with scissors, in many ways foretelling the role that portraiture would play in the city when it became the capital. (See Figure 1.3.)

The Swedish immigrant Gustavus Hesselius launched his American artistic career in Philadelphia in 1712. Catering to the needs of the populace, his major subjects consisted of portraits, in addition to a few religious and mythological scenes. His son John was joined by the Scottish painter John Smibert and Robert Feke who moved from Rhode Island to meet the growing demands for portraiture. As the thirteen original colonies underwent their transformation into the United States of America, the arts may have seemed secondary to the practical necessities of everyday life.

Nevertheless, by the 1780s the leaders of the newly formed government perceived the necessity of commissioning artists to honor its leaders and heroes with works that emulated the European tradition in educating the public, creating a native tradition of art, and honoring the valiant efforts of those who helped in the struggle for independence. As in England and France, the two countries where American artists refined their skills and deepened their knowledge of the heritage of their artistic ancestry, portraiture dominated as the genre most in demand as a means of disseminating national aspirations. In Paris, portraiture dominated all other subject matter in number at the Salon even while history painting was held in higher esteem. Portraiture remained the most patronized genre of art and in the early years of its founding, America would follow suit as it labored to document its material and intellectual growth and honor its war heroes and government leaders along with its allies from abroad. America's pictorial biography emerged from the hands of artists and craftsmen eager to advance the aesthetic and social needs of a new nation. The portrait both mirrored and formulated the culture of early America. As the nation developed, several artists pursuing the profession of painting were drawn to the art studios of France, eager to absorb the teaching and intellectual heritage of Paris, which in the nineteenth century dominated the art world.

Since the founding days of the nation in Philadelphia, France has played a significant role in the arts with its draw of great museums, art school training, and picture dealers and collectors. Benjamin West, John Singleton Copley, John Trumbull, and Charles Willson Peale, among others, made their way to Paris to advance their knowledge of the arts. Franklin and Jefferson fostered the love of French ideas and culture during their stays in Paris. Both were instrumental in commissions of works of art from French artists for American images, and their return to Philadelphia after diplomatic missions to Paris further disseminated a strong attraction to the cultivated aspects of French society. The political tug-of-war between America and France is often mirrored in the fine arts as the quest for a national cultural identity. As political, social, and economic issues were tightly entwined with aesthetic issues, the formation of a national style became a crucial concern. Ongoing business dealings and cultural transactions between the citizens of Philadelphia and France, especially when the city served as the nation's capital during the 1790s, made the city a strong magnet for innovation and entrepreneurship. As François Furstenberg noted in *When the United States Spoke French*, "it was the only time the United States had a single great metropolis the way France had Paris and England has London, and it made Philadelphia by far 'the most agreeable city for a foreigner.'"[15] Investigating examples of how the visual culture of the city has been formed in relation to France sheds light on the transformation of the idea of the visual arts as extraneous and perhaps dangerous to life in the colonies to an understanding of the impact the cross-cultural relations between France and Philadelphia had on our artists, museums, collections, and environment.

[2]

The Crucible

France and Revolutionary Philadelphia

During the last quarter of the eighteenth century, Philadelphia became the crucible for the creation of a new political and social order, one that would serve as a model for constitutional government down to the present day. It was in Philadelphia where the most powerful ideas, French at least as much as British, of the age of Enlightenment launched a new nation. Yet, ideas alone did not bring about a new and independent nation. The United States of America largely owes the success of its revolt against Great Britain to the military and diplomatic aid it received from both the court of Louis XVI and a number of individual Frenchmen inflamed by the desire to participate in creating a new republic, the first in the modern world.

Philadelphia's central role in early America had developed from the time of its birth and subsequent growth during the previous century. Like Athena springing from the head of Zeus, the plan for Philadelphia sprang from that of William Penn (1644–1718) in 1682. Soon after he set foot in the New World, Penn mapped out his City of Brotherly Love to stretch from the Delaware River to the Schuylkill River. Less than a century later, Philadelphia had become the largest and richest city in Britain's North American colonies, with a population of nearly thirty thousand people. The city sat roughly in the middle of British America, which nearly two million people called home. That made Philadelphia by 1780 the largest city in the English-speaking world apart from London, itself the capital of a kingdom of more than six million. Yet the rate of population growth in the colonies was much higher than in the mother country, a fact that might have explained much about events then roiling two continents.

Within less than a dozen years from the time the conflict erupted in North America, the Declaration of Independence (1776) and the Constitution of the United States (1787) were created in Pennsylvania's urban center. The first asserted the natural equality of all human beings and their right to decide for themselves how they wished to be governed. The second set forth a blueprint for government designed to thwart tyranny and ensure the expression of the peoples' will. Now, we take those documents and their ideas for granted, but they were like thunderclaps in their day.

Yet, they were not bolts out of the blue. A century earlier, the great English philosopher and Penn's contemporary John Locke (1632–1704) had laid the groundwork by arguing for the right of revolution, limited constitutional government, and the separation of church and state.[1] In the same decade when William Penn was launching Philadelphia, Locke had attended to the creation of a constitutional monarchy in Great Britain. In 1688, William and Mary were invited by Parliament to reign jointly over the island nation.[2] Even though Locke's writings on politics were of crucial importance to the success of that Glorious Revolution and to modern political theory, he was not much read in Britain after his death and the evident triumph there of many of his ideas. In the British colonies in North America, however, his seminal *Second Treatise on Government* was frequently cited, especially once it was published in Boston in 1773. Meanwhile, in eighteenth-century France, Locke was taken up by the philosophes. These brilliant thinkers in turn would profoundly influence the leading American revolutionaries.

In contrast to Great Britain, France remained one of Europe's most absolute monarchies in the eighteenth century, the roots of its ancien régime in the feudal past still reflected throughout the life of the nation. During the course of that century, Montesquieu (1689–1755), Voltaire (1694–1778), Rousseau (1712–1778), and Condorcet (1743–1794) led the way in calling for a new social and political order, drawing in part on what they learned from across the Channel to argue for constitutionalism in their own land.[3] Voltaire was lavish in his praise of William Penn, whom, he said, "might glory in having brought down upon earth the so-much boasted Golden Age, which in all probability never existed but in Pennsylvania."[4] (The assessment that they were the center of a golden age might have raised the eyebrows of many Philadelphians, then as now.) Yet Locke was perhaps their greatest inspiration—"le sage Locke," was how Voltaire called him.

In Britain's North American colonies, those same philosophes were avidly read by the men who were increasingly troubled by the restrictions their king and Parliament were placing on their own freedoms. Montesquieu's influence was among the most profound. His *L'Esprit des lois* (The spirit of the laws) was first published anonymously in 1748. It became the most frequently quoted authority, other than the Bible, on government and politics by America's founders. By 1756, the College of Philadelphia (today's University of Pennsylvania) placed Montesquieu's great work on a reading list for college seniors. Harvard and Yale soon followed suit.[5] Montesquieu had even predicted as early as 1730 that the British colonies in North America would rebel against the mother country because of their growing population, economic dynamism, and Britain's restrictions on colonial trade.[6] Half a century later, that prediction came true. (See Figure 2.1.)

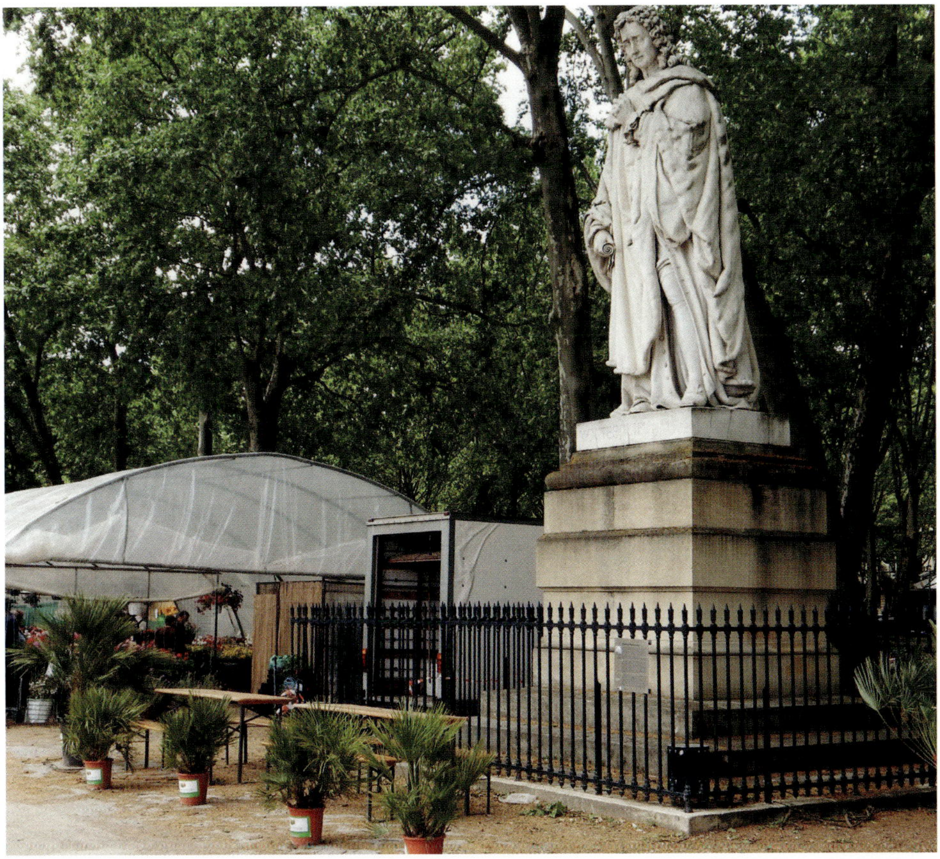

Figure 2.1 Dominique Fortuné Maggesi, *Charles Louis de Secondat, Baron de la Brède et de Montesquieu*, 1858, Esplanade de la Quinconces, Bordeaux, France. Montesquieu's writings had the deepest impact of any of the French philosophes on the framers of the Declaration of Independence. His likeness stands in his hometown of Bordeaux, France.

The First Continental Congress met in Philadelphia's Carpenters' Hall in September and October 1774. There the delegates consulted Montesquieu in their deliberations, having access to his work in the Carpenters' Hall library, and invoked his authority repeatedly in drafting their complaints to king and Parliament.[7] In the months that followed, their grievances went unassuaged. When the delegates to the Second Continental Congress met in the Pennsylvania State House (Independence Hall) through the summer of 1776, their leading figures, such as Franklin, Jefferson, John and Samuel Adams, Richard Henry Lee, and John Witherspoon, all had immersed themselves in Montesquieu's Laws. As later scholars have noted, it is no doubt true that Montesquieu's view of the British constitutional system was too benign: he thought he saw a more liberal government of checks and balances in England than was actually the case at the time.[8] But his rose-colored version was of almost exactly the kind of government the Americans wished for—and thought was being denied them. By this time, their view that their rights as Englishmen had been usurped by Parliament led them to declare their independence.

By the time the Second Continental Congress met on May 10, 1775, blood had been shed at Lexington and Concord. Now an army had to be raised. These events in North America did not go unnoticed in France, where the foreign minister for the government of Louis XVI, the comte de Vergennes, hoped to learn if there were opportunities in these developments to counter the imperial interests of Great Britain. To gather intelligence firsthand, Vergennes tapped an adventurous sometime-soldier from an ancient family, the chevalier Julien Alexandre Achard de Bonvouloir, to undertake a secret mission. He would travel to Philadelphia to meet with members of the Committee of Correspondence. Without divulging his ties to the French government—his cover was that he was an "Antwerp merchant"—he would assure the Americans of French sympathy for their cause. Because he spoke no English, Bonvouloir secured the assistance of an acquaintance, Francis Daymon, a Frenchman in Philadelphia who tutored locals in the French language and was secretary of the Library Company of Philadelphia (which was only one of Benjamin Franklin's many civic creations for his adopted city).

Late in December, Bonvouloir and Daymon met for three highly secret meetings with Franklin, John Jay, and John Dickinson in Carpenters' Hall. The Americans took pains to arrive separately under cover of darkness so as not to arouse the suspicions of British loyalists. They were not fooled by Bonvouloir's insistence that he had no connection to French officialdom but were encouraged to believe that they might find help there. Bonvouloir's reports back to Vergennes paved the way for what would turn out to be critical assistance for the revolutionary cause from the French court.[9] (See Figure 2.2.)

Meanwhile, matters were gradually coming to a boil in the State House. By July 1776, Congress voted to break with England. The members turned to a young planter and intellectual from Virginia to draft their Declaration of Independence. Thomas Jefferson (1743–1826) was a child of the Enlightenment through and through. He tackled his assignment at his boardinghouse at Seventh and Market Streets in Philadelphia. (See Figure 2.3.) His listing of the various tyrannical acts of the British monarch clearly reflected his reading of Montesquieu on tyranny. He was also well acquainted with the thinking of Voltaire, whom he regarded as the greatest philosophe of the century. The Declaration of Independence is based upon precepts fundamental to these and other French philosophers, such as the "self-evident" truth that all men are created equal and that they are entitled to the inalienable natural rights of life, liberty, and the pursuit of happiness, that last being Jefferson's felicitous substitute for John Locke's "right to property." Although Montesquieu was dead by the time the American Revolution broke out, Voltaire, Rousseau, Condorcet, and other philosophes in France rejoiced at the news. From the time American independence was secured more than six years later, it became an article of faith among French intellectuals that, in the words of Alexis de Tocqueville decades after that independence was achieved, "the Americans seemed to have executed what our writers had conceived."[10]

In 1776, however, that Revolution still had to be won. In the autumn of that year, Congress appointed Benjamin Franklin (1706–1790) to be its emissary to France,

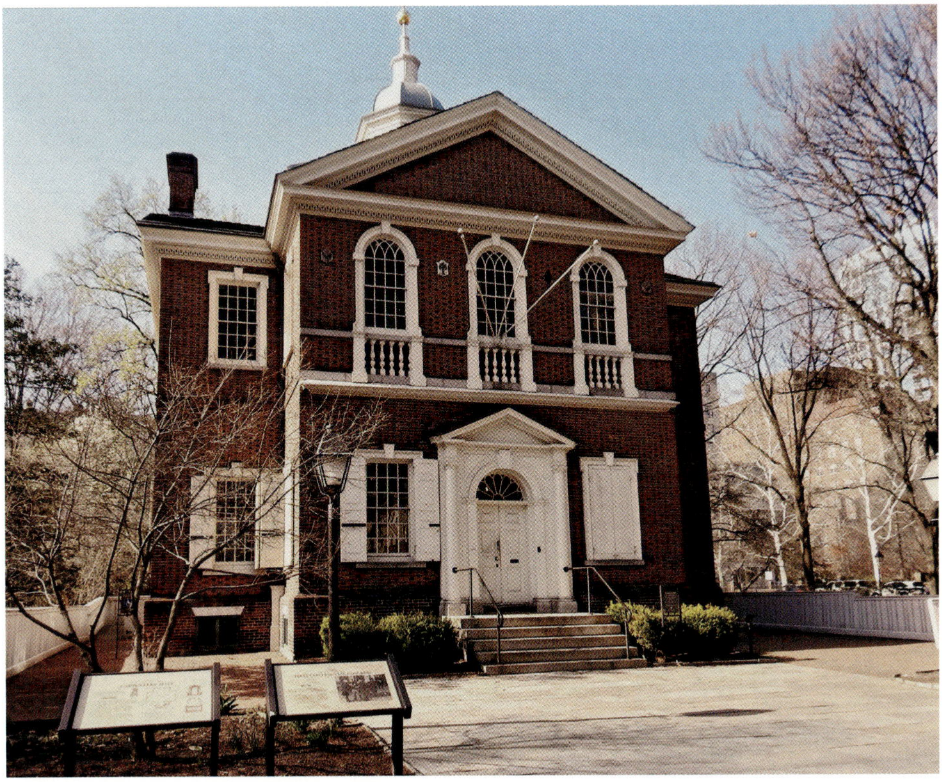

FIGURE 2.2 Carpenters' Hall in Philadelphia was the site of the First Continental Congress in 1774. In December 1775, Benjamin Franklin, John Jay, and John Dickinson met here secretly with emissaries of the French foreign minister to discuss possible French assistance to the revolutionaries' cause.

where his mission was to negotiate a treaty of assistance with the government of Louis XVI. Philadelphia's leading citizen, Franklin, a widower at age seventy, was one of the most famous men in the world, thanks largely to his pathbreaking studies of electricity more than twenty years earlier. This self-taught genius—who had also been a successful printer and publisher, inventor, and civic leader, among a dizzying list of accomplishments—would soon be lionized in Paris as one of the greatest men of his age. "Into Enlightenment Paris he rode on his own coattails," in the words of one of his biographers.[11] To many followers of the philosophes, Franklin seemed to embody Rousseau's "natural man," one uncorrupted by the evils of civilization. In his ambles about Paris, he famously wore a cap of marten fur and the clothes of a frontiersman. Soon, that startling dress sparked a fashion rage. From that point until revolution broke out in France itself a dozen years later, the upper classes increasingly dressed more simply; they discarded wigs and avoided finery to the point that it became increasingly difficult to tell a man's social class from his garb.[12] What could better show how fashionable were Enlightenment ideas than in their effect on fashion?

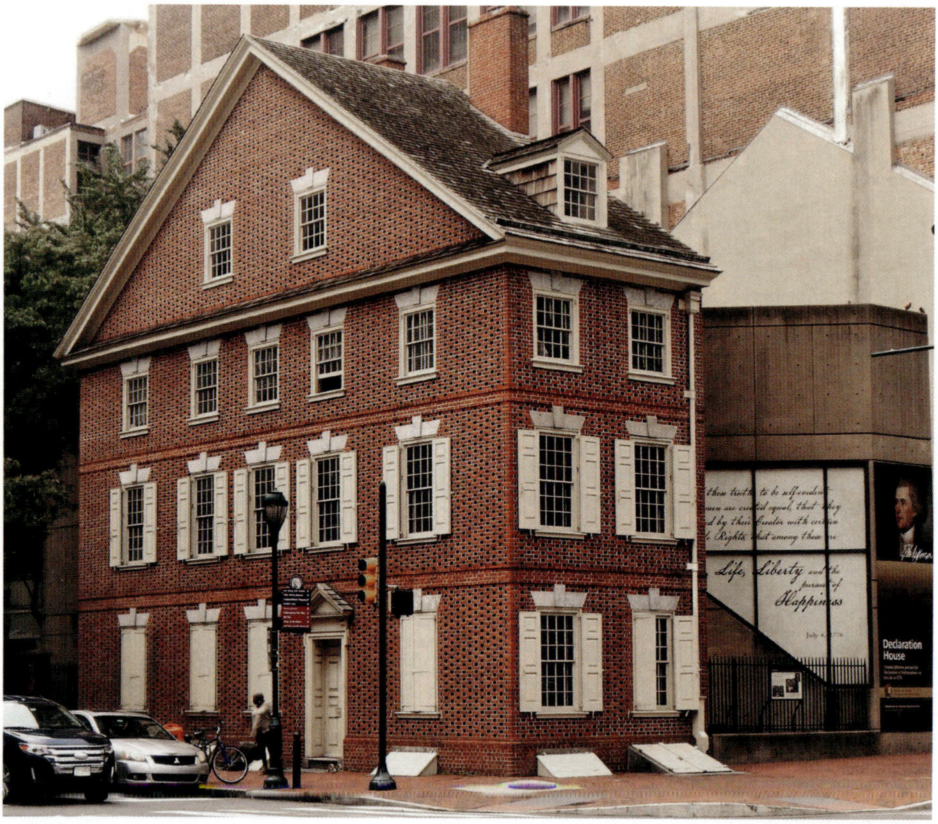

FIGURE 2.3 This little museum at Seventh and Market Streets is a replica of the boardinghouse where Thomas Jefferson resided during the Second Continental Congress in 1776. It was here where he wrote the Declaration of Independence.

Franklin's diplomatic task was nearly superhuman. At a moment when the rebellious colonies were almost totally unequipped to fight their way to freedom against the greatest military power in the world, it was his job to persuade the young French monarch to provide the substantial numbers of men and matériel needed to reverse the odds and secure defeat for their enemy, the British. On the face of it, that goal might have seemed absurd. Franklin had to beseech this greatest absolute monarch in the world to help create what was anathema to him: a republic. Yet, from his earlier discussions with Bonvouloir, Franklin knew that Louis's foreign minister, Vergennes, would welcome revenge against the English for winning French Canada as the result of the French defeat a decade earlier in the Seven Years' War. In an echo of Montesquieu's earlier warning, Vergennes had even noted soon after that defeat, "England will soon repent of having removed the only check that could keep her colonies in awe. . . . She will call upon them to contribute to the burdens they have helped to bring upon her, and they will answer by striking off all dependence."[13] Thanks largely to Franklin's persuasive abilities, Vergennes, and through him, Louis XVI, would conclude that it was now France's turn to make England repent. (See Figure 2.4.)

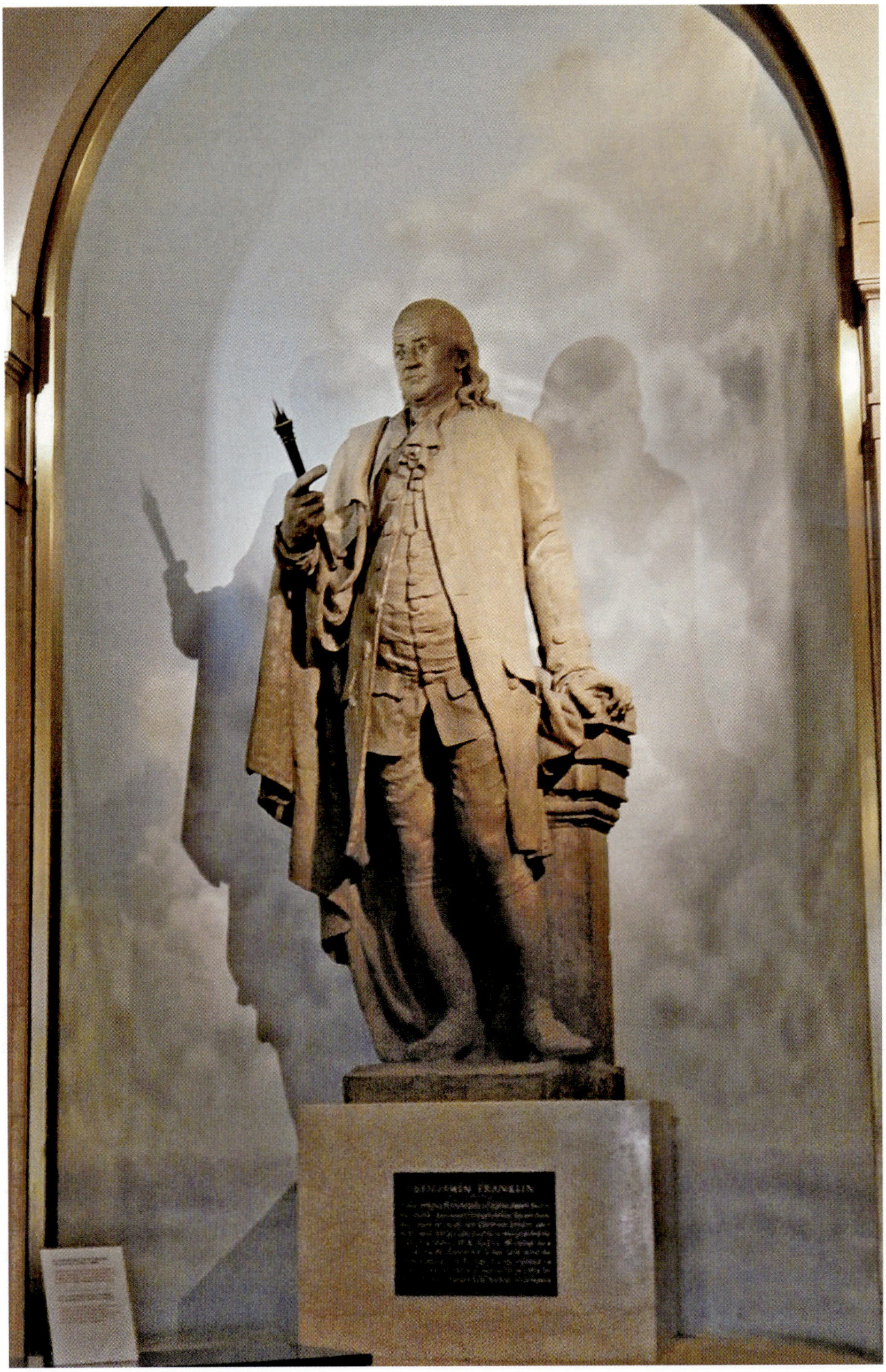

FIGURE 2.4 This full-length depiction of Benjamin Franklin is by the French-born Philadelphia sculptor Joseph Bailly. It greets visitors in the lobby of the Public Ledger Building across Sixth Street from Independence Square.

But to arrive at that eventual outcome required all of Franklin's skills as a worldly diplomat, and one who knew how to use his celebrity to advance his cause. The task was to coax France out of its neutrality in the war between Britain and its colonies. From the time he first arrived in France in December 1776, Franklin was made to understand the French government's unwillingness to acknowledge the assistance it might make to the Americans, even if assistance might be forthcoming. Some help in the form of munitions in fact was already underway, but secretly through a private emissary, the same Pierre-Augustin Caron de Beaumarchais who had recently triumphed in the theater with his play, *The Barber of Seville*.[14] Vergennes was at pains not to claim ownership of Beaumarchais's efforts so that he might maintain the pretense of France's neutrality in the face of accusations by the British ambassador.

While Franklin and the French court played a game of cat and mouse, Silas Deane, another American also representing Congress in Paris, was busy recruiting French officers to cross the Atlantic to aid the insurgents. Before long, the growing number of these unofficial volunteers was presenting a problem for the leader of the rebel army. In the view of General George Washington, who had to deal with those who made it to North America, they were for the most part ill fit to serve the American cause. In a February 1777 letter to the president of Congress, John Hancock, the annoyed general wrote, "You cannot conceive what a weight these kind of people are upon the Service, and upon me in particular," he wrote. "I wish it were possible to make them understand when Commissions are granted to them, that they are to make themselves Masters of the english Language in some degree, before they can be attached to any particular Corps."[15] What Washington needed above all were trained military engineers, not adventurers with claims to commissions as officers largely because of their aristocratic births. Eventually, a number of such experts—almost all French or French-trained—would provide critical help to Washington, although he could not know that when he wrote so despairingly to Hancock.

What might have been one more such highborn adventurer, and one just nineteen years old, arrived in Philadelphia the following summer, ablaze to serve the cause of freedom. Remarkably, rather than disdaining him, Washington soon made him his favorite. The Marquis de Lafayette (1757–1834) was a nobleman whose father had been shot and killed by an English soldier during the Seven Years' War, before the man had ever laid eyes on his infant son. That made the son, who was related to a host of prominent French officials, the heir to a vast fortune. Lafayette left his pregnant young wife and a distraught family at home to sail into the revolutionary cause in America. His trip had been opposed by his father-in-law, the duc de Noailles, who was so well-connected at court that he persuaded Louis XVI to issue a decree forbidding the headstrong teenager to go. Nonetheless, the young man went, on a ship for which he paid, and with an entourage of twelve officers. After a rough two-month voyage during which he was often seasick while he struggled to learn English, Lafayette landed in South Carolina and made his way to Philadelphia. Benjamin Franklin had written the members of the Continental Congress from Paris urging them to make use of the young man. After Lafayette offered to serve without pay, the Congress hastened to commission him a major general, on July 31, 1777.[16]

Days later, he met General Washington for the first time. The dinner they shared at the City Tavern in Philadelphia on August 5 would change both men's lives forever.[17] Washington was immediately impressed by the young man's enthusiasm and idealism. He showed him his military camp and soon invited Lafayette to join his staff. For his part, the marquis was simply swept off his feet by his boundless admiration for the older man. A month after this first meeting, while Lafayette recovered from a leg wound he had received at the Battle of Brandywine, that nearly catastrophic engagement for the insurgents, he poured out his feelings in a letter to his wife in France, in which he said of Washington,

> That respectable man whose talents and virtues I admire more and more as I know him better and better, is willing to be my intimate friend. His tender interest for me soon won my heart to him. I am established in his house, we live like two united brothers in the midst of a mutual intimacy and confidence. . . . When he sent me his personal surgeon, he told him to take care of me as if I were his son, because he loved me like one.[18]

After Brandywine, Washington commended Lafayette for his "bravery and military ardour" and recommended him in a letter to Congress for the command of a division.[19]

Even if the reserved Washington was slightly less effusive than his young admirer, his affection for the French aristocrat was clearly genuine. By the end of 1777, Washington had to answer congressional critics of his military accomplishments in what had, to date, been largely a losing campaign. Lafayette immediately sprang to his defense. Washington wrote to thank him, saying "It will ever constitute part of my happiness to know that I stand well in your opinion, because I am satisfied that you can have no views to answer by throwing out false colours, and that you possess a mind too exalted to condescend to dirty arts and low intrigues to acquire a reputation."[20] This from the commander of the Continental Army to a boy not yet out of his teens.

Meanwhile, Franklin in Paris continued his low-key but persistent effort to pursue an alliance with France. His first meeting with the foreign minister, the comte de Vergennes, on December 28, 1776, in Versailles, was clandestine. Only gradually and over time was Franklin able to persuade Vergennes and the court to enter into a semiformal, if still secret, alliance with the Americans. The secrecy did not end until February 1778 when a treaty of amity and commerce and a defense alliance were signed in Paris. The signing of the Paris pacts was of huge importance. Now the two parties were bound not to lay down their arms until the independence of the United States was secured.

The Franco-American alliance was secured at a moment when the Americans at last had demonstrated staying power in the military conflict. The early part of the war had brought little but dark days for the rebels. The British under the command of General William Howe defeated Washington's forces at the Battle of Brandywine south of Philadelphia on September 11, 1777, inflicting severe casualties on the Americans. Howe's troops then were able to march the few miles to occupy an undefended Philadelphia without incident. Ahead of them, the Continental Congress fled first to Lancaster, then York, Pennsylvania. Yet the occupation of their capital city failed to make the insurgents capitulate. Although the bedraggled Continental Army retreated to Valley Forge for the winter of 1777–1778, they emerged in the spring, having been trained by Baron von Steuben during their encampment to fight again. Meanwhile, a turning point for the Americans came in upstate New York in October 1777, in the Battle of Saratoga. There British forces under the command of General John Burgoyne were defeated by troops led by an American force, and Burgoyne surrendered the nearly six thousand troops under his command. Two engineers trained in France had played critical roles in the American success.

At almost the same time as that critical battle was taking place in upstate New York, General Washington in Pennsylvania dispatched two French officers, volunteers in the insurgent cause, to shore up entrenchments at the two forts on opposite sides of the Delaware River just below the southern boundary of Philadelphia. These experienced soldier-engineers, Major François Louis-Teissèdre de Fleury and Captain Thomas Antoine Maudit de Plessis, so improved the defenses of both forts—Mifflin on the Pennsylvania side of the river, and Mercer on the New Jersey shore opposite—that they were able to fend off attacks by British and Hessian forces until such time as a winter freeze made it impossible for British naval vessels to reinforce General Howe's forces occupying Philadelphia. Although both forts eventually had to be abandoned under the British onslaught, they held out for two months until the winter was so far advanced that the British were unable to launch a new offensive against Washington's troops. As at Saratoga, French-trained engineers were key to the successes of the Continental Army.[21] (See Figure 2.5.)

It was when the news of Saratoga reached Paris that the French were persuaded to formalize their support of the Americans.[22] The success of the revolutionaries at last seemed plausible. Vergennes had become alarmed when intelligence reached him (Franklin no doubt made sure it did so) that London was willing to make peace with the Americans on the basis of home rule within the empire. That offer might have been most welcome in North America two years earlier, but no longer. Back in Philadelphia, General Howe resigned his post and was replaced by General Henry Clinton at the head of the occupation forces. By the spring of 1778, with the threat of greater French involvement in the war, Clinton was ordered to evacuate the city and lead his army north to help fortify New York. With the departure of the redcoats, the Continental Congress returned to hold their meetings in Philadelphia's State House. Once news of the French alliance reached Philadelphia, it did much to reinvigorate the American cause, even though it still would be many months before the *Expédition Particulière*, as the French military mission was named, would actually arrive to join the fight in America.

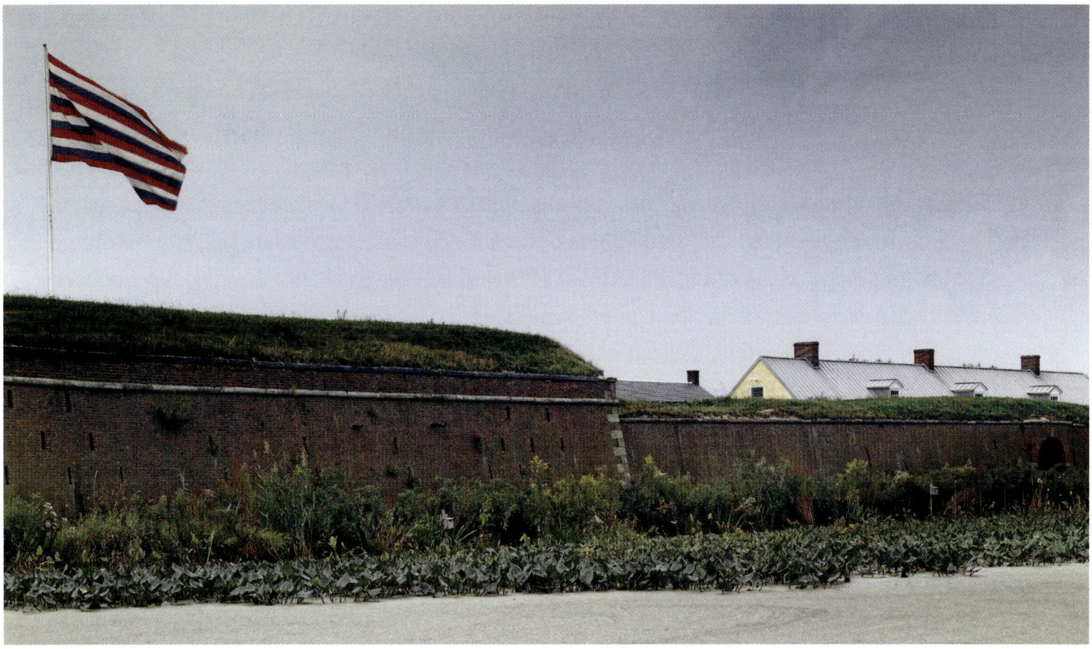

Figure 2.5 In 1777, two French engineers, volunteers in the French army supporting the American Revolution, improved the defenses of Fort Mifflin on the Delaware River. As a result, British naval vessels were unable to reinforce General Howe's forces occupying the city at the time. (Library of Congress, Prints & Photographs Division, photograph by Carol M. Highsmith. Reproduction Number: LC-DIG-highsm-12303.)

Once the treaties creating the Franco-American alliance were signed, they were placed aboard a ship bound for Philadelphia, where they would be ratified by Congress in May 1778. John Adams had arrived in Paris, replacing Silas Dean as commissioner, to join Benjamin Franklin at the point when the alliance was nearly ready to be sealed. He soon professed shock and disdain at his older countryman's willingness to adapt to what he regarded as decadent French manners while ingratiating himself with French society. Whereas the Philadelphian understood that the French way was to appear to do nothing much while working hard in private, through Adams's eyes, Franklin merely looked lazy and disheveled. He saw how the old man was being wined and dined by the upper crust of French society and was shocked at his behavior in his relations with various Parisian lady friends. After witnessing their interactions on a number of occasions, Adams was bemused if impressed at French women's "unaccountable passion for old age."[23]

Meanwhile, now that the alliance between France and America was out in the open, Vergennes authorized the publication of a print depicting Franklin allegorically as America's liberator, a thing that the government had prohibited only six months earlier.[24] The Philadelphian was more the rage than ever, with small busts and lockets bearing his likeness adorning mantelpieces and ladies' breasts across Paris. (Those bisque statues were not always carefully researched by their maker, however, for beneath Franklin's unmistakable likeness on some was stamped the name of Washington.)[25] Franklin had become the eighteenth-century equivalent of a rock star. Never had he known such acclaim at home, and he lapped it up, but without ever losing his customary common touch. He met the aged Voltaire, and the two appeared jointly at a meeting of the Académie des Sciences. The acclaim for them was so great—the assembled scholars demanding that the two repeatedly embrace—the scientific discussions were cut short that day. The two sages later appeared together at a late-night meeting of a Masonic lodge into which Franklin had recently been inducted. French newspapers hailed the American, never mind the hyperbole, as "the founder of the New World."[26]

The alliance brought with it recognition of the United States as a new nation, making the government of Louis XVI the first to do so. The career diplomat, Conrad Alexandre Gérard, had been the chief negotiator of the alliance on behalf of Vergennes, having served as his trusted principal secretary. Now he lobbied the foreign minister eagerly for an appointment as the first minister of France to the United States. That appointment made, he left for Philadelphia in March 1778 aboard a ship that was part of a fleet under the command of Admiral d'Estaing, who was determined to make trouble for the Royal Navy along the coast of North America. Once he arrived in the capital city, Gérard took up residence in the townhouse of John Dickinson, which became the French legation. Conveniently located at the northwest corner of Sixth and Chestnut Streets, the legation stood at the intersection diagonally across from the western end of the State House, where the Continental Congress once more met. Gérard engaged himself deeply in American affairs, working assiduously to promote good feelings toward France and the French alliance among the public and American officials—even to the point of lavishing gifts on members of Congress. Yet, due to ill health, Gérard reluctantly resigned his post in 1779 and was replaced by another aristocrat, the Marquis de la Luzerne, that September.

In May 1778, when General Howe and his troops began to evacuate Philadelphia and march toward New York, Washington sent Lafayette with some twenty-two hundred men to reconnoiter the enemy. Word soon came back to the British that Lafayette had camped nearby, some ten miles northwest of the capital city. Five thousand British troops moved to try to trap and capture him. On May 20, General Howe arrived with an additional force of six thousand to attack his left flank. Nearly surrounded, Lafayette organized a retreat, but feigned numerical superiority while he did so, his soldiers popping out of a forested hill periodically to fire at the enemy. His tactic succeeded, and he and his troops escaped the trap. This Battle of Barren Hill so secured Lafayette's reputation as a military tactician that years later the locality was renamed Lafayette Hill in his honor.

In the months that Lafayette spent in Washington's company, he absorbed the Virginian's deep convictions about the value of a free government. He, of course, had come from France because of his passion for what the philosophes taught, but it was from Washington that he drew the deeper education. Throughout the rest of his long and often difficult life, Lafayette would remain true to the principles he had learned to cherish at Washington's side.

In September 1778, after Lafayette had made known his desire to return for a time to France, Congress presented him with a ceremonial sword and invited him to rejoin the American cause as soon as he could, assuring him that his commission as major general in the Continental Army would continue in force. His last letter to Washington from American soil, dated January 11, 1779, made his feelings and his intentions plain:

> The sails are just going to be hoisted, my dear General, and I have but the time of taking my last leave from you. . . . Farewell, my dear General, I hope your French friend will ever be dear to you, I hope I schall soon see you again, and tell you myself with what emotion I now leave the coast you inhabit, and with what affection and respect I'l for ever be, my dear general, your respectfull and sincere friend.[27]

Back in France by February 1779, Lafayette hastened home to his wife, Adrienne, and young daughter. On December 14, Adrienne gave birth to a son. They named him Georges Washington.

Months later, in April 1780, Lafayette began his second visit to America. The circumstances were very different from those at the time of his first departure three years earlier. Now he came at the order of the king, as a representative of France. Yet, even though he was the monarch's own emissary, Lafayette was returning as both the symbol and the embodiment of the French Enlightenment's triumph in America. His arrival aboard his gorgeous new frigate, *l'Hermione*—which "sails like a bird," he exclaimed—was jubilant. When he disembarked in Boston harbor, he was met with thunderous acclaim. Vergennes had given him the honor of informing Washington and the Congress that the French Expeditionary Force under the command of General Rochambeau would soon arrive in North America. Before he left Paris, Lafayette had persuaded Vergennes and King Louis that the French force should be placed under the overall command of General Washington.[28]

The French soldiers landed in Newport, Rhode Island, on July 10, 1780. Seven thousand strong, they exceeded the number of men commanded by Washington in the Continental Army. Yet, for the next year, the force remained inactive while the war remained largely at a stalemate in the north. The British had blockaded French ports and effectively blocked Narragansett Bay as well with the arrival of Rochambeau's army there. Two months before the French came to Rhode Island, the British took Charleston, South Carolina, in a bruising defeat for the rebels. Although England had begun to withdraw troops from the north to counter French threats elsewhere, it was now the British goal to hold onto the south at all costs. Washington, meanwhile, gathered his troops at White Plains, New York, and waited.

While the stalemate lasted, Lafayette was a frequent and sought-after guest in Philadelphia. He entertained members of the Continental Congress aboard the *Hermione* and was wined and dined by the city's elite. The following winter, he was elected the first foreign member of the American Philosophical Society (which had been another

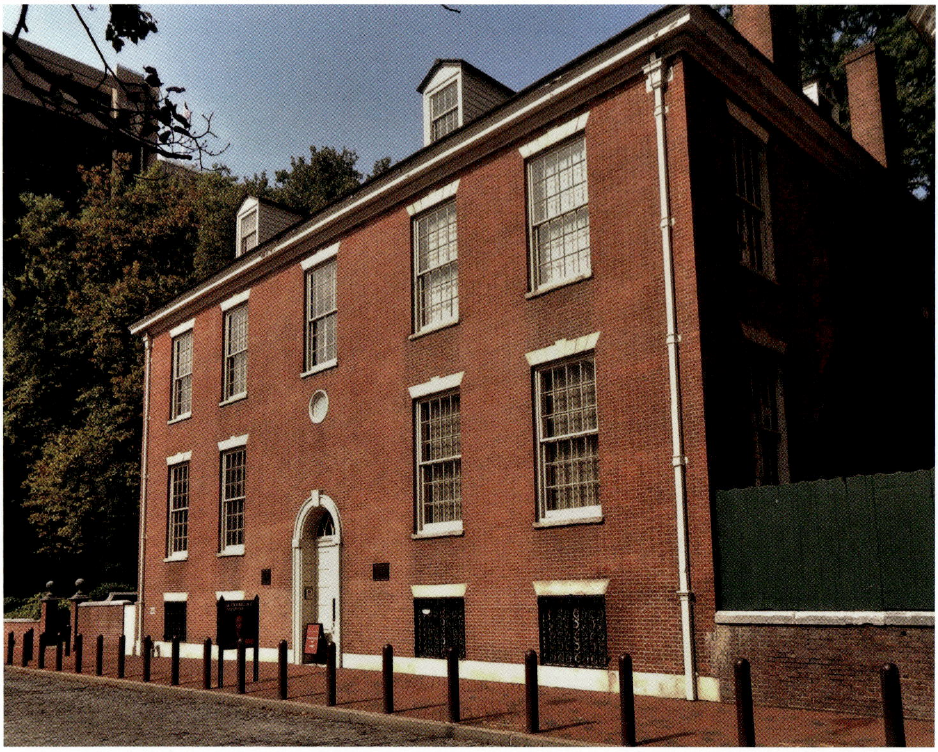

Figure 2.6 The American Philosophical Society is the oldest organization of learned individuals in the United States. Lafayette and other notable Frenchmen were members. Its original quarters adjacent to Independence Hall now house a museum.

of Benjamin Franklin's creations, back in 1743). Meanwhile, the marquis kept pressing Washington to attack the British, while the general continued to counsel prudence. "It is impossible, my dear Marquis," Washington wrote on October 30, "to desire more ardently than I do to terminate the campaign by some happy stroke; but we must consult our means rather than our wishes; and not endeavor to better our affair by attempting things, which for want of success may make them worse."[29] (See Figure 2.6.)

Early in 1781, Washington learned that the turncoat general, Benedict Arnold, had gone to Virginia on a raiding expedition and was destroying mills, supply depots, and other economic targets in the countryside. In February, he ordered Lafayette to re-form his force in Philadelphia and travel to Virginia to counter Arnold. Within another month, Arnold was receiving reinforcements from New York. Lord Cornwallis, the general second in command to Clinton in the British army, tried and failed to capture Lafayette in Richmond. Meanwhile, however, the marquis became convinced that Washington was planning to launch a decisive battle someplace in the north, and he began to move his troops back toward Philadelphia. At that point, Washington ordered him to return to Virginia to assume military command there. Lafayette protested, convinced that he was being left out of what he supposed was Washington's plan to act without him.[30]

Yet Washington's strategy, which he dared not spell out in a letter that he would have to entrust to couriers, was to trap Cornwallis in Virginia. In July 1781, Rochambeau led his army out of Rhode Island to march across Connecticut toward the Hudson River. At Mount Kisco, New York, he met up with Washington and his army and they then proceeded toward Philadelphia. On September 3, thirty-seven days after they began their trek, the French troops arrived outside the city. Wanting to look their best for the residents of the capital, they paused to brush and chalk their white uniforms and trim their grenadier hats with colored plumes. Their regimental chaplain, the abbé Robin, later gave his account:

> The arrival of the French army at Philadelphia was more like a triumph than simply a passing through the place. They marched through the town, up Chestnut Street to Center Square where they camped; with military music playing before them, which is always particularly pleasing to the Americans; the streets were crowded with people, and the ladies appeared at the windows in their most brilliant attire. All Philadelphia was astonished to see people who had endured the fatigue of a long journey so ruddy and handsome, and even wondered that there could be Frenchmen of so genteel an appearance![31]

The description of this scene suggests the pains taken by the French troops to ingratiate themselves with Americans, who were sometimes wary of the presence of a new set of foreign troops replacing the occupying forces of the British. Their effort was also accounted for by an aide-de-camp to General Rochambeau, who kept a journal describing the movements of the French army throughout its engagement in North America.[32]

During their stay in Philadelphia, the French officers and their guests were entertained at a gala dinner by the French minister, de la Luzerne. The abbé Robin was one of the guests. He reported the reaction when an express arrived:

> A disquieting silence immediately seized every guest. . . . Our eyes were fixed upon the Chevalier de la Luzerne, everyone endeavoring to guess what the message would turn out to be. "Thirty-six ships of the line," said he, "commanded by Monsieur le comte de Grasse, have arrived in Chesapeake Bay, and three thousand men have landed and opened a communication with the marquis de Lafayette." Joy and good humour immediately resumed their place on every countenance.[33]

The celebratory mood in Philadelphia anticipated what would be the decisive victory for the French and American forces six weeks later in Virginia. In August, when he arrived at Cap-Haitien in the Caribbean with his fleet, the rear admiral of the French navy, François Joseph Paul, le comte de Grasse, was met by a ship dispatched by Rochambeau and Washington requesting his assistance. He immediately set sail with his fleet for the Chesapeake, arriving there on August 30. Within days, his ships

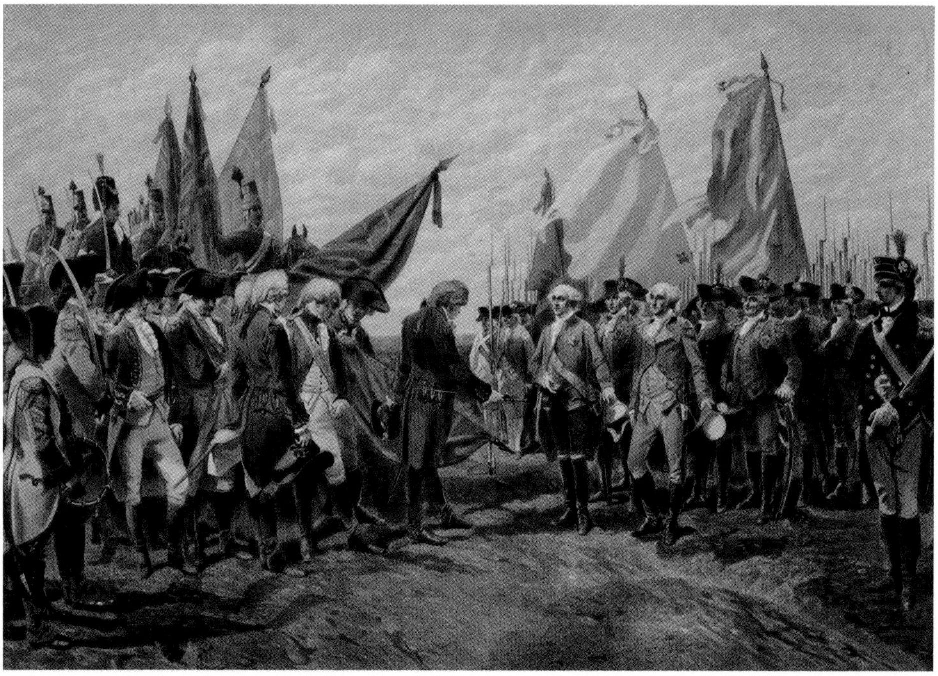

FIGURE 2.7 Illman Brothers, engravers. *The Surrender of Cornwallis at Yorktown A.D. 1781*, ca. 1870. General Cornwallis surrenders his sword to George Washington, commander of the Continental Army, at the close of the decisive loss for the British at Yorktown in 1781. (Prints and Photographs Division, Library of Congress. Reproduction Number: LC-DIG-01668.)

engaged those of the British in the Battle of the Chesapeake. While its outcome was indecisive, it effectively prevented the Royal Navy from reinforcing or evacuating the troops of General Cornwallis encamped in Yorktown.

Meanwhile, weeks earlier, Lafayette had stationed his troops around those of Cornwallis to contain them. That was the situation when de Grasse arrived, did battle with the Royal Navy, and prevented the enemy from assisting Cornwallis. Then, on September 14, after a march of 680 miles over the course of two months, Washington and Rochambeau arrived with their combined armies and joined forces with Lafayette. Two weeks later, with the French fleet still blockading the bay, the joint forces launched a siege of Yorktown. The British defenses were soon broken, their counterattack failed, and on October 19, Cornwallis surrendered.[34] The air was soon filled with cries of "God and liberty!" intermixed with "Vive le Roi!" Once news of the victory reached Paris, the city was illuminated by three nights of fireworks. Franklin drank in the details of how the campaign had gone and exulted at its perfect execution—even though the allied armies could only communicate through an interpreter. He marveled that the British army had actually "quit a situation from whence it might have escaped, and place[d] itself in another whence an escape was impossible."[35] (See Figure 2.7.)

Two months later, Lafayette again prepared to leave America now that his assistance was no longer needed. Ready to sail from Boston, he wrote one last love letter to his hero and substitute father:

> Adieu, my dear General, I know your heart so well that I am sure no distance can alter your attachment to me—With the same candor, I assure you that my love, my respect, my gratitude for you are above expressions, that on the moment of leaving you I more than ever feel the strength of those friendly ties that for ever bind me to you. . . . Your respectfull and tender friend, Lafayette.[36]

Before Lafayette left Philadelphia, Congress had appointed him to assist the three American envoys in Europe: Franklin in Paris, John Jay in Madrid, and John Adams, who by then was minister to the Netherlands. He also carried a congressional letter to Louis XVI commending the marquis for his service to America. Once Lafayette was back in France by late January 1782, the king expressed his "most favorable opinion" of the young nobleman. He then made the twenty-four-year-old a *maréchal de camp* in the French army, skipping him over several ranks. Franklin immediately begged Lafayette to try to persuade Vergennes to provide still more funds for the American cause now that Franklin found himself unable to persuade the court for greater largesse. The foreign minister had already let Franklin know that the treasury was being dangerously depleted. By Vergennes's accounting, the king had spent 28 million livres in gifts and loans to assist the rebels. But on March 1, Lafayette succeeded in talking another six million livres out of the king's pocket and into Franklin's. The old man heard the good news just when he learned that the British Parliament was disinclined to pursue the war further.[37] Now it would be possible to advance the final peace.

In the negotiations with the British that led to the Treaty of Paris and the official end of the Revolutionary War, Benjamin Franklin was once more the indispensable American. At first, the French alliance threatened to constrict what the Americans might accomplish. France was exhausted by the conflict and proposed confining the new nation to territory east of the Appalachians, allowing Britain to control the area north of the Ohio River. With that, the Americans turned directly to their English counterparts, who were becoming alarmed at the prospect of a long-term Franco-American alliance. Soon the English began to see a possible benefit in the loss of their empire in North America. They were persuaded to negotiate a more generous settlement, one that would encourage the growth of the United States as a trading partner responsible thereafter for the costs of managing and policing its large territory.[38] When word reached Vergennes at how the Americans had negotiated behind his back, he was outraged. But Franklin assured him sunnily that the last thing they intended was to offend their French friends or the king. The foreign minister was soon appeased—also at the prospect that a prompt peace would bring an end to the American raid on the treasury.[39]

The treaty was signed by Franklin, John Adams, John Jay, and Henry Laurens for the Americans on September 3, 1783. (Coincidentally, if ironically, both the New Yorker Jay and the South Carolinian Laurens were the grandsons of French Huguenots who had fled to America around the time of the 1685 Edict of Fontainebleau, which confiscated their property and banned Protestant worship in France.) After ponderously slow transfer of the pact back to America for ratification by Congress, then to Europe once more for the official approval of the other parties, the ratified versions were exchanged in Paris on May 12, 1784.

Over the previous year, however, unrest in the infant nation would unsettle its government and reveal the weakness of the confederation that gave it life. When Pennsylvania officials failed to protect the Congress from a mob of mutineers in June 1783, its representatives were hastily removed from Philadelphia to Princeton. That little college town became the nation's de facto capital for the next several months; but in December, Congress moved to Maryland's capital of Annapolis. Late in 1784, the French Arms Tavern in Trenton, New Jersey, became the seat of government. Finally, Congress moved to New York's city hall in January 1785. Not until 1787, when the states agreed to call a conference to amend the Articles of Confederation, would Philadelphia's State House again host delegates from throughout the infant nation. That body, however, would make the bold decision not just to amend but to remake the government of the United States with a new constitution.

All that still lay well in the future, however, during the years after the Revolution's triumphant success. Three days after Cornwallis surrendered at Yorktown on October 19, 1781, the queen of France, Marie-Antoinette, gave birth to her first child, Louis Joseph, heir to the throne. The news did not reach the Marquis de la Luzerne in Philadelphia until the spring of 1782. He then announced the happy tidings to the Congress. The following August, the marquis hosted a lavish party to honor the infant Dauphin. The affair was held at his rented house at Sixth and Chestnut Streets. For this occasion, the minister hired Pierre L'Enfant, an engineer serving in Rochambeau's army, to construct a large pavilion in the garden, which extended all the way to Seventh Street.[40] Philadelphia was abuzz as the city watched the construction of the grand, open-air structure with a decorated ceiling atop brightly painted pillars. On the morning of the event, whole squadrons of hairdressers styled the coiffures of women guests, some of whom reportedly had to have their hair dressed as early as four in the morning because of the demand.

One of the guests, the noted Philadelphia physician, Dr. Benjamin Rush, was effusive in a letter he wrote the next day describing the affair. After extolling the warmth and fine manners of the host and the delicacy of the dishes that made up the supper's "cold collection," he weighed in on the evening's social interactions:

> General and Mrs. Washington, Comte de Rochambeau, the marquis de Chastellux, Robert Morris, John Dickinson, General Thomas Mifflin and a host of distinguished men and women were there while an Indian chief or two lent variety to the scene—especially so when a Chief in his savage habits

> and the Comte de Rochambeau in his expensive and splendid uniform talked with each other as if they had been the subjects of the same government, generals in the same army, and partakers of the same blessings of civilized life. A most unique feature of the entertainment was an apartment fitted up by the thoughtful host for the reception of those Quaker ladies whose principles would not permit them to join in the gaiety, but who watched the dancers through a gauze curtain! This little attention to the curiosity of these ladies marks in the strongest manner the Minister's desire to please everybody.[41]

Back in Paris, once Franklin had helped complete the treaty that gave the United States its independence, he thought that his job at last was done. He was nearly seventy-eight years old when he signed that pact and was suffering from gout and gallstones. He had been serving his country in Paris for almost seven years and wanted to go home. He had also remained on excellent terms with Vergennes and the French court at a time when other Americans in Paris—most notably, John Adams and John Jay—were finding much to censure in their treatment by the French. No doubt, his weariness of Adams's prickliness added to the old man's wish to be discharged. He wrote to Robert Morris, "I hope that the ravings of a certain mischievous madman here against France and its ministers, which I hear every day, will not be regarded in America."[42]

So, Franklin could only feel pleased and relieved when Thomas Jefferson at last arrived in Paris in August 1784, nearly a year after the Treaty of Paris had been signed. Jefferson, he was reassured to know, was a fellow Francophile. Franklin had admired the younger man's abilities in drafting the Declaration of Independence eight years earlier. Jefferson reciprocated that respect, his admiration for Franklin growing as they saw each other frequently in Paris. For most of the next year, they worked together negotiating trade agreements while Franklin no doubt guided his younger friend through the pleasures of the French capital. They were both frequent visitors at Lafayette's new home in the rue de Bourbon in Paris, where they and other Americans—John and Abigail Adams, John and Sarah Jay among them—dined with the whole Lafayette family and liberal members of the French aristocracy.

Not until May 1785 did Franklin receive word from Congress that after almost nine years in Paris, he was relieved of his duties and might return to America at his convenience. Franklin set sail in July. After he said goodbye to the comte de Vergennes, the foreign minister noted to a member of his staff, "This minister has won the King's esteem . . . The United States will never have a more zealous and more useful servant than Mr. Franklin."[43] But it was the new American minister who paid him the enduring compliment. In his diplomatic and social engagements around Paris, Jefferson was often introduced as the man who had replaced Franklin. "No one can replace Dr. Franklin," he would interject, "I merely succeed him."[44]

Once back in Philadelphia, Franklin returned to the house he had built years earlier in a courtyard off Market Street. This compulsively curious, brilliant, and energetic man no doubt found the comparative quiet of his return difficult—even though he

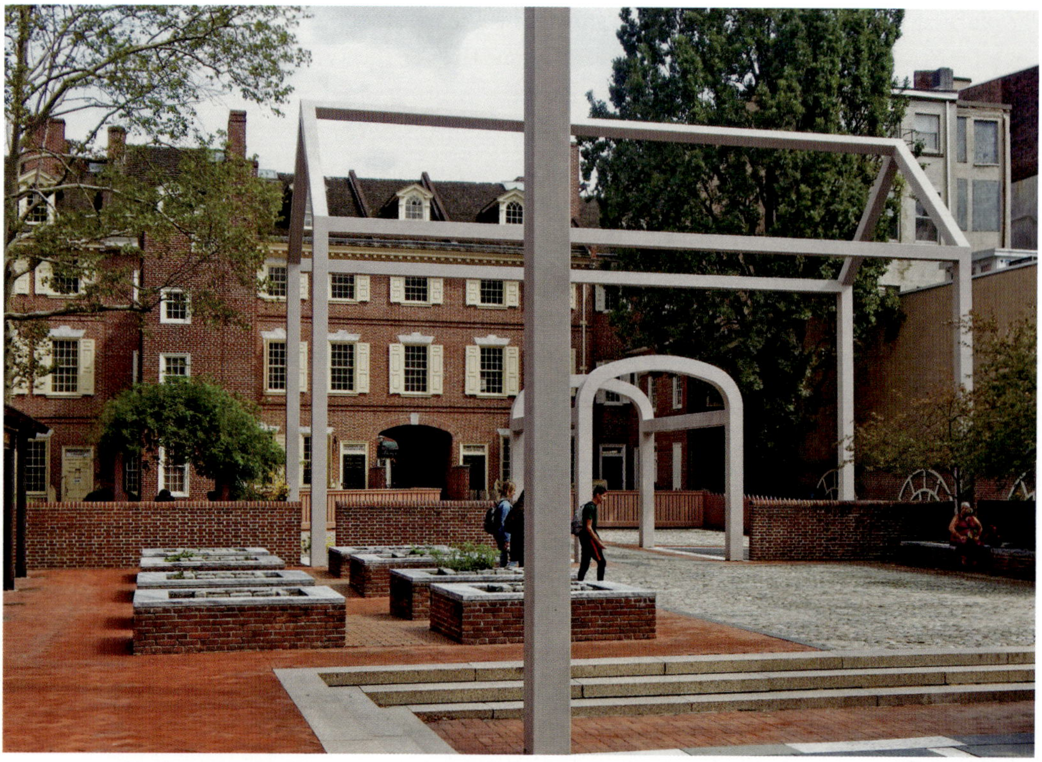

FIGURE 2.8 Benjamin Franklin's printshop is outlined in steel as is the passageway through it to his residence, which stood in the foreground of what is now a museum. The reconstruction was undertaken for the Bicentennial of the American Revolution in 1976. In the rear, the original brick buildings on Market Street were also Franklin's property.

was almost immediately elected president of the Executive Council of Pennsylvania, a mostly honorific post. He therefore amused himself by adding a large addition to the house in 1787, when he was eighty-one. His gout and gallstones were so painful that he was often carried about the city by prisoners from the Walnut Street Prison in his French-made sedan chair. He professed to be happy to be surrounded by his daughter, Sally Bache, and her children, who lived with him. But he admitted in October of that year, "as for everything else, I was happier in France."[45] (See Figure 2.8.)

Franklin's concern from Paris that the anti-French sentiment of Adams and Jay had infected others was not entirely misplaced. Some Philadelphians feared that their leading citizen had "gone native" during his long stay in France. After his return, Franklin never hesitated to refer to Louis XVI—the world's most powerful absolute monarch—as the father of American independence. He lived nine more months after the fall of the Bastille in Paris on July 14, 1789, but, given the debilities of his advanced age and the glacial flow of news from Europe to America, he knew little of that transformative event. He remained a friend of the France he had known until the end. Yet the outbreak of the French Revolution would have political consequences in the young United States, as well. Philadelphia would again become the crucible—as the place of refuge for large numbers of French people in exile, and the federal seat of government—where the friendship of France and the young nation would be tested.

Two centuries after America's Declaration of Independence, the ambassador of the French Republic to the United States summed up the remarkable way in which his nation had assisted in the birth of the new nation: "It was in arms of the French aristocracy that American democracy came into the world."[46] He may have intended to allude to the double meaning of the word *arms* in English, for in addition to the military support commanded mostly by members of France's aristocratic class, the fraternal bonds established during the conflict between such men as Lafayette, Rochambeau, and their American comrades were crucially important to the outcome of the struggle. With the conclusion of peace, officers from the Continental Army and their French counterparts formed the nation's first patriotic organization, the Society of the Cincinnati. The medallion awarded to its members was suspended from a pale blue-and-white ribbon, colors invoking both armies. The fraternal bonds of the two nations, sometimes strained but not forgotten, would continue to influence their dual affairs within the next decades as the result of the great upheaval that loomed on France's horizon.

During the years when the Franco-American alliance produced momentous events, the capital of what finally was recognized as the new United States flourished as the greatest urban center in the nation. While the Revolution was being won, another French-speaking transplant to Philadelphia was putting down roots and making a name for himself in his adopted city. Pierre Eugène du Simitière (1737–1784) spent most of his childhood in his native Geneva before immigrating to the West Indies. He landed in New York in 1769, then Philadelphia five years later. He soon made himself known in the city as an artist and a collector of all kinds of artifacts. Soon after the thirteen American colonies declared themselves a free nation, Congress invited artists to submit designs for a new great seal of the United States. Although Simitière's design was not accepted, his depiction of the *Annuit Coeptis* (He favors our enterprise) found its way into the final design, where it remains on the back of the dollar bill to this day. It shows the Eye of Providence within the triangle that forms the top of the pyramid representing the thirteen states. He is also credited with devising the nation's motto: "*E pluribus unum.*"

Within the next few years, Simitière began creating an important series of portraits of the heroes of the American Revolution. They were engraved in Paris by Benoit Louis Prévost with financial support from Conrad Alexandre Gérard.[47] Simitière was hired by the American Philosophical Society as its official historiographer. There he collected documents containing the personal recollections of a wide variety of Americans. He intended to write an exhaustive history of the United States and undertake a major exploration of the Missouri River basin while it remained a part of then-Spanish Louisiana. But his always precarious financial situation, not to mention the ongoing war in North America, held him back. Yet his insatiable habit of collecting—of specimens he had brought with him from the Caribbean and elsewhere, as well as political ephemera of all kinds—led him to establish the first museum in the nation. The American Museum opened in June 1782, in his house on Arch Street. Its "natural curiosities" included seashells, coral, and other creatures of the deep as well as the fossilized remains of plants and animals. The museum's "artificial curiosities" presented artifacts from West Indian cultures, paintings, the antiquities of North and South American Indians, along with "Various Weapons, Musical Instruments and Utensils of the Negroes, from the coast of Guinea, and the West-Indies."[48]

Unfortunately, his half-dollar admission fee proved too steep to attract sufficient visitors, and he was forced to close his museum not long before he died in poverty—and perhaps of hunger—in 1784. Many of the papers resulting from his projects, both finished and unfinished, are in the collection of the Library Company of Philadelphia.[49]

[3]

A New Nation Is Born

French Art in Philadelphia

The American Revolution of 1775–1783 provided copious dramatic events and distinguished heroes along with prime opportunities for artists to create a distinctive American imagery and style in art. When the nation emerged as an independent entity, it needed visual symbols to define its purpose and forge its new identity at home and abroad. In 1779, the Supreme Executive Council of Pennsylvania deemed that those who rendered distinguished services to their country should have their resemblances in statues and paintings. This was what "the wisest, freest and bravest nations" do "in their most virtuous times."[1] Aspiring artists in young America lacked access to art academies and museums where they could learn the rudiments of the trade. London and Rome beckoned as centers of training and repositories of the classic masterpieces. Paris attracted artists as well as statesmen due to the Enlightenment ideas articulated by the philosophes. Louis XVI's financial aid to the colonies in their fight for independence influenced style and manners, as did the subsequent presence of large numbers of French in Philadelphia. Diplomatic exchanges between France and America enabled the flow of ideas and images that would shape the imagery of the new republic.

Benjamin Franklin's many achievements as an inventor, writer, politician, and statesman to France made him a prime candidate for portrayal at home and abroad. The famous portraitist to Marie Antoinette, Madame Louise Élisabeth Vigée Le Brun (1755–1842), remarked about the American envoy in Paris: "His venerable aspect, his homely sayings, his republican simplicity of dress and manner, combined with the tact and politeness of his deportment, his anecdotes and his bon mots gained him among all classes of admirers, disciples, and friends. No man in Paris was more à la mode, more sought after, than Doctor Franklin. The crowd used to run after him in the streets and in the public resorts; hats, canes, snuff-boxes, everything was à la Franklin."[2] Leading French artists such as Jean-Jacques Caffieri (1725–1792), Jean-Baptiste Greuze (1725–1805), Joseph Siffred Duplessis (1725–1802), and Jean-Honoré Fragonard (1732–1806) captured Franklin's likeness during the years of his diplomatic ministry. His celebrity had become fixed so strongly in Paris that three images of him were exhibited at the 1779 Salon, the venue where the public could view works of painting, sculpture, and prints by emerging and established artists. The Salon was open to all and reports on its contents circulated throughout the major capitals of Europe.

In addition to the Duplessis oil and a sculpted portrait by Caffieri, a terra cotta bust by Jean-Antoine Houdon (1741–1828) portrayed the elder statesman. (See Figure 3.1.) So convincingly lifelike was Houdon's image that Frédéric Melchior, Baron von Grimm, warmly praised the work and the man in one exclamation: "What elevation of thought is seen in the bust of the legislator of the New World!"[3] Physiognomic readings that related facial features to character were being popularized in France through the writings of Johann Kaspar Lavater, who published his work between 1775 and 1778. These theories clearly influenced Pierre S. du Pont's evaluation of artistic representations of Franklin seen at the Salon of 1779 when he wrote that Franklin's large forehead manifested his strength of mind and the stout neck his firmness of character.[4] Although the elder statesman purchased several wigs when he arrived in France and was more than once depicted in his distinctive marten fur hat, Houdon depicted him bareheaded with a receding hairline that draws the eyes of the viewer to the broad expanse of the forehead and skull that covered the brain of the man who was an indefatigable inventor, writer, and political theorist, among just a few of his talents. The unadorned clothing with its simple folds serves as an effective visual foil to the creases around Franklin's eyes and mouth while the sagging flesh beneath the neck indicates the toll that seventy-three years had taken on the diplomat's body. But the deep cutting around the eyes highlights the sharpness of the mind that was poised to articulate something undoubtedly lucid that would emerge from lips that are just opening. Nothing superficial could be uttered from a face that held that much character. What Houdon made visible in this bust of Franklin was the internal state of mind of one who remained intellectually alert to the complexities of the tumultuous political times in which he lived.

No written evidence exists to confirm that Franklin ever sat for Houdon who executed two marble busts at his own expense and did other versions in terra cotta and plaster.[5] Nevertheless, both Houdon and Franklin were members of the Masonic Loge des Neuf Soeurs where they both attended a ceremony involving Voltaire on April 9, 1778. When Franklin and Voltaire embraced each other at the Académie des Sciences on April 29, the sharp-eyed sculptor had an opportunity to study both men's features. The French philosophe and the American Founding Father would have their busts joined by those of the great French playwright Molière and the Enlightenment philosophe Jean-Jacques Rousseau at the Salon of 1779. Undoubtedly, Houdon was shrewd enough to see the advantages of executing and exhibiting the likeness of an

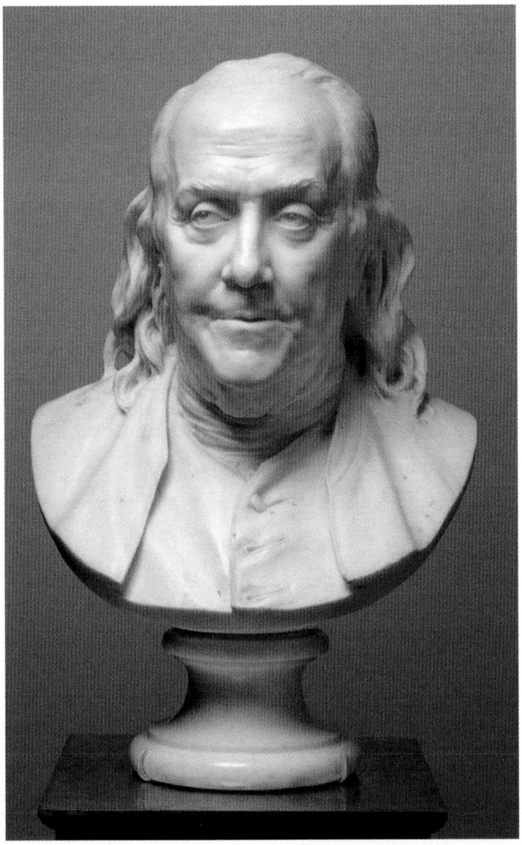

Figure 3.1 Jean-Antoine Houdon, *Bust of Benjamin Franklin (1706–1790)*, 1799. Marble, 21 × 13½ × 10 in. (53.3 × 34.3 × 25.4 cm). (Philadelphia Museum of Art, 125th anniversary acquisition. Purchased with a generous grant from the Barra Foundation, Inc., matched by contributions from the Henry P. McIlhenny Fund in memory of Frances P. McIlhenny, the Walter E. Stait Fund, the Fiske Kimball Fund, and with funds contributed by Mr. and Mrs. Jack M. Friedland, Hannah L. and J. Welles Henderson, Mr. and Mrs. E. Newbold Smith, Mr. and Mrs. Mark E. Rubenstein, Mr. and Mrs. John J. F. Sherrerd, the Women's Committee of the Philadelphia Museum of Art, Marguerite and Gerry Lenfest, Leslie A. Miller and Richard B. Worley, Mr. and Mrs. John A. Nyheim, Mr. and Mrs. Robert A. Fox, Stephanie S. Eglin, an anonymous donor, Mr. and Mrs. William T. Vogt, and with contributions from individual donors to the Fund for Franklin, 1996-162-1.)

illustrious American to compete with Caffieri's version. He could then capitalize on the rage for Franklin's image in Paris as mentioned by Franklin himself in a letter to his daughter that copies of his image on lids of snuff boxes, in prints and busts, sold at such a high rate that his face was as well known as that of the man in the moon.[6]

Caffieri believed that his success with the Franklin bust and a commission for a monument to the American General Richard Montgomery made him the uncontested recipient of future commissions from America, but Houdon had other plans. The execution of an equestrian monument marked the crowning achievement of a sculptor's artistic career, and from his early years Houdon aspired to create one. Many of his most important commissions had come from foreign courts in Russia and Germany, and now the prospect of subjects from the newly formed United States held great promise.

When America, England, and France signed the Treaty of Paris in 1783, the Virginia General Assembly decided to honor George Washington with a life-size bronze equestrian monument. They consulted with Thomas Jefferson, then living in Paris as Franklin's successor, who recommended Houdon. War debt caused the postponement of the equestrian monument, but in 1784 another vote secured the funding for a statue of General Washington with both Franklin and Jefferson endorsing Houdon for the task. Houdon canceled a commission from the empress of Russia in order to execute Washington's statue, claiming that it promised to be the brightest chapter in his history.[7] Since Washington declined to travel to France to pose for Houdon, Governor Benjamin Harrison of Virginia sought out Charles Willson Peale (1741–1827) to paint a life-size image to serve as a model. Peale's canvas arrived in Paris in April 1785, but Houdon insisted that he needed to take physical measurements of Washington and bring back a life mask of his face in order to sculpt a true image. He offered to come to America and consequently set sail from Le Havre with Franklin, who was at last heading home from his long mission in France. Together they docked in Philadelphia on September 14, 1785.

Houdon remained in Philadelphia for two weeks before departing for Mount Vernon in Virginia where he worked with three assistants from October 3 to October 15. The fifty-three-year-old future president recorded his fascination with Houdon's working methods in his diary. As Washington was lying on a table with two quills emerging from his nose to have his life mask taken, his granddaughter wandered into the room and was so startled that she thought her grandfather had died! Houdon remained in Philadelphia for a short time again before he returned to France, showing his plaster bust of Washington, along with others he brought with him when he returned to France in December. While in Philadelphia, he was entertained by Francis Hopkinson, one of the signers of the Declaration of Independence who wrote the following to Jefferson in Paris in a letter dated October 25, 1785: "This will be delivered to you by Mr. Hudon, the Artist who came over to make a Model for a Statue of G. Washington. I yesterday saw the Head he has model'd of that great Man. I am charmed with it. He is certainly a most capital Artist. There is no looking at this Bust without Admiration and Delight. The noble Air, sublime Expression and faithful Likeness evince the Hand of a Master. You will be charmed with it. Mr. Hudon having executed the Purpose of his Voyage is Impatient to return. I should have been happy in a further acquaintance with him, for I not only admire the Artist but love the Man. As he had given me so much Pleasure. I endeavoured to please him also in my Way. I played for him on my Harpsichord as well as I could. He was surprised at the Effect of the Instrument. I wish you would ask him what he thought of it."[8]

The wealthy Philadelphian William Bingham, who was sent on several diplomatic missions to France, purchased busts of Franklin, Voltaire, and Rousseau while he was in Paris in 1786 to be displayed in the mansion he planned to build on Third Street. As art historian Wayne Craven has observed, portrait busts in the homes of distinguished citizens and significant public spaces awakened Philadelphians to the potential of sculpture as a high art. They functioned not only as objects of decorative beauty but also as visual reminders of the men whose philosophical and political ideals formed the new nation.[9]

Jefferson had assured Washington that Houdon possessed "the reputation of being the first statuary in the world,"[10] alerting Washington to the sculptor's ambition to do an equestrian statue. He urged Washington to convince Congress to fund this work in the future. When Houdon returned to his Paris studio, he crafted two versions of the

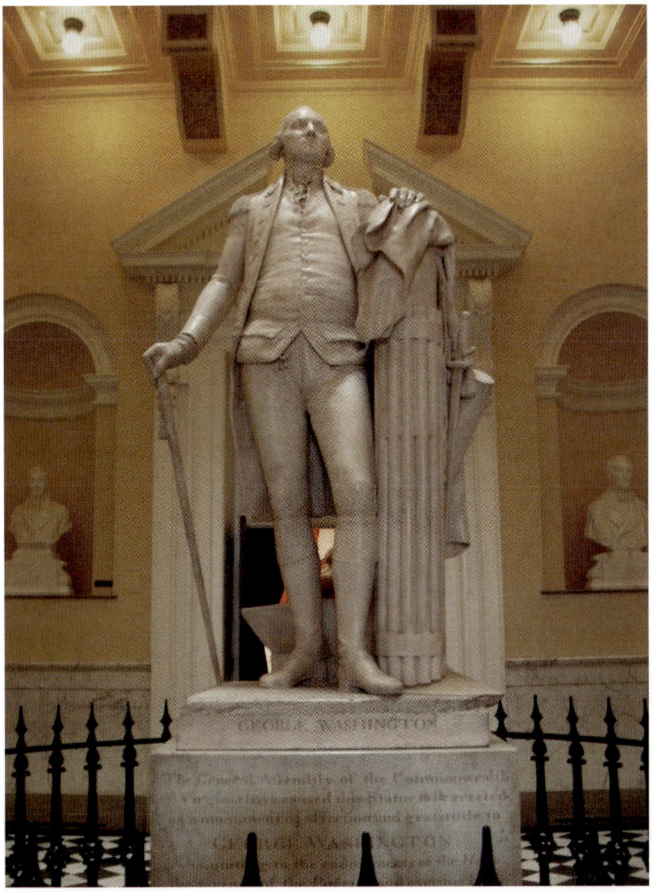

Figure 3.2
Jean-Antoine Houdon, *George Washington*, 1785–1792. Carrara marble. Virginia State Capitol. (Photo: Albert Herring for Wikipedia. Licensed under CC BY-SA 3.0, available at https://creativecommons.org/licenses/by-sa/3.0/legalcode.)

full standing figure—one in antique and the other in modern garb. (See Figure 3.2.) Houdon acceded to Washington's preference for contemporary dress but included a reference to republican Rome by depicting the general as a modern Cincinnatus, the valiant retired fifth-century Roman general who resumed active duty to his country against the invading Aequians. Having accomplished his task, Cincinnatus returned to his farm, leading a modest life. Likewise, Washington left his farm in Virginia to serve as the general of the Continental Army then resumed his life there once the war had been won. By posing Washington with a plow behind him, Houdon referenced how both men incarnated the ideal of public service over private gain. So convincing was the likeness of Washington that when he saw Houdon's work the Marquis de Lafayette declared: "That is the man himself. I can almost realize he is going to move."[11] Houdon had succeeded in balancing the symbolic import of Washington's role as a military leader with the specificity of features that made him recognizable to generations to come. Houdon completed the standing statue of George Washington in 1788 and considered it the most important commission of his career.[12]

Replicas of Washington's image in bronze and plaster proliferated throughout the nineteenth century. The molds, made from the original, allowed the image to be

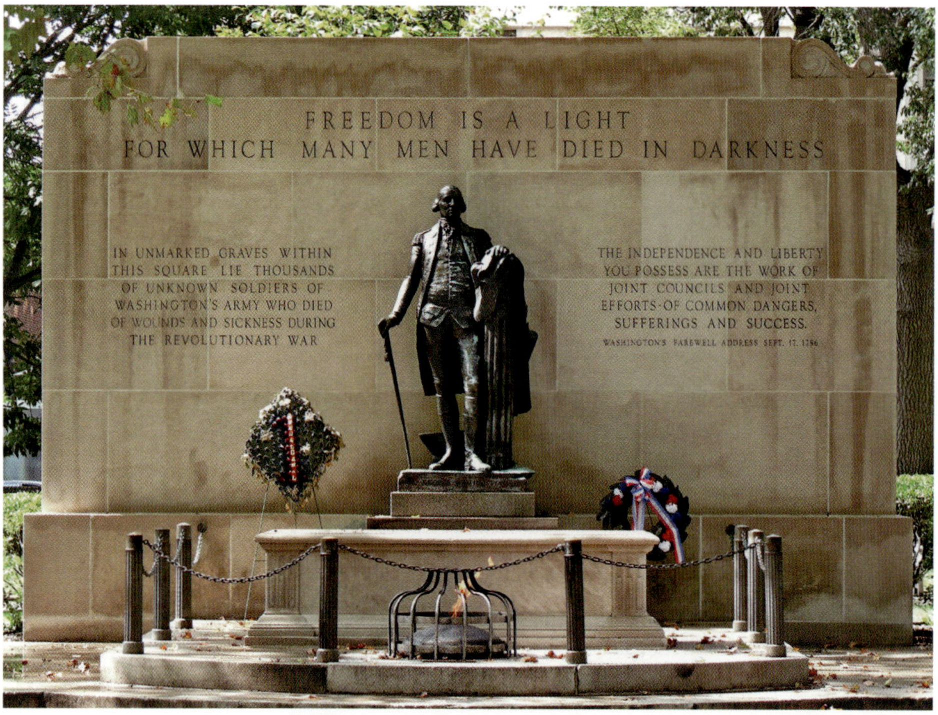

FIGURE 3.3 Cast by Jean-Antoine Houdon, *George Washington at the Tomb of the Unknown Revolutionary War Soldier*, Philadelphia, Washington Square.

situated in significant historical venues, which additionally would ensure the continued existence of the statue should the original be damaged, as occurred with Antonio Canova's statue of Washington that was destroyed when the North Carolina State Capitol burned in 1831. Today a replica of Houdon's statue can be found in Philadelphia's Washington Square, which was named in 1825 when a monument to the first president was proposed. This never came about, but in 1954 the Washington Square Planning Committee took up the project of creating a Tomb of the Unknown Revolutionary War Soldiers.[13] In 1957, G. Edwin Brumbaugh's monument was completed with an eternal flame and a bronze cast of Houdon's statue as the centerpiece. Another replica in Valley Forge National Park near Washington's headquarters reminds visitors of the father of our nation. (See Figure 3.3.)

Houdon commented that "one of the most beautiful attributes of the difficult art of statuary is that it preserves forms in all their truth and renders almost imperishable the images of men who have brought their nation glory or happiness. That idea has followed me constantly and encouraged me in my long labors."[14] Houdon combined profound psychological insight and a prodigious visual memory with virtuosic skill. He not only replicated physical anatomy with amazing accuracy but visually summarized attitudes of character that imprinted themselves on the facial features of the Americans whose impact on its founding was as deep and durable as the stone in which they were immortalized. His likenesses of Thomas Jefferson, whose profile remains on the American dime, and the bust of John Paul Jones, the celebrated naval hero of the American Revolution, provide stunningly lifelike images of these noted Americans.

It was not surprising that Governor Harrison turned to Charles Willson Peale to paint Washington's portrait as a model for Houdon in 1784. By that time, Peale had established himself as one of the foremost portrait painters of his time, receiving important commissions from the Continental Congress and several of the most prominent families. Like many young aspiring artists in America, Peale had studied in England under the tutelage of Benjamin West for three years, beginning in 1767. Born in Springfield and raised in Newtown Square, Pennsylvania, West moved to England in 1763 where he became known as the American Raphael. West had a well-established reputation as a history painter, but Peale found himself more drawn to portraiture. Nevertheless, Peale learned from West how to incorporate details that would serve as markers of symbolic import that elevated the image beyond the mere depiction of a figure.[15] West had flourished under the patronage of King George III, but Peale's patriotism to the American cause for independence became evident when he refused to doff his hat one day as the king passed by him. Peale eventually settled in Philadelphia in June 1776, just days before the signing of the Declaration of Independence. He enlisted in the Philadelphia Associators (the militia) on August 9th and was elected a second lieutenant on October 3rd. He commanded his company, fought with the Continental Army under Washington during the New Jersey campaign that defeated Cornwallis, and was promoted to the rank of captain on June 17, 1777. He wintered at Valley Forge where he formed a close friendship with Lafayette, delighted at the opportunity to practice his knowledge of the French language and boast of his Huguenot heritage.

Peale painted George Washington in 1772 at Mount Vernon, providing the only prerevolutionary portrait of the general. On January 18, 1779, the Supreme Executive Council of Pennsylvania commissioned Peale to paint a full-length portrait of Washington to be hung in the Council Chamber. The many opportunities Peale had to observe the general during battle inspired him to portray the commander-in-chief leaning on a captured cannon as a symbol of his victory. Peale had seen action with Washington at Trenton, Princeton, and Germantown. The Princeton battle forced Cornwallis and the Hessian mercenaries out of Pennsylvania, New Jersey, and New England, thus reinforcing America's confidence in the effectiveness of the Revolutionary War. Washington's relaxed pose and statesmanlike restraint in this portrait echo that assurance. Peale returned to Trenton and Princeton in preparation for the portrait to sketch the landscape. The artist could have posed Washington in a variety of battle venues, but he had joined Washington on the front lines at the battle of Princeton and took obvious pride in the victory. The blue sash of the commander-in-chief winds its way from Washington's shoulder down to the mouth of the captured cannon on which Washington lays a proprietary left hand. The captured Hessian flags occupy the right lower corner of the painting while to the left a British ensign rests on the ground, posed underneath Washington's upturned heel as if it had just been scoffed

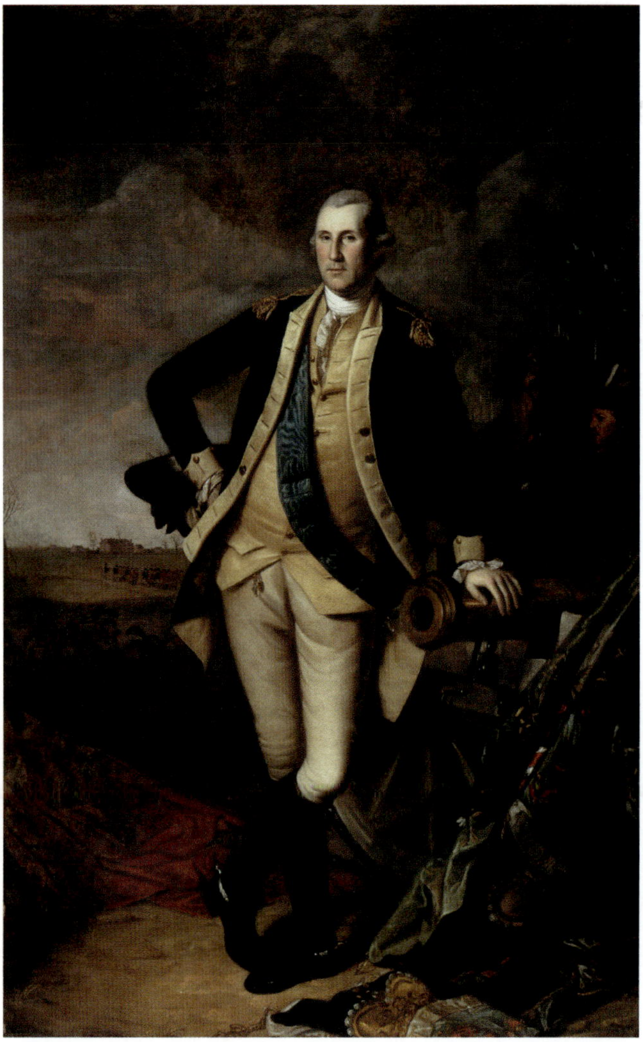

FIGURE 3.4
Charles Willson Peale, *George Washington at Princeton*, 1779. Oil on canvas, 93 × 58½ in. (236.2 × 148.6 cm.). Acc. No.: 1943.16.2. (Courtesy of the Pennsylvania Academy of the Fine Arts, Philadelphia. Gift of Maria McKean Allen and Phebe Warren Downes through the bequest of their mother, Elizabeth Wharton McKean.)

aside. Nassau Hall on the distant hill on the left marks the site where the battle ended. (See Figure 3.4.)

Portraits throughout history have played significant roles in statecraft and diplomacy as they honor the status of the sitter and secure their identity for posterity. They sometimes served as diplomatic tactics to forge alliances between nations, and this indeed was the case with Peale's portrait of *Washington at the Battle of Princeton*, which enjoyed such wide renown that the artist was inundated with requests for replicas. Conrad-Alexandre Gérard (1729–1790), the first minister of France to the United States who had been instrumental in negotiating the Treaty of Alliance and the Treaty of Amity and Commerce with the United States, purchased a copy. When he returned to Versailles, Gérard presented the painting to King Louis XVI who accepted it as an indication that the Americans remained firm in their commitment to free themselves from Great Britain's control.

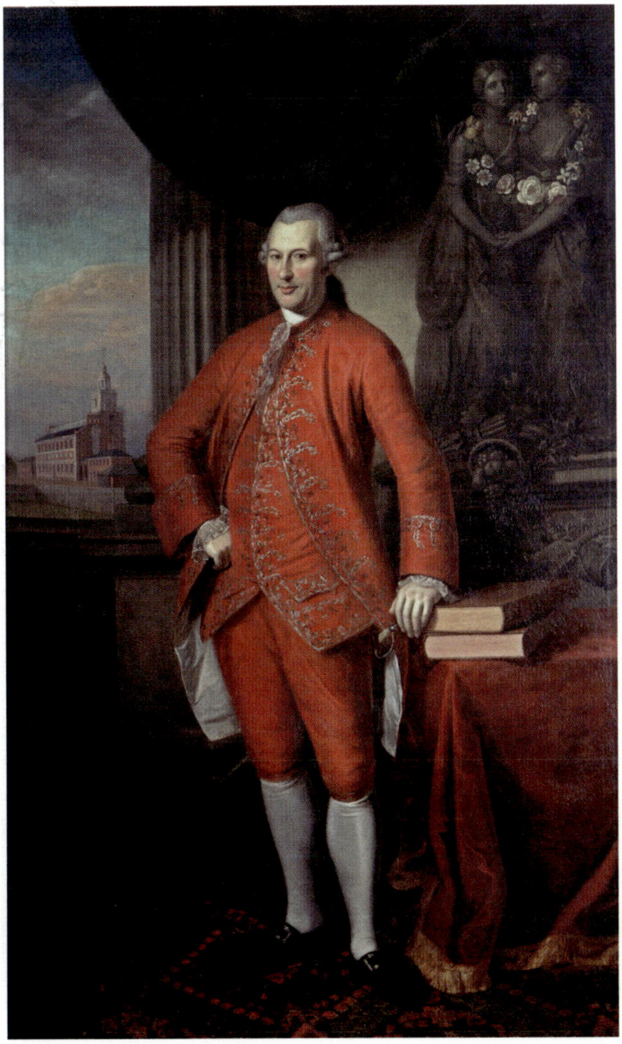

Figure 3.5 Charles Willson Peale, *Conrad Alexandre Gérard*, 1779. Oil on canvas, 241.3 × 150.11 cm. (Courtesy of Independence National Historical Park)

On September 3, 1779, the Continental Congress ordered a portrait of Gérard that Peale finished on September 18 of that year. (See Figure 3.5.) The success of the Washington portrait motivated Peale to repeat elements of the composition, adding appropriate differences. Gérard stands proudly in his study leaning his left hand on two large tomes resting on a draped table. Above Gérard's head two sculpted female allegorical figures representing France and America clasp hands and gaze lovingly at one another while encircled in a garland of flowers to personify the relationship between the two nations. The figure representing France clasps a protective arm around the personification of America who stands above bound fasces situated atop of a cornucopia that spills over the plinth and unites the figures to the space in which Gérard stands. The minister's right elbow points outward to an image of the Pennsylvania State House, thus locating the scene in America and echoing the depiction of Nassau Hall in the Washington portrait at the Battle of Princeton. The allegorical details such as the swag of curtain and column, surely questionable features of Gérard's home in Philadelphia, demonstrate Peale's training in England with West and his awareness of the customs of European court portraiture. Peale's depiction of Gérard visually relates him to a great American hero and role model along with appropriate allusions to the French royal heritage that it was the diplomat's duty to represent while on foreign soil. Gérard's portrait was originally destined to hang in the assembly room along with that of Washington, but Peale kept the portrait in the hope of making mezzotint prints later. When Peale moved his portrait collection from his residence to the former statehouse (later Independence Hall) in 1802, Gérard's portrait received the honor of being hung on one of the end walls of the Long Room next to the 1779 portrait of *Washington at the Battle of Princeton*.

Gérard's portrait would be one among several images of Frenchmen portrayed by Peale who had helped the cause of American liberty. From early in his career, Peale displayed a keen interest in French thinkers and the French language. Shortly after settling in London to study with West, Peale purchased Abel Boyer's *The Royal Dictionary, French and English, and English and French* to advance his education.[16] He read French novels and tutored members of the Polk family in the language in 1778.[17] After Peale showed John Adams some of his paintings, Adams wrote to his wife Abigail: "He is ingenious. He has vanity, loves finery, wears a sword, gold lace, speaks French, is capable of friendship, and strong family attachments and natural affections."[18] He maintained correspondence with Frenchmen, such as Étienne Geoffroy Saint-Hilaire, regarding his disagreement with the Comte de Buffon's ideas on animal degeneration. Peale's love of French culture remained with him throughout his long life, despite the political vagaries of France's relations with America.

During the summer of 1782, Peale erected an addition to his house at Third and Lombard Streets in order to display his ever-growing collection of portraits of those who had distinguished themselves in service to the American cause of independence. He sought to join commemoration with education in his desire to document the likenesses of his subjects for the public of his own time and for posterity. Peale's esteem for the French, whose contributions to the war effort played a significant role, impelled him to add their portraits with those of the American patriots he had painted. The October 13, 1784 issue of the *Freeman's Journal and Philadelphia Daily Advertiser* announced the opening of the Philadelphia Museum with forty-four portraits of "worthy personages" from the revolutionary era. Eight Frenchmen were listed as on display and can be seen today in their current location at the Portrait Gallery in the Second Bank of Philadelphia on Third Street.[19] These took the form of bust-size likenesses against a dark background, evoking Roman sculptures and coins as well as engraved frontispieces to biographies.[20] The forthright realism of Peale's style avoided the idealization found in European portrait busts with their dramatic characterizations and stylized mannerisms whose intent was to flatter the sitter, and where likeness needed to be subordinate to ennoblement. Peale's "plain style" recorded the features of the political and military figures without the traditional adulation seen in European portraiture.[21] In 1795, the artist cataloged sixty-one portraits accompanied by short biographical sketches. He framed the bust-sized oils in rectangular gilded frames with oval spandrels. No background detail distracted from the sitter's head and shoulders so that the uniqueness of character and the denotative apparel and military insignia could signify personality and achievement. As Brandon Brame Fortune has observed, their uniformity of appearance in the manner in which they were hung in his museum "contributed to the sense of collective honour as important for the message of the gallery as any individual likeness."[22] Peale's documentary style reinforced individuality while the similarity of mounting and presentation affirmed republican values of equality not dependent on rank or hierarchy.

Gérard was succeeded in Philadelphia by the Chevalier de la Luzerne who had trained since his youth for a military career. (See Figure 3.6.) By the age of twenty-one, Luzerne had attained the rank of major general in the cavalry and subsequently served as a colonel in the service of the French grenadiers. In 1776, he launched his diplomatic career in Bavaria. Three years later he arrived in Philadelphia to serve as second minister of France to America. An ardent champion of the young Republic, Luzerne reached into his own pockets to feed the troops in 1780. He enjoyed being the bearer of the report of official peace between England and America after the battle of Yorktown. A year later he delighted in bringing momentous news from his home country to the people of Philadelphia. Cannons thundered in the streets while Luzerne was led to the State House by the First City Troop on May 13, 1782 to deliver the official announcement of the birth of the Dauphin to Marie-Antoinette on October 22, 1781. Peale designed and decorated triumphal arches to celebrate this joyous occasion in France, collaborating with Luzerne on a triumphal arch to celebrate the event. The arch contained three transparencies with one in the middle representing the United States by thirteen stars. The ensemble was bordered with wreaths of laurel and accompanied by the motto, *Libertas lux optima nobis* (Liberty is our brightest light). The right panel bore the image of the arms of France, with this legend: *Lud XVI.* Fr. and Nav. *Rex defens Libertatis* (Louis XVI., King of France and Navarre, defender of Liberty). The whole was irradiated, and the motto was *Sole novo terras irradiat* (A new sunbeam on earth). The transparency on the left displayed a wreath of flowers, in the center of which contained a verse, presumably authored by Peale:

MARIA ANTONIETTA, *QUEEN OF FRANCE*

No emblems here her Tablet grace;
What Pencil can her Emblem trace?
Let Beauty, Wit, and Worth advance,
And joining form the Queen of France.[23]

Peale's portrait of Luzerne, done during this same period, captures the description of the chevalier as being "of good stature, rather large, plump, of a ruddy handsome countenance."[24] A faint smile marks Luzerne's lips, bestowing on him a benevolent appearance. Lavater's theories of physiognomy underscored this as an expression of

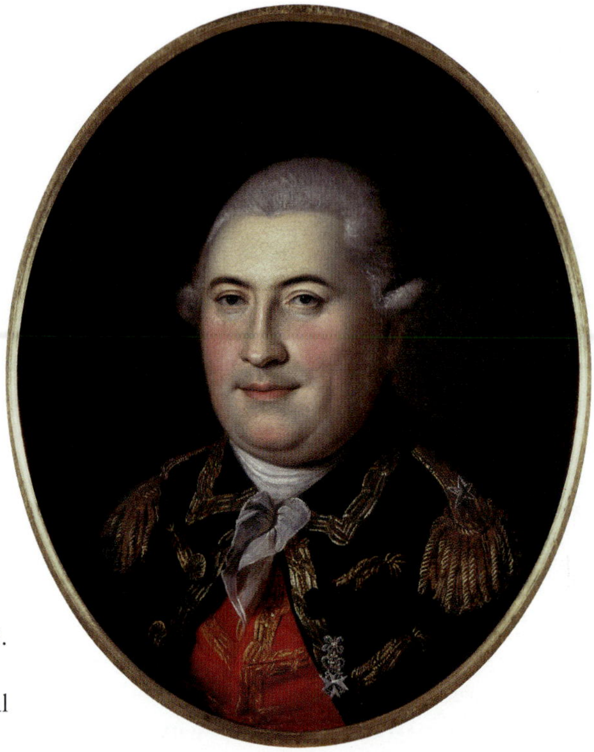

FIGURE 3.6 Charles Willson Peale, *Chevalier de La Luzerne*, 1781–1782. Oil on canvas, 55.88 × 48.87 cm. (Courtesy of Independence National Historical Park)

harmony and penetration of mind.[25] The combination of military and diplomatic dress worn by Luzerne summarizes the best of the chevalier's achievements in France and America. The American Academy of Art and Sciences, established during the Revolution by John Adams, John Hancock, James Bowdoin, and other scholar-patriots, made Luzerne an Honorary Fellow in 1781 in recognition of his service to the cause of liberty. Peale's portrait, done shortly after this, pays homage to the man and his service to the revolutionary cause.

On June 15, 1779, the American Congress had requested portraits of Louis XVI and Marie-Antoinette to be hung in place of the image of George III. Gérard informed Louis XVI's foreign minister Charles Gravier, Count of Vergennes, in a letter that they would be hung in the State House's Assembly Room. Benjamin Franklin, John Jay, and Robert Morris instigated the appeal as a signal of gratitude for French aid in the war effort and as a means to reinforce financial and commercial relations.[26] The atelier copies of Antoine-François Callet's *Louis XVI in Coronation Robes* (Madrid, Museo del Prado) and Élisabeth Vigée Le Brun's *Marie-Antoinette in Ceremonial Dress* (Vienna, Kunsthistorisches Museum) were not completed until 1784. They were then shipped to Philadelphia where Luzerne received the canvases at his home at Sixth and Chestnut Streets. In a letter to Congress of August 13, 1783, the king informed the Americans that the portraits testified to his continued friendship and functioned as a visual reminder of their obligation to sustain their cooperation with France.[27] Luzerne stored the royal portraits temporarily in his reception room, where they attracted

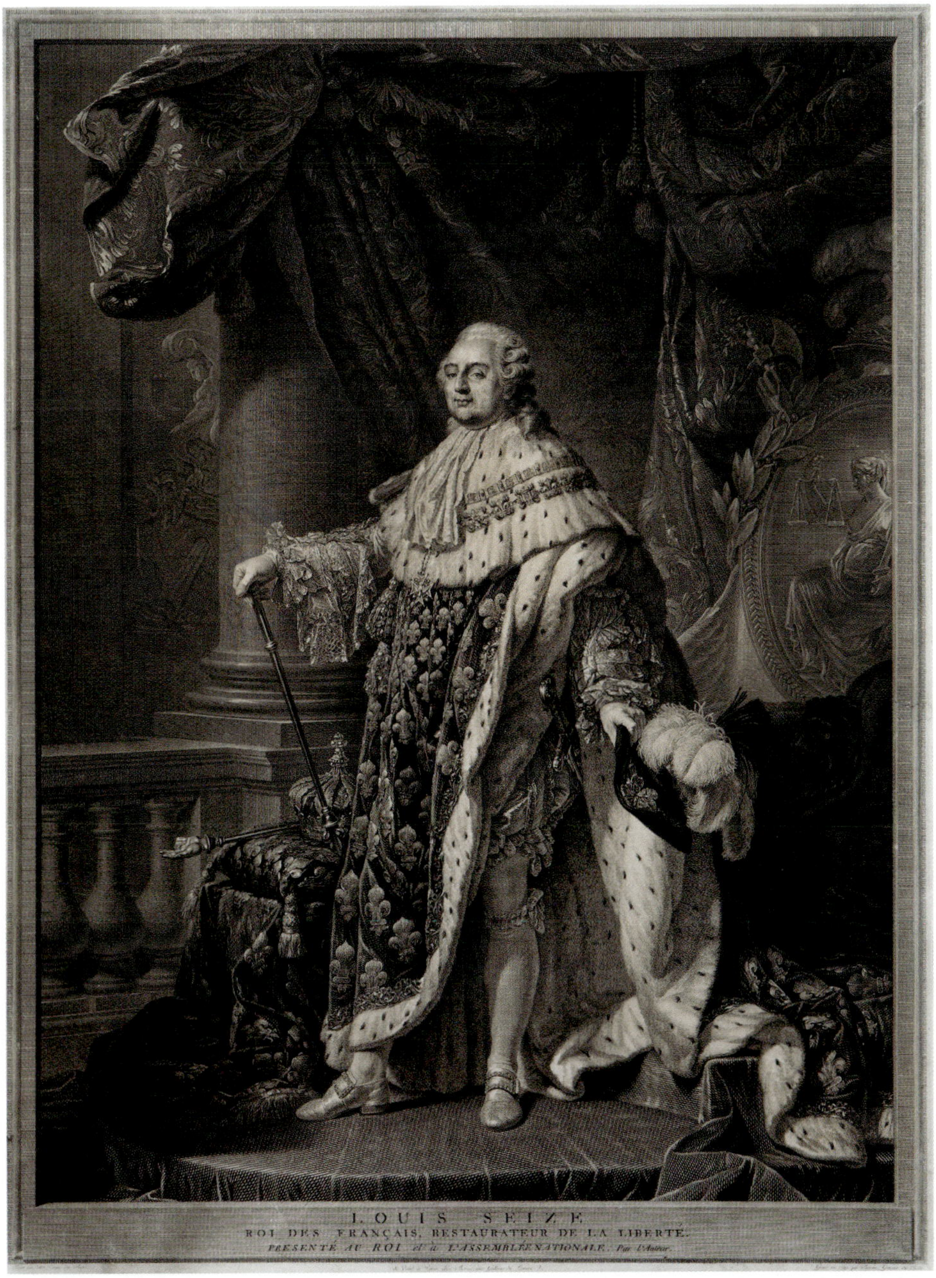

FIGURE 3.7 Charles Clément Bervic, after Antoine François Callet, *Louis Seize, Roi des Français, Restaurateur de la Liberté*, 1790. Engraving. Ink, laid paper, 28¼ × 21½ in. (71.76 × 54.61 cm). (Mount Vernon Collections, Purchase, 1939, W-767/A-B)

admiring crowds before they made their way to Federal Hall in New York City. On December 22, 1791, the French ambassador Jean-Baptiste Ternant presented a framed and engraved copy of Callet's portrait of Louis XVI to George Washington who displayed it in the state room of his home in Philadelphia. (See Figure 3.7.) The ornate frame, one of the prime examples of French palace-style framework, had been commissioned by Louis XVI in recognition of Washington's presidency. The royal crest of the kings of France is symbolically situated above the image with Washington's coat of arms at the bottom. The gift celebrated the harmonious relations between France and the new United States of America.[28]

The original portraits of the royal couple have not been located and were presumably destroyed in August 1814, when the British burned much of Washington during the War of 1812. President Giscard d'Estaing presented copies to Mayor Frank Rizzo while on a state visit during the 1976 Bicentennial. However, these reproductions do not represent what the Americans would have seen in Philadelphia in the eighteenth century. Instead, they are based on existing portraits that the D'Estaing government had immediate access to in the collections of the Musée Nationale at Versailles of the Duplessis portrait of Louis XVI dated around 1785 and the 1788 Marie-Antoinette by Vigée-Lebrun. These portraits once again hang on the second floor of Congress Hall in Philadelphia.[29]

When news arrived in Philadelphia that Rochambeau had joined Washington and Lafayette to defeat Cornwallis at Yorktown in October 1781, a young Frenchman, Alexandre Marie Quesnay de Beaurepaire, who had served as a captain with residence in Virginia during the war, hung in his window a scene of George Washington brandishing a spear while crushing the golden crown of "Brittish Pride" beneath his feet. He painted this on a translucent substance and lighted it from behind. The next night, Peale festooned transparencies in the windows of his home on Third and Lombard to celebrate the victory. On the ground floor the ship "*Cornwallis*" depicted the French flag flying over the British standard. The middle window on the second floor displayed large portraits of Washington and Rochambeau with rays of glory emanating from their heads beneath crowns of laurel. "SHINE, VALIANT CHIEFS" in large letters served as a salutation, and in a third-story window the words "FOR OUR ALLIES, HUZZA! HUZZA! HUZZA!" proclaimed the joy of the victory. Peale wrote that the ensemble "made so brilliant a display, that the People from all parts of the City came and so crowded the streets that if a Basket should be thrown out it could not meet with a vacancy to get to the ground within a considerable distance from the house."[30]

Peale subsequently set to work on his portrait of Rochambeau for his museum. (See Figure 3.8.) Reputed for his elegant dress, Rochambeau is portrayed in the garb of a French courtier with the Grand Croix of the Order of Saint-Louis that he had received in 1771 for his distinguished service in the Seven Years' War eminently on display. The ornate braid on the coat and the carefully tied jabot signal Peale's sensitivity to Rochambeau's concern for fashionable appearances. The red note of the *cordon rouge* beneath the white jabot indicates the highest rank in the Order of Saint-Louis and effectively sets off the deep blue of the jacket and the richness of the gold ornamentation.

As discussed in Chapter 2, Rochambeau played a significant role in the defeat of Cornwallis. Charles Coleman Sellers observed that, in spite of Rochambeau's own seniority in age and military service, the Frenchman "placed himself under the orders

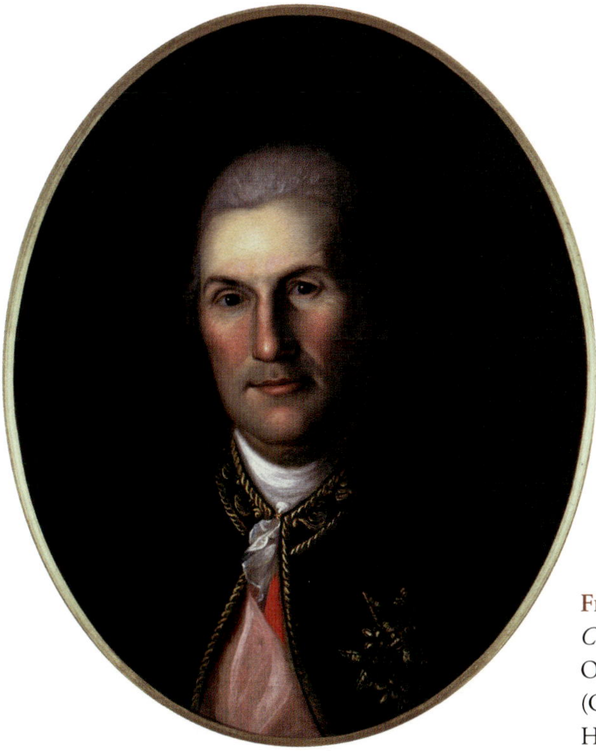

Figure 3.8 Charles Willson Peale, *Comte de Rochambeau*, 1782. Oil on canvas, 55.25 × 48.51 cm. (Courtesy of Independence National Historical Park)

of the American commander-in-chief, playing his part thereafter, but with completely self-effacing tact."[31] Cornwallis offered his surrender to Rochambeau when the British troops laid down their arms, but Rochambeau demurred, claiming he was only an auxiliary and sent Cornwallis to Washington. Peale's portrait caught Rochambeau's direct but unpretentious air, chin slightly tucked under and head tilted subtly to the side, communicating dignified reserve and the innate humility of the Frenchman. Rochambeau acquired a replica of Peale's *George Washington at the Battle of Princeton* in July 1782, taking it with him when he returned to France where it graced the walls of his ancestral château at Thoré-la-Rochette in the central Loire as a visual souvenir of the time he spent in America. Louis XVI paid homage to Rochambeau for his role in the American Revolution when he commissioned Louis-Nicolas van Blarenberghe to paint two gouaches to commemorate the victory at Yorktown for the ministry building at Versailles. The king had replicas made and presented them to Rochambeau in 1786.

Washington and Lafayette's deep friendship impelled them to commission portraits of each other in 1778 or 1779. The power of portraiture had struck Lafayette when he witnessed John Hancock giving the French Count d'Estaing a copy of Peale's 1776 portrait of Washington. Lafayette ordered a small copy from Peale and commissioned Pierre Charles L'Enfant to sketch Washington from life. When Washington learned of Lafayette's request for an image of him, he wrote to the Marquis on September 25 that "when you requested me to set for Msr. Lanfang [*sic*] I thought it was only to obtain the outlines and a few shades of my features, to have some Prints struck from. Could I have conceived that my Picture had been an object of your Wishes, or in the smallest degree worthy of your attention, I should, while Mr. Peale was in the Camp at Valley Forge, have got him to have taken the best portrait he could, and presented it to you."[32]

For his portrait of Lafayette, Peale used the three-quarter-length pose that he had used for his 1776 portrait of Washington that had so pleased Lafayette. (See Figures 3.9 and 3.10.) The artist may have wanted to allude to their close relationship with one another as he portrayed them with similar clothing and sashes with their hands tucked into their waistcoat. Before dispatching the finished portrait to Mount Vernon a year later, Peale made a bust replica of Lafayette's head for his museum and later executed a mezzotint print. (See Figure 3.11.) Lafayette's immense popularity made his image a desirable commodity for Americans who took more warmly to him than any other foreigner during the war.[33]

Peale used the occasion of the signing of the Paris peace treaty in 1783 to lobby for financial assistance from the Pennsylvania Assembly to construct a triumphal arch that would serve as a central feature for a public celebration. The structure made of wood, paper, and canvas stood forty feet tall and fifty-six feet wide and spanned Market Street. France took pride of place along with America as images of Washington and Louis XVI joined with allegorical scenes and Latin inscriptions on transparent panels. Peale portrayed Washington as Cincinnatus and Louis XVI's image was accompanied by a Latin inscription *Merendo memores facit* (His merit makes us remember him). The flags of the United States and France served as visual reminders of the political origins of the new Republic. Eleven hundred lamps were to light the panels and seven hundred fireworks were set off as a culmination of the celebration. Unfortunately, a rocket went off before the event was fully coordinated and ignited the structure. One person was killed, and Peale suffered severe burns as he was caught on the scaffolding. Undaunted, Peale re-created the arch after recovering from his injuries.

Peale's readings of Montesquieu, along with French scientists and naturalists such as the Comte de Buffon and Georges Cuvier, inspired him to create a museum as an addition to his house in 1782 that would combine both fine art and natural history. He modeled the scientific aspect of it on the National Museum in Paris. Labeling of exhibits was done in Latin, French, and English. He was convinced by his readings of Jean-Jacques Rousseau that instructing one's contemporaries was a high cultural ideal. In 1802, the Pennsylvania State House became the repository of the museum's collection when the Pennsylvania legislature relocated to Lancaster. The second-floor displayed specimens of a variety of fossils, insects, birds, reptiles, and minerals, along with the partial skeleton of a mastodon excavated by Peale in New York State in 1801. Peale's 1822 *The Artist in His Museum* portrays the eighty-one-year-old artist inviting the viewer to enter his collection where seventy portraits in two rows hung above the diverse biological and zoological specimens as the culmination of the highest class of

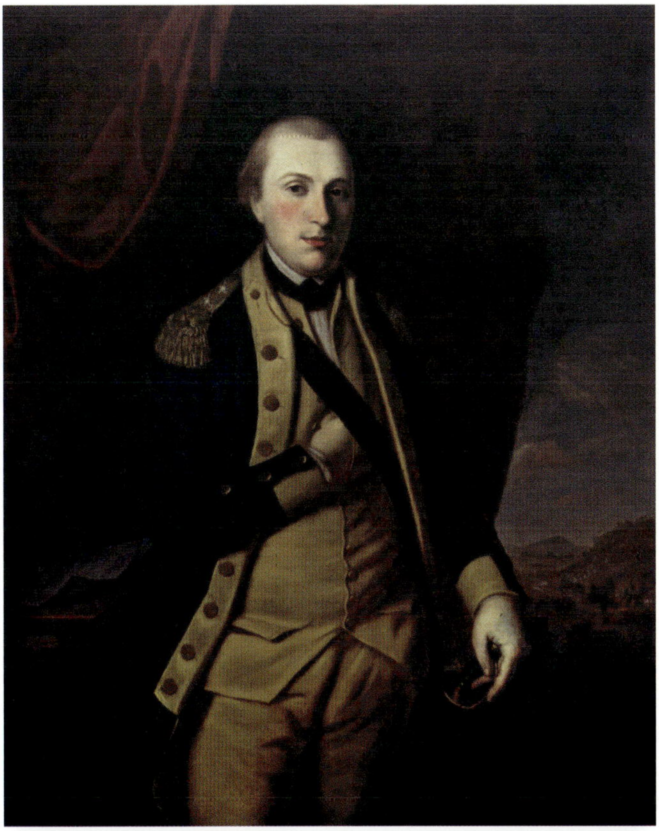

Figure 3.9
Charles Willson Peale, *Portrait of Marquis de Lafayette*, 1779. Oil on canvas, 48.5 × 40 in. (Courtesy of Washington and Lee University, University Collections of Art and History)

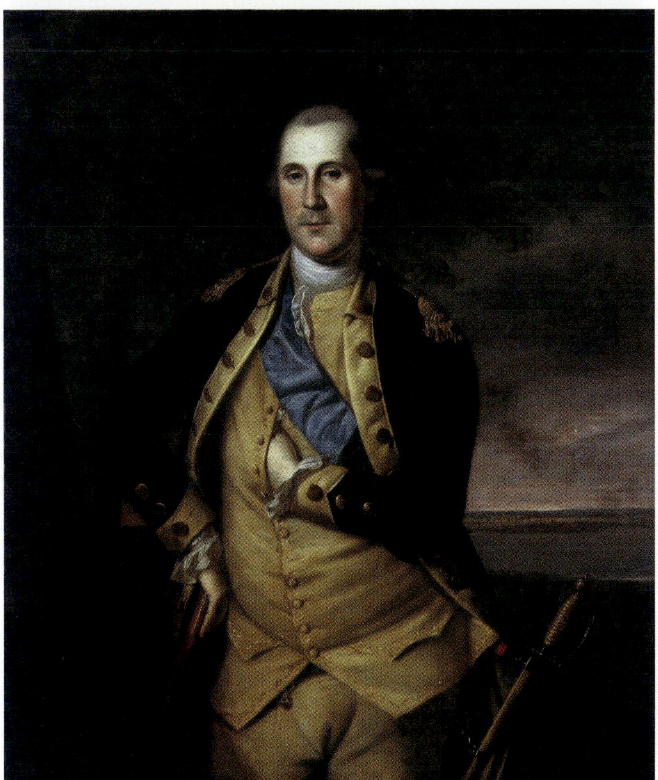

Figure 3.10 Charles Willson Peale, *George Washington*, 1776. Oil on canvas, 44 × 38⁵⁄₁₆ in. (111.7 × 97.3 cm). (Brooklyn Museum, Dick S. Ramsay Fund, 34.1178)

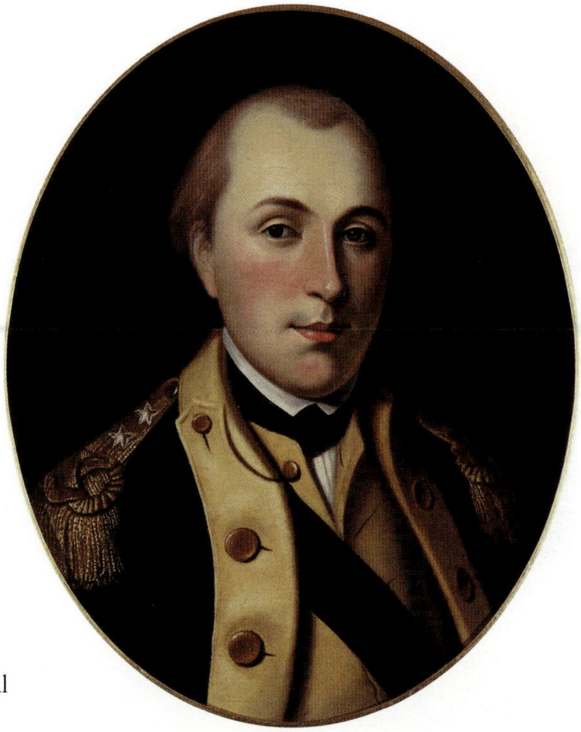

FIGURE 3.11 Charles Willson Peale, *Marquis de Lafayette*, 1781. Oil on canvas, 58.42 × 45.97 cm. (Philadelphia, Independence National Historical Park)

natural beings in the Linnaean system.[34] (See Figure 3.12.) Portrait busts by Houdon and William Rush also had an honored place in his educational display.

John C. Milley has suggested that Peale's self-image may have been influenced by a 1659 engraving of the painting *Cardinal Jules Mazarin Seated within the Gallery of His Palace* by Pierre Mignard, an image that was widely distributed in the seventeenth century.[35] (See Figure 3.13.) Madame Suzanne Necker, wife of the French statesman and finance minister to Louis XVI from 1777 to 1781, had sent Peale a packet of prints that included portraits of her husband and Buffon. Peale had executed prints of his works for public sale and much of his artistic education of older art came from imported prints, of which this may be one.[36] In this print, Mazarin is posed with a globe of the world anchoring the lower left corner of the image, a symbol of the expansion of knowledge of the world from Europe to foreign countries. The left corner of Peale's image holds a turkey and taxidermy tools. Peale learned much about taxidermy from Étienne François Turgot's *Mémoire instructif sur la manière de rassembler, de pré d'envoyer les divers curiosités d'histoire naturelle* (Paris 1758).[37] Using similar skills as the fine art portraitist, the taxidermist sought the most salient features of the species for public display. The world Mazarin lived in, as personified by the globe, saw the expansion of European might over the colonies by means of monarchical power and absolutist rule. The world Peale occupied had recently freed itself from such controls. The turkey and tools on the left side are echoed in shape by his palette and brushes

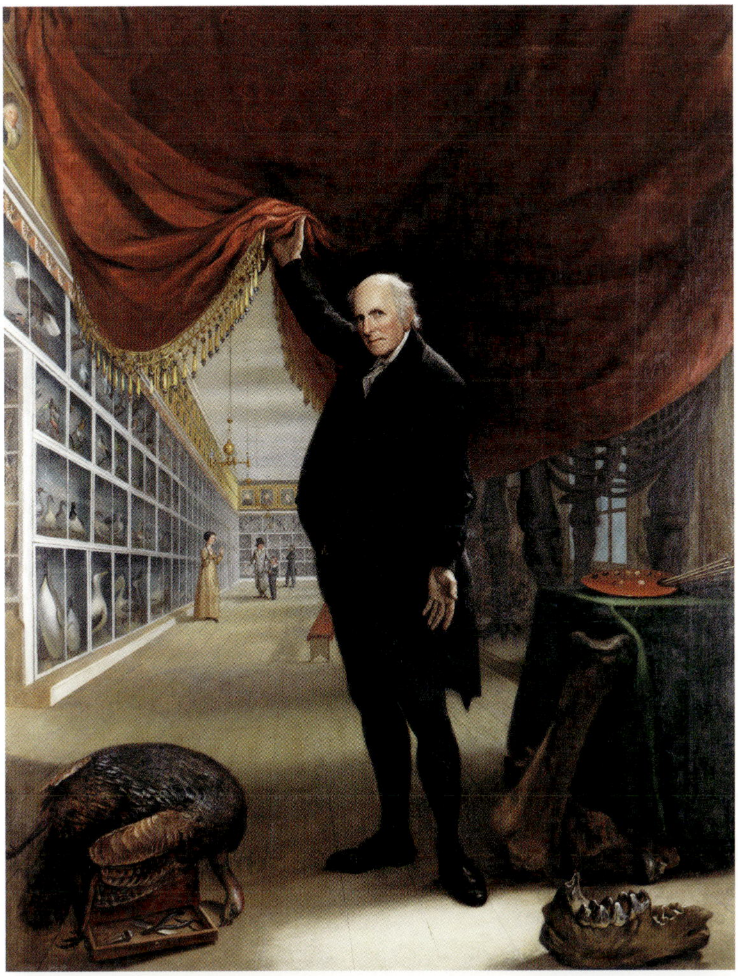

FIGURE 3.12 Charles Willson Peale, *The Artist in His Museum*, 1822. Oil on canvas, 103¾ × 79⅞ in. (263.5 × 202.9 cm). Acc. No.: 1878.1.2. (Courtesy of the Pennsylvania Academy of the Fine Arts, Philadelphia. Gift of Mrs. Sarah Harrison [The Joseph Harrison, Jr. Collection]).

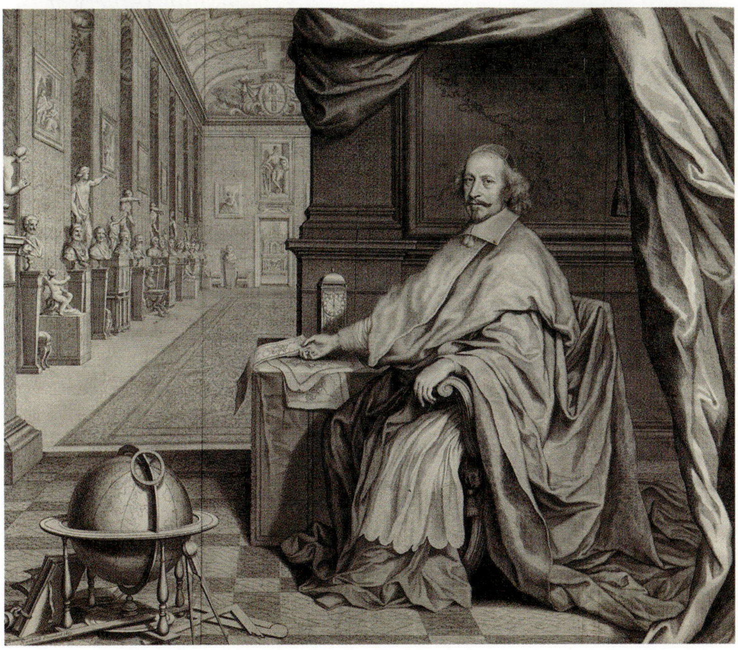

FIGURE 3.13 Robert Nanteuil, *Cardinal Jules Mazarin Seated within the Gallery of His Palace,* 1659. Engraving, 18¹¹⁄₁₆ × 26⁷⁄₁₆ in. (47.5 × 67.1 cm). (Metropolitan Museum of Art, Gift of Lev Tsitrin, 2000)

on the right, symbols of the painter's secular belief in the spirit of inquiry, spurred by Enlightenment ideals and the physical means by which he communicated his ideas to the public.

Peale believed that animal behavior provided a model for an economically productive, socially harmonious, and morally upright republic.[38] The portraits of statesmen and revolutionary heroes topping the specimens from the natural world stood as the apex of the notion of the Great Chain of Being in God's creation. Mazarin sits complacently in his ornate clerical robes with his vast collection of private art behind him in his study. The Cardinal, with the world figuratively at his feet, gazes at the viewer who has seemingly interrupted his reading. Peale, on the other hand, dressed soberly in black colonial garb, stands proudly with a beckoning gesture to welcome his visitor into the New World that summarized his artistic, philosophical, and intellectual pursuits. Mazarin epitomizes French aristocratic privilege in his image; Peale's self-portrait testifies to his effort to create an American culture where art and science served a newly formed nation.

"There is a penchant for our arts, our manners, our language," claimed Constantin François Chasseboeuf, comte de Volney whose portrait Peale painted in 1782.[39] Volney's observation about Philadelphia certainly rang true as the eighteenth century drew to a close, due to the increased presence of the French fleeing their own revolution, as is discussed in the next chapter. Americans returning from France also imported artifacts along with philosophical ideas. Jefferson shipped more than eighty packing crates when he moved from Paris to New York in 1789 to assume his position as the first secretary of state. His five years in France, considered by many historians to be the most memorable of his life, influenced his political ideals and his attitude to the role of the fine arts in a new nation.[40] Busts of John Paul Jones, Lafayette, Franklin, Washington, and his own image by Houdon moved with him from the Hôtel de Langeac in Paris to his home in Monticello, where they joined his collection of portrait miniatures and medals.

Following New York City, Philadelphia served as the nation's capital for the next ten years. When Washington relocated his New York residence from the former home of Elénor-François-Élie, the Marquis de Moustier, he took all the French furnishings with him to Philadelphia. Those visiting the newly inaugurated American president thus ate off of French china while seated on French furniture, surrounded by fine examples of French art.

Peale's portraits of the French joined his images of Americans whose words and deeds shaped the emerging nation. As David Ward observed, Peale's portraits "more than signaled achievement or heroism: they also had an educational and inspirational function, depicting what could be achieved when right-minded individuals, acting according to the dictates of their conscience, aspired toward a larger, transcendent goal."[41] France's impact on the political, social, economic, and religious conditions in America as they occurred in eighteenth-century Philadelphia can be tracked in the sculpture, painting, and architectural treasures that came about through intercontinental diplomacy and opportunity. Franklin had written to Peale in 1771: the "arts have always travelled westward, and there is no doubt of their flourishing hereafter on our side of the Atlantic, as the Number of wealthy inhabitants shall increase, who may be able and willing suitably to reward them, since from several Instances it appears that our People are not deficient in Genius."[42] France's role in the political transition of America from its colonial status to that of an independent nation penetrated the arts in ways that would impact the relations between the two countries well into the following century.

[4]

Federal Philadelphia in the French Revolution

PHILADELPHIA'S DECADE AS THE NATION'S CAPITAL, 1790–1800, corresponded with the most tumultuous social and political change in France's history. Its tremors reverberated loudly in Philadelphia, which, in absorbing many of those displaced from France and its empire, took on a more French coloration than it ever had before. At the same time, the tumult in France thoroughly upset the Franco-American alliance that had been so crucial in achieving the freedom of the United States. The result was more than one diplomatic crisis for the young republic, which nearly plunged the recent allies into war. But in the years immediately preceding, other issues took center stage.

In 1785, when Benjamin Franklin returned home after nearly a decade in France, he had come back to a city that no longer hosted America's political elite and to a new nation that, in spite of its hard-won freedom from British rule, looked as if it might disintegrate. The loose confederation that had emerged from the Second Continental Congress left virtually all political power in the capitals of the thirteen states. The unicameral Congress had no power to levy taxes or to regulate foreign trade or interstate commerce. The Continental Army had nearly starved during the war for independence when funds to supply the troops with basic needs were not forthcoming from the states. With the war concluded, all thirteen maintained militias of their own, and most, their own navies. Army officers, including Washington himself and his top aide, Alexander Hamilton, now were leading the call for a stronger central government.[1] Hamilton organized a convention of delegates to meet for several days in September 1786, in Annapolis. Only a handful of state representatives made the trip, but those that did called for a constitutional convention to meet in Philadelphia in the following year.

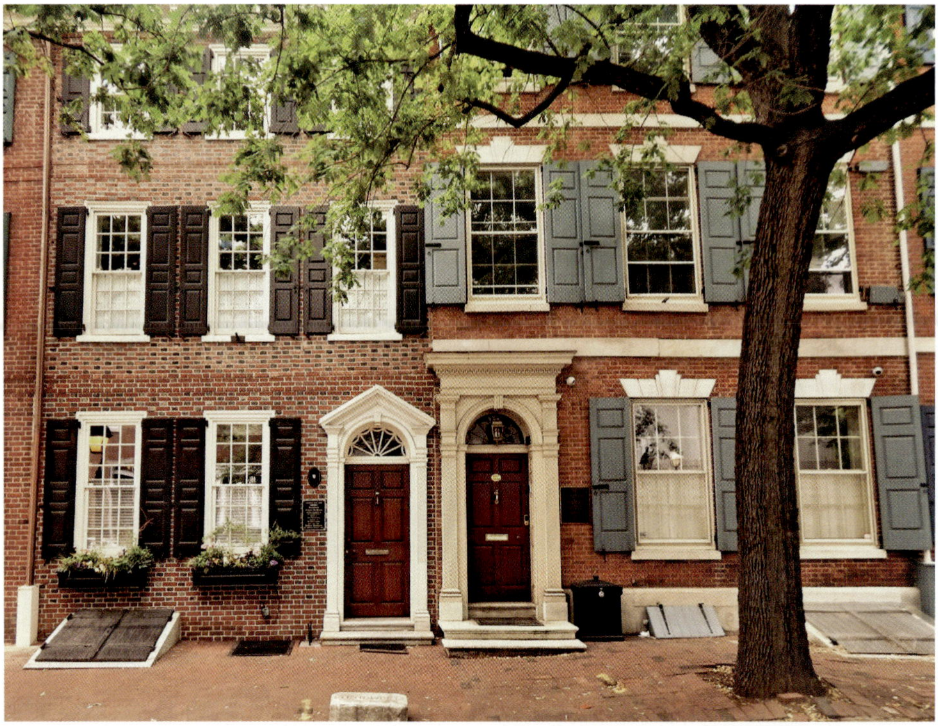

FIGURE 4.1 The house on the left was the Spruce Street residence of James Madison and his wife Dolley in 1796 while Madison served as a Virginia congressman. Next to it on the right was the home of France's consul general to the United States from 1791 to 1793, Williams-Mathurin. It is the sole surviving eighteenth-century diplomatic legation in the United States.

From May until mid-September 1787, Pennsylvania's State House became the birthplace of the second great founding document of the United States of America. The effort to make the young republic succeed by overcoming the weaknesses of the confederation would require, in the view of the delegates, a form of government like nothing ever seen before, a federal or compound system. Sovereignty would be divided between the states and the central government, which would share political power and governmental authority. A thirty-five-year-old Virginian, James Madison (1751–1836), drafted the basic plan for such a system in Philadelphia while he waited for the other delegations to arrive. Madison would be remembered as the father of the Constitution. Yet, the document that finally emerged in September was the product of many minds and the result of compromises that reflected the competing interests of large and small states and the sectional interests of the North and South. (See Figure 4.1.)

Like the Declaration of Independence, the Constitution of the United States was the brainchild of Americans who had read—and interacted with—the leading philosophes of the period. Madison himself was too young to have played a role in drafting the Declaration of Independence. But he had been the student of the Reverend John Witherspoon, the president of the College of New Jersey (today's Princeton University) and one of those signers of the declaration who had been an avid reader of Montesquieu. He was also the protégé of Thomas Jefferson when they both served in the Virginia legislature during the Revolution. After Jefferson became the American minister to France, he shipped boxes of the writings of the philosophes and others back to Madison, who absorbed their ideas on the various forms of government.[2] The youngest of these French intellectuals, the Marquis de Condorcet, was eight years older than Madison (as was Jefferson) and had already made a name for himself as the first to appreciate the application of quantitative methods to the study of politics. He would go on to leave as his greatest legacy what has been called the most influential formulation of the idea of progress ever written.[3] Condorcet and Jefferson met frequently in Paris, and the Frenchman's pamphlets on politics were among the writings Jefferson sent to Madison. Years before, Condorcet had struck up a correspondence with Franklin in Philadelphia, addressing him as *mon cher et illustre confrère*, so the two met as friends in Paris. They were dinner companions at the home of Madame Helvétius, where Franklin was a frequent visitor. Other guests at her salons included Louis XVI's former minister of finance, Turgot; Diderot, the *Encyclopédiste*; and the mathematician d'Alembert.[4] Republicanism, free trade, the rule of reason, and the rights of man were among their topics of conversation.

While Jefferson did not participate in the Constitutional Convention because of his assignment in France, his connections to Madison surely made his influence felt. When Franklin, the elder statesman among the delegates, became involved in the preparations for the meeting, he created a Society for Political Inquiry, which met weekly in the newly enlarged library of his house on Market Street. Among those who attended was George Washington, whom Franklin had persuaded to leave Mount Vernon to come to Philadelphia and involve himself in the deliberations at the State House. When it came to choosing a man to preside over the convention, Franklin and Washington were the two obvious candidates. Franklin deferred to the general, perhaps partly out of consideration for his own age and infirmities but mostly from his reckoning that Washington's stature as the military hero of the Revolution would boost the morale of all who hoped to create a stronger union.[5]

Once the Constitution was hammered out, it had to be ratified by the governments of nine of the thirteen states before it could come into effect. The debate over ratification played out between Federalists and anti-Federalists across the nation. By far the most important of the polemics in favor of the new arrangement came in what today we know as *The Federalist Papers*, a collection of eighty-five essays and articles published serially in two New York newspapers under the anonymous authorship of "Publius." The authors in fact were Alexander Hamilton, James Madison, and John Jay. Their arguments remain the standard for understanding the intent and philosophy underlying the Constitution and are, no doubt, the most important political essays ever penned in America. Number ten, by Madison, may be the most philosophical of the lot. It discusses how to prevent self-interested factions (i.e., "those activated by some common impulse of passion") from running roughshod over the well-being of the larger community. His solution is found in the representative structure of the proposed republic, because elected representatives are at one remove from factional interests and must be accountable to their larger constituencies. Scholars see the influence here of Condorcet, who developed a theory of social choice that supports the same republican argument.[6]

After the requisite number of states ratified the Constitution, the first national election was held. The members of the Electoral College met to cast their ballots for president of the United States on February 4, 1789. Their unanimous choice was George Washington. Following his inauguration in New York City on April 30, Washington set out to invent the office of the presidency.

The government would remain in New York for the next sixteen months and then move to Philadelphia in November 1790. At the time, this most cosmopolitan and central city in the new republic was the choice of many to become the nation's permanent capital. In the three years since the Constitution was created at the State House, two new wings had been added to that building. On the west side, what had been intended to house the Philadelphia County court was hastily remodeled to become Congress Hall, where the House of Representatives would meet on the ground floor and the Senate in the chamber above. On the east side of the State House, the new city hall became the home of the U.S. Supreme Court. The city began construction of a presidential palace on Ninth Street in the hope of derailing the recent plan to build a new capital farther south. (See Figure 4.2.)

That plan had been the centerpiece of a deal worked out by contending figures in the federal government several months before the capital moved from New York to Philadelphia. The secretary of the treasury, Alexander Hamilton, had been unable to persuade his colleague Thomas Jefferson, Washington's secretary of state, and Representative James Madison to accept his plan for the Treasury to assume the debts of the states, and thereby establish a strongly centralized mercantile state. During the work of the First Congress, that Assumption Bill had failed twice in the House of Representatives, thanks to Southern opposition. Then, an elegant and French-inspired private dinner hosted by Jefferson at his New York residence in June 1790 became the catalyst for compromise. That meal had been prepared by Jefferson's slave, James Hemings, whom Jefferson had taken with him to Paris in 1784 expressly to be apprenticed to a French chef so that he might learn French cooking.[7] Madison agreed that he would not again lead the opposition to the Assumption Bill when it came before the House of Representatives for a third time. In exchange, Hamilton agreed to concede to the strong desire of the Southerners to establish the permanent U.S. capital along the Potomac River border between Maryland and Virginia. That concession would gratify the South and permanently remove the capital from the nation's financial center, Philadelphia, thereby deferring at least symbolically to the Jeffersonian vision of a largely agricultural nation of yeoman farmers. The target date for such a move was set at 1800. Philadelphia would remain the political, social, and economic capital of the United States for just one more decade.[8]

Meanwhile, in the months when the new constitutional system was being fleshed out in America, revolution broke out in Paris. The electrifying event was the storming

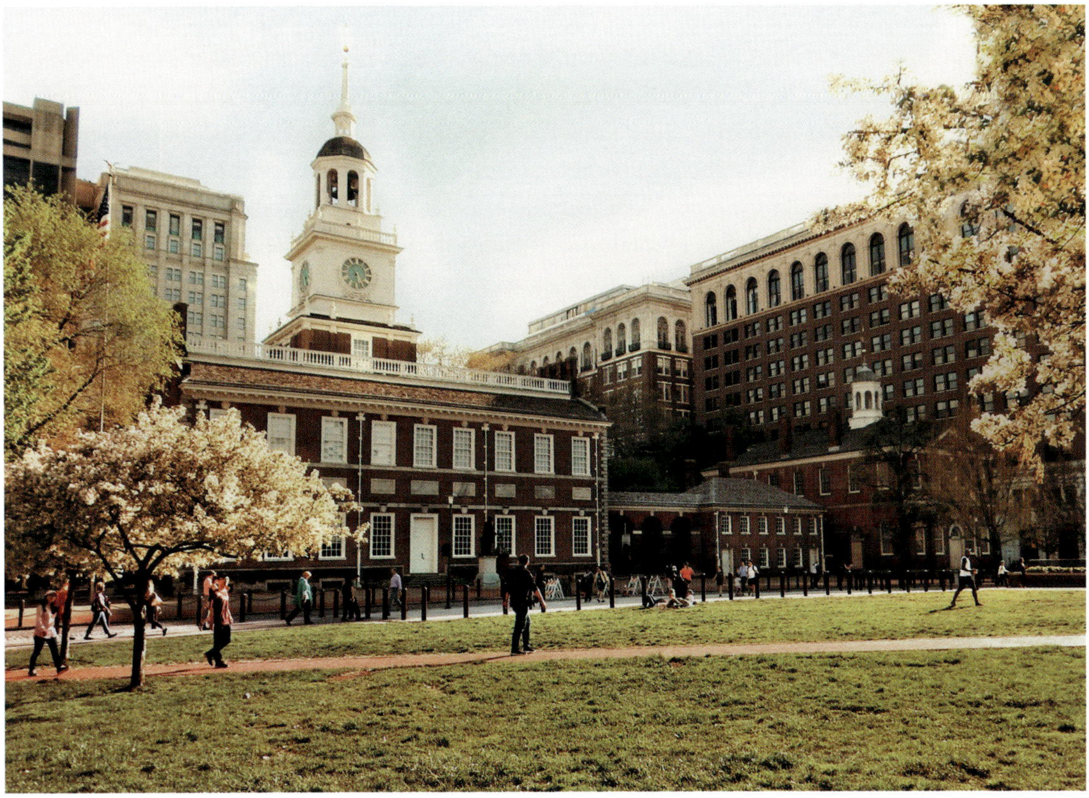

Figure 4.2 During the decade 1790–1800, when Philadelphia was the nation's capital, the U.S. Congress met in Congress Hall, the building topped by a small cupola on the right. The House of Representatives met on the ground floor, the Senate on the second floor. Independence Hall is the larger building on the left.

of the notorious Bastille prison, on July 14, 1789.[9] The next day, Lafayette was named commandant-general of the National Guard of Paris by the body of commoners and their friends among the clergy and aristocracy that had declared itself the National Assembly. Thanks to the fame and goodwill Lafayette had acquired among progressives because of what he had done for the American Revolution, he was an obvious choice to maintain order while supporting reform. He would play one of the leading roles during the French Revolution's first two years, which was the period when reform of the old order remained the goal of leading revolutionaries. The previous May, Jefferson—who would not leave his post as minister to France until October—had witnessed the opening ceremony of the Estates General in Versailles and watched the dramatic events that soon produced a National Assembly determined to create a constitution for the nation. In his farewell to France, he joined Lafayette and Condorcet to collaborate in drafting a document that set out the Enlightenment gospel of natural rights. Jefferson's own stamp was evident on all of it. Lafayette would introduce that document, the Declaration of the Rights of Man and the Citizen, to the assembly for its adoption in August 1789.[10]

If, within the next year or two, the French Revolution had succeeded at creating a constitutional system that satisfied most of the French people, its government might then have looked very much like that of the United States after 1789, albeit one with a constitutional monarch. Like Lafayette, virtually all the other liberal aristocrats who were the leaders of the initial phase of the revolution idealized the new American republic and sought to replicate it in France. Both nations declared that sovereignty rested in the people, while proclaiming the idea of the equality of all.[11] By June 1789, in response to the demand for a bill of rights to be included in the U.S. Constitution, such measures were introduced in Congress as the first ten amendments to the Constitution. The French declaration, in contrast, was adopted before the French republic's founding laws were established, which made them largely aspirational rather than part of the bedrock of the constitution. Yet, the impact of the American Revolution upon the French was clear to all. Both came out of the shared intellectual heritage of the Enlightenment and the writings of the philosophes.[12]

But the French Revolution did *not* end at a point when its outcome might have resembled that in America. Its original leaders, members of the elite, were overthrown by more radical figures backed by revolutionary hordes, especially in Paris. The most fortunate of those pushed aside survived prison or exile, while many more were slaughtered. (See Figure 4.3.) There was no turning back to the revolution's moderate phase after the king and queen tried to flee France, in June 1791, but were caught, brought back to Paris, and eventually imprisoned. Lafayette, still viewed by the right as a dangerous revolutionary, was increasingly vilified by the radical left as the protector of the monarchy. Robespierre called him a traitor for not having prevented the king's flight.[13] In 1792, France made war on Austria and Prussia when their rulers threatened to intervene in support of Louis XVI. Lafayette was made one of three generals—Rochambeau was another—whose armies were deployed to defend the frontier. Yet as the nation grew more divided, Lafayette's position became untenable. When he denounced the Jacobins, Danton ordered his arrest. By the late summer of 1792, Lafayette tried to make his way to America but was taken prisoner by Austrian forces. He remained a prisoner of the Austrian Empire for the next five years.[14]

On January 21, 1793, months after Lafayette was captured, Louis XVI was led to the guillotine. The upheaval launched by the revolution would play out over an additional two decades and more. France's military adventurism in Europe continued until the downfall in 1815 of the strongman who came to power at the end of the previous century, declared the French Revolution at an end, and tried to conquer much of the continent. The turmoil in France soon made Philadelphia a place of refuge for French people in exile. By 1792, the revolution also produced a slave insurrection in France's richest possession in the New World, Saint-Domingue, which brought another flight of French colonists to Philadelphia. France's upheaval also infected American politics throughout the last decade of the eighteenth century and reordered the nation's foreign policy during the decade in which Philadelphia was the nation's capital. By 1793, the European wars of the French Revolution would present the first major

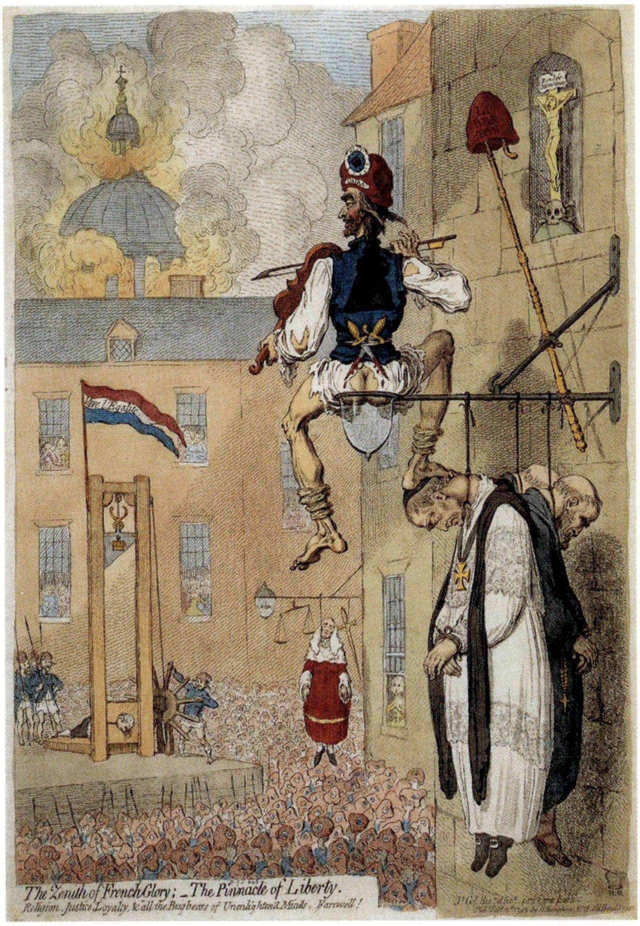

FIGURE 4.3 James Gillray, *The Zenith of French Glory—All the Bugbears of Unenlightened Minds—Farewell*, 1779–1895. Caricature. Accessed April 29, 2019. (The Miriam and Ira D. Wallach Division of Art, Prints and Photographs: Print Collection, The New York Public Library. New York Public Library Digital Collections.)

foreign policy challenge to President Washington. For a time, however, because of the vast ocean between America and Europe, those conflicts were like distant thunder.

In America, less than two weeks before Louis XVI was beheaded in Paris, the nation's top officials and common citizens alike gathered in Philadelphia to witness an event that impressed them not with France's troubles but with its technological prowess. On the morning of January 9, 1793, a magnificent balloon slowly rose from behind the wall enclosing the large courtyard of the Walnut Street Prison. Across that street to the north stood the State House and to the west across Sixth Street lay Southeast Square (today's Washington Square), where dead prisoners and soldiers killed in the Revolutionary War were buried in trenches. The diminutive man in the basket lifted by the balloon was Jean-Pierre Blanchard, who, along with the Montgolfier brothers, had repeatedly thrilled Parisians with this new invention. Benjamin Franklin had witnessed one balloon flight from his residence in Passy. This was the first time such a spectacle had been seen in America, and it attracted a crowd that filled the streets around the prison where the leaders of the nation were prominently assembled. In addition to President and Mrs. Washington and Vice President John Adams, three others were present who would also become presidents of the United States: Thomas Jefferson, James Madison, and James Monroe. Members of the growing French community were also among the dignitaries.[15]

For many, perhaps most, in the crowd, the display seemed a brilliant confirmation of France's progress in science as well as in politics, since France had followed the American example and overthrown tyranny. Yet, for the French minister in attendance, Jean-Baptiste de Ternant, the moment was filled with tension. Only days earlier had he learned of the murderous turn of the French Revolution during the past summer. Ternant himself had been Louis XVI's representative to the federal government in Philadelphia since August 1791. A dozen years earlier, he had served under Baron von Steuben as a soldier in the American Revolution. Lafayette had recommended him to Washington, who considered him "an old friend."[16] Now, on this January morning, Ternant was almost the last official anywhere on earth who still seemingly represented the now-extinguished ancien régime.[17]

The balloon was gradually inflated until it came into view above the wall. Once Blanchard indicated that he was ready, President Washington presented him with a passport he had written himself. Should his balloon descend where frightened and uninformed Americans might seek to do him harm, Washington begged them to "oppose no hindrance or molestation" to the Frenchman or his conveyance. The balloonist—who spoke no English—also had thought to carry a bottle of wine to show his hospitality to whatever strangers he might encounter in some distant place. Once he was safely aboard, he threw off the ballast and doffed his plumed hat as his conveyance lifted him above the scene. As one observer reported in a Philadelphia newspaper, "It was indeed a spectacle as magnificent as it was new to us, to see this intrepid aeronaut majestically rise from the earth."[18]

Blanchard's balloon carried him high above the city. He drifted first toward Philadelphia's northern limits beyond Vine Street before reaching the Delaware. Shifting winds then drew him south along the river for a time until he floated across it into New Jersey. After a flight of less than an hour, he descended gently next to a wooded area near Woodbury, New Jersey. A team was brought to help fold the balloon and load it onto a wagon. Blanchard shared his bottle with excited locals and then returned in triumph to Philadelphia before the day was out.

Some two months later, President Washington took the oath of office for the second time. His next, and last, four years in office would be dominated by events that had their origin in revolutionary France and divided the American nation, testing the president's leadership of the young republic. Yet, even while his and the nation's next agenda were being put into place, Philadelphia was suddenly visited by a natural catastrophe that terrified the city.

In the early days of August, yellow fever broke out when a ship sailed up the Delaware, docked at a city wharf, and released *Aedes aegypti* mosquitoes it had unknowingly carried from its starting point at an island off the coast of Africa. Once free to feast in Philadelphia's crowded streets, the mosquitoes soon took their deadly toll. Several lodgers at a boardinghouse were the first victims. Before the month was out, more than three hundred people had died, while all who had the means to do so fled the city in terror. President Washington, his family, and whatever part of the federal government that was still functioning decamped to Germantown. September brought more than a thousand additional deaths in Philadelphia; October, nearly two thousand. Meanwhile, nearly half the city's population had fled to other locations, leaving mostly poor citizens behind, many to become victims. Cooler weather and a frost, on October 27, finally began to kill the mosquitoes, and the epidemic gradually subsided. By the time it ended with the coming of winter, between four thousand and five thousand people had died, nearly 10 percent of Philadelphia's population.[19]

It was not yet understood that the disease was carried by mosquitoes. Frightened Philadelphians assumed their health was threatened by the generally squalid conditions along the waterfront, including refuse rotting in the streets. Many blamed the increased number of exiles pouring into the port from the upheavals in Saint-Domingue, for some of the displaced had indeed been aboard the ship that carried the mosquitoes, which had picked up passengers in the Caribbean, and were no doubt infected when they arrived.

Among those Philadelphians who refused to flee but stayed and tried to help the victims was a French immigrant who had established himself in the city nearly two decades earlier. Stephen (Étienne) Girard's (1750–1831) role was heroic during the weeks the epidemic brought terror to the city. He had arrived in Philadelphia largely by accident in the late spring of 1776, soon after representatives from all the colonies convened at the State House to consider independence. He in fact had intended to sail the merchant ship that he commanded to New York, but the British were tightening their blockade of American ports along the Atlantic. His schooner had also suffered considerable damage from a recent storm at sea. So, he turned up Delaware Bay and headed for Philadelphia instead. He would call Philadelphia home for the rest of his long life. A native of Bordeaux, Girard was already a seasoned seaman when he arrived in his adoptive city at age twenty-six and a man who was acquiring skills as a merchant and businessman. By the time of the yellow fever outbreak, he had become one of Philadelphia's leading citizens, trading across the world as the master of a fleet of merchant ships: *Montesquieu*, *Rousseau*, and *Voltaire* were the names he had given three of his vessels. (See Figure 4.4.)

When yellow fever broke out and other members of Philadelphia's elite fled the city, Girard stayed in Philadelphia and proceeded to assist the victims. He took charge of transforming an estate just outside the city's boundary, Bush Hill, into a hospital. He recruited staff and personally took on many of the menial tasks involved in caring for the sick and dying. Once the crisis subsided, Girard was acclaimed as a hero in a meeting at City Hall. It would not be the last time this French American citizen would come to the rescue in a way that would leave his mark on Philadelphia and the nation.[20] Girard's leadership in battling yellow fever was well supported by the assistance he got from several French physicians recently arrived in Philadelphia from the upheavals in France and the Caribbean. Unlike Philadelphia's own leading doctor,

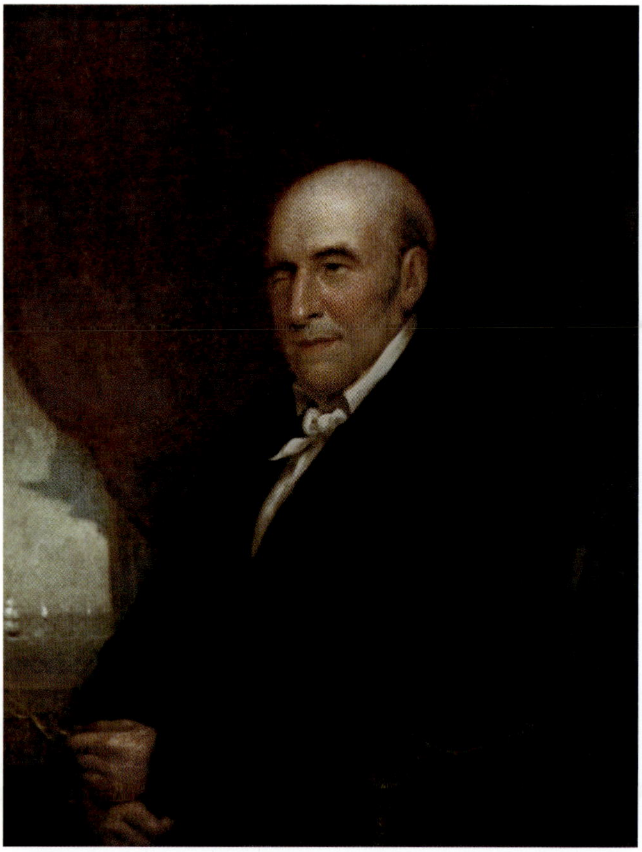

FIGURE 4.4
James Reid Lambdin, from a posthumous portrait by Bass Otis, *Stephen Girard*, in *The Life and Times of Stephen Girard, mariner and merchant*, 1918. One of Philadelphia's leading citizens at the time yellow fever decimated Philadelphia in 1793, Stephen Girard had emigrated from France nearly two decades earlier. By the time of his death in 1831, he was Philadelphia's greatest philanthropist and the nation's wealthiest citizen.

Benjamin Rush, who insisted on bleeding and purging the afflicted, the French doctors engaged in milder medicinal treatments with the result that many more of their patients survived. Among these exiles, Dr. Jean Devèze became the most important champion of these gentler techniques once the city established a quarantine center. He would eventually be recognized as one of the world's leading authorities on yellow fever.[21]

By the time of Washington's second inauguration, Louis XVI was dead, the monarchy abolished, and revolutionary France's wars in Europe included Great Britain as its adversary. Washington, with his cabinet's approval, proclaimed the neutrality of the United States. It would prove to be a difficult and controversial policy to maintain at a time when passions were already aroused in America at the news of the birth of a second republic, one at least initially inspired by the American example. For the most pro-French factions, American neutrality was a betrayal of the Franco-American alliance and gave tacit support to, because it did not oppose, the British monarchy from which the nation had so recently been liberated. Stephen Girard was one of those who loudly voiced his objection to the president's policy. On the other side were those who supposed that this nation's long-term interest was to continue to mend fences with the former mother country in the interests of peace and the cultivation of trade.[22]

The trigger for Washington's Proclamation of Neutrality came after the arrival of France's new minister. Soon after the previous representative, Jean-Baptiste de Ternant, had watched Blanchard rise into the winter sky over Philadelphia, he was recalled by the Girondins, who were determined to remind America of its obligation, as the revolutionaries saw it, to support France in its conflict with Britain. They replaced Ternant with a young member of the bourgeoisie, Edmond-Charles Genet. Citizen Genet, as he would become known, was blithely—even recklessly—determined to involve the United States in the war as the partner of France. On his voyage to America, Genet's ship captured an English brig near Bermuda and sailed with it into Charleston harbor as its prize, arriving there on April 8, 1793. Before he left that port, he commissioned four privateers to attack British merchant ships in the Caribbean. From Charleston, Genet's prolonged procession toward the nation's capital was, as he reported to the French foreign minister, "an uninterrupted succession of civic *fêtes*, and my entry into Philadelphia a triumph for liberty."[23] As he traveled, confirming the victories of French forces in Europe, many Americans greeted him with the new French *tricoulure* (an emblem that Lafayette had created) stuck in their lapels.

Arriving in Philadelphia in mid-May, he openly recruited Americans to join the French navy in the fight against Britain. He encouraged the establishment of pro-French Democratic Societies in American cities. Breaking all the rules of diplomacy, Genet's enthusiasm for his cause was so great that he spoke of stirring up the Canadians to throw off British rule and made plans to invade Spanish Louisiana. His dispatch to the French government of May 31, 1793, was exultant: "All America has risen up to recognize in me the Minister of the French Republic: the voice of the People continues to neutralize President Washington's declaration of neutrality. I live here amid perpetual feasts."[24] (See Figure 4.5.)

Washington grew alarmed. He and members of his administration increasingly feared that Genet's excitement of pro-French mobs would pull the nation into war in spite of his proclaimed policy. Some, Vice President John Adams among them, even feared that Washington might be bodily dragged from office by an inflamed public. Genet called on the president at his residence on High (today's Market) Street but argued with him when the chief executive demanded that the minister of France respect the nation's neutrality. Washington then sent Genet a long letter outlining the ways in which the minister's behavior was endangering the United States. Critically, that letter was sent on the joint advice of Jefferson and Hamilton, who otherwise remained adversaries within the president's cabinet. It was a defining moment in the history of the United States. Genet embodied the revolutionary sentiment that saw the republicanism of France and America as making them effectively one nation. Yet American officials, including such fervent republicans as Jefferson, knew that their first responsibility was to their own sovereign country rather than Enlightenment ideals. Months after the new ambassador's arrival, when his efforts to drag the young nation into France's wars had further inflamed the public, Washington demanded Genet's recall.[25]

Meanwhile, the most radical of the Jacobins had taken power in Paris in January 1794. In agreeing to Washington's demand, they ordered Genet to return to France.

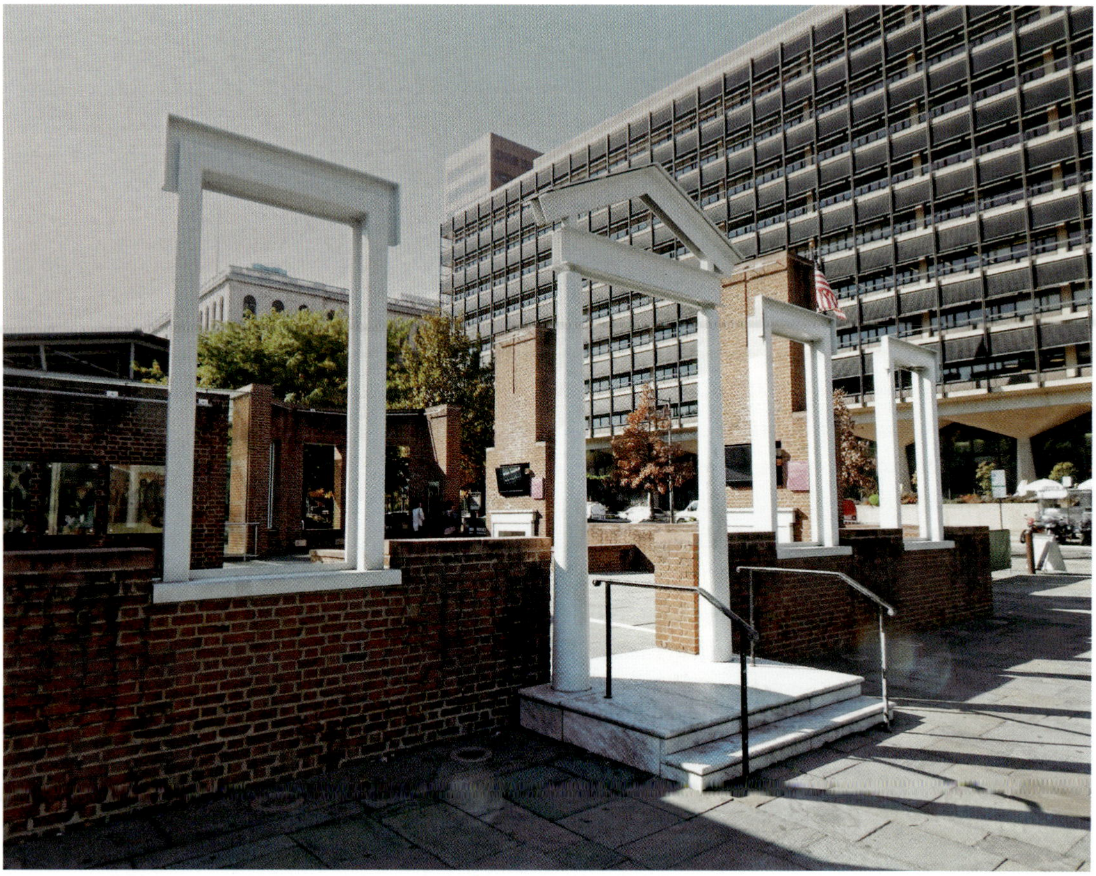

FIGURE 4.5 The large townhouse at Sixth and Market Street that became the home of the nation's first two presidents, George Washington and John Adams, was razed in the nineteenth century. Late in the twentieth, its suggested outlines were reconstructed adjoining a new Liberty Bell pavilion. Here Washington met with Citizen Genet and then demanded his recall.

Now Genet feared for his life at the hands of his own government, and he pleaded for asylum in America. Hamilton, his most fervent opponent in the cabinet, counseled Washington to allow him to stay. That permission granted, Genet's time at the center of the political vortex in America came to an end. He lived out the rest of his life as a gentleman farmer in upstate New York, marrying first the daughter of Governor George Clinton and, after her death, the daughter of the first postmaster general of the United States.[26]

A footnote to the Genet affair unexpectedly embroiled another distinguished Frenchman in American politics, at least for a time. André Michaux (1746–1802) had been appointed the royal botanist by Louis XVI and sent to the United States in 1785 to investigate native plants and determine how they might be of value in France. For the next six years, Michaux traveled with his young son throughout the nation and into Canada, researching the continent's plant life. He shipped some ninety crates of plants and seeds back to France. Along the way, he introduced the camellia, crape myrtle, and other plants to North America. With the fall of the monarchy in France, Michaux appealed to Thomas Jefferson for support from the American Philosophical Society. In 1793, Jefferson initiated a subscription within the society to finance an expedition in which Michaux might carry on his botanical studies in the west. Before he set out, however, Michaux volunteered to help Genet evaluate a scheme to raise a militia that might seize Louisiana territory from the Spanish. With that assignment, he went to Kentucky with Jefferson's knowledge, but without his approval, to assist Genet in the Louisiana effort. Meanwhile, news of his Louisiana scheme was bringing Genet into greater censure by the Washington administration. Michaux's role in it ended along with Genet's inability to raise the funds needed to recruit the militia. The would-be botanical expedition to the west also was aborted.[27]

In 1796, Michaux returned to France. But he left behind botanical gardens in New Jersey and near Charleston, South Carolina. Early in the nineteenth century, Michaux's son, François André (1770–1855), would return to America and carry on his father's work. In 1815 in Philadelphia, Southeast Square was declared a park. Ten years later, it was renamed for Washington and landscaped to resemble the downtown park still much in use today. Michaux fils was responsible for that redesign and for planting hundreds of trees there.[28] He continued his father's botanical studies and left a monumental work on the forest trees of America. At his death in 1855, he left a bequest to the American Philosophical Society. Several years later, that gift became the source of a memorial to father and son when some forty-four species of oak were planted at a site only recently incorporated into the newly expanded Fairmount Park west of the Schuylkill River. Established in 1870–1871, that grove and its descendants are now known to park visitors as Michaux Walk.[29] (See Figure 4.6.)

The end of the Citizen Genet controversy made clear that America's gratitude to France for its support during the Revolutionary War did not mean that the two countries would be perpetually joined when confronting the rest of the world. Genet and his supporters had in effect called for a revolutionary change in the conduct of world politics, wherein sovereign nations might virtually merge their sovereignty in the name of a shared ideology. President Washington's resistance was based on the traditional principle of statehood that independent states should never permanently combine their national interests or cede their authority to other nations. America's neutrality carried the day in 1793 and became the linchpin of American foreign policy. Washington's warning to the nation in his farewell address to refrain from entangling alliances remained dogma for the next century and a half. It also marked the beginning of the end of an era in which the democratic idealism that had briefly seized two nations seemed poised to transform the international system itself.

Still, at the personal level, ties forged with the French during the American Revolution continued to matter to important individuals while Philadelphia remained the nation's capital. Word reached the city that Lafayette had been moved to a prison in Austria and that his wife Adrienne and their two daughters were imprisoned in France. After their initial house arrest, the mother and girls were transferred during

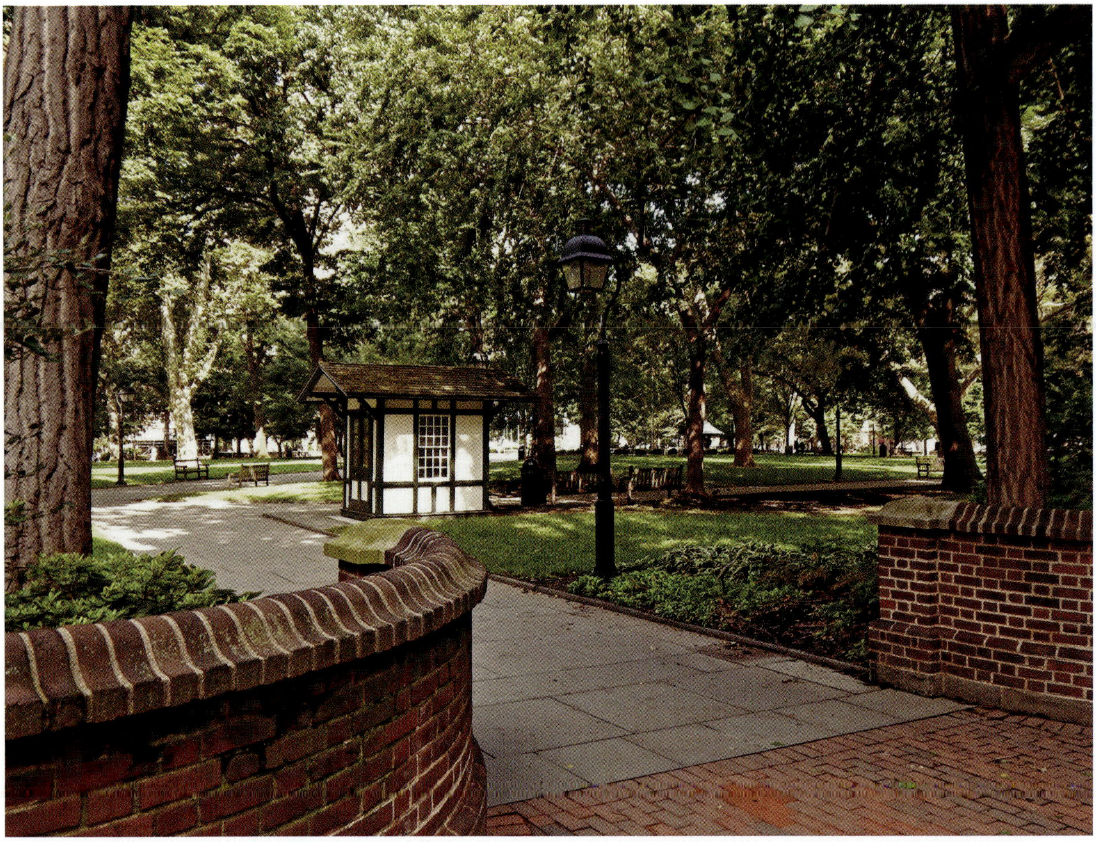

FIGURE 4.6 In the 1820s, François André Michaux redesigned and planted Washington Square, one of the original such open spaces laid out by William Penn in the 1680s. The square largely retains the Michaux design to the present day.

the Reign of Terror to La Force prison in Paris. They barely escaped the guillotine. Adrienne's mother, grandmother, and sister were not so fortunate; all three women were executed in July 1794 in the last days of Robespierre's rule. Meanwhile, Secretary of State Jefferson persuaded Congress to enact legislation allowing Lafayette to be paid for his services to the United States from 1777 to 1783. Once Robespierre himself was executed and the Reign of Terror ended, these funds eventually allowed the marquis and his family certain privileges while they remained incarcerated.

Their situation had been carefully watched, first, by the American minister to France, Gouverneur Morris, and, starting in 1794, by his successor, James Monroe. Monroe's wife visited Adrienne in prison. A plan was developed once Adrienne and her daughters were released in January 1795. Monroe was able to obtain passports from Connecticut for the Lafayette women, which had granted citizenship to the whole family.[30] Adrienne and the girls made their way to Vienna where they were given an audience with the Holy Roman emperor Francis II. He granted the request of the marquis that she and her daughters might join Lafayette in prison. They did so on

October 15, 1795, and the family lived together there for the next two years. A rising young French general, Napoleon Bonaparte, negotiated their release on September 19, 1797. Under Austrian escort, the family was handed over to the U.S. consul in Hamburg two weeks later.

With the rest of his family imprisoned, the fifteen-year-old Georges Washington Lafayette had been sent into hiding with his tutor at the start of the Terror. In April 1795, with help from American officials in Paris, he was smuggled out of the country to the United States. For much of the next three years, he would be a student at Harvard. Soon after his arrival in America, he was Washington's house guest in the presidential residence on the corner of Sixth and High Streets in Philadelphia. After Washington retired from office in March 1797, the young man visited him at Mount Vernon, where Washington must have taken special pleasure in the company of his namesake, and the son of the man who had been like a son to him. Once word was received that the rest of the Lafayette family were free at last, Georges returned to France in 1798.[31]

During that fraught decade in which Philadelphia was the nation's capital, French immigrants poured into the city, transforming it as never before. Although it was already the most cosmopolitan city in North America, it had been overwhelmingly an English settlement prior to the Revolution, with German-speaking immigrants creating communities they dominated, such as Germantown, close by. French immigrants in the previous century had largely been peasant farmers or other rural poor. Some were Huguenots, some Quakers; all were drawn to America by the promise of religious freedom and greater liberty. Seldom did they settle in Philadelphia or other urban centers. The upheaval that transformed France in the 1790s also brought a slave insurrection in Saint-Domingue with sweeping consequences for that island close to America's shores. Refugees from the Caribbean as well as from France itself were flung like storm-tossed birds to Philadelphia. In 1790, the city's population totaled just over forty-four thousand. Halfway through the next decade, with immigration surging, the French consul estimated the number of French people in Philadelphia at five thousand, or more than one in ten residents.[32]

Among those displaced persons were a great many in dire straits. Early in 1793, the first French organization to be created in the United States was founded by elite members of the French community in the city. The purpose of the French Benevolent Society of Philadelphia [La Société de Bienfaisance de Philadelphie] was to assist those residents of French extraction, mostly refugees from the upheavals in France and Saint-Domingue, who "have been . . . reduced to want by misfortune and not by bad conduct." Within months of the society's formation, the yellow fever outbreak hit French-speaking residents particularly hard, with more than 20 percent of those newly arrived in Philadelphia affected. From the time of that first crisis until the mid-twentieth century, the society served as the principal charity serving Philadelphia's French community by providing its members with economic advice and assistance.[33]

Revolutionary forces had cast French people from all walks of life into the port of Philadelphia. Even so, when the upheaval in France grew more radical, it was the upper classes who were mainly targeted. That was also true of many of those who fled Saint-Domingue, who were largely the privileged owners and managers of France's most productive colony, grown rich on the backs of slaves. But also from France came some of the liberal-minded aristocrats who had been driven out by the revolution they initially had led. Several of those who would land in Philadelphia had been born into the highest echelons of the French aristocracy, which was sufficient reason for the radicals now in charge of the revolution to regard them as enemies. Some of them had first taken refuge in England. But when the revolution turned more violent in France, the early refugees were joined by thousands more desperate people from all segments of society who fled across the English Channel into Britain. Once word reached London that Louis XVI had been executed and that the French had invaded Belgium, the government of the British Crown, fearing that revolution might come to its own soil, prepared to enter the war against France. At that point, the liberal French aristocrats who had become exiles there were viewed as a dangerous presence. Several of the most prominent among them saw that their most obvious haven was the United States.[34]

One of these already knew the country well, for he had served alongside his brother-in-law, the Marquis de Lafayette, and represented the government of Louis XVI in negotiating the surrender of Cornwallis and his army at Yorktown in 1781. The Viscount Louis-Marie Marc Antoine de Noailles (1756–1804) had become a close friend of Alexander Hamilton and an admirer of General Washington during his time in America. Back home in France, he served in the *Assemblée constituante* at the start of the French Revolution. In August 1789, as president of the assembly, he enthusiastically proposed eliminating all inherited privileges. By the time war broke out between France and Prussia in 1791, Noailles was a *maréchal* in the French army. But increasingly he recognized the danger stemming from his social position, relationship to the court (he had been a frequent dance partner of Marie-Antoinette in the 1780s), and the greater radicalism of the new French leaders. He had left his family to take up residence in England. No longer welcome there, he fled to Philadelphia, arriving in May 1793.[35]

Nearly a year later, another French refugee of impeccable birth and a less than impeccable reputation also came ashore in Philadelphia. Unlike the tall and heroically handsome Noailles, Charles-Maurice de Talleyrand-Périgord (1754–1838) was small, lean, and lame—*le diable boiteux* (lame devil) was one of his nicknames—and a man with a surprising résumé. Ordained a priest at twenty-five, he almost immediately became the representative to the crown of the French Catholic Church. A bishop at thirty-five, he represented the First Estate of the clergy at the meeting of the Estates General, which spawned the revolution. Yet, there he threw his support behind anticlericalism and, with Mirabeau, organized the appropriation of church properties. For that, Pope Pius VI excommunicated him in 1791. But a year later, like Noailles, he feared arrest by the new revolutionary establishment and fled to England. By 1794, he, too, was forced from that place of exile and set sail for America.[36] (See Figure 4.7.)

In the same period, other men of comparable rank, forced to flee the revolution they had helped launch, found themselves washed up in Philadelphia. Among any

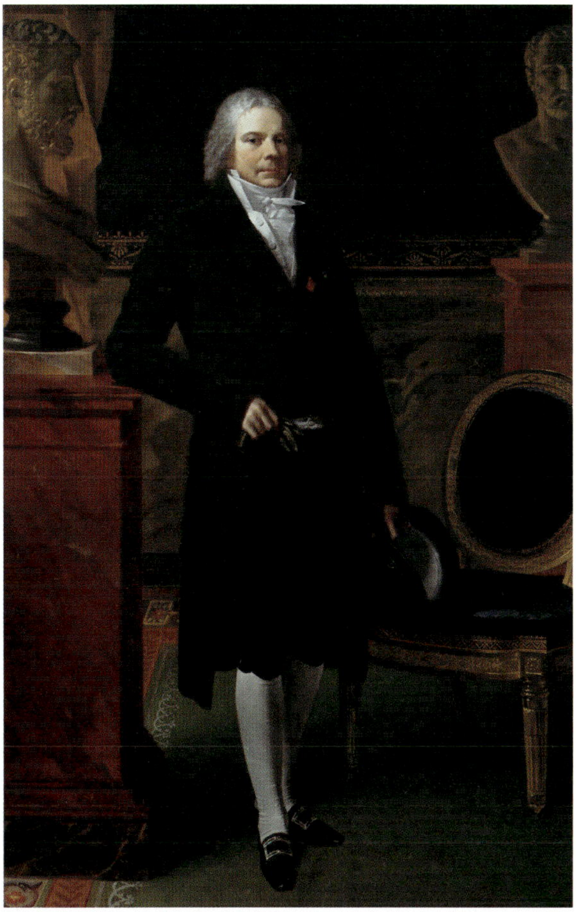

Figure 4.7 Pierre-Paul Prud'hon, *Portrait of Charles-Maurice de Talleyrand-Périgord (1754–1838).* Oil on canvas, 215.9 × 141.9 cm (85 × 55.8 in.). A resident of Philadelphia in the 1790s, Charles Maurice de Talleyrand would go on to serve as France's leading diplomat during the French Revolution when the XYZ Affair roiled Franco-American relations. Talleyrand then assumed a similar role when Napoleon Bonaparte came to power, assisting in the Louisiana Purchase. (Metropolitan Museum of Art, Purchase, Mrs. Charles Wrightsman Gift, in memory of Jacqueline Bouvier Kennedy Onassis, 1994.)

number of aristocrats, they included a duke: François-Alexandre-Frédéric, duc de la Rochefoucauld-Liancourt; a count: Constantin-François de Chasseboeuf, comte de Volney; a marquess: Henri-François-Lucrecius-Armand de Forest, Marquis de Blacons; and a knight: Louis-Saint-Ange Morel, Chevalier de la Colombe. In spite of their titles, they had abjured their feudal privileges in August 1789; yet, largely because of their titles, they were now refugees in America.[37]

Liancourt had served as master of the garderobe of Louis XVI at Versailles, making him one of the most privileged members of the ancien régime. He was forty-seven years old when he arrived in Philadelphia in 1794. He had lost his fortune and, while in exile in England, had learned that his cousin, the Duc de la Rochefoucauld-d'Enville, had been arrested and killed by revolutionaries.

Volney had been at the point of being sent to the United States as French consul when, thanks to the radical shift in the revolutionary government, he was instead imprisoned for ten months. As an Enlightenment philosopher, he had known Franklin in Paris and had traveled the world before arriving in America, where he almost immediately set off to explore its interior.

Blacons had been a friend of Jefferson's in Paris and a member of the Estates General. He, with a number of his countrymen, would create a town of French émigrés deep in Pennsylvania's interior, one planned in the forlorn hope that it might serve as a refuge for the royal family.

La Colombe had been Lafayette's aide-de-camp in America, then served with him during the French Revolution until both men were arrested. Soon released, La Colombe eventually made his way to Philadelphia. He visited Washington in his retirement at Mount Vernon in October 1797 and a month later sent the former president the news of Lafayette's release from prison.

These men were merely several of the wellborn elite of the French exiles in Philadelphia. Of these, it was Talleyrand whose behavior most scandalized Philadelphians. "In search of adventure in this modest city dominated by puritanical Quakers, he offered the spectacle of a Catholic bishop, walking flippantly about in broad daylight in the main street, tenderly holding on his arm a beautiful mulatto woman."[38] If, as some thought, he fathered a child by this woman, it would not be the first or last such accomplishment of this infamous libertine.

By the middle of the 1790s, a number of immigrants of varied backgrounds had set themselves up in businesses all over town. They included a French hatter, a hairdresser, a dancing master, several dentists, a writer, and a bookseller. The *Aurora General Advertiser*, a local newspaper whose editor was Benjamin Franklin Bache, grandson of the famous Philadelphian, published advertisements in both English and French for such varied services as French instruction, fencing lessons, or dental surgery.[39] Young Bache had learned French while being educated in Switzerland and France while his grandfather served as his nation's chief diplomat in Paris. At age fifteen, he had then apprenticed as a printer in the French capital in 1784–1785.

The arrival of French dentists contributed mightily to the oral health and hygiene of Philadelphians, since these Frenchmen were far more advanced in their training and practice than their counterparts in America or in England at the time. Pierre Fauchard, regarded as the father of modern dentistry, had published his landmark text in Paris in 1728.[40] In 1778, a young French naval surgeon, James (Jacques) Gardette (1756–1831), who had learned from Fauchard's text while studying anatomy and surgery in Paris, arrived in Plymouth, Massachusetts, on board a French naval vessel. He soon resigned from the French navy, then rejoined Rochambeau's army as a civilian in 1780. Determined to remain in the United States at the conclusion of the Revolutionary War, he settled in Philadelphia in 1784 and practiced dentistry there for the next forty-six years. He came to be highly respected for his work. Late in 1795 or early 1796, he created a set of dentures for President George Washington (they were made not of wood, as myth has it, but of hippopotamus ivory), shortly before the president sat for his iconic portrait by Gilbert Stuart. His stern-jawed visage is familiar to all from its reproduction on the dollar bill. In 1820, Gardette was awarded a medal for three "mechanical improvements" in his profession, and "for a simple lever instrument for the easy and expeditious extraction of teeth and stumps of teeth."[41]

The bookseller was Médéric-Louis-Elie Moreau de Saint-Méry (1750–1819), who had also played an important role in the early days of the French Revolution. Born in Martinique, he studied law in Paris, married in Saint-Domingue, and was making a name for himself as a writer on the law. That brought him back to Paris in time for him to participate fully in the revolutionary developments immediately after the fall of the Bastille. But after witnessing the increased violence against the moderates by 1792, he took his family to Le Havre. In November 1793, anticipating a warrant for his arrest, he fled with his family, first to New York, then to Philadelphia. His bookshop at the corner of Front and Walnut Streets became a gathering place for refugees from France and the Caribbean. For a time, he published a French language newspaper, *Courrier de France et des colonies*. In 1796, he published what would become a highly regarded study by Liancourt, *On the Prisons of Philadelphia by an European*.[42]

As his prison study made clear, Liancourt quickly became a diligent student of what he observed about America and was impressed at the relatively humane treatment meted out to inmates at the Walnut Street Prison. He attempted through his studies of American life to counter his perpetual depression at the circumstances that had driven him from France. Somewhat shy as well, he deferred to Noailles as the central social lion of the expatriate community. Noailles took an apartment on the estate of the grandest mansion in town, that of William and Anne Bingham, whose property filled the block between Third and Fourth Streets at Spruce. He joined the Bingham banking firm and began a determined effort to regain what he could of his lost fortune.

Back in 1776, in the weeks leading up to the Declaration of Independence, the twenty-four-year-old William Bingham had been dispatched by the Continental Congress to travel to Martinique to purchase a quantity of French muskets, solicit privateers to attack and plunder British merchant ships, and try to assess possible French support for the insurgents in their fight for independence. Back in Philadelphia in 1780—and already a very rich banker—he married, and soon he and Anne traveled to France. On their return, they furnished their house with the finest French furniture. The Binghams were members of a Philadelphia elite of leading lawyers, bankers, and businessmen that increasingly emulated French society and manners, especially when titled Frenchmen joined their social circle, as they often did. Having learned a great deal in Paris about how aristocratic French women starred in social gatherings of their own making, the young Anne Bingham created her own salon in which to dazzle Philadelphia society. Although the leader of the Republicans, Thomas Jefferson, was Anne's friend and admirer, her guests were more often leading Federalists who felt no pangs of guilt at joining in the aristocratic displays that marked an evening at the Binghams. George Washington was among those charmed by the sparkling conversation of his hostess.[43] (See Figure 4.8.)

Beyond the Bingham salons, the impact of France and the French was by no means limited to those at the top of Philadelphia society. People of French heritage left their imprint on every aspect of the city. Some of that impact is evident by examining a list of French residents during the 1790s on South Second Street between High (Market) and Spruce Streets. In the course of its few blocks, which cover scarcely half

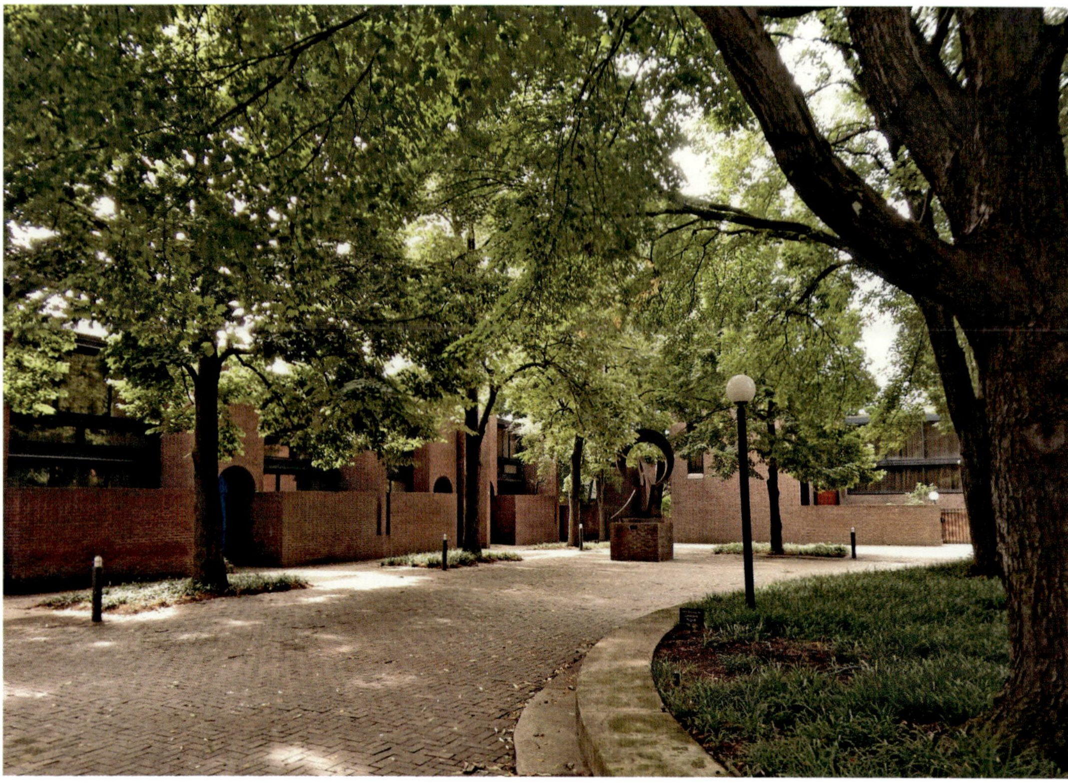

FIGURE 4.8 Today's Bingham Court, with twentieth-century townhouses, is on the site of the eighteenth-century mansion of William and Anne Bingham, who were prominent socialites whose salons included French aristocrats in exile as well as leading Americans residing in the capital city in the 1790s.

a mile, sixty-five French residents and their families occupied perhaps half the houses. Most lived above or behind their places of business. They included several hairdressers, shopkeepers, and umbrella- and dressmakers. Distillers and brewers were part of the mix, as were cooks and pastry chefs. There were goldsmiths, jewelers, and watchmakers, an engraver, two dancing masters, a schoolmaster or two, as well as a dyer, a hatter, and a paper manufacturer. The French owner of City Tavern resided in the street. So did a merchant engaged in the slave trade. They came from various places in France, from Quebec, and from Saint-Domingue and elsewhere in the French Caribbean. They had all settled in Philadelphia, at least temporarily, to begin new lives.[44]

Among them, a French sculptor left an enduring mark in the nation's temporary capital when the headquarters of the new First Bank of the United States rose on South Third Street from 1795 to 1797. That classical structure housed the central bank of the new federal financial system for the United States then being created by the Treasury secretary, Alexander Hamilton. For the tympanum shielding the columned portico, Claudius LeGrand carved an immense American eagle clutching the nation's shield in one talon, a cornucopia in the other. It marked perhaps the first architectural representation of the iconic image in the nation's history. (See Figure 4.9.) Today, the tympanum and the entire edifice are about to be restored. The building will house an important new museum within Independence National Historical Park to tell the story of the nation's financial system as it came into being in federal Philadelphia.[45] Also during the 1790s, Philadelphia's Insurance Company of North America commissioned LeGrand to create, again in the shape of an eagle, its fire mark, the tablet placed on property to signify that it was insured against fire damage.

Immigration of French-speakers also greatly increased Philadelphia's African American population. Although numbering little more than two thousand before the arrival of large numbers of French-speaking refugees, hundreds more, both enslaved and free, came from Saint-Domingue in the great influx from that island in the mid-1790s. Because Pennsylvania had by then enacted laws providing for the gradual emancipation of slaves, which also required any slaves imported into the state be freed after six months, manumissions became numerous. The new arrivals taught French to the local African American elite and added substantially to the city's labor force.[46]

The tumult in France and the Caribbean that had sent so many people of French heritage to Philadelphia overturned all their lives. Some of the most shaken, or romantic, soon shared a dream of a new Eden in America, one that might replace their golden memories of a France now lost to them. They would build a new settlement in the wilderness of northern Pennsylvania as a place of refuge for themselves and for the growing numbers of their countrymen now in flight to North America. In 1793, Stephen Girard and Robert Morris, two of the wealthiest men in Philadelphia, were

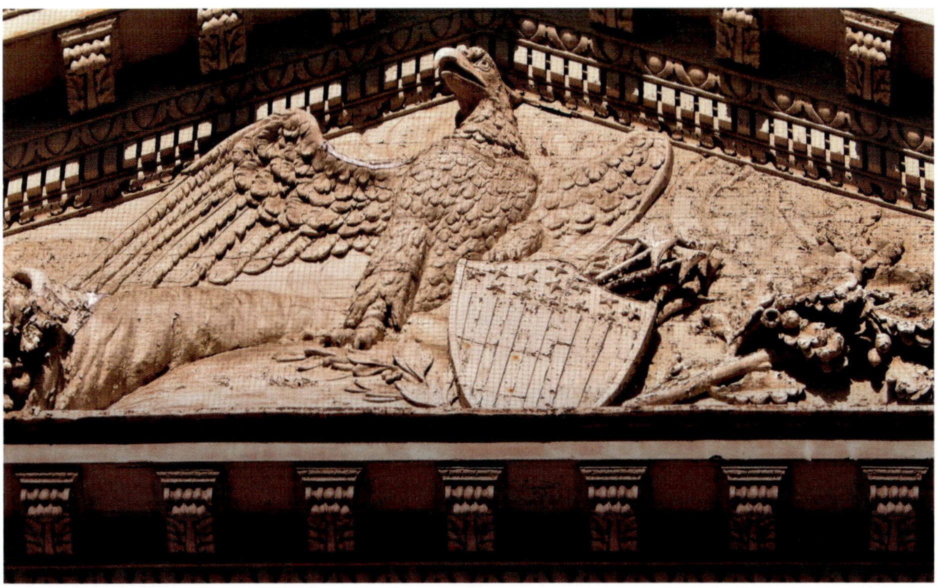

Figure 4.9 The first architectural depiction of the American eagle, ca. 1797, was the work of the French wood-carver Claudius LeGrand to decorate the tympanum over the entrance to the First Bank of the United States.

among those who backed the project. They bought sixteen hundred acres of land on a bend in the eastern branch of the Susquehanna River more than two hundred miles northwest of Philadelphia. Noailles, always looking for a way to improve his finances, was an enthusiastic recruiter of settlers. He proposed the name for the new town: Azilum, a coined word that seemed to fit the French tongue better than the English "Asylum." The town was laid out and opened for settlement by the refugees. The man who no longer styled himself the Marquis de Blacons, but simply Lucretius Blacons, made the journey there with a young woman who would become his wife in the new town. She had recently arrived in Philadelphia from Saint-Domingue after the murder of her father and the destruction of his plantation there. Within a year, some thirty houses had been built on land cleared for the town.[47]

Talleyrand visited for a week in the autumn of 1794. The next spring came Liancourt, but he soon moved on to continue his exploration of American life. One of the settlers, Antoine Orney Talon, who had been an early revolutionary but a confirmed monarchist, held out the hope after word reached him of the execution of Louis XVI, that Marie Antoinette and her children might soon be able to emigrate to safety in Azilum. A grand house was prepared for her. When word finally reached the settlement that the queen, too, had gone to the guillotine, it perhaps confirmed for some residents that theirs had been a fairy-tale dream from the start. Few of them were inclined to do the hard work required to create a livelihood from the wilderness. After achieving a population of some 250 people by 1795, the settlement began to decline gradually.[48] Noailles, in Philadelphia, was stunned when word finally reached him that his wife, parents, and mother-in-law had all been executed during the last days of the Terror.

At about the same time, three refugee princes from France visited Azilum for a brief stay. They were cousins of Louis XVI, but from the House of Orléans rather than Bourbon, between which there were serious differences. Their father was the man who had been known as Philippe Egalité; he had thrown his lot in with the revolutionaries after the fall of the Bastille and later voted for the king's execution, only to be put to death himself during the Terror. His eldest son, now Duc d'Orléans, would spend more than twenty years in peripatetic exile throughout Europe and America after fleeing France in 1793.[49] In 1796, the twenty-three-year-old Louis-Philippe, Duc d'Orléans, joined his brothers in Philadelphia, settling into a house at 322 Spruce Street. No one could yet know that more than thirty years later, Louis-Philippe would ascend the throne as the "citizen king" of France.

Azilum was on its way to a sputtering end even before Napoleon, in 1803, offered amnesty to many of the French exiles who had been forced from their homeland by the revolution. The experiment that launched that settlement had been motivated in part by the growing sense by English-speaking Americans that the ever-growing French presence along the Eastern Seaboard, perhaps especially in Philadelphia, risked destabilizing the nation. In fact, the divide in American politics that accompanied the drama of Citizen Genet grew even more virulent by the end of President Washington's second term and the presidency of his successor, John Adams. Newspapers in Philadelphia grew ever more scurrilous in attacking the perceived malfeasance of politicians from whichever party they opposed.[50]

France's war with Britain increasingly threatened the peace of America. The British navy began seizing U.S. merchant ships trading with France, often impressing their crews. Pro-French forces in the nation's capital pushed for a trade war with Britain, prompting President Washington in 1794 to send John Jay, chief justice of the Supreme Court, to London to negotiate a new treaty with the British. The pact that resulted was decidedly a half loaf from the American point of view. In it, the British did agree to withdraw from territory they still occupied around the Great Lakes and to concede better terms of trade to their former colony. But the issue of impressment was left unresolved. Madison and his allies were bitterly opposed, arguing that the treaty effectively repudiated the French alliance of 1778. Partisans heaped opprobrium on both Jay and Washington. A mob attacked the Bingham house to protest its residents' presumed sympathy for the Federalists' treaty. Yet, President Washington himself seemed to waver in his support for what Jay had negotiated until it was revealed that his secretary of state, Edmund Randolph, who had succeeded Jefferson in that position, had made damagingly indiscreet and pro-French statements in conversations with the French minister to the United States, Joseph Fauchet, the successor of Citizen Genet. With that, Washington forced Randolph to resign and made clear his support for the treaty. In the Senate, in June 1795, the pact was assented to by the minimum requirement of the Constitution: twenty senators in favor with ten opposed.[51]

John Adams narrowly defeated Thomas Jefferson for president in the election of 1796, the first in which two national political parties, Federalist and Democratic-Republican, were clearly engaged.[52] The fight over the Jay Treaty had deepened the cleavage between them. The Federalists were pro-British and anti-French (although the two leading Federalists, Adams and Hamilton, were already adversaries and soon would become bitter foes); the Democratic-Republicans, led by Jefferson and Madison, were defined by their reverse sympathies. The French government of the Directory made clear its distaste for Adams and the Federalists. Months before Adams's election, the French foreign minister had informed James Monroe, minister of the United States to France, that passage of the Jay Treaty had effectively nullified the neutrality principles laid down in the 1778 treaty between their two nations. Interfering directly in the election, the Directory's new minister to the United States placed several statements in Benjamin Bache's *Aurora* newspaper warning that the election of Adams could mean war with France.[53] Once Adams was elected, his administration reciprocated by refusing to repay its Revolutionary War debt to France on the grounds that the money was owed to the regime of the now abolished French monarchy. (See Figure 4.10.)

French privateers then stepped up their assaults on American ships. By 1797, conflicts between American and French vessels on the high seas grew to the point that the outbreak of war looked possible, even likely. The newly appointed French consul-general, Victor Marie du Pont de Nemours, arrived in Philadelphia from his previous diplomatic post in Charleston, but President Adams refused to receive him.[54] The young envoy thereupon sailed home to France, although he would return to America

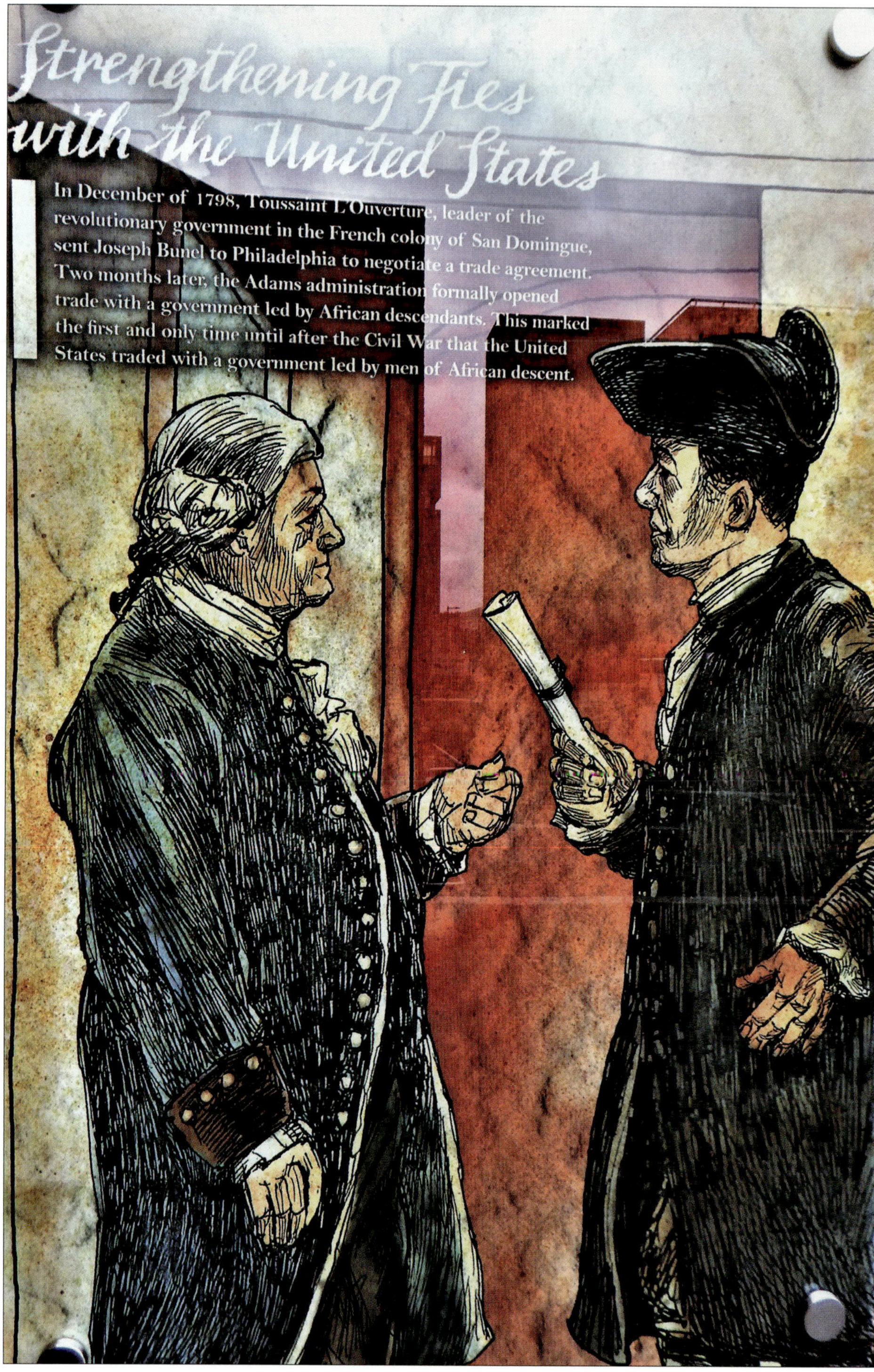

Figure 4.10 In December 1796, Toussaint L'Ouverture, leader of the revolutionary government in French Saint-Domingue, sent an emissary to Philadelphia to negotiate a trade agreement with the Adams administration. Once formalized, that agreement marked the first and only time until after the Civil War when the United States traded with a government led by men of African descent. (Artist: Unknown.)

several years later with his father and brother and their families to establish one of the premier companies in their adopted homeland.

In July of that year, Adams sent a diplomatic commission to Paris to attempt negotiations with the French that might restore peace. There they expected to meet with France's new foreign minister, a man known to all of them from his time in Philadelphia and who had now risen high. Talleyrand had left the United States in June 1796 to return to France. He immediately set to work to realize his ambitions. He was named foreign minister by the Directory early in 1797. But months after the American emissaries arrived in Paris, President Adams informed Congress, in April 1798, that French agents, acting on Talleyrand's order, had refused to meet with the Americans unless and until their government paid a very substantial sum and advanced a loan for the privilege of beginning substantive negotiations. Congress and the nation were incensed. "Millions for defence but not a cent for tribute!" was the toast at a congressional dinner in Philadelphia before it became the rallying cry of anti-French forces throughout the nation.[55]

Talleyrand had definitely been playing a cat-and-mouse game with the American diplomats, as would become clear when the evidence finally reached Congress. He may have thought that by stringing out talks, he could appease those in the Directory who were virulently anti-American. His duplicity and double-dealing would become hallmarks of his long career in charge of French foreign policy. At times, he seemed to delight in subterfuge for its own sake, and he had long been a confirmed cynic. His epicurean disdain for American life was evident when he reportedly said, after traveling through the new nation, "The United States are a country where, if there are thirty-two religions, there is only one dish, and it is a bad one."[56] For months in 1797 and 1798, he attempted to divide the American commissioners by dealing with them individually and privately, leaving the prize of an agreement always off in the distance. Eventually the emissaries returned to Philadelphia, their mission a failure.

But before that end came, many Republicans assumed that the president was pushing the nation toward war with France and openly doubted his portrayal of how the American officials had been received by Talleyrand. They insisted that Adams should disclose the dispatches the Americans had sent from Paris describing their treatment by the French foreign office. He did so, after the names of the French intermediaries for Talleyrand were redacted and replaced with the initials X, Y, and Z. The revelations made clear how badly the Americans had been treated. They were a stunning comeuppance for the Republicans, who found themselves accused of disloyalty to the nation while the clamor for war with France grew louder.[57] This XYZ Affair, as it was immediately known, marked the lowest point in American sympathy for France in the nation's history, before or since. In July 1798, twenty years after the Franco-American alliance gave succor to the American cause, Congress rescinded its treaties with France. Hostilities with French naval vessels in the Caribbean grew worse; more than three hundred American ships ultimately were taken. The events, which included battles on the open sea, came to be known as the Quasi-War. Adams struggled to keep it from becoming a full-fledged military conflict. His administration moved to build a new navy, since none had existed after the nation's independence.

Eventually, Talleyrand concluded that he had miscalculated in his dealings with the commissioners. He then threw his lot in with the new first consul, Napoleon Bonaparte, who overthrew the Directory in the Coup of 18 Brumaire (November 9, 1799). Bonaparte proclaimed the French Revolution at an end and moved quickly to end the Quasi-War with the United States as well. New negotiations began with the Adams administration and an end to hostilities between the two former allies was concluded on October 3, 1800, at Mortefontaine, north of Paris.[58] The site was the residence of Napoleon's brother, Joseph Bonaparte, who was one of those involved in the negotiations.

Meanwhile, however, the Federalist majority in Congress passed legislation in 1798 reflecting the mood of siege that gripped the nation. The Alien and Sedition Acts made it harder for immigrants to become citizens; they allowed the president to deport aliens he deemed dangerous as well as individuals from hostile nations; and they criminalized the making of false statements critical of the federal government. Of those soon to be prosecuted under the sedition act, Benjamin Franklin Bache was among the most prominent. He had accused "the blind, bald, crippled, toothless, querulous Adams" of nepotism in his *Aurora* newspaper and been arrested for it. Yet, before his trial could take place, another outbreak of yellow fever in the city in 1798 carried Benjamin Franklin Bache to his death at age twenty-nine.[59]

With the signing of the treaty of October 1800, the furies of the Quasi-War began to subside. Philadelphia's time at the center of national politics also came to an end. The nation's capital moved to the new little city being built on the Potomac. It would be named Washington, in honor of the father of the nation who had died the previous December, only days before the end of the century. Thomas Jefferson soon would be elected to replace John Adams as president. The Alien and Sedition Acts had turned popular sentiment against him. Alexander Hamilton, leader of the Federalists and the president's one-time ally, led those opposed to his reelection. Later, in his forced retirement, Adams wrote to a friend that the only inscription he desired on his gravestone was this: "Here lies John Adams, who took upon himself the responsibility of peace with France in the year 1800."[60]

[5]

Détente in Philadelphia and for the Nation

As the nation's capital and most important city in the 1790s, Philadelphia was also at the heart of growing strains with revolutionary France, leading to the Quasi-War late in that decade. The new century brought détente in that relationship as well as the removal of the Quaker City from its central place in the nation's political life. A number of individual Frenchmen were left to make their mark on the city's life and art. Some of them left a long-lasting influence, while at least one who flared brightly was soon forgotten, not to be acknowledged by the nation until the passing of another century, his Philadelphia legacy long gone. Meanwhile, a leading French Philadelphian played a decisive role in the nation's last major conflict with its former imperial power, which brought détente on that front as well.

Philadelphia's brief era as the nation's capital came to a close at about the time the Quasi-War between the United States and France was ending and, with it, the most serious conflict ever between the two countries. On the French side, one of the principal negotiators of the treaty of commerce that restored the peace at Mortefontaine in October 1800 was Joseph Bonaparte, whose brother was just then entering center stage to dominate European politics for the next decade and a half. That changing of the guard soon produced an amazing doubling of the territory of the United States and the start of a new era in both the New World and France. Yet, aftershocks from the upheaval that had rocked France since 1789 were felt in Philadelphia well into the new century, especially the impact of French and Francophone exiles from that storm. Joseph Bonaparte himself was eventually among them.

Months before Philadelphia ceased to be the nation's capital, its time as the capital of Pennsylvania also came to an end. That seat of government moved first to York in 1799, then to Harrisburg in 1812. Nonetheless, the city continued to thrive. Once

Congress left the west wing of the State House, that space became home to the county court, as had originally been intended; the east wing was transformed into Philadelphia's city hall after the U.S. Supreme Court decamped to the District of Columbia. In 1800, the University of Pennsylvania purchased for its educational mission the impressive house on Ninth Street that had been built as a would-be home for the president of the United States. Pennsylvania Hospital doubled, then more than tripled, its buildings between Spruce and Pine Street. The city's population grew at a remarkable pace: to more than forty-one thousand residents by 1800, nearly fifty-four thousand a decade later, and just short of sixty-four thousand by 1820. Yet the city was bursting from its original borders, which confined it to a mere two square miles. If residents from contiguous suburbs were included, those population figures were nearly twice as large. Philadelphia remained the nation's financial capital while the First Bank, then the Second, of the United States were headquartered in the city, as was the U.S. Mint.

The terrible epidemics of yellow fever in the 1790s led to a campaign to provide the city with a new and clean source of water, since it was thought that filth and contaminated water harbored the disease. As a result, by 1799, plans were underway to create the modern world's first municipal water system. Water was pumped from the Schuylkill River through a ditch along Chestnut Street to an elegant pump house in a new classical style (thereby starting a nationwide architectural trend) in the heart of Centre Square. Its steam engines raised the water to a reservoir from which water flowed through bored-log pipes to customers throughout the city. A public park was created to surround it.[1] Meanwhile, some men got rich. Stephen Girard's fortune increased multifold while this American transplanted from Bordeaux kept finding new ways to increase his wealth. He was more than ever one of Philadelphia's leading citizens.

Once Napoleon Bonaparte declared the French Revolution at an end, the aristocrats and other friends of the revolution who had fled to America generally found welcome once more in their homeland. Most of those who had taken up residence in Philadelphia returned to France, leaving only a few behind to try to make their fortune in the New World. One of the most notable of that group was Pierre Charles L'Enfant (1754–1825), who had been recruited back in 1777 by Beaumarchais to join the fight for America's independence. Trained as an engineer, he joined Washington's staff at Valley Forge, became a friend of Hamilton's, and showed his architectural skill (or, at least, that of a stylish builder) when he designed the large frame pavilion in Philadelphia in August 1782, which was commissioned by the French minister, the Marquis de la Luzerne, in honor of the birth of the Dauphin of France. After Yorktown, he settled in New York, established a civil engineering firm, and called himself "Peter" to make clear his new identity. In 1787, Benjamin Franklin's grandson, Temple Franklin, who was by then trying his hand at real estate in New York, invited L'Enfant to design a large structure for that city. L'Enfant's inspiration was his memory of the arcaded gallery of shops surrounding the Palais-Royal in Paris. The plan, like much else in L'Enfant's later career, never materialized.[2] But at about the same time, he was hired to redesign New York's city hall, turning it into the Federal Hall that would serve the First Congress of the United States when New York City became the capital under the new Constitution.

In 1791, L'Enfant's fortunes soared when he was named by President Washington to plan the new Federal City on the Potomac. To the surprise of most officials, including Thomas Jefferson, who had made a sketch of a fairly modest town, L'Enfant soon produced a grandiose plan on the scale of a European capital, complete with an enormous "Congress House" and a huge "President's House." Had the latter been realized, it would have been some five times the size of the White House that actually was built. His plan also showed great boulevards and a "grand avenue" rolling out from the base of the Capitol grounds. The government's commissioners put in charge of carrying out the building plan were skeptical of the costs of trying to build on such a scale and insisted on constructing the essential federal buildings first. L'Enfant soon proved to be a headstrong and difficult man to work with. Before long, his principal remaining advocate was President Washington, who admired the grandeur of what L'Enfant had conceived. But, eventually, even the president conceded that the man needed to be dismissed. So he was, although his plan was retained as the basis for the city that gradually arose.

After "resigning," as he insisted, from the Federal City project, L'Enfant once more sought his fortune in Philadelphia, arriving back in the city in 1793. His taste for the grandiose immediately appealed to the city's richest citizen, Robert Morris, who hired him to design a new mansion for his family. It would be, as both men agreed, "like none other in the city."[3] The property began to rise palace-like at what was still the edge of the city, occupying the entire block from Seventh to Eighth and Walnut to Chestnut Streets. L'Enfant's model was of the lavish *hôtels particuliers* that were home to Parisian aristocrats, set back from the street with elegant gardens to the rear. The redbrick and marble structure slowly rose, acquiring ever more costly embellishments in the process. After three years of work, it remained unfinished, its two grand wings largely open to the elements. (See Figure 5.1.)

Meanwhile, and unfortunately for the man who had largely financed the American Revolution, Morris rather suddenly lost his fortune from overly optimistic speculation in western land. By late in 1795, he could no longer accept L'Enfant's expenditures and delays. Morris and L'Enfant mutually agreed that the "unfortunate building in Chestnut Street" would not be continued.[4] Bankrupt, Morris spent three years in debtors' prison. The mansion—Morris's Folly, as it was known by then to Philadelphians—was never completed. The unfinished house, subject to a sheriff's sale, was sold in 1798 for the original price of the lot alone. The building was then demolished and all its embellishments sold off.[5] Shortly thereafter, the property gave rise to rows of houses built by a developer, William Sansom, whose name would be given to the new street bisecting the block from east to west.

Meanwhile, L'Enfant had tried his hand at two other major building projects in Philadelphia. His plan for the City Dancing Hall never moved from the drawing

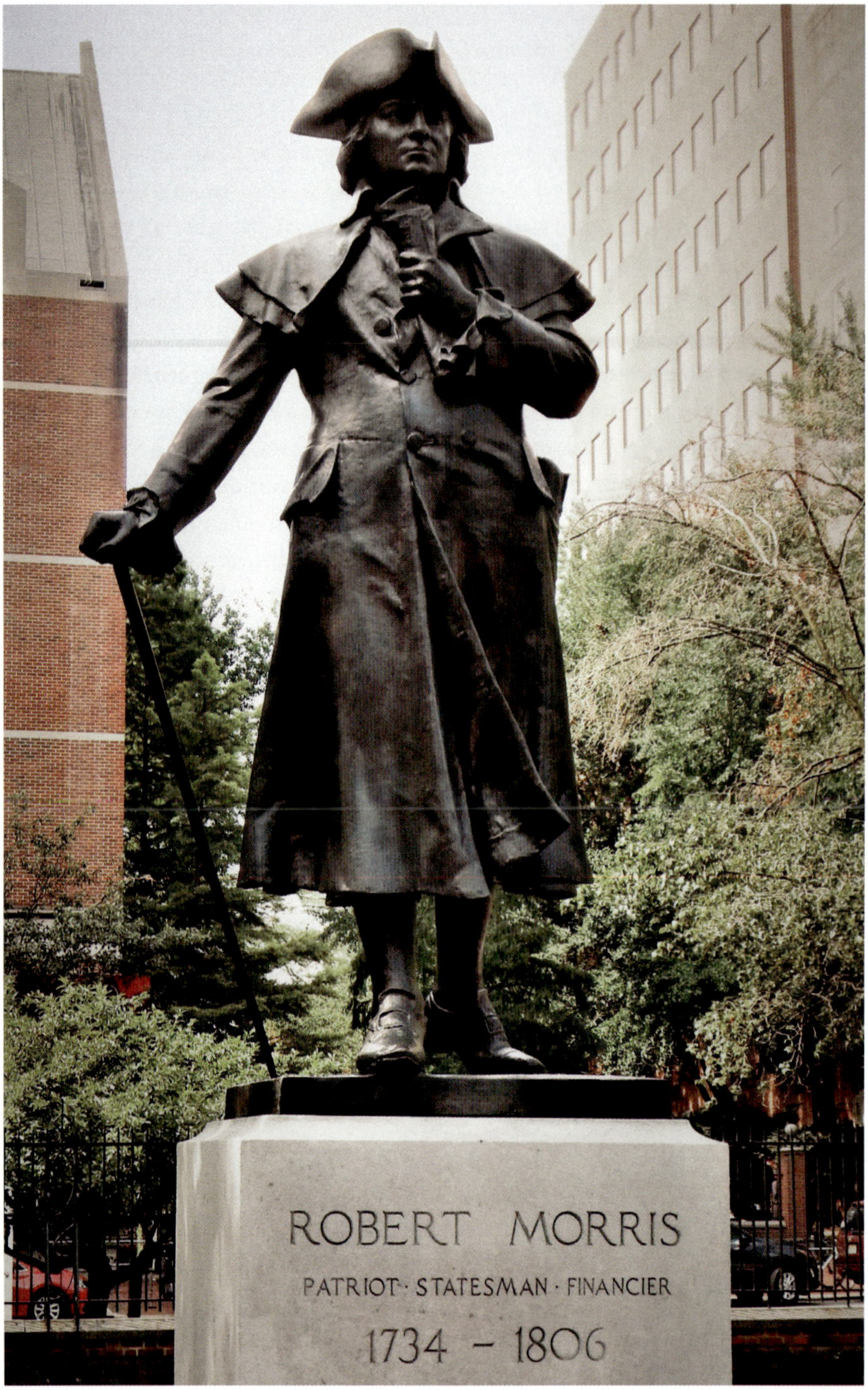

Figure 5.1 Paul W. Bartlett, *Robert Morris*, 1923. Bronze. Unveiled June 18, 1926, on the Chestnut Street steps of the Second Bank of the United States. Moved to the present site south of the bank, 1961. Robert Morris largely financed the American cause in the War of Independence. But in the 1790s, he lost his fortune speculating in western lands and was sent to debtors' prison. As a result, the Philadelphia mansion Pierre L'Enfant designed for him never was completed.

board because of accusations of his overspending. He was also hired to make improvements to Fort Mifflin, that essential fort in the Delaware River just below Philadelphia's southern boundary. That, too, ended in recriminations, with L'Enfant's critics arguing that his "improvements" were unsound, while he complained of interference from others. Eventually, that assignment went to another French engineer, Louis de Tousard, who had served under Lafayette in the Continental Army. By 1795, Tousard was a lieutenant colonel and an inspector in the U.S. Corps of Artillerists and Engineers. He supervised the successful completion of the repairs to the fort that L'Enfant had begun.[6] Stephen Girard, meanwhile, on his way to replacing Morris as the city's richest citizen, had considered hiring L'Enfant to design his new house on Water Street. But, after seeing more of his fellow-countryman's unrestrained expenditure on what was becoming Morris's Folly, he reconsidered. Instead, he had built for himself a large, but foursquare brick house in plain Quaker style.

L'Enfant never had much fit in with the other French émigrés living in Philadelphia, who, perhaps finding him nettlesome, seem mostly to have ignored him.[7] The Swedish consul with whom he boarded eventually sued him for bills he was charged with owing. After departing from Philadelphia for the last time, L'Enfant spent the rest of his life near the new capital city until he died in poverty in 1825. Nearly a century passed before a considerably more powerful United States, urged on by the then French ambassador to Washington, acknowledged him—once more Pierre L'Enfant—as the essential planner of the nation's capital.[8] By then, L'Enfant's grandiose planned city sat more easily on the nation's shoulders. His remains were reburied with honor in Arlington National Cemetery in 1909. Yet, in Philadelphia, where he labored through most of the 1790s but where none of his work survives, he is remembered, if at all, for having helped bring ruin to Robert Morris.

As Morris's financial downfall suggested, wild speculation in land in America's West was a recurring theme of the period, and one to which Frenchmen excited by their experience of America too often fell victim. The life of Louis le Bègue de Presle Duportail (1743–1802) provided a prominent example. Like Lafayette and others, he had met Franklin in Paris in 1777, and the American persuaded him to cross the Atlantic to fight in the Continental Army. Because of the young Frenchman's training as an engineer, Franklin named him colonel in chief of engineers for the insurgents. Duportail soon proved himself invaluable to General Washington, rebuilding the forts at West Point and working alongside the general at Valley Forge.[9] Once Rochambeau arrived in America, Duportail was attached to his army, then promoted to the rank of lieutenant colonel. He was taken prisoner when Charleston, South Carolina, capitulated to the enemy, and he was later freed in a prisoner exchange. At Yorktown, he was the director of work on the army's fortress and trenches in preparation for the siege of the British forces holed up there. Immediately after the American victory that brought an end to the conflict, Washington promoted him to the rank of brigadier general.[10]

Duportail returned to France in October 1783. We get a glimpse of some of his activities and interests several years later from a letter he wrote to the former general, now president, Washington on February 10, 1790, from Paris. He begins with this news:

> Twenty-three persons and myself we have acquired some lands on the ohio and we propose to make a setlement there. For that purpose we agreed to Carry or send over a certain number of Cultivators. this is a kind of experiment, which if successful, will be followed by a much greater one, so that a large french Colony may rise florishing [*sic*] in a few years.[11]

We now know that Duportail and his compatriots were among more than five hundred French investors lured to America by the Scioto Company's unscrupulous prospectus that held out to the settlers a tantalizing vision, falsely claiming that a tract of four million acres was cleared for settlement and cities already thrived there. Duportail himself would not be among the first group of settlers, as he made clear in his letter to Washington, because of "the critical situation of our affairs at home." His reference to the dramatic first months of the French Revolution would prove prescient:

> Probably your Excellency knows the extraordinary events which have taken place here. we are also struggling for liberty, but I do not know if our success will be as Compleat and perfect as that of the american. there is a very great difference between a young nation and an old one divided almost in two Classes, the one Corrupted by extreme luxury, the other by extreme misery.[12]

Within months after writing to Washington, Duportail would take on a major assignment in the hopeful early stage of the French Revolution. His work in the American cause had won him Lafayette's admiration, and it was he who was instrumental in having Duportail named France's minister of war in November 1790. In that position, he initiated reforms of the military. But in December 1791, with Lafayette's downfall, Duportail resigned his office. Soon, he was forced into hiding while under threat by radical Jacobins. In 1794, he fled to the United States. By then, it was surely apparent to him that the Ohio dream had dissolved in ruins. So, once he arrived back in Pennsylvania, he bought a farm near Valley Forge, where he lived and worked until 1802. In that year, no doubt aware of more promising prospects for men like himself in France, he decided to return. Unfortunately, he died during the voyage and was buried at sea.

In his contributions to America's liberty and his speculation in western land, Duportail's history was not very different from that of a number of his countrymen of his generation—or, for that matter, from that of some Americans, such as Robert Morris. But as younger people of French heritage settled in the Philadelphia area, other factors attracted them. One of those, Pierre-Étienne du Ponceau—or Duponceau, as he would soon prefer (1760–1844)—also arrived here in service to the American Revolution, at age seventeen and in the company of another foreigner who would play a critical role in turning the Continental Army into a respectable fighting force. Baron Friedrich Wilhelm von Steuben (1730–1794), formerly aide-de-camp to Frederick the Great of Prussia, was in exile from his native land largely because of improper behavior, so it was rumored, with young men. In Paris in 1777, he sought employment and a new start. He paid a call on the ever-perceptive Benjamin Franklin, who recognized Steuben's military accomplishments and persuaded him to go to America to assist in training Washington's troops. The fatherless young Duponceau, who had already proved himself to be an unusually able student of language, presumably was by then Steuben's lover. He was persuaded by the older man to accompany him to America to act as his interpreter and personal secretary. He seems to have felt at home in America almost at first sight. At age eighteen, he was made a captain in the Continental Army.

Steuben's work in training that army at Valley Forge made him something of a revolutionary hero. He laid out an orderly and sanitary camp where none had existed while transforming a rag-tag bunch of farmers and shopkeepers into a disciplined outfit. Duponceau's role was critical as well. The baron wrote out a portion of his drill instructions each day in French, a language in which he was fluent. Duponceau then translated the text into English and handed it over to Alexander Hamilton and John Laurens, whose job it was to turn the translation into proper military jargon. It then had to be hand-copied for each of fourteen brigade inspectors. The same arduous process was repeated every day. Eventually, in 1779, Steuben's manual was published in Philadelphia as *Regulations for the Order and Discipline of the Troops of the United States*. It remained the standard military manual for the American army through the War of 1812.[13]

Duponceau left the army due to illness in 1781, when he and Steuben also parted company. Settling in Philadelphia, now as Peter Stephen Duponceau, he was almost immediately made secretary to Robert Livingston, who was secretary for foreign affairs for the Continental Congress. He proceeded to pursue his studies in linguistics and to make himself an expert in international law, studying with the noted Philadelphia lawyer, William Lewis, who had been largely responsible in the previous year for the passage of Pennsylvania's Act for the Abolition of Slavery, the first such law in the nation. Duponceau remained in Philadelphia for the rest of his life and became one of its leading intellectuals. The practice of law became his profession; he eventually was made chancellor of the Philadelphia Law Association.

But it was his avocation, the exploration of matters linguistic, which secured his reputation. By 1791, after he married and began a family, he was asked to join the American Philosophical Society. In 1828, he became its president, remaining in that position until his death at age 84. As his stature in the city grew, he also presided over the Athenaeum and the Historical Society of Pennsylvania. He was prominent in the work of the French Benevolent Society as well. His contributions to the study of the language of indigenous people in America were pathbreaking and of great interest to Thomas Jefferson, who had also long served as president of the American Philosophical Society and, like Duponceau, was a student of Native American languages.[14] Late in his life, Duponceau was awarded the Prix Volney of the Institut de France for his *Mémoire sur le système grammatical des langues de quelques nations indiennes de l'Amérique du Nord* [Memoir on the grammatical system of the languages of several Indian nations in North America]. The Volney Prize, by the way, had been established by the same Constantin François de Chasseboeuf, comte de Volney, who had visited

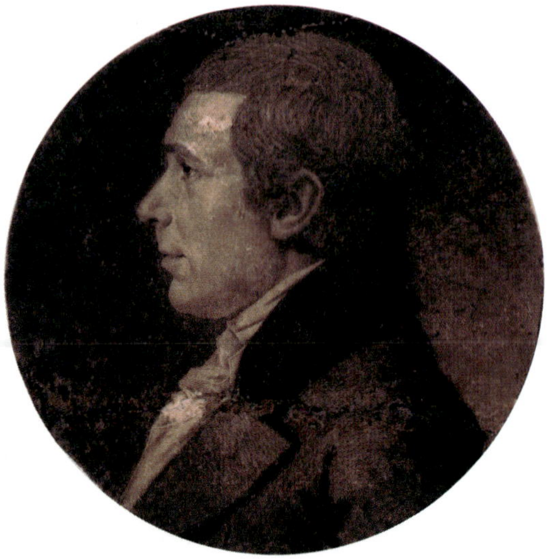

FIGURE 5.2 Charles Balthazar Julien Fevret de Saint-Mémin, 1770–1852, *Peter Stephen Duponceau*, ca. 1800, head-and-shoulders portrait, left profile. Engraving, 2036 × 2038 cm. As a young French immigrant, Stephen Duponceau had served alongside Baron von Steuben at Valley Forge. A lifelong Philadelphian thereafter and one of its leading intellectuals, he was for many years the president of the American Philosophical Society. (Prints and Photographs Division, Library of Congress. Reproduction Number: LC-DIG-pga-13339.)

Philadelphia and traveled through much of the United States during the 1790s. (See Figure 5.2.)

One of the last French families to flee to the Philadelphia region from the excesses of the French Revolution would eventually become one of the richest, most powerful, and influential dynasties in America. Pierre Samuel du Pont (1739–1817) had distinguished himself under the ancien régime, serving as Louis XVI's inspector-general of commerce. A friend of Voltaire and Turgot, his 1767 treatise on economics calling for low tariffs and free trade greatly influenced Adam Smith in Edinburgh, who would publish his *The Wealth of Nations* nine years later.[15] In 1783, du Pont was one of those who negotiated with the British to produce the Treaty of Paris ending the American Revolution. In the next year, the king ennobled him through *lettres patentes*, which added "de Nemours" to his title. Jefferson, in Paris, called du Pont "one of the very great men of the age."[16] He supported revolutionary reforms after the fall of the Bastille, but when a mob attacked the Palais des Tuileries on September 4, 1792, du Pont and his younger son sought to protect the royal couple. The elder du Pont was condemned to the guillotine but still awaited execution when the Reign of Terror ended in July 1794. Yet, three years later, on September 4, 1797, his house was ransacked and his belongings destroyed by a mob during the coup of 18 Fructidor V.

With that, at nearly sixty years of age, he and his two adult sons and their families began making urgent preparations to immigrate to the United States. (When a grandson was born in 1798, the hopeful name, "Philadelphe," was added to "Alfred Victor" at the child's christening.) The clan arrived in Rhode Island on the first day of the new century. Like several of their fellow-countrymen in Philadelphia, the du Ponts first aspired unsuccessfully to found a colony for French refugees in America.

Shortly after their arrival, the elder du Pont began a warm correspondence with Thomas Jefferson, which would continue through Jefferson's presidency and his retirement at Monticello. In February 1800, Pierre du Pont (see Figure 5.3) expressed his relief at recent news from France as well as his somewhat wry reaction to the new regime headed by Napoleon:

> So our friend Lafayette is back in his homeland. I am very relieved, and to know that several of his friends and mine have ceased being mistreated, and that they are even being consulted. But I should wish that it was all done according to forms less arbitrary and less Roman.

He made clear what had become his own political preference:

> The Gospel says that God gave the Kingdom of Heaven to the Ravishers. He does likewise with those of the earth. That is why I prefer proper Republics.[17]

Pierre's twenty-nine-year-old younger son, Eleuthère Irénée, had early shown an aptitude for chemistry, having studied in France with its greatest practitioner and exponent, Antoine Lavoisier, who had been executed at the guillotine in May 1794. Once in America, Irénée, as he was known, concluded that he might put his own knowledge of explosives to work in a new industry. According to local legend, he had seen for himself the poor quality of American gunpowder when he went hunting with Louis de Tousard, the same French engineer who had taken over the successful restoration of Fort Mifflin after Pierre L'Enfant was dismissed from the job. Du Pont's rifle misfired when he shot at a bird, which led him to investigate the techniques used

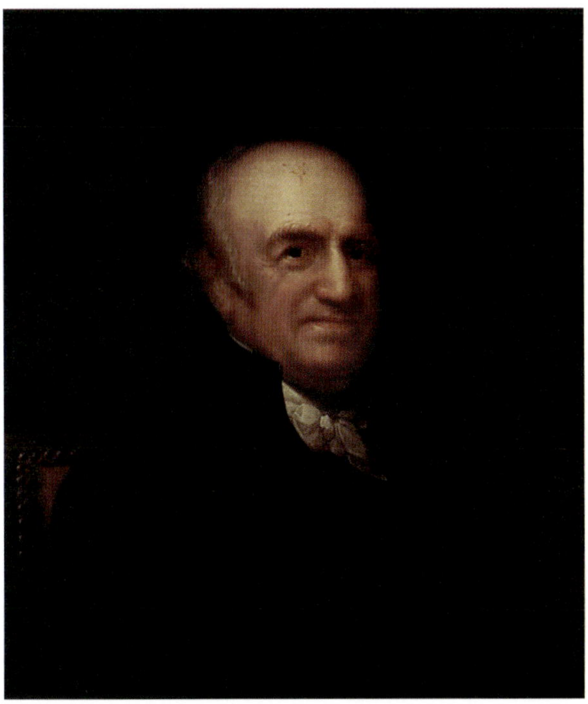

FIGURE 5.3 *Pierre Samuel du Pont de Nemours* (1739–1817), portrait, unknown artist. Oil on canvas, 1550 × 1810 cm. After immigrating to northern Delaware in 1800, the eminent economist, Pierre S. du Pont, became the head of one of the most prominent dynasties and important industries in America, E. I. du Pont de Nemours and Company. (Hagley Museum and Library, Wilmington, Delaware)

by the native powder industry. Convinced that what he had learned from Lavoisier gave him the knowledge to create a superior refining process, he and his brother Victor returned to France to assemble the needed capital and equipment to create their own firm.

Back in the United States, they acquired a site for the gunpowder factory on the Brandywine Creek a few miles south of Philadelphia in Delaware. Eleutherian Mills was established in April 1801, as the home of E. I. du Pont de Nemours and Company. The first gunpowder was produced three years later. Meanwhile, Victor—whom President John Adams had refused to recognize as France's consul-general several years earlier—turned first to trading, then farming in New York. But in 1811, he established a woolen mill across from Eleutherian Mills. Pierre S. du Pont died in 1814, Victor in Philadelphia in 1827. Eleuthère lived until 1834. By then, their E. I. du Pont Company was on its way to becoming one of the greatest corporations in America. It provided some 40 percent of all the gunpowder used in the Civil War and grew into a highly diversified conglomerate that described itself early in the twenty-first century as a global science company, which by then was employing some sixty thousand people worldwide.[18]

No company, and no family, has produced a more enduring imprint on northern Delaware and southeastern Pennsylvania than that of the du Ponts. Among the two thousand or more descendants of Pierre S. du Pont today, some have made their mark not only in business but in politics, the arts, and philanthropy. In the twenty-mile stretch between Philadelphia and Wilmington, a number of important public amenities and institutions are either entirely or largely the offspring of du Pont family members. They include the Brandywine Conservancy, the Delaware Museum of Natural History, Hagley Museum, Longwood Gardens, the Mt. Cuba Center, Nemours Mansion, and Winterthur. Farther afield, the National Trust for Historic Preservation and the restoration of James Madison's home, Montpelier, owe much to du Pont philanthropy.[19] In 2013, Lammot du Pont Copeland's Mt. Cuba Center near the Delaware-Pennsylvania border contributed $20 million to purchase land for donation to the federal government as a means to create the First State Historical Park. That new addition to the U.S. National Park system brings together a number of historic sites throughout Delaware, all illustrating the state's colonial-era contributions to the nation.

The rise of Napoleon in France with the dawn of the nineteenth century would again rearrange the map of Europe as it would also do, more unexpectedly and permanently, in North America. By then, the United States was increasingly populating its western lands between the Appalachians and the Mississippi River. That, in turn, meant ever more commerce on the Mississippi, the main highway from north to south along the nation's western frontier, and a far cheaper route for shipping goods than to send them overland to eastern ports. The vast lands of Louisiana had been under French rule from 1699 to 1762, when they were given to France's ally, Spain. The United States had an agreement with the Spanish government for the right to send its goods down the river to be stored in the port city of New Orleans. But, in 1800,

Napoleon reclaimed Louisiana for France in a secret treaty with Spain and revoked the "right of deposit" for American merchants to continue the free use of New Orleans. That worried President Jefferson who feared that, in spite of his own sympathies for the French, Napoleon's new policy would make New Orleans "a point of eternal friction with us." In the views of certain headstrong Americans—Pennsylvania's senator James Ross among them—the United States should move quickly to take possession of New Orleans by force before the mighty army of the French could cross the Atlantic to defend it.[20]

Jefferson, however, had been advised by Pierre S. du Pont that it should be possible to avoid a new conflict with the French. Du Pont had recently returned to Paris, where he was in touch with governmental officials acting as an informal liaison with the American government. He floated the idea that the United States might purchase New Orleans and eliminate this likely source of conflict with France. President Jefferson was persuaded to try. He sent the seasoned diplomat, James Monroe, to Paris to join the American minister, Robert Livingston, to make a financial offer to Napoleon to purchase the city along with some adjacent territory along the coast of the Gulf of Mexico. But the ruler of France astonished the diplomats by offering to sell *all* of the Louisiana Territory, an expanse of some 828,000 square miles extending from New Orleans and the Mississippi delta west to the Rocky Mountains and north well over a thousand miles (the exact boundaries had not yet been determined) to British Canada. The American negotiators, exceeding their instructions, took little time to accept the offer. It was done, on May 2, 1803, for the price of $15 million, which included a cash payment of $11.5 million and the forgiveness of $3.75 million in French debt. The cost of the deal which, at the stroke of a pen, at least doubled the size of the United States, worked out to something like three or four cents an acre. Although the U.S. Senate easily ratified the treaty, this enormous acquisition was not without controversy in America. Jefferson himself had to be persuaded that it was constitutional—he had always insisted on interpreting that document strictly—and New England Federalists, in particular, correctly foresaw that doubling the nation's territory would likely reduce their own influence in the America of the future. (See Figure 5.4.)

Napoleon's decision to rid France of this territory also met with opposition on the part of some who were close to him. His two brothers, Joseph and Lucien, were known to be strongly opposed. So was his foreign minister, the redoubtable Talleyrand. But Napoleon was at that point determined to marshal all his power to defeat Great Britain, he hoped, once and for all. With that as his goal, the dreadful French reversals he was just then learning about in Saint-Domingue in 1802–1803 no doubt convinced him to quit America and concentrate his forces in and around Europe.

It was an astounding about-face. He had come to power determined to reassert French control over Saint-Domingue, which had long been France's richest colony. For that, he sent an expeditionary force of thirty thousand to the island to wrest it from former slaves and mulattoes who had largely taken control of much of the territory; the French revolutionary government had proclaimed the abolition of slavery there in February 1794. Once it became clear to the local population that Napoleon's

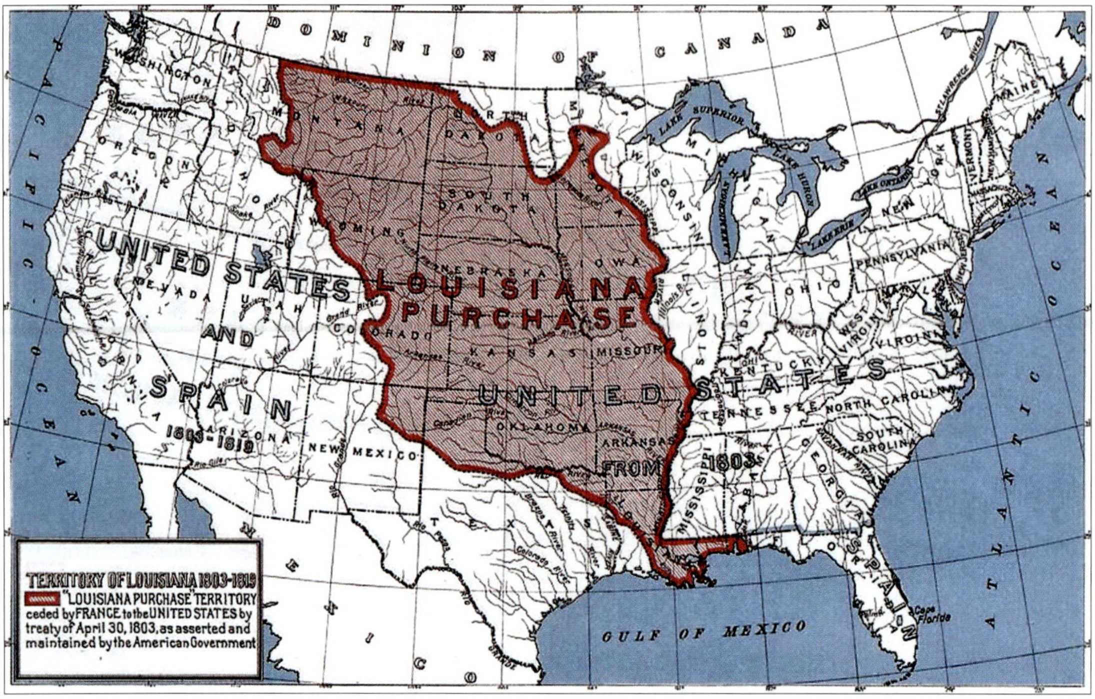

FIGURE 5.4 When the Jefferson administration purchased the Louisiana Territory from Napoleon in 1803, the United States was approximately doubled in size.

force intended to restore slavery, the people strongly resisted. Meanwhile, yellow fever began to take a terrible toll on the French troops. Their commander, General LeClerc, Napoleon's brother-in-law, fell victim, along with nearly fifteen thousand others, decimating the force to the point that it could no longer succeed at its mission. The last of what remained of the French expedition left the island at the end of December 1803. Saint-Domingue was finally lost for France. For the first and only time in history, a slave insurrection had succeeded. With it, a second republic was born in the New World, this one ruled by people of color.[21] Meanwhile, the British navy was attacking French vessels in the Caribbean, with more loss of life. One of the French officers who died in Havana after a battle with the British at sea was the vicomte de Noailles.

While events moved ineluctably toward the establishment of the independent Republic of Haiti, which was proclaimed on January 1, 1804, Napoleon saw little incentive to hold onto New Orleans, whose chief value to the French for years had been as an entrepôt and transit stop for the sugar and coffee shipped back to Europe from the Caribbean. Nor had there ever been much French settlement in the distant lands of Louisiana. Napoleon no doubt could see that American pressure on that territory would increasingly strain France's resources. Therefore, he rather quickly lost interest in attempting to defend French interests in the Americas. As both Napoleon and President Jefferson had hoped, once all of Louisiana became part of the United States, the tensions that had often roiled them since the early days of the French Revolution were finally relaxed.

That left Great Britain as the chief thorn in America's side. The independence for America that came with the Treaty of Paris in 1783 had brought a largely cold peace. Since then, the British government had repeatedly imposed trade restrictions on American ships, periodically seizing those vessels in international waters, impounding their cargoes and impressing their seamen. On the nation's western frontier, American settlers had been subject to harassment, and worse, by British forces, sometimes with help from Native Americans resisting their displacement from their ancestral lands. The Jay Treaty of 1794 had brought an interlude of relative calm between the two nations, but, in the years following the Louisiana Purchase, it became increasingly clear that most of these issues had merely been postponed rather than resolved.

James Madison succeeded Thomas Jefferson as president in 1809 and, like his predecessor, tried to persuade Britain to respect America's merchant fleet and its settlers in the West. But by the time he approached reelection in 1812, he concluded that stiffer action had become essential. On June 1, he sent a message to Congress outlining the nation's grievances against its former mother country. It made clear his willingness to sign a declaration of war should Congress ask for it. After debate, both houses did so, although narrowly, and, on June 18, Madison signed the bill declaring the nation at war.

Congress immediately recognized the need to build up the nation's army, and to do so quickly, if there were to be any prospect that the United States might hold its own with its powerful adversary. Bills were passed to provide bonuses for men to enlist and to award them land for their service. But, by the time Congress adjourned in July, it had passed no new legislation to pay for these incentives or for the war more generally. That would have to wait for the next Congress, which would not be elected until November. Meanwhile, the secretary of the treasury, Albert Gallatin, thought it expedient to explore how the United States might obtain a substantial loan for the war effort. He sent an emissary to Philadelphia to explore the matter with America's richest citizen, Stephen Girard.[22]

Within the previous months, Girard had put his already great wealth to unprecedented use, augmenting it further when he single-handedly bought the property of the First Bank of the United States in Philadelphia. The bank, which had been politically controversial since it was created in 1791, had closed on March 3, 1811, after Congress refused to renew its charter. The tie vote in the Senate had left Jefferson's vice president, George Clinton, to vote against renewal. The bank's trustees then had tried, and failed, to obtain a state charter that would allow the bank to reopen, but the Pennsylvania legislature refused to grant a charter. At that point, the bank's property was put up for sale. Girard moved quickly to purchase it—for cash. He thereby turned himself into a banker, and a unique one at that, inasmuch as he was sole owner of the business with neither shareholders nor a board of directors to answer to. Just one month before the War of 1812 began, Girard opened his bank for business. Almost

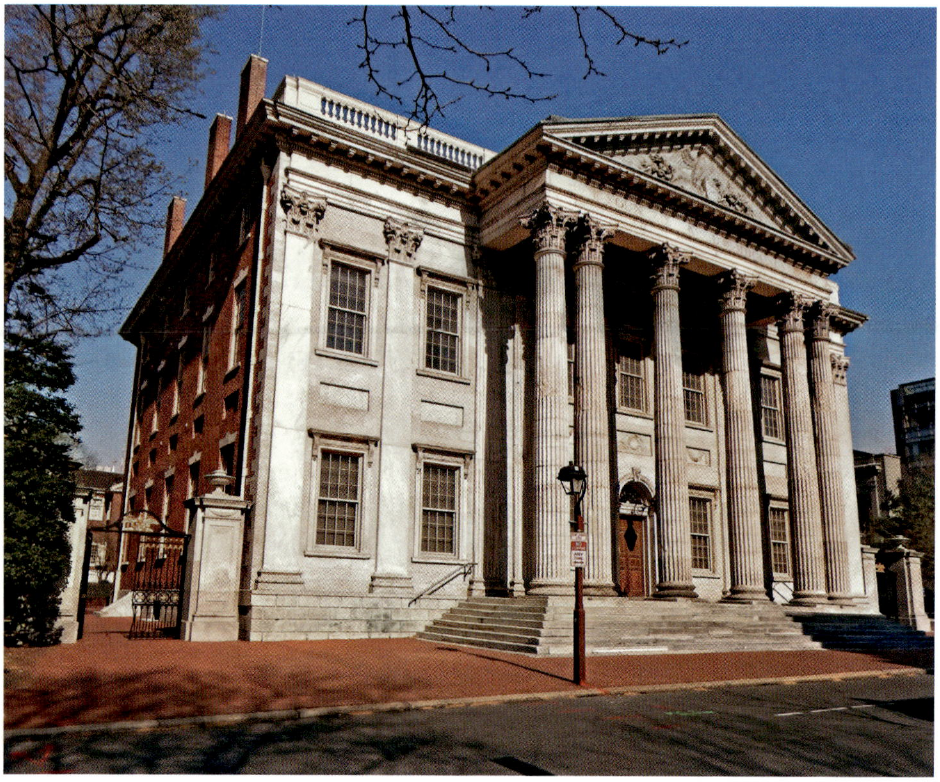

FIGURE 5.5 The First Bank of the United States was created by Congress in 1791 but closed in 1811 when Congress refused to renew its charter. Stephen Girard then purchased the bank's building and assets, thereby becoming the nation's most powerful banker.

overnight, Stephen Girard, at age sixty-two, became the most powerful banker in the nation.[23] (See Figure 5.5.)

During the first months of the war, the British captured American military outposts at Forts Mackinac and Detroit in Michigan Territory and destroyed Fort Dearborn, site of the future Chicago. Although the American navy had some modest successes at sea, America's prospect of winning the war seemed dim, especially so without the funds needed to finance the war effort. Napoleon was losing his grip on continental Europe, which meant that England would soon be able to devote more of its forces to the conflict with America. In February 1813, the new Congress authorized the U.S. Treasury to borrow $16 million, the largest loan ever for the federal government until then.[24] Although the interest rate was generous, subscriptions were fairly meager, even after Secretary Gallatin persuaded a number of rich individuals, Stephen Girard among them, to participate. When the subscription period ended on April 5, the loan drive had fallen terribly short: less than $6 million had been subscribed. The federal government, meanwhile, ran out of money. Stephen Girard also had bad news. He learned that two of his fleet of merchant ships had been seized by the British: one was held for ransom at the entrance to Delaware Bay; the other, attacked off the coast of France, had been taken to England.

At this dire moment, the secretary of the treasury came to Philadelphia to call in desperation on Stephen Girard, who was, in the words of his biographer, "the only person in America in 1813 who had millions of available and spendable dollars."[25] Gallatin had been born in Switzerland and, like Girard, was a native French-speaker. He presented a plan to the banker that included a conditional subscription by John Jacob Astor and others that would add some $2 million toward the loan's total. The condition was that Girard should advance all of the remainder, which was more than half the loan amount. Their meeting on April 5 ended with Girard agreeing to put up that enormous amount of money. His only requirement was that the residue of the loan be deposited in his bank and not in those of any of his rivals. Gallatin readily agreed. Girard's Bank then became the source for funding the war effort of the United States. Girard's action soon restored public confidence in the financial stability of the federal government and inspired other investors to participate in the loan. Within days, Girard was able to sell a substantial portion of his own obligation to others. His patriotic desire to come to the aid of his adoptive country was already clear; so was his business acumen.

The full amount of the $16 million loan went immediately to the war effort. Resources were rushed to commanders on the nation's western and northern frontiers. Victories followed in New York, Ohio, and Ontario. In September 1813, the entire British fleet on Lake Erie was sunk or captured. These military reversals for the British prompted them, some two months later, to propose a peace conference in which their emissaries would negotiate directly with the United States. President Madison promptly accepted. The city of Ghent in Belgium was the agreed-upon site for the conference. Yet, thanks to the slowness of communications, a long delay followed before the peace talks began. In April 1814, Napoleon abdicated and went into exile on the island of Elba in the Mediterranean, allowing Britain to turn its full attention to the war in America. Over the summer, the commander of British naval forces in Chesapeake Bay grew more aggressive and moved his forces toward the nation's capital. Following a British victory at the Battle of Bladensburg, Maryland, only two miles east of the border of the District of Columbia, President Madison and other top officials fled Washington on August 24.[26] Enemy forces quickly captured the city that night and set fire to its most important buildings, including both the Executive Mansion and the Capitol. Fortuitously, a ferocious rainstorm—possibly a hurricane—soon swept across the city, extinguishing the fires. After they razed much of the city, the British forces withdrew twenty-six hours after entering it, their eyes next on Baltimore and Philadelphia.[27] (See Figure 5.6.)

Understanding what might come, Stephen Girard took the precaution of sending wagonloads of specie from his bank, along with other valuables that included cargo from his ships, to warehouses in Reading, sixty-five miles northeast of Philadelphia. Fortunately for him and for the American cause, Fort McHenry outside Baltimore withstood "the rockets' red glare and bombs bursting in air" to prevent the British from reaching Baltimore.[28] Instead of moving on to Philadelphia, the fleet retreated back down the Chesapeake in September. In the north, the Americans also held off the British effort to cut New England off from the rest of the nation. News of these reversals reached Europe after the negotiators had already begun their work in Ghent. By then, both sides were ready to end the fighting. On Christmas Eve in 1814, they agreed on a treaty that largely restored the status quo at the time hostilities broke out, although with a sense on both sides that this "Second War of American Independence," as many saw it, put an end to the nearly constant tensions that had endured between the two nations since they had concluded the first war of independence more than thirty years earlier.[29]

Had it not been for Stephen Girard's willingness early in the conflict to finance the war, it is likely that it would have ended in a humiliating defeat for the United States, including, possibly, the loss of its independence. Instead, another détente would mostly rule U.S.-British relations in the future just as it did those between America and France.

The return of peace to the United States brought an even larger change in the American outlook. James Monroe, who had served every president since Washington, himself was swept into the White House as the result of the election in 1816, which seemed to obliterate the old political divisions. His two terms would soon be known as the "Era of Good Feelings" for the sense that many Americans felt that their nation had arrived, prosperous and successful, on the world stage.

After his inauguration, James Monroe and his wife were able to move back into a White House that had been largely restored after the 1814 fire, and the couple, therefore, undertook to redecorate and refurbish the mansion. Their taste ran strongly

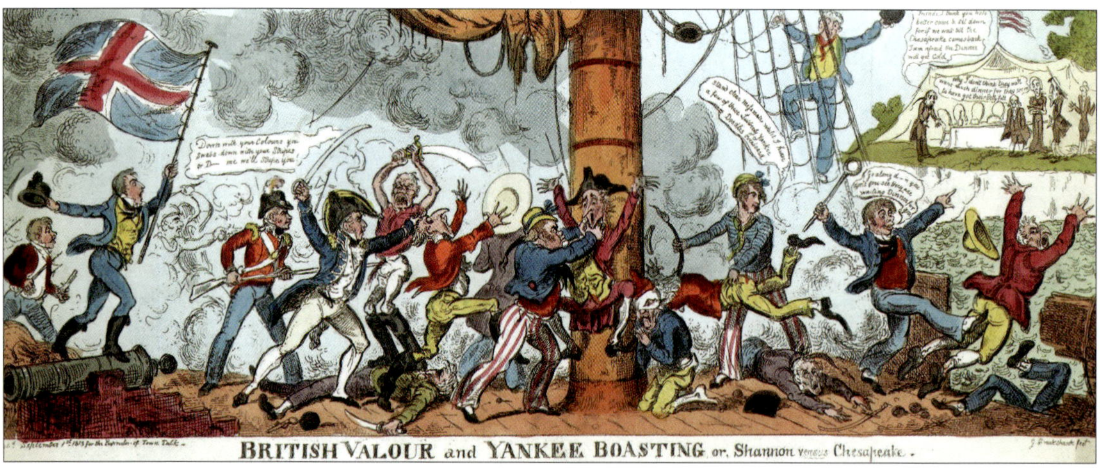

FIGURE 5.6 George Cruikshank, *British Valour and Yankee Boasting or, Shannon vs. Chesapeake,* published September 1, 1813. This English cartoon from the War of 1812 suggests that the Yankees were no match for the valorous British navy. (Prints and Photographs Division, Library of Congress)

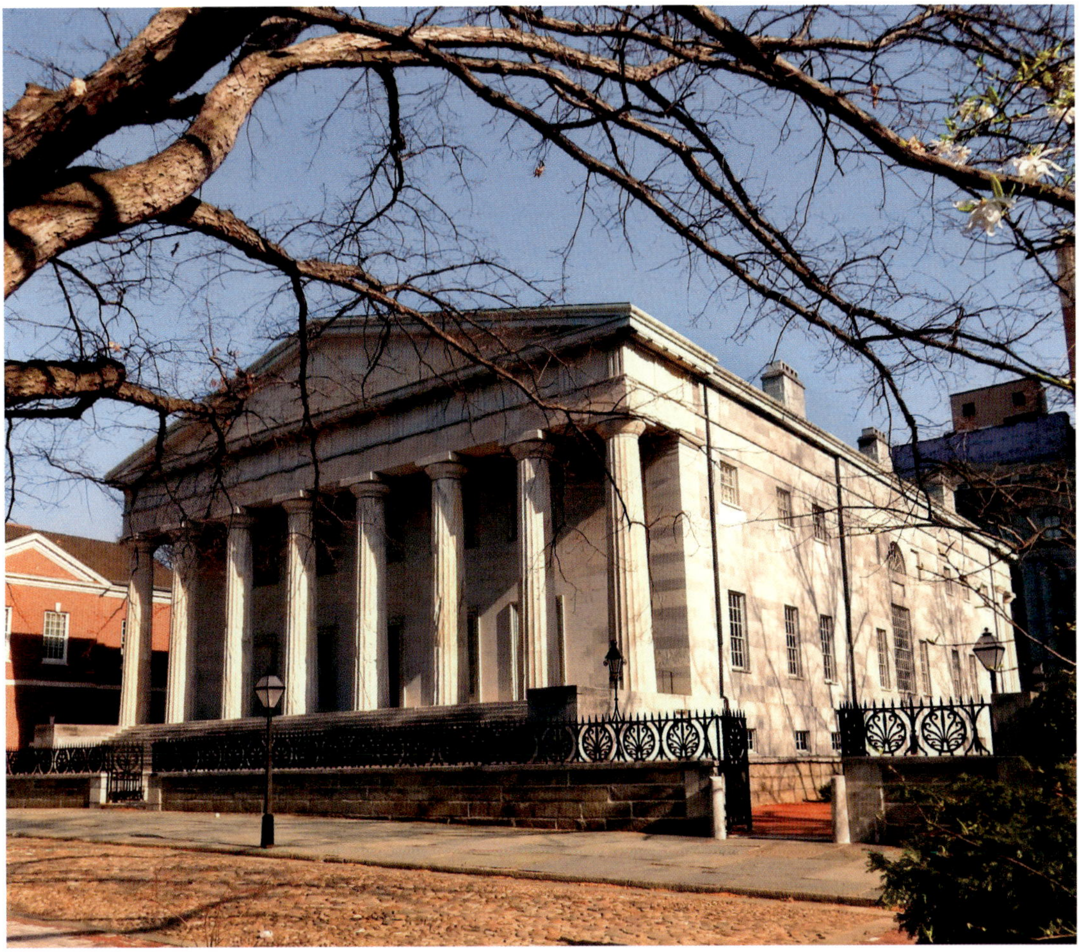

FIGURE 5.7 Built between 1818 and 1824, the life of the Second Bank of the United States was brief. Today it houses a national portrait gallery in honor of many figures from the Revolution. A number of French officers depicted by Charles Willson Peale are among them.

to the elegant French furnishings they had come to know during their years in Paris when Monroe was minister of the United States. They sold their collection of Louis XVI furniture, china, and plate to the federal government for use in the White House. They ordered additional goods from France for the oval drawing room (known today as the Blue Room) and for smaller rooms as well. The Monroe restoration still serves as the heart of the mansion's historic collection, and many of the items they selected remain in use and on display today.

The coming of the Era of Good Feelings had already been signaled in February 1816, when the outgoing President Madison signed the charter to establish the Second Bank of the United States, which seemed to indicate his and the public's new support for a strong federal government. The Second Bank, like the First, would be headquartered in Philadelphia for its lifetime. Yet, like that of its predecessor, its life would be brief; it would end twenty years later after the return of partisan politics and as the result of the opposition led by another president, Andrew Jackson. Yet, for a time, the outlook for the bank as for the nation remained balmy. For the last years of its brief life, the bank would be housed within two blocks of what had become Girard's Bank four years earlier, in a chastely elegant Greek temple designed by Philadelphia's leading architect of the era, William Strickland.[30] Its commanding presence suggested Philadelphia would continue to play a dynamic role in the nation's future. (See Figure 5.7.)

[6]

The Appeal of French Art for Early Nineteenth-Century Philadelphia

The relocation of the capital from Philadelphia to the banks of the Potomac in 1800 did not diminish Charles Willson Peale's determination to make his hometown a vibrant center for the arts and sciences. Along with his son Rembrandt Peale, the sculptor William Rush, and some business leaders, Peale founded the Pennsylvania Academy of the Fine Arts in December 1805 with the purpose of promoting the cultivation of the fine arts. Modeled on the Royal Academy of Arts in London and the New York Academy of Fine Arts, which had been launched in 1802, the Pennsylvania Academy sought to educate artists by familiarizing them with copies of paintings and sculptures from the great masterpieces of the past. Painting instruction in Europe had evolved from an apprenticeship system in the Renaissance to the establishment of official art academies that aimed at elevating the status of the artist from a craftsman to a practitioner of a liberal art where the intellectual content of art became paramount. To perfect their drawing skills, beginning artists copied first from prints, then from plaster casts of antiquities to keep the prominence of the classical archetype in mind, and finally advanced to sketching the live model. The French Academy had been established in 1648 and England's Royal Academy in 1768. Regular exhibition of works that demonstrated the accepted canons of subject matter and style educated the public to the refinements of aesthetic taste.

Eager to emulate the appreciation of the arts that existed abroad but still lagged in America, the founders of the Pennsylvania Academy set about importing casts of sculptures. Houdon's *Écorché*, a full-length standing anatomical rendering of a flayed figure in plaster, could be seen along with casts of the *Apollo Belvedere*, the *Laocoön* group, the *Venus de Medici*, and other works. Houdon's cast was the sole contemporary work selected in Paris by Nicholas Biddle and Houdon for display in Philadelphia. In

1807, the Academy held its first exhibition, which featured over five hundred works with nearly half by American artists.

European art students received strict instruction in copying masterworks as prime examples of adherence to standards of propriety and the transmission of ideals closely controlled by the academy and the state. This would ensure the training of their eye and hand for producing works that would take their place in the lineage of great masterworks. The importation of these casts to Philadelphia testified to the commitment of American artists to educate themselves on native soil and establish a school of art worthy of the ideals of the new republic.

The British model of portraiture and history painting remained dominant at the beginning of the nineteenth century and Americans aspiring to a career in the arts were drawn to London. This was largely due to the presence there of fellow Pennsylvanian Benjamin West (1738–1820), whose nascent artistic talent attracted the attention and support of Dr. William Smith, the provost of the College of Philadelphia, and William Allen, a wealthy Philadelphian. Together they sponsored West on a "Grand Tour" of Europe to foster his knowledge of the cultural treasures of the continent. While abroad, West stopped in England and decided to remain there. He enjoyed an illustrious career in London through the patronage of King George III, eventually becoming the second president of the Royal Academy of Art, following Sir Joshua Reynolds.

Despite the allure of London, Paris also attracted American artists to its vast repository of resources and academic training, with artists such as John Vanderlyn and Washington Allston establishing residences there. In 1802, West visited Paris where he exhibited his *Death on a Pale Horse* at the Salon to great acclaim. The art community celebrated him, and the following year Napoleon made him a foreign associate of the academy. Paris became a further desirable destination once the Louvre opened its collection to the public during the French Revolution when the National Assembly commanded that it function as a museum to exhibit the royal collection. Napoleon's marauding campaigns brought further treasures from Spain, Austria, Holland, Italy, and Egypt with the goal of making Paris the European center of art, science, and culture. Foreign national funding of the arts and the rigor of academic training served as an inspiration for American artists who desired the same respect and financial support from their newly minted government.

Rembrandt Peale (1778–1860), the third child of Charles Willson Peale and his first wife Rachel Brewer, learned his painting skills from his father as would his many siblings. Rembrandt traveled to New York City during late July and August 1807 to solicit work for an inaugural exhibition at the Pennsylvania Academy. Visits with Robert Fulton, who had more success in Paris with his career as an engineer than he did as an aspiring painter, and the diplomat and poet Joel Barlow, who had been made a French citizen in 1792, fired Rembrandt's determination to go to France. Rembrandt studied in London, during 1802–1803 with Benjamin West and Washington Allston, where he was exposed to the advantages of drawing from antique casts and the life model. Nevertheless, he returned from England convinced that Paris held more opportunity for him. He eventually convinced his father that he needed to expand his knowledge of the old masters and improve his technical skills by studying with the principal painters of France and by steeping himself in the treasures of the old masters held by the Louvre. Additionally, portraiture remained the most popular subject at the French Salon and held the promise of lucrative commissions.

Charles Willson Peale sent a request to President Jefferson in February 1808 to solicit contacts for his son to establish while in Paris. Jefferson provided eleven names along with a presidential passport that would furnish the painter access to American ministers and consuls living abroad.[1] Jefferson, deeply familiar with the encouragement of the arts in France, worried that the lack of patronage and support for the arts in America would result in Rembrandt's permanent move to Paris as more artists, including Samuel F. B. Morse, settled there for lengthy stays. America had lost the talents of John Singleton Copley and West to England and Jefferson feared further defections to France. Benjamin Latrobe expressed a similar apprehension about Rembrandt abandoning America: "Whether you will return or not neither you nor I can guess. If your horror at our barbarism in the arts should give way to your detestation of European barbarism in government, we shall see you again."[2] After some initial reluctance based on the same fears, the elder Peale endorsed his son's determination to hone his talents in France: "He is strong," wrote the elder Peale to the American minister General Armstrong, "but he will be stronger—He is now good but will become excellent."[3] Peale trusted his son to produce portraits for his "Gallery of Great Men" at his museum and subvented several excursions to France.

Rembrandt's first visit to Paris lasted a month or two in 1806, cut short by fears of the instability of the political situation in France, followed by a slightly longer stay from June to September 1808.[4] His portraits of the sculptor Jean-Antoine Houdon; the naturalist and zoologist Georges Cuvier; Jacques-Henri Bernardin de Saint-Pierre, who authored the influential 1788 novel *Paul et Virginie*; and Dominique Vivant, Baron Denon, diplomat, author, and first director of the Louvre, demonstrated his ability to gain access to the artistic, scientific, and cultural elite of Paris. In keeping with the format of his father's works for his museum, Rembrandt's images of these luminaries retain the bust-length format but demonstrate an advance in color and depth learned in France.[5] He posed Houdon with his arm extended as if in the act of creating a sculpture. Rembrandt's inclusion of the red drapery over Houdon's shoulder indicates the sculptor's status as an officer of the state while it simultaneously enhances the warmth of the complexion that unites foreground and background to give depth to the painting. (See Figure 6.1.) Houdon gazes with sharp-eyed scrutiny at the person painting him, thus creating an image of artistic camaraderie. Houdon's ability to imbue his sculpted busts with vivid character is matched by Rembrandt's grasp of the alert assessment of Houdon's face. Both men had proudly crafted Washington's image, and Houdon's sojourn in Philadelphia would surely have given the painter and sculptor more than one subject for conversation during the posing sessions.

When Jefferson replied to Charles Willson Peale in March 1808 about a list of names of people for Rembrandt to paint while in Paris, he highlighted Cuvier, commenting that the paleontologist was someone "whom you mention & whose eminence

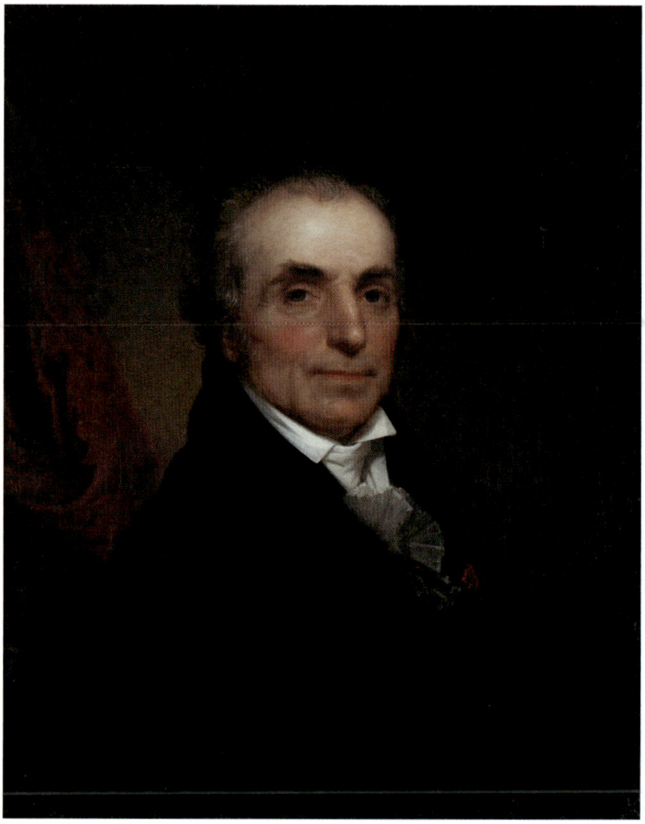

Figure 6.1
Rembrandt Peale, *Jean-Antoine Houdon*, 1808. Oil on canvas, 28 7/16 × 23 in. (72.2 × 58.4 cm). Acc. No.: 1854.1.3. (Courtesy of the Pennsylvania Academy of the Fine Arts, Philadelphia. General Fund)

you know."[6] The elder Peale had suggested Cuvier as a subject in his February 21, 1808, letter of solicitation to the president. In 1801, Charles Willson Peale obtained funding from then vice president Jefferson and the American Philosophical Society to excavate the bones of extinct mammoths discovered on a farm in Newburgh, New York. Peale assembled a team to drain the site and reconstruct the remains, bringing them back for display in his museum. Rembrandt and the sculptor William Rush filled in missing parts of the skeleton with wood and papier-mâché under the supervision of Caspar Wistar, the foremost anatomist of the time. Capitalizing on the dramatic impression this creature would arouse, Charles Willson Peale dressed his black servant Moses William in Native American headdress on Christmas Eve 1801, mounted him on a white horse, and sent him on a ride through the streets of Philadelphia to announce the display of the mammoth in the museum that could be seen for a fee. The exhibit quickly became a sensation, setting off competitions in a type of pre–Guinness Book of World Records manner when claims were made of mammoth breads and cheeses being produced and the discovery of a mammoth peach tree and parsnip. The Peales assembled a second skeleton from bones from the New York sites and held a dinner beneath the animal's enormous rib cage, where thirteen men were entertained by a musician playing "Jefferson's March" and "Yankee Doodle." Rembrandt and his brother Rubens took the specimen to London for exhibition in

1802–1803 with the goal of eventually selling it in France to Cuvier, but war between Britain and France impeded the transaction.[7]

Rembrandt published a ninety-two-page pamphlet in 1803 titled *Historical Disquisition on the Mammoth, or the Great American Incognitum* on the exhumation of the mammoth, and he cited Cuvier's paleontological work at length. Cuvier had obtained Rembrandt's drawings of the mammoth and in 1806 gave the creature the name of mastodon in a paper he published in Paris, where he disputed Rembrandt's claims that the animal had been a carnivore. Rembrandt's renderings of the mammoth had significantly advanced Cuvier's scientific knowledge, causing him to apply a separate genus to the creature and solidify his theory. Cuvier christened the newly discovered creature "mastodon" based on the visual nature of the bumpy tooth of the excavated mammoth.

American and French nationalism also entered into the scientific issues surrounding the mammoth as the Comte de Buffon in the fifth volume of his *Histoire naturelle* in 1766 declared that humans and animals in America degenerated due to the climate and were thus smaller and weaker than those found in Europe. Jefferson vigorously opposed these ideas in his *Notes on the State of Virginia* in 1785. At six feet, two inches tall, Jefferson towered over the five-foot, five-inch Buffon when they met in Paris, where the future president displayed an enormous panther skin and later the hide of a moose to prove his point and defend his country. The visual impact of these meetings alone must have silently countered Buffon's allegations.

Thus, for a variety of reasons, Charles Willson Peale had several compelling reasons to obtain Cuvier's image for his museum where it would reside adjacent to the room where the mastodon bones were displayed next to the skeleton of a mouse as a rebuttal to Buffon's demeaning comments. Rembrandt's portrait of Cuvier presents the scientist in a three-quarter profile that accentuates the scientist's elongated nose and protruding chin. (See Figure 6.2.) The extended opening of Cuvier's jacket emphatically echoes the sweep of the chin with the stiff white collar underlining Cuvier's elongated jawline. The stark whiteness of the ruffled shirt sets off the flesh tones of the face and serves as a kind of sculptural pedestal for the strong features of the renowned paleontologist who gazes thoughtfully but assuredly in the distance. The emphasis on Cuvier's jawbone could perhaps be a visual pun on the paleontologist's invention of the name mastodon. When Charles Willson Peale first saw this part of the mammoth when it was excavated he cried out: "Gracious God! What a jaw! How many animals must have been crushed beneath it!"[8]

Before leaving for Paris, Rembrandt obtained a letter of introduction from Joseph Allen Smith, a noted American collector of European art, to Baron Denon who had been appointed by Napoleon as director general of museums and head of the Musée Napoléon. Denon had accompanied Napoleon on his Egyptian expedition and continued to loot many works of art through Europe that eventually formed the nucleus of the Louvre. (The Denon Wing carries his name to this day.) Denon gave Peale wide access to the Louvre collections, where the painter carefully studied the works of Raphael, Correggio, and Veronese. The Flemish painters Van Dyck and Rubens also captured his attention with the Marie de Medici cycle at the Palais de Luxembourg.

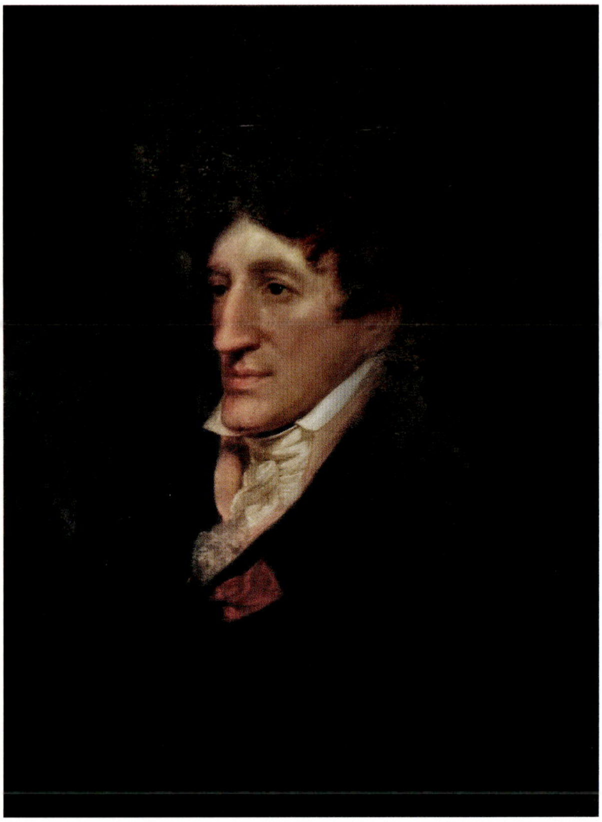

FIGURE 6.2
Rembrandt Peale, *Georges Cuvier*, 1808. Oil on canvas, 27½ × 22¼ in. (Philadelphia, Mütter Museum, the College of Physicians)

At the time Peale visited Paris, only Dresden, Amsterdam, and Florence gave the public access to their collections, which held examples primarily of works from their own countries.[9] The Louvre thus afforded Rembrandt a priceless international artistic education that influenced his career for the rest of his life. Peale later maintained that Denon had requested that he remain in France and would furnish him with commissions to paint imperial portraits, claiming that the man who was known as the "eye of Napoleon" preferred Peale's portraits to those of his native countrymen who had turned their attention to history paintings.[10]

Whether this offer was true or not, Denon proved helpful to the American painter by introducing him to the leading painters of the neoclassical school in Paris, led by Jacques-Louis David (1748–1825). Rembrandt considered David, along with François Gérard and Robert Lefêvre, to be the three principal painters in France. He carefully observed the style and techniques of neoclassicism with its emphasis on firm contours, strong contrast of colors, refined sensibility, and meticulous attention to detail, gradually incorporating these features into his own paintings. Rembrandt boasted about the endorsement of the French for his portraits, writing to his father: "My Pictures by the few who have seen them are much approved of—and what I am most flattered by & secretly hoped, are said to be in the stile of Vandyck."[11] His attendance at the distribution of awards given at the Institut National, where artists were applauded and given flowers, medals, and books for their accomplishments, deeply impressed him, igniting in him the ambition to have the American government demonstrate similar recognition. Despite the successes he reported to his father and his joy in studying the old masters, Rembrandt's unrelenting homesickness and the continued threat of war throughout Europe impelled him to return to America in October 1808.

A year later, Rembrandt returned to Paris with his wife and five children where they would remain until November 1810. Seeing the progress his son had made, the elder Peale was less apprehensive this time about his son's return to France and commissioned fifty portraits for which his son would be paid $100 each. Rembrandt completed twenty-three portraits during the thirteen months of his return to the French capital, among them images of the Marquis de Lafayette (lost), Pierre-Samuel du Pont de Nemours (Wilmington, DE, Hagley Museum), and the painter François Gérard (lost). Rembrandt was elated when David agreed to allow Peale to do his portrait, writing to his father and brother Rubens: "I have taken two sittings of David the painter, and he appears quite pleased. I believe I shall make a picture of him which will give me a great reputation, he has refused to sit to every painter—I shall exhibit it at the Louvre."[12] (See Figure 6.3.)

David had been scarred in a fencing incident, causing a tumorlike swelling that contorted the left side of his face. In his self-portraits of 1791 and 1794, David virtually eliminates the disfigurement whereas Rembrandt renders a straightforward record

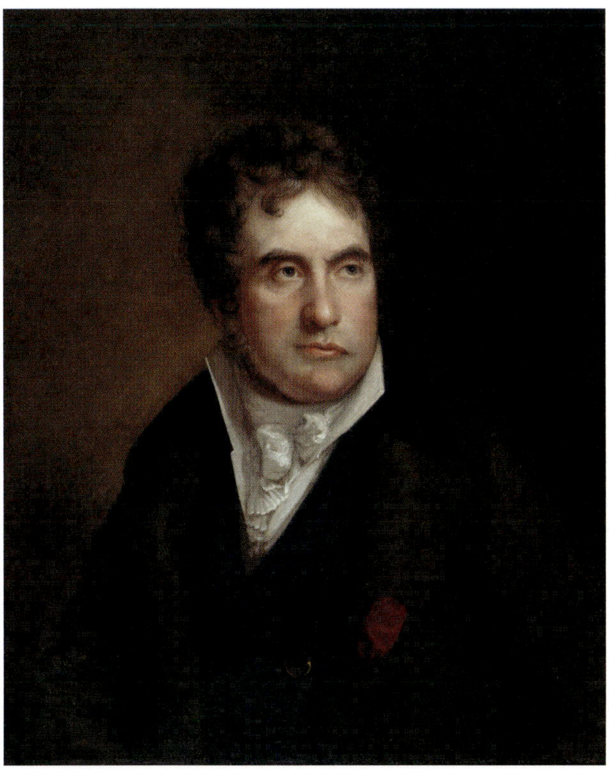

Figure 6.3 Rembrandt Peale, *Jacques-Louis David*, 1810. Oil on canvas, 28½ × 23³⁄₁₆ in. (72.4 × 58.9 cm). Acc. No.: 1854.1.2. (Courtesy of the Pennsylvania Academy of the Fine Arts, Philadelphia. General Fund.)

of the French artist's true appearance in keeping with late colonial American practice. Peale nevertheless tried to attenuate focus on David's downturned mouth by casting the upper right half of the portrait into relative darkness where the hair and dark jacket almost merge. The brightness of the red ribbon on David's jacket pulls the eye down from the distorted side of David's face. An aura of light on the left half of the portrait puts the focus on the regularity of the features on that side. The lively curl on the forehead functions as an animated marker that deliberately contrasts with the flattened lock of hair on the other side that leads the eye off into the shadowy depths of the right background. Wisps of curly hair on the right side of David's head visually rhyme with the overlapping lacy folds of the jabot at David's neck to keep the gaze on the more regularized side of the painter's countenance. No documentation exists of David's reaction to this painting, which he knew would be seen in America. Rembrandt may have conveyed his deep interest in and knowledge of science to convince David to allow him to portray the visual evidence of his facial features without enhancement or idealization, as in typical European academic practice.

David allegedly expressed his admiration for American art to Rembrandt in a conversation recalled many years later:

> When I was painting the portrait of the celebrated DAVID, he asked me, why it was that *all* the best painters in London were Americans? I replied, *not all.* He replied, "West, Copley, Trumbull, Allston." I told him that many American artists succeed, because of the *difficulties* they have to encounter. "How so, when our Napoleon gallery is to concentrate every facility to artists?" I told him, my opinion was that the American, strongly excited by all that he had read of European talent and excellence, exerts every means to reach the European seats of arts, and having little money and time to spend, studies with his whole soul, and therefore outstrips his more indolent and luxurious fellow students; and afterwards being visited by literary travellers, they distinguish themselves by lavish expenditures of patriotic praise.[13]

Clearly the disparity between the experience of being an artist in America with that of being a financially supported one in France resonated throughout the years in Peale's memory.

Rembrandt painted David's portrait in encaustic where molten wax was used as a medium for pigment instead of oil. He wrote of his intense excitement for this method of painting in a letter to his father and brother Rubens, which was published in Philadelphia in the *Port folio* in 1810. He praised the richness and transparency that the technique allowed. An added benefit was that the medium dried quickly and did not collect dust. Most pleasing to him was that painting flesh no longer proved so arduous. Given the pressure to produce portraits, these qualities allowed him to capitalize on his time in France and boded well for a productive career when he returned to America. On September 10, 1810, Peale lectured on encaustic at the Institut de France and demonstrated the technique with one of his own paintings.

When Pierre-Étienne Duponceau, a Frenchman who emigrated to America at the age of seventeen and became a prominent Philadelphia lawyer, learned of this he wrote enthusiastically—and chauvinistically for his adopted county—to Robert Livingston: "I am informed that Mr Peale at Paris has recovered the ancient mode of painting in encaustic, and that David is sitting to him for his picture. With such resources as we possess within ourselves, it is impossible to check our growth. America shall rise and flourish in spite of Europe."[14]

David's reputation in America had been established in the 1780s among the cultural elite of America and Jefferson's deep admiration of the artist was well known. He had been introduced to David by Trumbull in Paris and wrote to his friend Madame de Bréhan in 1789: "I do not feel an interest in any pencil but that of David."[15] After the opening of the Salon of 1787, Jefferson wrote to John Trumbull urging him to make the journey from London to see the exhibition's many offerings. He opined that David's *The Death of Socrates* was the "best thing" in it.[16] Rembrandt met David during his first stay in Paris in 1808, most likely through Denon, and had visited his house and studio. Their relationship continued during Rembrandt's second Paris sojourn, prompting David's subject matter and style to remain a spur to the American throughout his career. According to Peale scholar Lillian B. Miller, David's influence fostered Rembrandt's ability to project forms in space and capture the individuality of the sitter to express character and psychology. Rembrandt thus abandoned the eighteenth-century British tradition that had lingered in his work due to his father's authority and his own time studying in London in 1801–1803.[17] Most significantly, David's moralizing history paintings that swept away the rococo style associated with the aristocratic realm of Louis XVI, convinced Rembrandt that portraiture might be a means of making a living, but great artists aspired to depict heroic deeds that would elevate and instruct. This was a lesson carried back from his studies in London and greatly reinforced by his contacts with the neoclassical school of painting in Paris, especially David.

When Napoleon crowned himself emperor in 1804, he appointed David as first painter to the Imperial Court, keenly aware of the advantages of imagery for affecting public opinion. Truth to reality gave way to the power of propaganda in images such as David's *Napoleon Crossing the Alps*. (See Figure 6.4.) Napoleon led an expedition into Italy during the spring of 1800 to seize territory that had been confiscated from the French. The audacity of crossing the Saint Bernard Pass when climate conditions almost continuously rendered it unnavigable enhanced Napoleon's reputation. His decisive victory at the Battle of Marengo fortified his standing in Paris as first consul after his coup d'état in November 1799. David manipulated the visual record as Napoleon followed his troops rather than led them, rode a mule rather than a horse, and crossed in good weather rather than battling fierce winds and icy slopes. Napoleon refused to pose for the portrait but remained alert to the political propaganda inherent in visual imagery, insisting that he be portrayed "*calme sur un cheval fougueux*" (calm on a fiery horse). With one hand, David portrayed him steadily controlling his violently rearing steed, thus suggesting intellectual discipline matched with equestrian and

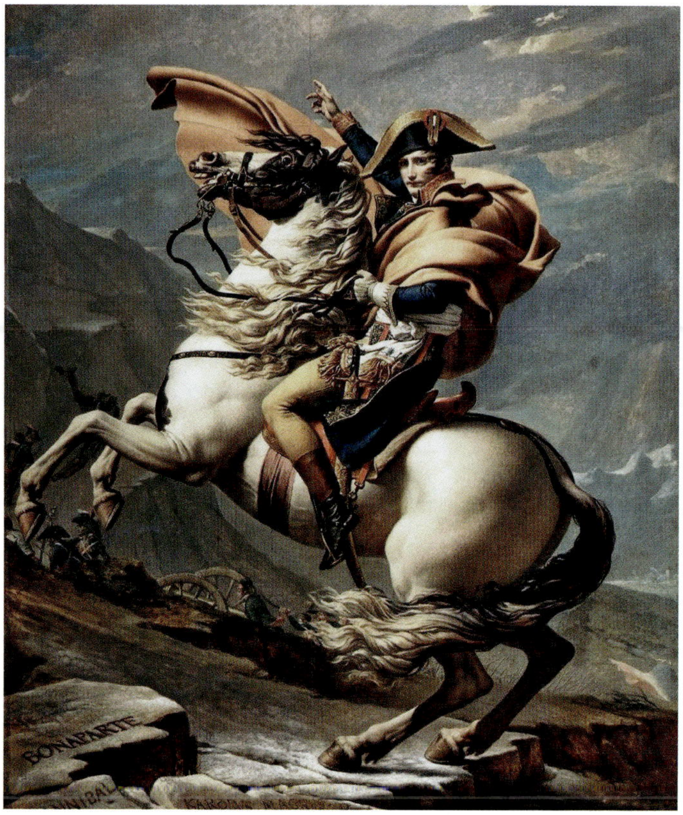

Figure 6.4
Jacques-Louis David, *Napoleon Crossing the Alps*, 1800. Oil on canvas, 259 × 221 cm (101.9" × 87"). (Château de Malmaison)

physical prowess. Paired with a commanding physique that gave lie to his nickname of "le petit Caporal," the image aspired to take its place among the lineage of great commanders and kings on horseback. David inscribed Napoleon's name in bold lettering on a large flat stone under the hooves of the horse with those of Hannibal and Charlemagne following in lighter script on rocks below, thereby creating a historical pedigree for the French victor. David made five copies of the painting and kept one in his various studios until his death in 1825.

The elder Peale had hoped his son could obtain a sitting from the emperor while in Paris, writing to Jefferson in 1808: "It would be a most fortunate thing for Rembrandt could he paint an Original Portrait of Buonaparte, yet so great a distinction could scarcely be expected, unless his study and residence in Rome and Paris were long and successful enough to place him at the head of Portrait Painters on the Continent; in which expectation I confess I do indulge, persuaded even at present that few can surpass him in the strength & fidelity of his Portraits, the force & nature of his colouring & the Individuality & expression of his Countenances."[18] Rembrandt did bring back a portrait bust of Napoleon, but one where he had to record the emperor's features while observing him on public occasions such as at the theater or addressing the Legislative Assembly. A long procession of deputies on the Champ de Mars where the emperor sat still for several hours provided a further opportunity for the artist to record his features.

Rembrandt first saw Napoleon at the theater and gave a detailed report of the emperor's features and character in a February 1810 letter published in the *Port folio*. Despite claiming that he was certain not to be dazzled by Napoleon's high rank and great achievements, Rembrandt gave a thorough biography of the emperor and obtained his autograph. Rembrandt had traveled to Italy a few weeks after Napoleon, collecting as many anecdotes as he could from people who encountered the emperor during his trip. Rembrandt's painterly eye detailed Napoleon's features as he described his "small, piercing, deeply sunk, dark grey eyes, a prominent nose, a chin out of proportion large, a good mouth, short coal-black hair, a forehead that would have satisfied Lavater."[19] According to the painter, Napoleon never looked in the face of the person to whom he was speaking and there was "nothing mean in Napoleon's countenance, but there is nothing inviting."[20] In an 1810 article for the *Port folio*, the painter characterized the emperor as "artful, selfish, arrogant, unfeeling, and inexorably vindictive."[21]

Peale painted Napoleon's image in 1810 and brought it home with him to America (Private Collection). Latrobe commented on the Napoleon portrait in a letter to Jefferson on May 19, 1811: "Mr Rembrandt Peale has returned from France much improved. But I do not know how it happens,—the portraits of eminent men in France of whom he has painted I think are much superior to any he has painted here. He has brought over a head of Napoleon of very striking character. He says that it was considered in France as the best portrait of the Emperor in existence. I do not doubt its being a good one. He possesses the talent of catching strong character."[22] John Neal, an important early American art critic, characterized it as one of the most remarkable portraits he had ever seen, describing Napoleon as "pale, earnest, and thoughtful, with a mixture of sadness and solemnity, such as you would expect from one who could see far into the future."[23]

Rembrandt was not to be long satisfied with a bust-length image of the emperor. Shortly after he returned to America in November 1810, he launched into his own version of Napoleon on horseback (now lost), finishing the picture and exhibiting it in Philosophical Hall the following April. What the public would see upon paying an admittance charge of twenty-five cents was a "Historical Portrait as large as Life, of Bonaparte Mounted on an Arabian charger, giving orders relative to a distant Engagement. Painted by Rembrandt Peale, who had various opportunities of seeing the Emperor, and offers this original likeness as a better one than any he could have copied in Paris."[24] David's influence on Rembrandt could not be denied, and John James Audubon called the painting *Napoleon Crossing the Alps* when he saw the work in 1812. The similarities prompted accusations of plagiarism, but Peale insisted on the originality of the design. John Neal called the image "a vigorous picture . . . the greatest of his workmanship."[25] The thirteen-by-eleven-foot canvas was Rembrandt's first attempt at large-scale history painting that resulted from his determination to rise in the ranks above portraiture. Benjamin West had hoped that Rembrandt would take up history painting when he returned from France in 1809,[26] but not everyone was convinced that his version of *Napoleon on Horseback* succeeded. Latrobe informed Jefferson that Rembrandt hated portrait painting but had unfortunately wasted time on the large image of a foreign dictator: "I regret exceedingly that a young artist of his merit should not go straight forward in the line that good sense points out as the only one leading to wealth & leisure and eminence on this side of the Atlantic, that of portraits, more or less historical, as his principal employ;—& of historical painting of *domestic* subjects as a *speculation* on public liberality."[27]

The October after his return, Rembrandt began an addition to his house at 155 Walnut Street for an Exhibition Room. The stimulus came from his experience in France: "On my return to America with improved knowledge and facilities in my art, I was abundantly patronized in portrait painting, but could not suppress an increasing desire to engage in greater works; I therefore built a Gallery."[28] It opened to the public in December 1811 with his equestrian portrait, a large-scale landscape of Harper's Ferry, a sampling of his portraits, a copy of West's *King Lear in the Storm*, his portrait of *Rubens with a Geranium* in order to demonstrate his ability at still life—all aimed at representing his mastery of the hierarchy of genres. Intent on making his career as a history painter, Rembrandt embarked on *The Roman Daughter* based on a story popular with artists and playwrights about a daughter breastfeeding her imprisoned father to prevent his starvation. (See Figure 6.5.) While French culture revered the nude as *la grande peinture* and the academic ideal, Americans arched at such representations. The critic for the *Port folio* hailed the design and execution but lamented that the subject matter was ill suited to public exhibition while the *Monthly Anthology and Boston Review* pronounced the painting disgusting.[29] With its well-defined outlines, strong color, pyramidal composition, and high finish, *The Roman Daughter* displayed Rembrandt's absorption of French neoclassical style and marked a decisive break from the British tradition. The prototype derived from Peter Paul Rubens's *Caritas Romana*, which he either knew from the original, a copy, or an engraving from it.[30] Rembrandt's choice of an artistic forebear and the subject testified to his ambition to distance himself from his reputation as a portrait painter and attach his name to the grand tradition.

Rembrandt never abandoned his determination to be a history painter although his financial support came from portrait commissions. Scholars of his work regard the Paris period and the following decade as the acme of his career. He renamed his Exhibition Room as the Apollodorian Gallery in June 1812 based on his experience of Parisian artists employing private exhibition spaces for the sale of works apart from the Salon. French references recur in his use of a French engraving for his 1812 *Jupiter and Io* that was destroyed in a fire in 1823. His 1820 *Court of Death* is rife with references to works by David, Lefèvre, and Gérard while an image of Homer at the Louvre inspired the depiction of the personification of Old Age in foreground beckoning to the lifeless figure.

Americans would learn more about French taste in art when Napoleon's elder brother Joseph Bonaparte (1768–1844) came to America in 1815 and settled in Point Breeze, New Jersey, bringing with him an extensive collection of paintings, sculptures, antiquities, and six thousand books. Surrounding his collection of Empire furniture were two hundred paintings with canvases by Rubens, Murillo, Canaletto, a Leon-

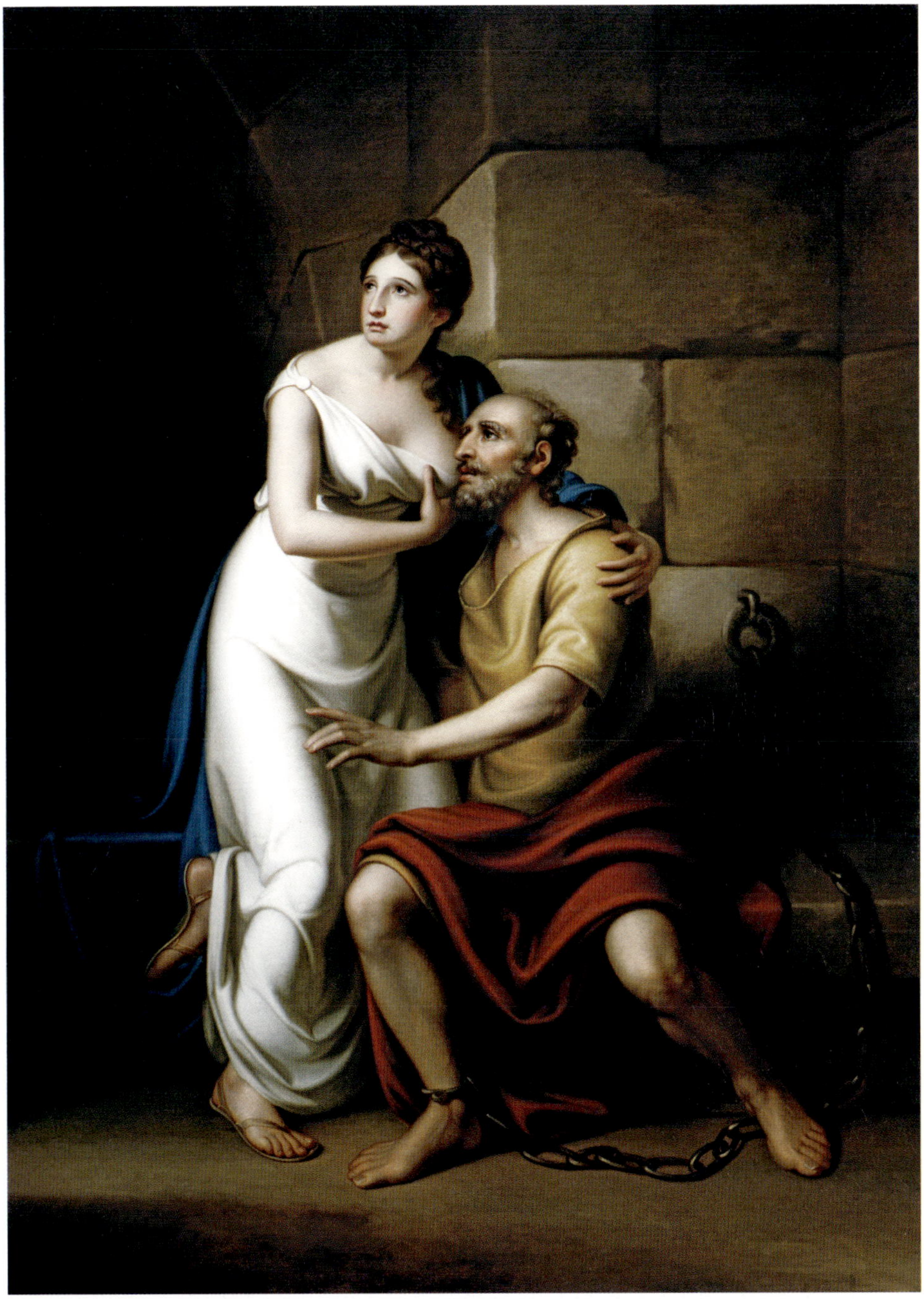

Figure 6.5 Rembrandt Peale, *The Roman Daughter*, 1811. 215 × 159.8 cm (84.6"× 62.9"). (Courtesy of Smithsonian American Art Museum, Gift of the James Smithson Society)

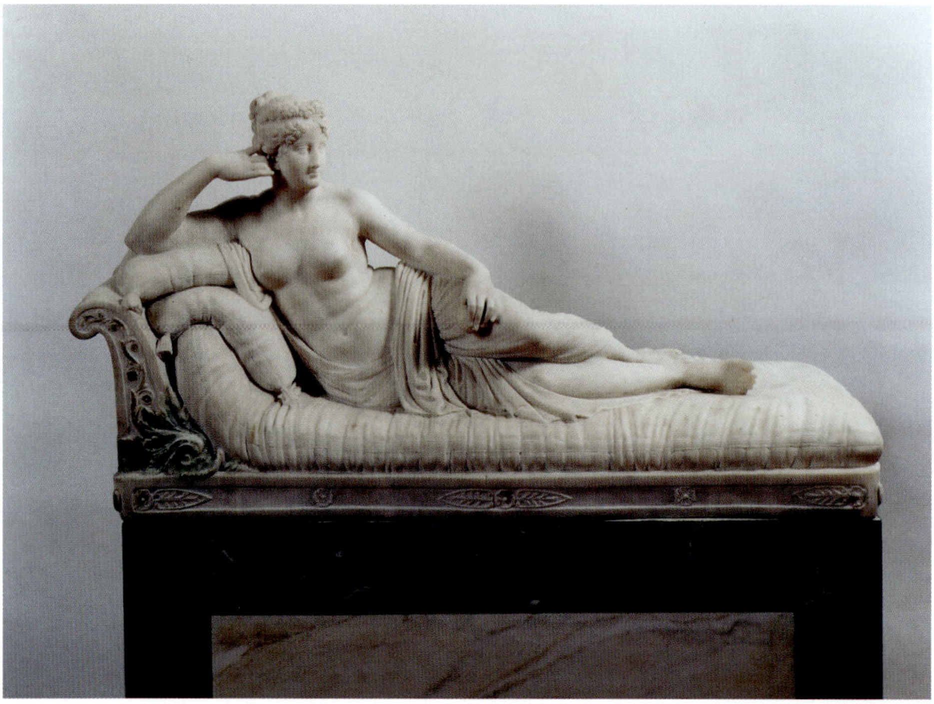

FIGURE 6.6 Antonio Canova, *Pauline Borghese as Venus Victrix*, ca. 1811. (The Athenaeum of Philadelphia)

ardo, and a Velázquez, along with several works from the Dutch school. David's *Napoleon Crossing the Alps* greeted visitors in the foyer and as they entered the main salon, they encountered François Gérard's portrait of the exiled emperor (now lost). Examples of sculpture resided in the Statuary Room where antique bronze castings from Pompeii were displayed along with marbles depicting the Bonaparte family, including a reduced version of Antonio Canova's seminude Pauline Borghese Bonaparte as Venus Victrix sensuously reclining on an antique daybed. (See Figure 6.6.)

Joseph kept a townhouse in Philadelphia and became close friends with eminent Philadelphians, among them Thomas Cadwalader, one of the founders of Pennsylvania Hospital and the Library Company of Philadelphia, as well as Joseph Hopkinson, a prominent lawyer and president of the Pennsylvania Academy of the Fine Arts. Stephen Girard gave Joseph a sixteen-oar barge for guests to be rowed up the Delaware River to the estate in Point Breeze. There they experienced the French attitude toward the history painting of mythology in works such as Charles Joseph Natoir's *The Toilet of Psyche* and Noël-Nicholas Coypel's *The Abduction of Europa*, whose proliferation of cavorting bare-breasted women made Rembrandt's *The Roman Daughter* seem almost Puritan in comparison. Helen Berkley visited Point Breeze with her husband and niece in July 1839 to view the works of art. The account of her reaction and the diffidence of her French host in the presence of so much female nudity effectively captures the gap between American and French attitudes to the body in art. Helen recalled that the "walls were covered with oil paintings, principally of young females, with less clothing than their originals would have found agreeable in our cold climate, and much less than *we found agreeable* when the count without ceremony led us in front of them, and enumerated the beauties of the painting with the air of an accomplished amateur."[31] Noël-Nicolas Coypel's *The Abduction of Europa*, considered to be his masterpiece, teems with numerous naked figures cavorting in the sea in a reenactment of Jupiter's capture of the nymph Europa. (See Figure 6.7.) So many bare breasts and buttocks had not been seen in America by those who had not visited the great collections abroad. Joseph Bonaparte gave the painting to Thomas Cadwalader as a gift when he left America in October 1839. The work continues to be a major attraction at the Philadelphia Museum of Art.

One of Rembrandt's encaustic paintings done in Paris in 1810 was of Lafayette (now unlocated) who was residing at La Grange. The Peale family would again enthusiastically encounter Lafayette when the marquis returned to America with his son Georges Washington de Lafayette as an honored guest of the nation at the invitation of President James Monroe. After an absence of forty years, Lafayette arrived in New

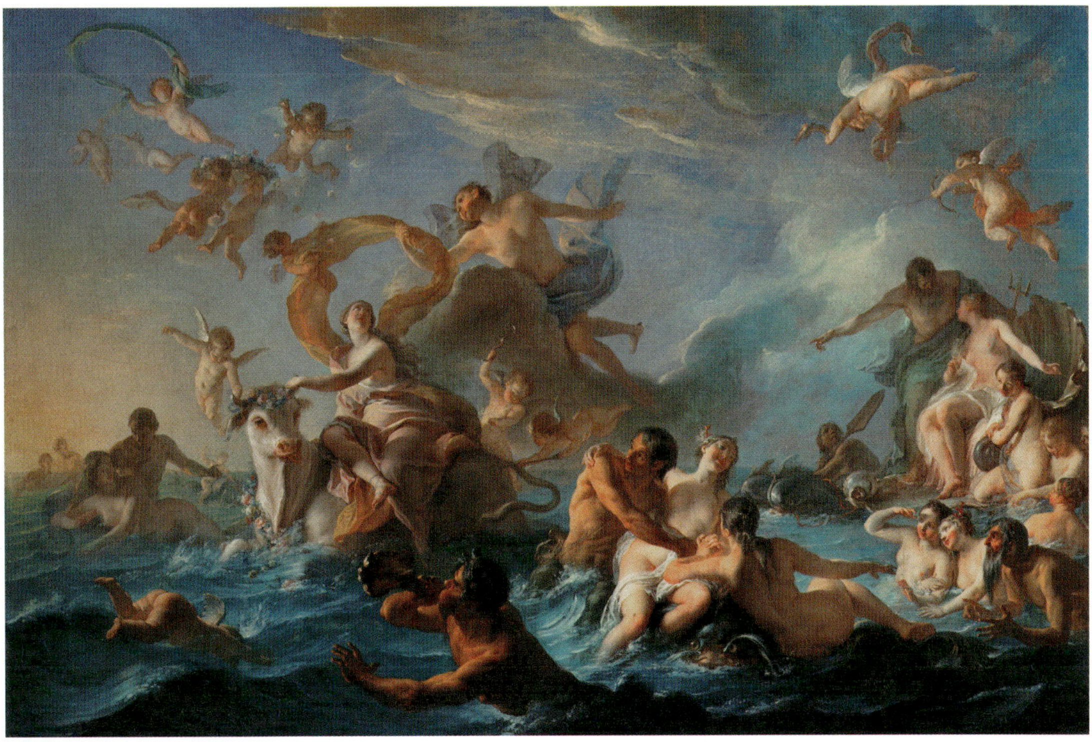

Figure 6.7 Noël-Nicholas Coypel, *The Abduction of Europa*, 1727. Oil on canvas, 50¼ in. × 6 ft., 4⅜ in. (127.6 × 194 cm). Framed: 58⅝ in. × 7 ft., 1 in. × 5 in. (148.9 × 215.9 × 12.7 cm). (Philadelphia Museum of Art, acquired with the kind assistance of John Cadwalader Jr., through the gift of Mr. and Mrs. Orville Bullitt [by exchange], the Edith H. Bell Fund, and other Museum funds, 1978-160-1.)

York on August 16, 1824. Philadelphia figured prominently on an itinerary that took him through twenty-four states. Philadelphia's excitement reached a fever pitch over the visit of the Frenchman who had played such a key role in American and French history. "Everything is Lafayette," the *Saturday Evening Post* reported on October 16, 1824: "There are Lafayette coats by day, blankets at night—La Fayette bread, butter, vegetables—and then the old veteran gets from his wife what she is pleased to tell him is a 'La Fayette kiss.' 'Pshaw, Ma,' cries the charming daughter, 'What's the difference between a La Fayette kiss and any other?' 'A La Fayette kiss,' answers the dame, 'is the kind I used to give him before you were born.'"[32]

On September 28, 1824, Lafayette made his dramatic entrance into the city in a resplendent barouche custom built for his visit. Six cream-colored horses paraded him down the streets and through the arches to the entrance of the State House. The east room of the building, where both the Declaration of Independence and the Constitution were signed, had been refurbished in anticipation of the visit and from that time on the State House came to be called Independence Hall. Eventually, the entire building took over the name. Charles Willson Peale and his family watched the arrival from the windows of the Long Room and then were greeted warmly by Lafayette. The Marquis asked the painter to stand beside him in front of the statue of Washington while the mayor made his address. Lafayette visited Peale's Museum after the completion of the formal ceremonies. There the portraits of the revolutionary heroes from America and France surely evoked sharp memories of former days of sacrifice and glory. When Peale showed Lafayette his own portrait, done when the Marquis was but nineteen years old, the elderly general graciously replied that it remained the best portrait of him.

Lafayette's claim that Peale's early portrait was the finest might have alluded to his likeness when he was younger because he was known to have said that his favorite image at the time of his tour was a full-length portrait he brought with him from France by Ary Scheffer. (See Figure 6.8.) Engravings were made after the painting, which Lafayette handed out liberally throughout his travels. Scheffer painted Lafayette from life and exhibited the portrait at the Salon of 1819. The artist shared Lafayette's liberal political views and generously donated a large copy of the portrait to the House of Representatives. By January 1825, it hung in the Capitol Rotunda where artists crowded their easels to copy the French master's work.

Lafayette was sixty-one when Scheffer painted his portrait and the resemblance was said to be remarkable. The Committee of Arrangement orchestrating Lafayette's farewell tour in Philadelphia also wanted to donate a portrait of the French aristocrat to the State House and commissioned the artist Thomas Sully to execute "a correct resemblance of the excellent and early friend of their country."[33] Although the committee wanted the portrait done before Lafayette's arrival so that they could use it during his visit, Sully only began working on it after the aging war hero had departed for Baltimore to continue his tour. (See Figure 6.9.) Sully's portrait mirrored Scheffer's with the standing pose and right hand holding a hat and walking stick. But Sully replaces Scheffer's somber backdrop with its darkened sky and gloomy landscape with

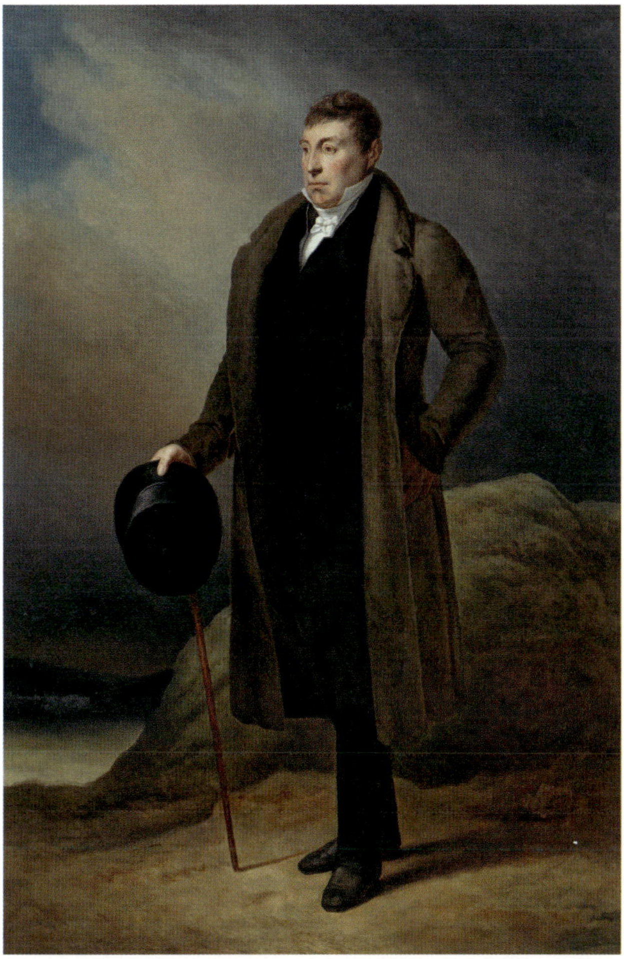

Figure 6.8 Ary Scheffer, *Gilbert Motier, Marquis de Lafayette,* 1822. Oil on canvas, 92 × 62 in. (233.7 × 157.5 cm). (Collection of the U.S. House of Representatives)

a colorfully animated scene. Scheffer's Lafayette looks serious and a bit wary, whereas Sully's Lafayette wears a slightly bemused and self-confident expression. The notes of red along the opened collar and lining of Lafayette's cape lends the figure a youthful animation. A slender gloved left hand with tapered fingers draws attention to the narrow waist that was the height of male fashion at that time in Paris. The high-rolled collar and "M-Notch" lapel function like a pedestal bust to the portrait head of the proud aristocrat. The Marquis stands proudly in front of Strickland's arch with Washington's Grays, who served as Lafayette's military escort, as he journeyed through the city, lined up behind him. A euphoric crowd stands in front of Independence Hall with its waving American flag echoing the raucously jubilant celebration.

Sully depicted Lafayette as significantly younger than his current sixty-seven years as can be seen in comparison with the Scheffer portrait. He merged contemporary events with a body and bearing that recalled the deeds of Lafayette's valiant past in America. James Fenimore Cooper's musings on Lafayette's tour four years later provide a literary equivalent to Sully's depiction of the noble bearing of the Marquis: "To

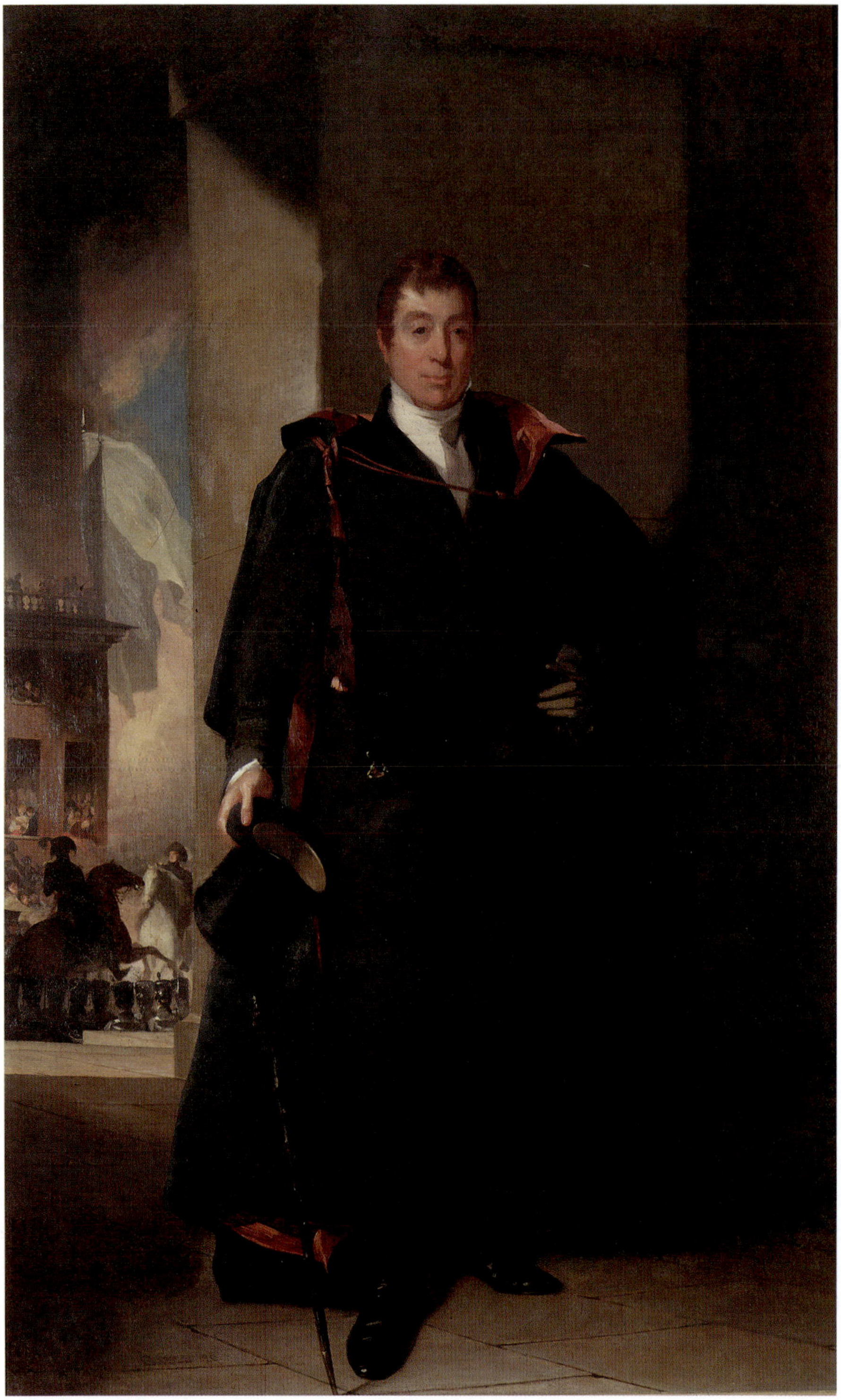

Figure 6.9 Thomas Sully, *Marie Joseph Paul Yves Roch Gilbert Motier, Marquis de Lafayette, 1825–1826.* Oil on canvas, 94⅜ × 59¼ in. Philadelphia, Second Bank. (Courtesy of Independence National Historical Park)

most of those whom he passed, his form must have worn the air of some image drawn from the pages of history. Half a century had carried all of his contemporary actors of the Revolution into the great abyss of time, and he now stood like an imposing column that had been reared to commemorate deeds and principles that a whole people had been taught to reverence."[34] Time could not erode the memory of what Lafayette had accomplished for the Americans. Sully's portrait of the great French revolutionary hero stood grandly at the end of the Assembly Room of Independence Hall, matched on the left side by Charles Willson Peale's portrait of George Washington, the man he claimed to be like a father to him. Thus, was the Frenchman who had accomplished such great deeds for the new nation so honored.

The place of art struggling for supremacy in both public and private realms can be tracked through the demand for paintings, monumental sculptures, and government buildings that reflected the aspirations of a new nation. The development of an image of the American national character between the colonial, revolutionary, and federal periods largely depended on portraiture. Charles Willson Peale and his son Rembrandt, along with Gilbert Stuart, were inundated with requests for replicas of his portraits of Washington. Thomas Jefferson brought sculpted busts from France to install in his gallery of worthies at Monticello and purchased sixty-three paintings during his stay in Paris in the hopes of stimulating his American citizens to appreciate the visual and intellectual effectiveness of the fine arts as a-tool for the betterment of the nation. Images of the Marquis de Lafayette who served as a pivotal figure allying colonial America and France that resulted in the surrender of Cornwallis at Yorktown emerged early in his successful involvement in the American war effort. His triumphal return in 1824 saw twenty original life portraits done with replicas disseminated throughout the country by eager copyists. As Marc H. Miller noted, this was a remarkable number, considering that Jefferson was portrayed only twenty-six times during his lifetime.[35]

In their translation of the British and French portrait tradition to America, Charles Willson Peale and his son Rembrandt helped formulate a national portrait style. Eighty-eight percent of Sully's prolific output consisted of portraits. The high demand in the early years of the formation of America for images of its most significant figures testifies to the emerging awareness of an individual culture of achievement to be transmitted to future generations. Government support of the arts in France became the hoped-for model for American artists when they returned to their homeland. The French art system with its schools and Salon exhibitions inspired the establishment of the New York Academy and the Pennsylvania Academy of the Fine Arts. Looking back at his career in his later years, Rembrandt acknowledged that he had "learned the rudiments of art with his father . . . but did not commence the study of its principles until he went to France."[36] He would be just one of an ever-growing number of American artists to cross the Atlantic to apprentice themselves to French masters, exhibit at the Salon, and ground their skills in the pursuit of creating an authentic American art.

[7]

All Manner of French Matters in Nineteenth-Century Philadelphia

The Era of Good Feelings that accompanied James Monroe's presidency (1817–1825) marked the arrival of the United States on the world stage as an actor much like the long-established players. The Quasi-War with France and the War of 1812 with Britain had both ended by recognizing that America would be treated like any other member in the society of nations. The British at last accepted the United States as a democratic republic, just as the French had earlier agreed to treat the young nation as a sovereign equal. Throughout the next half century, the impressions left on Philadelphia of French people and French culture grew more diverse. The period brought old friends as well as large numbers of new immigrants and visitors, among whom were those who would distinguish themselves in many areas of human endeavor. But during the nineteenth century's first quarter, Philadelphia, perhaps more than any other city in America, was still to feel the lingering effects of France's decades-long upheavals. The more negative impact of this new wave of French speakers was reflected in the condescending observation in a British publication in 1822, perhaps before unpleasant memories of the War of 1812 had completely faded from the writer's mind: "In Philadelphia and other towns frequented by the French exiles, society has rapidly deteriorated, both in morals and in manner, from its pure English origin, and . . . by taking, or attempting to take, the ton [*sic*] from these upstart mousequetaires, American high-life unfortunately unites the vulgarity of English simplicity with the ten-fold vulgarity of French refinement."[1]

First (and conceivably the most refined) among the new wave of exiles was Napoleon's older brother, Joseph (1768–1844), who had been the emperor's instrument before his own fall. Napoleon had made him, first, king of Naples, then king of Spain. The latter was a throne Joseph held reluctantly—three times he tried to abdicate—until

June 1813, when he fled to France from Spain after losing a battle against the Duke of Wellington. In March 1814, the forces allied against Napoleon reached Paris; Joseph fled with his family to Switzerland and bought a château on Lake Geneva. On April 12, Napoleon abdicated and was exiled to Elba. When, nearly a year later, he escaped and marched in triumph back to Paris from Cannes to begin his hundred-day rule, the ever-loyal Joseph rejoined him. Then came Napoleon's decisive defeat in the Waterloo campaign of June 1815 and his second abdication. Joseph, meanwhile, had chartered an American brig, the *Commerce,* so that he could escape from the port of Rochefort to the United States. He then offered to exchange places with his brother so that Napoleon himself might flee across the Atlantic. Napoleon seriously considered going into exile in America but ultimately decided to surrender to a British ship in hope of finding asylum in Britain. Instead, he was transported as a prisoner of war to far-off Saint Helena, where he would spend his lonely final years before dying of cancer in 1821.

Once Joseph learned of Napoleon's surrender, he set sail on the *Commerce* and arrived in New York harbor on August 28, 1815, accompanied not by his family but by an ordnance officer, an interpreter, his cook, and his secretary. His wife and two young daughters remained behind in Paris. Bonaparte had had the wit to carry much of his large fortune with him in his flight to America. The year before, while on the run at the time of Napoleon's first abdication, he had purchased a large tract of land in upstate New York, sight unseen, which he paid for with carts full of his own possessions he feared would be seized by the British.[2] He would not lay eyes on the New York property until 1817. When he began his exile in 1815, he gave himself the title of Count of Survilliers, for a village that was part of his estate of Mortefontaine north of Paris.

From the time Bonaparte stepped ashore in the United States, many—but not all—of the Americans he met were enchanted to find themselves in the company of a former king, and one who now seemed prepared to live as nearly like a monarch, but benignly and with grace, as exile in the New World would permit. New York's mayor was among those who viewed the Bonapartes with favor. He came to call on the count in his boardinghouse and suggested he should travel to Washington to ask President Madison for his protection. Bonaparte immediately set off. In Philadelphia, the Kentucky congressman (and leading war hawk against Great Britain in the recently concluded War of 1812), Henry Clay, offered him his rooms at the Mansion House hotel. Continuing his journey toward the capital the next day, Joseph soon learned that, however much he charmed many Americans, the name of Bonaparte still raised nervous memories for the nation's chief executive. At a tavern near Baltimore, Joseph was met by an agent of the president who made it plain that Madison "preferred declining" the foreigner's desire to pay his respects. His excuse was disapproval of Bonaparte's attempt to conceal his identity under an assumed name. Clearly, Madison and his secretary of state, James Monroe, feared angering the restored Bourbon monarchy in France if they were to receive Napoleon's brother.[3]

Turned back from Washington, Joseph was undaunted. He chose Philadelphia as the place where he would establish himself. He contacted Stephen Girard, who found

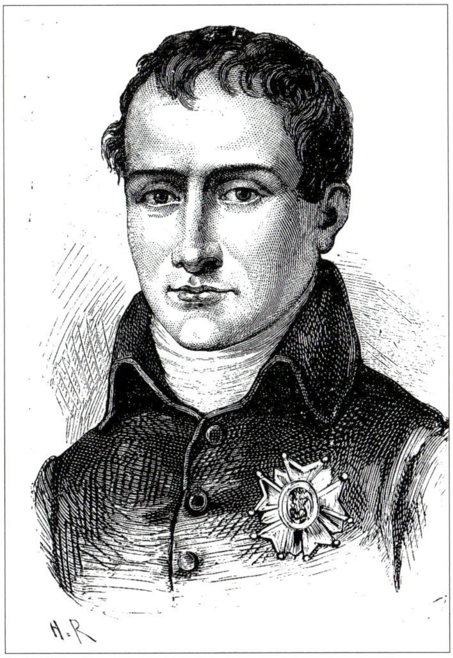

Figure 7.1 From 1815 until his death in 1844, Joseph Bonaparte lived much of the time in or near Philadelphia where he became a prominent member of the social elite and an admirer of American democracy. (H. Rousseau [graphic designer], E. Thomas [engraver]. *Joseph Bonaparte.* Engraving in Augustin Challamel, Desiré Lacroix, *Album du centenaire.* Paris: Jouvet et Cie, éditeurs, 1889.)

a spacious house for the exiled king to rent at Ninth and Locust Streets. Over the next several years, Girard was his invaluable banker and adviser, transporting much of Bonaparte's art and household furnishings across the Atlantic on his own ships.[4]

Bonaparte began to make plans for purchasing an estate where he might settle, live lavishly, and contribute his savoir faire to American culture and manners. Over the next year or two, he created a country manor from property he purchased north of Philadelphia on the east bank of the Delaware River in Bordentown, New Jersey. Point Breeze, as it was named, lay almost opposite William Penn's old plantation, Pennsbury Manor, on the Pennsylvania side of the river. Before he bought this property and began extensive renovations there, the Count de Survilliers leased one of the grandest mansions in the Philadelphia area as his temporary home. Lansdowne, in what is now Philadelphia's Fairmount Park, had been built by William Penn's grandson John in 1773 when he served as Pennsylvania's governor. Before the American Revolution, Penn and his wife made this greatest Middle Georgian house in the colonies Philadelphia's social center. It remained a fine if faded house through successive owners.[5] Bonaparte continued the tradition, entertaining both wellborn Frenchmen in exile and prominent Americans. The Philadelphian Charles J. Ingersoll, then the U.S. district attorney for Pennsylvania, was pleased to report that he had been told the former king preferred Philadelphia society to that of New York.[6] (See Figure 7.1.)

Joseph moved the existing house at Point Breeze into Bordentown, and then built a new and much larger home, landscaping the extensive grounds into what became the first major picturesque landscape in America. He almost single-handedly revitalized the local economy by employing so many from the Bordentown area to work on his property. Soon the estate was known locally as "Bonaparte's Park." There, as in Philadelphia, the count entertained lavishly. Among the friendships he made or continued, in addition to Ingersoll and Girard, were those with Peter S. Duponceau, Joseph Hopkinson, Nicholas Biddle, and Samuel Breck, who described Bonaparte as "devoid of pride and very sociable."[7] These Francophiles were all among the city's intellectual elite, active in the newly established Athenaeum of Philadelphia, the Pennsylvania Academy of the Fine Arts, and the professional life of the city. Several were also members of the prestigious American Philosophical Society, to which Bonaparte himself was elected in 1823. Meanwhile, the count added parcels to his New Jersey property over the years until it contained some 1,800 acres. Even while he made Point Breeze his principal estate, Bonaparte soon rented another Philadelphia mansion from Stephen Girard for those moments when his activities took him to the city.[8]

The house at Point Breeze was partially destroyed by fire in 1820 while Bonaparte was away. Upon his return he discovered that neighbors had rushed into the burning house to salvage what they could of his treasures. He was so touched that he sent a letter to newspapers across the country that revealed both his gratitude and his wonder at their selflessness: "This event has proved to me how much the inhabitants of Bordentown appreciate the interest I have always felt for them; and shows that men in general are good."[9] He rebuilt on a different site and on a scale that rivaled the White House in size and grandeur.[10] He enlisted Girard to ship his furnishings and paintings from Europe.

Bonaparte ordered additional furniture from a young Philadelphia cabinetmaker, Michel (Michael) Bouvier (1792–1874), who was already creating furniture for Girard's home on Water Street. Bouvier, a native of Pont-Saint-Esprit near Avignon, had been a soldier in Napoleon's army who fled to America from France in the aftermath of Waterloo. He would continue as one of Philadelphia's leading furniture makers through much of his long life. Bonaparte's rebuilt mansion contained, in addition to an eight-thousand-book library—the largest in America—a picture gallery, state dining room, and grand staircase. An artificial lake and causeway were constructed. Beside the lake, Joseph had a house built for his daughter, Zenaide, and her husband, Joseph's nephew, Charles Lucien Bonaparte, who would soon make a name for himself as an ornithologist. The young couple joined her father at Point Breeze a year after their 1822 marriage in Europe.

Already residing at Point Breeze was Zenaide's younger sister, Charlotte, who had arrived in the port of Philadelphia in December 1821. The girls, who were teenagers when their father came to America, had then remained with their mother in Europe. Although he pleaded with his wife to join him, she never did so throughout his lengthy residence in America, arguing that her health prevented it. Joseph made other arrangements for his domestic comfort. Long before his daughters arrived, he had taken a young American mistress with whom he had already fathered two children.[11] Nor would she be his last amour in America. In 1825, he became the reported father of the twin sons of a French woman, Emilie Lacoste, whose husband was away in Saint-Domingue.[12] Charlotte, meanwhile, developed into an accomplished artist during her time in the United States, exhibiting in Philadelphia at the Pennsylvania Academy of Fine Art. Charlotte returned to France in 1824; in 1826, she married another Bonaparte cousin, Napoleon Louis.[13] Both daughters' marriages were in keeping with the wishes Napoleon had expressed in his will (and very much approved by Joseph) that the family's inheritance—and the prospects for imperial succession—should remain in the family.

During their years at Point Breeze, the Bonaparte daughters grew close to the niece of Stephen Girard, Henriette, who married one of Napoleon's last generals, Henri Dominique Lallemand (1777–1823), in Philadelphia in 1817. After Waterloo, where he was wounded, Lallemand escaped to England under a false name, then to the United States. Settling in Philadelphia, he immediately became part of Joseph Bonaparte's entourage, which led to his courtship of the fifteen-year-old Henriette Girard. He was forty at the time of their marriage. In 1819, their daughter Caroline was born. Lallemand was engaged at the time in writing a treatise on artillery, drawing on his knowledge of the practice of Napoleon's army. The published work was adopted in 1821 as the standard manual for the United States army. Meanwhile, with his hot-headed older brother, Charles, also exiled in America, Henri traveled south in another attempt to establish a place of asylum for French refugees, this time in Texas. Like the plan years earlier in Pennsylvania, this one failed in short order. After initially advancing his nephew-in-law a substantial letter of credit, Stephen Girard refused the men more money, and the scheme soon died, having generated considerable ill will among Americans who encountered them in the South. Henri Lallemand died of dysentery in Bordentown in 1823. Stephen Girard had a tomb built for him in the churchyard at Holy Trinity in Philadelphia.[14]

Henri Lallemand was simply one of a number of former officers from Napoleon's army to choose exile in the United States after Waterloo. One of the most distinguished, General Emmanuel, Marquis de Grouchy (1766–1847), had served with valor and distinction throughout the Napoleonic wars. A supporter of the Revolution in spite of his noble birth, his sister Sophie was a noted feminist and the wife of Condorcet. Napoleon named Grouchy a marshal when he escaped from Elba and returned to rule France during the Hundred Days. But at Waterloo, Grouchy had declined to lead his troops from their nearby position to join the battle there, arguing that the emperor had not ordered him to do so. As a result, he was censured by Napoleon and his friends for having lost that all-important battle. For the rest of his life, he would have to withstand his Bonapartist critics, although he no doubt would have found it expedient to go into exile in any case with the Bourbon Restoration. He chose Philadelphia as his new home and took up residence in Society Hill. Whatever his differences with the former emperor, he was quickly reconciled to Joseph Bonaparte, whom he visited frequently at Point Breeze. He was a witness at the wedding of Lallemand and Henriette Girard. Grouchy remained in Philadelphia for nearly six years, then returned to France in 1821, when Louis XVIII restored his titles.[15]

The story of another French general exiled to America a decade earlier than Grouchy poses a what-might-have-been question for the nation's early nineteenth-century history. Jean Victor Marie Moreau (1763–1813) rose in the ranks of the French revolutionary army until, as a confirmed republican, he grew dissatisfied with the Directory's tyranny. That led him to assist Napoleon in his coup d'état of 18 Brumaire (November 9–10, 1799). But then, as Napoleon launched ever more aggrandizing conquests, Moreau grew disaffected from the man he had helped place in power. Eventually, his association with dissidents led to his seizure and trial. As first consul, Napoleon commuted his sentence of imprisonment to that of exile, and Moreau and his wife were banished to America. Their reception in New York, in August 1805, was enthusiastic, given the growing alarm of Americans at Napoleon's conquests. After extensive travels, the couple settled into a villa near Trenton, New Jersey. With the outbreak of the War of 1812, Moreau's military reputation was such that President Madison offered him the command of U.S. troops. Moreau reportedly was prepared to accept the post until word reached him of the disastrous retreat of the Grande Armée from Russia. With that, he returned to Europe in the hope that he might be of service in helping defeat Napoleon and return France to republican government. Before he could take direct military action against his fellow countrymen, however, he was mortally wounded at the Battle of Dresden in August 1813 and died several days later.[16]

The lengthy sojourn of Joseph Bonaparte in America scarcely altered Franco-American relations, either then or over the longer run. As his years in exile passed, it became increasingly clear to politically minded Americans that they need not fear their French guest was plotting a Bonapartist insurrection. His impact was almost entirely limited to Philadelphia-area society and the pleasure members of the social and intellectual elite took in his company. As he gathered ever more of his art collection at Point Breeze, he was generous in inviting the public to view it. He also loaned many of his paintings regularly to the Pennsylvania Academy of the Fine Arts at the behest of its president, Joseph Hopkinson.[17] His sociability generally won out over stern social disapproval of his sexual dalliances. More lastingly, the way in which the count accepted and to some extent fit into the democratic norms of his place of exile may have furthered Philadelphia's confidence in the rightness of the nation's experiment in democracy. Certainly, that experiment drew Bonaparte's approval. "Every day," he said, "that I pass in the hospitable land of the United States proves more clearly to me the excellence of republican institutions for America. Keep them, then, as a precious gift from heaven."[18]

Yet France for him was another matter. He remained hopeful that the day would come when Napoleon's own son would assume the throne in France just as the boy's father had intended. After Napoleon's final abdication in favor of the child known as Napoleon II, the boy's mother, Marie Louise of Austria, had fled with him back to Vienna. The Bourbon Restoration in France came to an end following the July revolution of 1830. Once word reached Joseph in America sometime later that Louis-Philippe of the House of Orléans had been installed as king, Bonaparte decided that the time had come to do what he could to return the throne instead to his nephew with himself as regent. He was sixty-four years old when he sailed from Philadelphia in late June 1832. Arriving in England on July 24, he learned that his voyage was in vain: Napoleon's son had died two days earlier in Vienna at the age of twenty-one.

For most Bonapartists, that death made Joseph himself the most logical claimant to a restoration of the former empire. But the Count of Survilliers, who then took up residence in England, remained convinced that such an event should only come as the result of a popular movement in his favor from the French people. Effectively turning his back on the prospect of leading the French nation, he returned to Point Breeze in 1835, but found its charms diluted both by his advancing age and the fact that the nation's first railroad now crossed part of his land. He considered moving into Philadelphia, but, by the summer of 1836, he left again for England. When his nephew, Louis Napoleon (the younger brother of Napoleon Louis, Charlotte Bonaparte's husband), attempted a coup against the government of Louis-Philippe in October of that year, Joseph was dismayed; he saw it as foolhardy and a damaging blow to any prospect of a possible Bonapartist restoration. His nephew sought to placate him, but Joseph replied harshly: "You have broken the ties that attach me to you in thinking yourself capable of taking my place and that of your father. From now on, I want you to leave me in peace in my retreat."[19]

Yet his retreat in England again proved unsatisfying. At age seventy, he set sail for Philadelphia once more, this time to settle his affairs. He stayed for just over a year before his final return to Europe in November 1839. Although he offered to sell his art collection—the largest in the nation at the time—to the federal government, Congress rejected the offer. Much of it returned with him to France, while the remaining contents of his household at Point Breeze were auctioned off after Joseph's death in two sales, in 1845 and 1847.[20]

Michel Bouvier, the young cabinetmaker who crafted furniture for both Bonaparte and Stephen Girard, was not the only French émigré skilled in that trade who settled in Philadelphia after Napoleon's fall. Antoine (Anthony) G. Quervelle (1789–1856) arrived in the city in 1816 or 1817 and soon established himself as a neighbor, friend, and rival of Bouvier. Their workshops made Philadelphia preeminent in the manufacture and sale of fine furniture in America during the next decades. When President Andrew Jackson redecorated the East Room of the White House in 1829, he turned to a new retailer of fine household goods in Philadelphia who was also of French heritage, Louis Veron. From his establishment at 98 Chestnut Street, Veron provided blue and gold draperies, a Brussels carpet, mirrors, and lamps for the renovation. It was probably at his recommendation that Quervelle produced a number of tables for the room.[21] He had already made a name for himself by winning prizes in the annual exhibitions of the mechanical arts sponsored by the Franklin Institute—an organization founded in Philadelphia in 1824. Some two centuries after the work of Bouvier and Quervelle was first sought by the nation's elite, it is still prized as among the finest produced in America.[22]

With their success as fine craftsmen of furniture, both Bouvier and Quervelle increased their wealth by acquiring real estate. By the time of his death in 1856, Quervelle owned, in addition to securities, a number of houses on Locust, Pine, and

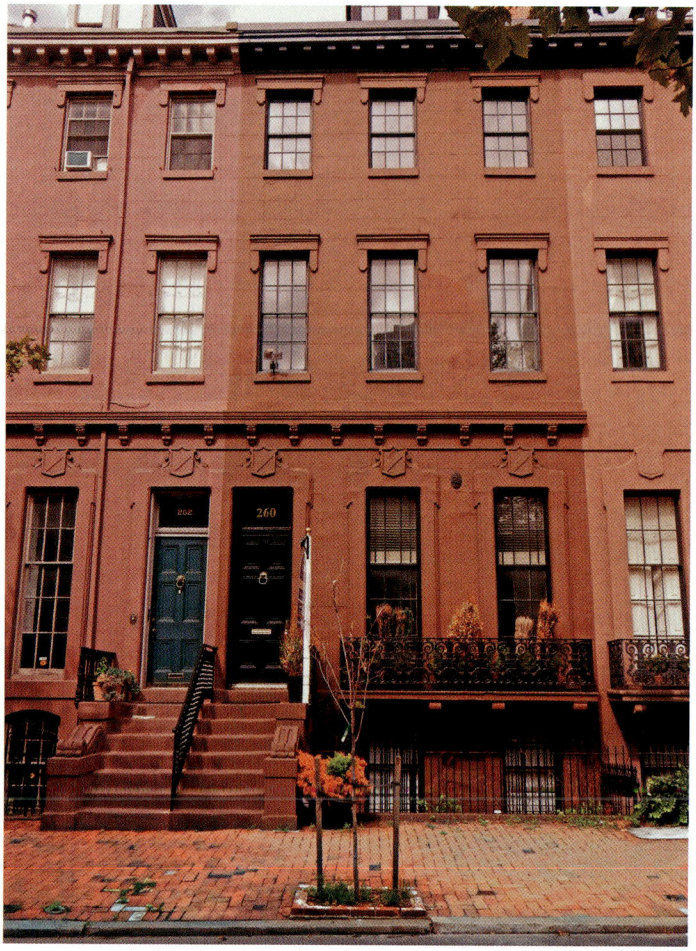

FIGURE 7.2 One of America's leading cabinetmakers of the nineteenth century, the French immigrant, Michel (Michael) Bouvier resided with his family in this large brownstone residence in Philadelphia's Society Hill neighborhood.

Lombard Streets and a partnership in the Bristol Iron Works. He was a member of the French Benevolent Society (Société de Bienfaisance de Philadelphie) and a stockholder in the newly funded Academy of Music then under construction in Philadelphia. Bouvier, who lived until 1874, was a director, then president, of the French Benevolent Society, which had been founded in 1793 to help the desperate refugees from the revolution in Saint-Domingue.[23] One of Bouvier's daughters married into the prominent Drexel family. Her stepdaughter, Katherine, raised millions of dollars during her lifetime to assist in the education of Native American and African American children. She was canonized in 2000 as Saint Katherine Drexel (1858–1955). One of Michel Bouvier's great-great-granddaughters, Jacqueline Bouvier Kennedy (1929–1994) would become first lady of the United States as the wife of President John F. Kennedy. Both Quervelle and Bouvier and their immediate families are buried in Saint Mary's churchyard on south Fourth Street.[24] (See Figure 7.2.)

During the period when Joseph Bonaparte's daughter Zenaide was living at Point Breeze, her young husband Charles became acquainted with an older naturalist and frontiersman with whom he shared, in addition to a French heritage, a passion for ornithology. Jean-Jacques (John James) Audubon (1785–1851) was the bastard son of a one-time plantation owner and privateer from Saint-Domingue. The boy's mother, a French chambermaid, died within months of her son's birth. Lieutenant Jean Audubon soon took another mistress, fathered another child, and remained in the colony until revolutionary unrest there led him to sell his property and buy a 284-acre farm twenty miles west of Philadelphia, a place called Mill Grove. But instead of moving to Pennsylvania, he returned to France in 1791, then had the young Jean-Jacques and the boy's half sister sent to him and the wife he had left behind years earlier. In 1794, the couple formally adopted the two children.

At first, Jean-Jacques seemed headed for a naval career, but when he reached the age of eighteen in 1803 and faced likely conscription into Napoleon's army, his father helped him with other arrangements. He sold off much of his plantation in Haiti to finance a lead mining operation at Mill Grove, secured a false passport for his son, then sent him to America to oversee that operation in Pennsylvania. John James, as he called himself by then, came down with yellow fever upon arriving in New York. He was nursed back to health and taught English by Quaker women in a boardinghouse they ran. Once he was able to travel to Mill Grove, he was immediately delighted with the natural environment in which he found himself. The lead mine was a mere distraction. As he later noted, "Hunting, fishing, drawing, and music occupied my every moment; cares I knew not . . ."[25] He found his calling in nature and soon began to draw the birds he shot, banding those he caught and released to study their behavior. He met his neighbor, William Bakewell, the owner of a property called Fatland Ford. Before long, he was in love with Bakewell's daughter Lucy, who shared his interest in the natural world.

In 1805, Audubon risked conscription by returning to France. He needed his father's permission to marry Lucy and to discuss the business about the mine. Lucy's father had been clear that young Audubon needed to prove himself financially to win his daughter's hand. While in France, John James met Charles-Marie D'Orbigny, a naturalist and physician who taught the young man scientific research methods and helped him with taxidermy.[26] Once back at Mill Grove, Audubon created his own little nature museum, his small tribute to the one Charles Willson Peale had built in Philadelphia. Soon, he convinced his father that the prospects for successful lead mining were slim and, with his blessing, sold part of the Mill Grove farm, investing the proceeds. Audubon moved to the Kentucky frontier to launch himself as a merchant, although his central occupation remained drawing and describing the birds around him. Finally, in 1808, Lucy's father consented to their marriage.

Following their wedding and the arrival over the next years of four children, the Audubon family moved several times through Kentucky and Missouri. John James frequently supplemented his meager earnings in business with the fish and game he provided his family. He dressed as a frontiersman and learned from the Native Americans he met around him, whom he grew to respect. Back in Philadelphia for a visit shortly after war with Great Britain was declared in 1812, Audubon became an American citizen. There followed some relatively good years as a frontier merchant, then bankruptcy and a stay in debtors' prison. He earned a bit from the portraits he did while continuing his work as a naturalist.

Meanwhile, in 1810, in the small general store he was then running in Louisville, Kentucky, he happened to have a fateful meeting with a Scottish immigrant, Alexander Wilson, who was then at work on an ambitious illustrated study of American birds. Audubon was too poor to pay the $100 that would have let him subscribe to Wilson's project even though he evidently admired the samples he was shown. His encounter with Wilson seems to have convinced him that the project he already had in mind would surpass the older man's in its scope. He may have brashly suggested as much to Wilson, who evidently harbored resentment toward the younger man that would have consequences in the future.

Fourteen years later, Audubon had largely completed his own study of the birds of North America. In the spring of 1824, he enlisted the assistance of Charles Lucien Bonaparte, who had been admitted to membership in Philadelphia's prestigious Academy of Natural Sciences (ANS) only two months earlier, at the age of twenty-one. The fact that he was a Bonaparte may have been a factor in Charles's admission to the ANS, but he was already well known in the city's scientific community for his ornithological studies. Now Audubon was eager to display his own work to the members in the hope that the academy would support its publication. Although Alexander Wilson was long dead, his colleagues in the academy still revered his memory, continuing to regard his work as the standard in the field. Audubon's perhaps florid presentation did not go down well. He may have criticized Wilson's work as lifeless. At least one member challenged Audubon's scientific credentials. The meeting ended disastrously for Audubon. Even so, Charles Bonaparte then offered to buy his pictures, if Philadelphia's leading engraver, Alexander Lawson, could be persuaded to engrave them. But a visit to Lawson also ended badly. When Bonaparte explained that he was willing to buy the paintings, Lawson replied sharply, "You may buy them, but I will not engrave them. . . . Ornithology requires truth in forms and correctness in the lines—here are neither!"[27]

Here were two devastating blows for Audubon. Yet, the experience may have prompted him to take greater care in the work he did afterward. Moreover, when he finally succeeded in having his work published in Great Britain, the results were prints much finer than any that might have been done at the time in Philadelphia.[28] Thomas Sully, Philadelphia's greatest portraitist of the period, became a friend and ally. Both he and Charles Bonaparte may have urged Audubon to take his paintings to Europe. With encouragement from Lucy, he began to prepare for such a trip. At last, in the autumn of 1826, he arrived in Liverpool with a portfolio of more than three hundred of his drawings. Armed with letters of introduction to prominent Englishmen, he was soon met with acclaim. "I have been received here in a manner not to be expected during my enthusiastic hopes," he wrote home.[29] He toured England and Scotland to enlist subscribers by exhibiting his work and painting portraits. He soon raised enough money to begin publishing *The Birds of America*, a project that would not be

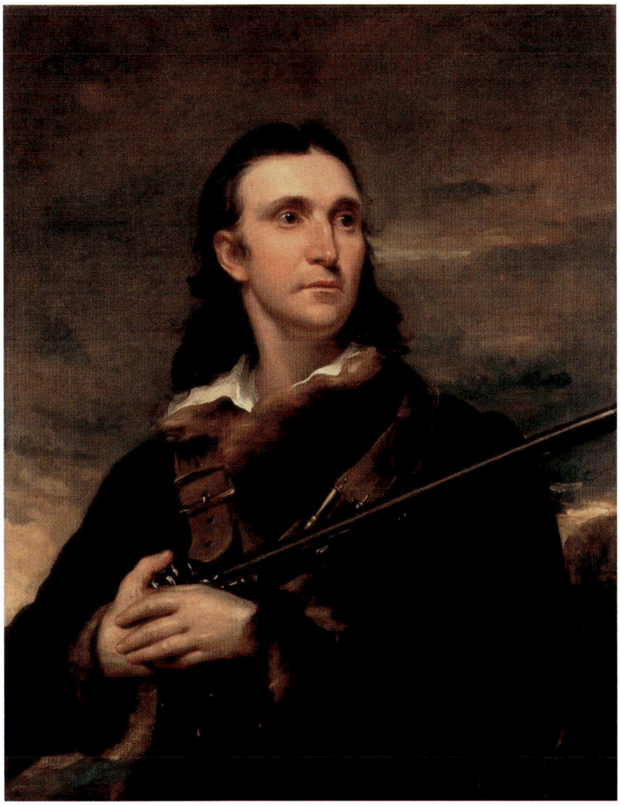

Figure 7.3 John Syme, *John James Audubon*, painting, 1826. Oil on canvas, 90.2 × 69.8 cm (35.5 × 27.4 in.). Jean-Jacques Audubon began to paint the birds that would make him an acclaimed artist and naturalist after he emigrated from France to a farm twenty miles west of Philadelphia. (White House Historical Association [White House copy of the 1826 painting])

completed for a dozen years. Audubon was lionized as "the American woodsman" in both Great Britain and France. A portrait done of him by John Syme shows him in rough frontier clothing, his dark hair shoulder-length, with a rifle cradled in his arms. That painting was placed at the entrance to exhibitions of his work.[30] To many Europeans, he must have seemed a latter-day incarnation of Benjamin Franklin. Soon, he would become the second American, after Franklin, made a fellow of London's Royal Society. (See Figure 7.3.)

In a felicitous coincidence, that same year of 1826 also marked the publication of a book in France that launched Romanticism in French literature. *Voyage en Amérique*, written years before by François-René de Chateaubriand (1768–1848), was a highly romanticized (and evidently fictionalized) account of his travels from Philadelphia and New York into the western wilderness and the Deep South in the early 1790s. Those locales had been the settings for two novels Chateaubriand had already published—*Atala* (1801) and *René* (1802)—and for a third, *Les Natchez*, which appeared in 1826.[31] Chateaubriand's idealized views of the American wilderness largely defined his contributions to the Romantic movement. The popularity of his writings renewed public awareness of Rousseau's Edenic archetype. Yet, for the monarchist and highly conservative Chateaubriand, Rousseau's "noble savage" of primeval nature was only ennobled through conversion to Christianity. Surely, at least some of what accounts for Audubon's enthusiastic acceptance in Europe was that he was seen as a living example of the unspoiled frontiersman at home in the American wilderness.[32] It was a myth that would resonate down through the years in the heroes of twentieth-century Hollywood westerns.

Such visions undoubtedly had *not* been conjured up by Philadelphia's staid scientific community two years earlier. Even after the first volumes of *The Birds of America* were being received with great acclaim in America as well as in Europe, Audubon's chilly relationship with the ANS continued. For years, he let it be known that he would not accept membership in the academy even if it were offered to him. But he finally relented in 1831 when he was informed that he had been elected a corresponding member—"*at last*," as he emphasized in a letter to his wife, nursing his injury by adding, "the papers say Unanimously."[33] His great accomplishment finally acknowledged, at home as well as abroad, he proudly listed his ANS membership in his future publications.

In the summer of 1824, months after Audubon's initial rejection by the ANS, America celebrated the return of the nation's hero, Lafayette, on a scale it had never seen before. President Monroe had invited him to come to America as part of the celebration of the fiftieth anniversary of American independence. It was an invitation Lafayette was eager to accept at a time when he hoped he might inspire republican friends in France to oppose the repressive policies of the Bourbon monarch, Louis XVIII. By then a widower, Lafayette arrived in New York on August 15, accompanied by his son, Georges Washington, and his secretary. For the next four days and nights, New Yorkers showered him with every manner of celebration, the first of an unending series of welcomes across all twenty-four states lasting thirteen months—more than three times as long as the marquis had originally intended to stay. At age sixty-seven, Lafayette was the last surviving general of the War of Independence. After touring New England, he arrived outside Philadelphia on September 27, where he was met by a six-thousand-man military escort. A hundred-gun salute boomed over the city at 8:00 a.m. the next day, and he entered the city in a carriage drawn by six white horses. The three-mile procession accompanying him passed under a dozen triumphal arches to end at the State House.

That building, which had fallen into disrepair over the years, had been dramatically renovated by William Strickland for the occasion. Starting with Lafayette's visit, the chamber where the nation's founders had met began to be referred to as the Hall of Independence, a name which soon came to be applied to the building itself.[34] Formal greetings from Philadelphia's mayor were followed by remarks from Lafayette extolling the virtues of the American republic and the wisdom of those who had founded it. His secretary later published an account of Lafayette's reaction to the ceremonies:

> In . . . recognizing this hall in which the declaration of independence was signed; this hall at whose door he had waited in 1777, with so much impatience to devote his life and fortune to an almost desperate cause, Lafayette felt

> an emotion he could scarcely conceal, and which several times showed itself in his eloquent answer.[35]

He remained in the city eight days, while Philadelphians waxed semidelirious at his presence. Thanks largely to the revived interest in the nation's history kindled by his return to the United States, the Historical Society of Pennsylvania was founded in Philadelphia in the year of Lafayette's visit.

The crowds were tumultuous wherever he traveled. Towns, cities, counties, parks, and squares throughout the nation were named for him. He visited the eighty-nine-year-old John Adams at his home in Quincy, Massachusetts, and eighty-one-year-old Thomas Jefferson at Monticello—where James Madison also came to call. He paid his respects to Washington's memory at Mount Vernon. He was in Washington, DC, when the deadlocked presidential contest of 1824 finally ended with the election of John Quincy Adams by the House of Representatives; afterward, he witnessed the defeated Andrew Jackson shake hands with the president-elect. He addressed Congress. He traveled up and down the country, returning again to Philadelphia for a longer, quieter stay in July 1825. When at last he and his son returned to France, he carried with him soil he had taken from the ground at Bunker Hill. Georges sprinkled it on his father's grave after the death in 1834 of America's greatest foreign hero.[36]

Lafayette's triumphal final visit to the United States helped validate America's experiment with democracy in the eyes of its citizens. A few years later, another French visitor—two generations younger than Lafayette—absorbed the sights, sounds, and every aspect he could plumb of the culture of American society. From that lengthy trip, he went on to produce the century's greatest analysis of what America's experience with democracy meant for the world. Alexis de Tocqueville (1805–1859) was a politically active young man from an old family who was working as a bureaucrat in the government of the Bourbon monarch Charles X when the July Revolution of 1828 forced the king's abdication and the eventual election of a new "Citizen King," Louis-Philippe, the duc d'Orléans, who had once lived in Philadelphia. For France, the change marked the definitive break from a hereditary monarchy with a claim to absolute power to a constitutional monarch created and supported by the bourgeoisie. The new king demanded an oath of allegiance from all who worked for him. Tocqueville and his close friend and fellow bureaucrat, Gustave de Beaumont (1802–1866), did so, although with reservations about the new regime. Soon, they conceived a proposal to travel to the United States in order to study the penal system there. Receiving a commission from the king, they sailed for America, landing at Newport, Rhode Island, on May 8, 1831.[37]

The two men traveled extensively over the course of nine months and visited many prisons across the country. Their penal study was published in two volumes in 1833.[38] But Tocqueville's ambition rose far beyond that project. He was the greater intellectual of the two, who, from the beginning, sought to discover everything he could about what made America distinctive and what lessons he might glean from the American experience that could apply to France. As he noted of himself, he was born after the French Revolution and the destruction of the ancien régime and before democracy had taken root in his native land. Perhaps as a result, dispassionate and sophisticated observation was his hallmark. Once back in France, he worked assiduously on his project. He published the first volume of his great work, *Democracy in America*, in 1835, the second volume four years later.[39] It was, as it remains, perhaps the most penetrating study of the subject ever undertaken, the work of a man who was at once a philosopher, political scientist, sociologist, historian, and moralist, with leanings both conservative and liberal.

No brief summary of the work can convey its scope or its keen and nuanced analysis.[40] Among the important ideas that emerge from his study are these: The coming of democracy to America was fortuitously built on the reforms already being established in England by the time North America was settled, in which the rule of law was superseding the arbitrary power of the throne. As a result, America—so unlike France, starting a decade later—underwent no real social revolution at all but simply made itself independent and therefore free of the ties to an aristocracy, since none existed in America, that still bound Europe. Tocqueville concluded that the idea of the equality of citizens in the American democracy motivates all its inhabitants, making them often restless and strongly bent on material gain, eager to achieve whatever they could from their own efforts. The tyranny of an absolute monarch has been replaced by the tyranny of a majority, which continually threatens the liberty so essential to the good life. When that tyranny is prevented, it is by applying constitutional protections for minorities based on the equality, and therefore the equal rights, of all citizens. Liberty, which also is threatened by the centralizing tendencies of government, is further protected in America by the very diffuseness of its federal system and the self-reliance of local groups.

Tocqueville thought that democracy in America was unique because of the historical circumstances that brought it about. But he was also convinced that the advance of democracy was a historical development that would continue to grow and spread throughout the world, overcoming the traditional social hierarchies based on birth and class. He avidly read Montesquieu, Voltaire, and other philosophes, but, given his knowledge of how repeated revolutions had brought violent results to France, he warned, as they had not, of what today we would call the unintended consequences of the social change they advocated. He summed up his creed as follows: "Je n'ai pas de traditions, je n'ai pas de parti, je n'ai point de *cause*, si ce n'est celle de la liberté et de la dignité humaine" [I have no traditions, I have no party, I have no cause at all other than that of liberty and human dignity].[41]

Philadelphia was fruitful ground for Tocqueville to continue his learning. For the prison study, he and Beaumont visited the newly built Eastern State Penitentiary, which, under Quaker influence, had initiated the newest doctrine in prison reform, solitary confinement. (See Figure 7.4.) Prisoners were left alone in silence with their Bibles for virtually every hour of every day, with the goal that they should become penitent for their sins. But the visitors' interviews of inmates found that many were

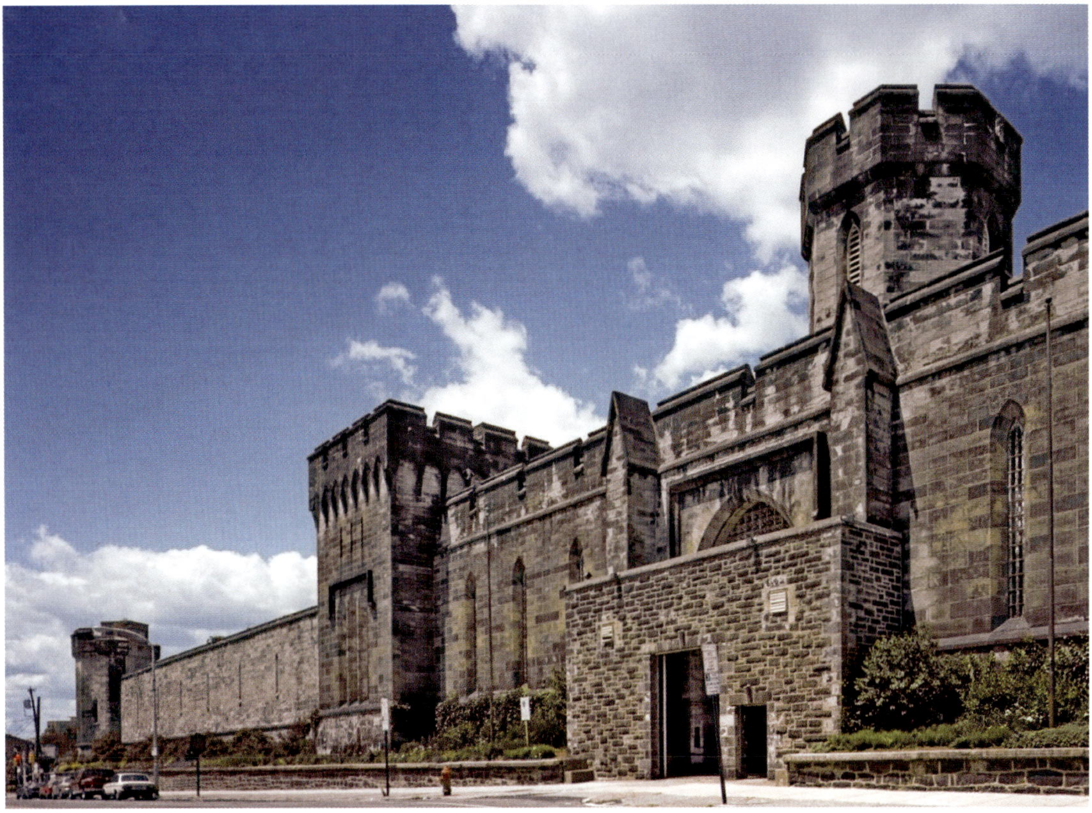

Figure 7.4 Philadelphia's Eastern State Penitentiary introduced the "progressive" idea of solitary confinement when it was opened in the 1830s. Yet, Alexis de Tocqueville concluded after his visit to the prison that this practice "does not reform, it kills." (Library of Congress, Prints & Photographs Division, photograph by Carol M. Highsmith. Reproduction Number: LC-HS503-3215 [ONLINE])

desolate from loneliness and driven nearly to despair from the lack of human companionship:

> The convicts had been submitted to complete isolation; but this absolute solitude, if nothing interrupts it, is beyond the strength of man; it destroys the criminal without intermission and without pity; it does not reform, it kills.[42]

Tocqueville also gleaned much for his larger study from his time in the city. He conversed with such leading citizens as Nicholas Biddle, Peter Duponceau, Philadelphia's mayor, and many others. Here, as elsewhere, he found that almost everyone he met regarded him as a member of the middle class. He was fascinated to understand the implications of a popular assembly, which had recently convened in Philadelphia. The convention had called together citizens from throughout the states to urge that the federal government adopt a practice of free trade. After its very public meetings had concluded with resolutions to that effect, Tocqueville was alarmed. "Of all that I have seen in America," he said, "it was that Convention which most struck me as being for us a dangerous and impracticable consequence of the sovereignty of the people." The "for us" must reflect his vision of mob rule during the worst excesses of the French Revolution. For Tocqueville, the danger lay in what seemed to him a too-direct democracy representing only some of the people but full of a passion that alarmed him. He was not entirely persuaded when the distinguished Philadelphian, Charles Ingersoll, argued that the convention's acts were merely opinions of a minority, meant to try to persuade Congress, not the legislation of a faction to be imposed upon the nation.[43]

The young Frenchman repeatedly examined racial attitudes and the impact of slavery. He tells of a "well-informed Quaker" in Philadelphia, who said that he was "perfectly convinced" that Negroes and whites were of the same race and that black children showed just as much intelligence as whites, adding that "they often learn faster." But when asked if the free blacks of Pennsylvania had the same citizens' rights as whites, the man explained that, although they do in law, they would be "ill-treated" if they actually tried to vote. Tocqueville protested: "What does that mean for the rule of law?" he asked. The man's response: "The law is nothing with us if it is not supported by public opinion." Taking further note of the social chasm between the races, as well as that between the law and practice, Tocqueville then noted that he had seen how white and black inmates were kept separate at the Walnut Street Prison, even when eating their meals.[44]

Yet he also heard examples in Philadelphia of black citizens who, in spite of great obstacles, had succeeded in making large fortunes. One he learned about was James Forten (1766–1842). Born free, he was educated at Anthony Benezet's school for African children and at age fifteen went aboard a privateer's vessel to assist in the American Revolution. He was captured by the British but refused to secure his own release by renouncing the cause for independence. After the war, he was apprenticed to a sailmaker. Within a few years, Forten was able to buy the business and expand it, thanks to the improvements he made to equipment used in the trade. Eventually, he was rich enough to buy several merchant ships, staffing them with black crews. Forten led the effort of free black citizens in Pennsylvania to turn back legislative efforts to prevent black migration into the Commonwealth or expel those already there.[45] As a fervent abolitionist, Forten was strongly opposed to the colonization movements for sending emancipated slaves to Africa that were then on the rise. He convinced William Lloyd Garrison to oppose colonization in his paper, *The Liberator*, to which Forten often contributed, and to fight instead to secure civil rights for African Americans in the land of their birth.[46]

Tocqueville sided entirely with Forten in his opposition to sending American blacks to Africa. He saw clearly that the central irony of American democracy was that the equal rights of citizens did not extend either to blacks or to Native Americans. He noted that, to rationalize that exclusion, even many educated whites viewed these minorities as inferior. Once Tocqueville and Beaumont traveled into the slaveholding states of the South, they concluded that slavery demeaned not just the enslaved but the whole slaveholding society.

> Slavery . . . dishonors labor; it introduces idleness into society, and with idleness, ignorance and pride, luxury and distress. It enervates the powers of the mind and benumbs the activity of man.[47]

Both men were convinced that, whatever the racism that existed in the North, the absence of slavery there at least made that region more vigorous and productive than the South. They also supposed that the very logic of democracy meant that slavery would eventually be ended and with it, they hoped, would follow the full assimilation of African Americans. They had no illusions that such a development would come easily.

The long life of Philadelphia's—and the nation's—richest citizen, Stephen Girard, came to an end in December 1831, while Tocqueville and Beaumont were still in America. Girard had never fully recovered from an injury he had received nearly a year before, when he was knocked down and run over by a horse and wagon while crossing the street. He left a carefully drafted will that bequeathed almost his entire fortune—an amount equivalent to about $50 billion today—to charitable causes. He left the City of Philadelphia a huge gift of money in trust, to be used for various public improvements. The will's centerpiece was the establishment of a boarding school for "poor, white, orphan boys," which would come into being as Girard College some years later. At the time, Girard's legacy was the largest single act of philanthropy ever made in America. The will was contested by a number of Girard's relatives, including his niece Henriette, who had remarried after the death of her first husband, Henri Lallemand, and moved to France. The case was appealed all the way to the U.S. Supreme Court, which produced a landmark decision upholding the will in 1844.[48]

At the time of Girard's death, his naming of "poor, white, orphan boys" as the intended population for his school was viewed as generous and unexceptionable. He made clear that what little instruction existed in his day for poor boys (poor girls were seldom thought to need formal education) he found deficient; hence, his bequest. Given the unequal treatment of blacks that was then the norm throughout society, he likely did not even consider including their sons as well. It was not until more than a century later, when America's views about race were rapidly evolving and after prolonged legal battles lasting for more than a decade, that Girard's restriction was overturned. In March 1968, a district court judge ruled that the language violated the clause providing equal protection of the laws to all U.S. citizens contained in the Constitution's Fourteenth Amendment. That meant African American boys who otherwise qualified must be admitted to the college. By the 1980s, Girard College decided to admit female students as well.[49] Girard's financial largesse to his adopted city, meanwhile, remains tangible in blocks of valuable real estate in the heart of Philadelphia.

Girard had written a codicil to his will that provided minute specifications about how and where he wanted the school to be built. It would be constructed on a forty-five-acre tract of land he owned a mile north of the city limits. The first building's dimensions, the height and thickness of the campus's enclosing walls, and the number of gates were all spelled out. Once the fight over the will was concluded, Nicholas Biddle, chair of the school's board of directors, moved to direct its construction. Twenty-one architects are known to have competed for the commission. Among them were the nation's two leading architects at the time, John Haviland and William Strickland, as well as one native of France, Michel De Chaumer. The latter justified his rather modest design on the grounds that the "architecture of a palace ought to find no place in a House of Charity."[50] Yet Biddle, whose view was all-important, disagreed, wanting a grand edifice. A champion of the newly popular Greek Revival style, he chose the Philadelphia architect, Thomas U. Walter (1804–1887)—who would later design the new dome and wings of the U.S. Capitol—to create the plan for Founder's Hall.

From the time of its dedication in 1848, the building has been regarded as one of the finest examples of that style in America. Though neoclassical, at least one observer has seen its French flavor, for, in his words, it creates "a kind of Parisian ensemble, the church of the Madeleine thrust into the Place de la Concorde."[51] Girard's remains had been interred at his death in Holy Trinity churchyard at Sixth and Spruce Streets. In 1851, they were moved in a great public ceremony to a marble tomb in the vestibule of Founder's Hall. Standing before it is a full-length marble sculpture of the benefactor by Nicholas Gevelot, a French artist then working in Philadelphia. In 1854, Philadelphia was greatly enlarged to make its new boundaries coterminous with those of Philadelphia County, where they remain to this day. A major new street, Girard Avenue, connected Girard College to the enlarged city to the east and west.

In the decade before the design of Founder's Hall was awarded to him, Thomas U. Walter was training a young man of French heritage in his architectural firm. Napoleon LeBrun (1821–1901) was the son of a man who had served as Napoleon Bonaparte's ambassador to the United States. After Napoleon's final abdication, Charles LeBrun and his wife settled in Philadelphia, where their son was born. Young Napoleon began his architectural training with Walter at age fifteen and established his own architectural firm a mere five years later. He began to receive commissions for new buildings in areas along the Schuylkill River as it underwent rapid industrialization upstream from Philadelphia. He also was hired to create a number of churches in the city. Among the earliest was Saint Patrick's (1841) on Twenty-First and Locust Streets in a then-new residential neighborhood.[52] In 1847–1848, he redesigned and rebuilt one of the city's first Roman Catholic churches, Saint Augustine, at Fourth and New Streets, which had been largely destroyed in the anti-Catholic, anti-immigrant riots of 1844. His 1848 design for an Episcopal church at 237 North Seventeenth Street is today the home of Saint John Chrysostom Albanian Orthodox Church. Over time, other churches by LeBrun have been demolished.

His most important buildings in Philadelphia were the Roman Catholic Cathedral of Saints Peter and Paul and the Academy of Music, both of which remain major landmarks. The Cathedral (1846–1864), today the Cathedral Basilica, is now the oldest building on Logan Square. LeBrun reworked the designs of two Catholic priests in a Roman-Corinthian style, then left the project for several years, when John Notman added the Palladian facade and dome to his design. But LeBrun returned to complete the construction of what remains both the largest brownstone structure in Philadelphia and the largest Catholic church in Pennsylvania. (See Figures 7.5 a and b.)

In 1847, LeBrun altered and enlarged Musical Fund Hall on Locust near Seventh Street. Since its construction in 1824, that hall had presented classical music to Philadelphians.[53] But the city was expanding so rapidly that by midcentury its center lay further west. It was LeBrun's 1854 design that won the architectural competition for a new opera house, named the American Academy of Music when it opened at Broad and Locust Streets in 1857. The Academy of Music, its interior planned to resemble that of Milan's La Scala, has functioned as such since its inauguration, making it the longest continuously operating opera house in the United States. Throughout all of the twentieth century, it was the home of the Philadelphia Orchestra. LeBrun's legacy, like that of Girard, continues to the present day to touch Philadelphians in their daily lives.[54] Although LeBrun moved both his practice and family to New York in 1864, at his death he was buried in Philadelphia's Laurel Hill Cemetery.

By the middle of the nineteenth century, Philadelphia was growing so fast that its remarkable plant for supplying the city with water could scarcely keep pace with the increased need. The waterwheels that pumped water from the Schuylkill River at Fairmount were no longer at the cutting edge of such technology. They were inefficient and also had to be stopped twice a day at high tide. The chief engineer of the Water Works, Frederic Graff Jr. became acquainted with a recent immigrant from France who had apprenticed with France's leading turbine maker, Nicolas Jonval. That young engineer, Emile Geyelin, had come to America to design turbines for the Du Pont company's black powder mills. Graff contracted with Geyelin to assist him in designing a hydraulic turbine for the Water Works. Their prototype proved a success, and, by 1862, a new mill house was built at the Schuylkill dam to house several of the Jonval-type hydraulic turbines. That so increased the water supply that the Fairmount facility continued as the provider of public water to Philadelphia for most of the rest of the century.[55]

Emile Geyelin (1825–1900) would soon marry the daughter of the last prefect to Louisiana, Pierre Clément de Laussat, who had overseen the territory's transfer from France to the United States in 1803. The Geyelins' descendants remained prominent in the Philadelphia region for generations. A son, Henry L. Geyelin (1857–1921), distinguished himself in track, rowing, and football at the University of Pennsylvania, where he would be remembered as the "Father of Penn Athletics." A great-grandson, Philip Laussat Geyelin (1923–2004), became a Pulitzer prize–winning journalist at the *Washington Post*, where, as editor of the editorial page, he led the newspaper's opposition to the Vietnam War, which included its publication of the Pentagon Papers in 1971.

French émigré dentists had brought their skills as the leaders in the field to Philadelphia beginning in the 1790s (see Chapter 4). It was, therefore, fitting that by the mid-nineteenth century, a native Philadelphian should begin a long and distinguished

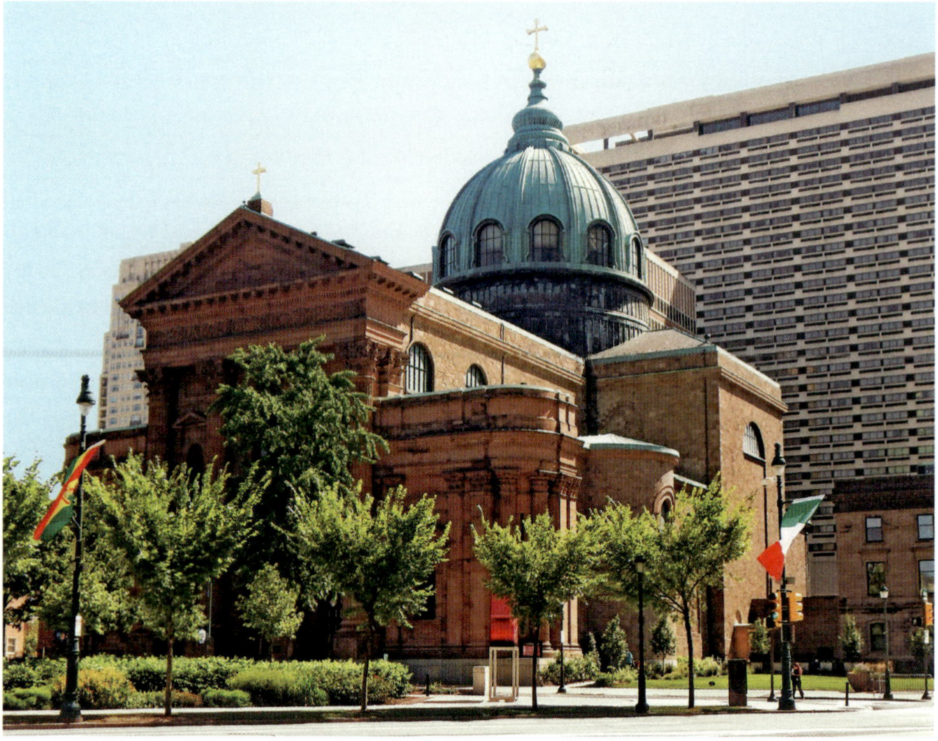

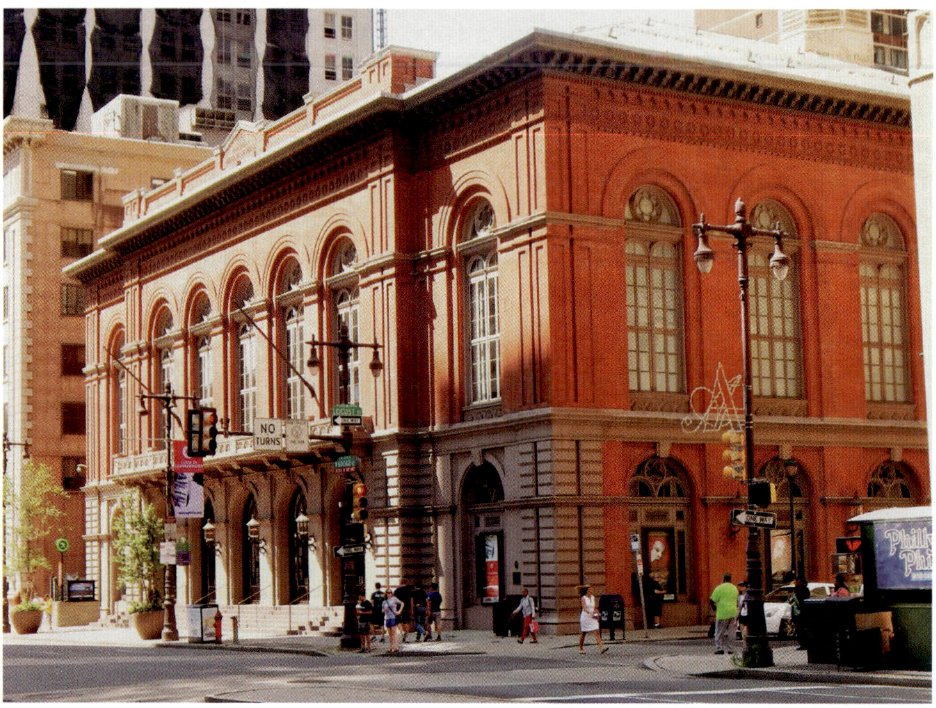

Figure 7.5a and **Figure 7.5b** Napoleon Le Brun, a Philadelphia architect whose father had served as France's ambassador to the United States, played leading roles in the 1840s and 1850s in the design of two of Philadelphia's most iconic buildings, the Cathedral of Saints Peter and Paul and the Academy of Music.

career serving as a dentist to Parisians, including the crème de la crème of French society. Thomas W. Evans (1823–1897) was descended from Welsh Quakers. At age fourteen, he became a student of local gold- and silversmiths whose business included the manufacture of dental instruments. At eighteen, he was apprenticed to a dentist and learned surgery by attending lectures at Jefferson Medical College. Once certified in dentistry, he soon established a reputation for his pathbreaking use of gold for filling teeth. At twenty-four, he was recommended as the assistant to an American dentist working in Paris. Knowing little French, he arrived there with his young wife in 1847 to begin a practice that would last for half a century, in the course of which he would achieve an international reputation.

Within a year of Evans's arrival in Paris, the bourgeois monarchy of Louis Philippe was overthrown and the Second Republic proclaimed (Alexis de Tocqueville was one of the authors of its constitution). That allowed the ever-hopeful Louis Napoleon Bonaparte, who had twice failed at attempts to overthrow Louis Philippe, to return from his exile in London and begin an electoral campaign that, by the end of 1848, resulted in his landslide election as president of the new republic. This Bonaparte—the same whom Joseph had castigated for earlier coup attempts—was the son of Napoleon's younger brother, Louis, and his wife, Hortense de Beauharnais, the daughter of Napoleon's first wife, Josephine, and her first husband. Within months after the new "Prince-President," as he styled himself, took office, he sent a message to Evans's mentor, the American dentist, calling him to the Elysée Palace to treat a toothache. Because the older man was unavailable, the young Dr. Evans went in his place and immediately impressed the leader of France with his skills. He performed a "slight operation" that gave the patient "great relief." The president summoned him again the next day, beginning an association that would last until Bonaparte's death nearly thirty years later. As the doctor put it years afterward, "I visited him often, for the relations between us were now not entirely professional having soon become friendly and even confidential."[56]

Some two years after their first meeting, the prince-president launched a coup against the Second Republic and declared himself Emperor Napoleon III.[57] Soon after, he made Dr. Evans surgeon-dentist to the Imperial Court, marking his arrival as a trusted intimate of the emperor. The next year, the monarch made him a member of the Légion d'Honneur. At the height of the American Civil War, when Napoleon III was increasingly pressed to extend diplomatic recognition to the Confederacy, he asked Evans for advice. Horrified at the prospect that France might give such a boost to the secessionists, Evans assured the emperor that the North would surely be victorious; he volunteered to return to America to assess the situation himself. After arriving in Washington, he conferred with Lincoln and Secretary of State Seward and with General Grant in Virginia, then toured several battlefields. When he returned to Paris, the emperor, evidently impressed at Evans's counsel, agreed not to recognize the Confederacy.

Evans was by then becoming perhaps the most famous dentist in the world. He led the way in the establishment of the kinds of practices that soon became standard

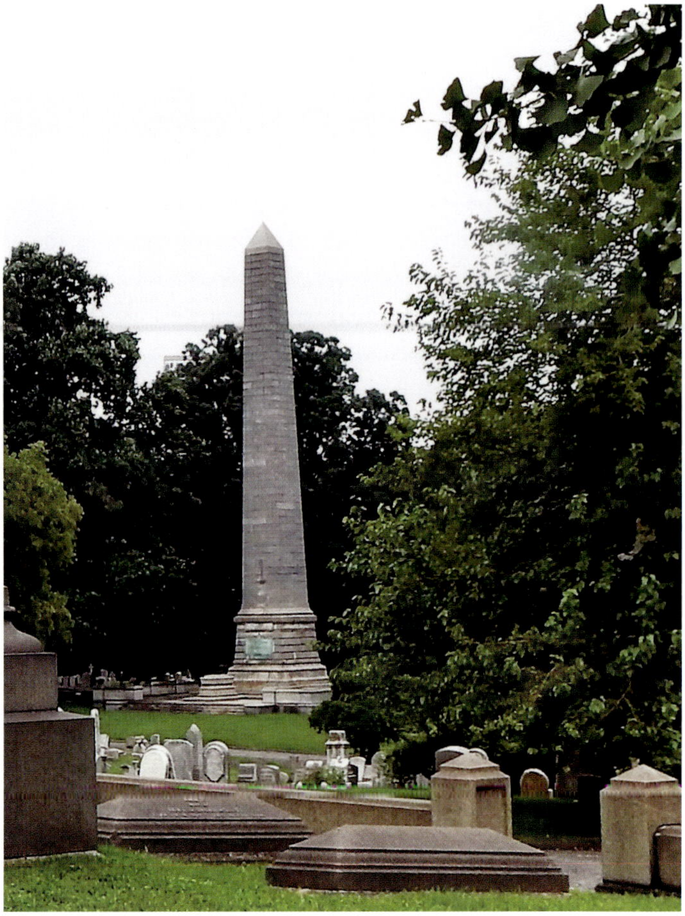

FIGURE 7.6
The obelisk marks the burial place of Philadelphian Thomas W. Evans, who became surgeon-dentist to the imperial court of Napoleon III. Penn Dental Medicine now houses the Evans Collection of his art and artifacts.

in the profession, such as the use of vulcanized rubber as the foundation for dentures. He first demonstrated the use of nitrous oxide as an anesthetic in tooth extractions at the Exposition Universelle in Paris in 1867, which made possible painless dentistry. His most indelible nonprofessional service came in the frantic hours in 1870 after Napoleon was defeated at Sedan, then imprisoned by the Prussians. With the collapse of the Second Empire, the Senate was dissolved and mobs poured into the streets of Paris. Her life threatened, Empress Eugénie turned to the trusted Evans for urgent help. He quickly made arrangements for her flight to Deauville in disguise. He and two others accompanied her in his own carriage, all the passengers traveling with aliases. Soon after they safely reached the coast, Evans managed to persuade a British yachtsman to carry the empress to England.[58] There, her husband and son eventually joined her. (See Figure 7.6.)

At the time of his death in 1897, the much-decorated Evans was laid to rest in Philadelphia's Woodlands Cemetery, alongside his wife. He left most of his property to create the Thomas W. Evans Museum and Dental Institute at Spruce and Fortieth Streets in Philadelphia, the site of his boyhood home. The museum was meant to house his substantial collection of art, much of it the gifts of European royalty who had been his patients. Included were several paintings by Édouard Manet, with whom Evans reportedly had shared a mistress. He specified that his estate should create a dental school "not inferior to any already established." As a result, the University of Pennsylvania's Evans Building was opened in 1915 and still thrives at the core of Penn Dental Medicine. Over time, much of the Evans art collection was either dispersed or relegated to storage. In 1967, the museum was closed and replaced with a new dental wing. The getaway carriage, which had been on display at the school for many decades, was loaned to France. It was eventually placed at the Château de Compiègne in Picardy.

Early in the twenty-first century, however, authorities at Penn determined to restore the Evans Collection as a prominent feature of Penn Dental Medicine. In 2015, the carriage was brought back to Philadelphia and again displayed in the atrium of the school's main entrance. At the same time, paintings, sculptures, and decorative art from the collection were featured in a temporary exhibition at the Arthur Ross Gallery, then much of it was displayed in the public spaces at the Evans building. Rotating exhibits from the collection are now also a feature of the school library's main reading room, so that today Thomas Evans's life and times are fully on view in Philadelphia.[59]

In 1876, Philadelphia attracted international attention as never before when it staged the first world's fair ever in North America. The Centennial Exposition, mounted in Fairmount Park in honor of the signing of the Declaration of Independence a century earlier, shone a bright light on modern art, invention, and manufacture from around the globe. Over its six months of life, the Centennial Exposition attracted nearly ten million visitors, or about one-fifth of the total population of the nation at the time. Among the more than two hundred structures erected for the fair, the enduring landmark today is Memorial Hall. This international art gallery for the exposition was the largest such structure for art in the United States when it was completed. It was also among the first in America in the French Beaux-Arts style that reigned triumphant in the design of monumental buildings here as it did throughout Europe over the next several decades. Memorial Hall was created by Hermann Schwarzmann, the fair's chief planner. He based it on the design of a French artist and architect, Nicolas Felix Escalier, who made it his project for a Prix de Rome.[60]

At the same time as the Centennial Exposition, a French Renaissance Revival building, Philadelphia's City Hall, was also rising at the crossroads of Broad and Market Streets, anchoring and inspiring what would unfold as a magnificent French boulevard early in the twentieth century. At the close of the Centennial Exposition, Memorial Hall became the permanent home of the Museum of Art and Industry until, renamed the Philadelphia Museum of Art, it moved into its new building atop Fairmount in 1928. In the interim, other structures in the Beaux-Arts style would dot Philadelphia's landscape.[61]

[8]

Philadelphia, Paris, and Thomas Eakins

In July 1795, the artist John Vanderlyn moved from New York to the corner of Fifth and Chestnut Streets in Philadelphia to become a copyist of Gilbert Stuart's works. Stuart had trained in England and remained abroad for eighteen years. He returned to America in 1793, moving in 1795 to Germantown where he established a studio. He painted George Washington in a series of iconic portraits that gained him great fame and created a heavy demand for copies. Vanderlyn's replica of Stuart's 1794 portrait of Aaron Burr, then serving as a U.S. senator from New York, caught the politician's eye. Burr, harboring deep-seated political resentment toward Great Britain, sent Vanderlyn to Paris in 1796 where the artist remained for five years, studying in the atelier of the neoclassical artist François-André Vincent and becoming the first American student to gain admission to the École des Beaux-Arts. Vanderlyn became the first of many artists throughout the nineteenth century to emigrate to the French capital to sharpen their skills in the atelier of a French master, steep themselves in the treasures of the Louvre, and attend the Salons to assess the merits of the juried selection of works of art sponsored by the government. The English painting tradition continued its hold on American artists in the first decades of the nineteenth century, but, as the century progressed, France drew more artists to its Salons and art studios. Vanderlyn alleged that "to acquire knowledge of the Arts, there is but one Paris in the Universe. I am certain, though, some of my countrymen have preferred London very foolishly, & to their own regret perhaps, had they known more of Paris."[1]

Due to its primacy in portraiture, England had drawn eighteenth-century American artists to its shores whereas the westward expansion and rise of nationalism under the Jackson administration gave American artists the incentive to seek inspiration in their native country in the 1820s and 1830s. English inspiration in art remained strong for landscapists such as Thomas Cole in the creation of his historical landscapes. Nevertheless, the restoration of the Bourbon monarchy in France (1815–1830) disappointed many Americans who began to turn against European style and subject matter as they sought to craft their uniqueness as a republican nation free from the trappings of royalty and independent of narratives derived from other cultures. The dramatic aspects of native topography and genre scenes of vernacular American life with their stock characters and quotidian experiences attracted antebellum artists and patrons more than erudite narratives of mythological tales, portraits of famous men, and large-scale deeds of valor.

Paris remained primarily a city visited as a stopover in the education of an American artist on the Grand Tour of European cities in the first decades of the nineteenth century. However, what had been a trickle of artists seeking artistic education in the early years became a veritable torrent of aspiring practitioners by the end of the century. Artists such as William Morris Hunt and John LaFarge began to seek apprenticeship with successful French artists whose works had been reported on by the American press and sold well to American collectors. The Salon exhibitions provided the greatest forum for international exposure and the potential marketing of art. The lack of experience in art training in America and the constant need for funds for the arts stood in sad contrast to the sophistication of the French art system with its state support, prizes, and esteem for an artistic career, making Paris a draw. Paris eventually replaced London and Rome as a destination to study art to the point where the twentieth-century philosopher and cultural critic Walter Benjamin dubbed it the capital of the nineteenth century.[2]

Under Napoleon III in 1853, the city underwent a massive urban transformation designed by Baron Georges-Eugène Haussmann that enlarged the city and created new boulevards, parks, buildings, and railroad stations. The emperor's desire to indicate that the visual arts played as significant a role as the new architecture became evident in the plan for the Universal Exhibition of 1855, which set out to rival London's Great Exhibition of 1851 in demonstrating France's supremacy in industry, technology, and the arts. London had accorded only a minor role to the visual arts in 1851, but Paris chose to erect a separate Palais des Beaux-Arts where the work of artists from twenty-eight countries could be displayed. The art exhibition saw nearly nine hundred thousand visitors between May 15 and November 15.

As transatlantic travel became easier, more Americans traveled to Paris. Earl Shinn began his career in Philadelphia as a property title investigator but was drawn to art and enrolled at the Pennsylvania Academy in 1859. He left for France in April 1866 among the first group of post–Civil War expatriate artists and soon began contributing a weekly column to the *Philadelphia Evening Bulletin* under the pseudonym "L'Enfant Perdu" titled "Rash Steps." He wrote an article for the *Nation* titled "Art Study Abroad," in which he claimed that a French friend told him that for "diplomacy, for the public idea, we fly to you; but for the toleration of taste, for the painter's dream, even America emigrates. She reverses the procession of empire . . . and comes to study of France the principles of liberty. You, monsieur, arrive for improvement in art."[3]

Shinn's words proved true for Thomas Eakins (1844–1916), his classmate at the academy. A year after graduating from Central High School in 1861, Eakins enrolled in the Pennsylvania Academy, which had been restructured in 1854, according to the recommendations of John Sartain, to align with the system of instruction given at the École des Beaux-Arts.[4] In his classes, Eakins encountered the Alsatian artist Christian Schussele who had emigrated to Philadelphia around 1848. For the next thirty years Schussele served as a significant proponent of the French academic system. He had trained in Paris under Adolphe Yvon and Paul Delaroche, academic painters who held history painting in the highest esteem. He began exhibiting paintings at the Pennsylvania Academy of Fine Arts in 1851 and, according to Shinn, was almost the only artist in Philadelphia to show any real interest in the academy's students.[5] Although he never studied directly with Schussele at the academy, Eakins most likely absorbed the Frenchman's advocacy of students perfecting their skills and artistic education by further training in Paris.

Drawing alone could be learned at the Pennsylvania Academy when Eakins attended, while anatomy lessons were taken at Jefferson Medical School. Training in painting and sculpture had to be pursued privately from professional practitioners. Encouraged by his father to pursue study abroad, Eakins left America for Paris on September 22, 1866, arrived in Paris on October 3, and remained in Europe until July 1870. With the exception of a month-long vacation with his father and sister Frances in Germany, Switzerland, Italy, and Belgium in August 1868, and a two-month visit back home later that same year, Eakins spent the majority of his time in Paris. A six-month sojourn in Spain shortly before returning to Philadelphia marked his longest stay out of the French capital. Sustained by a workable knowledge of the French language, Eakins fought his way through the bureaucratic system and gained admittance into the studio of Jean-Léon Gérôme (1824–1904), a highly esteemed painter who had been made a chevalier of the Légion d'Honneur in 1855 and was elected to the Institut de France the year before Eakins arrived in Paris.[6] Gérôme had experienced considerable Salon and commercial success with his meticulously detailed historical scenes of Greece and Rome along with ethnographic and neo-Greek subjects, all painted with a pristine surface finish. His works had been exhibited at the Pennsylvania Academy's annual exhibitions in 1860, 1861, and 1862, where Eakins would have had ample time to study them. Gérôme was married to Marie Goupil, daughter of a highly influential art dealership whose New York City branch helped promote his son-in-law's reputation and sales. Philadelphians such as Joseph Claghorn, Joseph Harrison, and Henry Gibson avidly collected Gérôme's work.[7] Monographs published in America in 1884 and 1892 sustained interest in his career.

Gérôme's studio remained a favorite among American artists for the forty years he taught there. He followed the standards of Beaux-Arts education where students had to master the essentials of drawing before advancing to figure drawing after a life model, who generally adopted a pose based on a classical work of art. Painting came only after the artists had perfected these skills under the stern scrutiny of the master. Eakins acknowledged in a letter to his father during his second week with Gérôme that the disapproval of his work had been harsh. Nevertheless, he had moved to Paris to learn and, therefore, accepted the criticism, recognizing that Gérôme wanted to see improvement in his pupil's work. Due to his prior drawing training at the academy that had been reorganized in 1854 on the model of the École des Beaux-Arts, Eakins was advanced into painting after five months. Gérôme's success at the Universal Exhibition of 1867, where he was awarded the Grand Medal of Honor, must have increased Eakins's awe for his teacher. Several of the works seen there found their way in one form or another into Eakins's paintings when he returned to America.[8]

Eakins's letters from Paris testify to his eagerness to capitalize on his European experience and broaden his aesthetic education. They also document his self-doubts and struggles. When Gérôme closed his atelier for the month of August in 1869, Eakins joined his fellow Philadelphian William Sartain in Léon Bonnat's studio. Bonnat (1833–1922) provided Eakins with a healthy alternative in painting technique with his combination of careful academic drawing with the use of strokes of paint brushed broadly and thickly on the canvas to capture the effects of light and shade, thus loosening the tighter technique taught by Gérôme. Bonnat had broader tastes than Gérôme when it came to the art of his day, championing the work of Gustave Courbet (1819–1877), Édouard Manet (1832–1883), and Edgar Degas (1834–1917). Eakins had learned at some point that during Bonnat's apprenticeship his teachers had little faith in him. One told him to stop painting but Bonnat went on to study with the Romantic history painter Paul Delaroche who recommended that he quit painting and become a shoemaker. Bonnat was only thirty-six when Eakins studied with him, so his success in overcoming his teachers' lack of confidence in his talent must have given Eakins some hope, especially since Bonnat had been elected a chevalier of the Légion d'Honneur, had been decorated at the Paris Universal Exhibition in 1867, and had won the Medal of Honor at the 1869 Salon.

Eakins's correspondence with his family aimed at easing their concerns about his progress in his studies. In the same letter to his father where he recounted Bonnat's experiences in his early career, Eakins mentioned that Thomas Couture (1815–1879) had also struggled with his teachers.[9] Although he never met Couture, whose masterpiece *The Romans of the Decadence* became the sensation of the Salon of 1847, Eakins admired his work immensely. He purchased Couture's *Méthode et entretiens d'atelier* in 1868, avid to learn more about Couture's painting techniques and ideas. He wrote to his sister Fanny asking her to inform Sartain that he would send him a copy after he got it back from an artist who was eager to read it. Couture aimed in his work and teaching at a balance between line and color, with a synthetic mixture of sketch and finish, that furnished Eakins at that moment with an alternative to Gérôme's painstakingly detailed drawing and polished surfaces. Another contrast with Gérôme's fastidious demeanor and disciplined professionalism was revealed by Eakins when he wrote about Couture's relaxed manner of dressing and his boldness in shocking women by exposing his chest and navel by wearing his shirt open during his summer visit to Écouen. References to Eakins's casual and sometimes slovenly way of dressing along with his undressing in front of female students when he began teaching are foreshadowed in these observations.[10] Eakins recounted how Couture clothed a dwarf in a Venetian costume and began painting him when he arrived in Écouen. But the dwarf went away after a few weeks and Couture never finished the painting, leading Eakins to inform his sister Fanny that Couture did not get a single thing done during the eight months he was away from Paris. A letter from Eakins to his father in October 1868 sought to calm his father's worries about his lack of progress in completing work, asserting: "There is a common mistake made by those who do not know drawing & that it [*sic*] that one should have the habit of finishing studies. This is a great mistake. You work at a thing only to assure yourself of the principle you are working on & the moment you satisfy yourself you quit it for another."[11] He admitted to having been dispirited by his father's criticism, so finding an example in a successful Parisian artist aimed to allay his family's concerns and perhaps even his own.

Bonnat's enthusiastic advocacy of the Spanish masters most likely prompted Eakins's three-month visit to Spain during the winter of 1869–1870 where the canvases of the seventeenth-century master Diego Velázquez drew Eakins's highest praise and further influenced his painting technique. The strong chiaroscuro and broad paint handling that had appealed to him in Couture's painting was confirmed in Madrid before the canvases of the Spanish master. When Eakins studied Velázquez's paintings in the Prado it was as if all the kaleidoscopic pieces of his artistic education fell into place and his future direction became clear. The simpering goddesses and mannered pretentiousness of Salon art collapsed like overinflated soufflés before the unaffected frankness and bold naturalism of Spanish art. He was done with drawing clavicles and ribs, ready to emerge from the chrysalis of his Parisian training. On January 26, 1870, he informed his father that his student work had ended, and he was ready to begin his professional career in America: "I am as strong as any of Gerome[s] pupils, and I have nothing to gain by remaining. What I have learned I could not have learned at home; for beginning, Paris is the best place."[12] He left France and arrived in Philadelphia on the Fourth of July in 1870, never to return to Europe.[13]

Throughout his years of apprenticeship, Eakins would accept and reject various aspects of his French teachers' examples and advice. Shortly before settling permanently in Philadelphia, Eakins claimed that Gérôme had done little for him and swore he would "never paint in the manner of the master."[14] Eakins labored with great difficulty when he transitioned from charcoal drawing to painting with Gérôme. Just months before leaving Paris he wrote to his father about his continued difficulties with the modeling of tones and the proper mixing of colors, lamenting the corrections of his teacher and the comments of his studio colleagues.[15] Most likely homesickness and burnout from his discouraging efforts in the studio prompted this repudiation as Eakins continued to correspond with Gérôme, send him works of art, and seek his counsel throughout his career. Gérôme's teaching remained a significant foundation of Eakins's entire career; Eakins took great pride when he was praised by his teacher in later years and recognized in the press as his former student. Photogravures of Gérôme's work hung in the Eakins's home and in his studio. His wife Susan expressed disappointment in Lloyd Goodrich's 1933 monograph because it failed to emphasize sufficiently Gérôme's impact on her husband's career.[16]

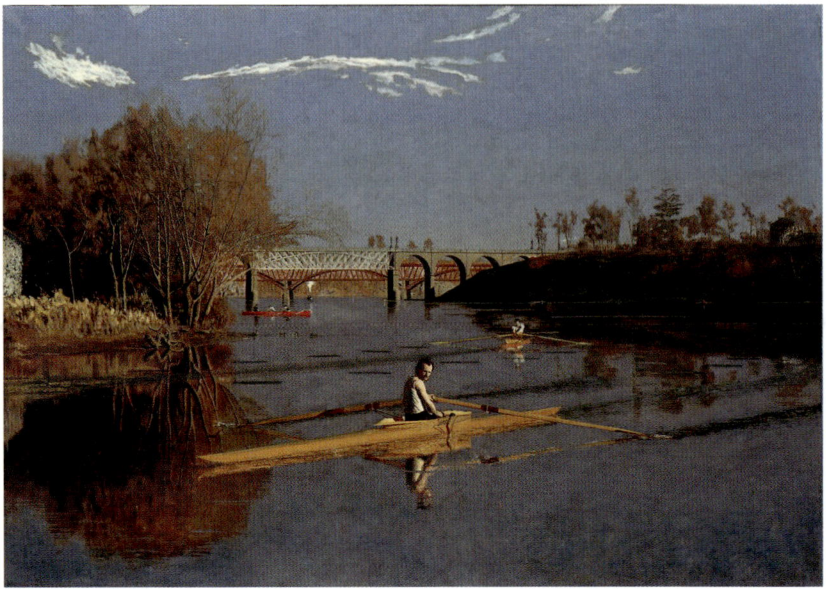

FIGURE 8.1
Thomas Eakins, *Max Schmitt in a Single Scull*, 1871. Oil on canvas, 32¼ × 46 ¼ in. (81.9 × 117.5 cm). (New York, Metropolitan Museum of Art, Purchase, The Alfred N. Punnett Endowment Fund and George D. Pratt Gift, 1934. Acc. No. 34.92.)

On his arrival home, Eakins set to work in the fourth-floor studio of his father's home on Mount Vernon Street. His first paintings consisted mainly of portraits, the genre he believed would help him earn his living and free him from his indebtedness to his father. His subjects were family and close acquaintances in domestic settings. When an opportunity to exhibit at the Union League occurred in the spring of 1871, Eakins submitted a portrait (now lost) of family friend and Philadelphia attorney Matthew Messchert along with a painting titled *The Champion Single Sculls*, also known as *Max Schmitt in a Single Scull.* (See Figure 8.1.) If successful, the portrait of an influential member of the Union League held the potential of future commissions for Eakins who had assured his father that, despite his struggles in the Paris studio, he could make his living painting heads. His exhibition of the painting of Max Schmitt aimed at demonstrating his assimilation and integration of his European experience. Eakins's choice of a sporting image afforded him several strategic opportunities to display his resolve to strike out on his own as an artist determined to announce his individuality and originality.[17]

Eakins's painting of Max Schmitt portrays his childhood friend pausing while rowing in his scull on the Schuylkill River. Schmitt had won the first single-scull championship of the Schuylkill Navy in a three-mile race on June 10, 1867. Eakins painted himself in the middle distance near the bank of the river, pulling on his oars. He signed and dated the painting with his name on the boat. In the far background, beneath the bridge, an older-style boat contains three figures dressed in traditional Quaker garb. As an avid rower himself, Eakins knew boating well and was particularly interested in Schmitt's achievements in regattas. He kept a close watch on Schmitt's activities while abroad, commenting in his letters on his friend's abilities and achievements in the sport.

A reviewer for the *Philadelphia Evening Bulletin* remarked that the painting of Schmitt dealt "boldly and broadly with the commonplace in nature."[18] He informed the reader that Eakins had recently returned from Europe and had been influenced by Gérôme. Scholars have pointed to the closely observed anatomy, perspectival rigor, and attention to detail—skills that were honed under Gérôme's tutelage. Eakins marked several of his preparatory perspectival drawings for this painting with notes in French. Gérôme's 1863 *The Prisoner* has been cited as an influence. (See Figure 8.2.) Yet Eakins's painting converts a gloomy Orientalist scene of exotic figures ferrying a captive in a heavy barge into a contemporary image of a scantily clad local hero in late autumn light.

Rowing was considered to be the first modern sport and Eakins witnessed the race on October 5, 1870, where Schmitt reclaimed his title of champion of the single sculls of the Schuylkill Navy. Having lived in Paris during its transformation under Haussmann, Eakins would have been well aware of the impact of modernization in the look of the city and the attitudes of its populace. Eakins's decision to launch his exhibition career with *Max Schmitt in a Single Scull* announced his intention to be a painter of contemporary subject matter rather than follow in Gérôme's footsteps with re-creations of events from ancient history or alluring scenes from Eastern harems that would be unfamiliar to many Parisians. While sporting images of racing champions had been published in journals and prints, they had not been the subject of a large-scale painting, which most likely prompted the reviewer from the *Philadelphia Evening Bulletin* to characterize *Max Schmitt in a Single Scull* as "peculiar."[19]

Eakins's letters from Paris dealt with personal and financial matters along with reports on his artistic growth, yet it is difficult to conceive that Eakins did not absorb what was happening in the art world around him. He remained aware of the contemporary art scene in Paris years after his return to America. His former student Charles Bregler remembered Eakins commenting: "Did you see those charcoal drawings by Degas? I saw one of a Ballet Girl putting on her tights. He had the wriggle of the foot. The action was good. It was done with a few strokes of charcoal. That fellow knew what

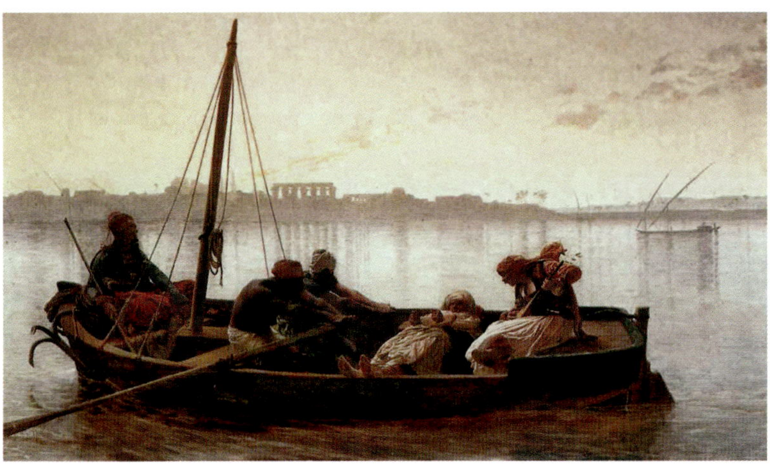

Figure 8.2
Jean-Louis Gérôme, *The Prisoner*, 1863. Oil on canvas, 45 × 78 cm (17.7" × 30.7"). (Nantes, France, Musée des Beaux-Arts)

he was about."[20] When William J. Clark Jr. commented on Eakins's innovative use of rowing as a subject, he noted that it came as "a shock to the artistic conventionalities" of Philadelphia.[21] Eakins embraced the subject matter of the painting of modern life that became the hallmark of Courbet and Manet in the Paris of the 1860s, who, along with the future impressionists, turned increasingly to popular imagery as visual sources of inspiration for their avant-garde works in order to modernize their subject matter.[22]

Eakins wrote to his father: "In a big picture you see what o'clock it is[,] afternoon or morning[,] if it['s] hot or cold winter or summer & what kind of people are there & what they are doing and why they are doing it."[23] The attention to weather and atmosphere became an essential part of Claude Monet's art and would be a hallmark of the *plein air* painting of the other impressionists. Eakins most likely saw Alfred Sisley's *Barges on the Canal Saint-Martin* at the Salon of 1870, where the thick paint and broken brushstroke of the water demonstrated the impressionist technique that flouted the smooth surfaces and tight drawing that had been the hallmark of academic art. Eakins shared the attitude to contemporary subject matter but ignored the spontaneous mark-making, the improvisational facture of fluctuating appearances, and the flattening perspectival picture planes of the emerging Parisian avant-garde. That Eakins inaugurated his public profession at home with a large-scale image more familiar from the pages of *Harper's Monthly* or a print from Currier and Ives affirms Goodrich's observation that Eakins's subject matter was eventually much closer to Courbet's, Manet's, and Degas's than to Gérôme's.[24]

Eakins may have intended to signal his awareness of the tensions between academic and avant-garde work he had experienced abroad at the outset in his painting of Max Schmitt, as old and new motifs combine in ways that signal his ideas on the trajectory of his art. The austere stone Roman arches of the Connection Railway Bridge in the background of the scene give way like a drawn curtain before the intricate trellis work and more modern look of the iron latticework of the Girard Avenue Bridge that will soon carry the train approaching from the right. Just beneath the bridges the bright red boat carrying the Quaker figures in their heavy garb and antiquated boat connote a bygone era. The specificity of the geographic markers and the subject of the work secure the image as a current event on the Schuylkill River. "At once painter, sculler, and embedded reporter," as Alan Braddock observed, "Eakins celebrated and identified with Philadelphia's quaint past, its progressive modernity, and its distinctive environment or milieu, all the while laying claim to an international academic pedigree in art."[25]

Achievement in a sport required many hours of grueling practice before a public performance. This provided a parallel to Eakins's years of having to master the drawing of antique casts, human anatomy, and correct perspective during his student days at the Pennsylvania Academy and his years in Europe. Gérôme's academic principle of concealing the action of the brush and the labor of the artist beneath a seemingly effortless surface finish matched the desired outcome of the accomplished athlete whose hours of disciplined preparation would result in an exhibition of skill that never betrayed the rigors of repeated hours of work that went into mastering the rudiments

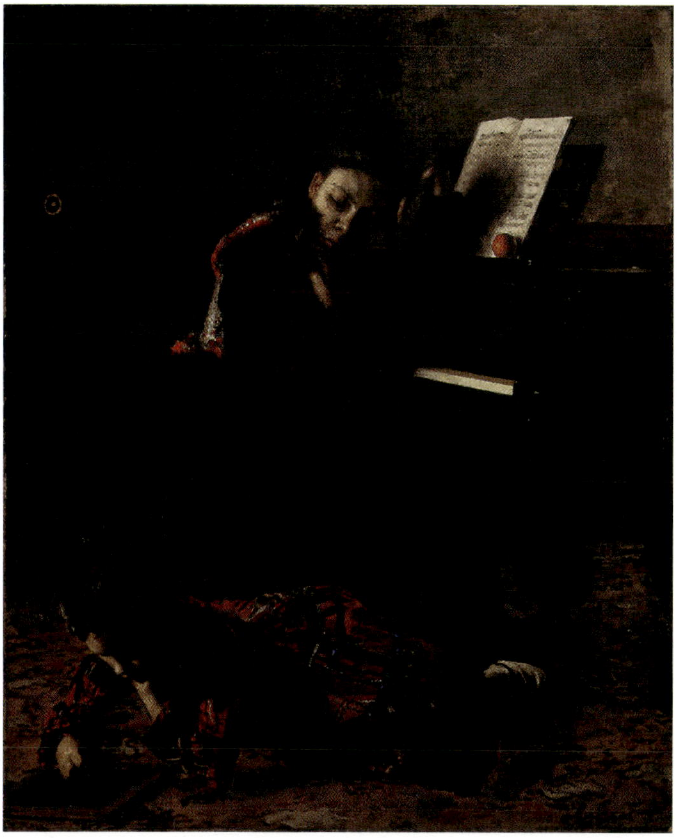

FIGURE 8.3
Thomas Eakins, *Home Scene*, ca. 1871. Oil on canvas, 21 7/16 × 18 in. (54.4 × 45.7 cm). (Brooklyn Museum, Gift of George A. Hearn and Charles A. Schieren, by exchange, Frederick Loeser Fund and Dick S. Ramsay Fund, 50.115)

of the sport. A few of Eakins's domestic paintings prior to his image of Max Schmitt imply the regimen of practice and its attendant struggles with which he identified. *Home Scene* portrays Eakins's sister Margaret leaning on a piano and turning to gaze down at her younger sister Caroline who is focused on drawing with chalk on a slate. (See Figure 8.3.) Margaret's weary look and slumped posture convey the boredom and fatigue of training and drills. She folds her awkwardly elongated left hand against her head to prop it up while she tucks her right hand under the collar of her dress and chin to play with the kitten on her shoulder. She seems to be relaxing her hand after practicing in order to take a break from repetitious chords, envious perhaps of her younger sister's alert energy and deft manipulation of the chalk as she draws on her slate.

Frances Eakins, at the Piano focuses on Eakins's sister Fanny actively performing. (See Figure 8.4.) Eakins took a keen interest in Fanny's piano playing. Shortly after departing for France, he wrote to his mother from the boat about his dreams where he heard one of Fanny's sonatas from beginning to end. A further episode in that dream had him rowing with Max Schmitt.[26] It is interesting that these would be the subjects of some of his first paintings four years later when he disembarked in Philadelphia. Fanny had expressed her frustration in a letter to her brother about conquering the technical difficulties of piano playing. Eakins sent her a long response in which he

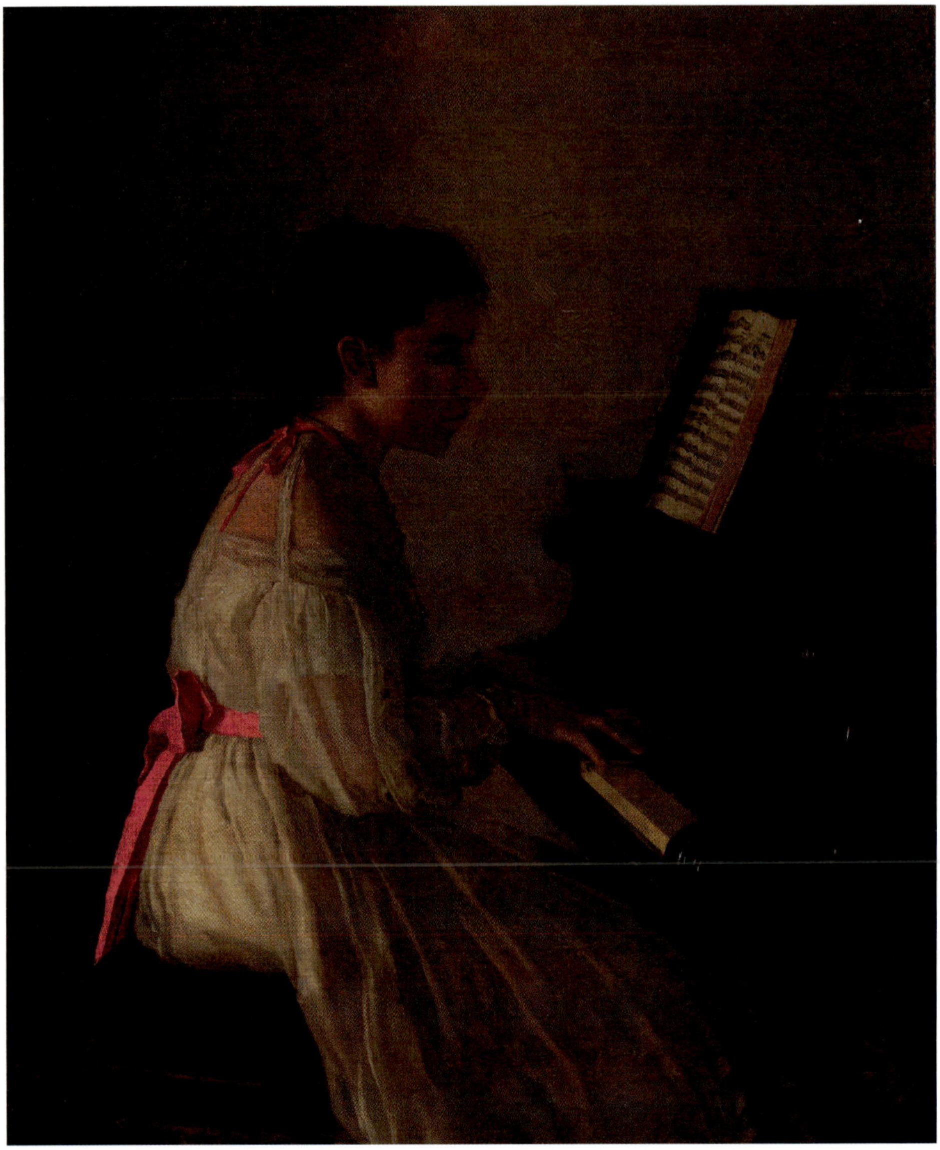

Figure 8.4 Thomas Eakins, American (1844–1916). *Frances Eakins*, ca. 1870. Oil on canvas, 24$\frac{1}{16}$ × 19$\frac{15}{16}$ in. (61.1 × 50.6 cm). (The Nelson-Atkins Museum of Art, Kansas City, Missouri. Purchase: William Rockhill Nelson Trust, 44-55/2. Photo courtesy Nelson-Atkins Media Services / Jamison Miller.)

recommended that she listen to another piano player, take a walk to Fairmount, or go rowing to get her out of her doldrums.[27] The gloomy concentration with which Franny plays the piano in his portrait several years later suggests that the struggle continued. Eakins blurs the notes on the music sheets, which are squeezed uncomfortably together and propped up like a canvas on an easel, whereas in *Home Scene* the notes on the page are crisply legible and the music accessible. Fanny is lit from behind, leaving her face covered largely by a dark shadow with only the fingers on her right hand and her ear—the bodily parts most technically involved in piano playing—to catch any illumination. Fanny's fancy white dress, alleviated only by the scarlet ribbons at her neck and waist, intimates that this is a public recital rather than a private practice session, where the somber atmosphere of the room seems to accentuate the laboriousness of the task, which she approaches with a look of grim determination. The style of her dress makes her shoulders look even more slumped than they actually may have been, thus enhancing the air of discouragement. He related his own trials in the studio with her own, when he admitted: "Don[']t think that you are the only one that has been down hearted. I have often wanted to die & I feel now plain it was my stupidity. I was playing my trills drawing from plaster casts."[28]

The intensity of Eakins's self-portrait in *Max Schmitt in a Single Scull* with his outstretched arms pulling mightily on the oars with a look of fierce resolve on his face could easily be matched with a mental image of him in the studio with his brushes, where he sought to become a champion in the craft of his own art. The competitive spirit ran deep in Eakins whether engaged in a sport or working in the atelier. In an early letter, he described a boxing match between two French art students who were egged on to fight once the studio model was on break. When another French student squared off at Eakins and challenged him, he eagerly accepted. Another student pulled Eakins's opponent away, saying, "My good man let me give you a piece of counsel: never box with an American."[29] He mentioned that Max Schmitt had taught him a little about boxing, which he had forgotten by that time, but he never shirked the challenge despite knowing his prowess was weak at that moment.

Eakins's Paris letters reveal his tracking of Schmitt's races, but his enthusiasm, though sincere, was decidedly cryptic. A June 1867 letter to his father acknowledged the receipt of his sister Maggy's letter about a race that Schmitt had won. He recorded his hope that Schmitt would be as fortunate in the next competition because the French papers were reporting that the sultan of Turkey and President Andrew Johnson planned to witness the event. Eakins revealed his political leanings when he dubbed President Johnson as "His Excellent Superfluity Andrew Johnson Esquire," thus disparaging the prestige of the audience before which Schmitt would perform.[30] Eakins informed his father that he would be glad if Schmitt could win the race without a trial but expressed his doubts, as he deemed Schmitt too excitable for a racer and who was in danger of pulling himself to pieces before he made half the race.[31] These comments come at the end of the letter where Eakins explained at great length to his father the competitive spirit in the Parisian art world for the Rome prize where the winning art student was awarded a stay in Rome for five years with expenses paid by the French government. Eakins recounted that the jury that year had been rigged and the winner chosen even before the paintings had been judged. The minister of fine arts appointed a new jury and the names of the offending jurors were printed in the newspapers. Americans could not compete for the Rome prize and at the same time that Eakins hopes that the winner will be one of Gérôme's students, he also expressed his disdain for such awards. Eakins letter to Fanny in July 1869 requested that she convey his congratulations to Schmitt on his victory but followed that up by asking, "Who was that Clark that run against him[?],"[32] revealing that he was as interested in measuring the competitor as he was the victor.

This rivalry can be read in the choices Eakins made in his insertion of his own image in *Max Schmitt in a Single Scull*, which he first exhibited under the title *The Champion Single Sculls* without the winner's name in the title. Schmitt is pausing after practice rather than crossing the finish line. His shoulders are hunched, his right hand rests on his thigh, and his eyes are cast downward as he looks over his shoulder in a rather ungainly posture. Even though he portrayed himself as diminutive in the middle distance, Eakins showed himself as athletically vigorous and energetically pulling on his oars in the heat of his workout. The smaller image of the aspiring Eakins is no threat to that of the accomplished sculler. Through hours of hard work and practice Schmitt has achieved his goal of a championship; Eakins is just beginning the pursuit of his own fierce ambition to succeed.

Eakins devoted nineteen oils, watercolors, and drawings to the subject of boats and racing. He focused several on John and Barney Biglin, brothers who came to Philadelphia from New York in April 1882 to compete in a pair-oared rowing competition with a purse of $2,000, a record sum for the time. (See Figure 8.5.) Pair-oared rowing required the strictest synchronization of the two rowers' bodies to propel their boat at the great speed that far exceeded that of the single sculler. Eakins painted them in a late-afternoon practice run as they pass the stone pillars of the Columbia Railroad Bridge in *The Pair-Oared Shell* and pulling ahead of another scull in *The Biglin Brothers Racing*. *The Biglin Brothers Turning the Stake* depicts the midpoint of a five-mile race on the Schuylkill River spanning the Reading Railroad Bridge to Connection Bridge just above Girard Avenue. The Biglin brothers won the race and were declared world champions in an event attended by a crowd estimated at thirty thousand. Eakins added himself into the painting as he did with his image of Max Schmitt, but in this one he is barely noticeable in the far-left background in his single scull with an arm raised.

Eakins several times used boating as a metaphor for his art. In a letter to his father in March 1868 from Paris, he wrote that once the artist masters light, color, and form "he's got a canoe of his own" and soon will be "sailing only where he wants to."[33] He compared the maneuvers that an artist needed to those that a skilled sailor makes through his experience, memory, and sense. Even though he felt he was ready to return home from Europe, Eakins still wrote to his father about the technical difficulties he experienced. From Spain he confessed: "The trouble of making a picture for the first time is something frightful. You are thrown off the track by the most contemptable [*sic*] little things that you never thought of & then there are your calculations all to the devil & your paint is wet & it dries slow, just to spite you, in the spot where you are the most hurried."[34] By choosing the moment of turning the stake, Eakins highlighted the strategy and competition required at the most crucial and difficult moment in the race when the rowers have to slow the boat to turn at the halfway mark. Mental concentration needs to match physical precision in order not to lose crucial time. Instead of pulling in coordination, the scullers must ply their strokes counter to each other for a few vital moments to rotate the boat around the stake. John Biglin stares over the stern with the sun underscoring the well-developed musculature of his

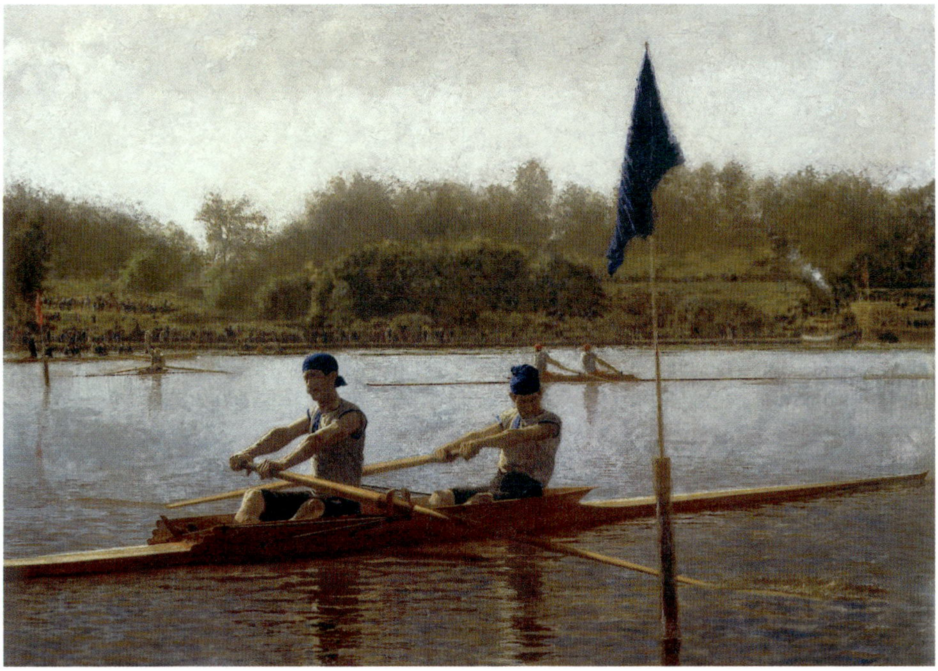

Figure 8.5 Thomas Eakins, *The Biglin Brothers Turning the Stake*, 1872. Oil on canvas: 101.3 × 151.4 cm (39⅞ × 59⅝ in.). (Cleveland Museum of Art, Hinman B. Hurlbut Collection 1984.1927)

arms and right leg. Confident in his brother's accuracy, he does not look behind him to calculate the distance of his oar to the stake. Barney looks intently at his brother's oar while plying his own oar deep into the water while he waits for the signal to start the next stroke. If done correctly, this movement will assure the success of the race as they are leaving their competitors behind them.

The Biglin Brothers Turning the Stake Boat was the largest painting in his series and Eakins made several elaborate perspective drawings in preparation for it. It may be significant that Eakins chose the moment when the brothers had to work against one another to achieve their goal. One can perhaps find an autobiographical similarity to the position Eakins felt himself in vis-à-vis his former teacher as he positioned his figures in the painting. He had worked for years in Paris with Gérôme to bend himself to his training. Now on the Schuylkill instead of the Seine, Eakins was ready to demonstrate his individual skills to the public and successfully turn his own stake.

In the spring of 1873, Eakins made a watercolor (now lost) of *John Biglin in a Single Scull* and sent it to Gérôme who responded favorably to the work, noting that his former pupil had made progress. He admitted he had experienced doubts about Eakins: "I will not conceal from you that formerly in the studio I was not without anxiety about your future as a painter, from the studies that I saw you make."[35] Suggestions for improvement ensued as Gérôme felt the figure lacked movement and appeared fixed on the water. Eakins then made another watercolor that he sent to Gérôme and made a replica for himself. This time Gérôme pronounced the results "entirely good" and, in words that Eakins may have thought he would never hear from his teacher, wrote that he felt "very pleased to have in the New World a pupil such as you who does me honor."[36] Eakins subsequently sent Gérôme four oils in early 1875 to be submitted to the May Salon. Two were accepted and labeled *Une Chasse aux États-Unis*. Most likely these were his hunting paintings *Pushing for Rail* and *Starting Out After Rail*. The tables were now turned as the French critic Paul Leroi found Gérôme's student to be the one who was "exotic" while the reviewer for the *Revue des deux mondes* wondered if the work with its photographic precision had been sent from America to frighten Jean-Baptiste Édouard Detaille, a painter of military scenes noted for the meticulousness of their realistic details.[37] Eakins was overjoyed and communicated Gérôme's praise to Earl Shinn who also had studied and admired the French master. Shinn highlighted Gérôme's admiration in an article in *The Nation* when Eakins had three watercolors shown at the Watercolor Society's Exhibition in 1875.[38]

Exhibition venues in America were scarce for Eakins in the 1870s as the Pennsylvania Academy was closed from 1870 to 1876 for renovations. An opportunity arose when Philadelphia planned to commemorate the first century of American independence with a centennial celebration. When he was studying in Paris, Eakins had his exhibitor's pass for the 1867 Universal Exhibition punched numerous times and clearly understood the benefits such exposure could provide. The Committee on Selection put out a call for paintings on March 5, 1875, requiring that all the works "must be of a high order of merit."[39] Eakins wrote to Shinn on April 13, 1875 that he had a new picture blocked in and "it is very far better than anything I have ever done. As I spoil things less & less in finishing I have the greatest hopes of this one."[40] Eakins had three oils and two watercolors on display in the Centennial International Exhibition galleries when they opened May 10, 1876, but not the one he had intended, which was *The Gross Clinic*. (See Figure 8.6.) The painting on which Eakins had staked so much hope could not be found in Memorial Hall or even in the secondary artists' galleries. It had been exiled to the Army Post Hospital located behind the U.S. Government Building where it hung like an illustration of a mock Civil War army hospital ward with papier-mâché patients occupying cots on either side of the painting.

If visitors to the Army Post First Aid Station needed help, they could perhaps be grateful that their injury might be less traumatic than that of the anonymous and anesthetized patient portrayed in Eakins's painting. Philadelphia surgeon Samuel Gross holds a bloody scalpel in his right hand while assistants hold open the gaping incision he has made. A female figure on the lower right, presumably the mother of the patient, draws back in horror at the sight of the wound. A scribe directly behind Gross takes notes on the procedure while on the right, buried deep in shadow, Eakins depicted himself among the onlookers in sketching the operation in the amphitheater at Jefferson Hospital.

Eakins had studied anatomy and dissection at Thomas Jefferson University prior to his moving to Paris. There he had access to cadavers in the dissection rooms as he attended surgical clinics at Paris hospitals and the École de Médicine.[41] Surgeons prac-

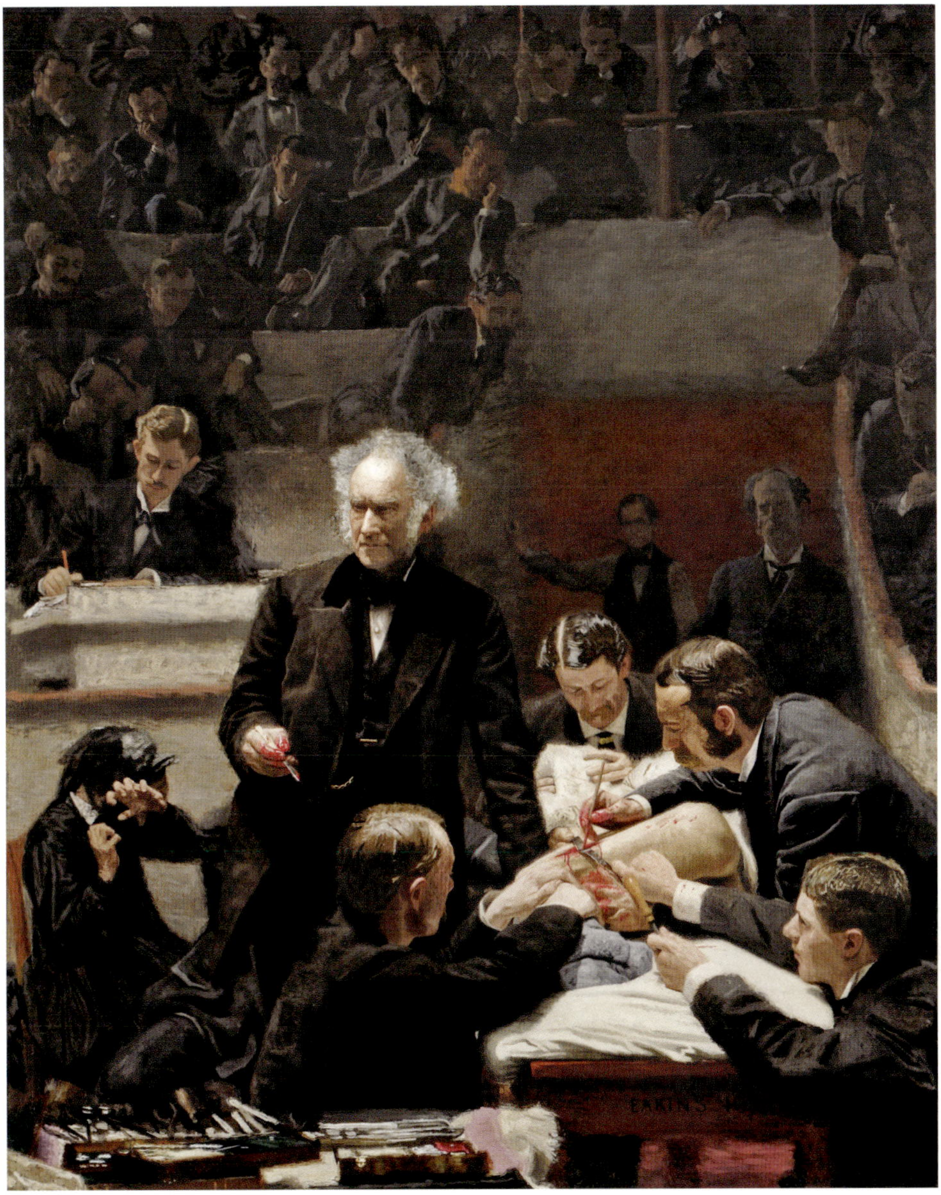

Figure 8.6 Thomas Eakins, *Portrait of Dr. Samuel D. Gross (The Gross Clinic)*, 1875. Oil on canvas, 96 × 78½ in. (243.84 × 199.39 cm). Acc. No.: 2007.2. (Courtesy of the Pennsylvania Academy of the Fine Arts, Philadelphia. Gift of the Alumni Association to Jefferson Medical College in 1878 and purchased by the Pennsylvania Academy of the Fine Arts and the Philadelphia Museum of Art in 2007 with the generous support of more than 3,400 donors.)

ticing in France after 1800 modernized their teaching and practice, drawing students and educated surgeons from Europe and America to learn the new procedures, thus providing a parallel to the same impetus artists felt to train there. When the surgeon George McClellan established Jefferson Medical College in 1825, he based it on the French model. Gross entered a year later and trained with Thomas Dent Mütter, who had also studied in Paris, and referred to his French masters frequently in his lectures as his "friends."[42] The importance of knowing French must have been ingrained in Gross during his training as he hired a private tutor and mastered the language. He earned extra money during the first lean years of his practice by translating French texts on anatomy, obstetrics, and surgery, boasting in his *Autobiography* about the speed with which he was able to expedite completion of the works. In 1861, he published *A Sketch of the Life, Character, and Services of Ambrose Paré*, the father of French surgery.[43] Gross held to the belief throughout his career that all medical students should study French for the sake of learning its admirable medical literature. Although Eakins mostly worked from his sketches and a photograph of Gross, the surgeon did come to his studio to model. One can imagine them sharing their love of the French language and culture during the sessions, which lasted so long that the impatient surgeon once told the painter "Eakins, I wish you were dead!"[44]

Eakins had attended Gross's lectures in 1874 and thus had ample opportunity to observe the man who asserted: "I have performed many operations, and flatter myself that I possess at least some of the qualities of a good operator—a steady hand, an unflinching eye, perfect self-control, and a thorough knowledge of relative anatomy."[45] Eakins could claim the same attributes for himself in his profession as a painter, especially in the accuracy of his anatomical studies.[46] He positioned himself in *The Gross Clinic* with his head glancing to the right in the same direction as Gross's head. He wields his sketching tool in a manner similar to how Gross holds his scalpel.[47]

Shortly before the Centennial International exhibition opened, William J. Clark hailed Eakins's work in an article where he championed the artist, noting the painter's success abroad:

> The fact is, Mr. Eakin's [*sic*] has been in the habit of sending his best things to Paris, where they have found a ready sale, and where his delineations of American sporting scenes especially have been greatly admired. The public of Philadelphia now have, for the first time, an opportunity to form something like an accurate judgment with regard to the qualities of an artist who in many important particulars is very far in advance of any of his American rivals. We know of no artist in this country who can at all compare with Mr. Eakins as a draughtsman, or who has the same thorough mastery of certain essential artistic principles.[48]

Clark called specific attention to the portrait of Samuel Gross, asserting that nothing greater had ever been executed in America.[49] But he was a voice crying in the wilderness as the only notice by an unknown writer in an unidentified newspaper commented: "The picture is painted in the modern French manner, with great mountains of paint, not dashed on with a trowel but laboriously and conscientiously piled up with the brush. Color there is none."[50] Critics pounced on *The Gross Clinic* when it went on display in New York at the Second Annual Exhibition of the Society of American Artists in March 1879. The writer for the *Herald* damned it with faint praise as "decidedly unpleasant and sickeningly real in all its gory details though a startlingly lifelike and strong work."[51] Clarence Cook in the New York *Daily Tribune* invoked French examples of death and gore, proclaiming it as "one of the most powerful, horrible, and yet fascinating pictures that has been painted anywhere in this century—a match, or more than a match, for David's 'Death of Marat,' or for Géricault's 'Wreck of the Medusa.'" Nevertheless, he condemned its admission to a gallery "where men and women of weak nerves must be compelled to look at it. For not to look is impossible."[52] Earl Shinn rallied to Eakins's cause by reminding his readers that the work "proceeds from the exact photographic realism of Gérôme, modified by the robust realism of Bonnat,"[53] hoping perhaps that the French pedigree could offset the negative attacks.

Eakins had set his scene in an amphitheater as did Gérôme in his *Ave Caesar* and *Pollice Verso* (*Thumbs Down*). Eakins incorporated Gérôme's *Ave Caesar* above the mantelpiece in his parlor scene *The Chess Players*, which he exhibited at the Centennial International Exhibition so that the visual references to Gérôme and his French training were made quite explicit. Eakins reported that Gérôme often brought out his painting *Pollice Verso* to demonstrate his principles. Little did Eakins know that so much of his work would meet its own thumbs down from many American critics during his lifetime. His motivation with *The Gross Clinic* was to create a picture "which may do me credit in my city and which if I may be allowed to exhibit in France may not lessen the esteem which I have gained there."[54] The work sold for a mere $200 to the Alumni Society of Jefferson Medical College in 1878. One hundred and twenty-eight years later, when Jefferson University announced in 2006 that the painting would be sold to the Crystal Bridges Museum in Bentonville, Arkansas, for $68 million, a successful fundraising campaign retained it for joint ownership by the Philadelphia Museum of Art and the Pennsylvania Academy of the Fine Arts. Eakins had written to Emily Sartain from Paris in 1866 about how proud he was to be a Philadelphian, and, with the purchase of the painting nearly a century after his death, Philadelphia returned the compliment.[55]

Civic pride featured again in *William Rush Carving His Allegorical Figure of the Schuylkill River*, where Eakins re-created a Federal Era scene in which the renowned Philadelphian sculptor and shipbuilder, William Rush, is shown fabricating his 1809 wooden figure for a fountain in the waterworks at Centre Square. (See Figure 8.7.) The original figure portrayed a nymph in a Grecian robe holding a bittern, a waterfowl that frequented the river. Eakins depicted Rush with a nude model posing for him while a chaperone, quietly attending to her knitting, sits slightly behind her. The model's clothes are brightly lit and take center stage on a chair in the center foreground of the work. Following Gérôme's example of thoroughly researching a subject, Eakins visited the site of Rush's former studio at Front Street below Callowhill, interviewed some elderly people who recalled details of the place, copied scrolls and drawings from a sketch-

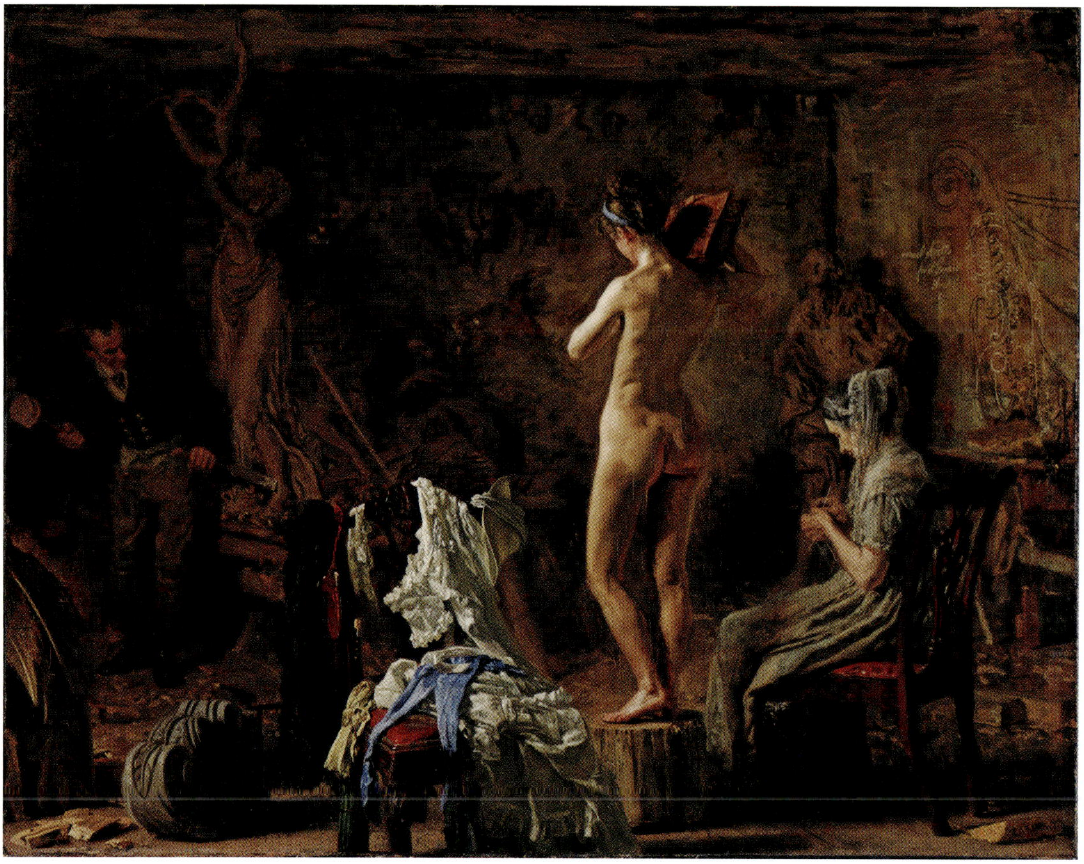

FIGURE 8.7 Thomas Eakins, *William Rush Carving His Allegorical Figure of the Schuylkill River*, 1876–1877. Oil on canvas (mounted on Masonite), 20⅛ × 26⅛ in. (51.1 × 66.4 cm). Framed: 29 9/16 × 32 5/16 in. (75.1 × 82.1 cm). (Philadelphia Museum of Art, Gift of Mrs. Thomas Eakins and Miss Mary Adeline Williams, 1929-184-27)

book once owned by Rush, and studied period costumes from John Lewis Kimmel's *Fourth of July in Centre Square*. Despite these efforts to secure historical data, it is now known that Rush did not use a nude model as such practices only came about at a later date. Nevertheless, Eakins's fabulation was taken for fact.[56] In his written statement on the painting, Eakins called attention to the European roots of Rush's work: "The statue is an allegorical representation of the Schuylkill River. . . . the wavelets of the wind-sheltered stream are shown in the delicate thin drapery, much after the manner of the French artists of that day whose influence was powerful in America."[57] Eakins saw Rush as intending to place himself in this heritage, and Eakins envisioned following suit. Thus, the figure of Rush has been read as autobiographical as much as historical.

The ostensible subject of Eakins's painting is William Rush, but it is the nude that draws the viewer's attention. Eakins's French training convinced him of the prime significance of the nude figure in artistic education. The realist treatment of the nude in the artist's studio has a precedent in Courbet's 1855 *The Painter's Studio: A Real*

Allegory Summing Up Seven Years of My Artistic and Moral Life. Eakins could not have seen Courbet's *Studio* as it remained rolled up in his studio from 1855 until 1881, but its lore was widespread, and caricatures were available. (See Figures 8.8 and 8.9.) Courbet had eleven paintings accepted for exhibition by the jury for the Universal Exhibition of 1855, but his *Studio* was not among them. He built a pavilion in the form of a circus tent across from the entrance to the Exhibition and produced a brochure titled *Realism*, which became legendary as a manifesto of his desire to translate the customs, the ideas, and the appearances of his time, a goal embraced by Eakins as well. The seven years included by Courbet in his title pointed to the culmination of his artistic ideas since launching his career, and Eakins could perhaps have identified with this in *William Rush* as it too was painted seven years after returning from Paris and establishing his position in the American art world. In both paintings, there are shadowy works of art in the background while the eye is drawn to the center of the paintings by a nude figure with discarded clothes.

Eakins's years in Paris working with the nude model convinced him of the artistic benefits of this practice. When the Pennsylvania Academy of the Fine Arts reopened in October 1876, Eakins taught Schussele's evening classes on a volunteer basis. Going back to the method of copying antique casts before the life model frustrated Eakins so he decided to set up his own school on Juniper Street in March 1877 calling the classes the Art Students' Union. A few weeks after Schussele's death on August 21, 1869, Eakins assumed the position of professor of drawing and painting at the academy, convinced that copying from the nude model taught the beginning art student more than copying from plaster reproductions of ancient works. When asked in an interview recorded in the September 1879 issue of *Scribner's Monthly Illustrated Magazine* why he departed from Gérôme's practice of preliminary drawing, Eakins replied that the student should learn to draw with color, thus emphasizing his individuality from that of his teacher. Sculptural modeling from the nude model assisted the academy student to give depth and weight to the human figure. Anatomy classes and dissections, unique to the academy in America, solidified an understanding of how the body was formed and functioned. What Eakins envisioned for the academy was freer access for female students of the nude model.

The free access to nudes that Eakins experienced in Paris exhibitions and in Gérôme's studio made him chafe against American prudery. Courbet was much in the art public's mind during the 1867 Universal Exhibition in Paris that Eakins visited several times. Courbet again built a pavilion as he had in 1855, mailed three thousand invitations, sent his catalog around the city, and exhibited over a hundred of his own paintings. Scholars of Eakins's have noted that he did not mention visiting either Courbet's pavilion or Manet's solo exhibition on the Pont de l'Alma during that time, but it seems unlikely that he would have missed the press coverage of these events and the discussion of their treatment of the female nude figure.[58] Neither did he comment on the eighty-two American art works on display. Not all of Eakins thoughts went into his letters; he was also known as a man who was private and his awareness of Courbet and Manet cannot be precluded entirely.[59] Gérôme and Manet

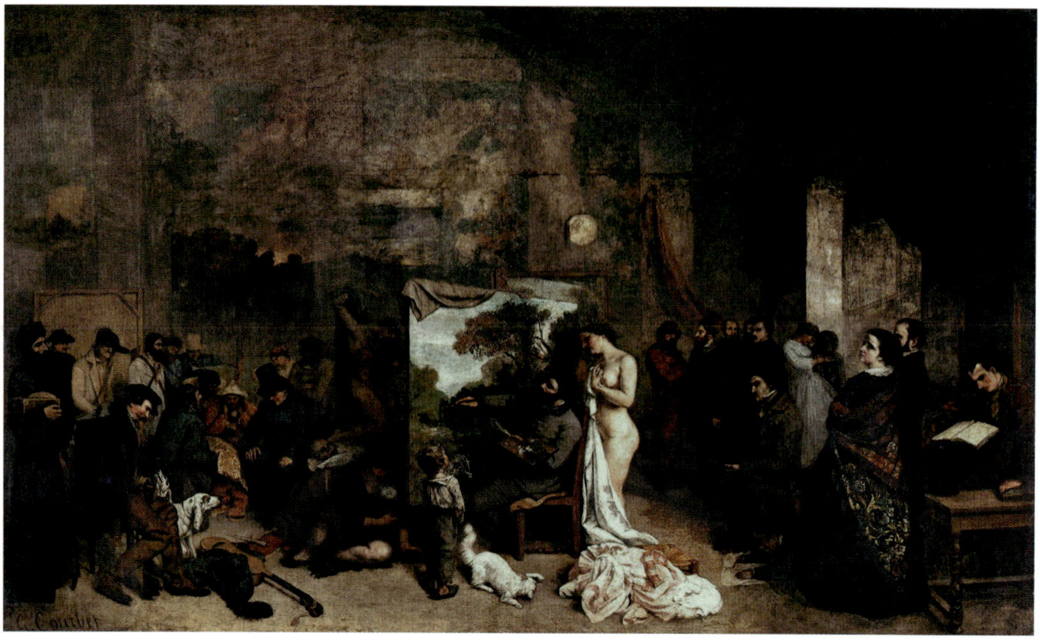

FIGURE 8.8 Gustave Courbet, *The Artist's Studio: A Real Allegory Summing Up Seven Years of My Artistic and Moral Life*, 1855. Oil on canvas, 361 × 598 cm (11.8 × 19.6 ft). (Paris, Musée d'Orsay)

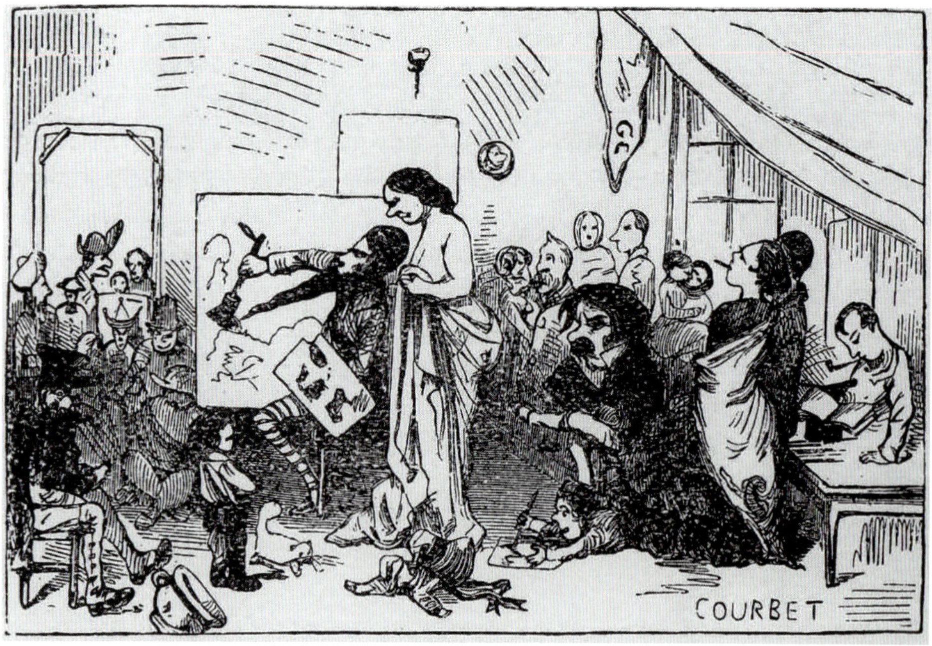

FIGURE 8.9 Quillenbois, *L'Atelier du Peintre de Gustave Courbet.* (*L'Illustration*, July 21, 1855. Work in the Public Domain.)

knew each other and borrowed motifs from each other in what began as a spirit of friendly rivalry.[60] Gérôme later became the determined enemy of Manet, opposing the posthumous exhibition organized after Manet's death at the École des Beaux-Arts and becoming enraged when his students began imitating Manet's style after their visit to the Manet retrospective in 1883.[61] Eakins, with his ties to the Goupil Gallery and his reverence for Gérôme, would have been circumspect in any mention of the artists his teacher so disdained so as not to offend his master.

Both Courbet and Manet rejected the rhetoric of the Salon nude to promote an art based on truth and nature. Courbet's nudes visually contravened the academic standard of alabaster perfection by their corpulent bulges and unsightly dimples. The standing nude figure seen from behind in his 1853 *Bathers* at the Salon horrified the public by its ungainly physique that caused one critic to sneer that "if this is a sample of M. Courbet's contribution to the development of the human race, we predict that he will have great success in Turkey, where females are sold by the pound. . . . "[62] In 1862, Marie Guichard recalled how the painting caused ladies to turn away in disgust and men to shrug their shoulders, just as viewers did in front of *The Gross Clinic* years later in Philadelphia.[63] Eakins rejected the polished perfection of flesh of Gérôme's female figures for the unidealized female body he painted in *William Rush*. The nude's dimpled lower back, thickened legs, and wide hips prompted one critic to state that Eakins "was no judge of the 'human form divine.'"[64] Another commented: "If belles have such faults as these to hide, we counsel them to hide them."[65] Eakins detested the affectations of Salon nudes that he saw at the Salon of 1868, describing them as "smiling, smirking goddesses of many complexions, amidst the delicious arsenic green trees and gentle wax flowers and purling streams a-running up and down the hills, especially up."[66]

The discarded clothes prominently facing the viewer of Eakins's *William Rush* shocked the reviewer of the *New York Times* because they signaled that the model was undressed rather than ideally nude as was the case with most allegorical treatments of the naked female in art.[67] Manet's *Luncheon on the Grass* aroused similar animosity at the 1863 Salon des Refusés, when he converted a pastoral scene into a picnic with a naked female sitting across from two men clothed in contemporary dress while a scantily clad female wades in the water behind the group. (See Figure 8.10.) A host of vexed aesthetic issues arose from this painting, which Pierre Bourdieu has called the most commented on after the *Mona Lisa*.[68] Critics attacked Manet's facture but also registered their distress at the profane nakedness versus the sacred nudity found in sanctioned academic art that was specifically pointed up by the discarded clothing at the seated figure's feet.[69] Louis Étienne complained in *Le Jury et les exposants*: "A commonplace woman of the demi-monde, as naked as can be, shamelessly lolls between two dandies, dressed to the teeth."[70] Manet exhibited this painting again in 1867 in a pavilion on the rue de l'Alma directly across the street from one of the entrances to the Universal Exhibition. He displayed fifty of his works, including the *Luncheon on the Grass* and *Olympia* whose notoriety continued to the point that they were caricatured by Randon in the pages of the June 29th issue of *Le Journal amusant*.[71] (See Figure 8.11.)

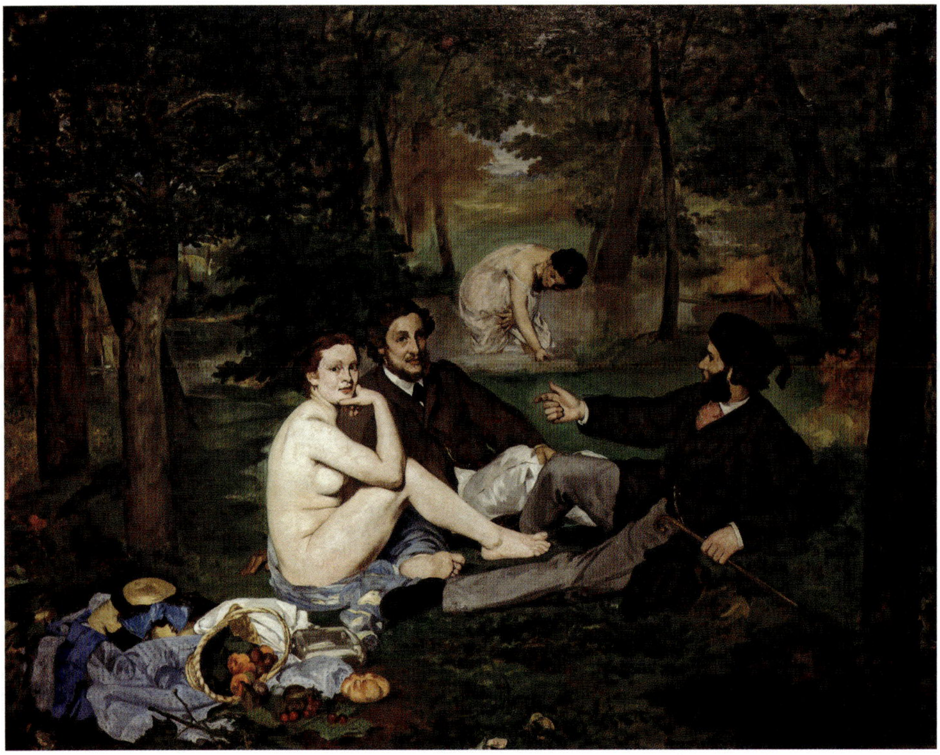

Figure 8.10 Édouard Manet, *Luncheon on the Grass*, 1863. Oil on canvas, 208 × 264 cm (81.8" × 103.9"). (Paris, Musée d'Orsay. Photo: Christopher Campbell.)

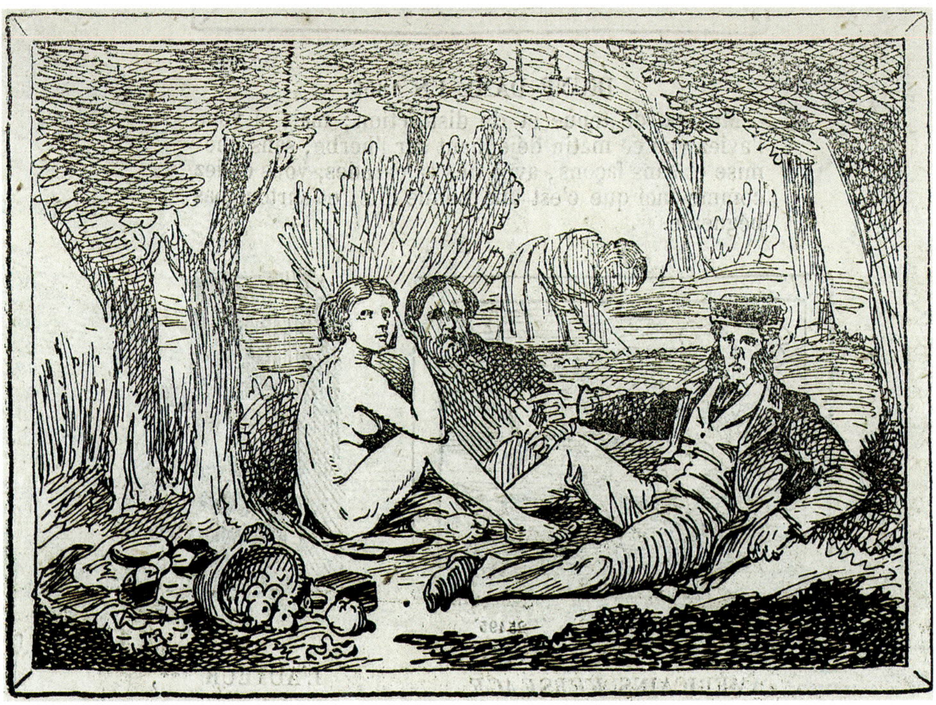

Figure 8.11 G. Randon, *Le Journal amusant*, June 29, 1867. (Work in the Public Domain. Photo: Christopher Campbell.)

If Eakins did not visit Manet's pavilion and its paintings, he might have read about Manet, whose name was appearing frequently in the press, and known that he had been taught by Couture whom Eakins admired. Émile Zola, in a series of articles titled "Mon Salon" written for the periodical *L'Événement* in April 1866, strongly defended Manet against the critical attacks of his work. Zola was fired for the articles but published them in pamphlet form in May 1866. In January 1867, the editor of *La Revue du XIXe Siècle* solicited an article on the artist, which Zola called *Une nouvelle manière en peinture: Édouard Manet*, which was distributed as a brochure for Manet's 1867 exhibition as *Édouard Manet, étude biographique et critique*. Zola ended his study by boldly predicting that the *Luncheon on the Grass* and *Olympia* would one day find their place in the Louvre, a preposterous assertion at the time. Years after his return from Paris, Eakins photographed his student and future wife seated naked outdoors. (See Figure 8.12a.) With the exception of the absence of her arm on her chin and her head turned to the viewer, her pose strongly echoes Victorine Meurent's in the *Luncheon on the Grass*. (See Figure 8.12b.) She, too, sits on a cloth and her hair is masked by the darkness of the foliage surrounding her head. The stones and foliage in the lower left of the photo bear an uncanny natural resemblance to the painted still life that anchors the lower left portion of Manet's painting. Imitation does not always mean admiration, but the visual impact and lore of the painting may have remained with Eakins. The similarities may have been coincidental—or not.

The discarded garments in Manet's *Luncheon on the Grass* are painted with skillful precision and conspicuously placed in the foreground of the work, contrasting with the broad handling of the modeling in the figures and landscape. Their presence signals that the female figure is naked rather than ideally nude, which is why the painting so inflamed the critics and public of his time.[72] As Henry Adams has noted, the focus of interest in Eakins's *William Rush* is the clothes on the chair, while the nude is more dimly lit and the figure of Rush is cloaked in shadow.[73] The reaction of the critic from the *New York Times* on seeing Eakins's *William Rush* in May 1889 paralleled what had been written in May 1863 about Manet: "What ruins the picture is much less the want of beauty in the nude model (as has been suggested in the public press), than the presence in the foreground of the clothes of that young woman, cast careless over a chair. This gives the shock which makes one think about the nudity—and at once the picture becomes improper."[74] Despite the distance of years and continents between Manet and Eakins, little had changed in the public acceptance of the realist representation of the undressed female body. Eakins adhered to the academic technique he had so diligently mastered in Paris and never adapted the flatness, broken brushwork, and unmodeled color that became the hallmark of avant-garde painting in Paris. Nevertheless, he shared their frank approach to the modern nude and its justification in art. William Clark in the Philadelphia *Telegraph* may have sensed this when he praised Eakins's work by citing a landscape artist who declared that "he had not believed there was a man outside of Paris, certainly not one in America, who could do painting of the human figure like this."[75] Mrs. Van Rensselaer wrote in 1881: "Of all American artists he is the most typically national, the most devoted to

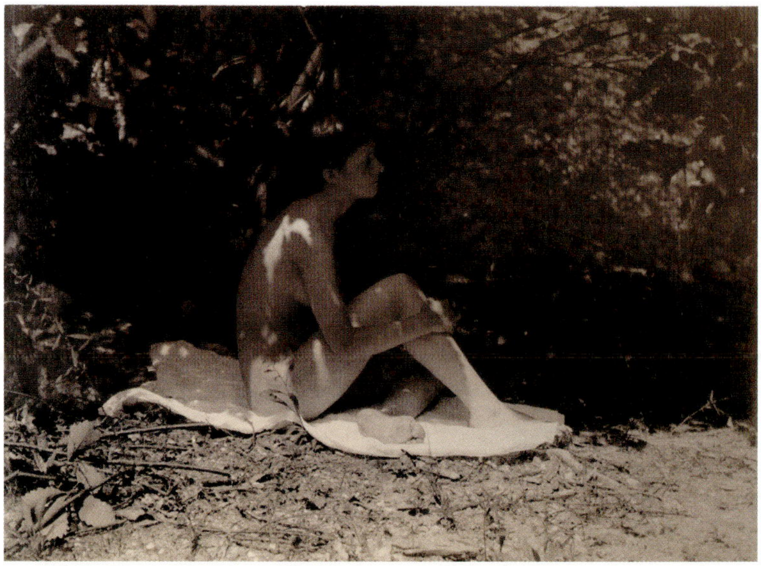

Figure 8.12a Thomas Eakins, *Susan Hannah MacDowell*, 1880–1882. Albumen print on paper, 3³⁄₁₆ × 4⁷⁄₁₆ in. (8.1 × 11.2 cm). (Gift of Joseph H. Hirshhorn, 1966. Digitally documented by Lee Stalsworth. Hirshhorn Museum and Sculpture Garden.)

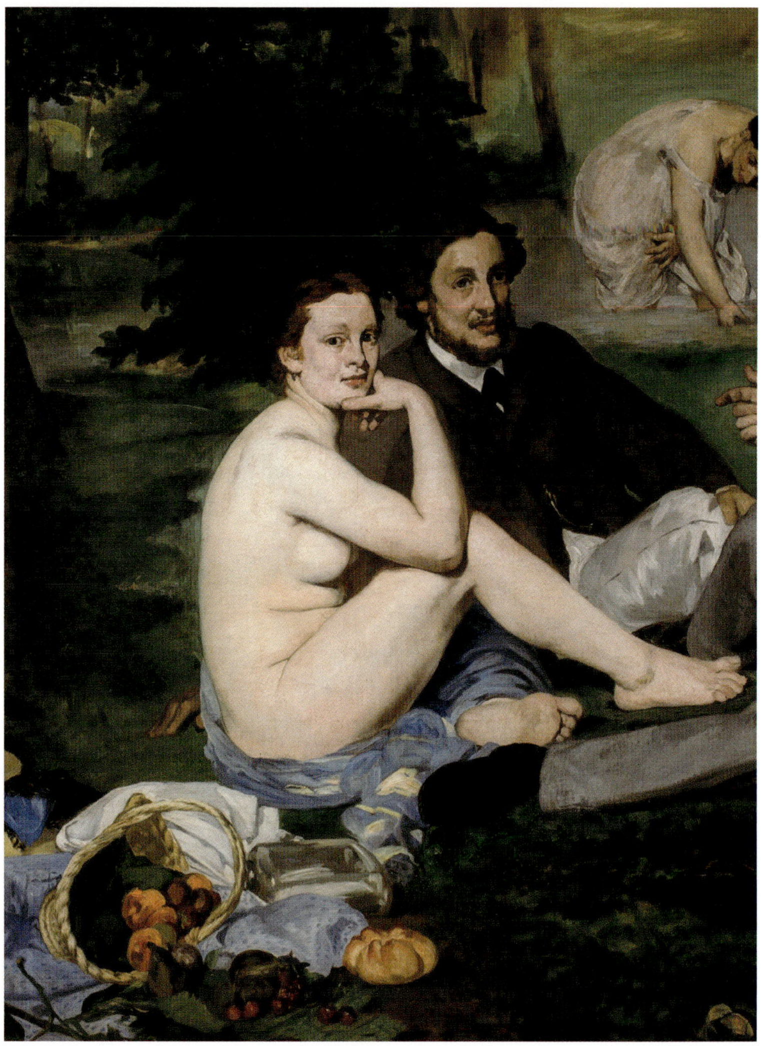

Figure 8.12b Detail of Figure 8.10. (Paris, Musée d'Orsay. Photo: Christopher Campbell.)

the actual life about him, the most given to recording it without gloss or alteration. That life is often ugly in its manifestations, no doubt; but this ugliness does not daunt Mr. Eakins, and his artistic skill is such that he can bring good results from the most unpromising materials."[76] Describing its qualities she found recourse in the French literary tradition, finding it as vivid, truthful, and naturalistic as a page of the novelist Honoré de Balzac.

The accusation of ugliness failed to intimidate Eakins who continued to take on controversial subjects. He may have learned how creating highly provocative work brought notice in the press as it had with French artists such as Courbet and Manet, and he wrote to Shinn in 1875 that exhibiting would call attention to his name and bring in some money.[77] This becomes most apparent with Eakins's 1880 image of *The Crucifixion* that received more critical attention than any other painting he had exhibited.[78] (See Figure 8.13.) Eakins sent the canvas to the Society of American Artists exhibition in New York in early spring of 1882 where it was initially rejected because of its large size. A subsequent exhibition in May included the work and opened it to mostly harsh criticism.

Eakins took on this subject not through any devotional impulse, as he claimed to be agnostic, but because the subject had ranking within academic history painting and an established lineage with European masters from ancient to modern times. His teacher Bonnat had created a stir in Paris in 1874 when, in the presence of Gérôme and some students, he nailed a cadaver to a cross to study the anatomy of the hanging corpse in preparation for his *Le Christ.* (See Figure 8.14.) Its exhibition at the Salon of 1874 solidified Bonnat's reputation as a realist and naturalist, prompting critics pro and con to discuss his work for years to come. Eakins's preparations for his rendition parallel those of Bonnat except that Eakins, familiar with corpses through extensive dissections, wanted to see how the anatomy of the live body looked suspended from a cross. He took his student J. Laurie Wallace to a secluded spot in southern New Jersey near Pennsauken Creek, where he suspended him on a wooden cross, gave him a crown of thorns, and proceeded to sketch him. Bonnat cast his suffering figure, head raised in prayerful supplication, against a darkened sky; Eakins's Christ, originally painted against a bright blue sky that was later covered with a gray and white impasto, has expired and his facial features are obscured by a dark shadow. Both men took the time-honored central symbol of Christian faith and recast it in modern naturalistic terms.

Bonnat's rendition of the Crucifixion dissatisfied the critics because it did not sufficiently emphasize the divinity of Christ.[79] Octave Mirbeau characterized it as a vulgar criminal attached to a yellow cross and painted with enough exactitude to pass an anatomy exam.[80] What was considered negative in the Bonnat most likely attracted Eakins. The year before Eakins painted his *Crucifixion* an article in the *Magazine of Art* on the Paris International Exhibition reproduced Bonnat's *Le Christ,* reporting that of all the paintings in the Central Pavilion Bonnat's attracted the most attention. The critic described the work as a "terribly realistic painting," where the artist failed to invest his subject with any dignity and grandeur, ignoring the divine nature of

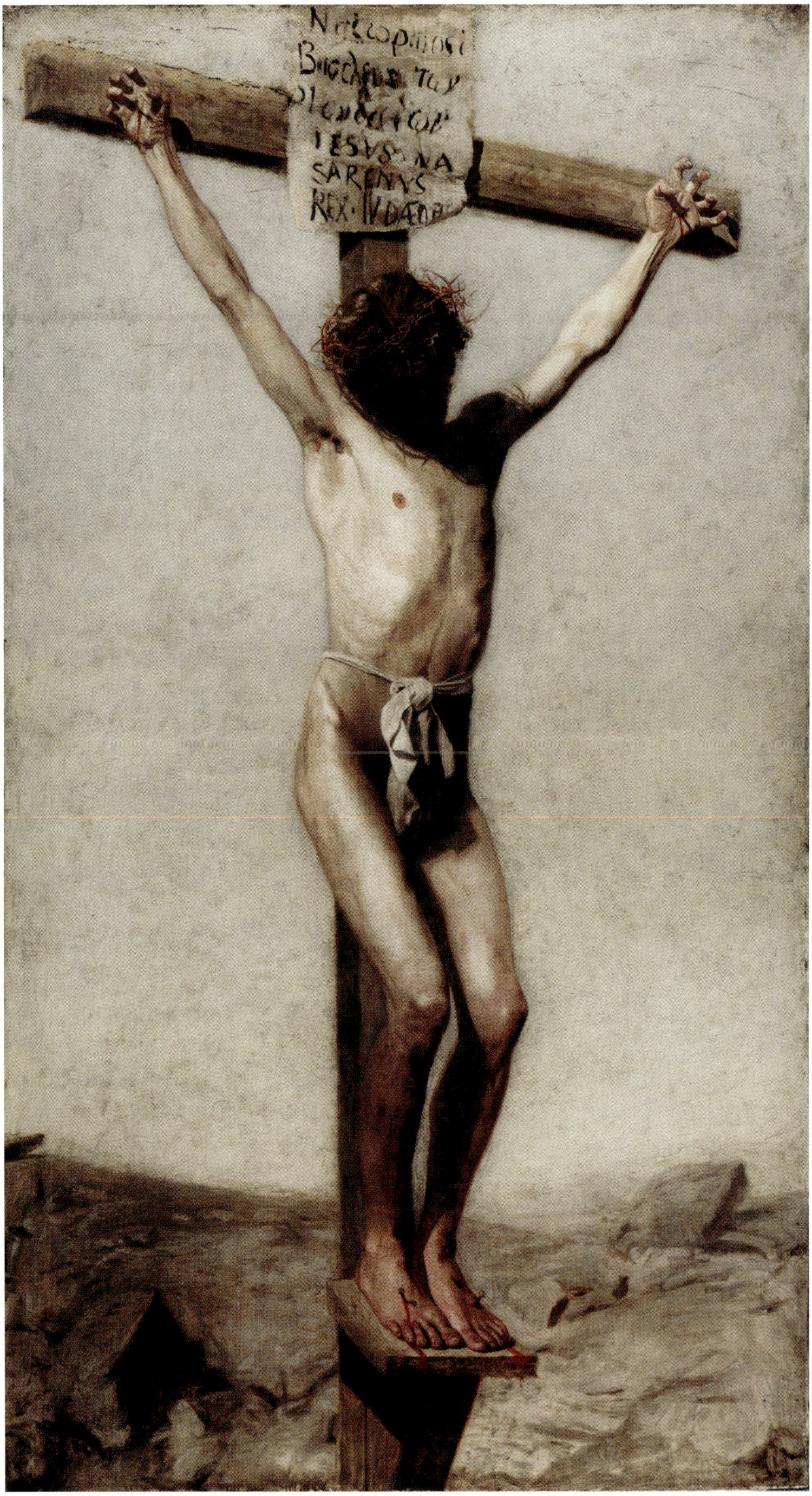
IESVS NA
SARENVS
REX

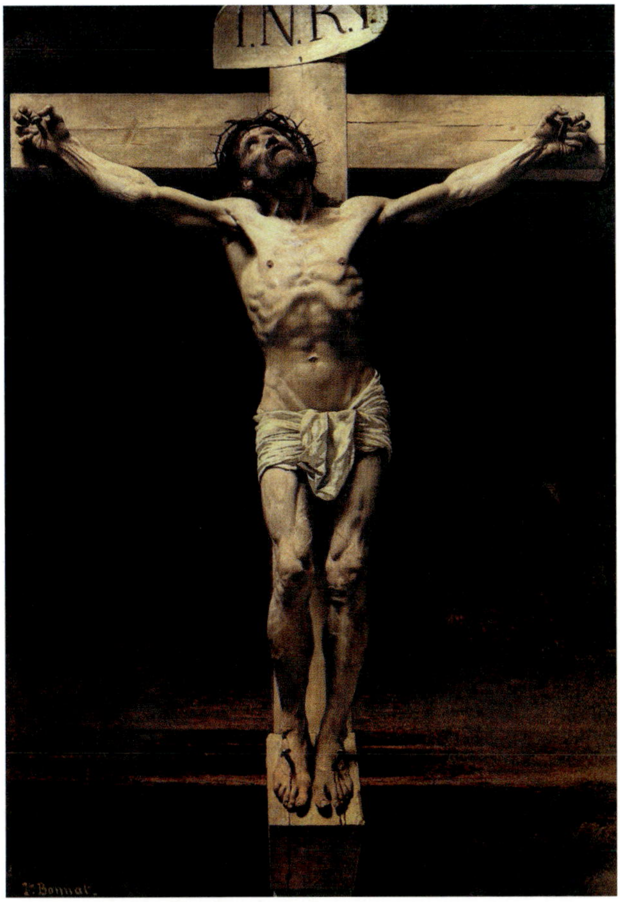

FACING PAGE:
Figure 8.13
Thomas Eakins, *The Crucifixion*, 1880. Oil on canvas, 8 ft. × 54 in. (243.8 × 137.2 cm). (Philadelphia Museum of Art, Gift of Mrs. Thomas Eakins and Miss Mary Adeline Williams, 1929-184-24.)

LEFT: Figure 8.14
Léon Bonnat, *The Crucifixion*, ca. 1874. Oil on canvas, 277 × 206 cm. (Paris, Petit Palais)

Christ: "He has, in fact, painted the limbs of a common laborer, the brawny sinews, and the boot-deformed feet; wonderful, no doubt, in their intense accuracy and truth to nature but deficient in the high qualities the artist could have impressed upon such a subject."[81] Eakins's *Crucifixion* came under similar censure a few years later by the critic of the *Art Journal* who complained, "When the feet are reached and one remarks the idiosyncrasies of the toenails, the ideal which everyone holds is degraded, and we realize that in an age tending so strongly toward realism, there are subjects which should be left untouched."[82] One critic found the work revolting beyond expression and more suited to the dissection laboratory than the walls of an exhibition.[83] As Kathleen Foster has observed, Eakins certainly knew of Bonnat's picture and its reception, and he may have wished to assert his allegiance to the radical battles about naturalism in the arts occurring in Paris.[84]

Drained of any devotional significance, *The Crucifixion* is essentially a nearly naked man suspended on a cross in daylight. After returning from the Salon of 1868 in Paris, Eakins expressed his ideas about nudity in art in a letter to his father: "I can conceive of few circumstances wher[e]in I would have to make a woman naked but if I did I wouldn[']t mutilate her for double the money. She is the most beautiful thing

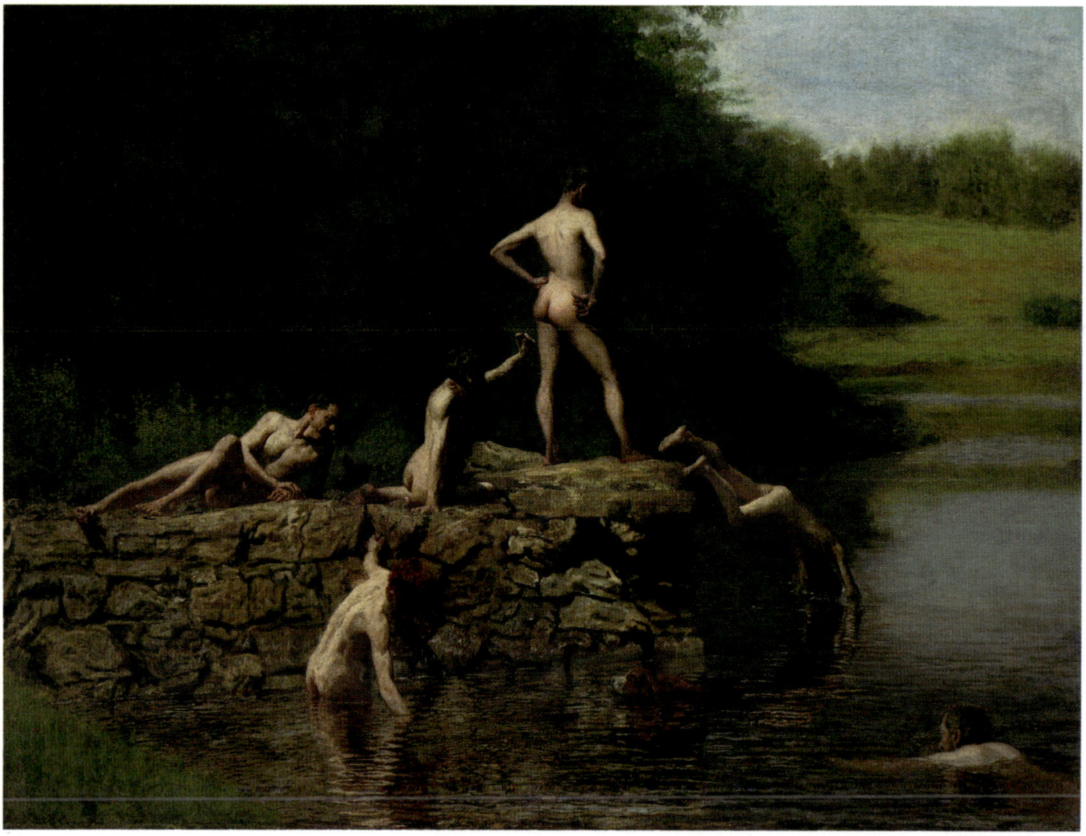

FIGURE 8.15 Thomas Eakins (1844–1916), *Swimming,* 1885, oil on canvas, 27⅜ × 36⅜ in. (Amon Carter Museum of American Art, Fort Worth, Texas, Purchased by Friends of Art, Fort Worth Art Association, 1925; acquired by the Amon Carter Museum of American Art, 1990, from the Modern Art Museum of Fort Worth through grants and donations from the Amon G. Carter Foundation, the Sid W. Richardson Foundation, the Anne Burnett and Charles Tandy Foundation, Capital Cities/ABC Foundation, Fort Worth Star-Telegram, The R. D. and Joan Dale Hubbard Foundation, and the people of Fort Worth, 1990.19.1.)

there is [in] the world except a naked man but I never saw a study of one exhibited. It would be a godsend to see a fine man model painted in a studio with bare walls."[85] Eakins fulfilled his own wish with his *Crucifixion* and multiplied the examples when he painted *Swimming* in 1885.[86] (See Figure 8.15.) He took his male students from the Pennsylvania Academy to Dove Lake in Bryn Mawr, Pennsylvania, near Mill Creek, where he and his colleague Thomas Anschutz photographed them in a variety of poses. Five naked men in a sylvan landscape on a rocky ledge sunbathe, dive, and climb out of the water while Eakins in the lower right corner swims toward them and his dog Harry.

Bathers had a long heritage in European art as seen in the works of Michelangelo, Titian, and Rembrandt, among others. Biblical figures such as Bathsheba or Susannah at the Bath provided artists with a narrative to justify nudity, which was largely focused on the female body. The male nude in art remained a revered topic of allegory and historical narrative until the last decade of the eighteenth century, whereafter it was largely jettisoned in favor of the female nude, which became a genre in itself.[87] Male bathers remained a rarity in art, but Eakins had an opportunity to study an example at the 1870 Salon with Frédéric Bazille's *Summer Scene*. (See Figure 8.16.) Bazille had moved to Paris from Montpellier to study medicine and began studying art in the studio of Charles Gleyre where he met Monet, Auguste Renoir, and Sisley. Like Eakins, he had been schooled in anatomy and dissection and sought to reconcile respect for tradition with subjects from modern life. Bazille had submitted *Fisherman Casting a Net*, a lifelike painting of two naked male figures, to the Salon of 1869, but it was rejected. Perhaps the note of contemporaneity in the discarded clothing, the pronounced sensuality of the male figure's buttocks, and the *plein air* effects of outdoor light and color,

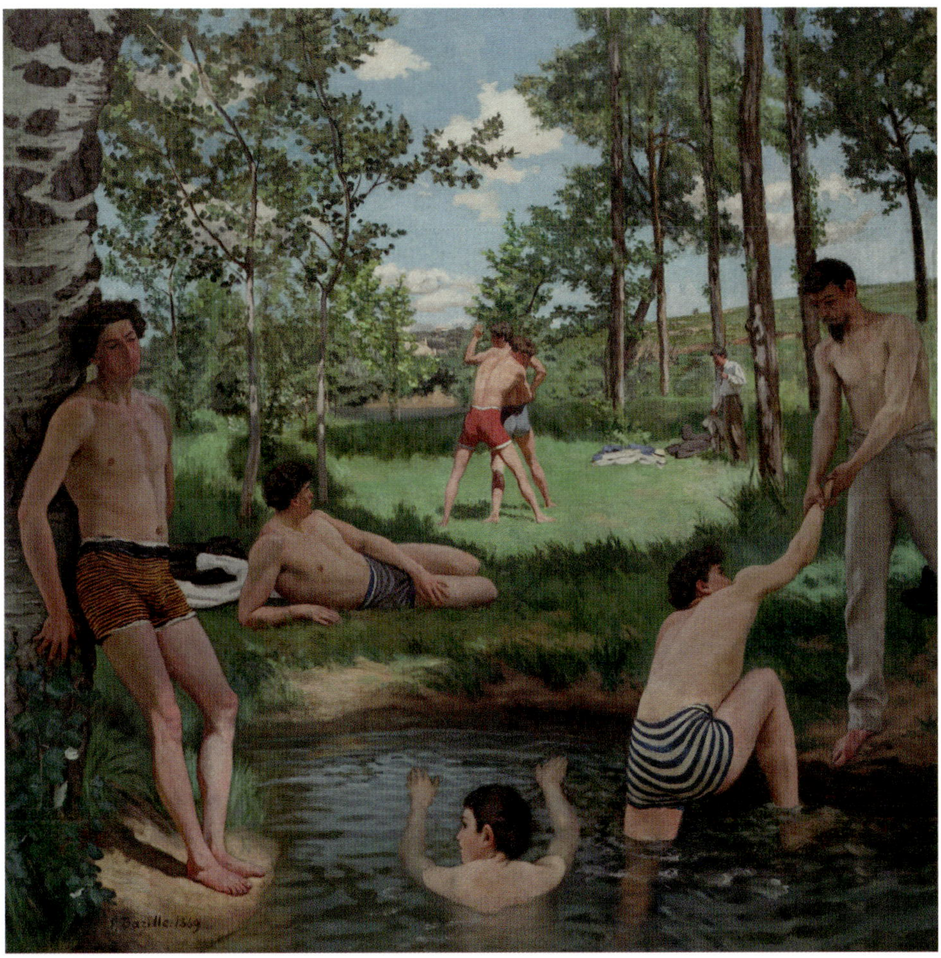

Figure 8.16 Jean Frédéric Bazille, *Summer Scene (Bathers)*, 1869–1870. Oil on canvas, 62.9 × 63.2 in. (106 × 160.7 cm). (Harvard Art Museums/Fogg Museum, Gift of Mr. and Mrs. F. Meynier de Salinelles Cambridge. Photo: Christopher Campbell.)

combined with a standard academic pose, caused the work's refusal. He had success the next year at the Salon with *Summer Scene* when he overpainted his originally nude male bathers with striped swim trunks. Here Bazille's figures supply an example of healthy homosocial behavior, though in a decidedly modern context due to the presence of bathing suits, clothes, and a top hat. Eakins may have known of Gérôme's strong antipathy to this work and that of the emerging impressionist group being exhibited in the Salon of 1870, as Bazille wrote to a friend: "It is Monsieur Gérôme who has done all the harm, he has called us a gang of madmen and declared that he believed it was his duty to do everything he could to prevent our paintings from appearing."[88]

Eakins sought to wed traditional art with the contemporary scene in *Swimming* by applying the academic clarity of drawing learned from Gérôme to a scene where male nudity would be plausible and acceptable. His setting is more Acadian than Bazille's as it avoids any discarded clothing or other signs of modern civilization. Nevertheless, the title and the portrait-like realism of his style, with its distinct clarity and definition, detach the work from any moralizing or political interpretation that would situate it within the genre of history painting.

Eakins undertook *Swimming* as a commission in 1884 from Edward Hornor Coates, chairman of the Committee on Instruction at the Pennsylvania Academy, who intended to donate the painting to the academy. Eakins and Coates shared an interest in the study of antiquity and the nude, but when Eakins completed *Swimming* and presented it to Coates, he rejected it and purchased *The Pathetic Song* from 1881 in its stead. Undeterred, Eakins exhibited the painting at the 1885 Fine Arts Annual, where it was met with almost total critical silence. Whereas the nude in art could be discussed freely in the Parisian press, attitudes toward nudity in America and the frank exposure of the male body differed from those acceptable at the Paris Salon. Eakins may have wanted the painting to be viewed in terms of the conventional *académie* that was at the heart of every art student's training, but the blatant homoeroticism of the painting proved too much for Coates and the critics.

Swimming produced a repertoire of poses that easily refer to studio sessions. Eakins insisted that the beginning art student could learn more from the living model in a given time than from the study of the antique in twice the period.[89] His ardent promotion of the nude model had triggered strong complaints at the Pennsylvania Academy, and his removal of a loin cloth from a male model in front of female art students in a classroom in February 1886, in defiance of the rules of the board, proved to be the final straw.[90] Coates informed Eakins on February 8 that a change in the management of the school was necessary, and the following day Eakins tendered his notice. His resignation made the news with the reporter from the *Philadelphia Evening Bulletin* asserting that Eakins's *Swimming* was "more than unusually bad" and that he had obtained his position at the academy primarily because the directors who appointed him "were being constantly informed by Mr. Eakins's friends that he was a pupil of Gérôme."[91] On February 15, a group of forty students from the life class at the academy marched in protest down Chestnut Street demanding that Eakins be reinstated, claiming that Eakins's methods patterned those in all art schools abroad. Nonetheless, the academy

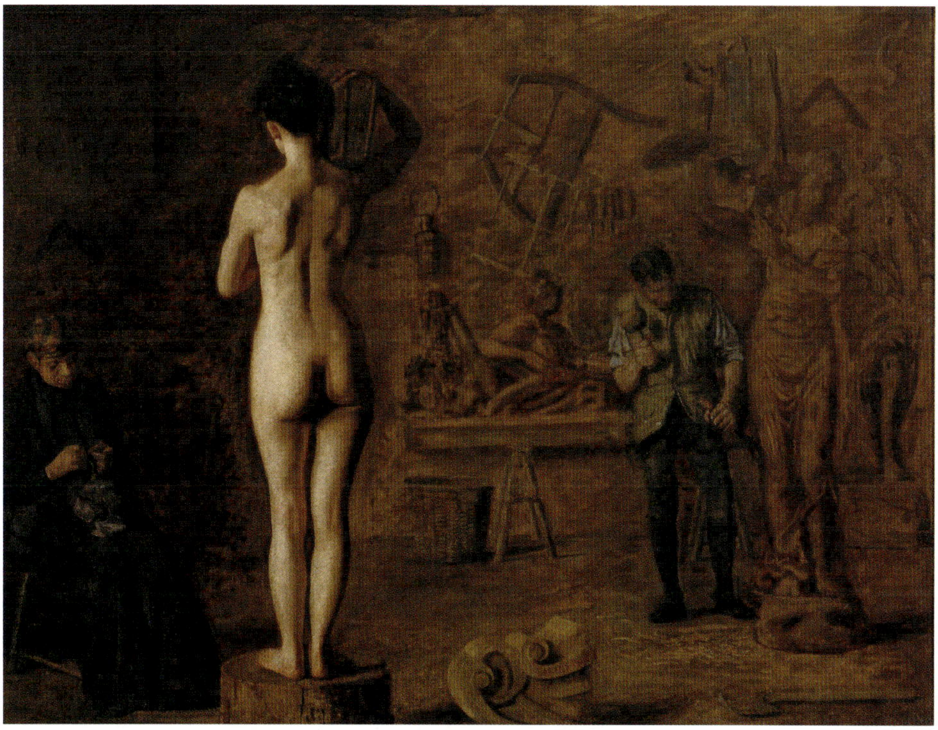

FIGURE 8.17 Thomas Eakins, *William Rush Carving His Allegorical Figure of the Schuylkill River*, 1908. Oil on canvas, 36¼ × 48¼ × 1¼ in. (92.1 × 122.6 × 3.2 cm). (Brooklyn Museum, Dick S. Ramsay Fund, 39.461)

held firm. Eakins, with the help of Lucien Crépon, a friend from his Paris days, along with H. T. Cresson, formed the Art Students' League. Cresson, who had also studied with Gérôme in Paris, insisted on the students' rights to study the nude and mentioned French training six times as a justification in a letter titled "Eakins Defended" published in the February 22, 1886, issue of *Philadelphia Evening Bulletin*. Nothing reversed the academy's decision and Eakins understandably suffered greatly from his termination. In the following years, he focused primarily on portraits of family, friends, clergy, and physicians. He retired fully from teaching in 1898 and launched into a series of academic figure paintings that, as Kathleen Foster has commented, revisited the themes of his youth and revived the memory of his "dear master," Gérôme.[92]

As he neared the end of his life Eakins revisited the topic of *William Rush* from 1876–1877. The year 1908 marked the centennial of Rush's sculpture of the Schuylkill and most likely brought back memories of all that had occurred in his life in the thirty years that had passed in his career, so much of it centered on the propriety of the nude figure as a subject for art. His 1908 version of *William Rush Carving His Allegorical Figure of the Schuylkill River* alluded to the autobiographical character of the earlier version. In his 1908 canvas Eakins rearranged the positioning of the figures and updated their clothes to the present day. (See Figure 8.17.) Instead of Rush working in

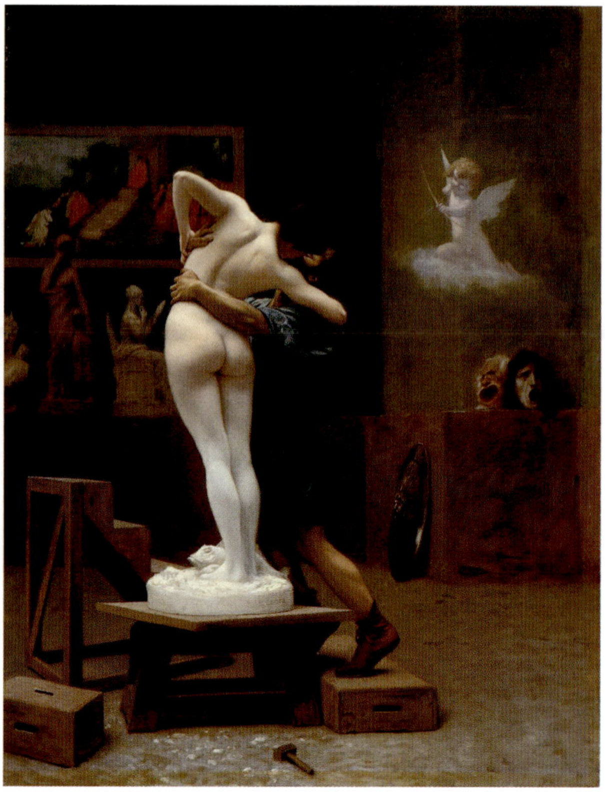

FIGURE 8.18
Jean-Léon Gérôme, *Pygmalion and Galatea*, ca. 1890. Oil on canvas, 35 × 27 in. (88.9 × 68.6 cm). (Metropolitan Museum of Art, Gift of Louis C. Raegner, 1927)

the gentleman's garb of the early nineteenth century, the figure in the 1908 painting, who has been identified as a self-portrait of Eakins, wears workman's clothes. The female attendant sits in front of the posing model and is African American. The model no longer holds the contrapposto pose but stands with two feet planted firmly on the pedestal. In lieu of the strongly illuminated chair in the foreground Eakins has placed a carved architectural scroll whose rounded forms lean toward and echo the buttocks of the standing model whose anatomy is more pronounced because her body is no longer partly concealed by dense shadow. The nude seen from behind is a clear reference to the works of Gérôme, such as his *Pygmalion and Galatea*. (See Figure 8.18.) In most of Gérôme's renderings of the female nude she is the object of the gaze of male figures in the painting, whereas, in his versions of the Rush paintings, Eakins has the sculptor and the maidservant concentrating their eyes on their hand work and thus on their craft.

Gérôme died in 1904, the year that Eakins won the Temple Gold Medal for his portrait of Archbishop William Henry Elder. The Pennsylvania Academy gave this prestigious award to an artist judged to have the best oil painting by an American in the annual exhibition. Previous winners included John Singer Sargent, James McNeill Whistler, William Merritt Chase, and Winslow Homer. Eakins accepted the medal, then set off on foot to the mint and had it melted down in a clear snub of the academy's recognition. His fit of pique surely arose from the late recognition of his talent and the Academy's rejection of his commitment to promoting the nude as an essential part of professional training and appropriate subject matter for art. Gérôme had sympathized with the artists who struggled against the prudery of American attitudes, writing to his American biographer: "As to the question of *nudity*, it is useless to argue about it in your country."[93] Visual allusions to Gérôme's *Pygmalion and Galatea* from around 1890 have been cited as inspiring the late Rush series.[94] The nude figure seen from behind may have played its part in the Brooklyn Museum canvas, but the theme of Pygmalion and Galatea had its own pertinence for Eakins. The story derives from Ovid's *Metamorphoses* where the sculptor Pygmalion has fallen in love with his ivory sculpture of a woman. He secretly wished for a bride as beautiful as his sculpture and was granted his wish by Venus, the Roman goddess of love. When he returned home from making an offering on the feast of Venus, he kissed his sculpture and the figure transformed in his embrace into his living ideal. Gérôme's painting portrayed this desire of the artist in his studio to bring the figure to life. Throughout his career and especially during his days in Gérôme's studio, Eakins detested copying from antique copies, always wanting the living nude human figure before him and his students.

Eakins left another unfinished version of *William Rush and His Model*, where the sculptor helps the nude model off her wooden pedestal. (See Figure 8.19.) The work, never exhibited in his lifetime, stands as a vivid summary of the aesthetic convictions of his artistic career. After visiting the Salon of 1868, Eakins wrote to his father: "The French court is become very decent since Eugenie had fig leaves put on all the statues in the Garden of the Tuileries & when a man paints a naked woman he gives her less than poor Nature herself did."[95] It was this type of deceptive prudery that Eakins railed against throughout his career and may have prompted him to recall Alexandre Cabanel's *Birth of Venus* that won the gold medal at the Salon of 1863 and was purchased by the emperor for his private collection, the very year Manet's *Luncheon on the Grass* was rejected and earned its notorious reputation at the Salon des Refusés for its indecency. (See Figure 8.20.) Eakins knew of Cabanel, referring to him in his letters from Paris, and by 1870 he would have seen the original when it was shown at the Universal Exhibition in 1867. A reproduction of the painting was made by the Goupil Gallery and sold for twenty thousand francs in 1871 to Henry C. Gibson, a major art collector and banker from Philadelphia. Eakins made a copy of the painting when it was exhibited at the academy in 1877, the year he worked on his original version of the Rush theme. Eakins's realistic depictions of his female nudes in his Rush series counter the feminine ideal of Second Empire Paris where he trained. Eakins represented Rush creating an allegory by means of the female body, but his figures bear the physical flaws of a living person. Cabanel's languorous nude wafted by the waves prompted Zola to describe her as a confection of rose and marzipan drowned in a river of milk, exactly the kind of painting Eakins despised.[96] Her marmoreal perfection and depilated body made her the popular sensation of the day, but Eakins's treatment of his subject aligns itself with the French critic Maxime du Camp who called Cabanel out in his review of the Salon of 1863: "A history painter takes a nude woman, makes a portrait of her with a few modifications most often inspired by vague recollections

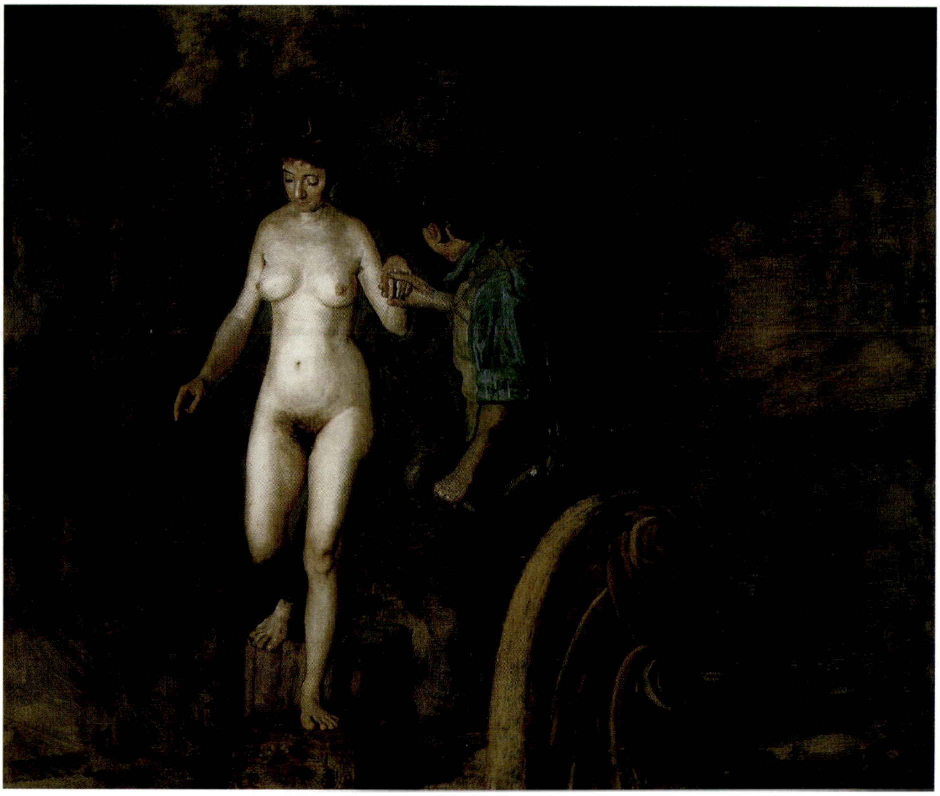

FIGURE 8.19 Jean-Léon Gérôme, *William Rush and His Model*, ca. 1907–1908. Oil on canvas, 35¼ × 47¼ in. (89.5 × 120 cm). (Honolulu Museum of Art, Gift of the Friends of the Academy, 1947 [548.1])

of the Old Masters, and then says 'It's a Venus!' Nothing of the sort; it's a model and nothing more. These models are only *académies*."[97] This was Eakins's very point in painting his frontal nude with her coarse hands, ungainly feet, bulbous breasts and detailed pubic hair, literally and figuratively defying the saccharine depiction of the female nude that prevailed in the academic painting of the time. No mask hides her face as it did in his charcoal drawing from his student days. He had argued for full corporeal honesty in art training and paid a high price for it in his career. With a gallant gesture the artist in this painting helps the un-self-conscious model off her pedestal, transitioning her from art to life as he had spent his career transitioning life into art.

Accused so often during his lifetime of salacious intentions, Eakins makes his point in his *William Rush* paintings that a posing nude is about art and nature, not voyeurism, as if to confirm Earl Shinn's statement made in *The Nation* in 1878 that "good sculpture, even decorative sculpture, can only be produced by the most uncompromising, unconventional study and analysis from life."[98] Eakins had been known to pressure his female students to pose nude for him and for each other while he was teaching at the academy, which prompted complaints that eventually added to the case for his termination. By placing the nude model in his painting of Rush's studio directly facing the seated female servant, thus giving her a full frontal view rather than the more discreet view of the earlier version, Eakins asserts his belief, articulated in a letter to Coates in 1886, by insisting that a female artist had to take on the right to examine naked men and women without the threat of the accusation of impropriety.[99] Rush is shown in his 1877 canvas carving the foot of the statue, but, in the 1908 rendition, Eakins has Rush fashioning the drapery of the allegorical figure of the Schuylkill. The gesture recalls Eakins's written explanation of his first version where he asserted that the delicately thin drapery of Rush's statue was done in the manner of the French artists of that day whose influence was powerful in America. His allusion to Gérôme in the nude figure seen from behind testifies to this continuing belief, at least in his own art.

Paris with its studios and Salons, teachers and traditions, and critics and camaraderie, added significantly to the aesthetic foundation of Eakins's formative years. Throughout his career he mined his cosmopolitan experience to create highly original images that captured the history of his own time in sporting images, imaginative portraits, a challenging interpretation of a religious scene, and self-referential images of William Rush plying his artistic skills in his Philadelphia studio. He followed his instincts rather than the crowd, bent on developing a singular style. Two years before his death, Eakins addressed the issue of study abroad in an article for the *Philadelphia Press*:

> If America is to produce great painters and if young art students wish to assume a place in the history of the art of their country, their first desire should be to remain in America to peer deeper into the heart of American life, rather

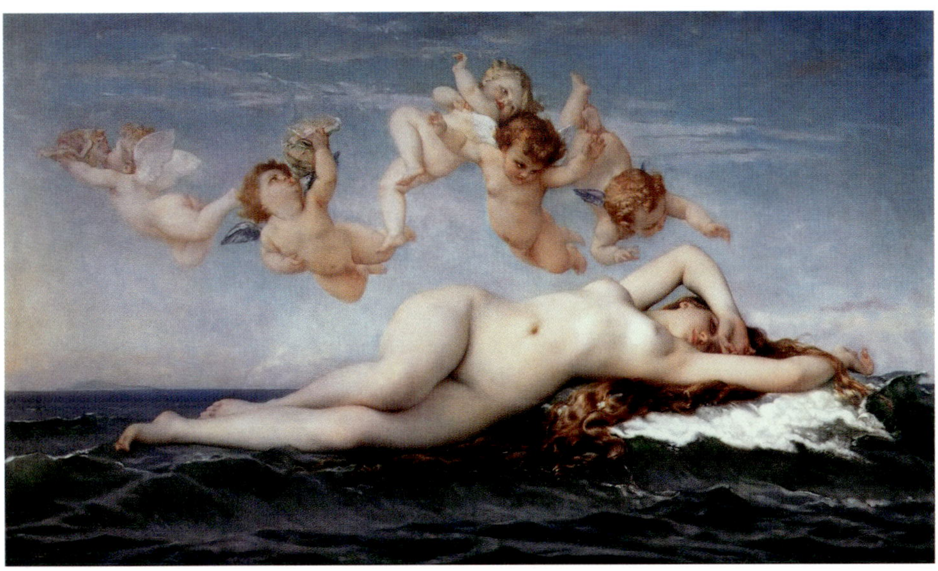

Figure 8.20 Alexandre Cabanel, *The Birth of Venus*, 1863. Oil on canvas, 130 × 225 cm. (Metropolitan Museum of Art, Gift of John Wolfe, 1893)

> than spend their time abroad obtaining a superficial view of the art of the Old World. In the days when I studied abroad conditions were entirely different. The facilities for study in this country were meagre [*sic*]. There were even no life classes in our art schools and schools of painting. Naturally one had to seek instruction elsewhere, abroad. Today we need not do that. It would be far better for American art students and painters to study in their own country and portray its life and types. To do that they must remain free from any foreign superficialities. Of course, it is well to go abroad to see the works of the old masters, but Americans must branch out into their own fields as they are doing it. They must strike out for themselves and only by doing this will we create a great and distinctly American art.[100]

And Eakins did just that.

[9]

From the Schuylkill to the Seine

Mary Cassatt and Henry Ossawa Tanner

For many Philadelphia artists such as Thomas Eakins, Paris served as an apprenticeship while others crossed the Atlantic to enhance their reputation by getting their work in the Salon and Universal Exhibitions. Reviews by French art critics provided a cachet of respectability and professionalism that could enhance sales in America and abroad. Opportunities expanded as American collectors grew in wealth in the post–Civil War era and American art began to achieve more cultural authority. As fascinating and absorbing as life was in Paris, most artists returned to their home country to pursue their careers. An American artist abroad primarily meant a white male artist. Women could journey to Paris to study with a master or attend classes at the Académie Julian but were denied access to the École des Beaux-Arts until 1897. Yet the woman artist was less an anomaly in Paris than she was in Philadelphia, where she often sought artistic training for social refinements rather than as a career path. An artist of color also found less prejudice in France than in America. These factors were among those that impelled two Philadelphia artists, Mary Cassatt (1844–1926) and Henry Ossawa Tanner (1859–1937), to spend the majority of their professional careers abroad. Neither renounced their American citizenship and both returned to Philadelphia on several occasions. Nevertheless, in an era of pervasive racism and sexism, they found that Paris allowed more freedom for their art to be evaluated apart from the social and cultural biases of the kind they met when they enrolled at the Pennsylvania Academy.

The Pennsylvania Academy of Fine Arts Charter of December 26, 1805, which was crafted by Charles Willson Peale, William Rush, and other business leaders, aspired to "promote the cultivation of the Fine Arts, in the United States of America, by . . . exciting the efforts of artists, gradually to unfold, enlighten, and invigorate the talents of our Countrymen."[1] By maintaining a museum, mounting annual exhibitions beginning in 1811, and establishing an art school in 1812, the academy served as a pivotal hub for the cultural life of Philadelphia and attracted national attention. Nevertheless, the experience of the art world for countrywomen differed considerably from that of the countrymen addressed in the charter. When the first building opened in 1807, women's classes were held one day a week and extended to three days in 1844. Copying from antique casts endured as a mainstay for artistic education, but in 1856 puritanical concerns for preserving women's innocence prompted the academy to affix fig leaves to the antique casts of male figures such as the Apollo Belvedere, the Laocoön, and the Fighting Gladiator. Only male students had the prerogative of drawing from the live model. Well aware of the advantages of life classes, Mary Cassatt and Elizabeth Haldeman, along with a few other female students, petitioned the Academy in January 1860 to provide a private room for them to model for each other for one hour four times a week. Their request was granted. Mary Cassatt's participation in this appeal manifested her early determination to distinguish herself as a serious professional artist rather than as an amateur seeking the feminine refinement of art skills deemed an appropriate accomplishment for society women at that time.

Cassatt spent the majority of her career in France but to the end identified as being from "the good city of P," as she called Philadelphia.[2] She was born in Allegheny County in 1844 to investment banker Robert Simpson Cassatt, a descendant of French Huguenots, and Katherine Kelso Johnston, who learned at a young age to speak and write in French. The Cassatts provided their offspring with the education and cultural privileges proper to their upper-class station in life. In 1849, the family moved to 408 Chestnut Street in Philadelphia. Two years later the Cassatts brought their five children to live in Paris and Germany, where Mary was schooled in French and German and first exposed to the art world that would be the focus of her adult career. The family returned to America in 1855, eventually residing in Philadelphia in 1858 at South Penn Square. One of Cassatt's principal biographers explained that since she lived there longer than anywhere else in her preadult life, "It would not be wrong to consider her 'from' Philadelphia."[3]

By the time she completed her course of study at the academy at the age of twenty-one, Cassatt had become eager to seek training in Paris. Despite opposition from her father and his insistence that she be self-supporting as an artist, Cassatt and her mother took off in December 1865 to live in Paris. Unlike her academy classmates Thomas Eakins and the sculptor Howard Roberts who arrived six months later, she was prohibited from studying at the École des Beaux-Arts, the most prestigious training ground for artists in Paris. Cassatt astonished her acquaintances in Philadelphia by being accepted by Jean-Louis Gérôme as a private pupil. As many of her letters from her first sojourn in France have not survived, we know little about her time with him. Along with Elizabeth Haldeman she attended Charles Chaplin's classes for women and obtained a permit to copy art works at the Louvre. A letter from Haldeman to her mother recorded Cassatt's comment that she intended to paint better than the old masters, praising her friend's work ethic: "I think she has a great deal of talent and industry. One acquires the latter living in France. The people study so hard and the results are wonderful."[4] Cassatt had also studied with Thomas Couture during a stay in the countryside in Écouen after the Salon of 1868, diligently seeking to improve her knowledge and technical skills.

The popular painter Charles Joshua Chaplin (1825–1891), known for his sensual neorococo renditions of young women, encouraged Cassatt and Haldeman to submit their work to the Salon of 1867. Both saw their work rejected, but in 1868 each got works admitted. Cassatt's *A Mandolin Player* achieved a coveted placement "on line"—at eye level—rather than "skied" like Haldeman's, where the work hung high over other paintings toward the ceiling. Exhibiting under her middle name, Cassatt received a favorable review in the June 7, 1868, issue of the *New York Times*: "A portrait of an Italian girl, by MARY STEVENSON, of Pennsylvania, has obtained a place on line, and well deserves it, for its vigor of treatment and fine qualities of color. MISS STEVENSON has been a pupil of Gérôme, and proposes shortly to visit Italy to improve herself."[5] As it had with Eakins, identification with Gérôme would enhance Cassatt in the eyes of the American public. Attaining an on-line position indicated jury approval as the paintings had to compete for attention with the dense hanging of the works and the jostling crowds.[6]

Encouraged by her recognition in 1868, Cassatt tried again for the 1869 Salon but was refused. Undeterred, she submitted a painting based on an Alpine trip to the Salon of 1870. It was accepted, but the outbreak of the Franco-Prussian War led her back to the States in the summer of 1870, where she settled temporarily in Altoona with her brother Alexander Cassatt, a manager and rising star in the ranks of the Pennsylvania Railroad, who had married Lois Buchanan, niece of President James Buchanan. Cassatt relocated with her parents and sister Lydia to Philadelphia in the fall of 1870, set up a studio, hired models, and began to paint. A move with her family in the summer of 1871 to Hollidaysburg, outside Altoona, sharpened Cassatt's awareness of the lack of an artistic community to nourish her ambitions and the difficulty of access to great museums. During a trip to market her paintings in Pittsburgh, she received a commission from the Catholic bishop to copy two paintings by the Italian Renaissance painter Antonio da Correggio for the cathedral. This provided her with the financial wherewithal to support herself abroad. With her friend and former classmate from the Pennsylvania Academy, Emily Sartain, she joyfully returned to Europe, settling in Parma, Italy, in the spring of 1872, to execute her commission. Lured by the opportunity to submit to the Salon of 1872, Cassatt put aside the Correggio assignment to create *Two Women Throwing Flowers during Carnival*. When word reached the art community that the work had been accepted and consequently sold, she was treated as a celebrity and invited to make Parma her home. After finishing her copies of the Correggios she headed to Madrid where she was captivated by Velázquez and Murillo, among others. She set up a studio in Seville in late October 1872, captivated by the colorful costumes of the bullfighters and the swarthy complexion of her hired models. Returning to Paris in April 1873, she had her *Torero and Young Girl* accepted at that year's Salon.

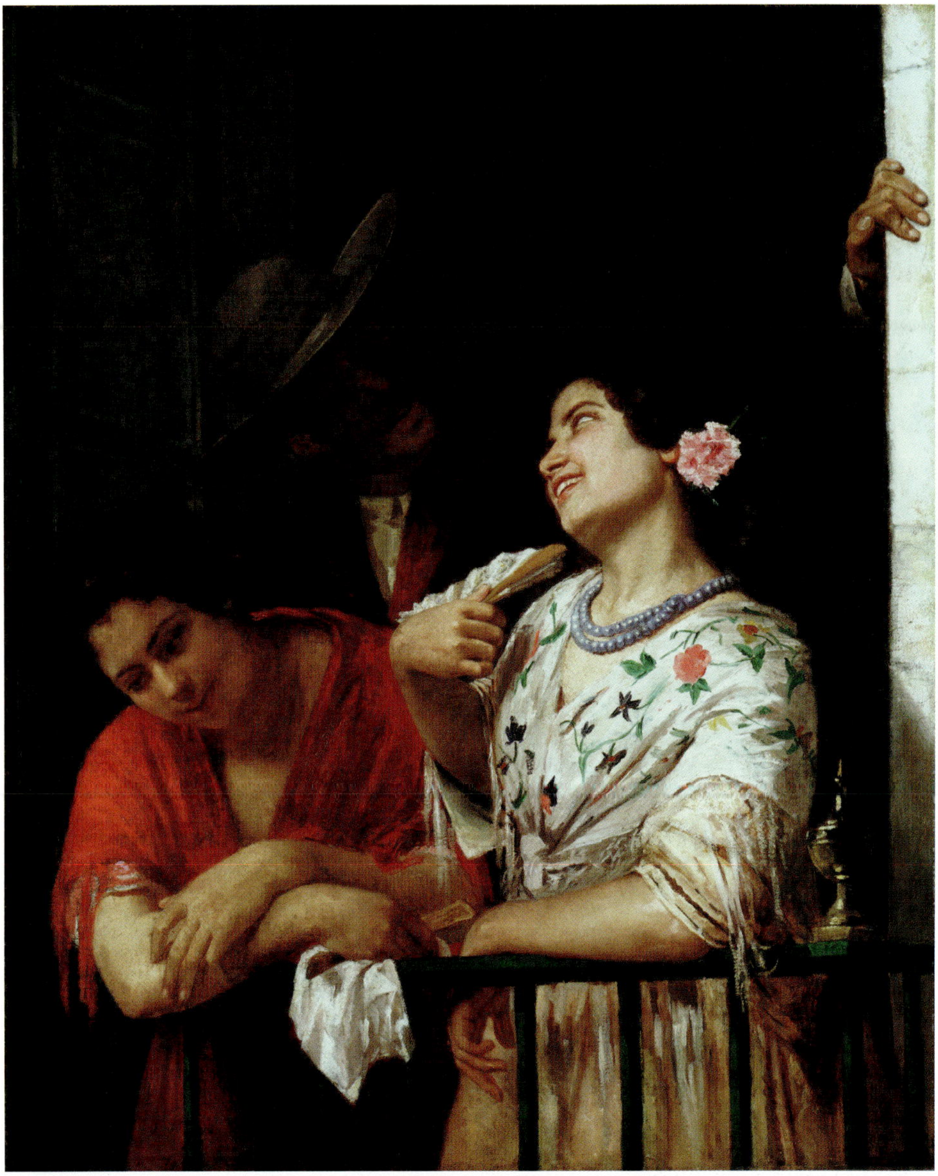

FIGURE 9.1 Mary Stevenson Cassatt, *On the Balcony*, 1873. Oil on canvas, 39¾ × 32½ in. (101 × 82.5 cm). Framed: 46¾ × 39¼ × 3½ in. (118.7 × 99.7 × 8.9 cm). (Philadelphia Museum of Art, Gift of John G. Johnson for the W. P. Wilstach Collection, W1906-1-7)

Capitalizing on the success of her Spanish-themed paintings, Cassatt sent *On the Balcony* to Bailey (see Figure 9.1) and Company's jewelry store in Philadelphia, where the public could view it alongside her *Spanish Dancer Wearing a Lace Mantilla*. The scene of flirtation combined her absorption of Murillo's *Two Women at a Window: A Young Girl and Her Duenna* along with Francisco Goya's *Majas on a Balcony* that had also inspired Manet's *Balcony* shown at the Salon of 1869. The critic William J.

Clark, a strong supporter of Eakins, highlighted Cassatt's painting in the June 16, 1873, edition of Philadelphia's *Daily Evening Telegraph*, praising its "intense vitality" and underscoring the ease and grace of the figures.[7]

Spanish themes had become increasingly popular in nineteenth-century France as travel accounts, such as Théophile Gautier's *Voyage en Espagne* that Cassatt had used as a travel guide, and studies of Spanish art were featured in illustrated periodicals such as *L'Artiste*, *Le Magasin pittoresque* and the *Gazette des Beaux-Arts*. Cassatt most likely visited Manet's 1867 exhibition on the Pont de l'Alma where twenty-eight of the fifty-three oils and all of the etchings on display featured his deep engagement with Spanish subject matter and style, prompting Jules Claretie to characterize him as "a Velázquez of the boulevards, or a Spaniard of Paris."[8] Cassatt engaged in a fairly stereotypical image of flirtation in *On the Balcony*, but it signaled her commitment to paint modern subject matter rather than produce the historical and mythological narratives that prevailed with Gérôme and the majority of academic painters at the Salon. Emily Sartain wrote to her father about Cassatt's disdain for the Salon paintings of Cabanel and Bonnat, justifying her opinion because of "the earnestness with which she loves nature and her profession. . . . Her own style of painting and the Spanish school she has been studying all winter is so realistic, so solid,—that the French school in comparison seems washy, unfleshlike, gray. Coming from Italy last winter, the salon made the same effect on me."[9]

Despite this disaffection, the Salon remained a necessity for emerging artists to get their work seen, to be critically evaluated in the press, along with the chance to be picked up by a dealer to represent them and facilitate the purchase of their work. Sales were not forthcoming for Cassatt's Spanish subjects, so she turned to portraiture. The Salon of 1874 admitted *Ida*, which found an admirer in Edgar Degas, who allegedly proclaimed, "Here is someone who feels as I do."[10] Prior to 1874, Cassatt had changed residences many times, traveling throughout Europe in search of motifs and steeping herself in the study of old master works to further her aesthetic education. Realizing that she needed to establish a studio in Paris to concentrate on work for the Salon and sales, Cassatt decided in June 1874 to put down roots in Paris rather than Philadelphia where her sales had been marginal. The jury for the Salon of 1875 accepted her portrait of a child leaning on the arm of a chair that got caricatured in the June 26, 1875, issue of *Le Journal amusant* but also rejected a portrait of her sister Lydia. She submitted Lydia's portrait the following year after having darkened the background in compliance with academic taste, and it was accepted. This only deepened her cynicism toward the Salon and its partisan jury system.

Refusal of her two entries to the Salon of 1877 both humiliated and angered Cassatt, but eventually proved fortuitous. She turned her back on the Salon and accepted an invitation from Degas to exhibit with a renegade group of disgruntled artists whose constant rejection from the Salon impelled them to band together and rent space in Nadar's photography studio on the Boulevard des Capucines in order to show their own work. They began advertising the exhibition in journals in January 1876, calling themselves the Société anonyme des peintres, sculpteurs et graveurs. More than two hundred people came the first day and, by the time the exhibit had closed a month later, more than thirty-five hundred had paid the one-franc admission price. They wandered through rooms displaying paintings that deviated significantly from the finely detailed and lacquered canvases that served as standard fare at the Salon that ran concurrently the last two weeks of the first show.

Many of the gallerygoers scoffed at the work, and Louis Leroy wrote in his review of the show in the April 25, 1874, issue of *Le Charivari* that Claude Monet had perhaps forgotten to use his brush and thus dipped his tongue in black paint and licked the surface of the canvas. "Then do I look like that when I'm walking along the boulevard des Capucines?" he asked incredulously.[11] Monet's painting, which the artist titled *Impression: Sunrise*, gave the movement its name when Leroy sneeringly commented: "*Impression.* I was sure of it. I was just saying to myself that, since I was impressed, there must be some impression in it. . . . And what freedom, what ease of workmanship! Wallpaper pattern in its beginning stages has more finish than this seascape."[12] (See Figure 9.2.) Leroy could not understand a painting being shown in public that looked like an unfinished sketch, whose brushstrokes seemed slapped carelessly on the canvas as if the artist had stepped out of the studio for a croissant and a café au lait and intended to return later to finish up his work. Monet reduced his palette to a range of blues, greens, and grays with yellow and black accents. The title *Impression: Sunrise* relates only to the time of day and therefore could not serve as a rationale for a painting that would elevate the mind of the viewer to some higher purpose. The background is so out of focus that it is difficult to tell if Monet is painting ships, smokestacks, or trees. By exhibiting this *pochade*, this sketchy impression of a Normandy harbor at sunrise captured spontaneously and on-site, Monet declared that *this* moment, *this* way of seeing held as much importance as an edifying subject that had been drawn from history or literature. Monet's graphic shorthand of strokes that signified rather than represented the ghostlike boatmen and the path of the sun across the water sought to convey the sensation produced by the early morning light and air. His aim was connotative rather than denotative, a poetic evocation of the present instead of a prosaic description of historical events.

When Degas contacted Cassatt in 1877 to join the impressionist group for their fourth exhibition she accepted with joy: "Finally, I could work with absolute independence without worrying about the eventual opinion of a jury! Already I recognized who were my true masters. I admired Manet, Courbet and Degas. I hated conventional art. I began to live."[13] Cassatt remembered vividly her first encounter with Degas's pastels, which she saw in the window of a picture dealer on the Boulevard Haussman in 1875: "I used to go and flatten my nose against that window and absorb all I could of his art. It changed my life. I saw art then as I wanted to see it."[14] Cassatt's innate attraction to the impressionist artists' radical departure from the detailed brushwork of Salon style, along with their embrace of contemporary subject matter, facilitated her transition to exhibiting with the impressionists. Additionally, two other female artists, Marie Bracquemond and Berthe Morisot, had shown with the impressionists from the beginning, thus easing Cassatt's acceptance into the group.

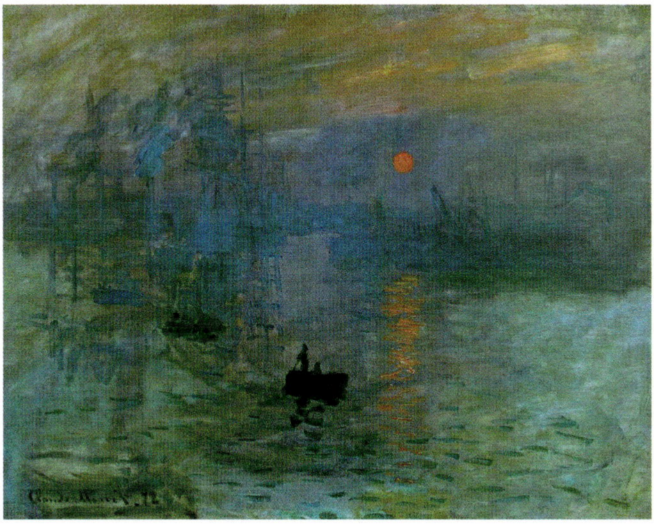

Figure 9.2 Claude Monet, *Impression: Sunrise*, 1872. Oil on canvas, 48 × 63 cm (18.8 × 24 in.). (Paris, Musée Marmottan Monet)

When Cassatt debuted April 10, 1879, at the fourth impressionist exhibition on the Avenue de l'Opéra she was given a room to herself with eleven works on display. Sixteen thousand visitors viewed the exhibition and the group turned a profit from entrance fees and sales. Her *Woman with a Pearl Necklace* attracted significant critical attention in Paris and America.[15] (See Figure 9.3.) A fashionably dressed young woman leans back on the red velvet seat in her loge, alert to the performance on stage. Her décolleté dress enhances the graceful sway of the balcony boxes reflected in the mirror behind her while a chandelier, described by a contemporary guide book as having the appearance of a crown of pearls, provides a visual pun on her necklace.[16] The subject of women at the theater attracted popular illustrators as well as painters interested in social settings, the effects of artificial lighting, and seeing and being seen.[17] Auguste Renoir's *La Loge* received much favorable commentary when it was shown at the first impressionist exhibition in 1874, and Degas's ongoing fascination with ballet dancers, musicians in the orchestra, and audiences at the opera continued throughout his long career. Cassatt's work fit perfectly within the ambit of impressionist subject matter, drawing critical approval in the pages of the influential weekly illustrated review *L'Artiste*. Critics hailed her paintings and pastel as a "symphony of color" whose compositions were "bold, mysterious, and fresh," signaling her *Woman with a Pearl Necklace* for special commendation.[18] The Italian art critic Diego Martelli praised the work highly, claiming that it was good enough to place its author in the ranks of the very best artists.[19] Georges Lafenestre associated her works with Degas, distinguishing them from the practitioners of "rough sketches and childish daubs" of the other impressionists, praising their skill in capturing the nuanced effects of artificial lighting on the skin of their models.[20] Cassatt's father wrote exultantly to his son Alexander, urging him to read the reviews for himself in the *Revue des deux mondes*, which he could access at the Philadelphia library. He exulted that the extensive coverage in French, English, and American papers practically guaranteed that "in short everybody

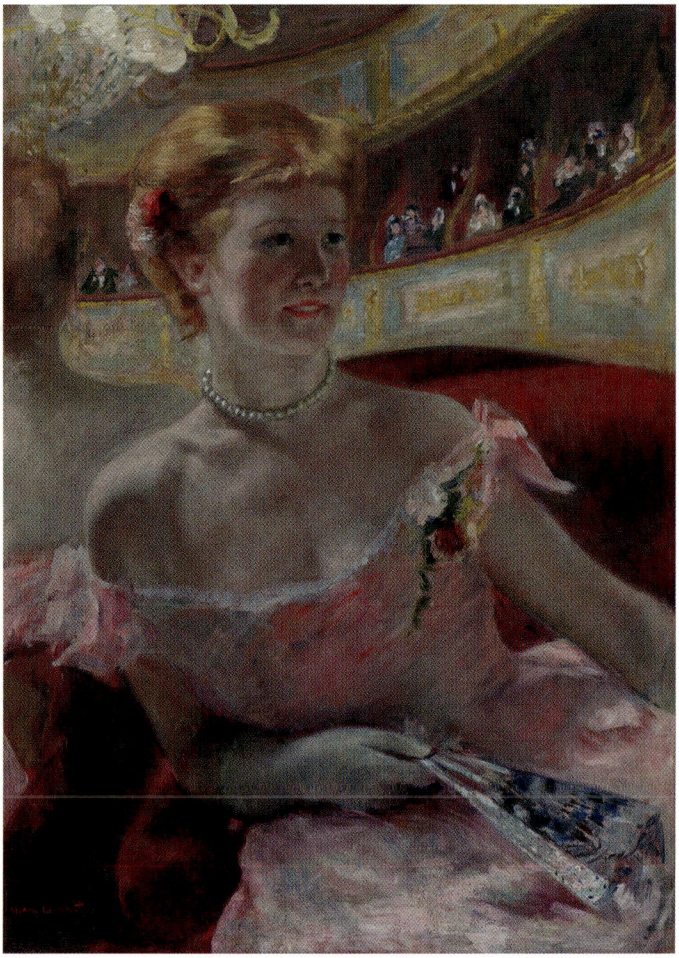

FIGURE 9.3 Mary Stevenson Cassatt, *Woman with a Pearl Necklace*, 1879. Oil on canvas, 32 × 23½ in. (81.3 × 59.7 cm). Framed: 42 × 33½ × 4½ in. (106.7 × 85.1 × 11.4 cm). (Philadelphia Museum of Art, Bequest of Charlotte Dorrance Wright, 1978-1-5)

says now that in [the] future it dont [*sic*] matter what the papers say about her—She is now known to the Art world as well as to the general public in such a way as not to be forgotten again so long as she continues to paint!!"[21] His initial reluctance to accept his daughter's choice of an artistic career had now yielded to pride in her success.

Cassatt's embrace of the new French style and subject matter can be seen by its congruence with the ideals set forth in an important essay "The Painter of Modern Life" published in 1863 by the poet and art critic Charles Baudelaire. He called for the depiction of contemporary life as an antidote to the academic subject matter that prevailed in the painting of his time, urging artists to depict women in the fashionable attire and social settings of the current day: "At one moment, bathed in the diffused brightness of an auditorium, it is young women of the most fashionable society, receiving and reflecting the light with their eyes, their jewelry and their snowy white shoulders, as glorious as portraits framed in their boxes."[22] Cassatt's *In the Box*, her 1879 version of two young women in evening dress at the theater, could serve as an

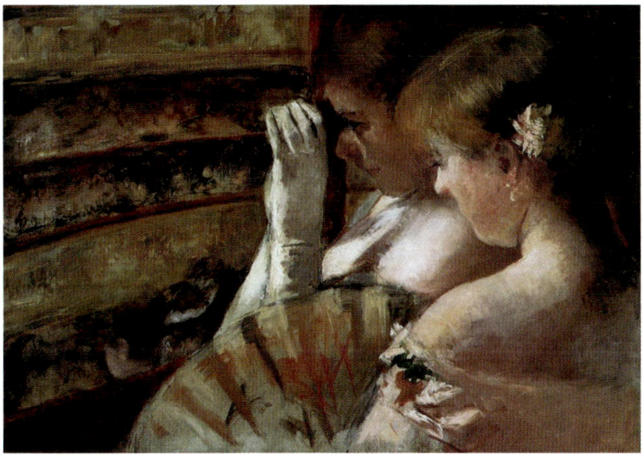

Figure 9.4
Mary Stevenson Cassatt, *In the Box*, ca. 1879. Oil on canvas, 43.1 × 60.9 cm (17 × 24 in.). (Private Collection)

illustration of Baudelaire's words as she emphasized the glare of the gas chandeliers on the bosom and shoulder of the women who gaze in rapt attention at the scene before them. (See Figure 9.4.)

Degas had the idea of uniting the fourth impressionist exhibition by suggesting that each of the participants contribute a fan-shaped painting. Cassatt declined to shape her works in the form of fans but featured them as decorative objects that could provide a shield of privacy from an intrusive gaze when needed. They also served as a visual sign language for women to greet, signal, and flirt from the privacy of their box. The fan portrayed in *In the Box* harmonizes the rounded shoulder of the figure holding it with the curved balconies occupying the left portion of the painting. (See Figure 9.5.) The fans in Cassatt's works also serve as pictures-within-pictures, as in her pastel *In the Loge* where its decorative surface and centralized position accentuate its flat colored shape as a modernist analogue of the surface of the pastel itself. With a flick of her wrist the figure could signal her presence to someone in the audience, quickly conceal herself, or engage in the multiple silent meanings conveyed by this fashion accessory. The green support of the fan stroked with red and gold calligraphic marks coordinates the dominant color scheme of this work, its unfurled curve a counterbalance to the rectangular format of the canvas as well as the strong vectors of horizontals and diagonals that structure the composition. Cassatt's colors avoid any cloying rococo sentimentality, enhanced by soft pastel pinks and blues, by the dominance of an apple green that probably caused one critic to compare looking at her work to the acidity of an unripe fruit.[23]

Although Cassatt largely experienced critical success in Paris, impressionist painting continued to have its enemies in France and America. Her participation in the impressionist exhibit and her new style stunned a critic at the *New York Times* who could not understand her defection from traditional academic painting: "She is a Philadelphian, and has had her place in the Salon. Why has she thus gone astray?"[24] Cassatt exhibited with the impressionists again in 1880, a period of transition for the

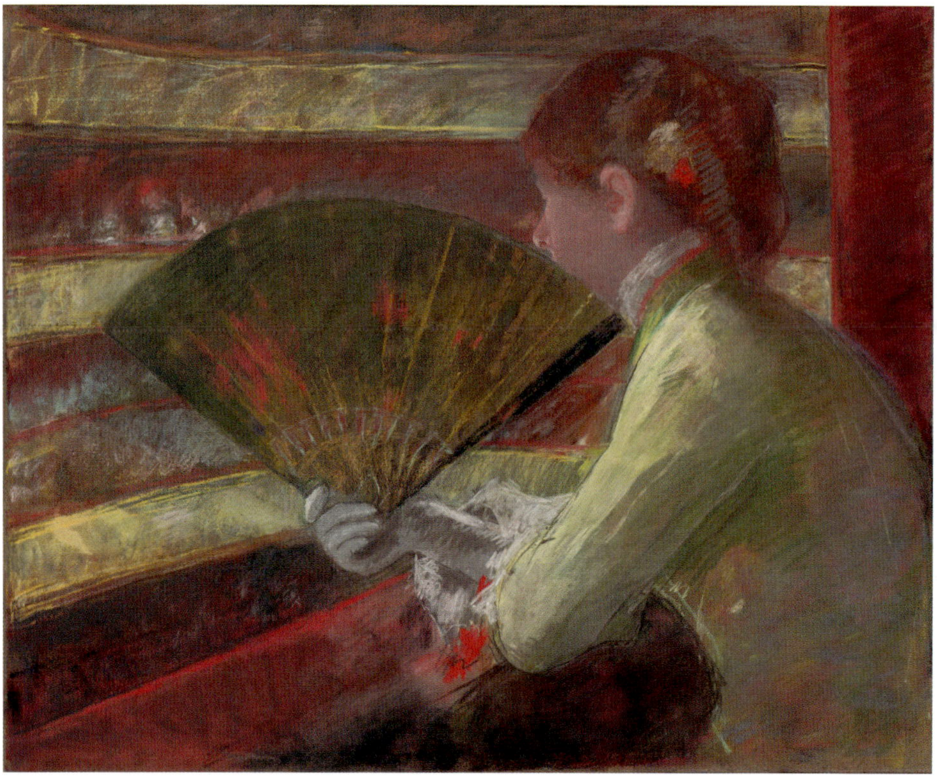

FIGURE 9.5 Mary Stevenson Cassatt, *In the Loge*, 1879. Pastel with gold metallic paint on canvas sheet: 25⅝ × 32 in. (65.1 × 81.3 cm). (Philadelphia Museum of Art, Gift of Mrs. Sargent McKean, 1950-52-1)

group as Monet returned to the Salon and Renoir, Cézanne, and Sisley also declined to participate. Critics perceived the group to be in disarray. The reviews were largely negative, and Cassatt's work was not spared. Philippe Burty noted that her much applauded work of the previous year had lost its strength due to lack of finish.[25] Undeterred, she contributed four oils and seven pastels to the 1881 exhibit, sold much of her work, and came to be represented by Paul Durand-Ruel, whose gallery became the major venue for sales of impressionists works in Paris, London, and America.

Cassatt's parents and sister Lydia moved from Philadelphia to Paris permanently in 1877, thus providing her with ample models for her work; Lydia willingly modeled for her sister as she sat in a garden and engaged in needlework or posed drinking tea while enjoying a social visit. Joris-Karl Huysmans highlighted Cassatt's images of Lydia in his review, commenting that they added a "fine odor of Parisian elegance."[26] *The Cup of Tea* so captivated the critic Gustave Geffroy that he described Lydia as "exquisitely Parisian," attentive to her fashionable attire and at ease in performing the ritual of a social call with friends, undoubtedly unaware that the model was a born and bred American.[27] (See Figure 9.6.)

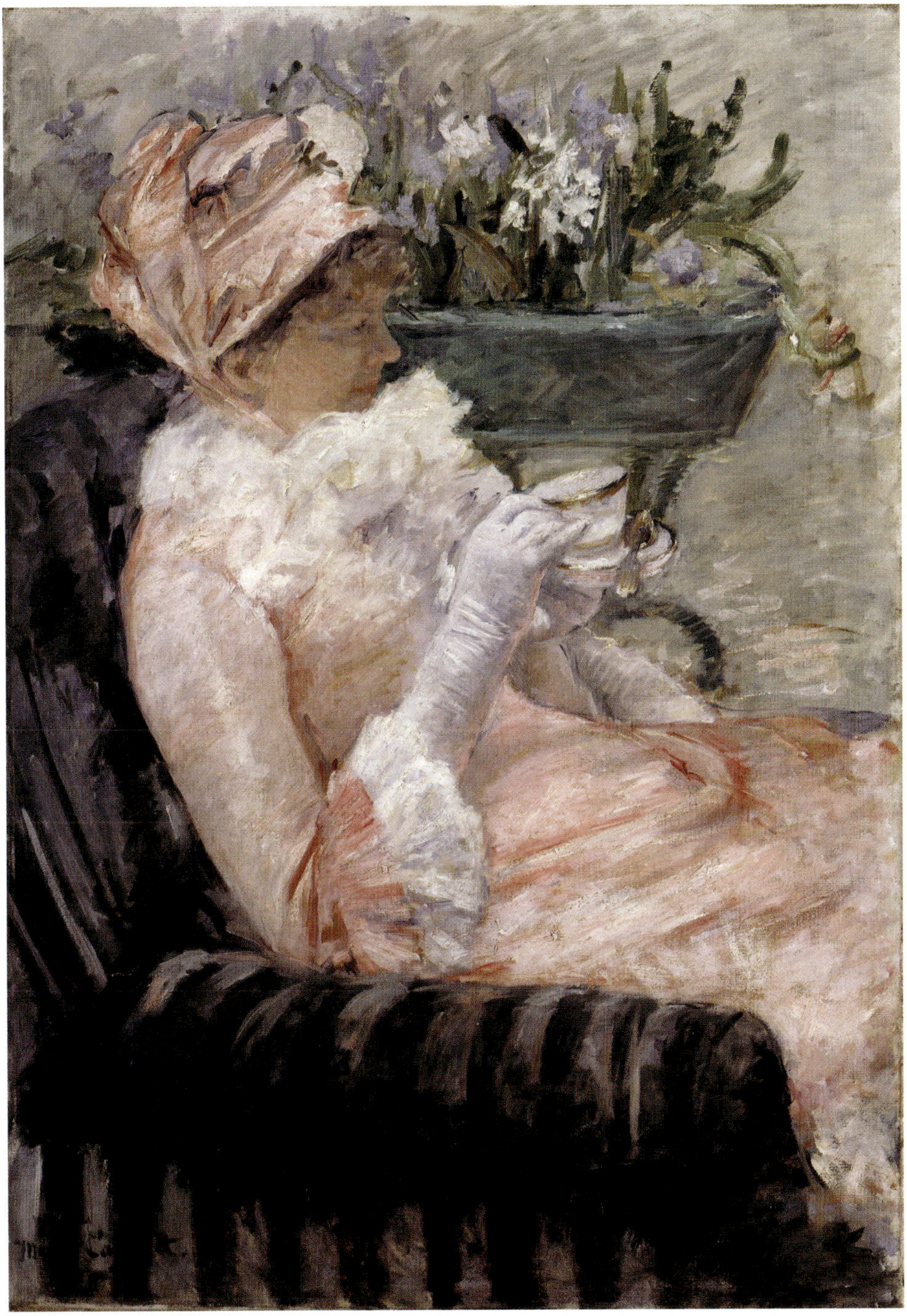

Figure 9.6 Mary Stevenson Cassatt, *The Cup of Tea*, ca. 1880–1881. Oil on canvas, 36⅜ × 25¾ in. (92.4 × 65.4 cm). (From the Collection of James Stillman, Gift of Dr. Ernest G. Stillman, New York, Metropolitan Museum of Art)

While these images might have been the stock-in-trade of bourgeois women at the time, Cassatt ventured beyond the norm in such images as *Woman and Child Driving* from 1881. (See Figure 9.7.) Lydia sits perched upright and alert as she controls the reins of a horse-drawn carriage while a young girl, posed by Degas's niece Odile Fèvre, sits next to her. Behind them a groom faces backward, his position a literal and psychological reversal of the traditional gender relations of the time. His dark clothing set against the deep green foliage of the background further emphasizes his subsidiary role and serves as a foil to the bright clothing of Lydia and Odile whose fashionable attire keeps the viewer's eye focused on them. Baudelaire had concluded his 1863 essay on Constantin Guys with a section on carriages as indicators of Parisian high-life society. The majority of Guys's many watercolor drawings and sketches of carriages conform to the traditional view of women as passengers and top-hatted grooms as the drivers. A rare exception is Guys's watercolor *The Team*, where one finds the same configuration of a woman, a child, and a groom in the rear of an open landau. (See Figure 9.8.) Cassatt's choice of the subject testified to her determination to be identified with the impressionist painters for whom Baudelaire's essay proved foundational. Cassatt focused tightly on the figures, boldly cropping her image at the sides and bottom so that one sees the work as if from the window of a passing carriage. The eye is drawn to Lydia's gloved arm where the creases in the material subtly suggest the discreet motion of pulling on the horizontal rein whose blurred outline above the rump of the horse indicates the effect of her gesture. Horizontals and verticals strongly structure the composition, thereby augmenting Lydia's businesslike attitude and sense of authority and control. Baudelaire had praised Guys's knowledge of harness and coachwork, and, as an experienced equestrian herself, Cassatt also displayed her own expertise in endowing her sister with the correct upright posture to supervise the vehicle while securely manipulating the riding crop with the same deft assurance as Cassatt wielded her paint brush.

Cassatt sent six paintings and a pastel to the eighth and final impressionist exhibition in 1886. Her presence at the exhibition could also be seen in Degas's pastel *At the Milliners* for which she posed. (See Figure 9.9.) Degas liked to visit fashionable shops with Cassatt, and she informed Louisine Havemeyer that she posed for Degas "only once in a while when he finds the movement difficult, and the model cannot seem to get his idea."[28] Three of Cassatt's works in this exhibition featured children at the beach, in the garden, or in their mother's arms. Parental bonds, especially those between mother and child, dominated Cassatt's painting and printmaking thereafter and she has since been as closely associated with the theme as Degas has been with ballerinas. He was a professional colleague and they shared an interest in similar subjects, although expressed from different viewpoints. In 1879–1880, they collaborated on a print journal, *Le Jour et la nuit*, which ultimately was never published. French and American critics more than once mistook Degas as Cassatt's teacher, which was not the case. When Cassatt participated in a 1915 exhibition in support of woman's suffrage at the gallery of M. Knoedler and Company in New York, Louisine Havemeyer took the opportunity to correct the misperception: "She could do without him,

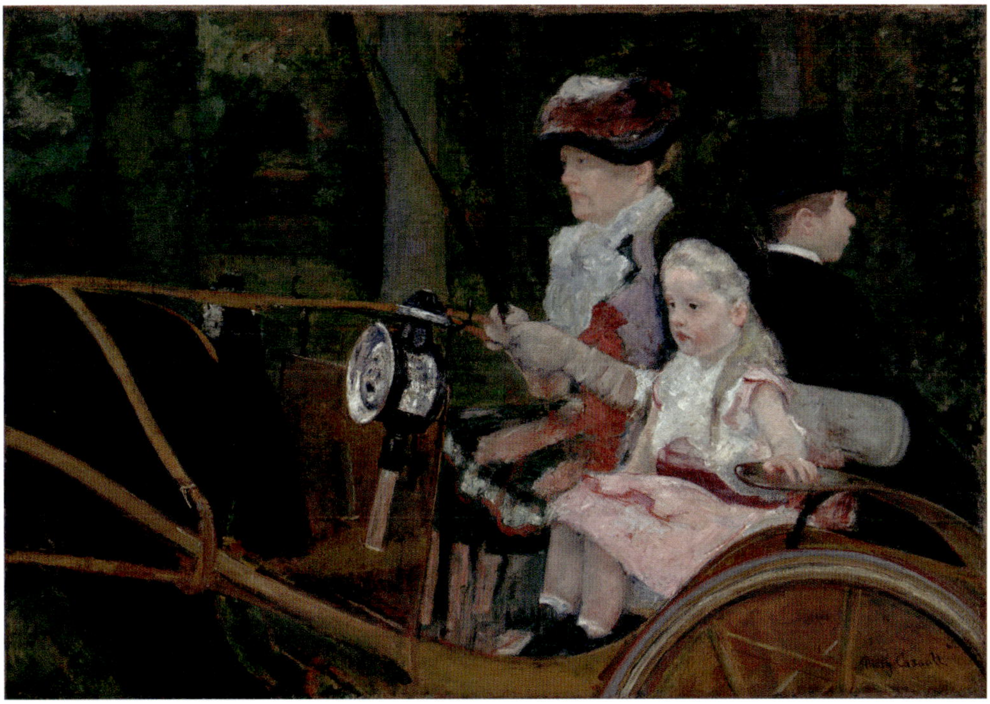

FIGURE 9.7 Mary Stevenson Cassatt, *A Woman and a Girl Driving*, 1881. Oil on canvas, $35\frac{5}{16} \times 51\frac{3}{8}$ in. (89.7 × 130.5 cm). (Philadelphia Museum of Art, purchased with the W. P. Wilstach Fund, W1921-1-1)

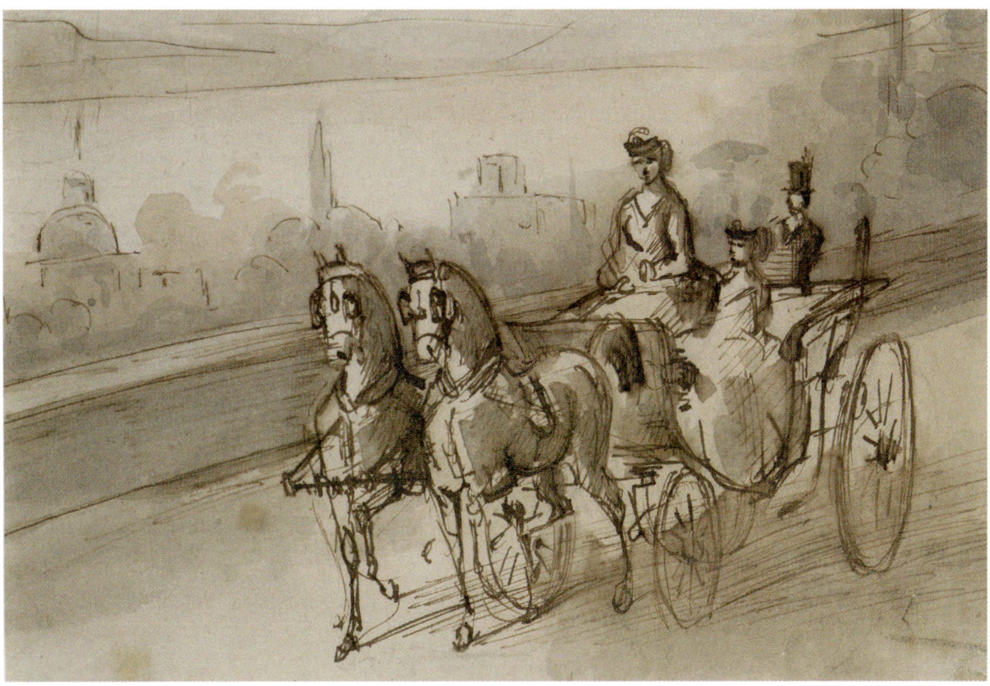

FIGURE 9.8 Constantin Guys, *The Team*, n.d. Ink and washes on paper. (Washington, DC, Phillips Collection)

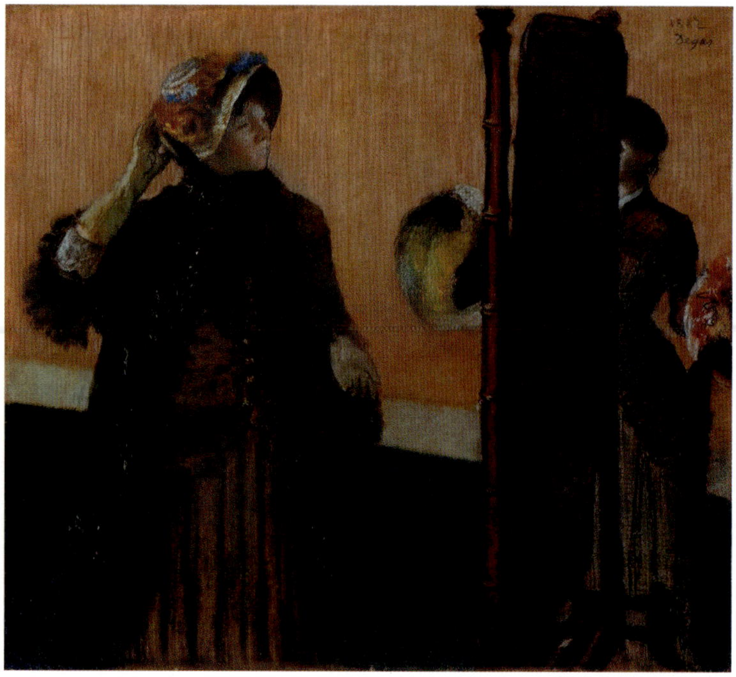

FIGURE 9.9 Edgar Degas, *At the Milliners*, 1882. Pastel on pale gray wove paper (industrial wrapping paper), laid down on silk bolting. 30 × 34 in. (76.2 × 86.4 cm). (Metropolitan Museum of Art, H. O. Havemeyer Collection, Bequest of Mrs. H. O. Havemeyer, 1929)

while he needed her honest criticism and her generous admiration."[29] Cassatt saw the opportunity of having her work hung next to Degas's as an opportunity to showcase her originality, commenting "I cannot open a catalogue without seeing stealings from me."[30] They frequently exchanged works of art with one another and Cassatt influenced Henry and Louisine Havemeyer in eventually owning sixty-five works by Degas, many of which were bequeathed to the Metropolitan Museum of Art.[31]

A one-person exhibit of Cassatt's work at the Durand-Ruel Gallery in the fall of 1893 elicited favorable criticism and quick sales and resulted in copious requests for portraits of children. She foregrounded the child in several works, partially obscuring the mother's face as in *Maternal Caress* as if to imply that the child is the future. One critic praised Cassatt's ability to capture "the innocent awkwardness of certain gestures, the transparent beauty of certain looks," which this work demonstrates.[32] Cassatt's exposure to the long tradition of old master images of the Madonna and child through her extensive travels to the great museums of Europe informed her imagery, but never infringed on her originality. She avoided the saccharine coloring of sentimentalized images of mothers and children, preferring the fresco-like tonalities of the Italian Primitives. Félix Fénéon once noted "these large, beautiful masculine hands that Cassatt liked to give her women"[33] that one sees in *Maternal Caress*. (See Figure 9.10.) She deliberately sacrificed superficial allure for sureness in execution that some critics found more suited to works produced by a man.[34] The critic from the *Daily Evening Telegraph*, reminding readers that Cassatt hailed from Philadelphia, claimed: "Miss Cassatt has for years been one of our painters who inhabit Paris. She has an unmistakable individuality, notwithstanding her entire subscription to the canons of the impressionists. An ardent admirer of Degas, not to say Manet, she nevertheless has a wholly virile point of view, rather than imitation of the manner of her masters, that characterizes her work."[35] Perhaps this is what made Degas one day exclaim, while looking at her work: "No woman has a right to draw like that!"[36]

Degas's remark would have annoyed Cassatt, who never wanted to be identified as a "woman painter" but as an artist who painted women. A commission from America in 1893 allowed her to express her mindset as a proponent of the role of woman in society and her growing feminist convictions. Along with Mary MacMonnies, Cassatt was invited to contribute a mural to the Woman's Building at the Chicago World's Fair. Her *Modern Woman* (now destroyed), executed on three panels, faced MacMonnies's interpretation of *Primitive Woman*. Cassatt's central panel featured *Young Woman Plucking the Fruits of Knowledge or Science* with the left panel showing *Young Girls Pursuing Fame*. The right panel, *Arts, Music, Dancing*, contained young women performing. Cassatt met with harsh criticism for her exclusion of men from her painting and her work was dismissed by one female critic as a ghastly joke in the worst taste.[37] Henry Fuller of the *Chicago Record* used his critique of her style to attack her association with the impressionists: "The impudent greens and brutal blues of Miss Cassatt seem to indicate an aggressive personality with which compromise and cooperation would be impossible. Indeed, Miss Cassatt has a reputation for being

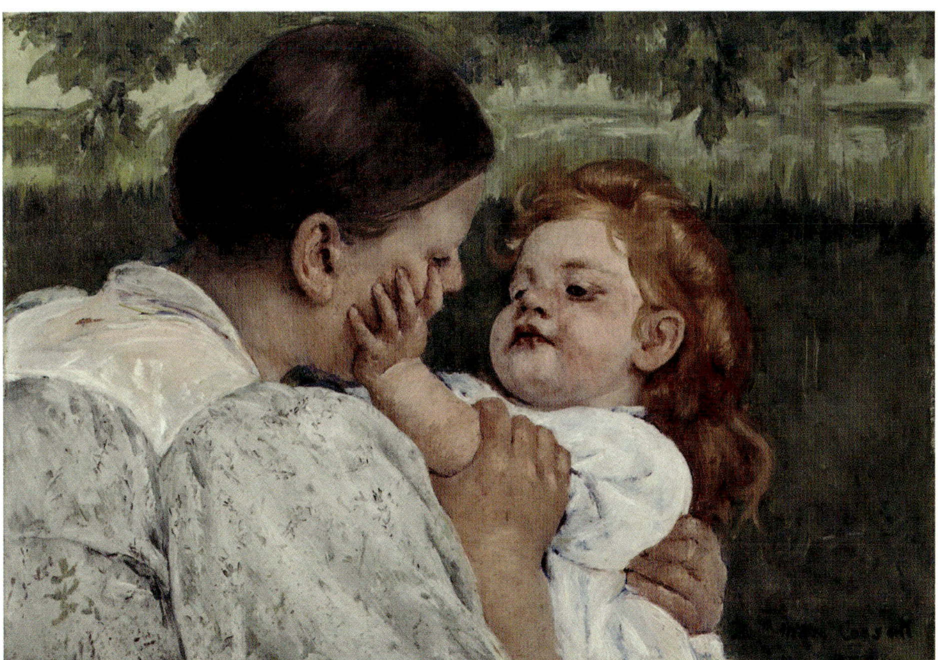

Figure 9.10 Mary Stevenson Cassatt, *Maternal Caress*, 1896. Oil on canvas, 15 × 21¼ in. (38.1 × 54 cm). Framed: 25½ × 31⅝ × 4¼ in. (64.8 × 80.3 × 10.8 cm). (Philadelphia Museum of Art, Bequest of Aaron E. Carpenter, 1970-75-2)

strong and daring; she works with men in Paris on their own ground."[38] Awareness of expanded opportunities for women in art served as a major impetus for Cassatt to spend her professional career in France rather than in America. "After all give me France," Cassatt wrote at the time of the Chicago Mural. "Women do not have to fight here if they do serious work . . . women should be *someone* and not *something*."[39]

Women in Cassatt's time were held responsible for the transmission of knowledge and skill through childcare and education, a subject Cassatt had pursued throughout her career in paintings of figures perusing reading material in books or newspapers. Although figures reading remained a familiar genre in traditional art as well as in the paintings of Manet and Renoir, Cassatt underscored women's interest in reading as an intellectual pursuit. An early portrait from 1878, *Reading Le Figaro*, shows Katherine Cassatt engrossed in the front page of the journal, where the political news of the day was reported. (See Figure 9.11.) Her mother is no decorative object with the newspaper as an accessory but an American woman fluent in French who intently seeks knowledge of current affairs rather than casually flipping through the pages of a fashion journal. The painting is as much a portrait of her mother's mind as her mother's features.

In her later life, Cassatt guided her nephews and nieces to schools during their stays in Paris, ever concerned for their learning. Her 1898 painting *Family Group Reading*, with the child's hands perched on those of the adult woman while another looks closely on, visually communicates the transmission of knowledge from one female generation to the next. (See Figure 9.12.) Cassatt fostered her own education to the point that her father wrote to Alexander in 1878: "Her circle amongst artists and literary people is certainly extending and she enjoys a reputation among them not only as an artist but also for literary taste and knowledge, which moreover she deserves for she is uncommonly well-read especially in French literature."[40] The symbolist poet Stéphane Mallarmé (1842–1898) dined at her home with Degas and had such confidence in her understanding of poetry that he invited her to contribute illustrations to a volume of his verse.

After more than two decades abroad, Cassatt returned to Philadelphia in January 1898, staying with her brother Gardner at his home at 1418 Spruce Street. The demeaning announcement of her arrival in the *Philadelphia Ledger* confirms Cassatt's ultimate decision to live in France rather than America: "Mary Cassatt, sister of Mr. Cassatt, President of the Pennsylvania Railroad, returned from Europe yesterday. She has been studying painting in France and owns the smallest Pekingese dog in the world."[41] Cassatt, portrayed here as an appendage of her brother, had been doing more than "studying" in France and, for the record, her dog was a griffon. Fortunately, the January 15, 1898, issue of the *Daily Evening Telegraph* took pride in her local roots as an internationally acclaimed artist: "[Cassatt's] contributions to the leading exhibitions of the world are everywhere received with the high consideration due to the work of an artist of the first rank, and while we of Philadelphia may take just pride in claiming her as a member of our community, she is one of the brilliant galaxy of cosmopolitan painters whose fame is worldwide and who are citizens of the world of

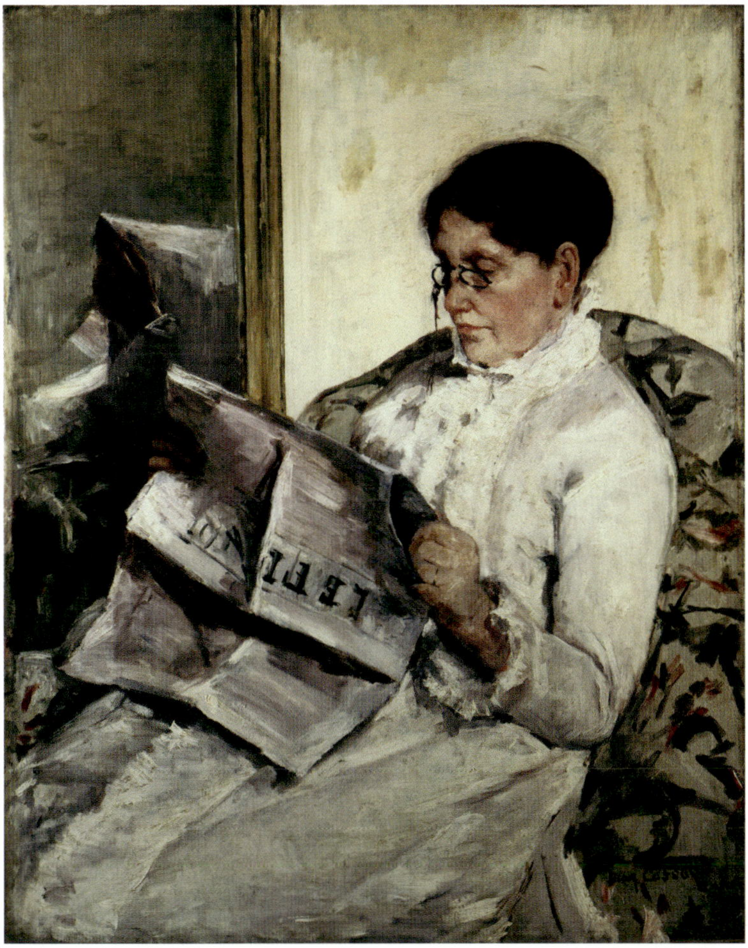

FIGURE 9.11 Mary Stevenson Cassatt, *Reading Le Figaro*, 1878. Oil on canvas, 104 × 83.7 cm (40.9 × 32.9 in.). (Private Collection)

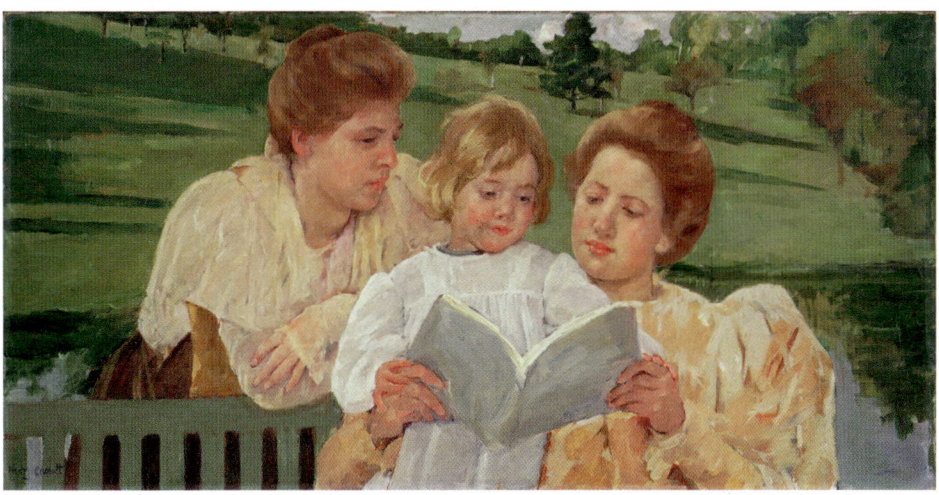

FIGURE 9.12 Mary Stevenson Cassatt, *Family Group Reading*, 1898. Oil on canvas, 22¼ × 44¼ in. (56.5 × 112.4 cm). (Philadelphia Museum of Art, Gift of Mr. and Mrs. J. Watson Webb, 1942-102-1)

art."[42] The Pennsylvania Academy honored her in 1904 with the Walter Lippincott Prize for her painting *The Caress*, which also took the Norman Walt Harris Prize when it was sent to the Art Institute of Chicago. When Harrison S. Morris, the director of the Pennsylvania Academy of the Fine Arts, wrote to Cassatt informing her that she had won the Lippincott prize, he sought to claim her for Philadelphia rather than France: "We are most happy that [*The Caress*] should have received [the Walter Lippincott Prize] as denoting an honor paid to a distinguished artist who is also our townswoman."[43] Cassatt refused both prizes, wanting only young artists to benefit from such honors. The rejections in her early years from the Paris Salons made her distrustful for her lifetime of all juries and awards. But when the French government named her Chevalier of the Légion d'Honneur on December 1, 1904, a high privilege for a woman and a foreigner, she accepted gratefully.

Cassatt sat for a series of interviews with Achille Segard in 1912–1913, which resulted in the first biography of her, titled *Mary Cassatt: Un Peintre des enfants et des mères* where he wrote: "Miss Mary Cassatt is French by adoption, but she remained an American. One must consider her work from this double point of view."[44] Although Cassatt spent the majority of her life in France and was buried there in 1926, she always claimed Philadelphia as her legal domicile.[45] While in Paris she banked at the Philadelphia-based Drexel Harjes branch and trusted her 1916 cataract surgery to the Philadelphia ophthalmologist Louis Barsch. Her paintings hung annually at the Pennsylvania Academy exhibition in the 1870s, with a hiatus in the 1880s, but resumed again from 1898 to 1920. Between 1873 and 1927, her work could be seen in some forty exhibitions. When she was awarded the Lippincott prize, the *Inquirer* informed its readers: "She holds a high place among the *pleinair* painters of France, though she maintains the stoutest allegiance to her native city."[46] French writers such as André Mellerio also highlighted her American heritage: "She remains exclusively of her people. . . . Hers is a direct and significant expression of the American character."[47] At the 1895 exhibition of her work in New York, organized by Durand-Ruel, the critics focused more on Cassatt's nationality than her gender. She was credited with retaining her powerful personality and originality despite her association with the impressionist group. Her reliance on drawing to structure the forms in her work rather than dissolve them in a flurry of strokes was seen as an American trait that allied her with the rising tide of nationalism in the early years of the twentieth century.[48] Her determination that America should possess great art equal to that of Europe made her a strong advocate and art adviser to the Havemeyers in New York, Sarah Choate Sears in Boston, Theodate Pope in Connecticut, and Bertha Honoré Palmer in Chicago, among others.[49] The Havemeyers eventually collected over five hundred works of art and dubbed Cassatt the "godmother" of the collection, and it is here and in the art she created that the fruits of her artistic fertility should be located.

Mary Cassatt was not the only Philadelphia artist to relocate permanently to Paris in the late nineteenth century. As an African American, Henry Ossawa Tanner also found France more compatible to his race and his talents than America. Tanner was the eldest of seven children born in Pittsburgh to Benjamin Tucker Tanner, then a minister in the African Methodist Episcopal Church (A.M.E.), and Sarah Elizabeth Miller, who had been born into slavery in Winchester, Virginia. The family moved to Philadelphia in 1868 where, at the age of thirteen, Tanner spotted someone painting a landscape in Fairmount Park when he and his father were on a walk. He watched the painter for an hour and returned home, grabbed an awning that hung over the kitchen door, and made a palette from an old geography textbook. With fifteen cents in his pocket, he went out the next day and purchased some meager paint supplies at a local shop and returned to Fairmount Park. He returned home that night, viewed his efforts from all points of view, and, despite the fact that he felt his first painting looked best upside down, he never wavered from his determination to become an artist. Tanner attended the Robert Vaux Consolidated School for Colored Students, then considered the most elite secondary school for black students in Philadelphia. However, the artistic training there only provided drawing as a practical skill solely to ensure good penmanship, make maps, or render mechanical drawings. Tanner eagerly studied the art displayed in the windows of James S. Earle and Sons on Chestnut Street and in the window of Bailey's jewelry store, rushing home to copy what he had seen. His first artistic success and public confirmation of his talents came with the award of a premium in the juvenile section of the 1876 Philadelphia Centennial International Exhibition. After graduating as valedictorian of his class at Vaux in 1877, he worked as a flour merchant but fell ill. His parents yielded to his resolve to pursue an artistic career, never wavering in their support of him thereafter.

Tanner registered at the Pennsylvania Academy on December 4, 1879, the only student whose presence in the studio had to be approved by the antique class because he was black.[50] He worked with Eakins for four or five years, and subsequently with Thomas Hovenden who took over after Eakins was dismissed. Both of these instructors most likely stimulated Tanner's desire to study abroad as they had done. After abortive efforts to establish a photography studio in Atlanta and a stint in the Art Department at Clark University in 1889, Tanner set sail for Rome via Liverpool and Paris in January 1891. When he arrived in Paris, however, he decided to stay, claiming that "after having been in Paris a week, I should find conditions so to my liking that I completely forgot that when I left New York I had made plans to study in Rome and was really on my way there when I arrived in Paris."[51] At a café, he encountered Robert Henri whom he had met at Earle's Gallery in Philadelphia. Henri had also studied at the Pennsylvania Academy in 1888 and had come to Paris to attend the Académie Julian.[52] He convinced Tanner to enroll at Julian's, an open-minded studio that accepted women and foreigners without making them pass a rigorous French language examination. The teaching differed from that of the École des Beaux-Arts in its flexibility regarding style and subject matter. A weekly competition each Sunday held the promise of a medal and a purse of one hundred francs. Tanner's religious convictions initially prevented him from submitting on the Sabbath until he negotiated to do his sketch on another day, and have it judged on a Sunday. The success of this strategy resulted in his winning one of the two prizes and drawing him to the attention of his teachers Jean-Joseph Benjamin-Constant and Jean Paul Laurens.

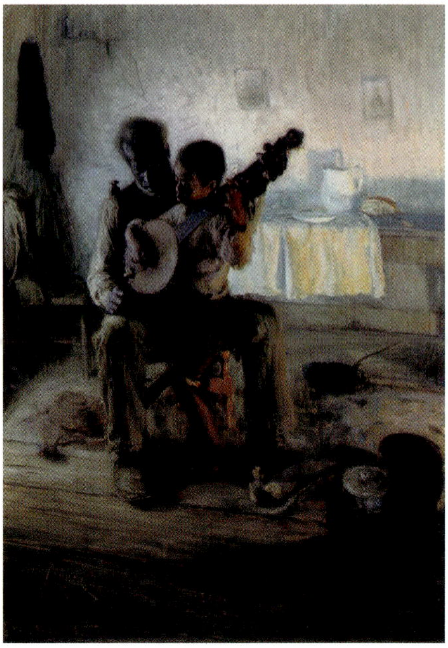

FIGURE 9.13 Henry Ossawa Tanner, *The Banjo Lesson*, 1893. Oil on canvas, 49 × 35.5 in. (124.4 × 90.1 cm). (Hampton University Museum)

Oddly enough, Tanner remained ignorant of the Salon until one Sunday he happened upon the crowds attending it:

> As I now look back, it seems curious to me that I should have been able to arrive at thirty years of age with two years in Paris and never to have heard of the Salon or, having heard of it, not to have at all realized its importance in the art world. Its discovery came to me in this manner: I had been to Dr. Thurber's church, and was on my way home when, near the Palais d'Industrie, I saw great crowds making their way into this building . . . such crowds as you might see going into Madison Square Garden to some great sporting event. To my question, it was Le Salon and, to see for myself, I joined that good-natured throng. What a surprise awaited me in the court of that old palais! Hundreds of statues that appeared to me nearly all of them fairer than the "Venus de Milo" and upstairs the paintings—thousands of them—and all of them much more to my taste than were the old masters of the Louvre—not that they were really as fine, but they were more within my range.[53]

Spurred on by what he had seen, Tanner submitted *The Bagpipe Lesson*, a painting of Breton peasants (1892–1893), to the Salon, but it was rejected. This did not deter him from pursuing his goal of being admitted there in the future. He was also confident that the Salon jury vetoed his painting on the basis of perceived quality rather than any racial bias, as he later stated: "In Paris questions of race or color are not considered—a man's professional skills and social qualities are fairly and ungrudgingly

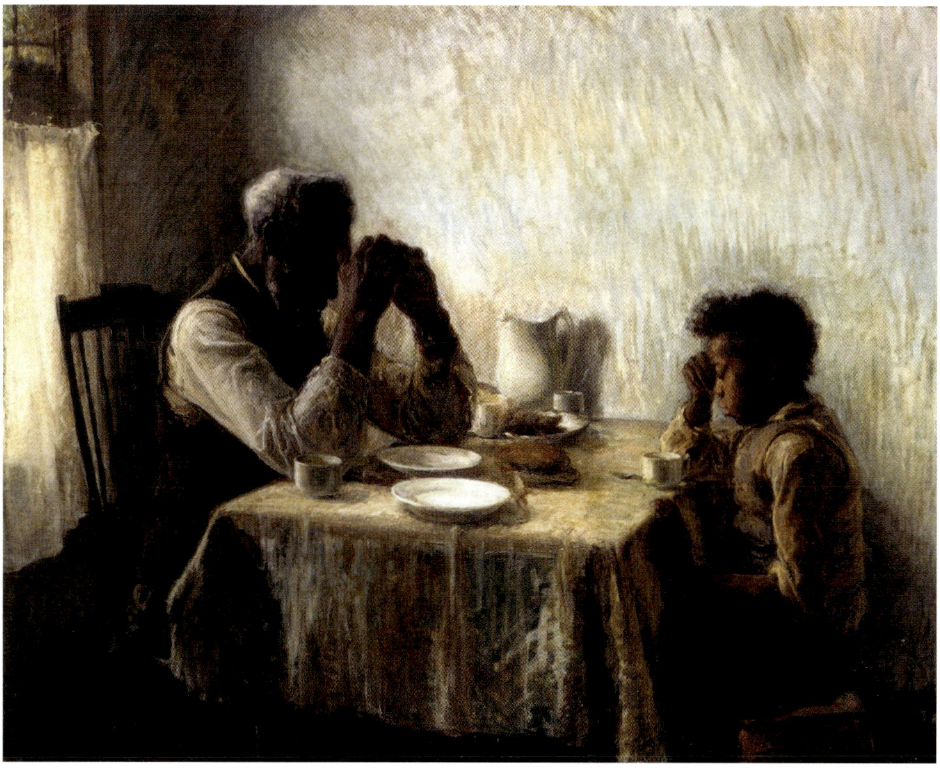

FIGURE 9.14 Henry Ossawa Tanner, *The Thankful Poor*, 1894. Oil on canvas, 35.5 × 44.2. in. (90.1 × 112.4 cm). (Private Collection)

recognized. No one who had not carefully observed the art world of Paris could have any clear idea of its broad and deep race admixture."[54]

A case of typhoid fever in the early months of 1893 sent Tanner back to Philadelphia, but he had recovered enough to attend the Congress on Africa that August at the World's Columbian Exposition in Chicago, where he was an invited speaker. Consciousness of his race and its depiction in paintings and popular imagery impelled him to create what would become two of his most iconic paintings—*The Banjo Lesson* (see Figure 9.13) and *The Thankful Poor* (see Figure 9.14). Images of blacks with banjos most often served as the fodder for caricaturists as manic performers for white audiences in Tanner's time. He sought to counter the cliché with *The Banjo Lesson*, a tender image of an elderly gentleman, presumably a grandfather, cradling his grandson on his lap to instruct him in the rudiments of a musical instrument by which his race has been identified.[55] The honest tenderness of the image, along with the lack of mawkish sentimentality, provided a counterimage to stereotyped portrayals of blacks as ignorant and clownish members of a lower class. Serious education rather than frivolous entertainment resonated from the painting whose initial title was *The First Lesson*.

Teaching and setting an example also infuse *The Thankful Poor*, where the older gentleman transmits religious values to the young boy whose eagerness to eat is subtly indicated by the cup pulled close to the edge of the table just beneath his closed eyes. His left hand grips the edge of the table on which the meager bowl of food rests. The total absorption in prayer of the elderly man whose arms form a gothic arch of support for his forehead is only half-echoed by the youth whose right hand is poised in imitation and could possibly hide a quick peek at the anticipated meal. No hint of satire or exaggeration of racial features mars this quietly intimate scene of ethnic piety. Tanner conveyed the dignity and humility of a generational lesson with a restrained Rembrandtesque palette of browns and ochres that connects back to the Dutch master's paintings of Christ sharing meals with his disciples. French art also influenced the image. Tanner had spent the summer of 1892 in the French countryside of Brittany and Concarneau, where he was exposed to peasant life. In Paris, he had access to the popular genre paintings of Jean-François Millet and Jules Breton whose genre scenes of rustic life with its simple mores captured the unpretentious lifestyle of country people that contrasted so markedly with the chic sophistication of metropolitan Paris.[56] The ethos of Millet's *The Angelus*, one of the most frequently reproduced images in nineteenth-century France, sets an example of simple devotion and solidarity with the working class. (See Figure 9.15.) A sketching trip to North Carolina may have inspired these images, and Tanner combined this with his exposure to French aesthetics and cultural values to create this memorable painting.[57] Tanner's transposition of foreign influences into the American vernacular foreshadowed his successful future as a painter of religious images. Earle's Gallery in Philadelphia displayed *The Banjo Lesson* and *The Thankful Poor* in its windows from April 28 to May 5, 1894, where an admiring crowd was noted in the pages of *The Christian Recorder*.[58]

When Tanner learned that *The Banjo Lesson* had been accepted for the Salon of 1894, he planned his return to Paris. The painting was skied—hung high up on the Salon walls where study of the painting was difficult to almost impossible. It received no critical attention, unlike in Philadelphia, but in 1895 he succeeded in getting three other paintings accepted at the Salon. That year he also joined the American Art Association of Paris whose president, Rodman Wanamaker, son of the Philadelphia department store magnate, John Wanamaker, presided as president. Rodman would eventually play a significant role in Tanner's career. In 1896, Tanner briefly took on the job as an art correspondent for a Philadelphia newspaper, but lost the job when he declined to return to Philadelphia to paint American subjects: "I refused to come home and paint things I was not drawn to, nor did I like quitting the helpful influences by which I was surrounded."[59]

Tanner's decision proved to be the right one for his emerging career as he achieved his first major success at the Salon of 1896 with *Daniel in the Lion's Den*, where the work received an honorable mention. (See Figure 9.16.) He had made studies of lions at the Philadelphia Zoo for an unfinished painting of the legend of *Androcles and the Lion* while he was at the Pennsylvania Academy in 1885. He converted the folktale into a depiction of an Old Testament figure and submitted it to the Salon. The hang-

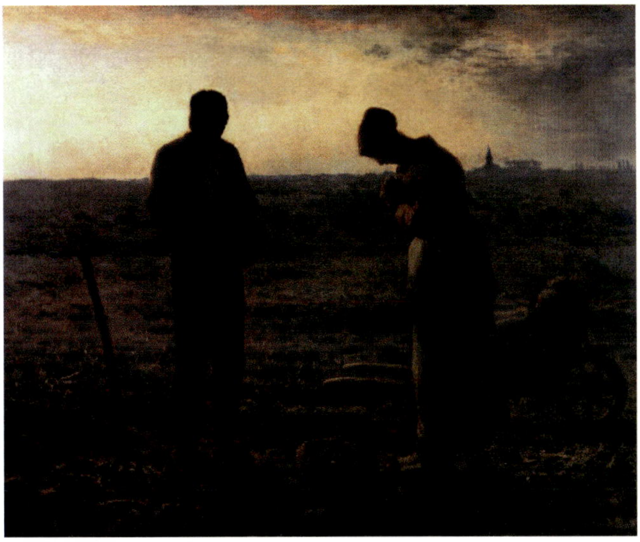

Figure 9.15
Jean-François Millet, *The Angelus*, 1857–1859. Oil on canvas, 55.5 × 66 cm (21.8 × 25.9 in.). (Paris, Musée d'Orsay)

ing committee skied it as they had with *The Banjo Lesson*, but Gérôme's intervention secured it a coveted "on-line" position, which meant that the painting hung at eye level in acknowledgment of its artistic qualities. This recognition convinced Tanner to continue with religious subject matter in lieu of the genre scenes that had been ignored by the press: "So it was that this first little 'mention honorable' gave me a courage and a power for hard work, and also a hope that I had never before possessed."[60] Praise from the *New York Times* for the critical success helped enhance his growing reputation in America. The Pennsylvania Academy exhibited the painting in 1896 and Harrison S. Morris, the managing director, informed the artist that the work just missed receiving the Walter Lippincott prize of $300 bestowed annually to an artist from Philadelphia. Morris encouraged Tanner to persevere and expressed confidence that a future work would garner the award.

In preparation for the Salon of 1897, Tanner painted the *Resurrection of Lazarus*. (See Figure 9.17.) Before submitting the work to the jury, Tanner brought the canvas to his teacher Benjamin-Constant who rightly predicted that it would certainly be accepted by the Salon, adding that Philadelphia "will yet put up a monument to you. You have not done it yet but you will."[61] Tanner earned a third-class gold medal and the Luxembourg Museum purchased the work, a significant honor bestowed on living artists. The museum once held revered old master works, but in 1818 these were transferred to the Louvre and the museum was declared a museum of contemporary art. His work would thus be held there until his death whereupon it would be permanently placed in another French museum. High praise poured in from France and America for Tanner's achievement, and Morris informed the artist that the mayor of Philadelphia was contemplating a commission. Although this never materialized, the enhanced recognition set Tanner on his path to devote himself to religious painting. Tanner received news of his award at the Salon while he was in Venice, unaware of

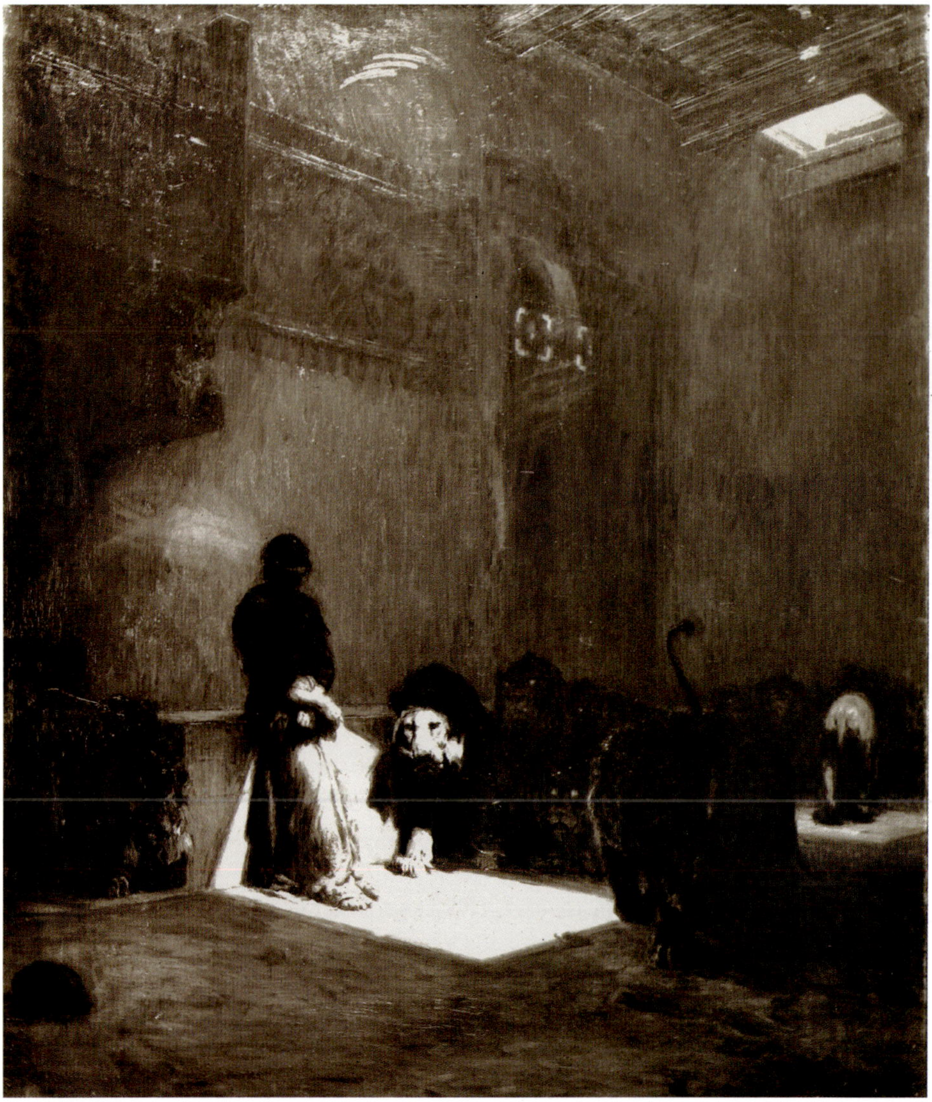

FIGURE 9.16 Henry Ossawa Tanner, *Daniel in the Lions' Den*, 1896 (lost). (Courtesy of the Pennsylvania Academy of the Fine Arts, Archives, Philadelphia)

the mounting praise for his accomplishment. A letter from a friend in Paris implored, "Come home, Tanner, to see the crowds before your picture."[62] The August issue of the *Quartier Latin* classed the artist among the "envied ranks of the arrived," informing its readers that "Mr. Tanner is resting on his well-earned laurels in Philadelphia, and is no doubt gathering inspiration for another *tour de force*, to be executed on his return to Paris in the autumn."[63]

The French press remained oblivious to the issue of Tanner's race, but not so in his home country. The *Baltimore Herald* reported on the purchase of the painting by the Luxembourg Museum, noting that "Americans have been thus honored twice or thrice before but never since the Luxembourg was established has this distinction been

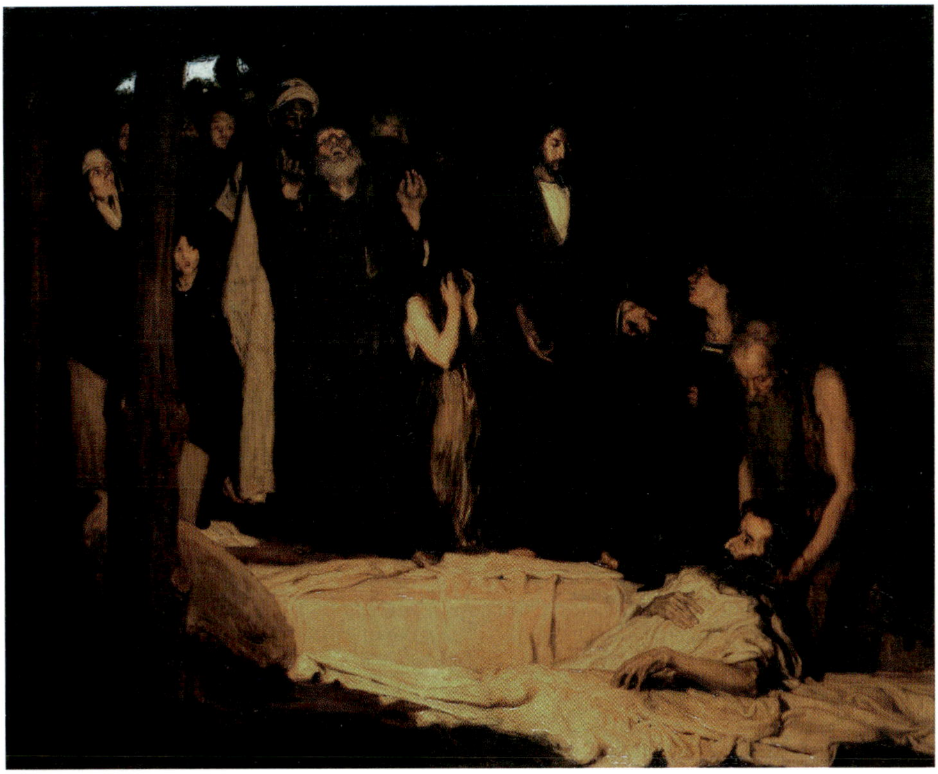

Figure 9.17 Henry Ossawa Tanner, *The Resurrection of Lazarus*, 1896. (Paris, Musée d'Orsay)

conferred on a man of Mr. Tanner's race."[64] The newspaper wanted a photo of the artist to accompany the article but found they had none. Years later Tanner recounted that the newspaper sent out a photographer who photographed "the first dock hand they came across & it looked like it may be some of my distant ancestors when they were come from Africa."[65] Justification for Tanner's repatriation to France can be easily discerned in Tanner's claim that in Paris "no one regards me curiously. I am simply 'M. Tanner, an American artist.' Nobody knows nor cares what was the complexion of my forbears. I live and work there on terms of absolute social equality."[66]

Tanner exhibited *The Bagpipe Lesson* at Wanamaker's department store in 1894, thus acquainting Rodman Wanamaker more closely with his work. So impressed was Wanamaker when he saw the *Resurrection of Lazarus* in Tanner's Paris studio that he sponsored a trip for him to Palestine and Egypt so that the artist could immerse himself in the history and culture of the Holy Land. The Salon of 1898 received the first fruits of this experience in *The Annunciation.* (See Figure 9.18.) Tanner's summers in Pont-Aven in Brittany exposed him to the tenets of the Symbolist movement that turned away from the style and subject matter of realism and impressionism to subjective imagery where visions, mysteries, and dreams replaced contemporary scenes of modern life and mass culture. In *The Annunciation*, Mary contemplates the Angel Gabriel who appears as a dramatic abstract column of white light in a simple

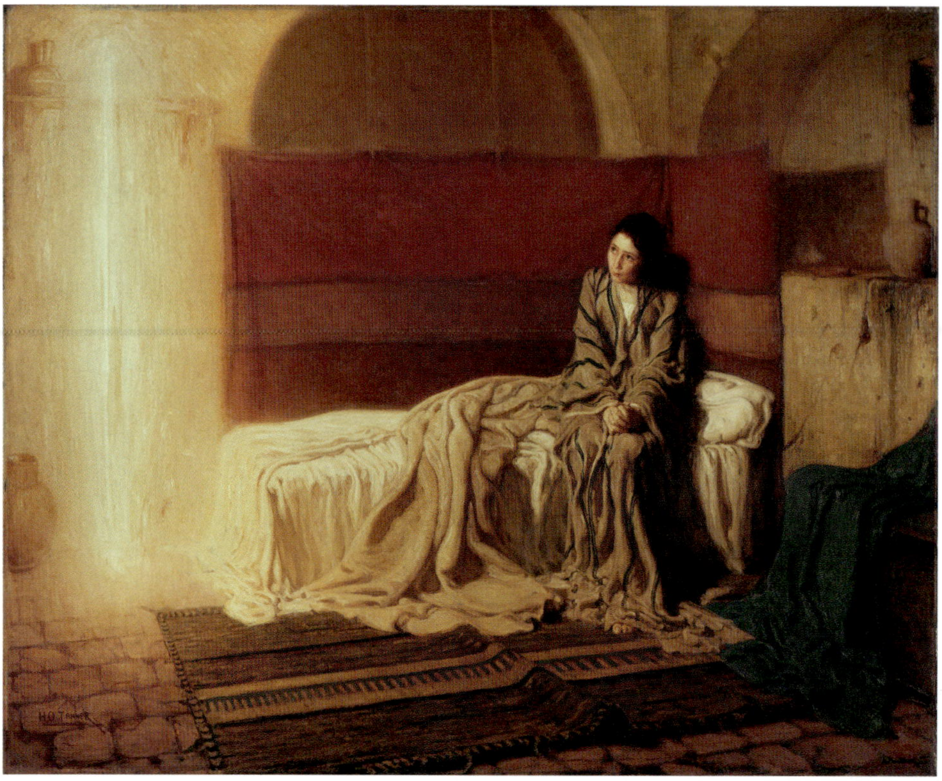

FIGURE 9.18 Henry Ossawa Tanner, *The Annunciation*, 1898. Oil on canvas, 57 × 71¼ in. (144.8 × 181 cm). Framed: 6 ft., 1¾ in. × 7 ft., 3¼ in. (187.3 × 221.6 cm). (Philadelphia Museum of Art, purchased with the W. P. Wilstach Fund, W1899-1-1)

domestic Middle Eastern interior. Tanner's imaginative take on a subject that had a long visual lineage in the history of art demonstrated his stylistic independence by his combination of a realist rendering of drapery and decor with an abstract handling of the light that suggests rather than defines the angel. According to one reporter, the painting elicited shouts of "bravos" when presented for submission to the Salon jury.[67] Eager to have the work at the Pennsylvania Academy, Morris wrote to Tanner: "Please believe that we earnestly want this new picture for the next [annual] exhibition, and after our abortive efforts of last year, you should let us have it without fail. You owe it to yourself and your growing fame that this second success should be seen in your native city and elsewhere in your native land which is becoming proud of you."[68] Morris had tried to obtain *The Resurrection of Lazarus* for exhibition at the academy but was denied because of the restrictions of the Luxembourg Museum once they had purchased the work. This time Morris was successful, and when *The Annunciation* went on display at the Sixty-Eighth Annual Exhibition in 1899 the *Philadelphia Inquirer* hailed it as a brilliant masterpiece, declaring that "Americans may be proud that this country has produced a painter of Mr. Tanner's ilk. They are not numerous."[69]

Morris's prediction that one of Tanner's paintings would win the Pennsylvania Academy's Lippincott Prize came true in 1900 with *Nicodemus*. (See Figure 9.19.) Wanamaker had subsidized a second trip to the Holy Land for Tanner from October 1898 to March 1899. On this trip, Tanner's palette and brushstroke evolved to accommodate the landscape and the moonlit nights he had observed in Jerusalem. As he had with *The Annunciation*, Tanner combined natural lighting with spiritual luminosity that here arises from the disembodied incandescent light rising from the steps on the right side of the painting. The glow also radiates from the heart of Christ, subtly highlighting his features in the darkened setting. Tanner's ethnographic Christ contrasts with James Tissot's images that had been presented in Paris in 1894 to widespread acclaim. Tissot (1836–1902) had trained at the École des Beaux-Arts and had a successful career as a portraitist and a painter of contemporary Parisian life and fashion. In 1885, he claimed to have experienced a vision in the church of Saint Sulpice and devoted the rest of his life to religious subject matter. His three hundred and sixty-five gouache illustrations of the life of Christ were highly acclaimed in

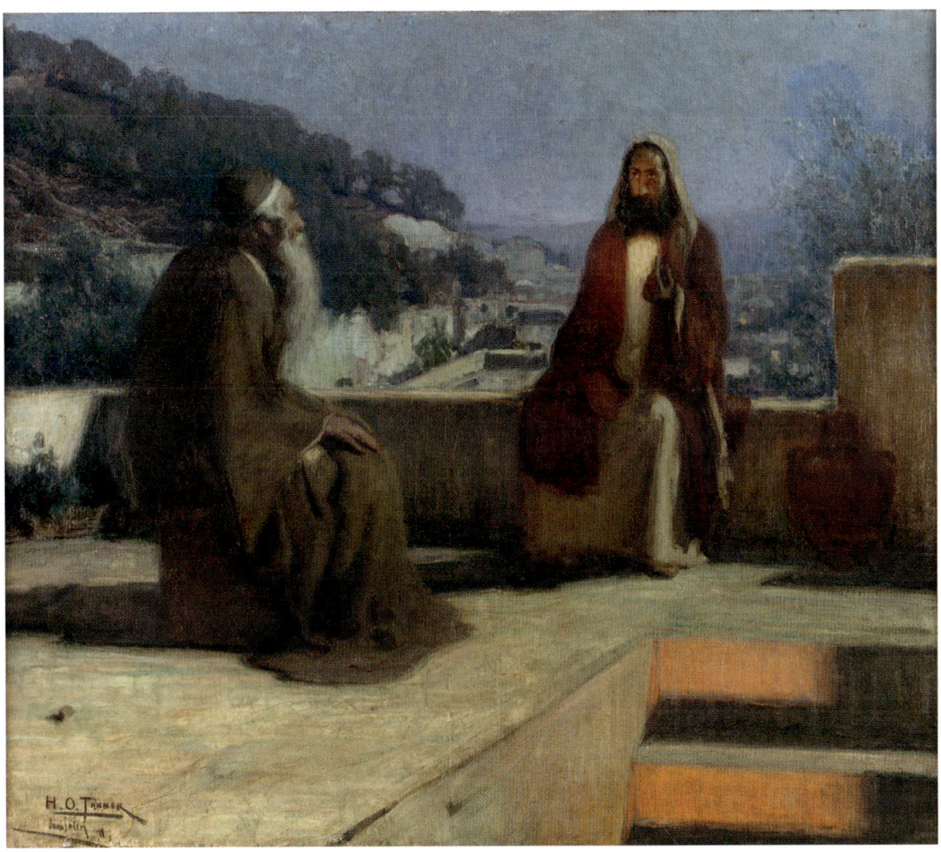

FIGURE 9.19 Henry Ossawa Tanner, *Nicodemus*, 1899. Oil on canvas. 33¹¹⁄₁₆ × 39½ in. (85.6 × 100.3 cm) Acc. No.: 1900.1. (Pennsylvania Academy of the Fine Arts, Philadelphia. Joseph E. Temple Fund)

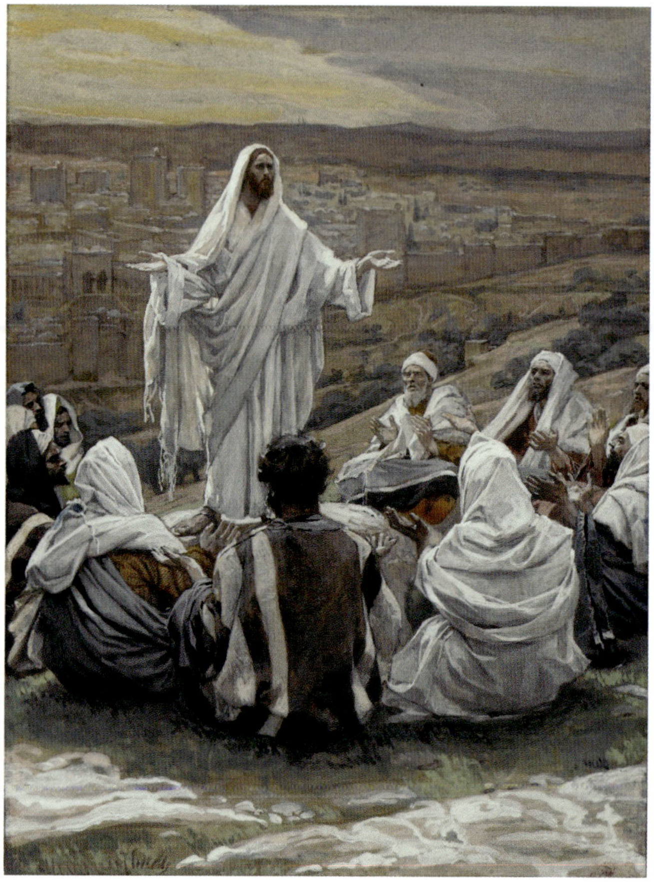

FIGURE 9.20
James Tissot, *The Lord's Prayer*, 1886–1896. Opaque watercolor over graphite on gray wove paper. Image: 8½ × 6 7/16 in. (21.6 × 16.4 cm). (Brooklyn Museum, purchased by public subscription, 00.159.167)

exhibitions in the late 1890s in Paris, London, and New York. As can be seen in Tissot's *The Lord's Prayer* (see Figure 9.20), Christ retained the white European features that would appeal to the public whereas Tanner's *Nicodemus* depicted an Arab Christ who was neither European nor African, thus asserting his originality and refusing to pander to popular public conceptions and stereotypes on Christ's ethnicity.[70]

Tanner's work continued to grow in popularity in France and America. The Pennsylvania Academy purchased *The Annunciation* in 1899. Tanner's *Daniel in the Lion's Den* received silver medals at the 1900 Universal Exposition in Paris and the following year at the Pan American exhibition in Buffalo, New York. Tanner married a Swedish American opera singer in 1899. The following year they moved to Trépied in the Pas-de-Calais region of northwestern France, where they alternated with residencies in Paris and continued their frequent visits to the States. Tanner painted scenic images of the Seine but did not exhibit them, and, after a negative review of his genre scene *The Cello Lesson* by the French press in 1902, Tanner resolved to compose only religious paintings. He painted over *The Cello Lesson* with an image of *The Pilgrims of Emmaus* and submitted it to the Salon of 1906. (See Figure 9.21.) The jury awarded it a second-class medal—the highest a foreigner could earn as the first-class gold medal could only be conferred on a French citizen. Tanner's prices rose and the demand for his work outpaced his ability to produce them. Tanner's 1907–1908 painting of *The Wise and Foolish Virgins* (lost), commissioned by Wanamaker for his Philadelphia department store, hung in the 1908 *Salon d'Honneur*, affirming the prestige of Tanner's work and garnering him an invitation by the president of France to a dinner at the Elysée Palace. His first major solo exhibition opened that year in New York at the American Art Galleries and in 1909 a lengthy autobiography titled "The Story of an Artist's Life" appeared in the June and July issues of *World's Work*. Tanner was at the top of his game.

Life and work progressed steadily and happily for Tanner and his family until the outbreak of World War I in 1914 when Trépied was evacuated. Travels with his family between Rye, England, Trépied, and Paris left little time for painting. What he did manage to produce seemed worthless to him, and he sank into a period of depression and self-doubt. He joined the American Red Cross in 1917, first employed as a lieutenant in the Department of Public Information and then as an assistant director of Farm and Garden Services. During this time, he made several images of the front lines and the daily lives of soldiers. He celebrated the end of the war with *The Arch*, which recorded a cenotaph erected beneath the Arc de Triomphe to honor fallen French soldiers. (See Figure 9.22.) France recognized Tanner's exceptional contributions by conferring on him the prestigious award of Chevalier of the Légion d'Honneur in 1923. Despite the acclaim for his career in France and America, the deaths of his wife and family members, along with the crash of the stock market in 1929, strongly

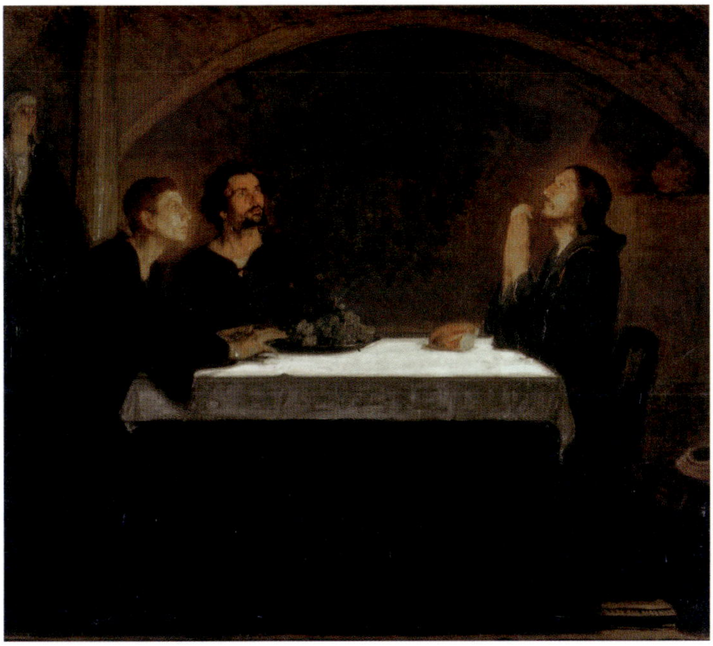

Figure 9.21
Henry Ossawa Tanner, *The Pilgrims of Emmaus*, 1905. Oil on canvas, 185.42 × 210.82 cm (73 in. × 83 in.). (Paris, Musée d'Orsay)

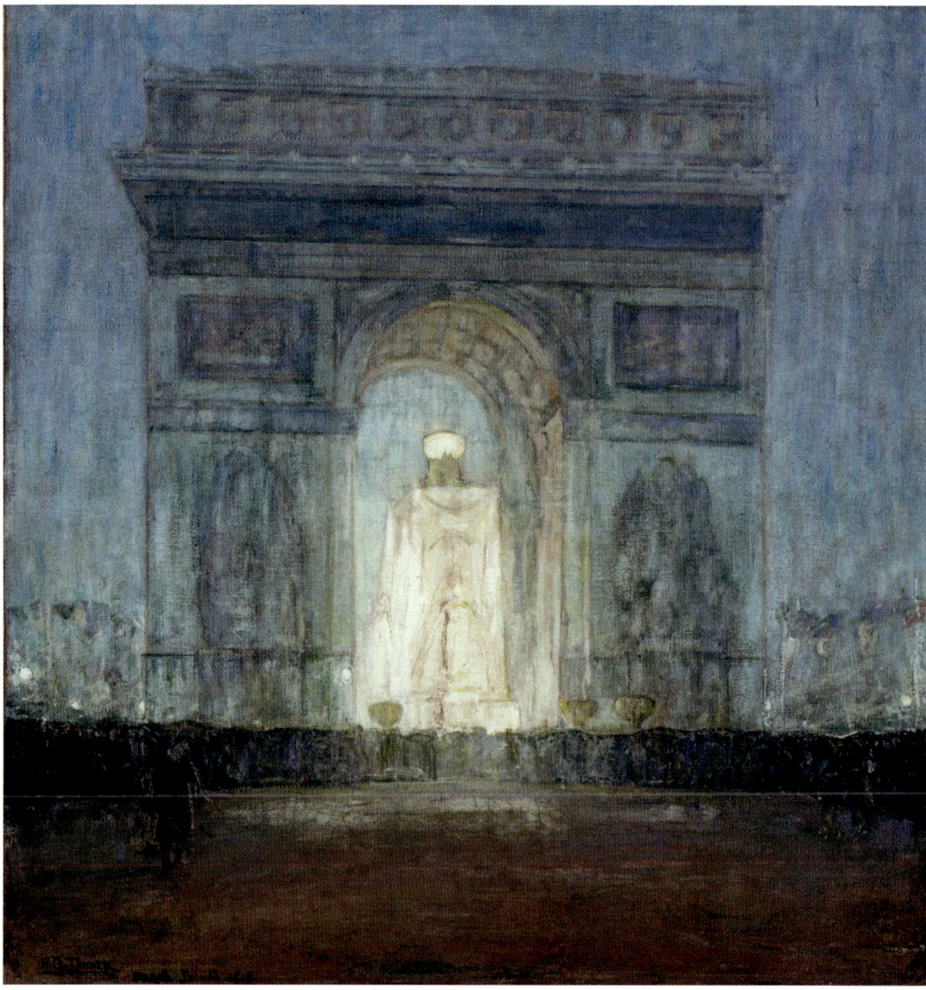

FIGURE 9.22 Henry Ossawa Tanner, *The Arch*, 1919. Oil on canvas, 39¼ × 38³⁄₁₆ in. (99.7 × 97 cm). (Brooklyn Museum, Gift of Alfred W. Jenkins, 32.10)

impacted Tanner in his last years as he had been dependent on the strong American economy of the 1920s for sales. Tanner died in his sleep in Paris on May 25, 1937, and was buried next to his wife and her parents in the cemetery at Sceaux, Hauts-de-Seine.

France provided Eakins and Tanner with artistic training along with exposure to great masterpieces of the past and contemporary trends in the current art market. Tanner remained freer of the influence of his teachers at home and abroad than did Eakins, charting his own stylistic course between academic realism and modernism, seeking to avoid racial and aesthetic typecasting in France and America. Tanner never renounced his American citizenship and was several times throughout his career torn between staying in France or repatriating to the States. Nevertheless, race remained a constant throughout his critical reception in the American press, whereas France judged Tanner on his artistic merits. As Tanner maintained: "There is a breadth, a generosity, an absolute cosmopolitanism about [France's] recognition of the fine arts which bars no nationality, no race, no school of variation of artistic method. All she asks is that the art shall be true, in other words that it shall set forth life."[71]

Mary Cassatt and Henry Ossawa Tanner, the first deemed a minority in America because of her gender and the second because of his race, both found that they could negotiate their careers with fewer distractions in France than in America. The Parisian art scene allowed each of them more autonomy to direct their career choices in particular ways. The Pennsylvania Academy of the Fine Arts provided the training in their basic technical skills and conceptual underpinnings. Living and working in Paris offered them exhibition possibilities that they felt America, and especially Philadelphia, lacked. Philadelphia-based artists would continue to travel abroad to steep themselves in the artistic richness of the museums and keep themselves current on the Salon scene. It would not be long until the lack of exhibition opportunities rankled enough artists that they forcibly rebelled against the New York National Academy of Design that in the early years of the twentieth century had become increasingly conservative. Mary Cassatt's renouncement of the Paris Salon and her alliance with the renegade impressionists in 1877 set an example for American artists to proclaim their independence in their home country.

[10]

Philadelphia's Champs-Elysées and Other French Inspirations

Creation of the Benjamin Franklin Parkway in the first decades of the twentieth century brought into being a district influenced by a French aesthetic and carried out by French architects. It marked the culmination of a period of Gallic architectural and artistic influence that transformed Philadelphia's landscape and brought French-style châteaus to its most affluent suburbs. Fittingly, over the course of the next century, the parkway gave rise to institutions holding many of the greatest masterpieces of modern French art while serving as a model of urban planning. French-trained Americans were also at the fore in creating much of the sculpture visible in the parkway district.

Philadelphia became an industrial powerhouse in the aftermath of the Civil War, enriching many of its business and professional leaders while drawing tens of thousands of newcomers—mostly immigrants from abroad—to work in its factories. The city's population soared, from 674,000 in 1870 to more than a million two decades later. Philadelphia's dynamism was symbolized in the construction of a vast new municipal building during this same period. City Hall, under construction from 1874 to 1901 on William Penn's Centre Square, was the largest and tallest all-masonry building anywhere in the modern world when it was planned. More than a century after it was finally completed, it maintains that distinction as the largest *habitable* such structure, although during its long birth, its height was surpassed (slightly) by the Washington Monument in the nation's capital and (considerably) by the Eiffel Tower in Paris; the latter, however, is constructed of iron, not stone.[1] City Hall had more floor space than any other office building in the world until 1940, when it was surpassed by completion of the Pentagon, across the Potomac from Washington, DC.

Still, it is the largest municipal building in the nation, and larger than the U.S. Capitol. Its more than six hundred rooms cover more than 14.5 acres of floor space.

City Hall is thoroughly French in style, its sweeping mansard roofs and rectangular components reflecting a heritage that stems from the Renaissance architecture of the Louvre, while its soaring tower, paired neoclassical columns, statuary, swags, and other ornaments from various architectural periods borrow directly from that style's revival in the Second Empire. It was Baron Haussmann's wholesale rebuilding of Paris at the direction of Napoleon III that identified the style with a new urban ethic. French Renaissance Revival architecture soon dominated the look of many public buildings erected in America during the latter decades of the nineteenth century.[2] But Philadelphia's City Hall has remained perhaps the grandest icon of them all, sprawling over four-and-a-half acres of the most central block in the city. Some 250 pieces of sculpture adorn its facade, all of them from the studio of Alexander Milne Calder (1846–1923), whose 37-foot bronze statue of William Penn looks out on the city he founded from the top of the building's tower. Penn's perch is precisely at the center of the city he founded; although City Hall has been eclipsed in height by several buildings constructed in recent years, they can never usurp its pride of place at the center.[3] (See Figure 10.1.)

By the time City Hall was under construction, the fruits of Haussmann's massive rebuilding of the city of Paris were being noticed around the world. His creation of broad, straight boulevards connecting landmarks looked to some Philadelphians as a stunning way to bring light and greater order to their city's cramped and crowded streets. A growing issue was how better to connect the city's park to its commercial center. The creation and gradual enlargement of Fairmount Park earlier in the century had provided a large area of open space as an amenity for all Philadelphians. By the 1870s, the park extended for some three hundred acres along the Schuylkill River from the Water Works at Fairmount and up the Wissahickon Valley. Although it spread for miles from its starting point, where it faced the city it remained largely enclosed by the grid of streets that grew from Penn's original plan.

In the 1870s, a city engineer for the Fairmount Park Commission, Lewis Haupt, was first to propose that diagonal roads might be superimposed over the grid, with one or more of these leading from Broad Street to the park.[4] It was an idea taken up by others over the next decades. Once the construction of City Hall was underway, a route from Centre Square to the south end of the park eventually received the endorsement of prominent citizens. In 1891, a bill to create such a boulevard was introduced into city councils. An architectural plan was drawn up, and once approved by both councils and the mayor, it was signed into law.[5]

That initial plan failed to bear fruit, thanks in part to the financial Panic of 1893, which prompted the mayor to veto parkway legislation. But in that same year, Chicago's Columbian Exposition appealed to a mass audience by presenting the kind of vision Haussmann had fathered as a model for American cities. A great plaster "white city" surrounded the exposition's central lagoon with monumental buildings and broad vistas. The aesthetic was largely that of the long-dominant École des Beaux-

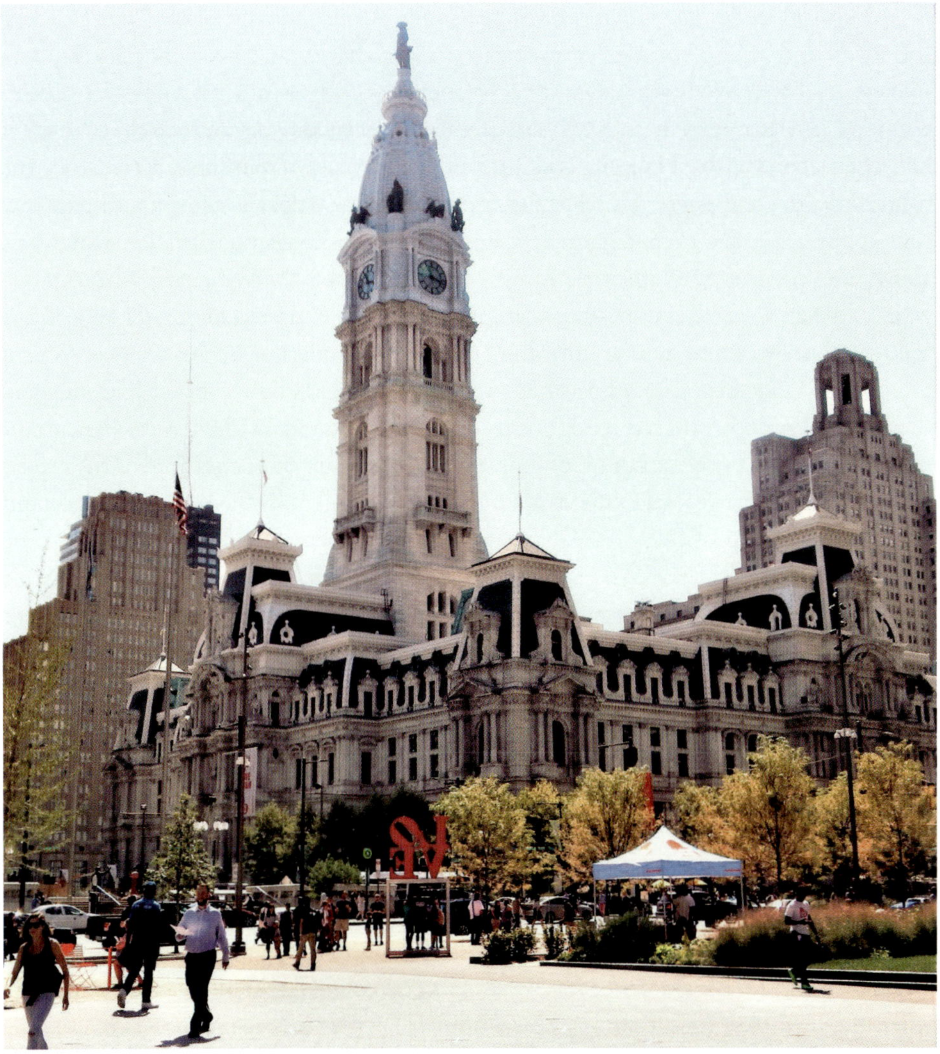

Figure 10.1 Philadelphia's French Renaissance–style city hall anchors the southeastern terminus of the Benjamin Franklin Parkway in much the same way its counterpart in Paris, the Louvre Museum, stands at the visual end of the Champs-Elysées.

Arts in Paris, which promoted highly decorated neoclassical structures surrounded by open and balanced spaces to encourage a harmonious social order. The Chicago exposition spawned a "City Beautiful" movement in America as a response to the crowded and unhealthy conditions that industrialization had brought to many cities across the continent. That movement grew, in effect, as the American version of the French Beaux-Arts architectural tradition, which had culminated in Haussmann's transformation of Paris. This Americanized vision would endure into the twentieth century, prolonging the influence of the École des Beaux-Arts in the United States past the time when European nations were increasingly turning away from French academic models to build on their own national traditions.[6]

In Philadelphia, the movement increasingly motivated civic leaders to return to the ideas underlying the earlier parkway project that would connect City Hall to Fairmount Park. While the original proponents of City Beautiful might have been regarded as urban reformers, hard-headed businessmen also began to appreciate what had been achieved by Haussmann's imprint on Paris: a remarkable increase in the value of nearby real estate. This was the argument in an article favoring a new parkway that appeared in the *Philadelphia Inquirer* in 1894: "That American city which first appreciates the utility of mere beauty will ultimately lead our Western civilization," it asserted.[7] A new architectural plan was commissioned, revised, and finally adopted so that the route was returned to official maps of Philadelphia in 1903.[8]

For the next several years, various stakeholders contested the exact placement of the route. Should it proceed straight through Logan Square to the foot of Fairmount or break its axis at the Cathedral of Saints Peter and Paul, then continue to the Green Street entrance to the park? In 1907, a new mayor, John E. Reyburn, took office and made construction of the parkway his priority. His trump card was the promise he received from one of the richest members of the city's elite, P.A.B. Widener, to pay for the construction of a new art museum on condition that it be built on the summit of Fairmount. That also settled the question of the parkway's terminus. It would proceed on a straight line from City Hall through Logan Square to the foot of Fairmount.[9] Yet another architectural plan was soon commissioned, this time, from more than one prominent architect or architectural firm.

Enter Paul Philippe Cret (1876–1945). This native of Lyon, France, attended that city's École des Beaux-Arts before moving to Paris, where he studied in the atelier of one of the leading practitioners of the Beaux-Arts style, Jean-Louis Pascal. Already well known for his work at age twenty-seven, Cret joined the faculty of the architecture department at the University of Pennsylvania in 1903, having been recruited largely so that he would bring his Beaux-Arts sensibility to Philadelphia. By 1907, when the new plan for a parkway was completed with Cret as one of its creators, he prepared a bird's-eye view of the architects' vision for the boulevard.[10] His drawing reveals the connections from the École des Beaux-Arts to Chicago's White City and City Beautiful. Cret took his cue from the great diagonal slash of the Champs-Elysées and, like that boulevard, ended his Philadelphia avenue in an open space similar to its counterpart's terminus at the Place de la Concorde. As in that landmark, Cret depicts a formal grand plaza, in this case, at the foot of Fairmount, with monumental buildings at each side and an obelisk at the center.[11] A domed art museum stands atop Fairmount in a classical mode. While new public buildings are placed around the great plaza, they also extend down the broad boulevard to Logan Square and on toward City Hall. From a small square at the base of Fairmount on its northeast face, another avenue runs straight into the east park before it curves back toward the Schuylkill at Boathouse Row.

The anticipated costs of such a huge project brought further debate, but, in April 1908, voters approved a $1 million loan to move it forward. Before Mayor Reyburn left office at the end of 1911, the Department of Public Works had created a model of the parkway for the public to inspect (a photograph of that model is today part of an outdoor display near the Market Street entrance into Dilworth Park, which abuts the west side of City Hall).[12] Further delays would follow, largely as the result of the conflicts between the Republican machine and would-be reformers. When the latter controlled the mayor's office, they were unable to obtain the needed appropriations from the two city councils, dominated as the councils were by the party machine from which political patronage flowed throughout this period. The delays also killed that 1907 pledge from P.A.B. Widener to pay for the construction of a new art museum at Fairmount. That project would largely remain on hold until well after Widener's death in 1915 and the near completion of the parkway several years after that.[13] (See Figure 10.2.)

Meanwhile, World War I broke out in Europe in 1914. Paul Cret, though long a Philadelphia resident, happened to be back in France at the time. At age thirty-eight, he enlisted in the French army, in which he served to the end of the war in 1919. For his contribution, the French government awarded him both the Croix de Guerre and the Légion d'Honneur. Yet for the duration of the war—which the United States only entered in April 1917—the parkway project in Philadelphia was evolving without the participation of Cret, its leading designer. By 1916, a new machine-favored mayor in City Hall pushed demolition of buildings in the boulevard's path. By that time, Philadelphia's city councils had determined that the parkway should be made a part of

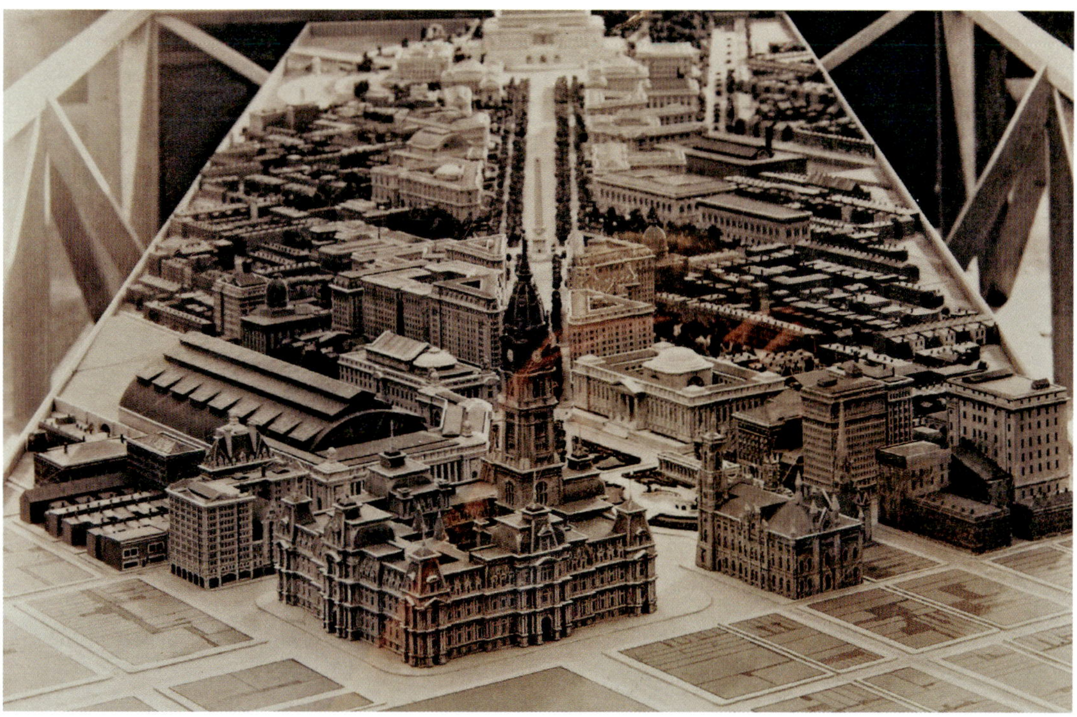

FIGURE 10.2 A model of the Fairmount (today's Benjamin Franklin) Parkway dating from 1911 is seen in this photograph near the western entrance into Dilworth Park.

the city's park system. Since the parks were governed by the independent Fairmount Park Commission, that gave the commission the right to control construction within two hundred feet of the proposed boulevard. Given that change, the commission soon drafted land-use regulations differing from those for the city.[14] That in turn called for revisions to Cret's 1907 plan.

The landscape architect chosen to make those changes was, once again, a native of France. Jacques Gréber (1882–1962)—like Cret, a graduate of Paris's École des Beaux-Arts—was then in the process of creating a stunning interpretation of a French classical garden at a private estate outside Philadelphia.[15] The property named "Whitemarsh," in suburban Elkins Park, was that of Edward T. Stotesbury, president of the Fairmount Park Commission, who recommended Gréber for the new parkway assignment. Gréber had recently completed another lavish garden for Stotesbury's late friend, neighbor, and fellow commissioner, the same P.A.B. Widener whose offer to fund a new art museum had come and gone in the previous decade.

Once appointed, Gréber prepared a set of drawings modifying the 1907 plan. They remained true to Cret's vision in their Beaux-Arts imprint, but with two major modifications. What had been a boulevard lined with monumental buildings now was drawn from Fairmount down to Logan Square as a tree-lined wedge of green, reflecting the district's new status as an extension of Fairmount Park.[16] That meant moving the reference to the Place de la Concorde from the foot of Fairmount to Logan Square—the halfway point along the new boulevard—which, in Gréber's plan, would contain a traffic circle. The square surrounding that circle would become the focal point of important public buildings. Already, the Cathedral of Saints Peter and Paul and the Academy of Natural Sciences loomed at the east and south borders of the square. Cret's grand plaza at the foot of Fairmount was replaced with a more modest oval from which automotive traffic could proceed around the hill to the east and west sections of the park beyond. The Gréber plan was approved early in 1918.

At last, the long effort to build a parkway was in sight. By the end of that year, work on the boulevard was largely complete.[17] After he heard repeated comments on the parkway's resemblance to Parisian counterparts, Gréber showed France's gratitude for the American war effort in this response:

> If by this work the city of Paris may be enabled to bring its sister in America the inspiration of what makes Paris so attractive to visitors, it will be the first opportunity of Paris to pay a little of the great debt of thankfulness for what Philadelphia and its citizens have done for France during the last three years.[18]

Although Paul Cret, still in France, was unhappy with reports of how his plans for the parkway had been superseded by a fellow countryman, his friends in Philadelphia assured him that his original conception remained basically intact. Once Cret returned to Philadelphia, Gréber worked assiduously to cultivate the older man's favor. As a result, in the 1920s, the two collaborated on the design for a new museum to nestle among the trees on the upper parkway.

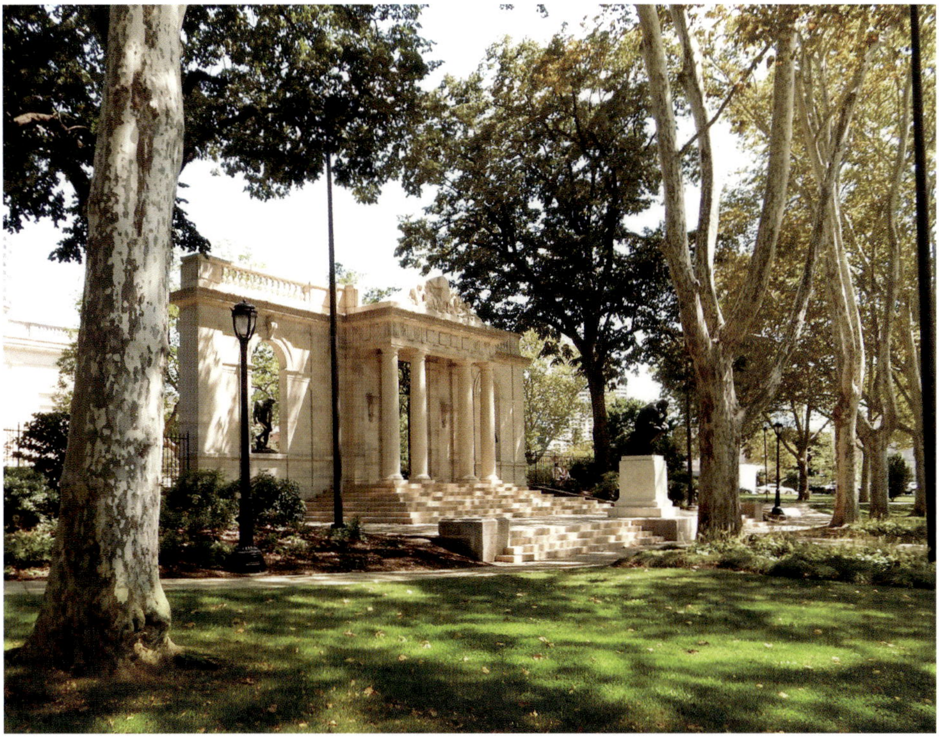

Figure 10.3 The Meudon Gate marks the entrance on the Benjamin Franklin Parkway to the Rodin Museum, the work of French architects Paul Philippe Crét and Jacques Gréber.

The Rodin Museum, which opened in 1929, came about because of a bequest from a local philanthropist and theater magnate. Jules Mastbaum (1872–1926) owned the largest chain of movie theaters in the world, having begun with a nickelodeon at Eighth and Market Streets in Philadelphia. By the 1920s, he had also built several of the largest and most glamorous movie palaces in his native city. In 1926, he approached Gréber to design a museum for his remarkable collection of the work of Auguste Rodin (1840–1917), some of whose sculptures he had initially exhibited in a number of his theaters. Soon after he engaged Gréber, Mastbaum died unexpectedly, leaving Philadelphia nearly 150 sculptures and casts of work by Rodin, one of the largest such collections outside Paris. Meanwhile, Gréber asked Cret to join him in designing the museum. In spite of disagreements during their collaboration, Gréber was gracious in the face of widespread praise when the building opened: "If the general composition and layout of the garden is my work, the building itself . . . ought to bear more the signature of Cret, than mine."[19] (See Figure 10.3.)

Visitors are greeted at the parkway entrance by the brooding bronze *The Thinker* before the facade of the classical Meudon Gate, so named to refer to Rodin's burial place at his villa in Meudon, Île-de-France, just outside Paris. Two niches in its wall hold Rodin pieces. Beyond the gate lies the formal garden, where gravel paths diverge past a reflecting pool and flower beds to a raised terrace and the Beaux-Arts-style museum at the far side. The bronze casting of *The Gates of Hell* on the doorway into the museum was the first ever done from the artist's plaster cast of the work and was installed here at the museum's opening in 1929. Large sculptural groupings flank the building to the rear of the garden.[20]

An abortive plan from 1921 might have completed some of Paul Cret's most ambitious visions for the parkway within the next few years. Philadelphia's leaders had decided to hold a world's fair in 1926 in honor of the sesquicentennial of the Declaration of Independence. Cret proposed making the parkway and adjoining land along the Schuylkill River the site of that exposition. His plan assumed the completion of new public buildings to become permanent institutions in the neighborhood as well as a number of temporary exhibition halls lining the boulevard from Logan Square to Fairmount. Although his proposal was endorsed by the Fairmount Park Commission, Philadelphia's Art Jury, and the city's leading newspapers, important members of the city's Republican machine held out for a largely undeveloped site, one from which some of them might profit personally, around marshy League Island in south Philadelphia. That site was eventually chosen for a world's fair that—plagued by delays in completing exhibition space, rainy days, and meager attendance—would be remembered as a failure.[21] Once the parkway was bypassed as the site for the sesquicentennial, the addition of new buildings along its route proceeded much more slowly.

In the 1930s, Gréber reflected on what had been accomplished with the construction of the parkway, and what it suggested about urban planning in his time. He regarded the planner as the effective coordinator of contributions from many disciplines, just as the medieval "maître d'oeuvre" was responsible for bringing together the work of the various building trades to construct Europe's great cathedrals. He also noted how property values had increased in Paris "a thousand-fold" as the result of Haussmann's projects, adding, "This principle has been applied quite recently to the creation of Fairmount Parkway, the green wedge of Fairmount Park in the heart of Philadelphia. And we do hope that, in spite of temporary hard times [his comments came during the Great Depression], the opportunity perhaps unique in the world, of carrying out its original layout will not be spoiled."[22] More than eight decades after Gréber expressed that hope, it is clear that even though the vision he and Cret together held was not fulfilled for many years—perhaps not entirely so to the present day—it has not been spoiled but continues to guide plans and visions for the parkway today, and no doubt will do so in the future as well. (See Figures 10.4 a and b.)

Philadelphia's homage to Parisian counterparts has become ever clearer from the time the parkway itself was completed in 1919. To this day, visitors from Paris remain struck by that resemblance.[23] Between 1927 and 1941, Philadelphia's tribute to the Place de la Concorde at Logan Square emerged from the construction of two new public buildings on the square's north side. The Free Library and Municipal (later, Family) Court buildings are closely modeled on the two great structures that anchor the Paris square: the Hotel de Crillon and French Maritime Ministry.[24] Their neoclassicism is echoed in the Franklin Institute on the north side of Logan Square at

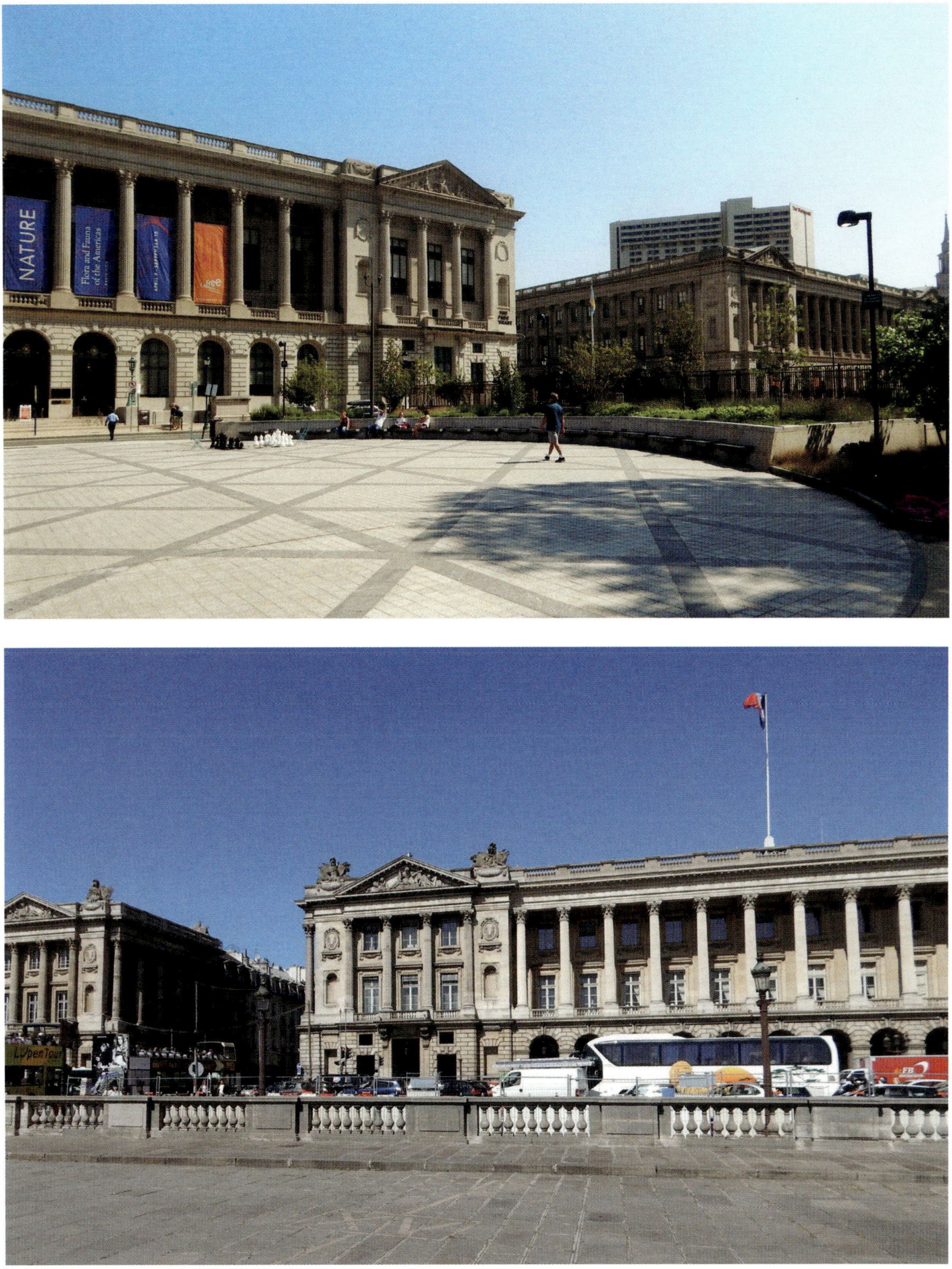

Figure 10.4a and **Figure 10.4b** The Free Library and Family Court building on Logan Square closely resemble the Hôtel de Crillon and Maritime Ministry on Paris's Place de la Concorde.

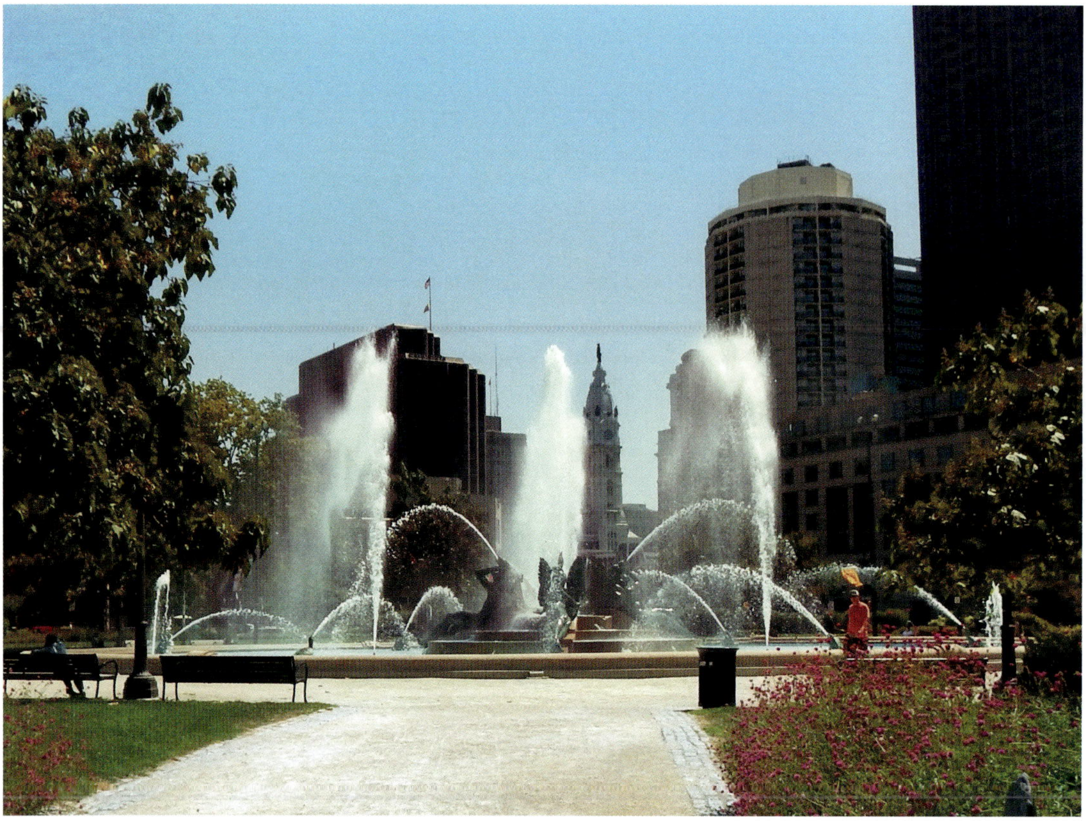

FIGURE 10.5 The Fountain of the Three Rivers, or Swann Fountain, is the centerpiece of Logan Square on the Benjamin Franklin Parkway. Its creator, Alexander S. Calder, studied at the École des Beaux-Arts in Paris.

Twentieth Street, and again in the School Administration Building just to its west, as well as in the neighboring Philadelphia Council headquarters of the Boy Scouts of America. Although none of these was designed by a French architect, their forms and civic purposes grow directly from the tenets of the French Beaux-Arts tradition.[25] As filtered through the City Beautiful movement that included building structures whose elegant forms might uplift citizens while housing functions to help educate them.

The central features of the Place de la Concorde are its two monumental fountains flanking an Egyptian obelisk, all of which were installed there between 1836 and 1840, during the reign of King Louis-Philippe. At Logan Square, the 1907 design by Cret and his associates had also placed an obelisk at the center, but that totem disappeared in Gréber's reworking of that plan, leaving a single monumental fountain in its place. The *Fountain of the Three Rivers* (more familiarly, the Swann Fountain) was installed in 1924. Like its two counterparts at Concorde, it pays tribute to nearby waterways—here the Delaware, Schuylkill, and Wissahickon.[26] (See Figure 10.5.)

The creator of the Swann Fountain, Alexander Stirling Calder (1870–1945), had also been trained at Paris's École des Beaux-Arts. This Calder was the son of the man whose bountiful sculpture, including the statue of William Penn, adorns City Hall, and who had studied in Paris as well early in his career. Directly in front of the Free Library on the north side of Logan Circle stands his Shakespeare Memorial, a large bronze depicting Hamlet (tragedy) and Touchstone (comedy), installed here in 1929. In the third generation, the grandson of the first Calder, also Alexander, but known as Sandy (1898–1976) would become the most famous artist in the family as the inventor of stabiles and mobiles.

His sister, in her biography of the family's three sculptors, argued that "it was the experience of Paris at a crucial, formative stage that puts its seal on the way each of these men approached his work."[27] Although Sandy was born just outside Philadelphia, he lived and worked for much of his life in France. In the early 1930s, his first acclaim came in Paris for his miniature circus of figures he created from wire and other materials, which earned him the sobriquet, *le roi du fil de fer* (the king of wire). As he later reported, "I got the first impulse for doing things my way in Paris."[28] It was there where he developed friendships with Fernand Léger, Jean Arp, LeCorbusier, Theo van Doesburg, and Piet Mondrian, and soon joined their group, which they called Abstraction-Création. After seeing his work, Marcel Duchamp arranged a Calder show in 1932 at Galerie Vignon near the Madeleine.[29] It was Duchamp who soon after gave the name "mobiles" to Calder's moving sculpture. According to a recent biographer, Calder became "the only American to be accepted on equal terms by artists of his radically innovative generation in Paris."[30]

There are still further resemblances between the Champs-Elysées and Philadelphia's Benjamin Franklin Parkway, as it was renamed in 1937. At the parkway's southeastern terminus, City Hall, with its clear references to the Louvre, is the focal point much like its counterpart in Paris; at the northwestern end, not the Arc de Triomphe but the neoclassical Philadelphia Museum of Art, rises at the summit of Fairmount. That building's inspiration is clearly Greek, not Roman, and Roman antecedents were more often a part of the Beaux-Arts vocabulary. Yet, it is very much a tribute to the Greek Revival tradition in the United States that had left so important a mark on public architecture in the young republic, when the reference to ancient Greek democracy was meant to inspire citizens of the new nation. Elements of that style, in fact, became the virtual visual symbols of American democracy, as is evident in the architecture of Washington, DC, and nearly every state capitol building in the nation.

In 1965, the Philadelphia Museum of Art acquired Sandy Calder's huge white mobile, *Ghost*, which hangs from the ceiling in the museum's great stair hall. From that vantage point, it is possible to look down the Benjamin Franklin Parkway to take in both A. S. Calder's "Swann Fountain" at Logan Square and A. M. Calder's statue of William Penn atop City Hall. A quip acknowledges the importance to the city of the three generations of Calder artists, noting that the view takes in the works of Father, Son, and Holy Ghost.[31] This trinity of Calders unquestionably makes them members of a Philadelphia pantheon, but with an overlay of Paris.

Where the northwest corner of Logan Square meets the greensward of the upper parkway, two granite and marble pylons flanking the boulevard commemorate the

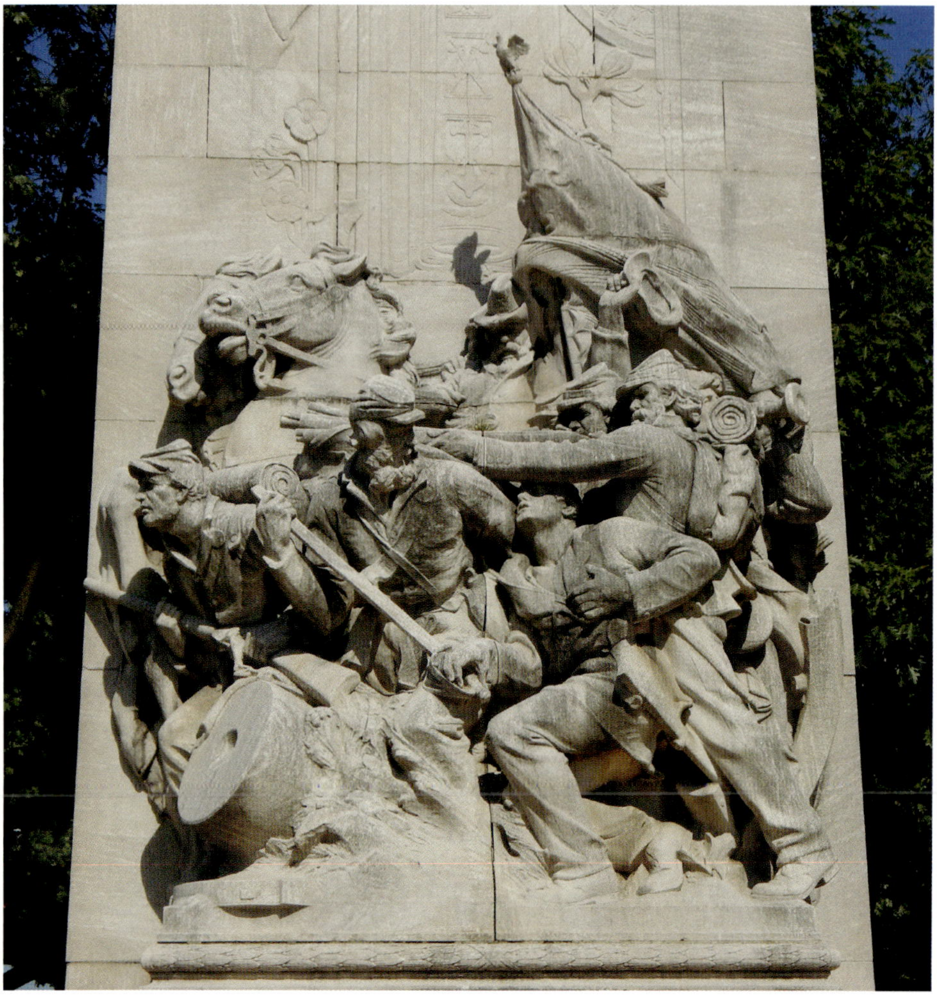

FIGURE 10.6 The Civil War Memorial by Hermon A. MacNeil consists of two pylons flanking the upper Benjamin Franklin Parkway above Logan Square. The relief sculptures are reminiscent of those on the sides of the central arch of Paris's Arc de Triomphe.

sacrifices of the soldiers and sailors of the Civil War. Their creator was the American sculptor, Hermon Atkins MacNeil (1866–1947), who had refined his artistry as a student at the École des Beaux-Arts in Paris from 1889–1891. He returned to Paris for further study ten years later. The swirls of heroic figures in his Civil War memorial, completed in 1927, have reminded some of the reliefs on each side of the central arch of the Arc de Triomphe in Paris.[32] Those four depictions of recent French history were done by three artists from 1833 to 1836 and would have been well known to MacNeil. His Civil War pylons may most resemble François Rude's *The Departure of the Volunteers* or *La Marseillaise*, which, when facing the arch from where the Champs-Elysées begins at L'Étoile, is the bas-relief on the right. (See Figure 10.6.)

Across the street to the north of the art museum, where the roadway sweeps around Fairmount from the end of the parkway into Kelly Drive, stands another reminder of the comparable district in Paris. A gilded equestrian statue of Joan of Arc riding into battle looms above the Twenty-Fifth Street intersection. The sculpture was installed at the eastern end of the Girard Avenue Bridge in 1890, but in 1959 it was moved to its current location facing the Fairmount acropolis (see Chapter 12).[33]

Although Paul Cret had collaborated with the architectural firms of Horace Trumbauer and Zantzinger and Borie in creating the bird's-eye view of the 1907 plan for the parkway, he played no role in devising the vast Grecian temple that would house the art museum. The Frenchman evidently made known his distaste for Trumbauer's work, which he apparently viewed as derivative in the way it appropriated the grand styles of the past with eclectic abandon, even though that was a practice that had already made Trumbauer rich as the designer of palatial mansions for "robber barons" of the Gilded Age. By 1907, Trumbauer had completed Widener's vast Lynnewood Hall and William Walsh Harrison's Grey Towers Castle, both in Philadelphia's northern suburbs and The Elms, perhaps the most extravagant summer "cottage" yet built in Newport, Rhode Island.[34]

Sure enough, the design for the Philadelphia Museum of Art produced by the Trumbauer firm is an unabashed, if huge, near replica of a Greek temple, or, more accurately, of several temple-like rectangular pavilions connected to form an E-shape embracing a central plaza in a configuration unknown in ancient Greece.[35] Nonetheless, its architects clearly were inspired by the acropolis of Athens.[36] While under construction from 1919 to 1928, the museum was known derisively to some Philadelphians as the "Greek garage," thanks in part to the fact that the two outer wings were built first to ensure that appropriations would be forthcoming to complete the central connecting concourse. Ever since it was completed, most observers have seen it as complementing, even if it does not incorporate, the more distinctive Beaux-Arts-derived flourishes of Cret's mature work. For nearly a century, its chaste neoclassical form atop Fairmount has provided an unforgettable image from every vantage point along Philadelphia's Parisian parkway. (See Figure 10.7.)

From the time it opened there in 1928, the Philadelphia Museum of Art has become one of the world's richest depositories of French art, starting with the purchase in the next year of the collection of a French art connoisseur, Edmond Foulc, containing some two hundred objects from the Gothic and Renaissance periods. Included was an exquisite sixteenth-century marble and alabaster choir screen from the chapel of the Château de Pagny. At the time, the Foulc acquisition was the largest single purchase ever made by a museum.[37]

Nearly eighty years later, in 2007, the Philadelphia Museum of Art expanded into the Ruth and Raymond G. Perelman Building across the Benjamin Franklin Parkway between Twenty-Fifth and Twenty-Sixth Streets. That Art Deco building was constructed in 1928 by the firm of Zantzinger and Borie, partners in the original parkway plan as well as that for the Philadelphia Museum of Art, to house an insurance company headquarters. To transform it for the museum, a long concourse, galleries, and a café were added across the back of the building, doubling its size. This building now houses

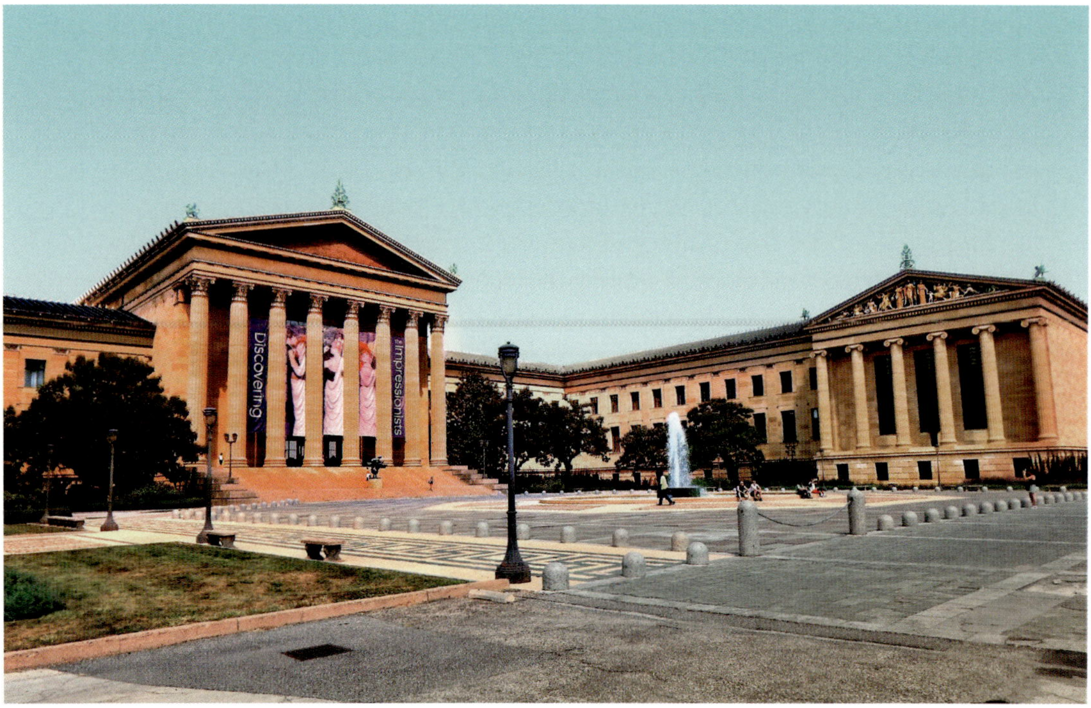

FIGURE 10.7 The Philadelphia Museum of Art crowns Fairmount, which acts as the northwestern terminus of the Benjamin Franklin Parkway.

the museum's library and administrative offices in addition to the new galleries. The opening of the Perelman Building followed the announcement in 2006 that the museum would launch a long-term project to expand its main building on Fairmount to provide some eighty thousand square feet of new public space. The plan produced by the renowned architect, Frank Gehry, does not disturb the familiar silhouette of the neoclassical museum but eventually will add some 30 percent more gallery space beneath the central plaza facing the parkway.[38] By 2019, construction was nearing completion on the first stage of the project, which reconfigures much of the space in the lower levels of the original building and provides access to the underground galleries to come.

In 2012, the Philadelphia Museum of Art was joined on the parkway by the new headquarters of the Barnes Foundation, whose collection of nineteenth- and early twentieth-century French art is perhaps the largest outside of Paris (for discussions of French art in all the parkway museums, see Chapters 8, 9, 11, and 12). The original headquarters, designed by Paul Cret and opened in the Philadelphia suburb of Lower Merion in 1925, features, in addition to the art that Albert Barnes had collected over many years, the cubist bas-reliefs he commissioned from Jacques Lipchitz for the building's portico entrance. Cret himself painted two landscape frescoes in the style of Cézanne for arched spaces in one gallery. The facility remains as the Barnes Foundation's school. The adjoining Cret-designed house for Albert Barnes is now the administration building. An arboretum surrounds the property.

The coming of the Barnes Foundation to the parkway brought another world-class cultural institution to the boulevard that had always been intended as just such a focal point.[39] Its move to the parkway was contentious because of Albert Barnes's well-known antipathy to Philadelphia's art establishment in his day and his insistence that his collection remain always in the building Cret had designed for it. A court decision famously allowed the Barnes trustees to move the collection but only on the condition that the interior galleries and arrangement of the artwork conform exactly to the Barnes-Cret arrangement of galleries at the Merion campus.[40] As a result, Paul Cret's interior design for the Barnes Foundation lives on in its new headquarters on the parkway.[41] (See Figure 10.8.)

At about the same time that the Barnes Foundation's new quarters were being built, the city of Philadelphia launched a major renovation of the upper parkway to improve and provide greater access to its underused spaces, calm traffic, and carry out as much as possible of what remained undone from the district Cret and Gréber had envisioned originally. Because the surrounding area had become increasingly residen-

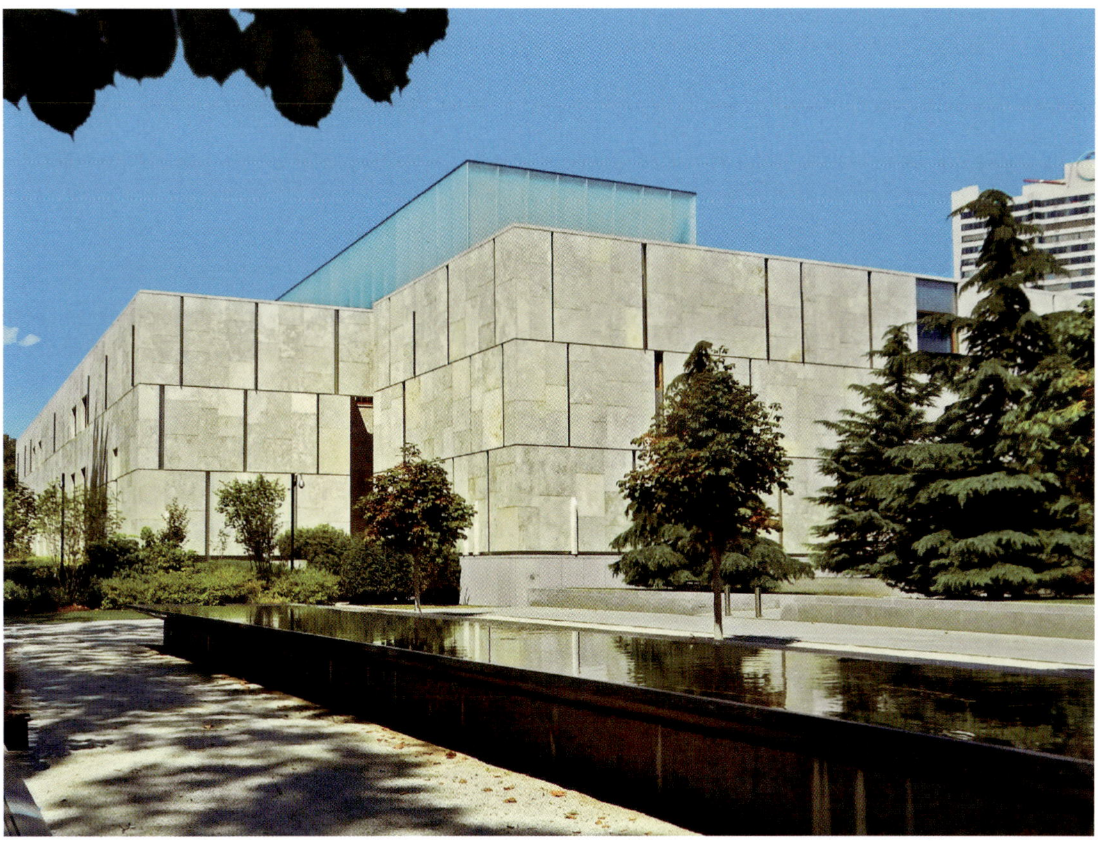

FIGURE 10.8 The Barnes Foundation moved to its new headquarters on the Benjamin Franklin Parkway in 2012. There it houses one of the world's largest collections of nineteenth- and early twentieth-century French art.

tial in recent decades, much of that effort was to enhance the parkway's open spaces as parkland and to improve access for pedestrians. Even the Eakins Oval at the foot of Fairmount was transformed into a pleasure ground in summer. Cret was honored with the creation of the Café Cret at Sixteenth Street and the parkway, where light refreshments and tourist information were available.[42] The triangular plot had remained empty since the decision by the American Philosophical Society in the 1930s not to move its headquarters to a building Cret had designed for the society's new headquarters at that site. (See Figures 10.9 a and b.)

These early twenty-first century developments on and around the parkway are remarkable in several respects. First of all, they are a response to the revitalization of the city's urban center after decades of a decline in its commercial and tax base when the flight to suburbs had been the norm. Like other northeastern cities, Philadelphia has not only stemmed a half century of population loss but begun to grow again, particularly in and around its downtown core, whose residential population has also increased in the first decades of the new century. As we have noted, new parks and amenities along the parkway are, in part, a response to that growth in population in nearby neighborhoods. In addition, in recent years the parkway itself has still proven to be, as from the time it was completed, a vitally important artery serving Philadelphia. It remains a useful and attractive avenue leading from the city's heart into one of the nation's greatest urban parks and on to the city's western suburbs. It is the first link in a chain that knits together the finest vistas within and of the city. Finally, it now comes closer than ever before to reaching its creators' goal of becoming the locus of the region's most important civic and cultural institutions. Its conception as half park and half avenue for civic buildings has kept it from acquiring the kind of high-end commercial glamor of the Champs-Elysées. But, like its Paris counterpart, it is a primary destination both for residents and visitors, and more so today than ever before.[43] Moreover, the Benjamin Franklin Parkway is now increasingly connected to the Broad Street Avenue of the Arts, so that these two major avenues leading to City Hall should continue to showcase the city's cultural offerings and give birth to still more.[44]

Paul Cret himself left additional important landmarks in Philadelphia, starting with a public park that he transformed into a Beaux-Arts jewel. As a direct result of his 1907 plan for the parkway, he was hired by the Fairmount Park Commission and the Rittenhouse Square Improvement Association to redesign that original square from William Penn's plan for the city. By the end of the nineteenth century, Rittenhouse Square was the center of Philadelphia's most affluent residential neighborhood, one that had grown and flourished in the aftermath of the Civil War.

The landscaping scheme that Cret's plans brought into being between 1913 and 1918 remains almost completely in place a century later.[45] Pedestrian traffic is directed through the square on walkways forming an X from each corner. The route leading from the northeast—the direction of City Hall—to the southwest passes around both sides of a long, narrow oval adorned with plants, flowers, and sculpture. As it

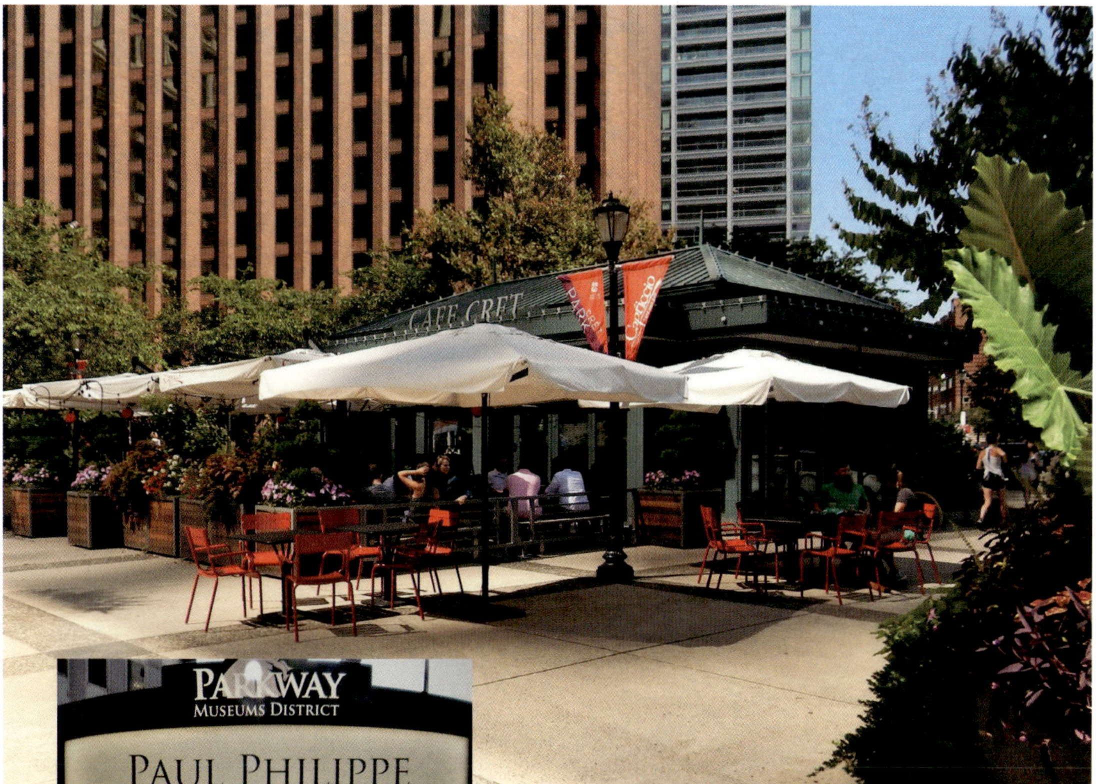

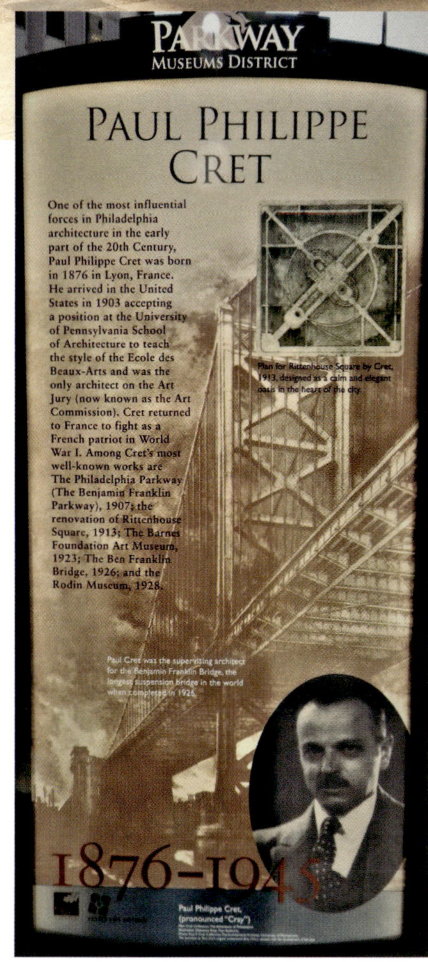

FIGURE 10.9A and **FIGURE 10.9B** This casual restaurant at Sixteenth Street and the Benjamin Franklin Parkway honors Paul P. Cret, the principal architect of Philadelphia's grandest boulevard.

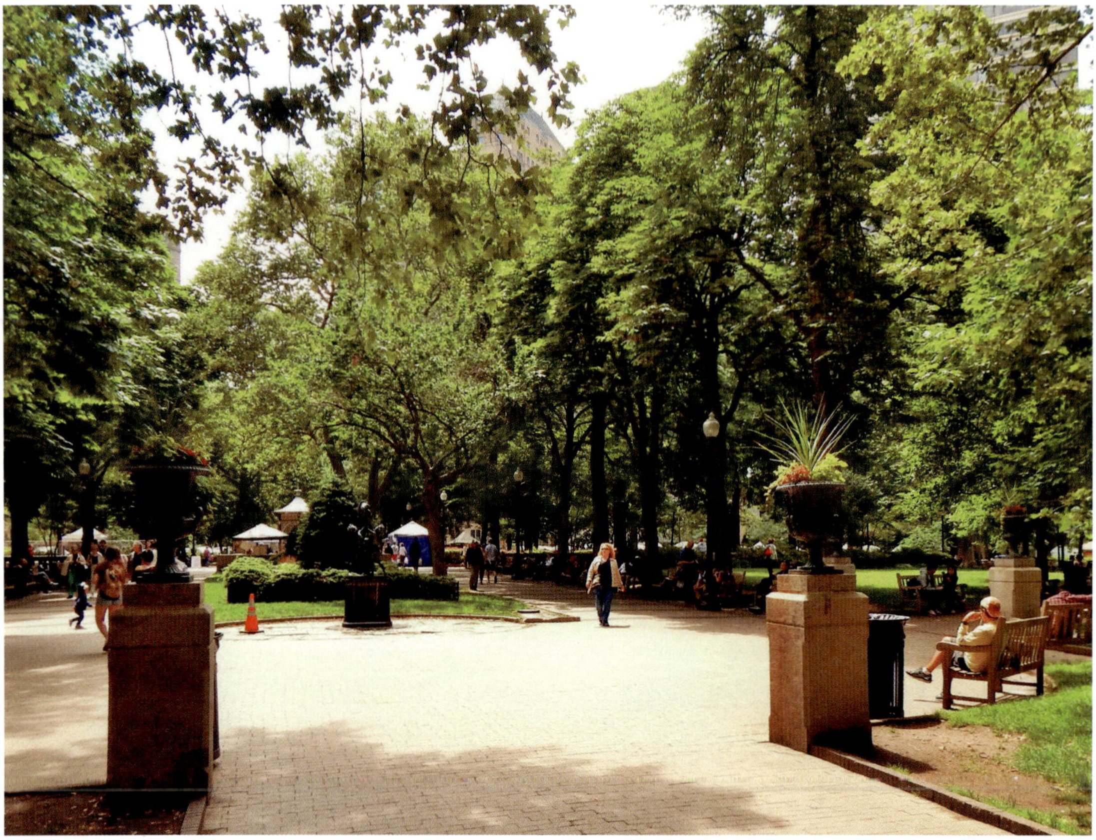

FIGURE 10.10 The architectural features and landscape plan of Philadelphia's Rittenhouse Square are those Paul P. Cret designed for the square's renovation between 1913 and 1918.

approaches the center, the double walkway swells and crosses through a much broader oval that lies across the other axis. A low stone balustrade encloses the wide central plaza that is created where the two ellipses meet. A pool and fountain, which Cret designed in conjunction with Joe Allen of Enfield Pottery and Tile Works, are tucked into one curved end of the wide oval, a flower bed with boxwood into the other. A popular sculpture among those plantings is the bronze *Lion Crushing a Serpent* by the nineteenth-century French sculptor, Antoine Louis Barye.[46] At the very center of the plaza, a Victorian sentry box today stands guard. Another path encircles the ellipse near the square's outer boundaries for walkers whose only aim is to stroll within the park; walkways arc away from it toward the central plaza and park entrances. Numerous benches line all the walks; scattered pieces of sculpture are landmarks. The square remains an elegantly refined example of Beaux-Arts principles of design. (See Figure 10.10.)

A landmark on the northwest side of the square at Walnut Street is the Church of the Holy Trinity, which opened its doors in 1859 to Episcopalian worshippers. The pastor of Holy Trinity from 1862 to 1869 was Phillips Brooks, an ardent preacher against slavery, who is best remembered today as the author of the lyrics for the Christmas favorite, "O Little Town of Bethlehem." Among the notable stained glass windows added to the church's sanctuary late in the nineteenth century is a pair in the middle of the north wall, to the right when entering from the narthex. This depiction of Christ with Mary and Martha was the work of the noted French artist, another product of the École des Beaux-Arts, Luc-Olivier Merson, who also created the mosaic in the chancel vault of the Basilica of the Sacred Heart (Basilique du Sacré-Coeur) on Paris's Montmartre.[47]

During the same years when Cret was refashioning Rittenhouse Square, he was also commissioned to create a new memorial at Valley Forge. The result was his National Memorial Arch, which resembles Paris's Arc de Triomphe but that Cret described as a simplified version of Rome's Arch of Titus—itself the prototype for the Paris landmark. Cret's monument, constructed from 1914 to 1917, memorializes the eighteenth-century soldiers and officers of the Continental Army who fought for America's independence. In France, starting soon after the conclusion of World War I, Cret's legacy of war memorials is extensive. They began with that erected in the village of Chamery in memory of Lieutenant Quentin Roosevelt, the twenty-year-old son of Theodore Roosevelt, who was killed when his plane was shot down here during that war. Others were sponsored by the American Battlefield Monuments Commission to mark other fallen Americans from that conflict.[48] During his wartime service in France, Cret had been brought to the attention of General John J. Pershing, commander of the American Expeditionary Force on the western front. It was Pershing who recommended Cret for the Roosevelt memorial, also endorsing him for the Battlefield Monuments projects that followed.

As his style matured, Cret drew from modernism as well as the tradition in which he was trained. He named it the New Classicism. It simplified the Beaux-Arts approach, stripping down the classical orders while maintaining an emphasis on proportion, balance, and symmetry.[49] After World War I, Cret received many important commissions for work around the city and the nation. In center city Philadelphia, two outstanding examples of his mature style are his Integrity Trust Company Building (1929), on Walnut between Fifteenth and Sixteenth Streets, and the Federal Reserve Bank (1932) at 925 Chestnut Street. By the time those buildings came into being, Cret's New Modernism was beginning to spread across much of Europe—and, ironically, was adopted in support of political ideologies that ran counter to his own.[50] That irony was so great as to border on the tragic when one considers that Cret and the American modernists he inspired considered the monumentality they sought for public spaces to be inherently democratic. (See Figure 10.11.)

Ten years after he was named chief architect of the Philadelphia Zoo in 1930, Cret designed the Pachyderm House in the style of a mammoth Pennsylvania barn with modernist touches. That structure was converted into the Children's Zoo in 2006. His 1940 design for a chemistry building at the University of Pennsylvania

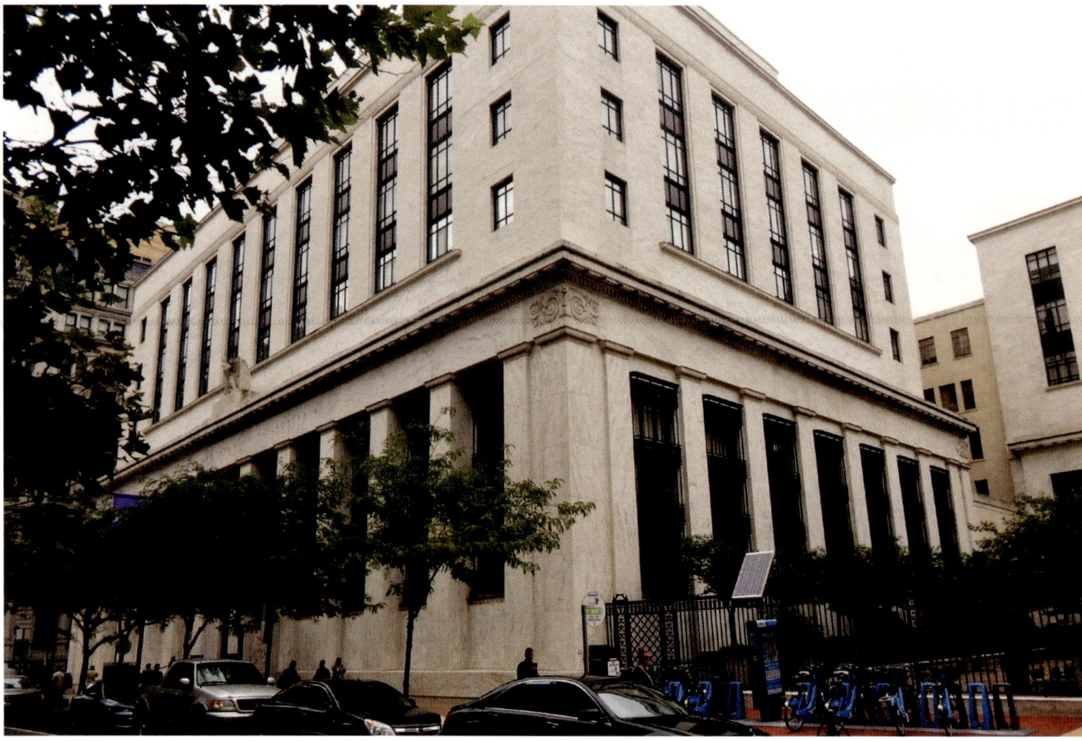

FIGURE 10.11 The Federal Reserve Bank of Philadelphia exemplifies Paul Cret's new classicism. It dates from 1932.

remains as the Cret Wing of today's Chemistry Laboratories. His two towering Philadelphia landmarks, however, are both monumental bridges. The Benjamin Franklin Bridge (1922–1926), which spans the Delaware from central Philadelphia to Camden, New Jersey, is the principal entrance to downtown Philadelphia from the east. When this suspension bridge was completed at the time of the U.S. sesquicentennial in 1926, it held the longest single span of any bridge in the world. As the structure's architect, Cret worked alongside the chief engineer, Ralph Modjeski, a Polish immigrant to America who had also trained in Paris. The Henry Avenue Bridge (1930–1932) over Wissahickon Creek towers over every traveler on Lincoln Drive. Its enormous central arch flanked by multiple smaller arches makes it a landmark for those passing between downtown Philadelphia and Germantown and Chestnut Hill.[51] Closer to center city in Fairmount Park is Cret's design for the three terraces bordering the Schuylkill of the Ellen Phillips Samuel Memorial, which showcases prize-winning sculptures from international contests sponsored by the city in 1933, 1940, and 1949.[52]

As these varied and enduring projects attest, Cret had become the designer par excellence of Philadelphia's built landscape during the last decades of his life. He left many more notable structures elsewhere in the nation and in France. Additionally, as a professor at the University of Pennsylvania—where he was voted the university's most popular teacher as early as 1910—he trained generations of architects, many of whom became notable in their own right, who carried on his legacy. In 1938, Cret's architectural accomplishments led the American Institute of Architecture to award him its most distinctive honor, the gold medal. As an important figure in Philadelphia, Cret also contributed to the welfare especially of the local French community. During the 1920s, he served as president of the French Benevolent Society, the charitable organization that, since 1793, had assisted French people in the area who were in need through no fault of their own. By Cret's day, one of the society's chief forms of assistance was to provide coal to heat the homes of those without the means to buy it. The society also owned properties to generate income for its endowment.[53]

At the time he was chosen to design the final plan for the Benjamin Franklin Parkway, Jacques Gréber was already setting the standard in the Philadelphia area for elegant, French-inspired landscapes, an accomplishment that, as we have noted, is what garnered him the commission for the parkway. The gardens he designed for Edward T. Stotesbury's Whitemarsh Hall in 1916 covered 275 acres and featured a mile-long axial vista from the main house in the style of the formal geometry of the grounds at Versailles. In 1922, the man who had led France as its president throughout World War I, Georges Clemenceau, was a guest of the Stoteburys at Whitemarsh and remarked on how the garden reminded him of that below the great French palace in which, several years earlier, he had participated in writing the peace treaty at the war's conclusion.[54] One authority has said of the Whitemarsh Hall gardens that "they may have been the finest example of French classical landscape art in America."[55]

Formal, French-style gardens were one thing, but other wealthy Philadelphians in the period sometimes used grand or romantic French houses as the inspiration for the design of their homes. An example that might have sprung from a storybook was Laverock Farm, just beyond Philadelphia's northern boundary in Montgomery County. The original house, built in 1895 by an investment banker, Arthur E. Newbold, was transformed in the next generation by his son, Arthur Jr., who had inherited the property. He informed his architect, Arthur Ingersoll Meigs, that he wanted the estate to serve as a working farm. Meigs, as a captain in the U.S. Army in World War I, had participated in the Aisne-Marne offensive and had been deeply affected by the destruction of simple farmhouses and villages in that campaign. He proposed a mock French village on Newbold's estate as a setting for the livestock—mainly sheep and horses—the owner wished to keep there. While the estate was reshaped from 1919 to 1925, the main house was enlarged into a near replica of a Norman Revival manor house.[56]

The fanciful result was widely acclaimed, and, in 1925, Meigs received the Gold Medal for Excellence in Design by the Architectural League of New York. Yet, it also had its critics. In one contemporary review, Lewis Mumford described Laverock

Farm as a case of "architectural anaesthesia." He added, "The weakness of the romantic architect is that he is employed in creating an environment into which people may escape from a sordid workaday world, whereas the real problem of architecture is to remake the workaday world so that people will not wish to escape from it."[57] Meanwhile, some wags were describing such escapist domestic architecture as "Wall Street Pastoral." During the decade of the 1920s, grand Norman-inspired dwellings became the rage in the Philadelphia neighborhoods of Mount Airy and Chestnut Hill. They include a cluster known as the French Village, whose architect was a former student of Cret, Robert McGoodwin, and George Howe's High Hollow, the design for which may have been inspired by the Château de Chantilly north of Paris. Both architects had also been students at the École des Beaux-Arts.[58] Escapist or not, the French-inspired architecture that became so popular in the region during the decade after America's participation in World War I surely also reflects the participation of a number of its practitioners in that conflict. However difficult it was to endure the many months of trench warfare in northeastern France, it allowed American soldiers, including future architects, to appreciate and absorb the built environment around them.

One of the grandest estates in the region arose on the outskirts of Wilmington, Delaware. Its creator, Alfred I. du Pont (1864–1935), came from old money by American standards, that of the du Pont family that had immigrated to the region in 1800, where they founded what would become an industrial empire.[59] In 1909–1910, Alfred, the great-great-grandson of the patriarch Pierre S. du Pont, created a virtual château in the style of the late eighteenth century as a gift to his second wife. He named it Nemours for the French village that became part of the family name when the founder was ennobled by Louis XVI in 1784. Unlike the lost baronial mansions of P.A.B. Widener and Edward Stotesbury, Nemours has been restored as a museum, which reveals to the public of today the opulent lifestyle of its original owner. The mansion itself contains one hundred and two rooms and is framed by the largest formal French gardens in North America, some three hundred acres. They are landscaped to resemble the grounds surrounding the Petit Trianon at Versailles. The house's furnishings reflect periods from the eighteenth to the early twentieth centuries and include a great many French pieces. Among several examples of French statuary in the gardens are two life-size likenesses of elk, the work of Prosper Lecourtier (1855–1944); they stand guard beside the Long Walk.[60]

Paul Cret, that French architect whose greatest impact was in America, and whose authenticity was never in doubt, left a lasting reminder of architecture's importance: "If there is any truth in the saying that every people has the government it deserves, it is even truer that every civilization, every race, every epoch finds itself reflected as in a mirror in its architecture."[61] For Philadelphia in the first decades of the twentieth century, much of its architecture and new urban aesthetic strongly reflected the heritage of France. Two first-rate architects, reared and trained in France, led the way with their designs for a new urban masterpiece. Their Benjamin Franklin Parkway

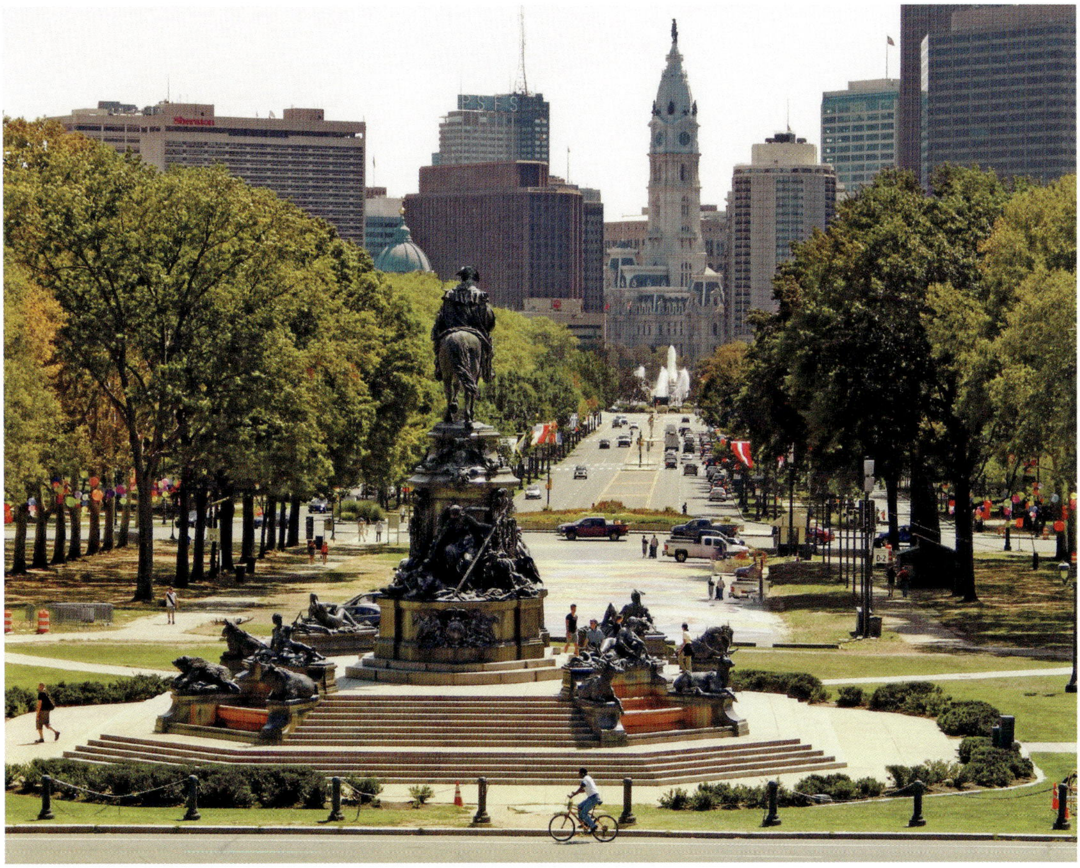

FIGURE 10.12 From the art museum at Fairmount, the view down the Benjamin Franklin Parkway takes in the Washington Monument in the foreground, the Swann Fountain at Logan Square, and City Hall's tower in the distance.

was both inspired by and radiated the presence of a French patrimony in the region's built environment. (See Figure 10.12.)

The architectural critic Paul Goldberger has named the Benjamin Franklin Parkway the greatest achievement of its kind in America. Unlike the City Beautiful landmarks of other cities, which are mostly individual buildings or groups of buildings centered about a plaza, the parkway is, in his terms, like a river, enhancing both the idea and the reality of connecting distinct urban neighborhoods.[62] It accomplishes beautifully the goal first imagined soon after the Civil War: a monumental boulevard from the city's governmental and commercial heart to its great urban park, thereby uniting the contrasting but essential elements of advanced urban life.

[11]

Moving into Modernism

The last impressionist group exhibition occurred in Paris in 1886 but the movement debuted in America when Paul Durand-Ruel exhibited nearly three hundred impressionist works in New York City at the invitation of James Sutton and the American Art Association. The show had a lasting impact on the artists and art market in America. The first American impressionist work to be exhibited publicly in Philadelphia took place in 1889 when Childe Hassam's *Grand Prix Day* was shown at the Pennsylvania Academy. Hassam had lived in Paris and studied at the Académie Julian between 1886 and 1889, eventually adapting the impressionist vision and tonality to his own way of seeing. Two years later, one of Monet's works found its way to Philadelphia in the Pennsylvania Academy show and, in 1892, four works by Monet were on display. The Pennsylvania Academy's faculty during the 1890s featured European-trained artists such as William Merritt Chase, Cecilia Beaux, and Robert Vonnoh. Along with Thomas Anschutz, Eakins's successor at the academy who encouraged his students to paint outdoors, the academy became a leading hub of American impressionism.[1] Students at the Academy continued to migrate to Paris, as had Thomas Eakins, Mary Cassatt, and Henry Ossawa Tanner, to study with French masters, visit the museums, experience the Salon, and attempt to get their work exhibited and sold. Artists such as Edward Redfield (1869–1965), William Schofield (1867–1944), and Daniel Garber (1880–1958), all of whom studied at the Pennsylvania Academy, became known as the Pennsylvania impressionists and settled around New Hope after spending time in France. Robert Henri (1865–1929) and William Glackens (1870–1938), both products of the Pennsylvania Academy, lived in Paris and returned there often during their careers. These artists are just a few who studied together in Philadelphia and returned from France to draw on what they learned abroad to advance painting in America. They knew each other, often traveled together, and were united by their concern for creating an art that was authentically American.

Art critic and painter Guy Pène du Bois attached the term Pennsylvania impressionists to the artists in a 1915 article for the periodical *Arts and Decoration*. Du Bois contrasted the aristocratic Boston impressionists such as Edmund Tarbell, who focused on figure paintings and urban themes, with the Pennsylvania School whose members demonstrated a vigorous, unsentimental approach to subject matter. Du Bois characterized the Pennsylvanians as more authentically American in their vernacularizing of the French impressionist aesthetic.[2] Redfield and Schofield can be considered the rural counterpart to the urban focus of The Eight, sometimes known as the Ashcan School, discussed later in this chapter.[3]

In 1898, Edward Redfield and William Lathrop moved to Centerville, Pennsylvania, in Bucks County. Centerville's convenient location close to Philadelphia and New York facilitated their continued exposure to French and American impressionist works and more importantly, offered countless beautiful vistas as sources of subject matter. Both Redfield and Lathrop had spent time studying and painting in France, grafting what they had learned onto a uniquely American voice. They soon attracted other young artists to the New Hope area through their growing reputation, successful sales, and presence on important art juries. As Brian Peterson has observed, the Bucks County painters were unified by their love of the local landscape rather than a rigorous adherence to any formalized group aesthetic.[4] Returning home, Redfield and Lathrop settled in the New Hope area, pursuing their individual style and manner of working as they employed the impressionist syntax and its conceptual underpinnings to picture their surroundings. For them, the Delaware River valley could provide as many scenic pleasures as the banks of the Seine.

Pennsylvania impressionism's definition can perhaps best be found in the works of Edward Redfield, considered the central figure of the group.[5] Guy Pène du Bois claimed that the "Pennsylvania school born in the Academy at Philadelphia or in the person of Edward W. Redfield is a very concise expression of the simplicity of our language and of the prosaic nature of our sight."[6] Redfield attended the Pennsylvania Academy from 1887 to 1889. Similar to many of his classmates, he journeyed to France and attended classes at the Académie Julian in Paris, where he studied with William-Adolphe Bouguereau (1825–1905). However, Redfield declared that it was not possible to learn painting in art schools. He claimed nature as his greatest teacher, as "real art comes from feeling."[7] When he was in France, he declared that the old masters in the Louvre attracted him less than the contemporary works of Claude Monet, Edgar Degas, and Camille Pissarro.

Although trained to paint the figure in a classical manner at the Pennsylvania Academy and in Bouguereau's studio, Redfield devoted his career to landscape, a genre that ranked beneath history painting and portraiture. America accorded an increased importance to landscape as it imaged the western frontier and expansion of the states with its vast prospects as a visual image of Manifest Destiny. Thomas Cole and the Hudson River School depicted American scenery in epically sized canvases that celebrated the

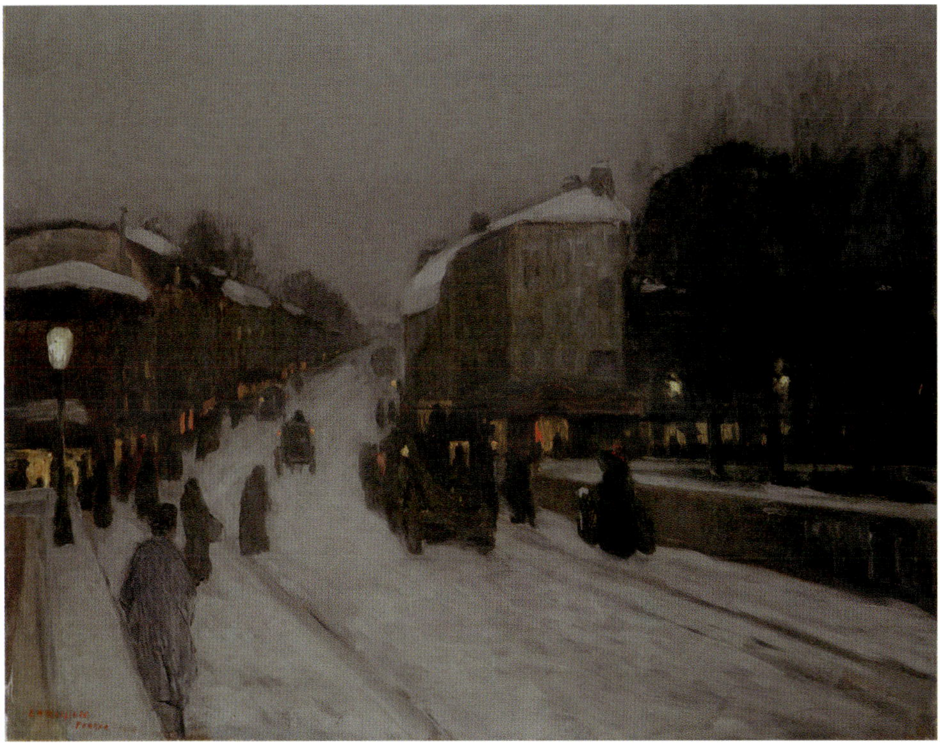

Figure 11.1 Edward Redfield, *France*, 1898–99. Oil on canvas, 31¼ × 40 3/16 in. (Photography © Terra Foundation for American Art, Chicago. Daniel J. Terra Collection, 1992.126)

grandeur and natural beauty of the nation. Their idyllic views optimistically promoted the idea of man living in harmony with the environment. After the Civil War, the Barbizon School influenced painters such as George Inness whose poetic interpretations of nature inaugurated the Tonalist movement with a loose brushwork that evoked subtle light effects to capture nature's various moods. Only in 1881 did the Pennsylvania Academy award a prize to the best landscape painting shown at their yearly exhibition. Landscape artists had to wait until 1902 until an annual prize was guaranteed. American collectors in the latter part of the nineteenth century eagerly purchased Barbizon art, supported by the advocacy of Durand-Ruel in Paris, London, and New York.

In 1891, Redfield moved to France and settled in the village of Bois-le-Roi in the forest of Fontainebleau. He became fascinated by snow scenes and began painting outdoors. He made the decision to abandon portraiture in order to dedicate his art to landscape. In a later interview he explained his rationale: "With landscape, if I can make it good enough, there are many who will appreciate it. Portrait painting must please the subject as a general thing—or no pay! It's a hired man's job!"[8] Redfield exhibited twice at the Paris Salon. He had his first acceptance in 1891 with a snow scene of the forest of Fontainebleau, and in 1893 he had a nocturne on display. He and his wife settled in America but returned to France in 1898 after the tragic death of their young daughter who was killed by a swinging barn door. His bleak rendering of a gray Paris street that year with its figures turned away from the viewer, its gray pall of weather cloaking the scene, communicates the evident grief he was experiencing. (See Figure 11.1.)

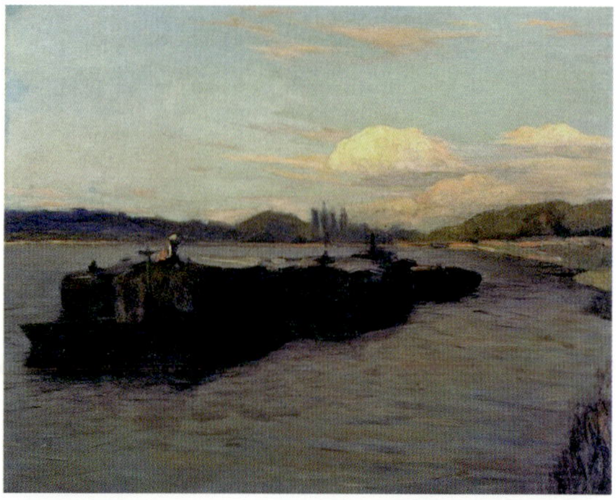

FIGURE 11.2 Edward Redfield, *Evening on the Seine*, ca. 1899. Oil on canvas, 81.28 × 101.6 cm (32 × 40 in.). (Private Collection)

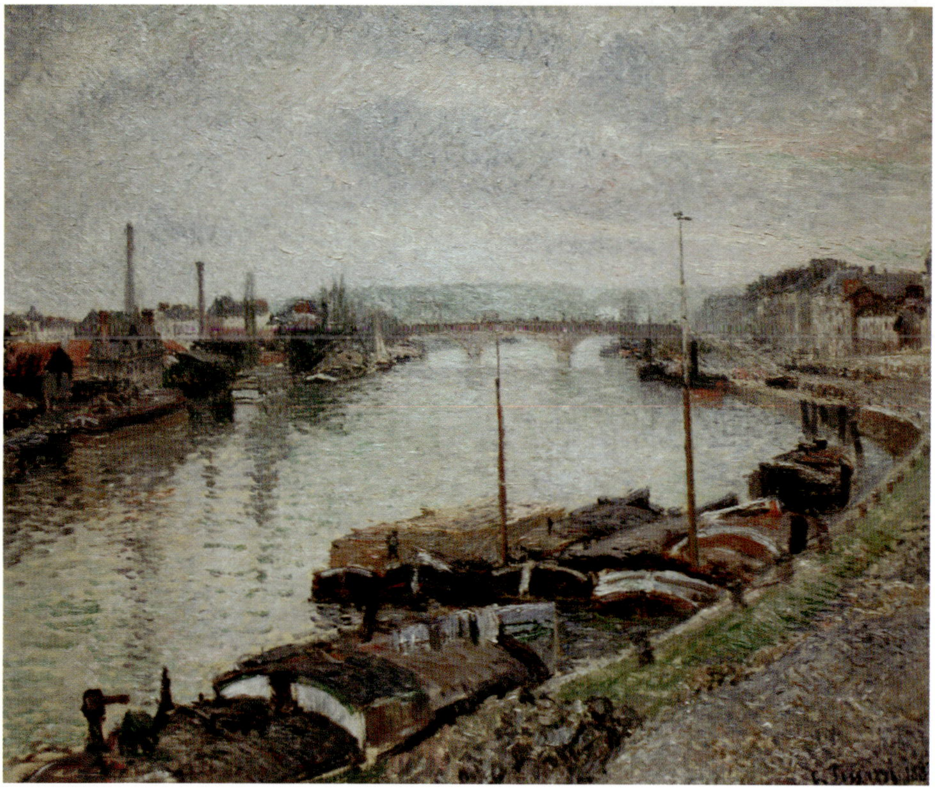

FIGURE 11.3 Camille Pissarro, *The Stone Bridge and Barges at Rouen*, 1883. (Columbus Museum of Art)

Redfield and his wife settled in the village of Alfort on the Seine, not far from Paris, where they stayed until the summer of 1900. Redfield's 1899 *Evening on the Seine* (see Figure 11.2) captures the effect of the setting sun's reflections on the water and bears a resemblance in motif to one of Camille Pissarro's (1830–1903) works, *The Stone Bridge and Barges at Rouen* (see Figure 11.3), with its focus on river commerce and the adaptation of a broken brushstroke. Both artists avoid any sentimentality or notion of the picturesque, with their motifs connoting industrial work. The massive brown hulk of Redfield's barge draws the attention of the viewer as it sits in the water like a giant animal at rest after a hard day's work. Redfield's interest centers on communicating the simple truths of the scene at a certain time of day. He once said, "When I first began to work, most artists used models in studios. What I wanted to do was to go outdoors and capture the look of a scene, whether it was a brook or a bridge, as it looked on a certain day."[9] This statement firmly allies Redfield with the impressionist aesthetic, and he remained true to it throughout his productive career.

Redfield's wife gave birth to a son in 1900 and the couple returned to America that summer. He found that the barges on the canals on the river in New Hope could be used as a pictorial motif just as easily as the ones on the Seine, and he settled into his signature style. Redfield was less attached to the specifics of a place than he was to record his immediate perception of a motif with his forceful brushwork. As Brian Peterson has observed, Redfield's canvases "are rarely invested with the spiritual intensity that comes from the inward contemplation of objects and one's relation to them."[10] This becomes evident in a comparison of Redfield's *Hillside at Center Bridge* (see Figure 11.4) with an early work from 1870 by Paul Cézanne called *L'Estaque, Melting Snow* (see Figure 11.5). Cézanne's trees writhe with baroque imbalance as they teeter on the hillside under a glowering sky. Cézanne infuses his work with a barely controlled passion whose intensity is enforced by the scudding clouds and the precipitous decline of the hill. Redfield adopts a similar viewpoint on a hillside, but the firmly rooted tree in the upper left corner of the painting provides a needed stability, while the view of the river with its horizontal bridge and its softly rising plain on the other side of the banks secures a visual foothold so that the spectator can take in the view of Center Bridge. Redfield aimed at a direct transcription of outward appearances rather than an expressionist view of a translated sensibility. He has captured a specific moment in early spring when the light is soft and blond. The next day this scene will look different as more of the snow will have disappeared. Redfield counted on, and succeeded in, giving us the imprint of the passing moment in a transitional season, fixing its sensations in pale pigmented color that remained true to Pennsylvania spring light.

In spirit, Redfield was closest to Monet who devoted himself to painting outdoors in order to capture the transient effects of light and atmosphere. Monet complained that the sun set so quickly that his hand could not keep up with his eye. In his later years, he worked on multiple canvases at once, painting on one and then advancing to the next as the light changed. Conversely, Redfield worked on one canvas at a time outdoors but challenged himself to capture the sensations of the landscape and its light "at one go," as he said.[11] If needed, he would strap his canvas to a tree on windy days so that he could finish his work on site. Snow scenes first attracted Redfield in 1891 when he lived in the village of Brolles near Fontainebleau, an interest he shared with Monet who painted almost 140 snow scenes, attracted by the colored shadows created by the changing light conditions. Monet's *Snow at Argenteuil* sacrificed detail as the artist blanketed his scene in tones of gray and blue to create a hazy atmospheric

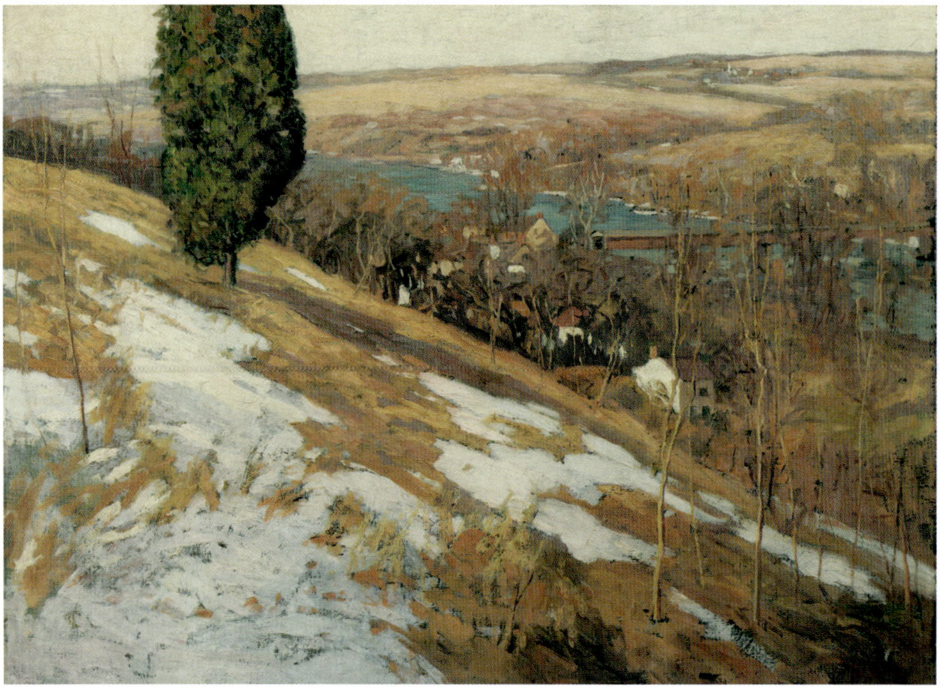

FIGURE 11.4 Edward Redfield, *Hillside at Centre Bridge*, 1904. Oil on canvas, 36 × 50 in. (91.4 × 127 cm). (Photo Credit: The Art Institute of Chicago / Art Resource, NY)

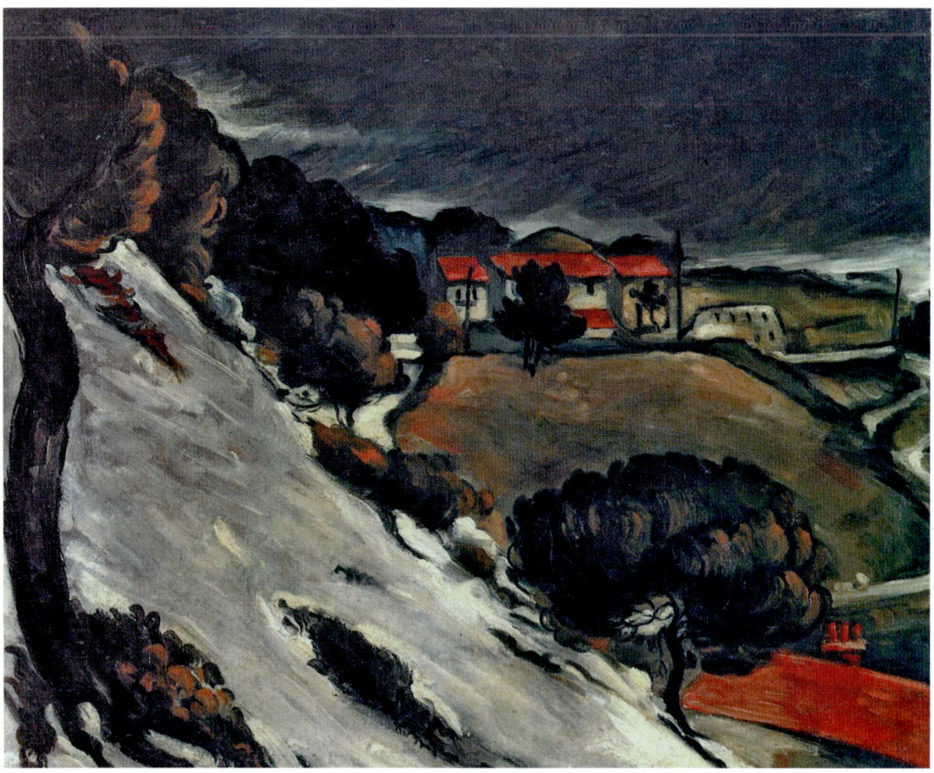

FIGURE 11.5 Paul Cézanne, *L'Estaque, Melting Snow*, ca. 1870. Oil on canvas, 73 × 92 cm (28.7 × 36.2 in.). (Zurich, Foundation E. G. Bührle)

effect of snow and fog. (See Figure 11.6.) Redfield's *Late Afternoon* accentuated the long blue shadows of the sun on the snow to denote the crisp frosty feel of winter weather. (See Figure 11.7.) Both sought in different ways to communicate the cold atmosphere of the season and avoided the traditional black shadows that academic art deemed realistic. Redfield's interest centered on communicating the simple truths of the scene at a certain time of day.

In 1909, the French government purchased their first American landscape, Redfield's *Canal in Winter* for the Luxembourg Museum. Frank Jewett Mather praised its American truthfulness, its "crisp, direct naturalism" that has been "saved from banality by thoughtful selection and elimination."[12] Redfield's work drew its inspiration from what he had learned in France, but his truth to vision, his vigorous touch, and his freedom from academic artifice were authentically American. What Redfield absorbed from France, he also individualized with a native creativity of style by the forceful application of his brush. J. Nilsen Laurvik was correct when he wrote: "Among the men who have done the most to infuse an authentic note of nationalism into contemporary American art, Edward Redfield occupies a prominent position. He is the standard bearer of that progressive group of painters who are glorifying American landscape painting with a veracity and force that is astonishing in the eyes of the Old World, long accustomed to servile aping of their standards."[13]

Pissarro remained one of Redfield's favorite artists whose devotion to visual truth was so great that he once declared that the Louvre should be burned down. This radical statement came from his belief that the return to nature could be successful only by "observing nature with our own modern temperament."[14] Richard Brettell observed that Pissarro preferred the little-known and informal aspects of landscape, because he wanted to avoid close competition with other landscape painters.[15] Pissarro's *Orchard* from 1872 convincingly portrays the temperate sunshine on a spring day where peasants gather the produce. (See Figure 11.8.) Pissarro varied the tempo of his brush, using short flecked strokes of white paint dabbed on the canvas to suggest the white blooms on the trees while he overlaid broader broken strokes of paint over the surface of the field to depict shadows, shrubbery, and harvested soil. Redfield's painting of *Plum Blossoms* exudes a similar warmth of the spring season. (See Figure 11.9.) He pushed the figure working in the field to the background so as to privilege the tender shoots of growing crops emerging from their regularly planted rows. Redfield's kinship with Pissarro most likely was rooted in a shared love of the rustic environment, the luminous spring light, and devotion to painting outdoors. Neither man wanted to read symbols in their landscapes and thus avoided tourist sites or the romantic image of distorted trees outlined by livid skies.[16] Guy Pène du Bois described the Pennsylvania impressionists as a "body of plain men to whom the artistic spirit is a myth, an extravagance or a frivolity."[17] Redfield's rudimentary figures derive from his own vision experienced in his New Hope environment. While Pissarro experimented constantly throughout his career with different styles, Redfield comfortably found his groove and changed little throughout his productive career.

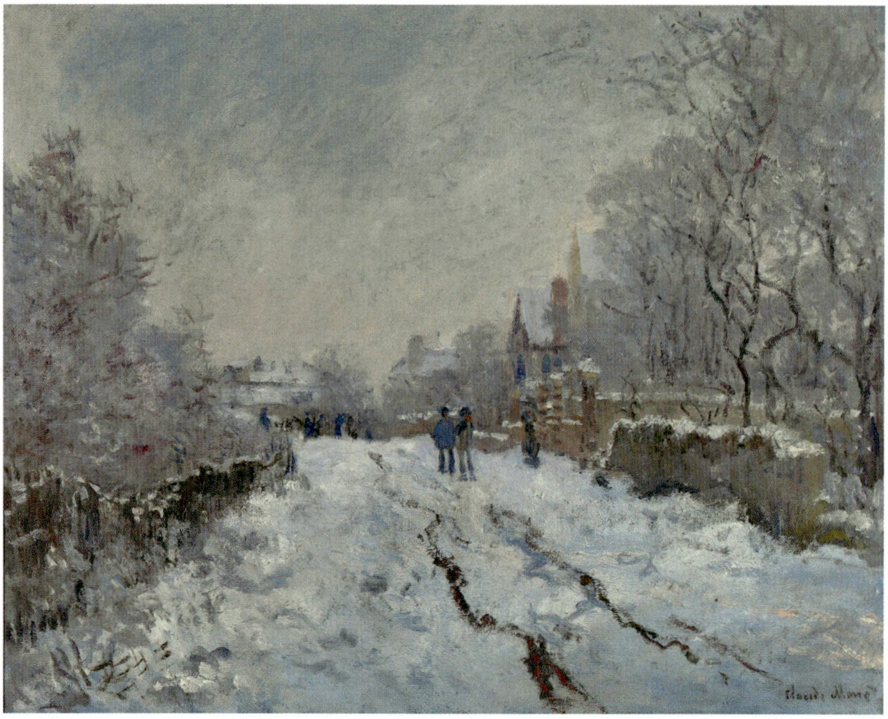

Figure 11.6 Claude Monet, *Snow at Argenteuil*, 1875. Oil on canvas, 71.1 × 91.4 cm (27.9 × 35.9 in.). (London, National Gallery)

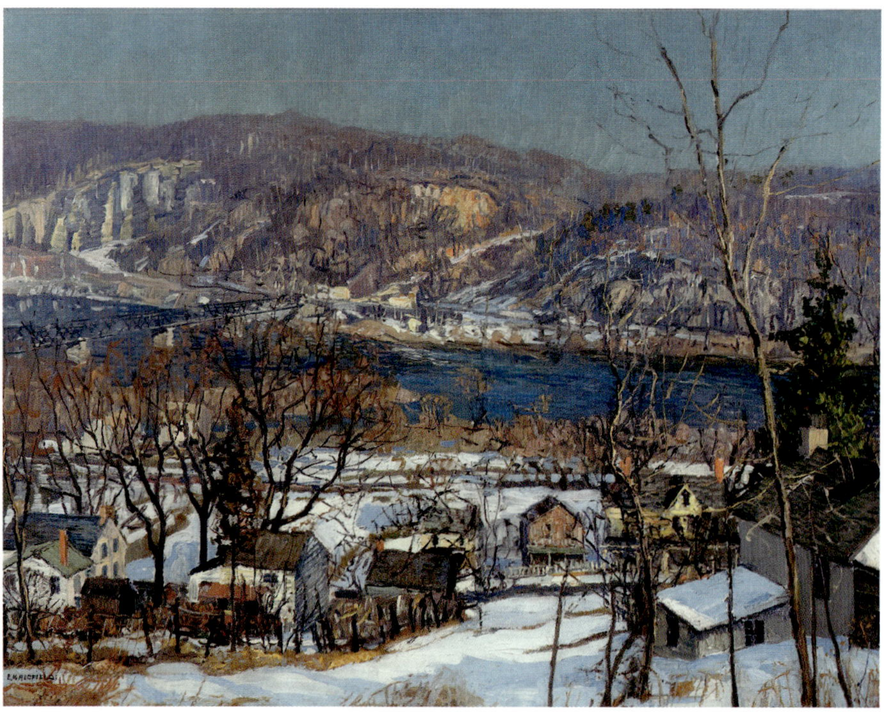

Figure 11.7 Edward Redfield, *Late Afternoon*, 1925. Oil on canvas, 38.125 × 49.875 in. (Photograph courtesy of Woodmere Art Museum: Museum purchase, 1959. Photograph by Rick Echelmeyer.)

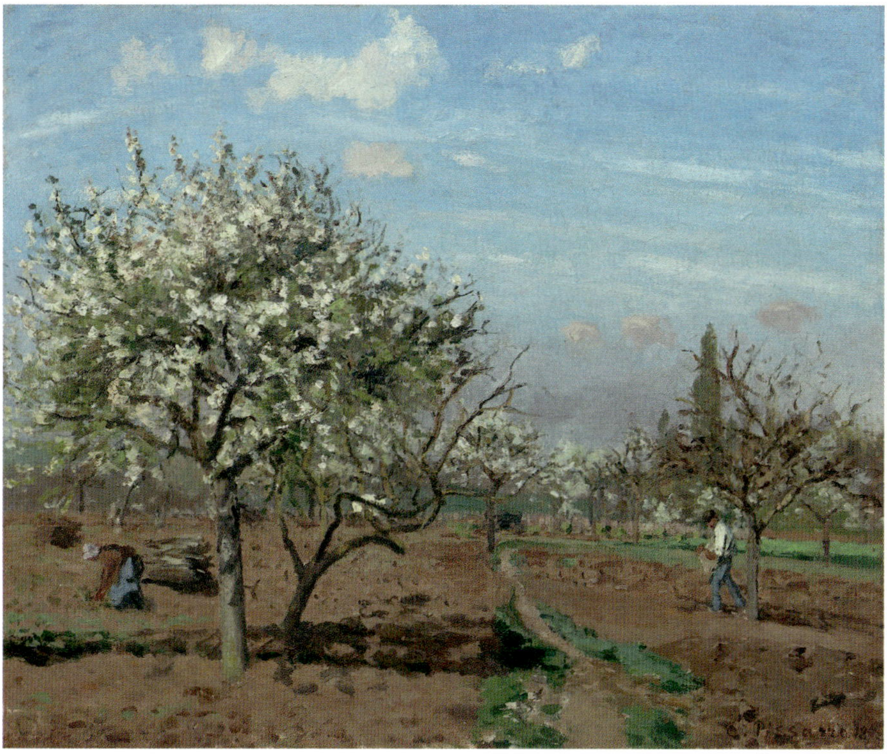

Figure 11.8 Camille Pissarro, *The Orchard*, 1872. Oil on canvas, 45.1 × 54.9 cm (17.7 × 21.6 in.). (Washington, DC, National Gallery)

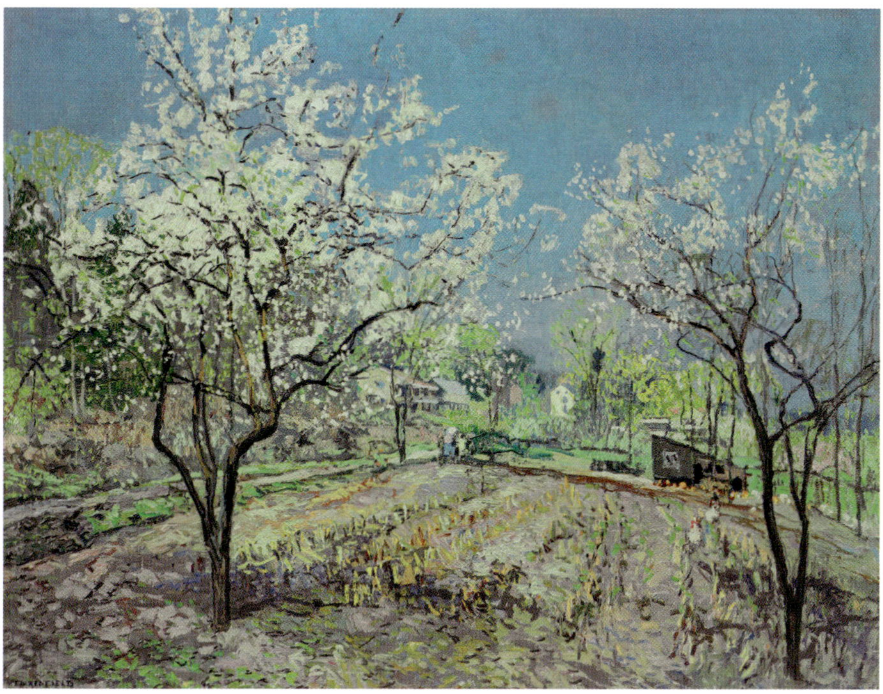

Figure 11.9 Edward Redfield, *Plum Blossoms*, ca. 1920. Oil on canvas, 38 × 50 in. (96.5 × 127 cm). (Private Collection. Photo: Christie's Images/Bridgeman Images.)

Constance Kimmerle sees Redfield's self-reliant character, disciplined deliberate methods, emphatic brushwork, and large robust canvases as connected with the ideas of many Americans as the country emerged as a world power.[18] Redfield's popularity during the early years of the twentieth century rested on the authenticity of his American vision. Lloyd Goodrich in his essay "What Is American about American Art" summarized its characteristics as displaying "adherence to facts, avoidance of subjective emotion, directness and simplicity of vision, clarity, solidity,"[19] all of which can be distinguished in the indigenous scenes vigorously brought to life by Redfield's thickly loaded brush.

Another artist credited along with Redfield for being "thoroughly American, thoroughly local" was Walter Elmer Schofield whose paintings demonstrate his affinity with motifs popular with the French impressionists. After graduating from Central High School in 1886, Schofield attended Swarthmore College for a year before moving to San Antonio, Texas, for a year and a half. He returned to Philadelphia and in 1889 began studying at the Pennsylvania Academy, where Glackens and Redfield were also in attendance. He became involved in Robert Henri's circle of friends before going to France in 1892 to attend the Académie Julian and work with Bouguereau. Schofield spent two years in France, staying largely in the Fontainebleau area where the landscape art of the Barbizon painters had flourished. He joined Henri and Glackens in 1895 on a bicycling tour through Belgium and Holland to study the old masters. Schofield married and eventually settled in England, but generally stayed in America between October and April each year. Despite his long absences from the States, critics recognized him as belonging to the New Hope group of painters.

Schofield's 1896 *Montmartre* depicts a street scene in the section of Paris where many artists lived and had studios due to affordable rents in the arrondissement. (See Figure 11.10.) Many of the impressionists painted café scenes, but they tended to focus primarily on the patrons. The figures in Schofield's painting serve as staffage, accessories that provide a sense of scale and suggest the animation of street life rather than the focus of an implied narrative. Schofield avoided the tourist views of the city that sold so well; neither did he portray the newer buildings that marked Baron Haussmann's renovations. He proclaimed his modernist stance in the manner in which he painted the building by the spontaneity of the brushstroke with its abbreviated marks daubed on the awnings over the café fronts. The massive solidity of the building is relieved by the animated French flags whipped by the wind, their forms suggested rather than defined.

Schofield's snow scene *Morning Light* (see Figure 11.11) recalls in its simplicity Monet's *Magpie* (see Figure 11.12). Both men exploit the transparent blue shadows contrasted with the stark white of the snow to convey the atmospheric chill of the scene. They restricted their palettes to focus the viewer's attention on the simplicity and elegance of the design elements. The snow in Monet's *Magpie* is flecked with multiple tiny touches of color to suggest the various effects of color and light on a white expanse. Schofield's touch is thicker and bolder, applied with vigor instead of delicacy. He seems interested in challenging himself to maximize the wintery topography with a restricted palette. Monet wrote: "I go out into the country which is so beautiful

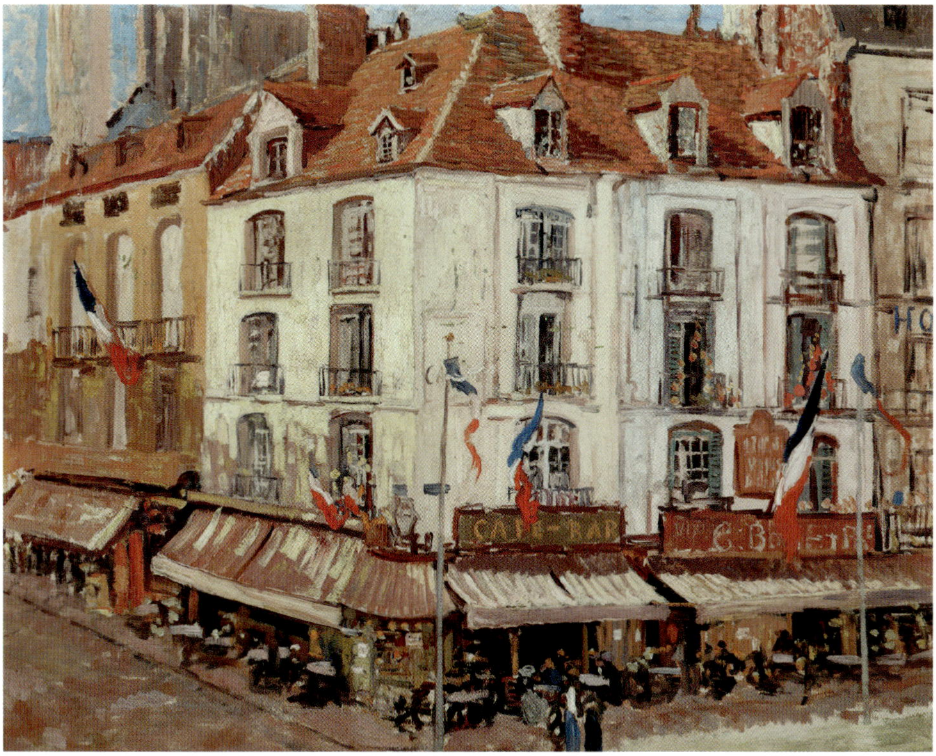

Figure 11.10 Walter Elmer Schofield, *Montmartre*, ca. 1896. Oil on canvas, 37 × 47 in. (94 × 119.4 cm). (Woodmere Art Museum: Museum purchase with funds generously provided by the Walter Elmer Schofield Legacy Fund of the Philadelphia Foundation, 2019)

here that I find the winter perhaps more agreeable than the summer, and naturally I am working all the time, and I believe that this year I am going to do some serious things."[20] Schofield held a similar attitude as he commented: "The landscape painter is of necessity, an outdoors man. . . . For vitality and convincing quality only come to the man who serves, not in the studio, but out in the open where even the things he fights against strengthen him, because you see, nature is always vital, even in her implicit moods and never denies a vision to the real lover."[21] The French government purchased Schofield's *Morning Light* in 1922, an American cousin to Monet's *Magpie*, which is considered the most popular painting at the Musée d'Orsay.

The beauty of Bucks County also attracted Daniel Garber to its landscape, where he produced works that have secured his reputation as the most original and accomplished of the Pennsylvania impressionists who settled in the New Hope area.[22] He grew up in Indiana and began his art studies at the Art Academy of Cincinnati before moving to Philadelphia in 1900 to attend the Pennsylvania Academy. He studied primarily with Thomas Anschutz who was noted for encouraging his students to develop their individual voice in art. When Garber was awarded the prestigious William H. Cresson traveling scholarship by the Pennsylvania Academy in 1905, he and his wife

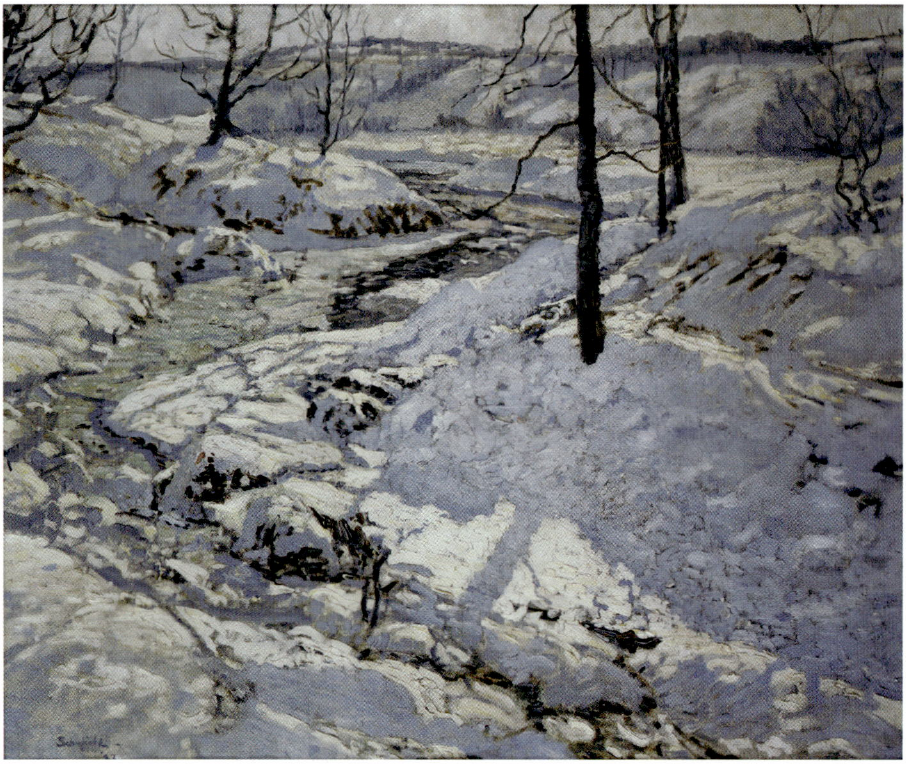

Figure 11.11 Walter Elmer Schofield, *Morning Light*, 1922. Oil on canvas, 101.5 × 122 cm (39.96 × 48.03 in.). (On deposit from the Musée d'Orsay. Château Blérancourt, France. © RMN-Grand Palais / Art Resource, NY.)

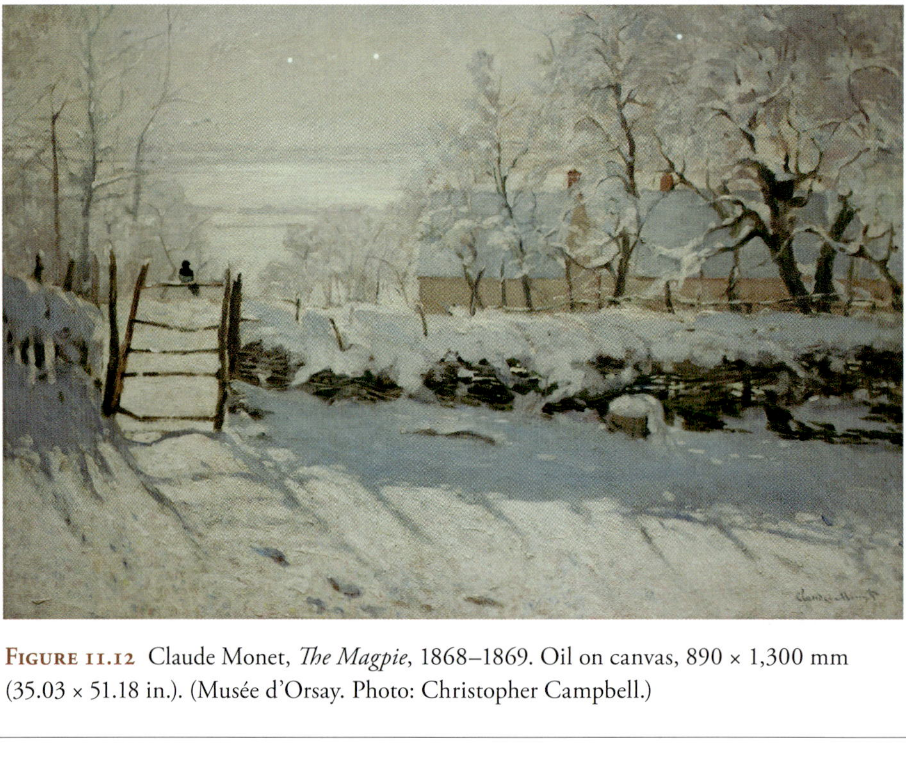

Figure 11.12 Claude Monet, *The Magpie*, 1868–1869. Oil on canvas, 890 × 1,300 mm (35.03 × 51.18 in.). (Musée d'Orsay. Photo: Christopher Campbell.)

departed for Europe. Garber decided against enrolling in art classes while abroad, preferring to experiment with the light and atmosphere of the cities where he stayed. Few of his works from this period survive as he later destroyed many of them.

Despite being funded for a third year abroad, Garber and his wife returned to Philadelphia in 1907 with their newborn daughter, Tanis. The family settled in Lumberville, Pennsylvania, six miles from New Hope up the Delaware River. Garber had visited the area before moving to Europe and needed little encouragement to move to the region with its scenic streams, quarries, and picturesque landscapes. A thriving art colony around Phillips Mill became the artistic center of the Pennsylvania impressionists. Redfield and Schofield had each developed their unique style of painting their surroundings in the area. Garber would do the same at his farm, which he named Cuttalossa. The Garbers also maintained a home in Philadelphia as Daniel taught at the Philadelphia School of Design for Women (now Moore College of Art) and, from 1909 on, at the Pennsylvania Academy for forty years.

As did Redfield and Schofield, Garber concentrated on landscapes in the New Hope area. *The Quarry, Evening* with its view across the Delaware River to New Jersey, demonstrates how Garber coordinated the horizontal and vertical lines of his autumnal landscape to support the classical serenity of the scene. (See Figure 11.13.) While including details of the workers, Garber reduced them almost to the point of invisibility, thus avoiding any pastoral narrative. The rectangular buildings, screened by foliage beneath the quarry, merge in color with the foliage and the rugged rock formations towering over them. Reading the planes of the painting from bottom to top suggests an almost contrapuntal rhythm starting with the rounded forms of the orange tree and the small hay mounds in the lowest register. These are followed by the parallel plane of the green meadow and squared silhouettes of the structures that lead the eye to the curvilinear shapes and irregular striations of the rock face, crowned by the slightly undulating row of trees that cap the quarry, their staccato procession across the upper register the final cadence before the serene rest of the sky is reached. A comparison to Cézanne's *Mont-Sainte Victoire Seen from Bibémus Quarry* (see Figure 11.14) demonstrates how Garber adjusted his brushstroke, composition, and palette to adhere to principles of realism rather than following the more modernist trends that had emerged in France with their abstracted forms leaving naturalism. It is as if the large triangular shape embedded just slightly right of center in the rock face in Garber's quarry mimics the peak of Mont-Sainte-Victoire, having yielded its dominant position to be humbly enfolded in the luminous American landscape, a subtle grace note rather than a thundering crescendo.

Garber's implementation of impressionist and postimpressionist techniques to make them his own emerges in his 1916 landscape *Buds and Blossoms.* (See Figure 11.15.) Garber professed a deep love of painting trees, often using, as he did in this painting, a prominent tree in the foreground against which he constructed the background as a kind of curtain or decorative backdrop. Many impressionist and postimpressionist painters became fascinated with the stylistics of Japanese art with its flat areas of bright exotic colors, bold outlines, cropping of the image, and suppression

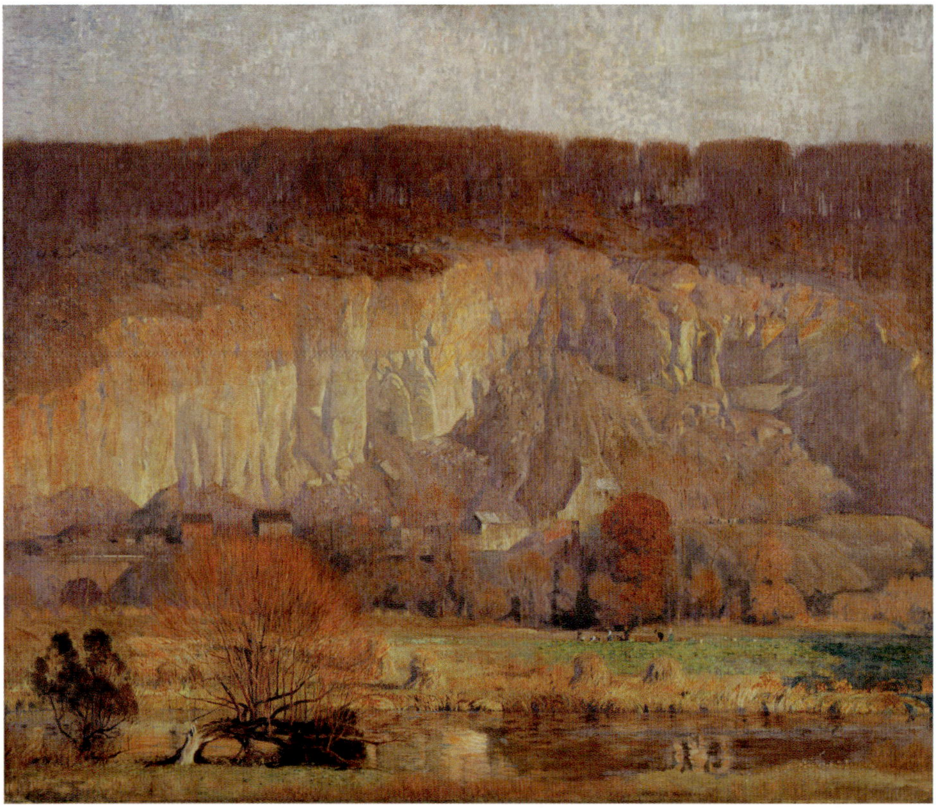

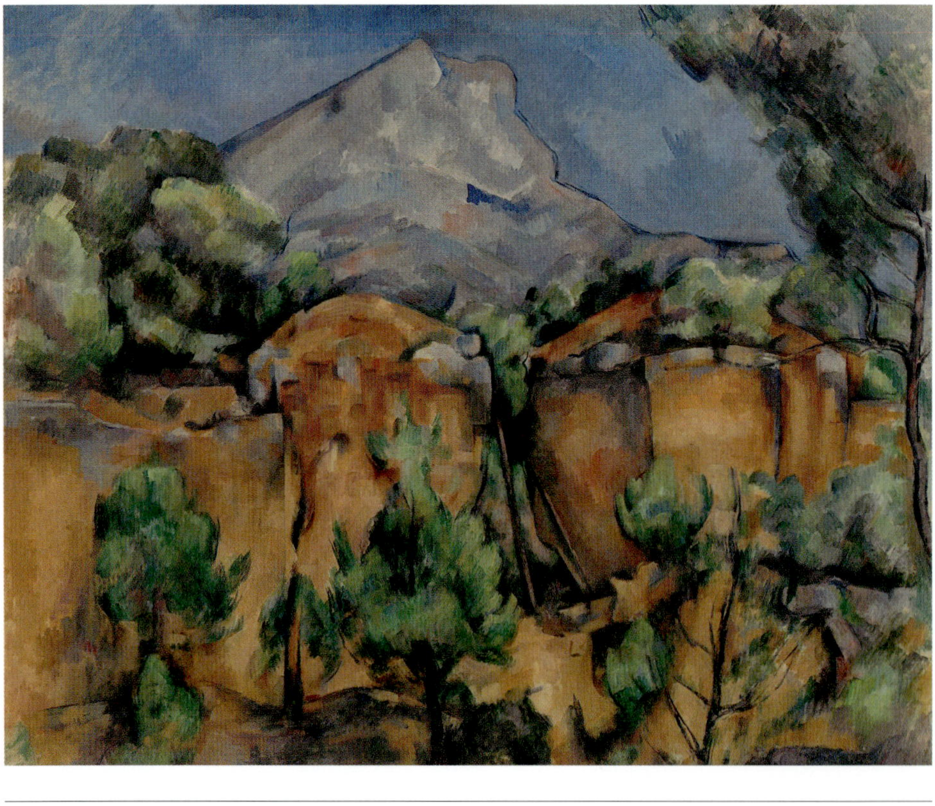

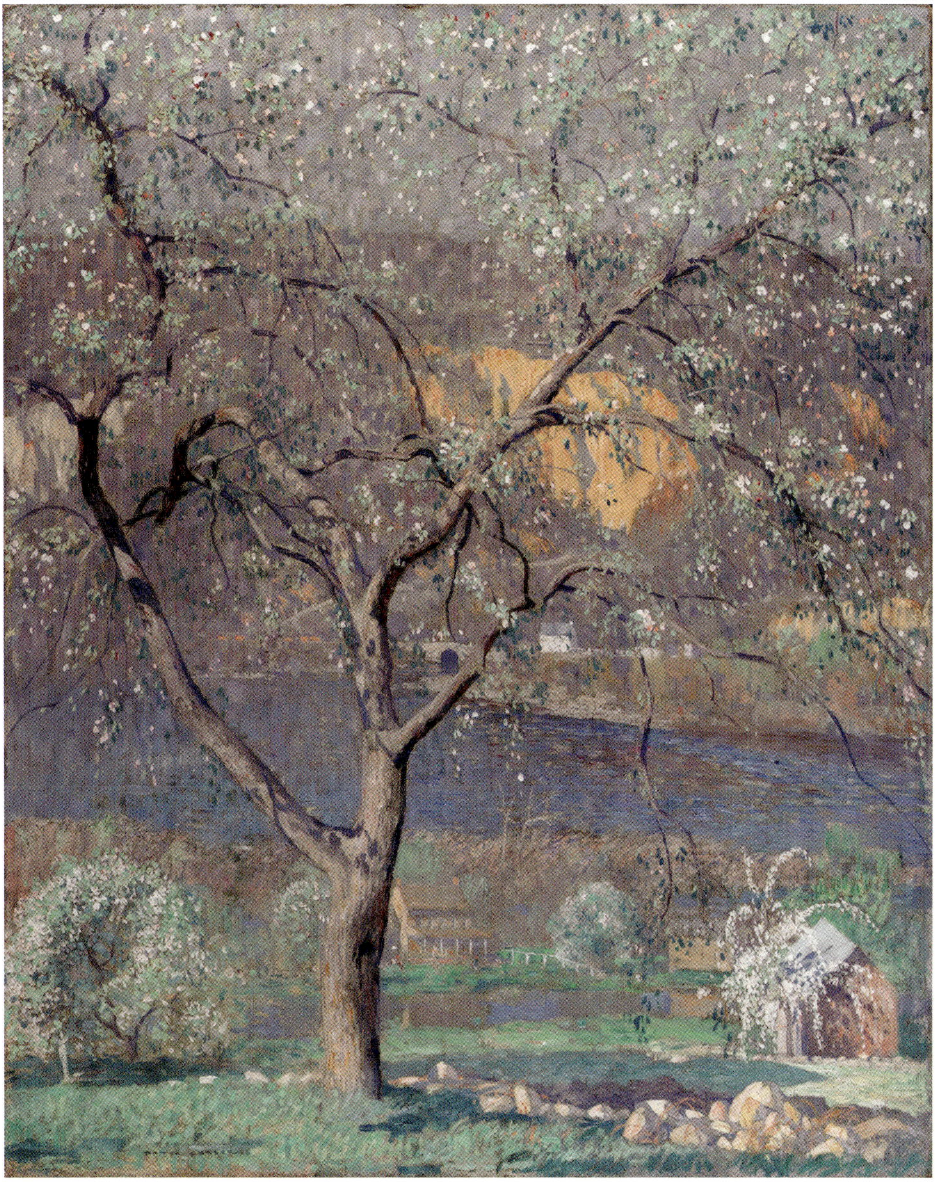

Figure 11.15 Daniel Garber, *Buds and Blossoms*, 1916. Oil on canvas, 44¼ × 36¼ in. (112.4 × 92.1 cm). (Philadelphia Museum of Art, Gift of Marguerite and Gerry Lenfest, 2019-2-2. Copyright: © Estate of Daniel Garber.)

FACING PAGE:

Figure 11.13 Daniel Garber, *The Quarry, Evening*, 1913. Oil on canvas, 50 × 60 in. (127 × 152.4 cm). (Philadelphia Museum of Art, purchased with the W. P. Wilstach Fund, W1921-1-3. Copyright: © Estate of Daniel Garber.)

Figure 11.14 Paul Cézanne, *Mont-Sainte Victoire Seen from Bibémus Quarry*, 1897. Oil on canvas, 65.1 × 81.3 cm (25.6 × 32 in.). (Baltimore Museum of Art)

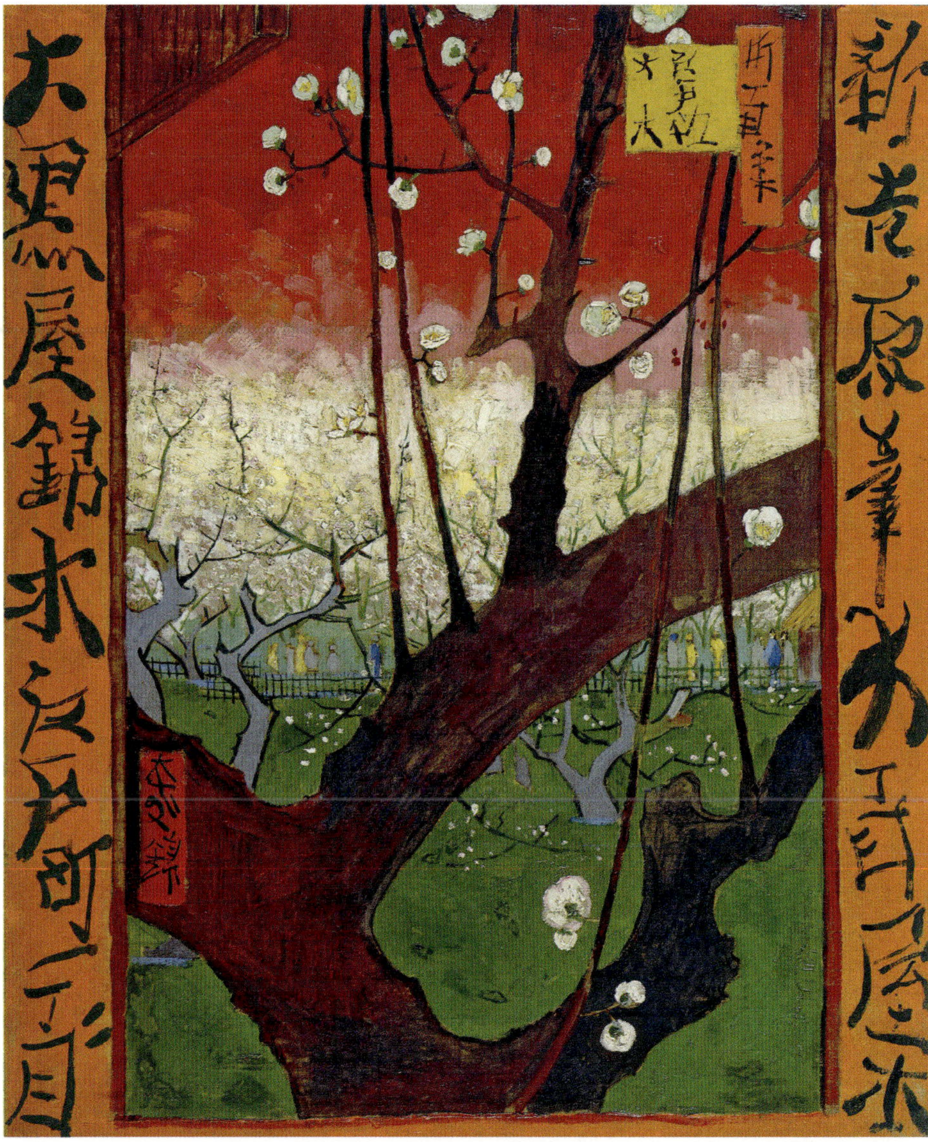

FIGURE 11.16 Vincent Van Gogh, *Flowering Plum Trees in Blossom*, 1887. Oil on canvas, 55 × 46 cm (21.6 × 18.1 in.). (Van Gogh Museum)

of the illusion of depth. Vincent van Gogh's painting *Flowering Plum Orchard (after Hiroshige)* duplicates a Japanese print he admired. (See Figure 11.16.) He added the flat strip of lettering to the border of his canvas to enhance the decorative effect of the image with its rejection of tonally modeled forms and western illusionism. Garber shared this admiration for Japanese art with its emphasis on surface design, adapting several of the visual strategies in his painting as can be seen, for instance, in the comparison of his *Buds and Blossoms* with Vincent van Gogh's *The Pink Peach Tree*. (See Figure 11.17.) Both artists asserted the two-dimensionality of the canvas by tightly

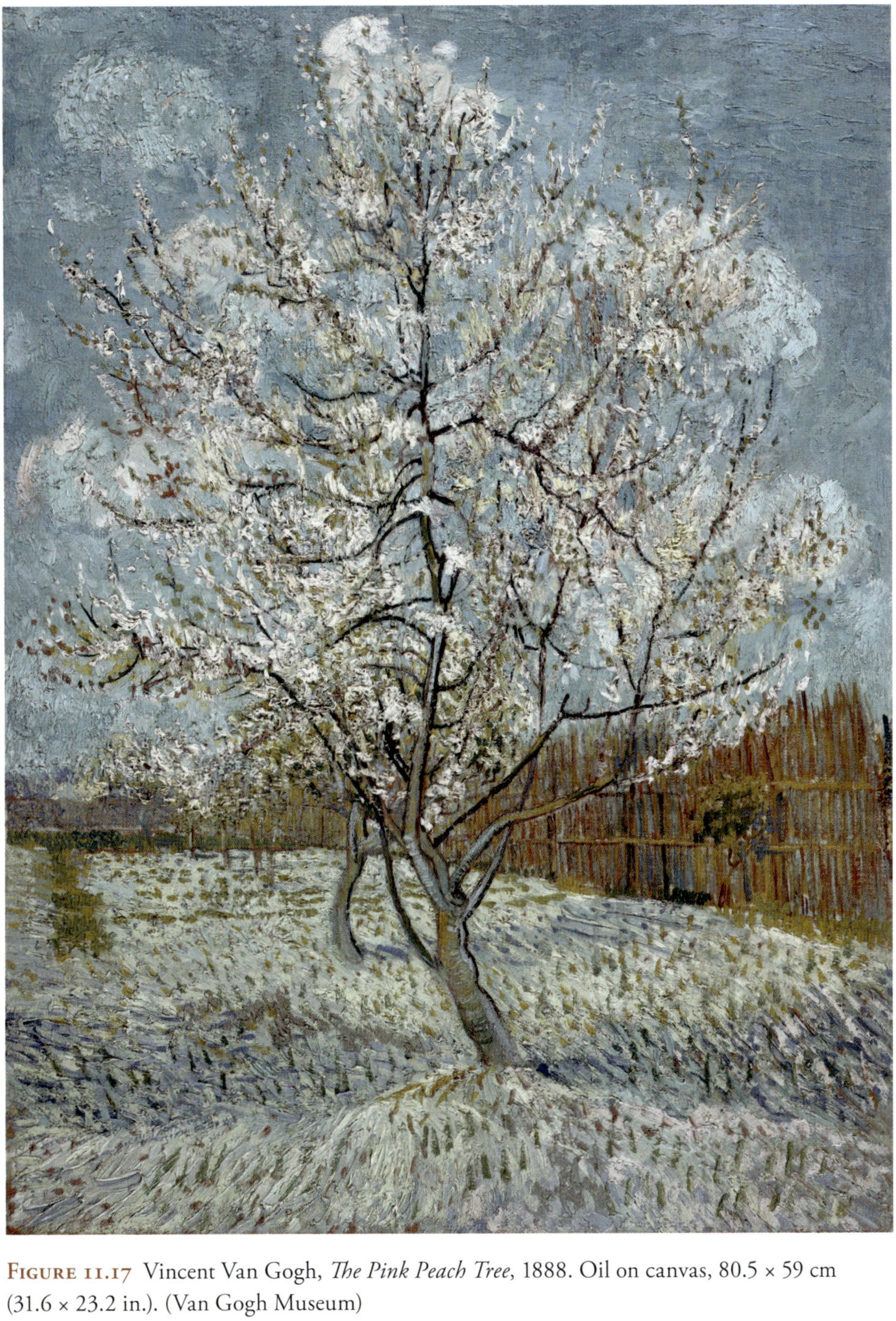

FIGURE 11.17 Vincent Van Gogh, *The Pink Peach Tree*, 1888. Oil on canvas, 80.5 × 59 cm (31.6 × 23.2 in.). (Van Gogh Museum)

framing the central tree with little space allowed beyond its branches at the edges of the painting. The quickly dappled strokes of paint that define the leaves in both works emphasize the flatness and surface effect of the canvas, a hallmark of modernism. Garber's tree branches protrude beyond the edge of the work and are cropped at the top to obscure any deep perspectival view that would distract from the daubs of white paint that create the decorative effect of the flecked upper region of the work with its delicate blossoms. Garber achieved a balance between modernism and realism, refusing throughout his career to yield to the abstract movement that American avant-garde painters embraced. He once told a journalist: "I want to paint things as I see them. I have too much respect for the trees that I paint, and their true forms, to make something out of them that I do not feel exists in them."[23]

Early in his career, Garber had earned income as a portrait artist and illustrator. Although his reputation remained largely based on his landscapes, he also excelled at figure painting. This can be seen in Garber's portrait of his daughter *Tanis*, which he painted over several months during the summer of 1915. (See Figure 11.18.) Like the impressionists, Garber used vibrant color and a varied brushstroke to distinguish his art from the academic manner. He posed his daughter in an open doorway in front of a garden drenched in brilliant sunlight. Her back-lit dress becomes translucent as she transitions between the exterior and the interior, her left knee bent in an understated indication of movement. Her feet are already shrouded in the darkened light of the room she will enter. Yet, the image goes beyond any fleeting impression as Garber painted the figure in a solidly realist manner, confining the animated impressionist brushstroke to the background. He clearly delineated Tanis's face and profile against the shimmering diffuseness of the foliage, her right hand pressing on the jamb of the French door between inside and outside. The dominance of blue and gold, along with the dazzling light that crowns her head, makes her seem like an updated Renaissance angel. The white flowers in the lower right corner could be seen to function as a substitute for the lilies that frequently accompanied Gabriel in scenes of the Annunciation as a symbol of the Virgin's innocence and purity.[24] (See Figure 11.19.) Tanis's highlighted hand almost mimics the pointing gesture often found in depictions of the archangel while the brilliant translucency of her summer dress makes her seem ethereal. The lush garden behind Tanis is reminiscent of the *hortus conclusus*—the enclosed garden—that became a verbal and visual trope as an emblematic attribute of the Virgin in medieval and Renaissance art and literature. Garber portrayed Tanis as both eternal and contemporary. Her liminal position on the threshold acts as a perfect metaphor for what Kathleen Foster has characterized as the most glorious convergence of academic and impressionist style in Garber's work.[25]

Religious symbolism may be detected again in *The Orchard Window*, the painting that won Garber the Temple Gold Medal from the annual exhibition of the Pennsylvania Academy in 1919. (See Figure 11.20.) Garber resumed several aspects of his 1915 portrait of his daughter with his use of translucency in the curtains and the similarity of her white tunic over a blue skirt. Again, he placed Tanis in front of a garden that fills the background. Her seated position with a book recalls familiar images of the

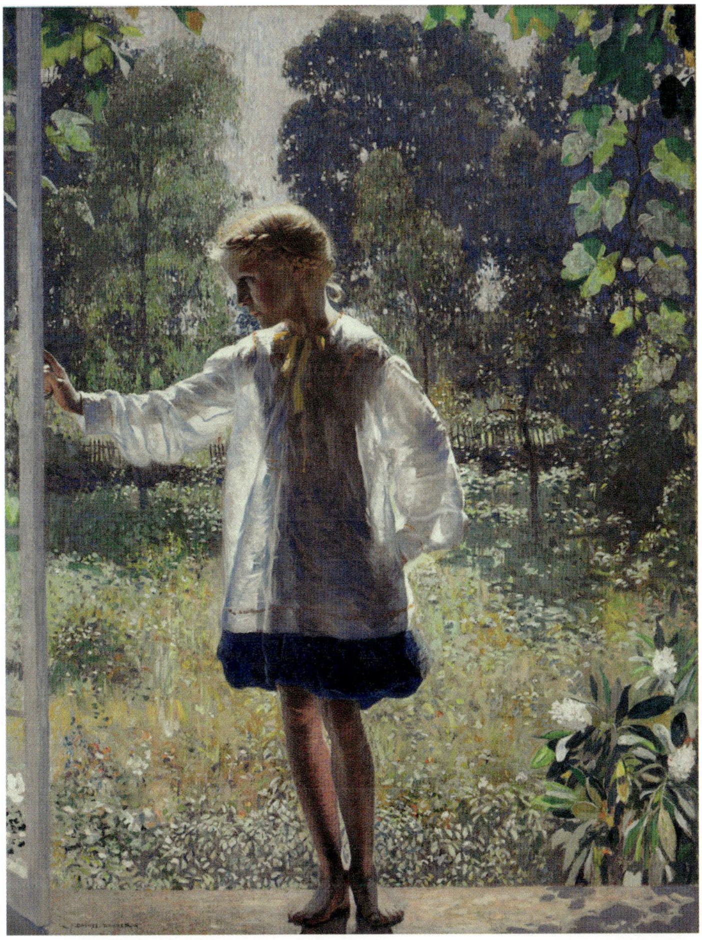

Figure 11.18
Daniel Garber, *Tanis*, 1915. Oil on canvas, 60 × 46¼ in. (152.4 × 117.5 cm). Framed: 71½ × 57⁵⁄₁₆ × 3⅝ in. (181.6 × 145.6 × 9.2 cm). (Philadelphia Museum of Art, purchased with funds contributed by Marguerite and Gerry Lenfest, 2011-60-1. Copyright: © Estate of Daniel Garber.)

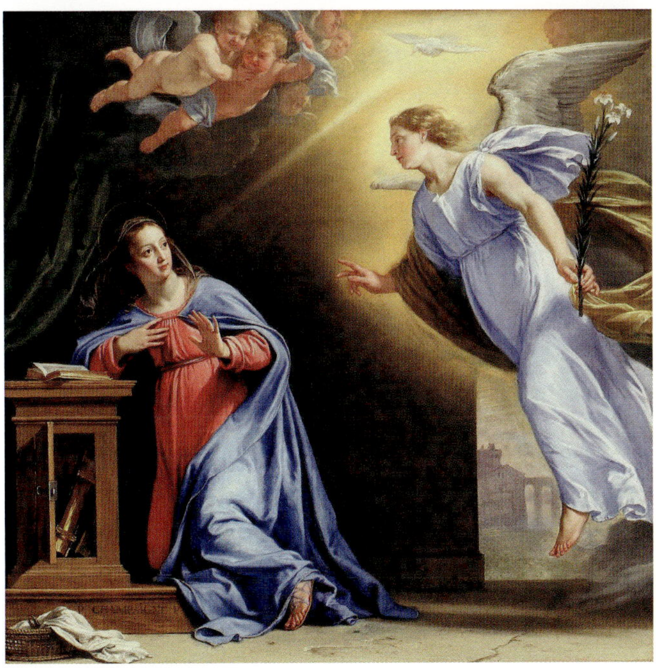

Figure 11.19
Philippe de Champaigne, *The Annunciation*, 1644. Oil on oak, overall, 28 × 28¾ in. (71.1 × 73 cm); painted surface, 27¼ × 27¾ in. (69.2 × 70.5 cm). (Metropolitan Museum of Art, Wrightsman Fund)

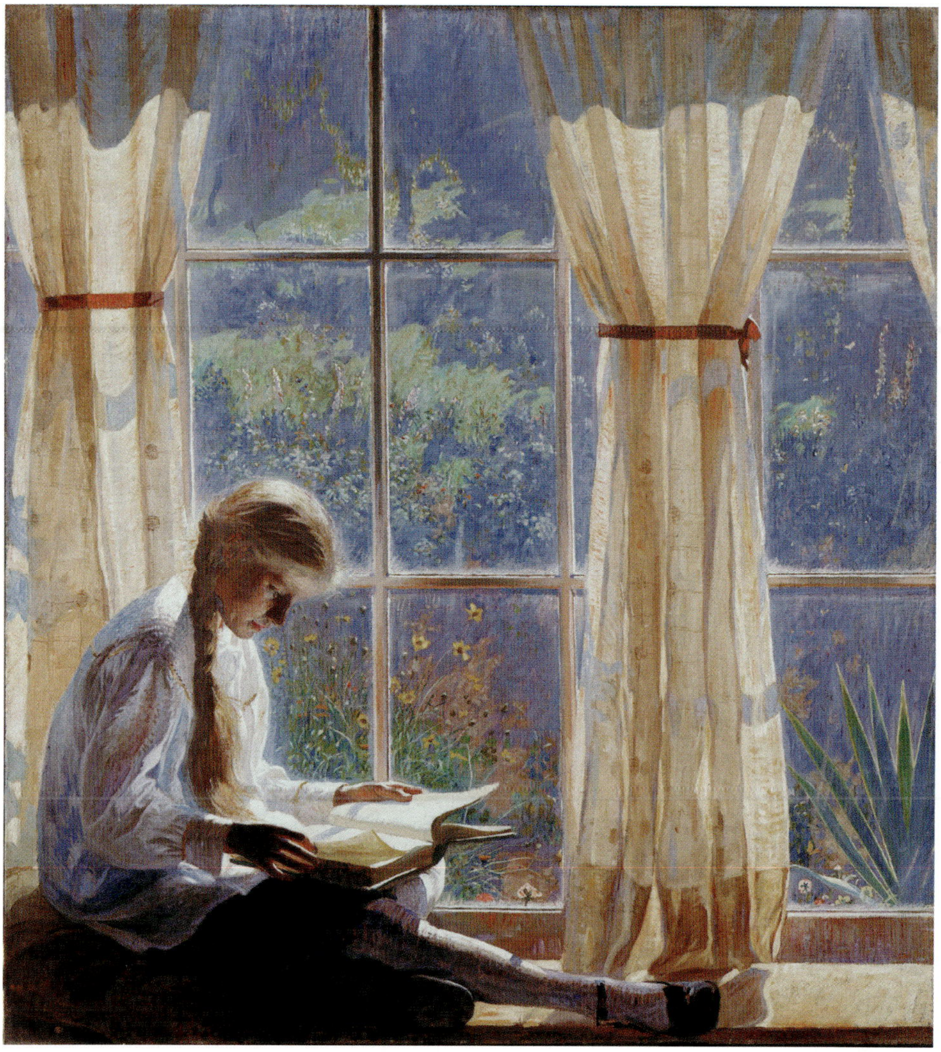

FIGURE 11.20 Daniel Garber, *The Orchard Window*, 1918. Oil on canvas, 56 7/16 × 52¼ in. (143.4 × 132.7 cm). Framed: 61 × 57 × 2¼ in. (154.9 × 144.8 × 5.7 cm). (Philadelphia Museum of Art, centennial gift of the family of Daniel Garber, 1976-216-1. Copyright: © Estate of Daniel Garber.)

Virgin reading the Bible in older art. Tanis's right hand becomes a shadow, backlit in a manner that became a signature device in the art of the French Baroque painter Georges de la Tour. (See Figure 11.21.) The tapering of the curtains behind Tanis suggests a Gothic arch. Lance Humphries has pointed out how Garber's construction of the image encourages the idea of a sanctuary. He observed that the sash bars of the windowpanes above Tanis's head form a cross. Garber edged them with the same light that creates a halo on Tanis's head and illuminates the pages of the book she is holding. Humphries also observed how the hillside flattened on the picture plane could suggest that the window is not clear glass but stained glass, heightened by the effect of the curtains pulled back as if to reveal a vision.[26] Garber largely remained silent on his religious beliefs, but this does not discount his knowledge of the religious art he had experienced in Europe and America.[27] Garber remained alert to what the art of the past—the old masters as well as the impressionists and postimpressionists—could supply him in the way of motifs and technique, but he did not allow these to limit the creative expression of his individuality.

Guy Pène du Bois claimed that the paintings by the Pennsylvania impressionists manifested "our first truly national expression," observing that their "realism, which began as being French is now essentially American. [Theirs] is a painting of great breadth, almost brutal in the extent to which it carries the gospel of the insignificance of detail."[28] Yet, as Kathleen Foster has observed, the Americans did not push their motifs as far into abstraction as did the French: "American painters retained their hold on their subject, on the solidity of objects; they felt a need for 'the quiet observation of fact' that appears to be one of the major differences between French and American Impressionism."[29] The sojourns in France taken by the Pennsylvania impressionists,

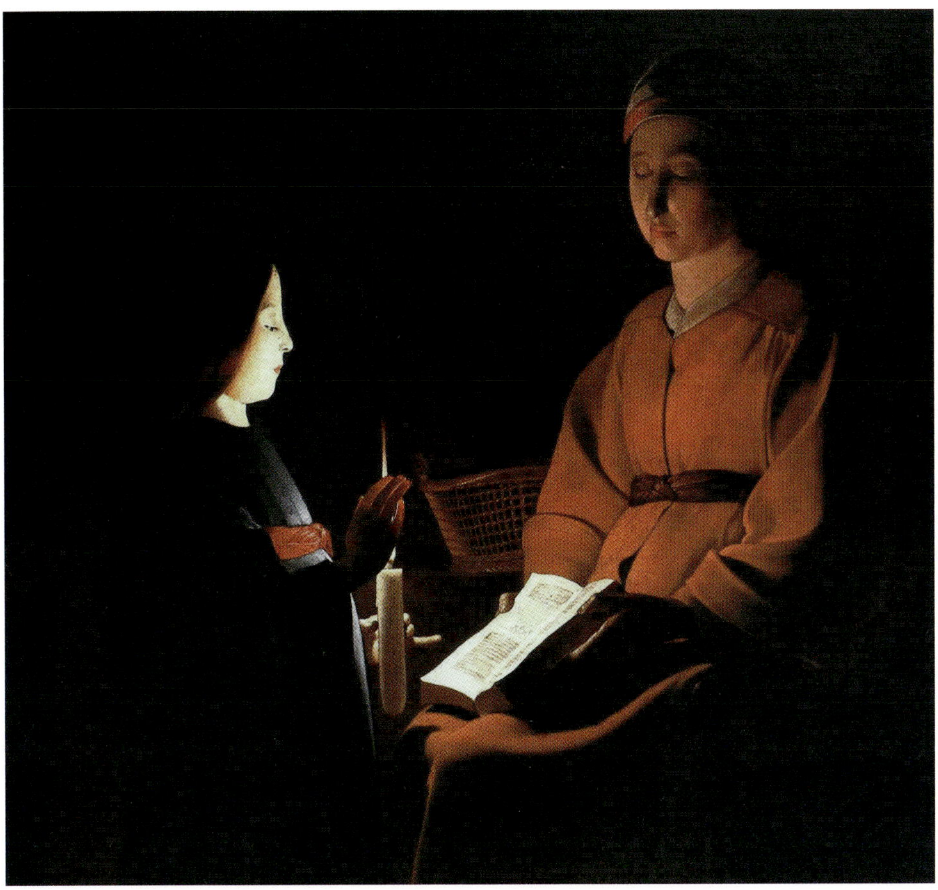

Figure 11.21 Studio of Georges de la Tour, *The Education of the Virgin*, ca. 1650. Oil on canvas, 83.8 × 100.3 cm (32.9 × 39.4 in.). (The Frick Collection)

their exposure to the French impressionist aesthetic through the Durand-Ruel Gallery in New York, and their contact with other American impressionists, helped them see the potential of conveying their American subject matter in newly expressive ways. Their depiction of seaside pleasures, secluded rural roads softened by snow, and quiet villages gently warming to the sun of late winter gained authenticity from their exposure to foreign art. They saw how they could infuse the feel of their home country, its particular light and native plantings, its colonial architecture and handcrafted farm implements, with a sense of their native rituals. They wed practical knowledge learned from hours in the studios at the Académie Julian, encounters with Monet at Giverny, and painting campaigns in the forests of Fontainebleau, with their observations of the farmhouses, local streams, and quiet villages of their native Bucks County environment to create a body of work that resonated with uniquely American freshness and spontaneity. If some of the technique of their art originated in a French syntax, the prose that emerged from their work was decidedly American. As Richard Harding Davis wrote, the best American painters were the ones who "made use of Paris, instead of Paris making use of them."[30]

Pennsylvania impressionism, as with other works of American impressionism, once so visually challenging, began to lose its radical edge as its innovations came to be seen as mainstream and conservative in the second decade of the twentieth century.[31] Rural scenes failed to satisfy some of the restive artists who lived in the bustling city and witnessed the societal and political changes brought about by industry and technology. Motifs were no longer sought in the pristine snow scenes and sunny landscapes of Monet or the intimate images of mothers and children by Berthe Morisot and Mary Cassatt. Historians of the movement agree that American impressionism had reached its peak at the Panama-Pacific International Exposition, held in San Francisco in 1915. Impulses of new stylistic innovations incited artists who had studied in Paris to turn to urban subjects as they gradually rebelled against impressionism, which had become the new academicism. This can be seen in the careers of Robert Henri and William Glackens who played leading roles in redefining American art in the early years of the twentieth century. The time they spent in Philadelphia and Paris played a crucial role in their artistic formation, providing them with training and significant personal contacts that they mined to forge their careers.

Robert Henry Cozad was born in Cincinnati to parents of French, English, and Irish ancestry. His father, a riverboat gambler and real estate speculator, got embroiled in a fight where he shot and seriously wounded his adversary who died two months later. Although cleared of any felony, his father feared the lingering taint of scandal and decided the family should change names. Robert changed his name to Robert Earl Henri, adopting the French spelling of his Huguenot heritage but pronouncing it "Hen-rye" to avoid any affectation. He moved with his family to Atlantic City in 1884 where he eventually met James Albert Cathcart who had studied at the Pennsylvania Academy and convinced Henri to pursue a career in art. Henri applied to and was accepted at the Academy in the autumn of 1886, enrolling the same day as Redfield and the sculptor Alexander Stirling Calder. Henri began in the antique class where he studied with Thomas Anschutz who had replaced Eakins. By November, Henri had been promoted to the life class—much to his relief—as he hated drawing from casts. His attraction to scenes from everyday life emerged in the composition class where original designs were encouraged. He shunned the scenes from history and mythology done by his classmates and soon helped organize a portrait class, a genre in which he won praise from his instructor Thomas Hovenden. Henri, often accompanied by Redfield, regularly stopped in at Earle's and Haseltine's commercial art galleries in the city to keep up with American and European art, both old and new. When he saw Eakins's *Gross Clinic* at Jefferson Medical College, he declared it to be the most wonderful painting he had ever seen.[32]

As were so many of the art students at the Academy, Henri was drawn to Paris to improve his technical skills and steep himself in the art treasures of Europe. He sailed from New York in September 1888, taking a brief stay in London before heading to Paris, where he exclaimed, "This is what I have hungered for!"[33] He enrolled at the Académie Julian, receiving critiques of his painting and drawing twice a week with Bouguereau and Tony Robert-Fleury. Both masters had enjoyed successful careers at the Salon with their academic subject matter and style based on Renaissance and Baroque models. Their training focused on having their students draw from the nude model and compose subjects adhering to themes from history and mythology. Before leaving Philadelphia, Henri asserted that there "are none or few of the works of the [old masters] that are equal to the moderns according to my way of seeing."[34] His exposure to modern works at the Luxembourg Museum, the Salon of 1889, and the International Exposition that year solidified his opinion.

The academic painting at the spring Salon of 1890 began to foster a revolt in him against its stylistic principles. Yet the works of Van Gogh, Gauguin, and the Symbolists that he saw at the 1890 Salon des Indépendants seemed too radical to him. Stylistically, Henri was at a crossroads, but a trip to the Mediterranean coast with Redfield led him to do more painting outdoors, trying to capture the site before the light and atmosphere changed, thus forcing him to work quickly as opposed to the meticulous finish required of work at Julian's. His *Misty Effect, Paris* (see Figure 11.22) demonstrates his rejection of the tightly controlled brushwork of academic art and his experimentation with the type of atmospheric cityscape such as that depicted by Pissarro in his *Boulevard Montmartre on a Winter Morning.* (See Figure 11.23.)

Despite his experiments with impressionism, Henri's desire to be accepted at the École des Beaux-Arts in Paris never waned. He stood for the rigorous entrance exam, failing four times before finally learning he had passed on February 23, 1891. He spent the mornings at Julian's and the afternoons at the École in the early months of 1891. Outings with Redfield to Fontainebleau immersed him in dialogue that stimulated his mind and helped forge lasting friendships. Despite his praise for and admiration of Monet's haystacks that he saw at the Durand-Ruel Gallery that spring, Henri still found himself drawn to academic artists and their exhibitions. He submitted two landscapes to the Salon but had them rejected. An excursion with Redfield to Venice in May 1891 failed to reconcile Henri's warring attractions: conforming to the

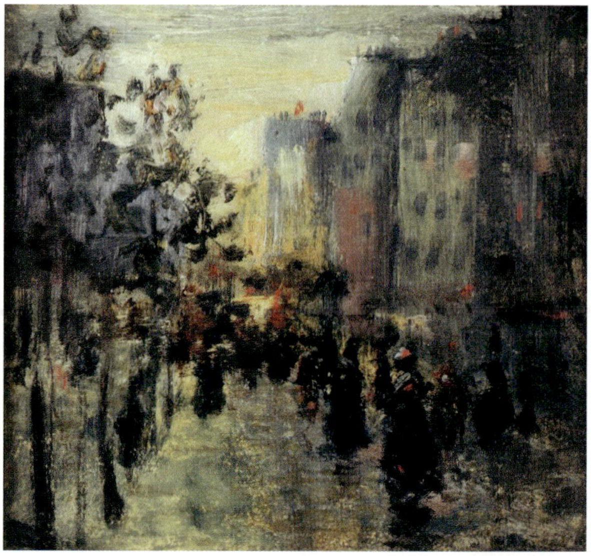

Figure 11.22 Robert Henri, *Misty Effect, Paris*, n.d. 6.25 × 6.88 in. (15.88 × 17.46 cm) (Private Collection)

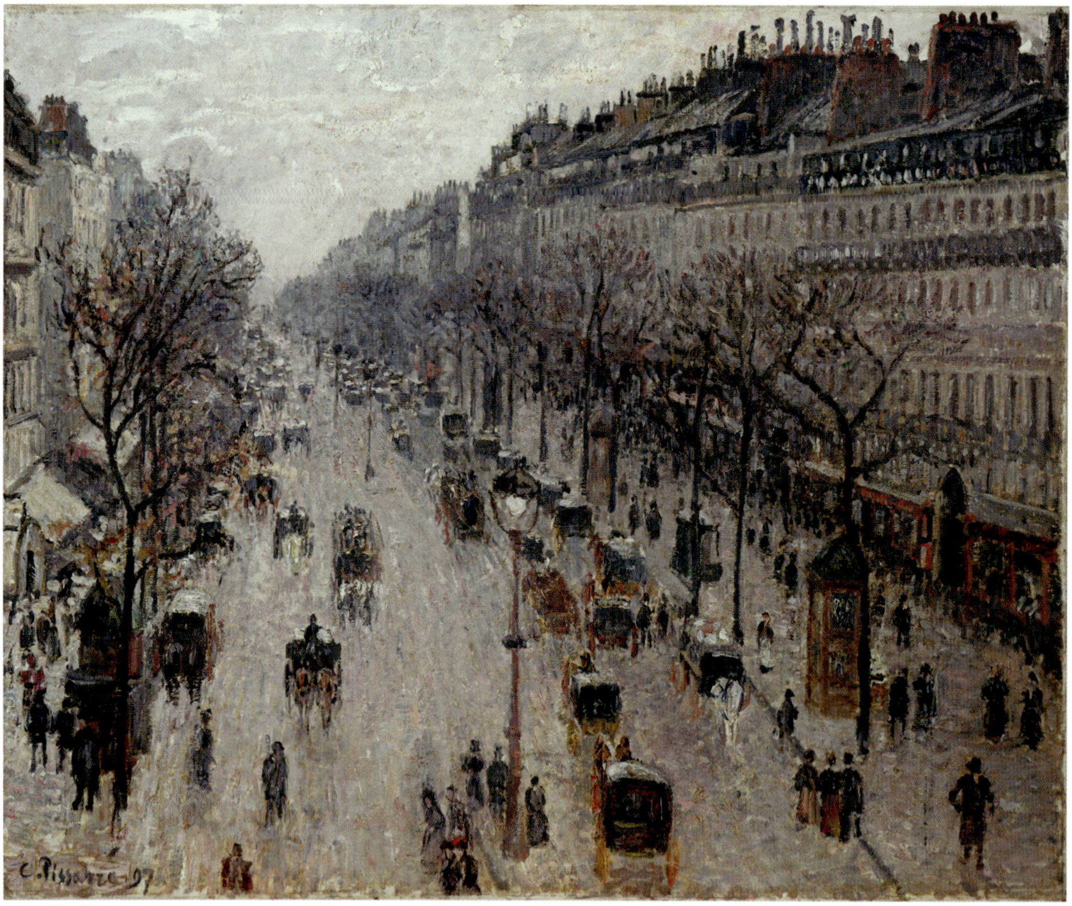

Figure 11.23 Camille Pissarro, *The Boulevard Montmartre on a Winter Morning*, 1897. 25.5 × 32 in. (64.8 × 81.3 cm) (Metropolitan Museum of Art, Gift of Katrin S. Vietor, in loving memory of Ernest G. Vietor, 1960. Acc. No. 60.174.)

type of execution of his academic training with his love of the impressionist freedom and color of rapidly sketched work observed on the spot that depicted contemporary life. Just as Eakins eventually tired of Gérôme's instruction shortly before returning to Philadelphia, so Henri rebelled against Bouguereau's emphasis on finish: "I am working for the big impression—but he demands the careful completeness. I believe I am right to do so."[35]

After three years in Paris, Henri sailed to Philadelphia in September 1891. He reenrolled at the Pennsylvania Academy in January 1892, determined to continue improving his craft. The academy's annual exhibition that year featured landscapes by Monet. When Henri's Venetian scenes hung with them, he and several of his other colleagues who displayed impressionist tendencies felt the sting of disparagement from critics and academic painters. The discrepancy between art's reception in Paris compared to Philadelphia irked Henri who wrote in a letter: "There's no wonder Philadelphia artists are lifeless—lack of public interest makes them ask themselves if it is not an idle fancy that theirs is a great art—and perhaps begin to wonder if their lives are not wasted. How different in Paris where the Artist is the *Great Man*."[36] Fortunately, not everyone in Philadelphia ignored Henri's talent. His plans to return to Paris changed when Emily Sartain offered him a teaching position at the Philadelphia School of Design for Women, where she served as principal. Financial necessity proved to be the mother of invention in launching Henri into a successful teaching career for which he would become legendary.

Henri's friendships with John Sloan (1871–1951), William Glackens, Everett Shinn (1876–1953), and George Luks (1867–1933) evolved into the Charcoal Club, also known as the "Philadelphia Four," a cooperative where artists competed for having the best work of the week. The group met at Sloan's studio but disbanded after a few months. Nevertheless, the acquaintances made there formed lifelong friendships and the core of a future group of painters whose shows would eventually be as disruptive to the American art scene as the impressionist exhibitions had been in Paris. Artists gathered weekly in Henri's studio at 806 Walnut Street, where they sketched from the life model and engaged in reading and discussing the works of Ralph Waldo Emerson, Henry David Thoreau, Walt Whitman, and Émile Zola. Henri expounded on his artistic idols Diego Velázquez, Frans Hals, and Francisco Goya, whose style presaged his commitment to realism, while his preference for modern masters centered on James McNeill Whistler (1834–1903) and Manet. These weekly meetings furnished a space to practice life drawing and a forum for Henri to lead discussions on ethics, politics, and the arts—literature and music included. The studio also served as a stage for theater lampoons such as *Twilbe*, the send-up of George du Maurier's *Trilby*, a best-selling novel about an artist's model set in bohemian Paris. Everett Shinn played the expatriate painter "James McNails Whiskers" while Henri, as Svengali, meets his fate by being bitten to death by Jersey mosquitoes.[37] Sloan later recalled the impact of Henri on the lives of his friends and students because he "brought us his experience of years of contact with European living and European painting. This background was an intangible thing and meant a lot to those of us who had few pictures save those in our museums and through engravings and photographs. It was before the day of half-tone printing, and color reproduction."[38] Sloan remembered that Henri's copy of George Moore's *Impressionist Paintings* supplied an important account in English of contemporary French practice: "Manet—as far as modern times and the immediate antecedent or our work was concerned, was the parent—through Henri."[39]

Three years of teaching in Philadelphia had depleted Henri of energy and sufficient time to pursue his own painting. He headed back to France in June 1895 along with Glackens, Schofield, and two other painters. After a summer of touring the Low Countries and Italy to visit museums, he returned to Paris where he took a studio on the boulevard du Montparnasse and eagerly resumed painting along with Glackens in the city and countryside. No longer did he feel the tension of choosing between the conservative style of the École des Beaux-Arts and the style of modernism. His 1895 *Place in Paris* affirmed his embrace of the more spontaneous and broadly brushed style of Manet and the impressionists that he had experienced during his first stay in Paris. (See Figure 11.24.) The Salon of 1896 accepted one of his portraits (unknown), and the following year two more works (also unknown) received the cachet of approval by the jury.

Buoyed by his Parisian success, Henri proposed a one-man show at the Pennsylvania Academy when he returned to Philadelphia in September 1897. Eighty-seven paintings and thirty small sketches on wooden panels covered the walls at the academy in October and November 1897, meeting with the critical success so lacking in his showing in the 1892 annual exhibition. Despite his triumph with the press, sales of his work were not forthcoming in Philadelphia. He approached the art dealer William Macbeth in New York who agreed to represent him and in 1898 showed a small selection of Henri's work from his academy show. Former doubts about Philadelphia's

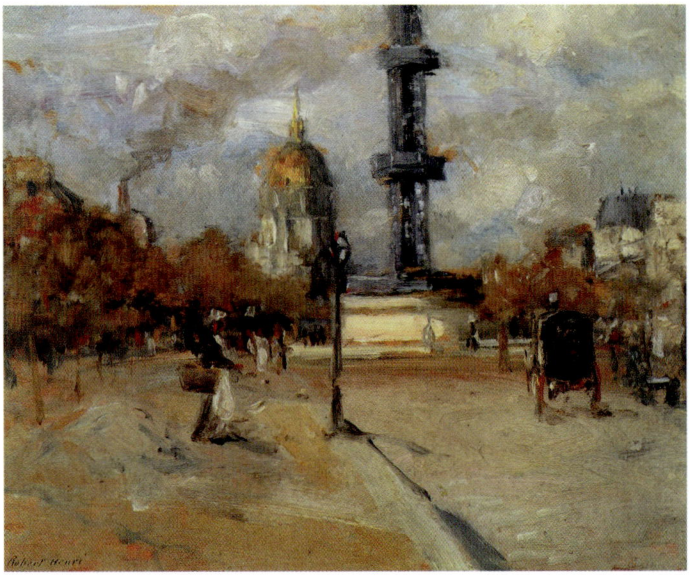

FIGURE 11.24
Robert Henri, *Place in Paris*, ca. 1895–1897. 10½ × 12¾ in. (26.7 × 34.9 cm). (Private Collection)

viability for an art career resurfaced as Henri wrote in his diary: "New York is so different from here—one feels alive over there."[40] Henri also submitted canvases and had them accepted by the Society of American Artists and the National Academy of Design in New York, the American counterpart of the École des Beaux-Arts in Paris and the Royal Academy in London.

Henri married his art student Linda Craige at Ashbourne in Elkins Park, Pennsylvania, on June 2, 1898. They set off for their honeymoon to Paris, spending the next two years there. His growing reputation earned him a visit from a former pupil who provided a calling card as an opportunity to "make it possible for Mr. Henri to pay his homage to Madame Manet, Mr. Henri being himself one of the greatest painters in the Manet school."[41] Henri focused on preparing work for the Salon of 1899 where he had four canvases accepted. After taking some time on the Brittany coast, Henri and his wife returned to Paris, where a letter informed him that his painting *La Neige* had been purchased by the French government for the Luxembourg Museum. The Philadelphia press expressed its pride in Henri by announcing—mistakenly—that he had been awarded the Legion of Honor. The hoped-for recognition by the Parisian art world had arrived, bringing financial assistance and, even more importantly, the assurance that he could succeed as a professional artist. Success in America also began to materialize when twelve of Henri's paintings sold to a Philadelphia entrepreneur while the Carnegie Institute and Chicago Art Institute also purchased his work.

Henri and his wife returned to America in August 1902 and decided to settle in New York, where Henri reconnected with Glackens. To support himself and his wife, Henri took on a teaching position for several days a week at a girl's private school. Claiming he was anxious to keep up his relations with Philadelphia, he frequently returned to the city to submit to exhibits at the academy and visit with his friends Sloan and Redfield. The year 1902 saw Henri return more frequently to the city as his wife recuperated from an illness at her parent's home in West Philadelphia. Letters to her between visits document his growing aversion to French academic art and his ever-increasing admiration for Manet, Renoir, and Degas. Eakins, Redfield, and Glackens, among other Americans, also earned his esteem.

Henri's one-man shows in 1902 at the Macbeth Gallery, the Pratt Institute in New York, and the Pennsylvania Academy drew critical praise but few sales. He became a juror at the National Academy of Design, advocating for a broader viewpoint than the traditionalist norms it promoted and exhibited. In 1903, he was elected to the Society of American Artists that had been founded in 1877 by a group of artists who rebelled against the conservatism of the National Academy. Henri was elected to the National Academy in 1905, where he used his influence to get his paintings and the works of his friends into shows at the academy and society, which merged in 1906. He had a special gift for teaching and organizing exhibits. While these activities would often pull him away from his own painting, they established his reputation as a leader in the art world.

Henri came to loggerheads with the National Academy of Design in March 1907 when fellow jurors marked down two of his paintings that had previously been accorded a high ranking. Entries by several of his friends had also either been rejected outright or severely downgraded. Henri withdrew his work from the exhibition, which caught the attention of the press. Henri received praise for confronting the jury and standing up for newer trends in art. The following month the academy eliminated his name from the jury list for the following year. Meetings with artists in Henri's studio spearheaded the idea for a group exhibition at the Macbeth Gallery on Fifth Avenue. Thus was born the group christened by critic James Gibbons Huneker as The Eight that opened their show on February 3, 1908.[42] The members of the Eight were Robert Henri, William Glackens, Everett Shinn, John Sloan, George Luks, Arthur B. Davies (1862–1928), Ernest Lawson (1873–1939), and Maurice Prendergast (1858–1924). The Philadelphians were Henri, Glackens, Sloan, Luks, and Shinn. Henri promoted the jury-free exhibition as a revolt against the academy and a rejection of the traditional art that it favored. The exhibit did not intend to showcase a group style—because there was none—but aimed to allow each artist to express his individuality without censure. The exhibition drew more than seven thousand visitors and then traveled to the Pennsylvania Academy in March 1908, followed by eight other showings in American cities. Out of the eight painters, five of them had lived and trained in Philadelphia before relocating to New York City. Years later, the group became known as the Ashcan School due to several of the members' predilections for expressively painted scenes of urban poverty with dark tonalities.[43] Despite being grouped together under one title, the purpose of the exhibition foregrounded the desire to display to the public their individual interpretations of contemporary art rather than a group aesthetic as the impressionists in Paris had done in 1874.

The expected critical division erupted in the press, divided between scorn and praise. W. B. McCormick in the *New York Press* derided the notion that, despite the show being advertised as a new direction in American art, the work presented "the most foreign, the most Frenchified show of paintings that we had seen in New York in recent years."[44] What good did it do, he asked, to follow in the footsteps of Manet, Degas, and Monet who had been the rage twenty years ago. What McCormick failed to understand was that French avant-garde art had functioned as a catalyst and springboard rather than an end point for the artists as they worked to achieve their distinctive style. Press reports nevertheless remained largely positive and noted that the work was not as radical as the French art of the last years of the nineteenth century. The French canvases that had served as inspiration impelled the Americans to embrace the modern technique and subject matter that rebelled against the academic norms of their day and the strictures of the Salon jury. Henri's 1908 depiction of *Jessica Penn in Black with White Plumes* (see Figure 11.25) demonstrates his admiration for Manet's portraits, such as *La Parisienne.* (See Figure 11.26.) Following Manet at that time was considered risky as the artist had been characterized in the Metropolitan Museum's catalog as "an eccentric realist of dubious talent."[45] Around 1904, critics such as Charles FitzGerald began to associate the emergence of the bold paintings of the young New York painters with the school of Manet.[46] Just as Manet took inspiration from Frans Hals, Velázquez, and Goya, among others, in order to develop his modern

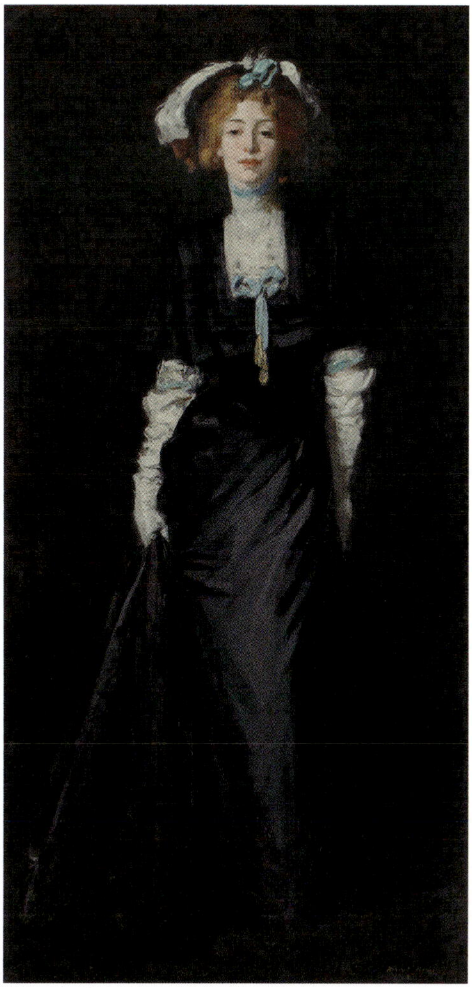

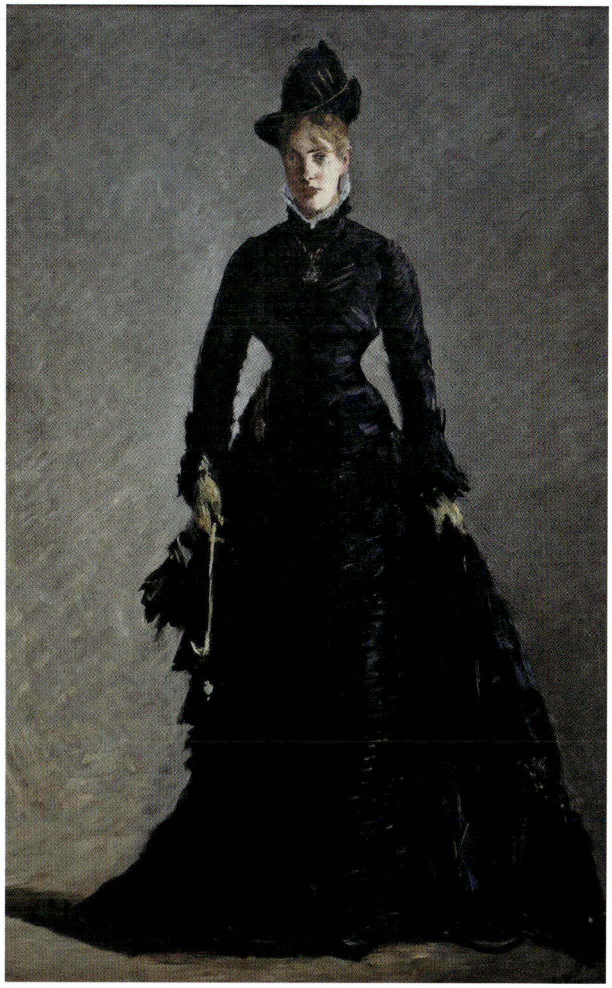

ABOVE LEFT: Figure 11.25 Robert Henri, *Jessica Penn in Black with White Plumes*, 1908. Oil on canvas, 77 × 38 in. (Crystal Bridges Museum of American Art, Bentonville, Arkansas, 2010.105. Photography by Susan A. Cole, Seattle Art Museum.)

ABOVE RIGHT: Figure 11.26 Édouard Manet, *La Parisienne*, ca. 1876. Oil on canvas, 192 × 125 cm (75.5 × 49.2 in.). (Credit: Nationalmuseum, Stockholm, Sweden/Bridgeman Images)

technique, Henri engaged in an artistic dialogue with these same masters in order to nurture his creativity in finding his distinct American voice, refusing to be bound by the authority of traditional academic practice. Manet had refused to follow the academic norms of beauty of his day, creating an art enamored of contemporary fashion and urban life in a style whose swift brushstroke mirrored the speed and immediacy of a bustling city. Guy Pène du Bois explained the negative reaction to Henri's art: "America is shocked by Henri as Paris was by Manet. He dares to express his opinion, and that is an error from the popular point of view. The populace demands pretty portraits."[47] Not surprisingly, Henri came to be called the "Manet of Manhattan."[48]

The confrontation of the academy by the exhibit resulted in the recognition that American subjects of everyday urban life in a realist style had pushed aside the impressionists' rural scenes. As Elizabeth Milroy has asserted, The Eight "transformed the art exhibition into political statement and media event and shifted forever the relationship between the American artist and the American public."[49] Encouraged by the impact of the exhibition of The Eight and frustrated by continued rejections by the National Academy in 1910, Henri, Sloan, Davies, and Walt Kuhn planned another show, the Exhibition of Independent Artists. Henri affirmed that the show would have no connection to the National Academy other than to rival it in size and importance, giving artists who had not been exhibited the opportunity to have their work seen and to showcase their individuality. The purpose of the exhibit would allow the American public to "learn the means of expressing themselves in their own time and in their own land."[50] The jury-free and prize free show drew nearly two thousand visitors who showed up at the opening on the evening of April 1, 1910. Henri soon came to be known as "the high priest of the seditionists."[51]

The incentive for organizing invitational shows free from the conservative jury of the National Academy of Design culminated in the February 1913 International Exhibition of Modern Art, known as the Armory Show. The event became a touchstone in American art during a moment of significant political and social change prior to the eruption of World War I in 1914. Over three hundred American and European artists displayed nearly thirteen hundred works of painting, sculpture, and decorative objects. Despite the fact that two-thirds of the works on display were American, the critics largely focused on the works of the postimpressionists, fauvists, and cubists. Marcel Duchamp's 1912 painting *Nude Descending a Staircase* served as a lightning rod for the howls of protest against the visual threat of its fractured forms and radical departures from naturalism. (See Figure 11.27.) Ridiculed as an explosion in a shingle factory, the painting spawned numerous cartoons, an investigation into immorality when the show traveled to Chicago, and the scathing derision by President Theodore Roosevelt who found the Navajo rug in his bathroom more pleasing than the cubist-inspired Duchamp.[52] A faction associated with the National Academy created fake European modernist works and announced that the exhibition would be held in the Lighthouse for the Blind.

The Armory Show adopted the image of an uprooted pine tree as its visual emblem, which had been adopted from the Massachusetts flag carried into battle during the Revolutionary War. The image connoted the new declaration of independence—"The New Spirit"—for American artists to cultivate their freedom to move beyond academic styles and realism, allowing them to pursue an openness to style and subject matter. It is highly appropriate that Duchamp's *Nude Descending a Staircase*, which became the eye of the critical storm of the Armory Show, now hangs in the Philadelphia Museum of Art in the city where freedom from tyranny was accomplished with the aid of the French. If the artistic revolution used palettes and posters instead of bullets and sabers, the rebellion against authoritarian rules was no less effective.

Plans to exhibit foreign art in the Armory Show fed into Henri's fears that, despite his great admiration for French art, the European work would overshadow American

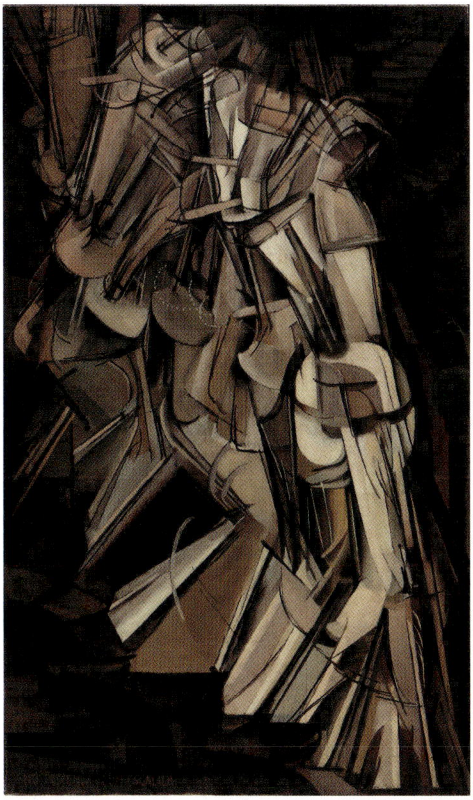

Figure 11.27 Marcel Duchamp, *Nude Descending a Staircase*, 1912. Oil on canvas, 57⅞ × 35⅛ in. (147 × 89.2 cm). Framed: 59¾ × 36¾ × 2 in. (151.8 × 93.3 × 5.1 cm). Philadelphia Museum of Art, the Louise and Walter Arensberg Collection, 1950-134-59. (Copyright: © Association Marcel Duchamp / ADAGP, Paris / Artists Rights Society (ARS), New York 2019.)

achievements. Indeed, this did happen, and 130 foreign works were purchased in contrast to only 35 by Americans. The American work in the show looked derivative and provincial when compared to the advanced art of the fauvists and cubists. The corner had been turned and the progress of modern art could not be silenced in the aftermath. Henri had been contacted by the organizers to choose European work for the show while he was in Spain and Paris from May until October of 1912. Reluctant to cede his leadership reputation, he refused unless he was given full authority as he sensed his control begin to be eclipsed along with his ideas on the direction American art should take. Although he encouraged his students to look at and try to understand the newest trends in French art, he decided not to follow the avant-garde into the level of abstraction that the new generation of painters embraced. Eakins's art now held more inspiration for him than that of Matisse and Picasso. Henri admired Eakins for his depiction of contemporary American life in the Whitmanesque spirit of democratizing art for America.[53] He bemoaned the fact that Eakins's had not achieved public recognition during his lifetime: "I venture to say that Thomas Eakins will be spoken of in times to come as one of the very great men in all American art, but he died practically unknown and received only an 'honor' or two."[54] For a decade through the nineteen-twenties Henri tried—unsuccessfully—to raise funds in Philadelphia to establish a permanent gallery for Eakins's work in the city. Henri died in 1929, the year before the Philadelphia Museum of Art first acquired and exhibited Eakins's paintings to the public.

The Armory Show wedged a divide in the road between those artists who became "ultra-moderns" and those who were considered middle of the road, neither too conservative nor too avant-garde.[55] Just as Henri earlier in his career felt divided between academic art and impressionism, so now he found that he could not embrace the intellectual side of cubism or the vividly abstracted colors of fauvism. He devoted the last part of his career largely to portraiture and teaching, where he exerted significant influence on artists such as George Bellows, Stuart Davis, and Edward Hopper. As his student Helen Appleton Read wrote, "The Henri class became a rallying cry for eager youth."[56] He gathered many of his ideas on art in *The Art Spirit*, whose advertisement brochure in 1923 succinctly characterized his art and influence. It announced him as "one of the very few men today who has the real dignity of the old masters, he is thoroughly modern, and expresses in his book the conceptions that dominate the minds of the best modern painters."[57]

In his later years Henri's friendships with the members of The Eight such as Glackens, Lawson, and Shinn continued, despite his refusal to embrace the more progressive modernist styles of expressionism and abstraction. Sloan called Henri "the Abraham Lincoln of American Art," an apt moniker for the artist who championed freedom from the enslavement to the hidebound laws and prescribed rules of painting.[58] The relationships Henri made in Philadelphia sustained him throughout his career. Sloan, for one, remarked: "I feel certain that the reason our group became painters is due to Henri."[59]

One of the artists who would have confirmed Sloan's sentiments was William J. Glackens who was born at 3214 Sansom Street on March 13, 1870. After graduating from Central High School in 1890, he began working the following year as an artist-reporter, first for the *Philadelphia Record* and then in 1892 for the *Philadelphia Press*. In 1891, he enrolled in evening classes at the Pennsylvania Academy where, at the press and the Academy, he formed lasting friendships. Also, in 1891, Henri returned to Philadelphia from study in Paris. Glackens visited the Metropolitan Museum of Art twice with Henri in 1894 where they both expressed keen admiration for Manet and Whistler whom Glackens would later deem the great artists of the century.[60]

Sharing a studio with Henri in November 1894 undoubtedly influenced Glackens on the advantages of working in France. In June 1895, Glackens, Henri, and Schofield sailed to France and headed for Paris where they immersed themselves in the art scene. Henri informed his parents: "We have nearly *killed* ourselves regularly every day in our efforts to see the Salons before they close. . . . There are many good things and hundreds and thousands of bad. There is lots of room at the top in art. . . . Glackens thinks Paris a wonderful place."[61] The following October, after traveling through Belgium, Holland, and Italy to study the old masters, Glackens rented a studio in Montparnasse where he stayed for a year. Glackens did not study with anyone in Paris, preferring to forge his own path through his study of the works of the modern school in Paris and the works in the Louvre, which he proclaimed "a wonderful gallery," concluding that there "is no need of any other school."[62] His 1895 *Bal Bullier* (see Figure 11.28) demonstrates his borrowing of motifs from Manet as he adapted the pose of *The Absinthe Drinker's* (see Figure 11.29) legs to the central male figure's dancing stride. He

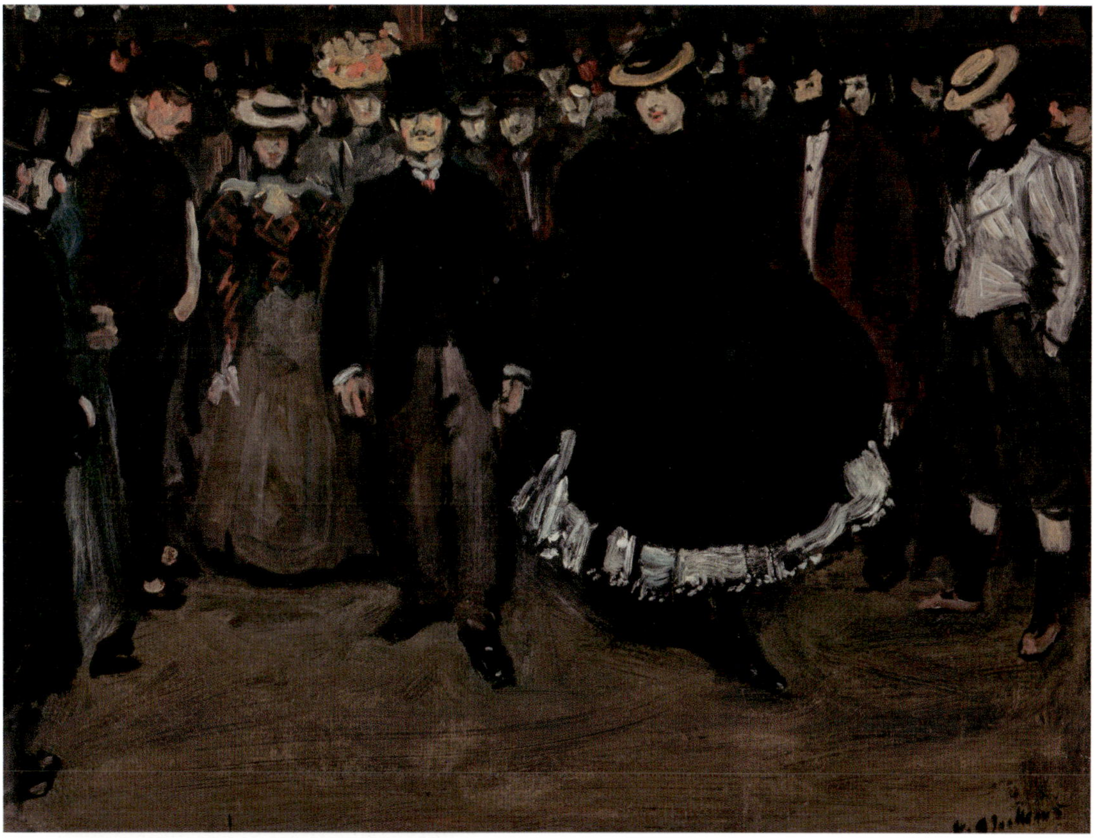

Figure 11.28 William Glackens, *Bal Bullier*, c. 1895. Oil on canvas, 23 13/16 × 32 in. (60.5 × 81.3 cm). (Photography © Terra Foundation for American Art, Chicago. Daniel J. Terra Collection, 1999.59.)

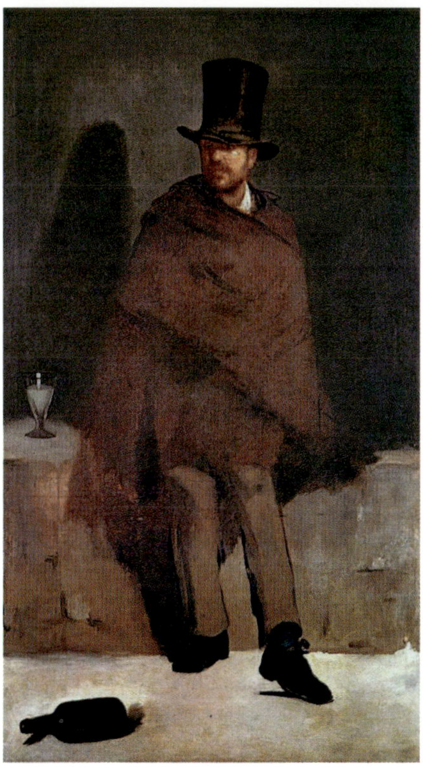

Figure 11.29 Édouard Manet, *The Absinthe Drinker*, 1859. Oil on canvas, 178 × 103 cm (70 × 40.5 in.). (Ny Carlsberg Glyptothek)

had a painting of the fashionable Luxembourg Gardens accepted for exhibition at the 1896 Salon of the Société Nationale des Beaux-Arts. The preference for the painting of everyday people and sites by the Parisian modernists in rejection of academic subjects of history and mythology greatly appealed to the Glackens whose profession as an illustrator for newspapers trained his eye to observe events of contemporary urban life.

Unlike other artists who destroyed most of the work they had done in Paris, Glackens returned to Philadelphia in October 1896 with what he described as "stacks of paintings."[63] He accepted a commission to create mural-size paintings for the Pennsylvania Academy's lecture room and exhibited five of his French canvases at the Sixty-Sixth Annual Exhibition at the academy that opened on December 21, 1896. But Philadelphia could not retain Glackens for long after his return from Paris. He was contacted by George Luks, a fellow student at the Pennsylvania Academy with whom he had worked at the *Pennsylvania Press* as an illustrator. Luks had moved to New York in April 1896 and had taken a position as an artist for Joseph Pulitzer's *New York Sunday World*, persuading Glackens to join him at the paper. Glackens moved to New York in late 1896 and resumed making newspaper illustrations.

In 1902, Glackens accepted a commission to illustrate the novels of Charles Paul de Kock (1793–1871), a prolific nineteenth-century French writer whose novels depicting French life and its mores enjoyed greater popularity abroad than they did in their own country. The fifty-four etchings and drawings done for the stories continued to stoke Glackens's Francophilia. When Henri relocated to New York in August 1900, Glackens turned once again to painting as Henri became actively engaged in arranging group shows. The 1901 exhibition at the Allan Gallery provided Glackens's first critical review in the *New York Evening Sun* by Charles FitzGerald who hailed Glackens's pronounced individuality while noting the influence of Manet.[64] The painters in the January 1904 exhibition organized by Henri at the National Arts Club gained recognition for their stylistic innovations and again the impact of Manet and Degas drew notice in the press.[65]

Glackens wrote to a friend in 1895 that the Paris cafés served as a never-ending source of inspiration to him.[66] The first Parisian café opened in the seventeenth century and continues today as a hub of social and culinary life. Manet and Degas sharpened their aesthetic and political ideas with other painters at the Café Guerbois and the Nouvelle Athènes. They frequently chose the subject of the café to demonstrate their commitment to painting the contemporary aspects of modern-day Paris. Glackens gave visual testimony to his love of modern café life in his 1905 painting *Chez Mouquin*. (See Figure 11.30.) The artist and his friends frequented the Café Bordeaux, known as Mouquin's, a restaurant that vicariously transported its clientele to Paris with its decor, music, and cuisine and was ranked as the most authentically French in New York City. Glackens posed the wife of the proprietor, Jeanne Louise Mouquin, and his friend James B. Moore, at a table. He played a variation on Manet's *A Bar at the Folies-Bergère* (see Figure 11.31) by adopting the indifferent boredom of the female figure, the mirror with its scumbled reflections, and the still life on the white table of flowers and glassware. Glackens largely avoided the contradictions and ambiguities of

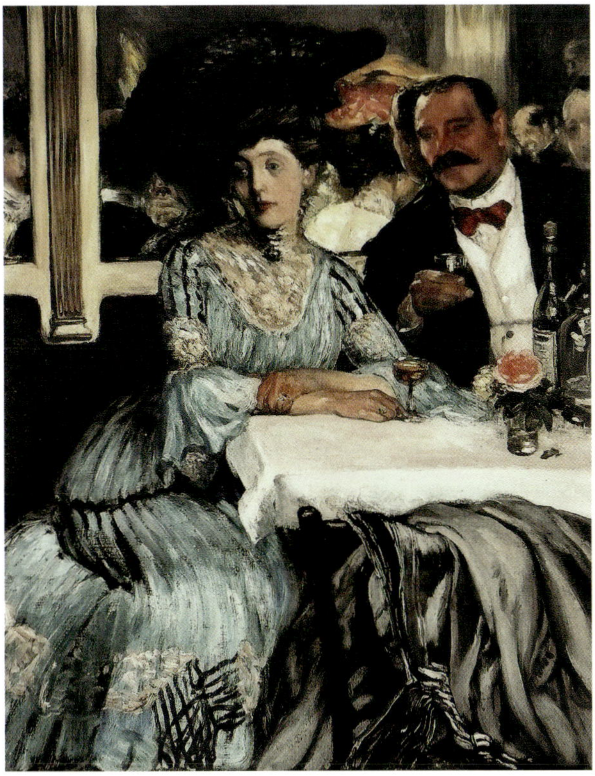

Figure 11.30 William Glackens, *Chez Mouquin*, 1905. Oil on canvas, 48⅛ × 36¼ in. (122.4 × 92.1 cm). (Art Institute of Chicago, Friends of American Art Collection)

Figure 11.31 Édouard Manet, *A Bar at the Folies-Bergère*, 1881–1882. Oil on canvas, 96 × 130 cm (37.7 × 51.1 in.). (The Courtauld Institute)

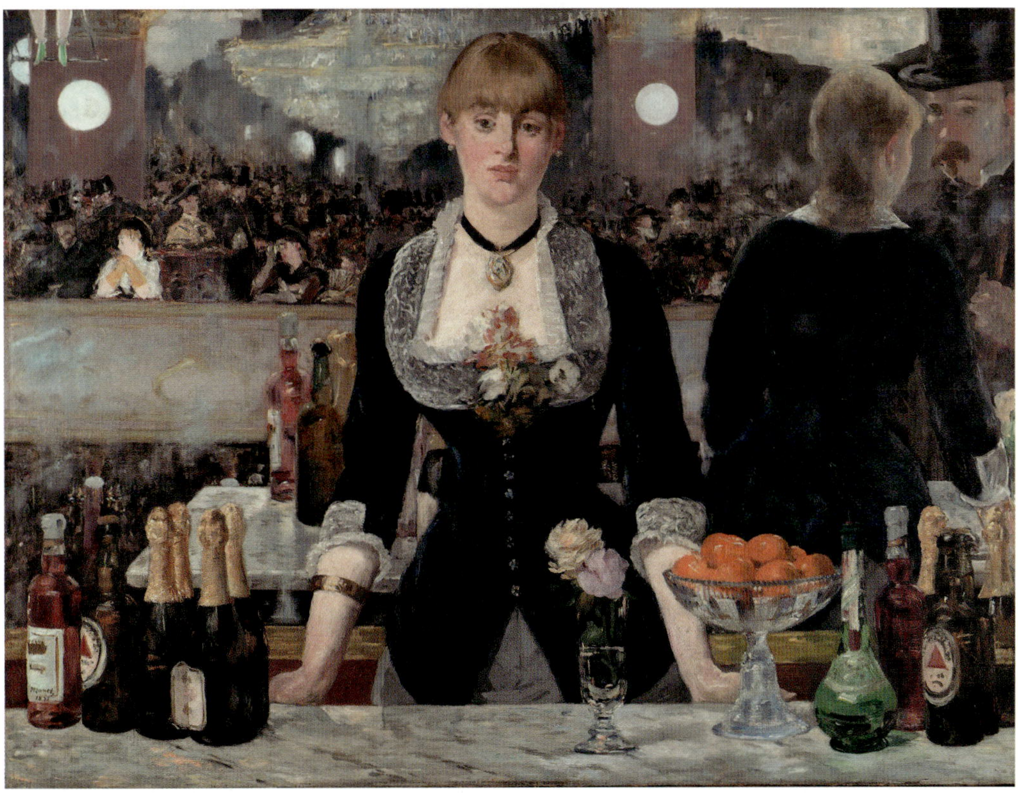

Manet's mirror, whose reflections refused to adhere to optical truth. Manet skewed the perspective of the barmaid and her customer, and the bottles in the foreground refuse to align with their reflected counterparts. Manet's strategy of emphasizing the disjunction between the figure and objects on the counter with their cognate reflections in the mirror deliberately undermined the tenets of naturalism and imitation in art. His violation of traditional pictorial protocols and abrupt dislocations rejected the traditional perspective of academic correctness, ignoring illusionism and mimesis in order to call attention to how the work was painted. Glackens's retained the illusion of depth by painting Madame Mouquin's gray cloak tossed over a chair in front of the table and the figures. He nevertheless made the cloak's creases and folds a swathe of painterly virtuosity and freedom that suggest rather than define the object, thus indicating his understanding of the modernist principles underpinning the avant-garde. Manet depicted a petit bourgeois barmaid whose working status has caused her to be read as a woman of easy virtue. Glackens's provided his female sitter with a wedding ring, thus avoiding the social innuendo of serious urban problems such as prostitution that swirled around the criticism of Manet's painting.[67]

Glackens married in 1904 but postponed his honeymoon to May 1906 when he and his wife Edith Dimock journeyed to Spain and France. When they returned home from their honeymoon, Glackens submitted canvases to the National Academy of Design's 1906 winter exhibition where every one of them was rejected. The following year he had only one accepted. Following Henri's lead, Glackens joined the exhibit at the Macbeth Gallery and became known as one of The Eight. His *Chez Mouquin* and *The Shoppers* (see Figure 11.32) depict middle-class pleasures and avoid any direct social propaganda. James Huneker affirmed that *The Shoppers* was "contemporary with a vengeance."[68] Degas had depicted female shoppers trying on hats and interacting with the milliners in a series of pastels and paintings from the 1880s.[69] "Think of a treatise on ornament for women or by women," Degas wrote, "based on their manner of observing, of combining, of sensing their fashionable outfits and all things. On a daily basis they compare, more than men, a thousand visible things with each other."[70] Glackens's dramatically large-scale painting with its women glancing in different directions visually fulfills Degas's recommendation. Fashionable hats and a mink coat replace the Roman helmets and togas that had been the mainstay of academic art. The narrative is a mundane scene from contemporary consumer culture rather than chivalrous deeds from a long-gone era, as if following Whitman's advice to "find great things in the littlest things of life."[71]

Glackens played a significant role in the Armory Show as chairman of the Committee on Domestic Exhibits. He rightly predicted that the American section of the show would pale in comparison to the foreign work. His explanation sheds lights on the rationale for his own attraction to French art: "American art is like every other art—a matter of influence. Art, like humanity, every time has an ancestry. . . . Everything worth while (*sic*) in our art is due to the influence of French art. We have not yet arrived at a national art."[72] After the Armory Show he began to put some distance between his subject matter and style from his colleagues who had organized the show

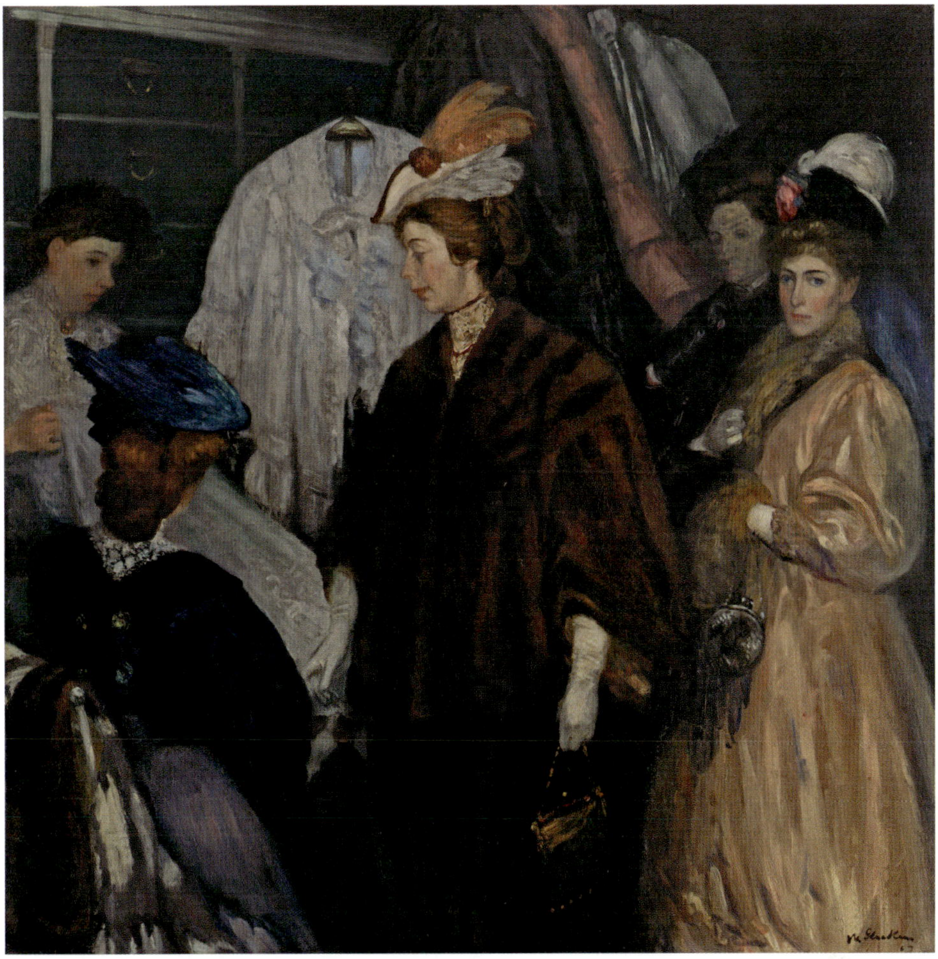

Figure 11.32 William James Glackens. American (1870–1938). *The Shoppers*, 1907–08. Oil on Canvas, 60 × 60 in. (152.4 × 152.4 cm). (Chrysler Museum of Art, Norfolk, VA. Gift of Walter P. Chrysler, Jr. 71.651.)

and who had split into two groups between the realists and the more progressive painters.

While Glackens never embraced abstraction and disliked cubism, his preference for impressionist light and color had already begun to replace the darker palettes of Manet and Degas as Renoir's art came into its ascendancy in his aesthetic preferences. Durand-Ruel's 1908 exhibit of forty-one Renoirs at his gallery in New York and Glackens's association with Maurice and Charles Prendergast, both of whom had adopted a lighter color palette and a more spontaneous brushstroke, provided him with the incentive to change his style. This became evident in his 1910 painting *Nude with Apple*. (See Figure 11.33.) Glackens invoked Manet's most notorious work, his *Olympia* (see Figure 11.34) that outraged the Salon critics in 1865 for its representation of a prostitute and its radical rejection of academic style and subject matter.[73] Glackens

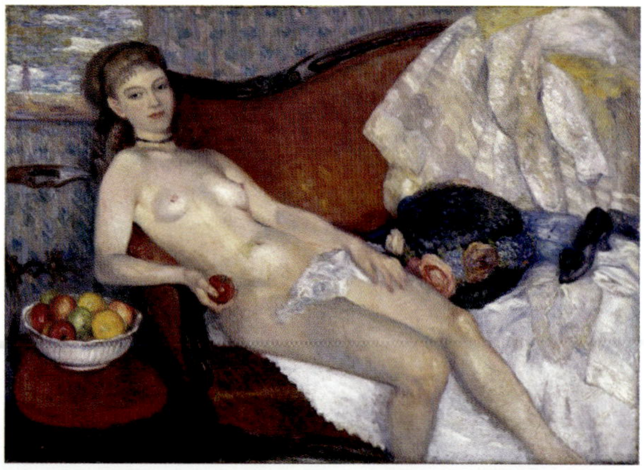

FIGURE 11.33 William Glackens, *Nude with Apple*, 1910. Oil on canvas, 39 7/16 × 56 3/16 in. (100.2 × 142.7 cm). (Brooklyn Museum, Dick S. Ramsay Fund, 56.70)

FIGURE 11.34 Édouard Manet, *Olympia*, 1863. Oil on canvas, 130 × 190 cm (51.1 × 74.8 in.). (Paris, Musée d'Orsay. Photo: Christopher Campbell.)

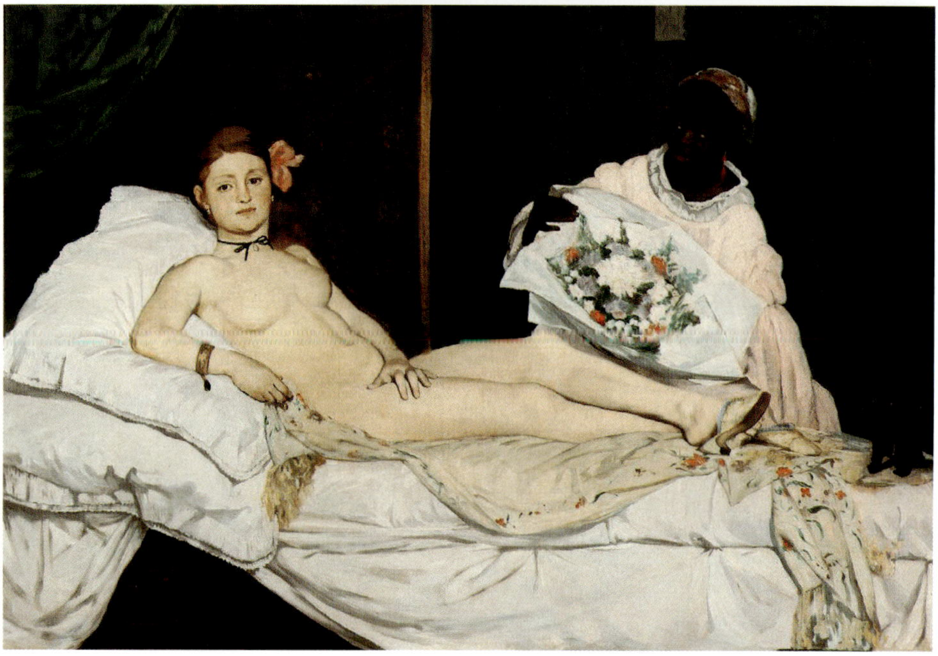

converted Manet's figure into a modern Eve reclining on a red sofa instead of a bed, substituting the bouquet held by the black maid with a flowered hat and placing a fashionable shoe where the cat in Manet's work stood. Gone are the dark palette and outlined figures in the Manet. Instead, one can easily detect the feathery touch, bluish tints in the cloth, and softened palette as seen in Renoir's *Reclining Nude*, for example. (See Figure 11.35.) As Glackens developed his painting after 1910, critics labeled him a "Renoirino,"[74] drawing parallels between his preference for genial subject matter and a variegated color palette. *Nude with Apple* marked a distinct change and was immediately noticed by Henri who observed the French influence but distinguished Glackens's originality from his models: "He shows a wonderful painting of a nude that has many of the qualities that you notice in the Neo-Impressionist movement. But

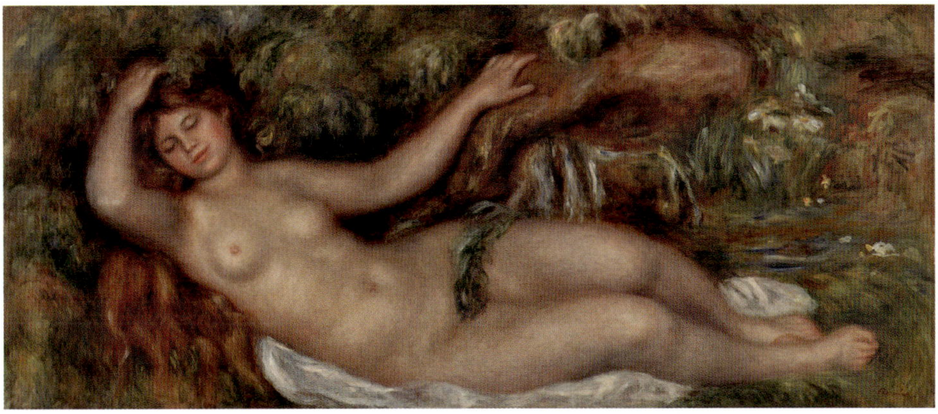

Figure 11.35 Auguste Renoir, *Reclining Nude (La Source)*, ca. 1895. Oil on canvas, 25 13/16 × 61 7/16 in. (65.5 × 156 cm). (Philadelphia, The Barnes Foundation)

Glackens seem to me to have attained a greater beauty and a more fundamental truth. There is something rare, something new in the thing that he has to say."[75]

Nude with Apple served as a signpost toward Glackens's future painting as after the Armory Show he focused more intently on the figure in the interior and the still life where one can discern Glackens's absorption of aspects of the art of Pierre Bonnard, Henri Matisse, and other French painters. But his attraction to Renoir, especially his late work, remained a force in Glackens's work. This became apparent in 1913, when Glackens exhibited five nudes at a solo show at New York's Folsom Gallery. A critic noted that here was "something monumental in his nudes, a bigness, a solidity, a sound firmness of flesh."[76] The similarities can easily be seen in Glackens's *Back of a Nude* (see Figure 11.36) when compared to Renoir's *Bather in Three-Quarter View*. (See Figure 11.37.) Both nudes are situated in timeless rather than contextual settings with their monumental scale and sumptuous physicality, with their lack of narrative and cropping giving them a primal force that dominates the canvases. Both artists layered their nudes with short fluid strokes of paint that build the sculptural form of the figures. Forbes Watson characterized Glackens's art in 1923: "There is no tormented, morbid struggle with profound life facts disturbing him. He doesn't delve deeply into psychology. The color of the world makes him thoroughly happy, and to express happiness in color has become his first and foremost natural impulse."[77] The alliance with Renoir becomes clear as the Frenchman had declared: "For me, a painting should be a loving, joyous, and pretty thing, yes pretty."[78]

Glackens had abundant access to Renoir's paintings at the Barnes Foundation in Merion, Pennsylvania, which is discussed in Chapter 12. Glackens and Barnes had attended Central High School along with John Sloan. In 1912, Barnes sent Glackens to Paris on a buying trip to purchase works of art that launched his growing collection. Eventually Barnes would amass one 181 Renoirs and credited Glackens for initiating his passion for the painter.[79] These, along with numerous works by Cézanne, Matisse, and Picasso, nourished Glackens's eye and imagination with artistic styles and motifs

FIGURE 11.36
William Glackens, *Back of a Nude*, ca. 1930–1938. Oil on canvas, 76.2 × 63.5 cm (30 × 25 in.). (NSU Art Museum Fort Lauderdale; gift of the Sansom Foundation, Inc.)

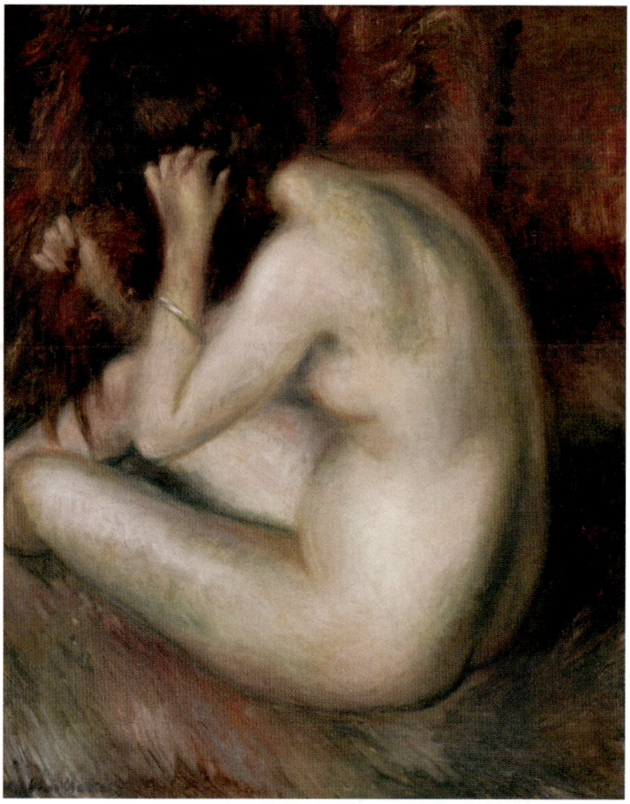

FIGURE 11.37
Auguste Renoir, *Bather in Three-Quarter View*, 1911. Oil on canvas, 32$\frac{5}{16}$ × 26 in. (82 × 66 cm). (Philadelphia, The Barnes Foundation)

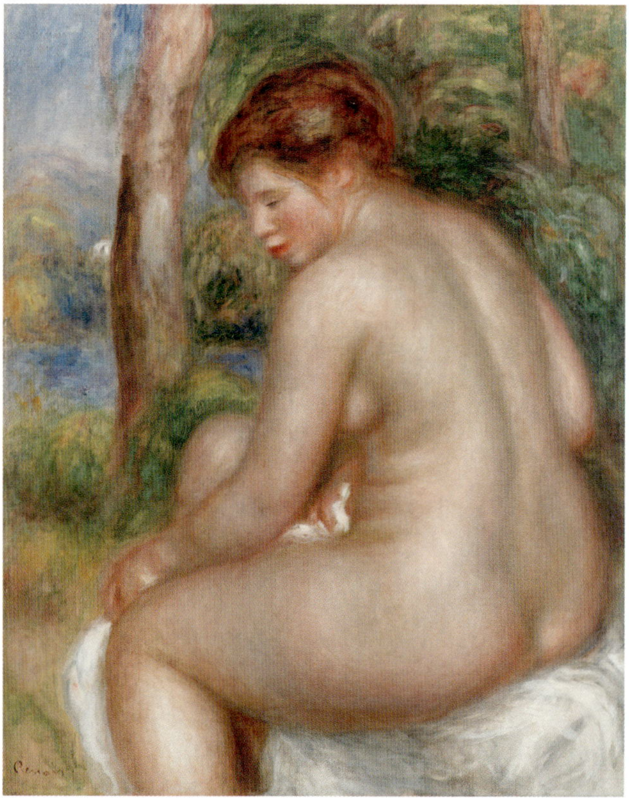

FACING PAGE, FIGURE 11.38
Robert Henri, *Nude in Motion*, 1913. Oil on canvas, 77¼ × 37¼ in. (196.2 × 94.6 cm). (Photography © Terra Foundation for American Art, Chicago. Daniel J. Terra Collection, 1992.126.)

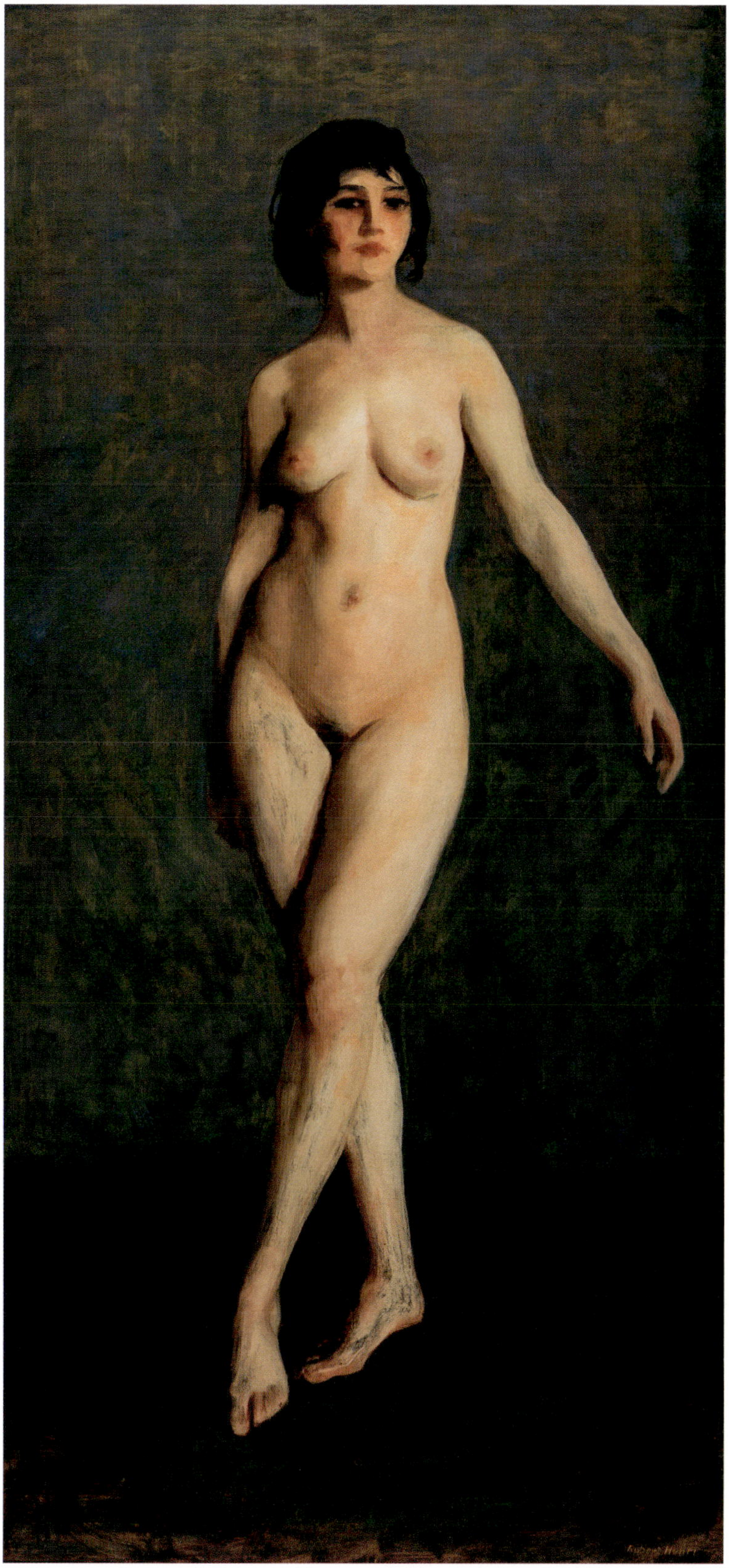

that he assimilated into a uniquely vernacular style that made him a significant figure in the history of American modernism. Glackens may have left Philadelphia while still a young artist, but he often returned to the city to visit with Barnes and traveled with him to Europe on purchasing trips. Barnes, whose irascible personality constantly alienated those who dealt with him, considered Glackens a lifelong friend and credited him with being "the most valuable single educational factor" in his knowledge of modern art.[80] The Barnes Foundation contains seventy-one of Glackens's works, more than any other American artist. Glackens's impact on Barnes and his collection makes him an irrevocable part of the history of the connections between France and Philadelphia.

Glackens's son Ira testified that "Paris was always my father's favorite city, and France his spiritual home. Everything suited him there, the food, the wine, the people in the streets and public gardens, whom he loved to sketch. . . . No other country seemed to invite his pencil and his brush."[81] Glackens avoided the complex references to older art that vexed Manet's critics and shunned the somewhat cynical side of the hardships depicted in so many of Degas's urban scenes. He experimented with and absorbed the advances of European and American modernism while remaining attentive to the lessons of the old masters. By studying their motifs and incorporating their pictorial strategies into his own methods, he created a unique and original body of art.

By the end of the second decade of the twentieth century, the art world largely ignored the paintings of the Pennsylvania impressionists and the works of The Eight. As the avant-garde artists embraced the new visual tactics seen in the Armory Show the work of the New Hope Colony and the Henri group seemed old-fashioned. An example of what the future would hold can be seen when both Henri and Duchamp showed a nude figure in motion at the Armory Show. Duchamp fractured the forms of the nude, that hallowed subject of art so dear to the academy, while Henri's demure balletic figure, *Nude in Motion,* adheres to the truth of the visual model. (See Figure 11.38.) Duchamp's shattered forms presaged the demise of impressionism and realism in America. With her plummeting passage down the staircase, her fleshy curves converted to a series of mechanical cylinders and cones, Duchamp's nude matched another French nude *succès de scandale*—Manet's *Olympia*—in the outrage it caused and the changes it engendered in the generation of artists that followed. Duchamp's nude slammed the door on naturalism, impressionism, and realism. With her appearance at the Armory Show, Duchamp's figure initiated an adventurous foray into modernist developments in American art. Her clanking, cantankerous footsteps can still be heard to resound in the present day.

[12]

Barnes and Mastbaum Enrich the Parkway, and Philadelphia's French Outdoor Art

After the Civil War, Philadelphia became a major industrial city with its factories and manufacturing industry earning the city the moniker "Workshop of the World." Diversified trades such as textiles and metalworking had their products shipped along with the output from carpet and yarn mills from the city's ports or laded them onto the Pennsylvania railroad system. As fortunes were made, wealthy entrepreneurs and successful businessmen and families sought to acquire works of art for their estates. Many turned to collecting paintings from Europe to display a social cachet of sophistication in imitation of families with inherited wealth. The increase in the number of art galleries began to rival independent exhibitions and facilitated knowledge of contemporary art at home and abroad. The 1876 Centennial Exposition provided the American public with its first widespread exposure to the visual treasures of Europe. This spurred the culture of collecting in Philadelphia, aided in the following years by the growth in the number of art auctions and dealers such as Paul Durand-Ruel whose gallery in New York brought impressionism to America.[1] By 1880, French painting became so avidly sought after by collectors in the United States, Germany, and Russia that the French government began to be concerned that few examples would remain on their native soil.[2]

Earl Shinn's three-volume work *Art Treasures of America* (1879–1881) documented the taste of collectors that conservatively tended toward the acquisition of French academic painters and landscape paintings of the Barbizon School. Around the turn of the twentieth century, Philadelphia displayed such an active culture of collecting that the city was compared to the Florentine Renaissance.[3] The businessman and inventor William L. Elkins (1832–1903), who formed his collection between 1887 and 1900, largely preferred seventeenth-century Dutch and eighteenth-century English portraiture. Joseph E. Widener (1871–1943) inherited an extensive collection of old master paintings from his father Peter that included a dozen or more paintings by Rembrandt that he housed at Lynnewood Hall in Elkins Park outside of Philadelphia. In 1939, he donated his collection, which by that time had grown to more than six hundred works, to the National Gallery in Washington, DC.[4] Old master paintings and academic Salon art sold easily, while the more radical modern art of the impressionists and postimpressionists proved more challenging to conservative American taste.[5]

None of this deterred Albert Coombs Barnes (1872–1951), one of the most avid and successful collectors of French art. His collection on Latch's Lane in Merion, and now on the Benjamin Franklin Parkway, has made Philadelphia a destination city for lovers of impressionist and postimpressionist art. With 181 Renoirs and 69 Cézannes, the Barnes Foundation can boast of having more of these masters' works than any other collection in the world. Additionally, the 59 works by Matisse and 46 Picassos make it a prime repository of early modernist art. Barnes became known as the Medici of Merion for his vast acquisition primarily of French painting, along with African sculpture, Pennsylvania German furniture, a variety of ceramics, wrought iron, Native American jewelry, and early twentieth-century American art.[6]

Barnes first saw the light of day in a small townhouse in the hard-scrabble section of Philadelphia's Kensington neighborhood. His father had worked as a butcher along with Peter Widener who grew very rich supplying meat to the Union Army during the Civil War. Barnes's intellectual acumen earned his acceptance into the academically rigorous Central High School where he met William M. Glackens and John Sloan, two painters who played a significant role in the modernist movement in early twentieth-century New York.[7] Barnes soon recognized that his attempts at making paintings and drawings could not produce the same results as those of his talented classmates. This early insight demonstrated Barnes's keen eye for quality and assessment. At the age of twenty he enrolled in the University of Pennsylvania Medical School, supporting himself by tutoring, playing semiprofessional baseball, and boxing. The competitive nature of the sports he engaged in would emerge in his combative personality as he sparred with dealers, collectors, universities, and the public throughout his lifetime.

A variety of internships in medicine convinced Barnes that he was not suited to clinical practice as a physician. He left Philadelphia for Berlin in 1896 to immerse himself in the study of chemistry for eighteen months. He returned to Germany in 1898 to study at the Ruprecht-Karls-Universität in Heidelberg under the sponsorship of the H. K. Mulford pharmaceutical company. There he recruited Hermann Hille to return with him to Philadelphia in 1900 to work for the Mulford firm. Two years later, they both left Mulford when they had invented Argyrol, a silver nitrate solution that treated eye infections and prevented infantile blindness caused by gonorrhea. Hille ran production while Barnes oversaw marketing and sales in their partnership. Their collaboration ended in a bitter legal dispute in 1908 with Barnes enlisting as his attorney John G. Johnson, the founder of the law firm Saul Ewing, who had acquired notable examples of early Renaissance Italian, Spanish, Flemish, and Dutch paintings.[8] Johnson's yearly trips to Europe yielded acquisitions of canvases by Courbet,

Manet, and Monet, which he stored in his Broad Street Mansion, along with works by John Singer Sargent, James McNeill Whistler, and T. Alexander Harrison, all of whom had lived and painted in Paris.[9] Johnson's collection, less focused on France than Barnes's but partnering with its riches, now resides at the Philadelphia Museum of Art. Both Johnson and Barnes, whose fortunes resulted from professional accomplishments rather than inherited wealth, preserved their collections from dispersal, thus making Philadelphia a major destination for art lovers.[10]

After Johnson obtained a legal severance from Hille for him, Barnes established factories in Philadelphia, London, and Australia, launching a direct-marketing campaign to physicians and hospitals under the solo name of A. C. Barnes Company. Argyrol's silver nitrate solution turned into financial gold for Barnes, whose millions freed him to pursue his interest in philosophy and art. In 1905, he began purchasing paintings in New York, mostly work from the French Barbizon School that had achieved significant popularity in America. He displayed these, along with works by William Glackens, Alfred Maurer, Maurice Prendergast, and Ernest Lawson in his Philadelphia factory where the racially mixed workers also participated in discussion groups for two hours a day, studying the writings of William James and John Dewey, among others. A circulating library was also at the disposal of his factory employees, thus manifesting Barnes's early determination to educate those with little opportunity for advanced study in aesthetics and art. Barnes's continued interest in chemistry remained entrepreneurial rather than investigative as his fortune allowed him to concentrate on building his collection. Its only trace might be recorded in his habit of mixing cocktails at his home with chemistry beakers.

In February 1912, Barnes sent William Glackens to Paris with $20,000 to purchase art for the estate he had built on nearly three acres in Merion with his wife Laura Leggett Barnes. Glackens scoured the galleries and found the assignment taxing but returned to Merion with twenty paintings, among them Cézanne's 1878–1880 *Towards Mont Sainte-Victoire* (see Figure 12.1), Van Gogh's 1889 version of *The Postman Roulin*, Picasso's 1901 Blue Period *Woman with a Cigarette*, and a Renoir. The following April, Barnes purchased a Corot landscape, a Renoir, and a Monet from the Paul Durand-Ruel Gallery in New York. In June, he visited Paris and when he returned again the following December he met Gertrude and Leo Stein who sold him two Matisse works. Barnes shared a deep love for Renoir and, in March 1913, informed his friend in a letter that he now owned a dozen of the painter's canvases. A year later, the number of Renoirs had doubled and were joined by a dozen Cézannes. Throughout the years, these numbers would swell exponentially with a concentration on Renoir, Cézanne, Matisse, and precubist Picassos.[11] It took an adventurous spirit of risk to invest in canvases disdained by critics for images and lifelike details obscured by strokes of paint dabbed quickly on the canvas. Heroic narratives on large canvases meant to commemorate historical events and serve as edifying lessons to the viewer yielded to common scenes from everyday life. Perspectival depth disappeared, keeping the viewer focused on a surface whose finish was no longer hidden under layers of varnish. The window of illusionism had been slammed shut.

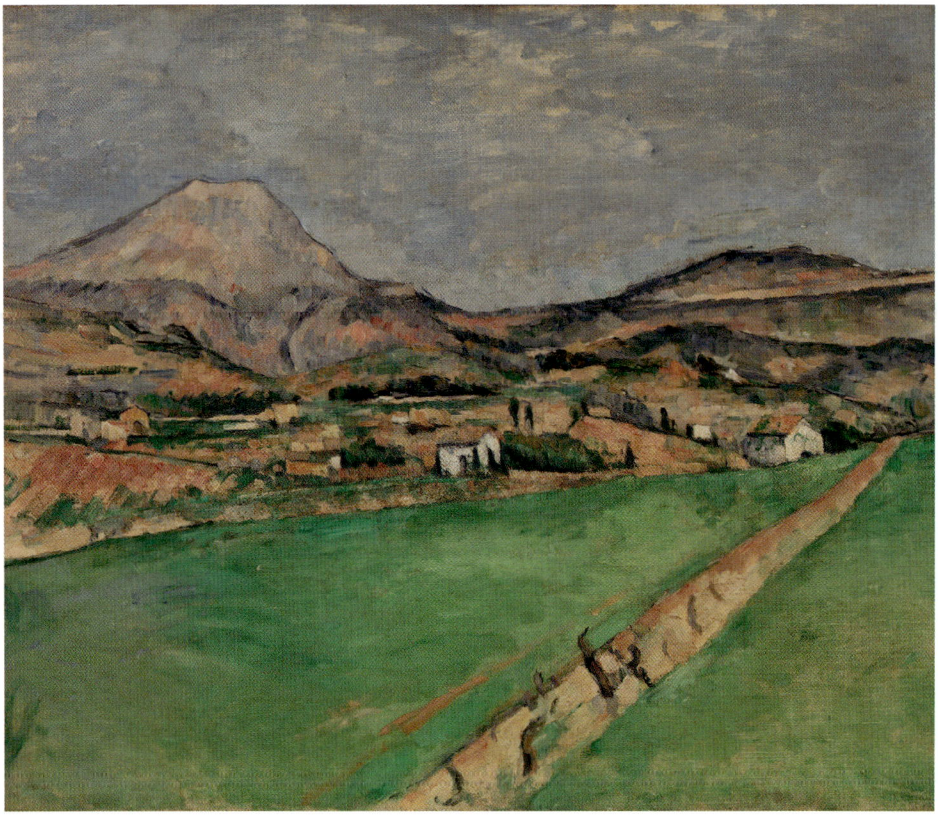

FIGURE 12.1 Paul Cézanne, *Towards Mont Sainte-Victoire*, 1878–1879. Oil on canvas, 18⅛ × 21⅝ in. (46 × 55 cm). (Philadelphia, The Barnes Foundation)

An encounter with Roger Fry, the English painter and art critic, in Paul Guillaume's art gallery in Paris resulted in a conversation on Renoir and Cézanne that Barnes said he would remember for the rest of his life.[12] Fry had coined the term *postimpressionism* when he organized an exhibit that he titled "Manet and the Post-Impressionists" at the Grafton Galleries in London in 1910. He perceived that works by Manet, Seurat, Cézanne, Van Gogh, Gauguin, Matisse, and others advanced beyond the fugitive painterly effects of impressionism to explore color, line, and form to convey highly personal emotional expressions. Fry's deep attraction to Cézanne's art informed his aesthetic principles, and Barnes had developed ideas along similar lines. Both men were among the first to grasp the revolutionary potential of French modernist art.

Fry's postimpressionist exhibition in London in 1910 evoked an outrage similar to the reaction to the first impressionist exhibition in Paris in 1874. Accusations of madness were flung at the artists and Fry himself, with cruel reminders that his wife was in an insane asylum. Critics deemed Cézanne's paintings the equivalent of children's doodles while the critic for the *Morning Post* described the exhibition in 1910 as a "widespread plot to destroy the whole fabric of European painting."[13] The second London show at the Grafton Galleries in 1912 fared little better. The press in America covered the tumultuous response to the exhibitions, and word of it would certainly have reached Glackens and Maurer as they purchased for Barnes the works of the very artists Fry promoted and the public scorned. Barnes attended the Grafton Galleries exhibit in 1912 and, furthermore, was never one to be swayed easily by public opinion or bow to controversy. He would remain as undeterred by critical drubbings as Fry was. If anything, they spurred his stubborn determination to prove the critics wrong.

Barnes read John Dewey's 1916 *Democracy and Education*, which led him to enroll in Dewey's philosophy seminar in 1917 at Columbia University. A lifelong friendship ensued that deeply engaged both men in aesthetics, psychology, and art education. They maintained a prolific correspondence, visited with each other, and traveled to Europe twice together. Their interactions fostered their mutual development in their aesthetic theories, and they dedicated books to each other. Although they understandably held different opinions on art and its function, they shared a belief in learning through lived experience. Barnes focused intently on the formal and expressive values in art—line, color, light, and space—to the exclusion of social history, biography, or chronological context, which he felt detracted from the intrinsic value of the work. When he first hung his art in his home and eventually in his gallery, he ignored period style and country of origin. He displayed his paintings in arrangements, known as ensembles, where he surrounded them with wrought-iron metalwork, Native American pottery, Pennsylvania German furniture, and Navajo textiles, to name just a few of the eclectic objects he amassed during his lifetime. The French poet and art essayist Paul Valéry characterized the arrangements as "a strange organized disorder."[14] The ensembles aimed to inculcate in the viewer a sensitivity to the formal and expressive affinities inherent in the juxtapositions. He eventually invested his commitment to establishing his attitudes for evaluating a work of art into five books that expounded on his method of looking at, analyzing, and appreciating works of art. The primary lessons of these books, three of them focused individually on Renoir, Cézanne, and Matisse, demonstrate the impact of French art on his aesthetic formations and convictions.

Barnes's combative nature came prominently to the fore when the Pennsylvania Academy of Fine Art displayed works from his collection. Barnes had congratulated Arthur B. Carles on an exhibit he had organized in 1921 at the Pennsylvania Academy titled *Paintings and Drawings by American Artists Showing the Later Tendencies in Art*. All but one of the eighty-eight artists were still living, and their work displayed progressive tendencies. Barnes praised Carles for making "the first real move to shake Philadelphia out of the lethargy which has been the reproach to us from artists and collectors of other cities."[15] In December 1922, Barnes proposed to Carles that he mount an exhibition of some of the acquisitions from his recent buying trip to Paris. This resulted in *Contemporary European Paintings and Sculpture* at the Pennsylvania Academy that displayed seventy-five paintings and sculptures that were on view from April 11 to May 9, 1923. Works by Chaim Soutine, André Derain, Amadeo Modigliani, along with seven sculptures by Jacques Lipchitz, met with a fury similar to that experienced by Fry a decade earlier. A physician named William H. Wadsworth asserted that the drawings of insane patients were superior to the "alleged" works he saw at the exhibition and suggested that legal action should be taken to suppress such works.[16] Edith Powell of *The Public Ledger* concurred with him, specifically attacking Chaim Soutine's canvases as "the creations of a disintegrating mind."[17] Barnes, ever the pugilist, responded to his critics with blistering letters, informing Powell in a letter that she would never be a bona fide art critic until she had sexual relations with the ice man. Barnes battled with the Philadelphia academic establishment and the press for decades to come, convinced of the rightness of his methodological ideas and aesthetic choices. "I am trying to do the biggest thing for Philadelphia that any one man has ever attempted," he wrote in the *Public Ledger*.[18]

Barnes hired Paul Cret to design the building for his foundation on Latch's Lane in Merion.[19] The Philadelphia press continued to deride his collection once his plans were revealed. "Merion to House Art of 'Radicals'" proclaimed the *Evening Bulletin* on January 13, 1923. On April 29, 1923, the magazine section of the *Philadelphia Inquirer* featured an article titled "America's $6,000,000 Shrine to All the Craziest 'Art.'" Undaunted by the rejection of his artistic selections, Barnes opened his foundation on March 19, 1925, all the while seeking to establish relations with Philadelphia-area public schools, colleges, and universities to fund professorships that would foster his ideas. His tenacity in insisting that his ideas be implemented without deviation led to conflicts with the University of Pennsylvania, Haverford College, and Sarah Lawrence, whose president he insisted should travel to the foundation for weekly lessons from Yonkers, New York. Barnes articulated his ideas in *The Art in Painting*, which he published the same year that he established his foundation, but he met with much resistance when he sought to fund professorships at institutions that balked under the yoke of his dogmatic method.

Barnes continued to collect on his several annual trips abroad. In Paris, he dealt with Ambroise Vollard whose early exhibitions of Cézanne, Renoir, Picasso, and Matisse considerably heightened their reputations and careers. Vollard described Barnes in the act of choosing art for his collection: "Mr. Barnes comes to see you. He gets you to show him twenty or thirty pictures. Unhesitatingly, as they pass before him, he picks out this one or that one. Then he goes away. In this expeditious fashion, which only a taste as sure as his made possible, Mr. Barnes brought together [his] incomparable collection."[20] Barnes purchased so much art from Durand-Ruel that he joked in a letter that his collection practically became an annex to his gallery.[21]

In 1926, the Republic of France named Barnes a Chevalier of the Legion of Honor. Brittany especially appealed to Barnes, and he was made an honorary citizen of Port-Manech where he adopted a dog that he named Fidèle de Port-Manech. The elegantly named canine even "signed" Barnes's letters, such as the one to the drama critic and actor, Alexander Woolcott, member of the famed Algonquin Round Table, who wrote to seek admission to the foundation. He was informed that Barnes was on his front lawn singing to the birds and could not be disturbed.[22] Perhaps Woolcott fared a bit better than T. S. Eliot who received a similar refusal, but with only one word: "Nuts!"[23] Barnes restricted entrance to his collection to students taking his prescribed courses and a few favored friends. Vollard avowed that a visit to the Barnes Foundation was itself worth a trip to America.[24] Barnes never intended his collection of French masterpieces to be used for entertainment, only education. Eminent scholars of impressionist and postimpressionist art such as Erwin Panofsky, Meyer Schapiro, and John Rewald were denied access, but Barnes did not hesitate to bring a truck driver into his gallery to engage in a discussion about Cézanne with him.

In 1930, Barnes invited Henri Matisse (1869–1954) to view his foundation that held at that time the largest collection of the artist's works in the world. Matisse had come to America to judge the Carnegie Medal in New York and welcomed the opportunity to see the famed collection in Merion. During the visit, Barnes negotiated with Matisse to decorate the three lunettes in the main gallery. The artist settled on the theme of dance, a motif he had explored in his *Joy of Life*, a significant work from his fauve period that was a jewel of Barnes's collection. (See Figure 12.2.) Its buoyant curves and rhythmically expressive lines inspired him to tackle the challenges of the architectural lines of the space in the room where his new work would have to hold its own high above among famed works by Renoir, Cézanne, Seurat, and Picasso that hung along with his own *Seated Riffian* from 1912 to 1913. After working on the painting in Nice for a year, Matisse discovered that he had executed his canvases with the wrong dimensions. (See Figure 12.3.) In May 1933, Matisse completed his work and traveled back to Merion to supervise the installation. Matisse informed his son in a letter about his experience: "It has a splendor that one cannot imagine unless one sees it—because both the whole ceiling and its arched vaults come alive through radiation and the main effect continues right down to the floor. . . I am profoundly tired but very pleased. When I saw the canvas put in place, it was detached from me and became part of the building."[25]

On July 24, 1951, Barnes ran through a stop sign at an intersection on Phoenixville Pike and collided with a ten-ton trailer truck. He died instantly. His beloved dog Fidèle, seated in the car with him, was so severely injured that he had to be put down on the scene. Directorship of the foundation passed to Laura Barnes until her death in 1967, when Violette de Mazia assumed directorship until her death in 1988. After years of bitter legal battles and considerable controversy, the foundation was relocated to the Benjamin Franklin Parkway in 2012. The reinstallation adhered to Barnes's beloved ensembles and exactly replicates the rooms in Merion. Only Matisse's *Joy of Life* found a new location in a room that allows better viewer access. In Merion, one passed it on the stairway to the second floor, which discouraged any prolonged appreciation due to a lack of any adequate viewing distance. Its present location, in a separate alcove opposite a balcony where one can look down to the main room and Matisse's *Dance*, allows one to experience the colorful dynamism and expressive vitality of Matisse's style in two of the most important paintings of his career that are major monuments in the history of modernist art.

Anne Distel's affirmation that "Barnes' single vision is behind each of the extraordinary works that greet the visitor" defines the impact of how one man's tenacity in

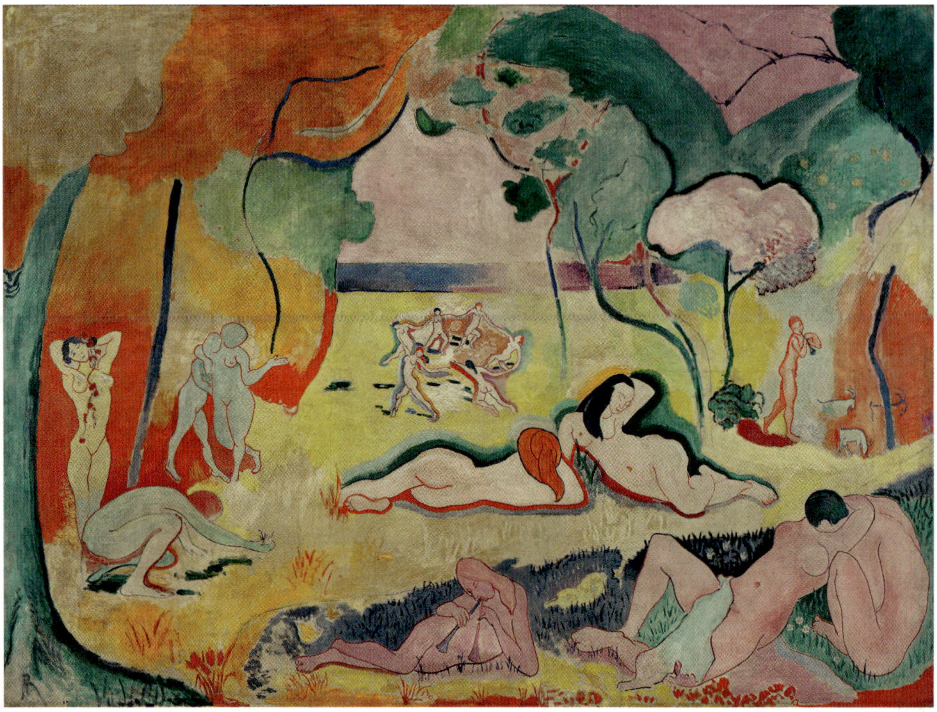

FIGURE 12.2 Henri Matisse, French, 1869–1954. *Le Bonheur de vivre*, also called *The Joy of Life*, between October 1905 and March 1906. Oil on canvas, 69⅛ × 94¾ in. (176.5 × 240.7 cm). (BF719, The Barnes Foundation, Philadelphia, Pennsylvania. Image © 2019 The Barnes Foundation / © 2019 Succession H. Matisse / Artists Rights Society (ARS), New York.)

holding to his aesthetic convictions produced a priceless art collection that shaped new contexts for understanding and interpreting art and cultural artifacts that had suffered condescension and contempt at the hands of others.[26] Barnes functioned as collector and curator in shaping the works he intended as his legacy, motivated by his convictions on how art should be viewed and experienced. As an autodidact, he combined vast amounts of reading and study in art and aesthetics with close analysis of the paintings he acquired. He aimed not to amass art for investment but to educate the viewer's eye to how the formal elements and expressive affinities of the relationships between paintings and objects develop an emotional capacity to be observant to the aesthetic potential of everyday things for everyday people. Seeing became an active creative process rather than a passive absorptive experience. He parlayed the proceeds he made from preventing physical blindness into an educational institution aimed at changing what he perceived to be the intellectual and aesthetic blindness of viewers of art. Barnes's sight and insight thus anchored Philadelphia as a peerless

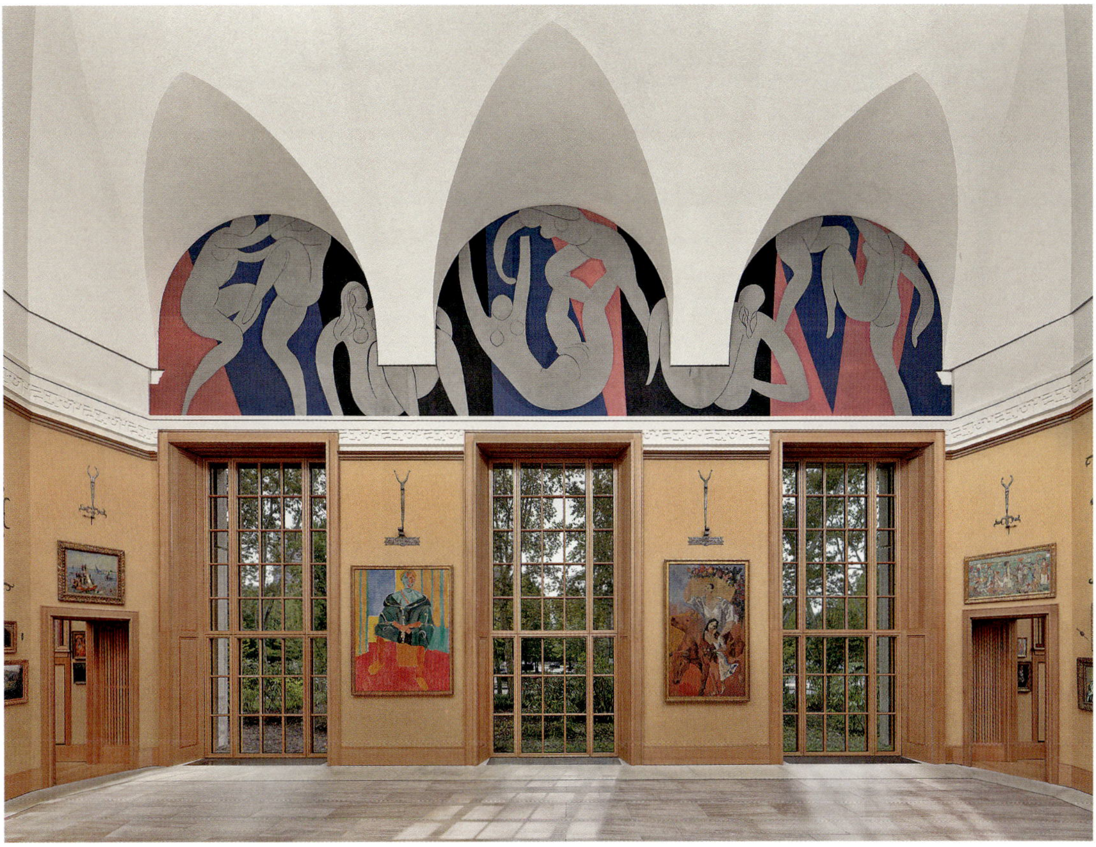

Figure 12.3 Henri Matisse, *The Dance*, 1932–1933. Ensemble view, Room 1, south wall, Philadelphia, 2012. (Photo © 2019 The Barnes Foundation, Philadelphia Location, 1912. © 2020 Succession H. Matisse / Artists Rights Society (ARS), New York.)

repository and the largest intact collection anywhere of French postimpressionist and early modern painting.

The year after Barnes opened his foundation to the public, Jules Mastbaum (1872–1926) (see Figure 12.4), another significant collector of French art in Philadelphia, contacted the Fairmount Park Commission regarding his plans to build a museum dedicated to the sculptor Auguste Rodin (1840–1917). In his application of April 26, 1926, Mastbaum requested that his museum be located on the Benjamin Franklin Parkway, pledging to maintain the building at his own expense. Unlike Barnes, he wanted his collection to remain "freely available for the study and enjoyment of my fellow citizens of Philadelphia."[27] He hired the architects Jacques Gréber and Paul Cret who played major roles in designing the parkway.[28] Cret had recently finished his building for the Barnes Foundation and accepted the commission to collaborate with Gréber in the creation of another structure to house works by a significant French artist.

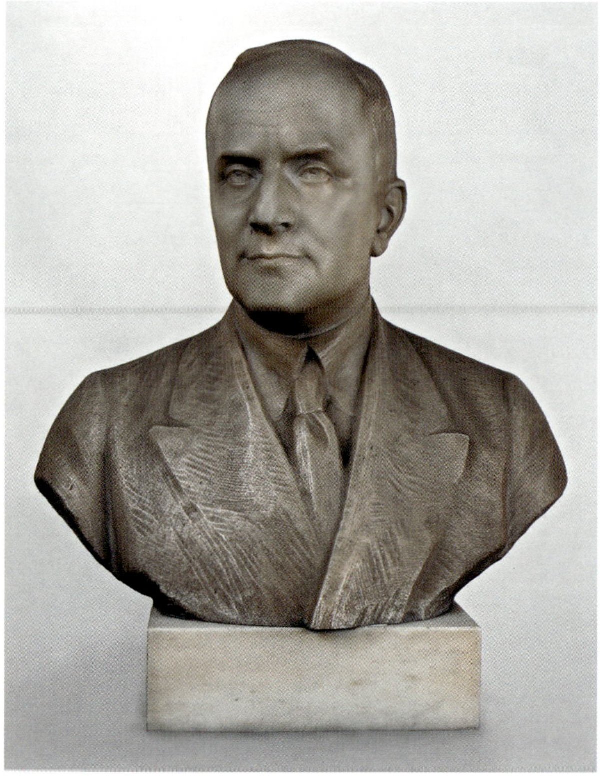

Figure 12.4
Henri Gréber, *Bust of Jules Mastbaum*, ca. 1927–1928. Marble, 20¾ × 20½ in. (Philadelphia Museum of Art, Bequest of Jules E. Mastbaum, F1929-7-130; The Rodin Museum)

Barnes, Mastbaum, and Joseph Widener, all born within a year of each other, came from working-class backgrounds rather than inherited money. Mastbaum was born at Thirteenth and Green Streets and attended public schools before gaining a scholarship to the University of Pennsylvania where he earned a degree in finance from Wharton. Clerkships at Gimbels department stores in Illinois and Wisconsin eventually led him back to Philadelphia where he became the store's European representative. Jules and his brother Stanley formed a successful real estate business with Albert W. Fleisher. The Mastbaum brothers saw the potential of the moving picture business that had been created in France by Auguste and Louis Lumière, the brothers who invented the cinematograph and projected their first film in Paris in 1895. The Mastbaums founded the Motion Picture Company of America and began to build movie theaters, eventually becoming the largest operators in the United States with more than 250 cinemas by the middle of the 1920s.

When Stanley died suddenly in 1918, Jules renamed his business the Stanley Company of America in honor of his brother. Proceeds from the company provided Jules with the wherewithal to become a prominent philanthropist in the city. Around 1923, he demonstrated his growing interest in French sculpture with small bronzes by Antoine-Louis Barye acquired for him by the Philadelphia portraitist and art collector Albert Rosenthal and Gilbert White, a muralist who had studied at the Académie Julian and with James McNeill Whistler. In 1924, Mastbaum and White traveled to

Paris where a visit to the Rodin Museum initiated Mastbaum's enduring fascination with the sculptor. Rodin had authorized that bronze casts of his work could be fabricated after his death. Mastbaum put in an order for seven casts and returned to Philadelphia with a bronze bust that launched what would become the largest collection of Rodin's works outside of Paris.

Living with Rodin's works in his home and office stimulated Mastbaum's desire to commission more casts, and just a year after his first acquisition, he had accumulated over a hundred of them. He originally thought of placing the sculptures in his theaters, but he realized that massive works such as *The Burghers of Calais* and *The Kiss* belonged more appropriately in a gallery. Thus, what had started as a private passion launched Mastbaum's mission to erect a museum solely dedicated to the work of the man who became known as the father of modern sculpture. Along with Rosenthal, Mastbaum worked with the Galerie F. and J. Tempelaere in Paris to secure ownership of Rodin's notebook, drawings, plaster casts, and marbles to extend his collection beyond sculpture.

Mastbaum's investment in Rodin significantly enriched France as well as Philadelphia. Rodin had been commissioned in 1880 to create a pair of bronze doors for a decorative arts museum in Paris. Rodin took his inspiration from Dante's *Inferno* and began what would become the major work of his career, *The Gates of Hell.* Despite the fact that the decorative arts museum never opened, Rodin continued work on the doors for thirty-seven years, investing his key ideas in the more than two hundred figures that writhed tumultuously across the surface of the work. The plaster model that remained in his studio in Meudon outside of Paris at the time of his death had never been cast in bronze as Rodin intended. A visit to Meudon prompted Mastbaum to contribute to the restoration of the sculptor's house and studio. He also commissioned two bronze casts of the doors, one for his museum in Philadelphia and the other for the Musée Rodin in Paris, thereby becoming a generous benefactor both at home and abroad. (See Figure 12.5.)

Mastbaum would not live long enough to see his museum completed. He died on December 7, 1926, at Jefferson Hospital after having been ill for only one week. His devoted widow Etta Lit Wedell Mastbaum, whose mother and uncles founded the Lit Brothers department store in Philadelphia, saw her husband's project through to completion along with her three daughters. Continuing the philanthropic generosity of her husband, Etta donated the museum to the city of Philadelphia in 1929. The city requested that the Philadelphia Museum of Art maintain and oversee administration of the museum. Fiske Kimball, the Art Museum's director, and Francis Henry Taylor, its curator of decorative arts, willingly agreed. France recognized Etta's significant role by having the French ambassador Paul Claudel, a renowned poet, award her the Legion of Honor at the Rodin Museum's inaugural ceremonies on November 29, 1929. Claudel knew Rodin well as his older sister, Camille Claudel, had served as the sculptor's studio assistant beginning in 1884, eventually becoming his lover, model, and muse. In his citation at the inauguration, Claudel acknowledged how Philadelphia and Paris would henceforth be inextricably linked to each other: "But the success

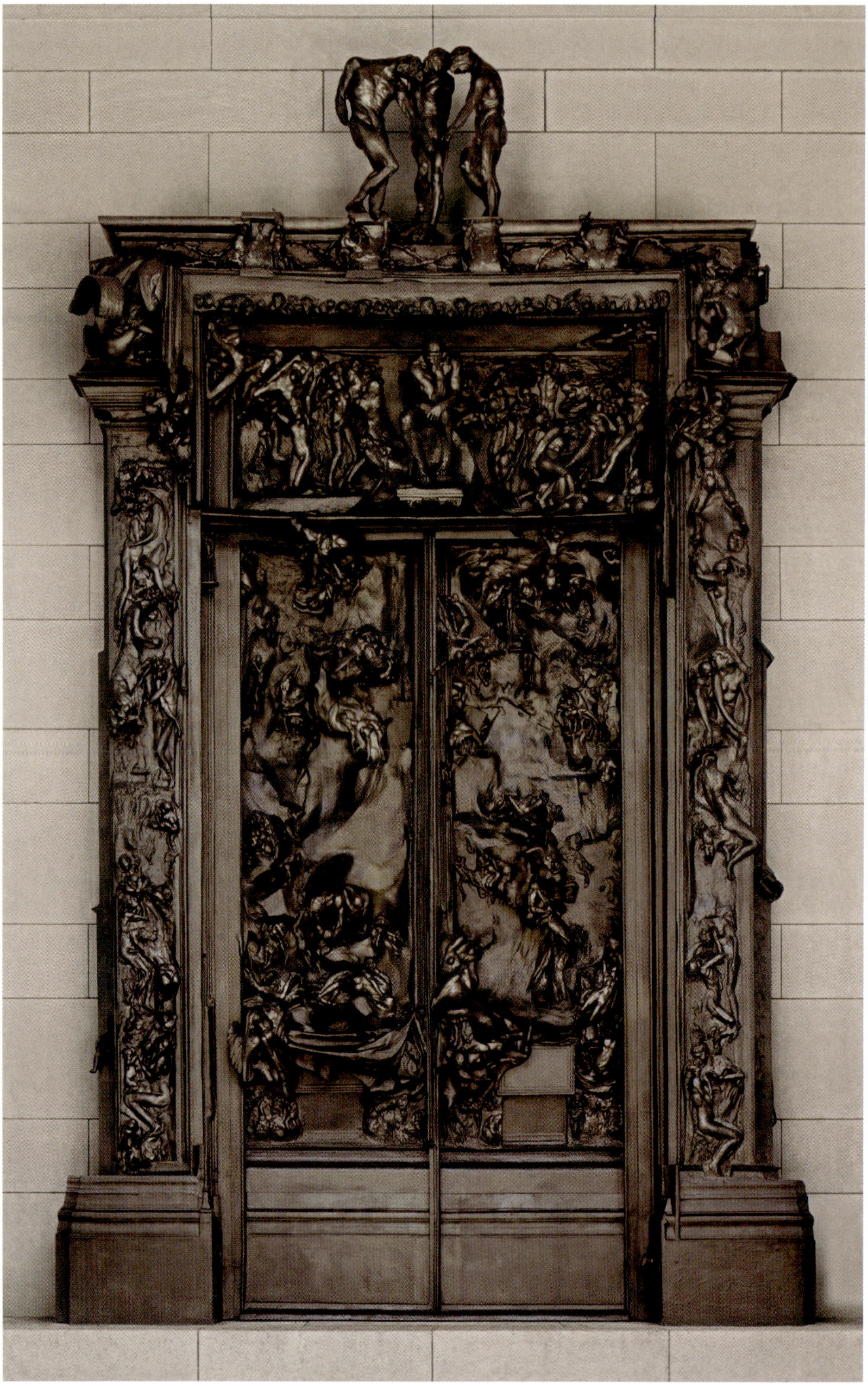

Figure 12.5 Auguste Rodin, *The Gates of Hell*, 1880–1917. Modeled 1880–1917; cast 1926–1928 Bronze. 20 ft., 10¾ in. × 13 ft., 2 in. × 33⅜ in. (636.9 × 401.3 × 84.8 cm). (Philadelphia Museum of Art, Bequest of Jules E. Mastbaum, F1929-7-128; The Rodin Museum)

of the new generation is made of the pain and sorrow of the preceding ones, and such a witnessing as this one of the great French sculptor Auguste Rodin deserves to be carefully kept in that fine city of art, which is Philadelphia. The sculptor had a great part in the edification of the ancient city and he has a great part in the new one."[29]

Neither Barnes nor Mastbaum had any formal education in art before they started collecting, nor did they come from a family tradition of acquisition. Impelled by their visual acuity and sustained by their self-made fortunes, both men invested in modern art that challenged entrenched taste and older traditions. They ignored the critical disdain centered on the artists they chose and traded future economic security for intellectual and aesthetic convictions. Through their intellectual adventurousness their collections had a significant influence on the artists who pioneered modernism. Fortunately, for the history of art, and for Philadelphia in particular, their instincts proved that the financial risks they undertook in their allegiance to provocative contemporary work sustained an influential and lasting legacy of some of the finest products of modernist art.

The sculptures contained in the Barnes Foundation and the Rodin Museum took their place in a lineage of works reaching back to colonial days. Philadelphia became the first American city to integrate sculpture into, and continuously use it in, its private and public spaces to embellish architectural facades and adorn parks.[30] Jean-Antoine Houdon's arrival from Paris to Philadelphia in 1785 to execute a statue of George Washington for the Virginia Legislature instilled in the citizenry the awareness of sculpture as a fine art as distinguished from the crafts of wood carving and stone cutting.[31] Portrait busts of famous figures began to populate the homes of notable Philadelphians such as William Bingham and David Rittenhouse. Charles Willson Peale included sculpted images of himself, his teacher Benjamin West, and Edmund Jennings, an early patron, in the portrait of his family that he finished in 1809.[32] (See Figure 12.6.) The busts rest on a shelf overlooking the family, bestowing a cachet of intellectual sophistication by their classical style to the family gathering where the arts are highlighted by an easel, a palette, and a figure drawing a woman and child seated opposite to him.

Early in its history Philadelphia placed public sculpture in squares and parks to adorn the city. One sees this in John Lewis Krimmel's 1812 painting *Fourth of July in Centre Square*. (See Figure 12.7.) Krimmel placed his scene in front of Benjamin Latrobe's neoclassical Water Works, built to purify water that was blamed for the yellow fever epidemic that had gripped the city in 1793 and again in 1798. The true focal point of the painting, however, is William Rush's figure of the *Water Nymph and Bittern* rising in white splendor over the heads of the celebrants. Carved in pine and painted white to imitate marble, the figure resembles the *Venus de Medici*.[33] The bird she holds spews water from its mouth and a spray from jets suggest her mythological origins from the sea. Rush was considered the father of American sculpture. The statue had been installed in 1809 and, along with the pump house, served as a source of civic pride in overcoming the pestilence of the yellow fever.[34] The 1809 installation of Rush's statue on Centre Square—now the site of Philadelphia's City Hall—marks an

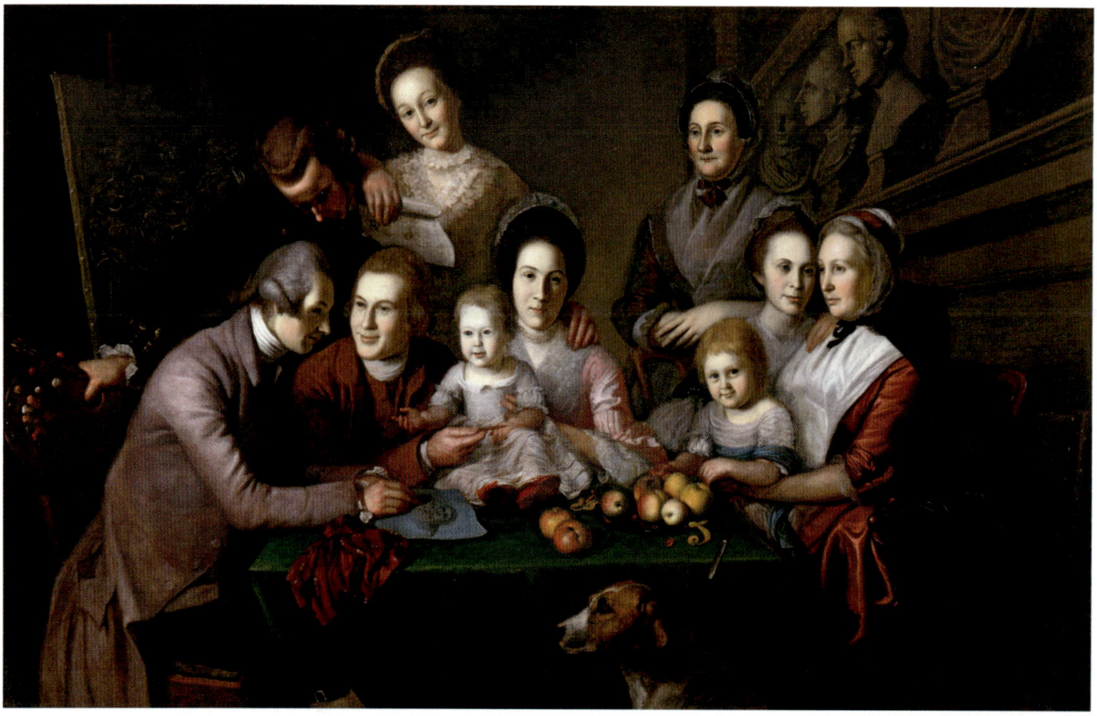

FIGURE 12.6 Charles Willson Peale, *The Peale Family*, 1773–1809. Oil on canvas, 56½ × 89½ in. (143.5 × 227.3 cm). 1867.298. (Photo © New York Historical Society)

originating impulse for installing outdoor sculpture. As Wayne Craven claimed: "One looks in vain for anything comparable to it in any other American city during the period around 1810 to 1820. It added immensely to the growing sculptural heritage of Philadelphia and encouraged additional commissions for such work."[35] The work inspired Thomas Eakins's 1877 painting *William Rush Carving His Allegorical Figure of the Schuylkill River* where he noted the influence of French art on Rush.[36] (See Figure 8.7 in Chapter 8.)

Rodin's work on the parkway resides not far from one of the works of Antoine-Louis Barye (1796–1875) who had instructed him in zoological drawing at the Museum of Natural History. Barye's dramatic presentation of a *Lion Crushing a Serpent* holds center stage in Rittenhouse Square where it was the first sculpture installed there in 1892 through the auspices of the Fairmount Park Art Association, today's Association for Public Art. (See Figure 12.8.) Barye's lifelike work had created a sensation at the Salon of 1833; a plaster cast of it so enthralled King Louis-Philippe that he acquired the work, which was subsequently cast in bronze and installed in the Tuileries Gardens in 1836. The king made Barye a knight of the Légion d'Honneur in 1833, obviously pleased with the implied symbolism of the work. Barye embedded in his staging of the king of the beasts combating the traditional symbol of evil an allusion to the advent of the House of Orléans and the defeat of the Bourbon dynasty. The reign of Charles X had come to an end after three days of fighting known as *Les*

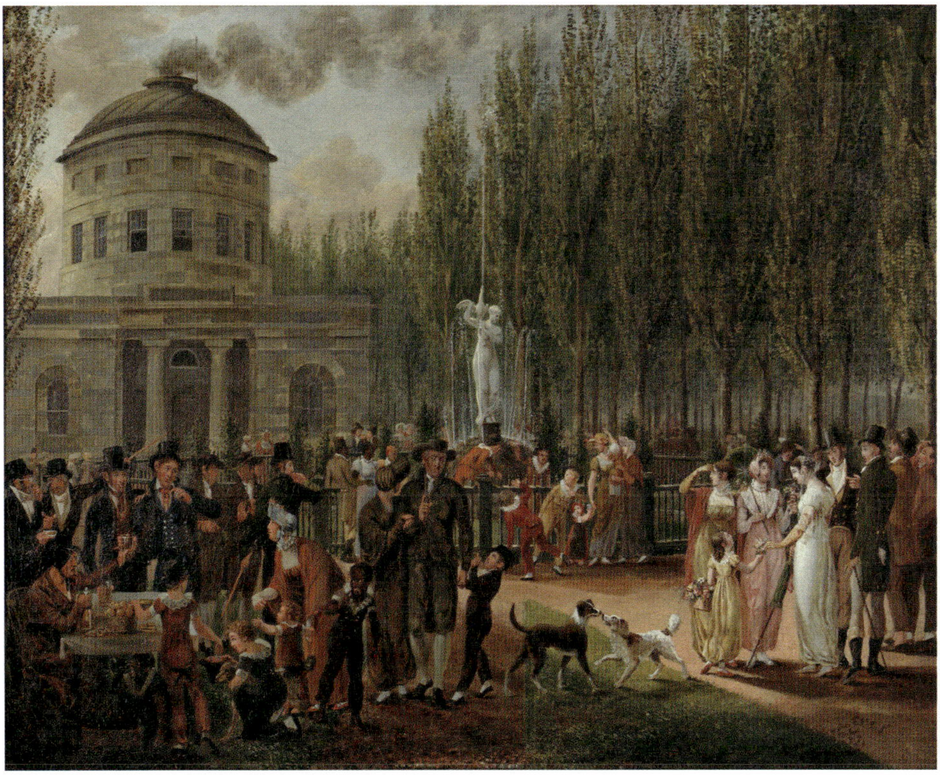

Figure 12.7 John Lewis Krimmel, *Fourth of July in Centre Square*, 1812. Oil on canvas, 22¾ × 29 in. (57.785 × 73.66 cm). Acc. No.: 1845.3.1. (Pennsylvania Academy of the Fine Arts, Philadelphia. Pennsylvania Academy purchase [from the estate of Paul Beck, Jr.].)

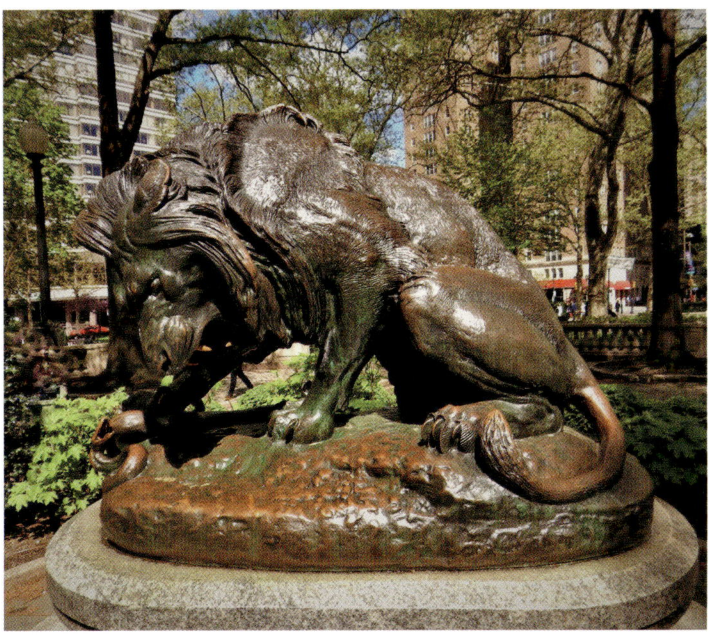

Figure 12.8 Antoine-Louis Barye, *Lion Crushing a Serpent*—original 1832, cast in bronze in 1891, and installed in Rittenhouse Square in 1892.

Trois Glorieuses that took place from July 27 to July 29, 1830 wherein Louis-Philippe assumed control of France and launched the July Monarchy (1830–1848). Lions had often served as emblems of royalty in heraldry, but Barye capitalized specifically on the astrological imagery of Leo and Hydra that marked the constellations of the days under which the revolution took place.[37] The fierce combat between the lion clutching the writhing open-mouthed serpent in its claws allegorized the dominance of the liberal regime over the dynastic powers of the older reign.

The attention paid to this work was unprecedented as animal sculpture traditionally ranked lower in academic esteem than representations of figures posed in dramatic reenactment of heroic deeds or commemorations of notable figures. The convincing realism of the work captivated the critics. Théophile Gautier, who christened Barye the "Michelangelo of the menagerie," wittily reported that the bronze had been "released" rather than installed in the Tuileries gardens.[38] He later remarked that the convincing simulation of Barye's lion made other sculpted images of the animals in Parisian parks look as if they wore marble wigs from the time of Louis XIV.[39] Critics reacted to the convincing dynamism of Barye's work by attributing acoustic potential to the inert bronze. In his review of the Salon of 1833, Charles Lenormant returned more than once to view Barye's *Lion Crushing a Serpent.* At first he thought it moved, but then he heard it roar.[40] Auguste Jal claimed he strode by the sculpted lions in the Tuileries gardens but only looked at Barye's from a distance because it so frightened him.[41] Alfred de Musset also heard the lion growl and the serpent hiss when he saw it at the Salon of 1836, imagining the muffed snarl emitting from the lion's muzzle with its lunging pose and praising the thirst for combat in the coiled snake with its gaping jaw.[42] As one writer commented, only the cage was missing.[43]

Barye's work came to Philadelphia through the advocacy of Ferdinand Barbidienne who had cast the *Lion Crushing a Serpent* in his foundry. He approached Thomas Hockley, chairman of the Fairmount Park Art Association's Committee of Works of Art and engaged his interest in the work. Hockley began fundraising in 1885 and in 1891 the commission of the cast resulted in Barye's work being brought to Philadelphia where it became the first sculpture erected in Rittenhouse Square.

Rodin had once proclaimed Barye the French nation's glory, calling him "the great man of our century."[44] This admiration was shared by Emmanuel Frémiet (1824–1910), who succeeded Barye as a professor at the Museum of Natural History. Frémiet also began his career doing animal sculptures, debuting at the Salon of 1843 with an Algerian gazelle. He received numerous state public commissions for monuments and eventually became director of sculpture at the Louvre. After the 1870 defeat of France by Otto von Bismarck's army in the Franco-Prussian War, the French government contracted with Frémiet to create a statue of Joan of Arc (1412–1431) who had been declared a national symbol of France by Napoleon in 1803. Joan had achieved victory in 1429 over the English and their Burgundian allies in the Hundred Years War. A year later she was captured by the Duke of Burgundy's troops, tried, convicted as a heretic, and burned at the stake in Rouen in May 1431. As a symbol of the dedication

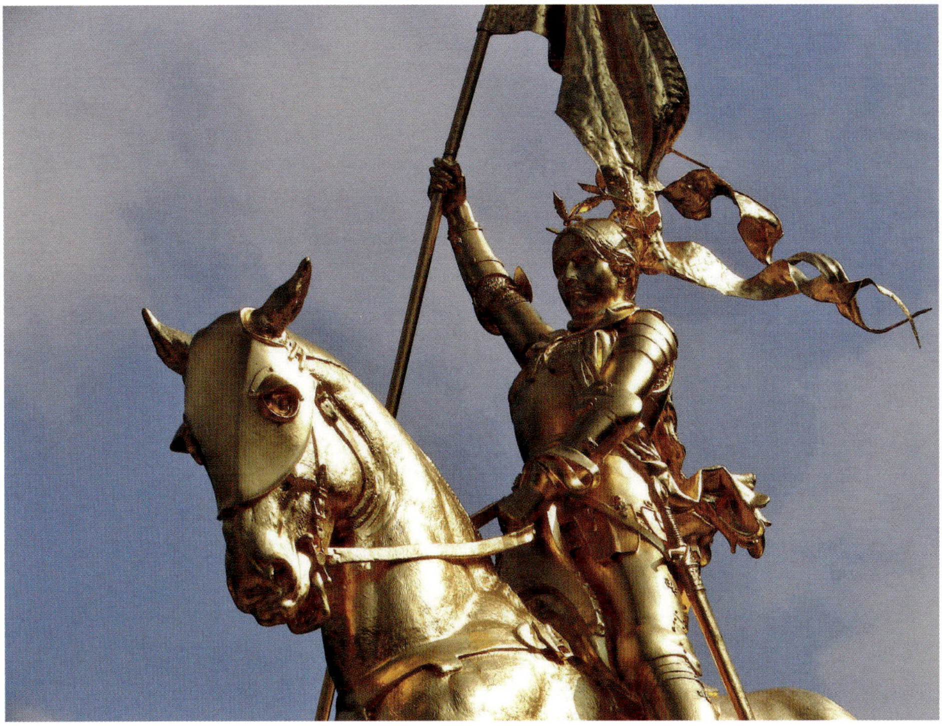

Figure 12.9 Emmanuel Frémiet, *Joan of Arc*, 1874. (Paris, Place des Pyramides. Photo by Francois Trazzi. Licensed under CC BY-SA 3.0: https://creativecommons.org/licenses/by-sa/3.0/legalcode.)

to the preservation of French identity against foreign invaders, Joan's image served as an emblem of victory and reunification, a much-needed reminder after the ignominious defeat of 1870. The Third Republic government situated Frémiet's statue in 1874 on the Place des Pyramides where Joan had led the newly crowned King Charles VII into Paris. (See Figure 12.9.) It stood opposite the ruins of the Tuileries, the residence of the French monarchy until it was burned in 1871 during the suppression of the Paris Commune. The remnants remained on the site for eleven years, a potent visual reminder of the defeat of former imperial regimes. Giuseppe de Nittis's 1876 painting *La Place des Pyramides* vividly records the juxtaposition of defeat and renewed hope in his documentation of the view of the rue de Rivoli where Joan's banner seems to call forth the light from the gray clouds scudding above the scaffolding of the Tuileries, suggesting hope and recovery. (See Figure 12.10.)

A replica of Frémiet's statue came to its present site in Philadelphia in 1890 through the auspices of the Fairmount Park Art Association Committee. (See Figure 12.11.) The members had responded to an appeal from the French residents of the city to obtain a copy of the statue, promising to raise the needed subvention. Conshohocken stone provided a foundation for the granite pedestal, and, on October 6, 1890, the statue was pronounced ready for unveiling. Russell Thayer, the superin-

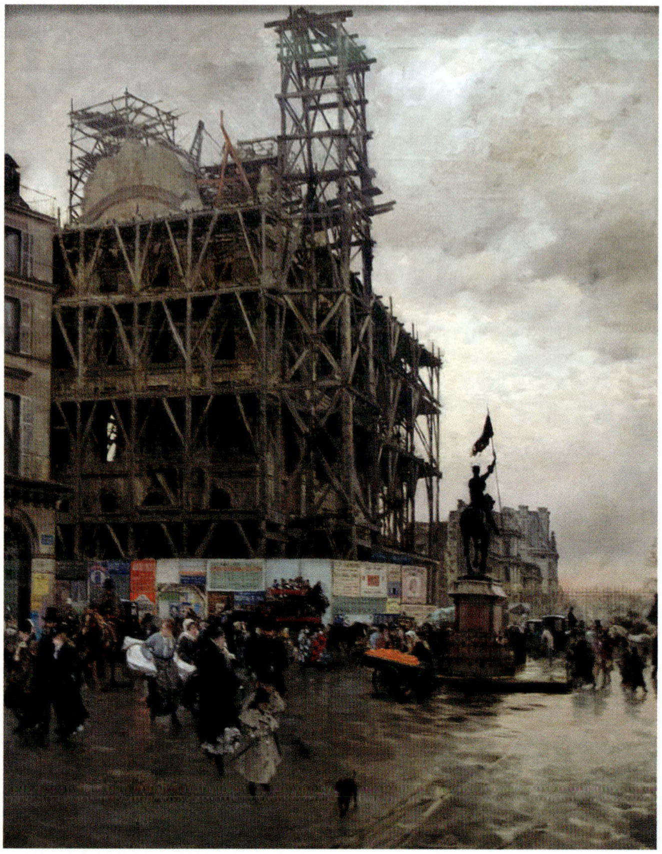

FIGURE 12.10
Giuseppe de Nittis, *La Place des Pyramides*, 1876. Oil on canvas, 92.3 × 75 cm (36.3" × 29.5"). (Paris, Musée d'Orsay)

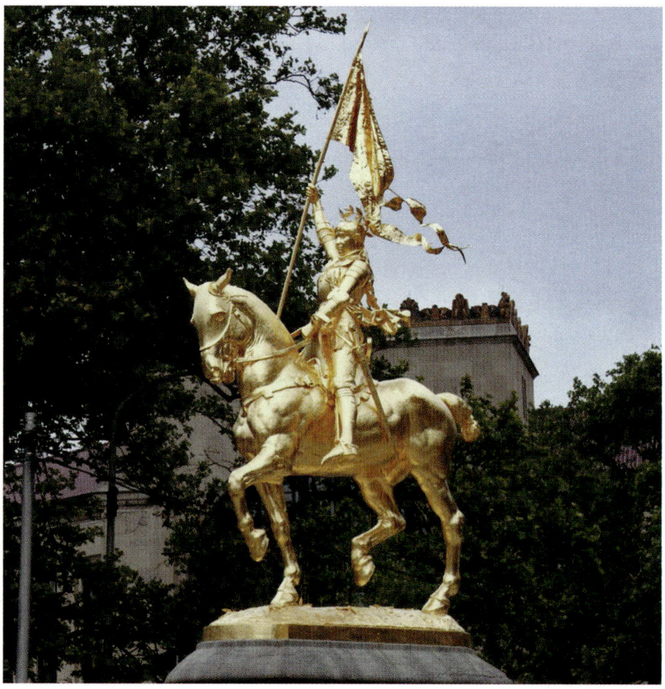

FIGURE 12.11
Emmanuel Frémiet, *Joan of Arc*, 1890. East River Drive at the Philadelphia Museum of Art.

tendent and chief engineer of Fairmount Park, wrote that he thought it to be by far the "most beautiful work of art yet placed in the Park."[45] The official unveiling took place on November 15, 1890, at its original location near the Schuylkill River at Girard Avenue. As the bunting was removed from the statue, the Girard College Band played the *Marseillaise* while French and American flags lent by John Wanamaker's department store blew in the wind. During his speech Samuel Gustine Thompson, a Supreme Court Justice for the state of Pennsylvania, made reference to Barye's work already in place: "Most of the works of art placed in public parks are made to represent destruction in some form or other. In such works we see the lion, the king of the forest, with his prey in his grasp ready to destroy it. . . . Far better it would be that these works in public places should represent subjects that will tend to advance and elevate the public mind."[46] After a speech by Victor Rigueur, a professor of French literature, the French consul Louis Voission praised Philadelphia as possessing a work that spoke specifically of France:

> When, in future years, the ships of our navy will visit your friendly shores, and drop their anchors in the blue waters of the Delaware; when our tourists, travelers, artists, merchants and writers will come . . . all, without exception, will be delighted to salute, with a throb of their hearts, Joan, the virgin of Domrémy, on her pedestal of marble, holding in her hand the lance and the oriflamme. The genius of Bartholdi created the beautiful statue of "Liberty Enlightening the World," which adorns so splendidly the entrance to New York harbor. But it is an emblem, a figure that may well belong to all the civilized nations, and symbolize the progress of the human race. Frémiet, in his Joan of Arc, which will now forever decorate your beautiful Fairmount Park, has created something exclusively illustrative of France; and it can well be said that in no place in the world, outside of France, could that noble statue be better placed than in Philadelphia, the Mecca of American liberties.[47]

The statue arrived in its original bronze state in 1890 and was first gilded in 1959 when the Fairmount Park Association relocated it to Kelly Drive across from the Philadelphia Museum of Art. When a crack in the pedestal caused the statue to be stored in the Milner and Carr Conservation studio, the French Heritage Society joined with the city's public art program to have the statue restored and regilded before having it remounted in 2010. The Barnes Collection, the Rodin Museum, the Barye sculpture, and Frémiet's *Joan of Arc* stand as fitting reminders of the bond of the city of Philadelphia with France, from the earliest days of its founding to the ongoing contributions of French culture to our civic and national heritage.

[13]

Three Centuries of French Cuisine, Plus Recent Gallic Contributions

During the years from 1784 to 1789 when Thomas Jefferson was living in Paris as the U.S. minister to France, he grew deeply appreciative of French cooking and French wines, making himself a connoisseur of both. He apprenticed his young slave, James Hemings, to a fine chef to learn the art of French cuisine. Hemings soon became sufficiently accomplished that he prepared feasts hosted by Jefferson for leading French progressives in Paris—Lafayette, Condorcet, and the duc de la Rochefoucauld-Liancourt, among others. When Jefferson left Paris in September 1789 to return to his native land, the eighty-six crates of household goods he shipped separately included a variety of French kitchen utensils, as well as a waffle iron, a machine for making macaroni (pâtes), and recipes for the vanilla ice cream he had come to love. He also had sent hundreds of bottles of French wines, cheese, olive oil, and Maille Mustard.[1] Because of his continuing prominence in America throughout the rest of his life, Jefferson led the elite among his countrymen in spreading the taste for French cooking.

When Jefferson arrived back in Virginia after his long residence in Paris, he learned that President George Washington had nominated him to serve as the nation's first secretary of state. The new federal government just then being formed was still based in New York (the capital would only move to Philadelphia in November 1790). So, to New York Jefferson reluctantly journeyed (he had made clear to Washington that he preferred to return to France as the U.S. minister), with Hemings in accompaniment to continue to serve as his French-trained cook. During the summer of 1790, Hemings prepared the meal for an occasion that would become particularly notable for the new republic. Over dinner, Jefferson and his guests, Alexander Hamilton and James Madison, resolved one of the thorniest issues facing the First Congress of the United

States. They agreed to what already had failed to reach agreement twice in the House of Representatives: the two Southerners accepted Hamilton's plan for the federal government to assume the war debts the states had incurred during the Revolution. In return, Hamilton concurred that the nation's permanent capital should be built along the Potomac River on the border between Maryland and Virginia.[2] For the occasion that resulted in such harmony, James Hemings prepared French-inspired dishes, including roasted capon stuffed with truffles and artichokes and *boeuf à la mode*, with Hermitage, Bordeaux, and Chambertin wines to accompany each course, along with champagne to quaff with sweets at the end.[3]

Once they moved to Philadelphia, Hemings continued to make Jefferson's table a font of French-inspired cuisine for the Virginian's frequent guests. Then, nearly three years later, when Jefferson gave the president his resignation as secretary of state, he wrote a contract setting forth the conditions whereby he would emancipate James. That document, written in September 1793, promised that, once back in Monticello, Jefferson would free James as soon as "he shall have taught such person as I shall place under him . . . to be a good cook."[4] Jefferson's promise to free Hemings finally was carried out in February 1796, after more than two years in which James trained his younger brother, Peter, to take his place as chef of Monticello.[5]

James soon left for Philadelphia, then Baltimore, where he was employed as a cook in a tavern. In the weeks before Jefferson was inaugurated as the nation's third president, on March 4, 1801, he tried to get in touch with Hemings to invite him to become the chef at the executive mansion. An intermediary reported back that James wanted Jefferson's request in writing. Some weeks later, the president replied to the same intermediary that he took Hemings's delays and request for a written invitation as indicating his unwillingness to move to the new capital in Washington, DC. Jefferson had evidently learned, meanwhile, that Hemings was by then drinking heavily. Although James did come to Monticello for several weeks during Jefferson's vacation that summer, he returned to Baltimore. Shortly thereafter, he committed suicide after several days of very heavy drinking.[6] He was thirty-six years old.

Apart from that unfortunate death—the curse on a "free" man released from a lifetime in slavery—the experience of Jefferson and James Hemings marked an important example of how, since the time of Louis XIV (1638–1715), French cuisine had served as the ultimate standard for all of Europe. In the new United States, the centrally important role of Philadelphia soon led French cooking and French tastes to take root in the city. The decade when the city was the nation's capital also marked a period of growing wealth and cosmopolitanism in the city's elite class. Contributing to both was the arrival of many of the well-to-do landowners and aristocrats from revolutionary upheavals in France and Saint-Domingue, which also brought other French refugees, including artisans and tradespeople, drawn to serve the elite. Among those landing in Philadelphia to escape the Reign of Terror was the lawyer and economist, Jean Anthelme Brillat-Savarin (1755–1826), who would become posthumously famous as a gastronome with the publication of his treatise on the art of dining, *La*

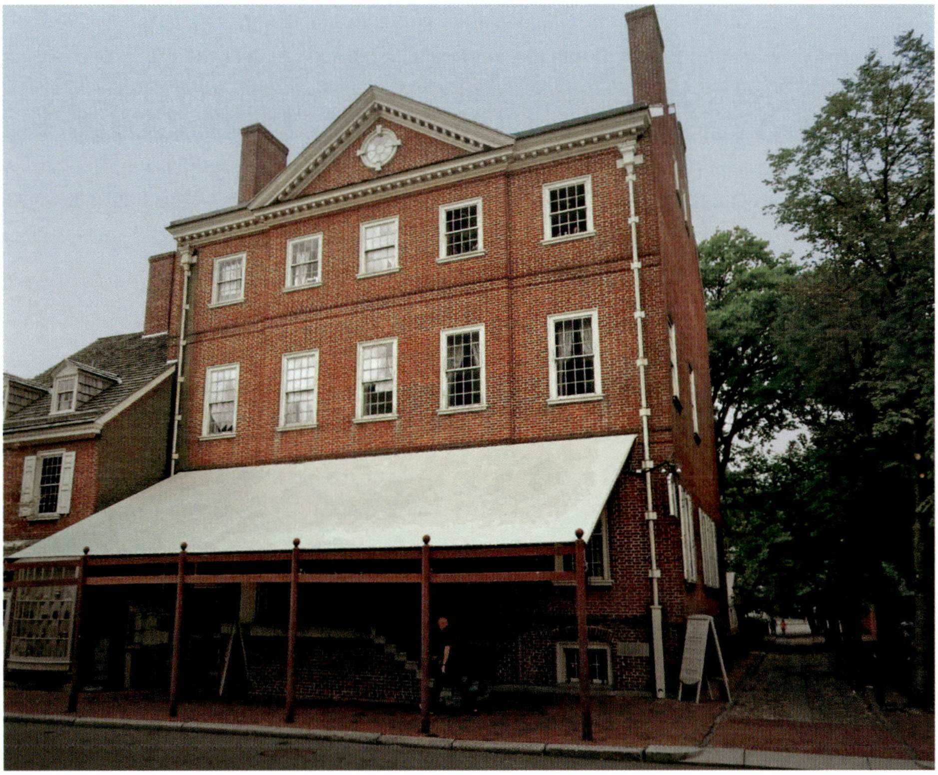

Figure 13.1 "This 1773 tavern was a center for political discussions, business transactions, and social events. Members of the Continental Congress lodged, dined, and celebrated here" (signboard outside the reconstructed City Tavern).

Physiologie du goût, near the end of his life.[7] In the American capital, he provided French language and violin lessons while also demonstrating how to prepare local fare in the French manner.[8] (See Figure 13.1.)

Jefferson himself played a role in popularizing ice cream, which he had learned to love in France. In 1791, he wrote to the chargé d'affaires in Paris, his protégé William Short, to ask him to send fifty vanilla pods so that he could make his favorite flavor (it is not known whether Short found this an odd request coming as it did at the height of the French Revolution). Others introduced new French foods, including French pastries. A Frenchman, Samuel Richardet, oversaw the kitchen of the Franco-Dutch banker Théophile Cazenove before he took charge of food preparation at City Tavern, that central hub of social dining in the city. Nearby, a tavern, café, and boardinghouse run by French émigrés catered to fellow refugees. Moreau's bookshop and a lending library provided French-language publications. Peter Stephen Duponceau was, by then, secretary of the newly founded French Benevolent Society, which held meetings in the tavern. A French Masonic chapter was established, the Loge Française L'Aménité, no. 73. A new and grand public house, Oeller's Hotel, contained a handsome ballroom that hosted any number of meetings, balls, and entertainments serving the French community. There French dancing masters gave lessons, French musicians performed concerts, and French delicacies were served.[9]

Philadelphia's native-born social elite also took on a thoroughly French inflection during the decade when the city was the nation's capital. That was partially due to the presence of the various French aristocrats and other wellborn refugees from the Revolution in France. At the pinnacle of that society, hosting all the others, reigned a rich American couple, Philadelphia born and bred. William and Anne Bingham were connected by blood or marriage to virtually every leading family in the city. Their tastes were largely those of the French aristocracy they had come to know. Early in their marriage, the Binghams had lived in France for several months during the 1780s. Their time in Paris was an extended stop on their grand tour of Europe. They schooled themselves in Paris's salons to learn the conduct of high society, its manners and its methods for influencing the affairs of state. While in Paris, Anne, a dazzling beauty, won the admiration of John and Abigail Adams and Thomas Jefferson, among many others in French society. After the family was domiciled again in Philadelphia, President Washington and other leading Americans joined her list of admirers.[10] The Bingham mansion, completed in 1788, was begun before they arrived home from Europe. It was built on more than three acres of land that sprawled from Third to Fourth Streets and across most of the land from Pine Street to Willing's Alley in Society Hill. They hired as their maître d'hôtel a French chef, Étienne Lemaire.[11] The vicomte de Noailles took apartments on the Bingham's property during his exile in Philadelphia.[12]

Among the next generation of Philadelphia's elite was the French-educated Samuel Breck Jr. (1771–1862) who entertained many notables during his long residence at Sweetbriar, the mansion he had built in 1797 on the west bank of the Schuylkill north of the city.[13] He socialized with Talleyrand, Joseph Bonaparte, and the future king Louis Philippe. He was also Audubon's patron. On July 24, 1825, he hosted the Lafayettes, father and son, when the marquis extended his stay in Philadelphia during his grand tour of the United States. Nicholas Biddle was also a guest. For the occasion, he hired a chef able to provide French-inspired cuisine, in order, as Breck reported to his diary, to remedy the "lamentable deficiency of our common cooks" for his distinguished guests. Unfortunately, however, that cook died on the very day of the dinner party, and Breck had to find a replacement at the last minute.[14] During his long life, Breck served in government; as a Pennsylvania legislator, he introduced a bill to provide a public school system in Pennsylvania before he was elected a U.S. representative for the Eighteenth Congress in 1823–1825. He was also a director of several canal companies and a bank, as well as a civic leader. An amateur artist and musician, he was the longtime president of the Athenaeum of Philadelphia, a trustee of the University of Pennsylvania, and president of the Pennsylvania Institution for the Blind.[15] (See Figure 13.2.)

From its earliest days, Philadelphia had played a central role in establishing a culture of beer manufacture and consumption in the colonies. Small breweries, often operated out of the brewers' homes, were seen as essential to public health at a time

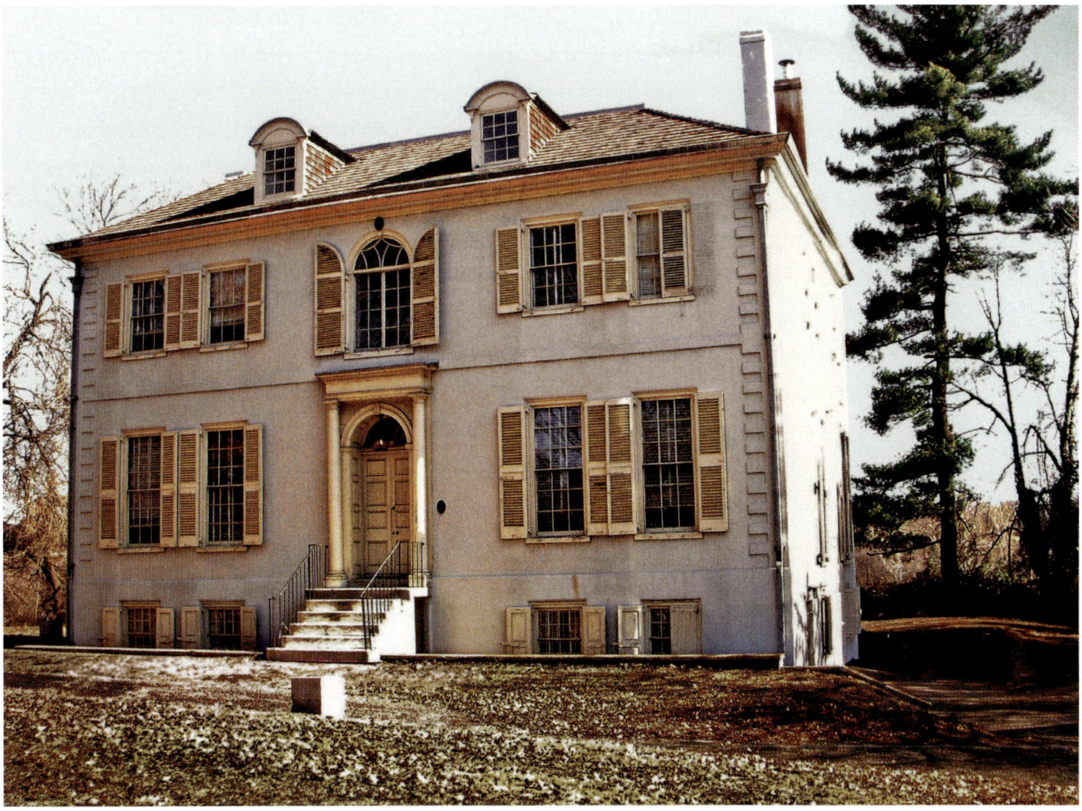

Figure 13.2 The French-educated Samuel Breck Jr. was a leading member of Philadelphia's elite during the first half of the nineteenth century. He entertained a number of distinguished French visitors in his home, Sweetbriar, located in today's Fairmount Park.

when water supplies were often contaminated and the carriers of waterborne illnesses. William Penn himself insisted on including a brew house on his plantation when he supervised the construction of his manor on the Delaware north of Philadelphia.[16] Although beer-making would come to be associated largely with the region's German immigrant community, a brewery with roots extending to the 1680s was operated by the descendants of French Huguenots during its nineteenth-century heyday. In 1811, young Francis Perot apprenticed at the Morris Brewery, which had been maintained by several generations of the progeny of Anthony Morris from the time he started the business in 1687. Perot opened his own beer-making establishment in 1818, but, after marrying one of the Morris daughters, he incorporated the Morris establishment into the company he ran with his brother. As the Francis Perot's Sons Malting Company, it remained an important Philadelphia enterprise until the early twentieth century, when it was relocated to Buffalo. It ranks among the oldest continually operating family businesses in American history.[17]

Samuel Breck's food-inspired lament in 1825 suggests that elite Philadelphians continued to regard French cuisine as the ideal standard, but one that was not often met at their tables. In fact, for much of the nineteenth century, traditional French cooking was most likely to be found in the various *pensions* run by French émigrés largely for the benefit of French visitors to the city. One of the more notable of these lasted from the latter years of the nineteenth into the early part of the twentieth centuries. The pension, Chez Madame Allard, in the 3400 block of Walnut Street, was actually run by the lady and her husband, who settled in Philadelphia after leaving their native Bordeaux. Situated as it was near the University of Pennsylvania, the lodging attracted professors and other professionals who frequented the Allard table to carry on conversation in French led by Monsieur Allard, who also gave French lessons.[18]

Philadelphia grew from a town of some fifty thousand in 1800 to a metropolis of well over one million a hundred years later, but, throughout the same period, the city lost its standing as the nation's most cosmopolitan center. While new, especially industrial, fortunes were made in the aftermath of the Civil War, the men who made them increasingly moved out of the city into the new suburbs from which they commuted by train and did their dining and entertaining largely in private clubs when in the city. Few public restaurants obtained much of a reputation for their quality; none with a French flair left a mark. Pennsylvania's Quaker heritage had much to do with that. For most of Philadelphia's history, the desire to quaff wine or spirits with one's meal was seriously hampered by the Commonwealth's "blue laws" prohibiting the sale of alcohol (as well as forbidding work, gambling, or hunting) on Sundays. The first of these was enacted in Philadelphia in 1682. Such laws purported to regulate the behavior of Pennsylvanians for nearly another three centuries; not until 1978 did the state's Supreme Court conclude that they had become largely unenforceable because of their many exceptions and discriminatory application.[19]

Compliance with these laws, which forbade the Sunday sale of alcohol in public restaurants, taverns, and bars, meant that many of the city's restaurants shut their doors every Sunday. That helped impel the creation of private eating clubs for Philadelphia's establishment. One of your authors recalls hearing this tongue-in-cheek admission by a local citizen when he first arrived in the city in the late 1960s: "Philadelphia is a city of gracious dining—or can be, if it's done in your own home."[20]

Shortly after that wry assessment, however, Philadelphia began to enter a restaurant renaissance that within a few years transformed it from a culinary desert to a city resounding with acclaimed new restaurants. Broadly speaking, that change marked the start of Philadelphia's transition into a postindustrial city after years of decline in the kind of economic activity that had made it a powerhouse of industrial production during the previous century. Although that renaissance was by no means exclusively French-inspired, it was the arrival in the city of a young Frenchman who was a native of Lyon that would have the greatest and most lasting influence.[21]

In 1970, at age twenty-four, Georges Perrier opened what would soon become one of the most highly rated restaurants in America, Le Bec-Fin, in a row house at the edge of the business district on Spruce Street. Perrier had begun his culinary training in France at age fourteen under the tutelage of several of his nation's most notable chefs. In 1967, Perrier arrived in Philadelphia at the invitation of Peter von Starck, a Philadelphia native who had trained alongside Perrier at the legendary La Pyramide in Vienne, to serve as head chef at von Starck's new restaurant, La Panetière. Three years later, when that restaurant moved to larger quarters, the two men parted company and Perrier opened his own restaurant in the vacated space.

Le Bec-Fin drew such favorable attention that by 1976 Perrier was made a *Maître Cuisinier de France*, one of some two hundred such honored chefs worldwide. A dozen years later, his fellow cuisiniers awarded him the Silver Toque, the most coveted trophy in the world of haute cuisine. Meanwhile, in 1983, Perrier moved his restaurant to larger quarters on Walnut Street. That permitted him to add a private banquet room and eventually the informal Bar Lyonnais downstairs. By the time he retired and sold the business in 2013, Perrier had received many awards, including the Légion d'Honneur in 2009. Within the previous decade, *Esquire* magazine had named Le Bec-Fin the nation's best French restaurant;[22] a Condé Nast readers' poll went further, calling it simply the finest restaurant in America.[23] Perrier's restaurant received the highest, five-star, rating from the Mobile Travel Guide for twenty-three years in a row. A film about his life and career, *King Georges*, was released in 2015.[24]

Over the course of his long career, Perrier trained a number of others in the fine art of French cuisine. As a result, many restaurants in the Philadelphia area continue to reflect the Perrier legacy. That legacy is more likely to show in the careful preparation of distinctive, flavorful dishes than in a mere copying of recipes from Le Bec-Fin's kitchen. In keeping with shifts in cultural tastes over the past half century, the kind of elegant haute cuisine for which Le Bec-Fin set the standard has become increasingly a thing of the past, not just in Philadelphia or America but in France as well. Dressy attire, for diners as well as servers, has largely given way—along with crystal chandeliers, starched tablecloths, silver chargers, even a universally followed sequence of multiple courses—to more casual dining.

Nonetheless, French-inspired cuisine still thrives in Philadelphia. When Jean-Marie Lacroix opened his eponymous restaurant on the west side of Rittenhouse Square at the start of the twenty-first century, he was already highly regarded as the executive chef at the city's Four Seasons Hotel, a position he had held for two decades. At the Hotel Rittenhouse, his restaurant, which looks out over the treetops on the square, soon won the highest possible rating from the food critic of the *Philadelphia Inquirer*, as well as top honors from *Esquire* and the James Beard Foundation. Lacroix was far from alone. By the second decade of the century, more than four dozen French eating places—bistros, cafés, *crêperies*, *tapisseries*, wine bars as well as fine dining establishments—offered their wares throughout Philadelphia. The names of several of the most acclaimed—among them, Bibou, Bistrot La Minette, Caribou Café, Parc, and Rouge—reveal their Gallic bent. At least an additional two dozen cafés and restaurants reflected the French-inflected cuisine of Francophone regions across the globe. Among them were Cajun, Creole, Haitian, Moroccan, and West African establishments. Some served their immediate neighborhoods—often where significant numbers of residents were part of the Francophone diaspora—while others had much

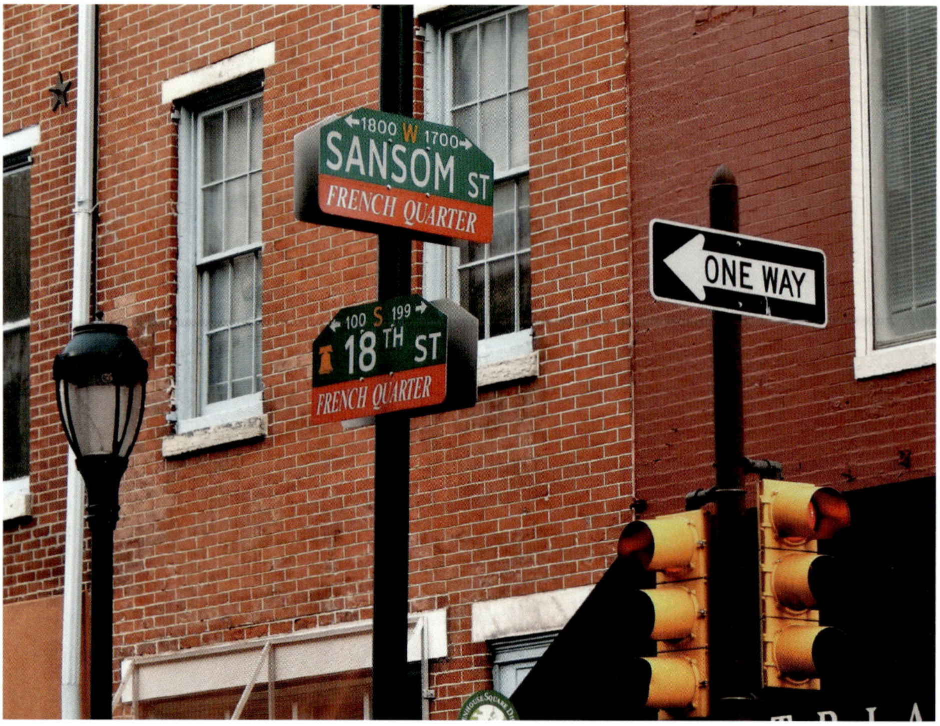

FIGURE 13.3 This intersection near Rittenhouse Square is in the heart of the neighborhood dominated by French restaurants and hostelries. Many other purveyors of French food are scattered throughout Philadelphia's neighborhoods.

wider appeal. Most of the latter were located within the center city business district and Queen Village. Many others were scattered throughout other sections of the city as well as in the suburbs. Several receiving acclaim appeared on East Passyunk Avenue, a street that became a multifaceted restaurant destination soon after the turn of the century. Reportedly, Philadelphia today may have more French-inspired restaurants on a per capita basis than any other American city.

In 1999, several blocks just to the north of Rittenhouse Square were officially designated by the city as a "French Quarter," thanks to the growing presence of French establishments there and in other streets nearby. (See Figure 13.3.) At that point, the French-owned hotel, Sofitel, anchored the quarter at Seventeenth and Sansom Streets. A decade or more after the French Quarter designation, the Kimpton Hotel Palomar opened across the street, facing Sofitel. The Palomar is situated in what had been the Architects Building, a slim art deco high-rise designed by Paul Cret in 1931. Another hotel with a French brand, Le Meridien, is several blocks away, at 1421 Arch Street. One may dine there at the French-themed aMuse restaurant or, at the Sofitel, in Chez Colette. Facing Independence Mall at Fifth and Chestnut Streets, a second Kimpton Hotel, the Monaco, now beckons from a landmark structure, the Lafayette Building, originally constructed by the Girard Estate in 1906–1907 to house offices.

It is a reminder of the ongoing importance of Stephen Girard's legacy to the city. The original architect was an alumnus of Girard College, James H. Windrim, who also designed other important buildings in late nineteenth- and early twentieth-century Philadelphia.[25]

Apart from the impressive number of restaurants in the Philadelphia region that today can be regarded as definitively "French," there are a great many more whose offerings may constitute "fusion" cuisine, cooking that deliberately borrows from more than one tradition. In Philadelphia, as in many other cities, this phenomenon grows out of the addition of new immigrants and their cultures to a cosmopolitan social mix. Fusion cuisines are increasingly the standard for fine restaurants everywhere. Because of the long historical appeal of French cooking, that mix very often displays unexpected French influences. For example, early in this century, a native of Francophone Haiti came to Philadelphia from New York to train with Stephen Starr, one of the city's best-known restaurateurs, in Starr's "game-shifting" Asian-themed restaurant. "I just fell in love with it," the newcomer, Sylva Senat, said of Philadelphia. As soon as he was able, Senat opened his own "sleek French-inspired restaurant and lounge," as the *New York Times* described the two-story space of his well-regarded Maison 208 on South Thirteenth Street in the heart of center city.[26]

Several articles in the "Food and Dining" section of the *Philadelphia Inquirer* on a single day early in 2018 also illustrate how immigrants are affecting Philadelphia's food scene. One explains that a new bakery in the city's Chinatown, Paris Baguette, is not so much an anomaly as its name suggests, since the firm is operated by Koreans, a country where French baked goods are beloved. (See Figure 13.4.) A number of other fine French bakeries in the city are also run by Asian immigrants. The article notes that colonialism brought French cuisine to Indochina. Now that substantial communities of people from Southeast Asia have been established in the Philadelphia region, so have their culinary borrowings from the French. "It's a story about immigrant entrepreneurship," the writer adds, "the cultural cachet of anything French, and the globalization of French cuisine."[27] Elsewhere, the newspaper's food editor writes a favorable review of the cassoulet then on offer at Bistrot La Minette, while another piece profiles the owner of a new Creole-Cajun restaurant that is about to open.[28] French-influenced cooking remains the gold standard worldwide.

In the three-and-a-quarter centuries since Philadelphia was first brought to life by William Penn, countless changes have occurred in the development of this American city and its place in the world. That has been just as true for France. Today, the Pennsylvania city still interacts with individuals and institutions within the French nation in ways that long have mattered, as when Philadelphians seek out French models for cuisine. Now they do so in novel fashion as well. The increased globalization of production and commerce has brought a number of French enterprises to establish their regional headquarters in the metropolitan area. Among them are a producer of chemicals for food preservation, a manufacturer of specialty chemicals, a purveyor of homeopathic medicine, and a provider of food and facilities management services.[29]

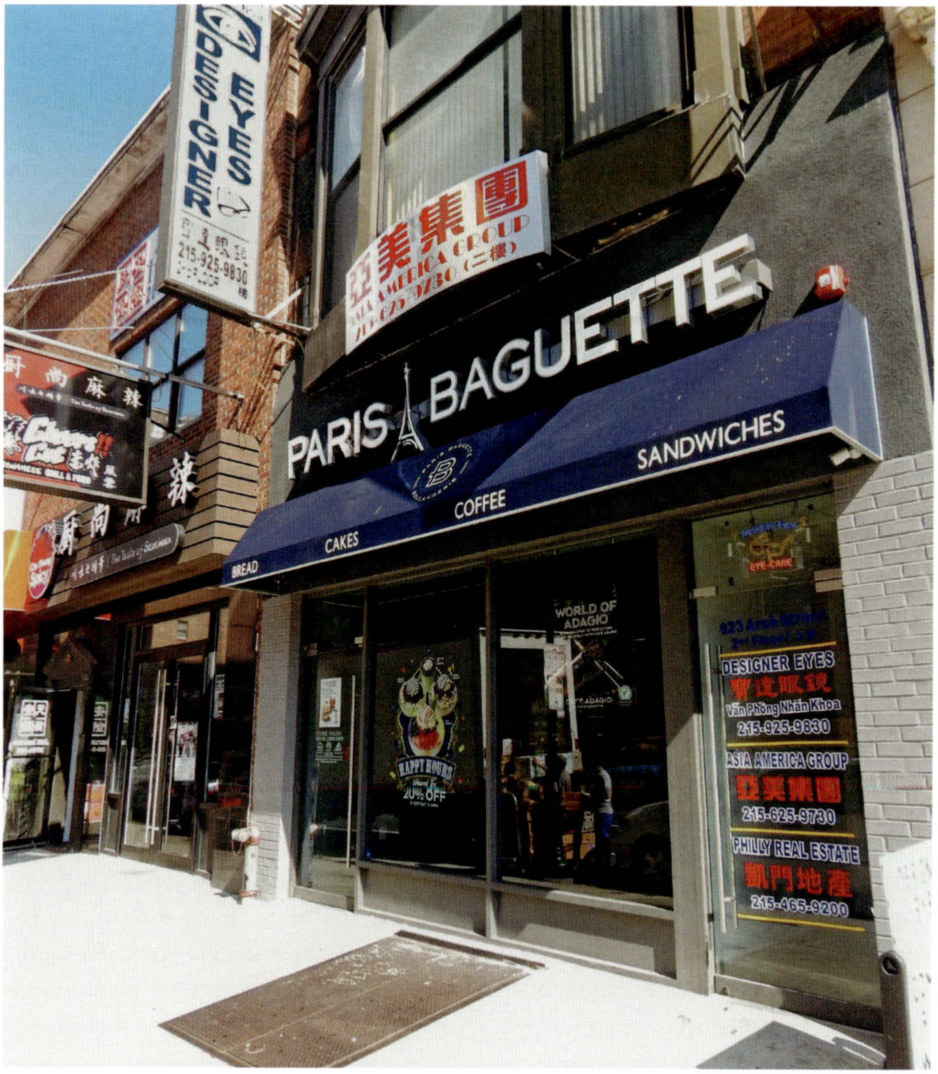

FIGURE 13.4 This bakery in Philadelphia's Chinatown reflects the appeal of French-style food and baked goods throughout the world.

In the second decade of the twenty-first century, nearly twelve thousand French people lived in the Philadelphia region. Many of them have commented favorably on the general quality of life they found in the area, including what they perceive as a rather European air in Philadelphia's built and cultural landscape. Most, but not all, of these individuals are expatriates brought here for reasons of employment. A considerable number of them came as the result of their connections to the chemical industry and their prior work in that field, especially in France's Rhone Valley. Such enterprises remain among the most important among French companies here. Substantial numbers of others are connected to food production, both in preparing and preserving it on a large scale and in providing it as artisans: bakers, cheese makers, and other purveyors of edibles.

Given the large number of French and Francophone expatriates in the area, an organization that began its work in 2000 now assists them. Philadelphie Accueil welcomes these newcomers to the Philadelphia region, offering to help them become acculturated and settled in their new American environment. They serve more than 180 families in the area today. Philadelphie Accueil is a member of the Fédération international des Accueils français et francophones d'expatriés (FIAFE).

Many of those of French heritage who have succeeded in their various business and professional fields are now active in the French Benevolent Society, which continues the mission it assumed when it was created on February 6, 1793, the anniversary of the Franco-American alliance. The society's mission today is much the same as when it was founded, namely, to help French people in the area who are in need through no fault of their own. The society assisted victims of yellow fever in the early years—Michel Bouvier served as a nineteenth-century president—and gave lavish balls at Musical Fund Hall to raise money for its charities in the years before the Civil War. During and after World War I, it assisted children orphaned by the war and supported the wives of men who enlisted in the French army. In the 1920s, when Paul P. Cret was its president, the society supplied coal to French immigrants without the means to buy it. The Great Depression ended the society's ownership of properties to generate income for its endowment, out of which scholarships have been offered to deserving postsecondary students.[30]

In 1884, an Alliance Française de Paris was created "for the propagation of the French language in the colonies and abroad." Its board of directors included such prominent figures as Ferdinand de Lesseps, Louis Pasteur, Ernest Renan, and Jules Verne. The mission soon spread to countries outside France. The Alliance Française de Philadelphie, founded in 1903, was among the first such associations formed in American cities at the start of the twentieth century, all making the promotion of French culture and the French language their mission. Also, in 1903, the Fédération des Alliances Françaises des États-Unis was created to collaborate in the work of various American branches. Now there are more than one hundred branches in the United States and more than eight hundred in 133 countries. All are run independently as nonprofit organizations.[31] They receive no financial support from the French government.

Today, the Alliance Française de Philadelphie offers French language instruction for students at every level, including classes for children and for adults at all stages of language competency. Immersion classes and private tutoring are also offered. Well-trained instructors typically are native speakers of French. The alliance is an official French language examination center providing four different competency tests. Members and students also may participate in a variety of social and cultural activities related to French culture, including lectures, French tables, wine and cheese tastings, concerts, movie nights, and a book club. The annual Bastille Day celebration is a gala fundraising event.[32] An Alliance Française publication, *French Philadelphia* (*Philadelphie à la française*, in the French language edition) is a guide to French sites and historical connections to the Philadelphia region.[33]

The greater Philadelphia chapter of the French American Chamber of Commerce (FACC) lists some eighty institutional members with ties to the local French community.[34] Its mission is to support strong trade relationships between the United States and France. The Philadelphia-area chapter is the second-largest among twenty-three chapters in America.[35] From both its institutional members and others, a number of French nationals serve as chief executive officers or board chairs of businesses located in the region. Corporate lawyers are part of that mix. Between 1997 and 2017, FACC every year honored individuals for their contributions to the commercial life of the Philadelphia region. Eight of those honored during that period were French nationals heading French corporations or their regional offices; four others were French nationals in charge of U.S. companies; still another was an American citizen at the head of a French company. Additional honorees included French officials resident in the United States and locally based American philanthropists and arts administrators with strong ties to France.

In addition, other firms dotting the landscape are either generated by or deeply connected to France and the Francophone world. Some have global reach, some regional, while others appeal almost entirely to local markets. Barry Callebaut USA Inc. is among the largest cocoa producers in the world; it maintains several plants and distribution centers in the Delaware Valley. Boutique Wine Collection is a Philadelphia-based importer of fine wines from Europe and South Africa that markets its products widely in North America. Carré d'Artistes, a locally franchised art gallery that is part of a network of such shops with headquarters in Aix-en-Provence, France, is a retail promoter of the original work of French and Francophone artists.[36] Its impact, like that of small businesses everywhere, may be largely restricted to a somewhat localized community, although one with global connections through its network of artists. Other French-inflected retail outlets in the area no doubt reach specific communities of consumers, suppliers, advertisers, and the like.

Occasionally, larger French firms might undertake a project in the region with wide appeal and influence. An example in 2015 was an elaborate interactive exhibition created and sponsored by the Saint-Gobain Group to celebrate its 350th anniversary. The company's North American headquarters, designed to comply with strict standards for energy efficiency, are in the Philadelphia suburb of Malvern.[37] Named "Future Sensations," the display filled several pavilions on Eakins Oval at the Fairmount end of the Benjamin Franklin Parkway, thereby providing a French vision of the future on a boulevard inspired by Paris and created by Frenchmen. For eight days that spring, tens of thousands of visitors could view Saint-Gobain's dazzling vision of futuristic structures and the kinds of materials used to construct them.[38] The company was founded in 1665 by Louis XIV to manufacture glass for the Hall of Mirrors the king was creating at his Palace of Versailles. Today, Saint-Gobain is a world leader in the manufacture of glass and a variety of other building materials. Philadelphians learned in 2019 that what had once been a visitor center at LOVE Park would become a restaurant, Loveluck, with new floor-to-ceiling windows created for it by Saint-Gobain.[39] The company also made

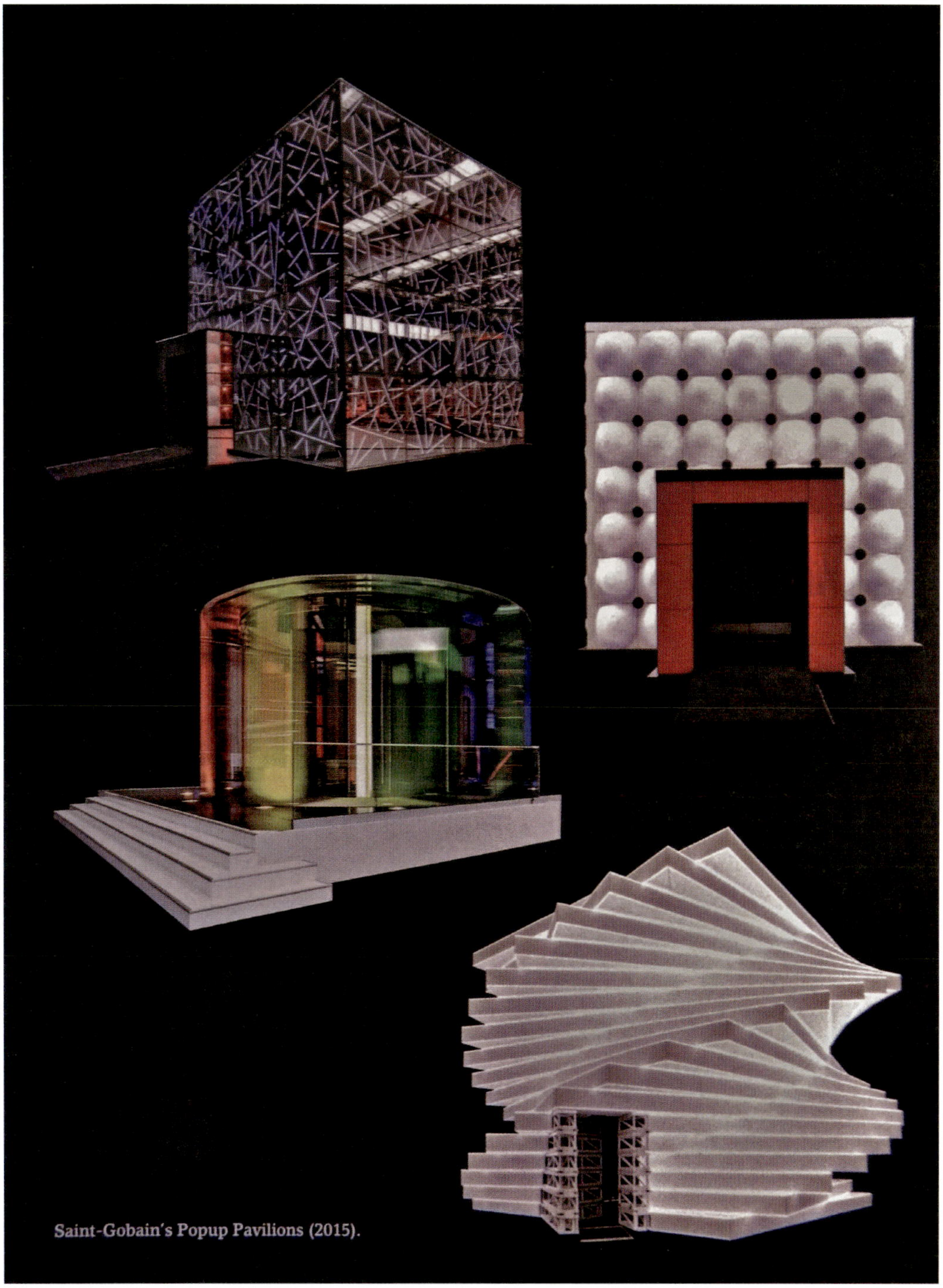

FIGURE 13.5 Saint-Gobain's Popup Pavilions. During its 350th year, this French maker of glass products, whose North American headquarters are outside Philadelphia, brought its interactive exhibition to the Eakins Oval on the Benjamin Franklin Parkway. (Photo courtesy of Saint-Gobain)

a substantial donation to the project. Thus, the French connection to the French-inspired parkway was again renewed. (See Figure 13.5.)

Outside the commercial world, other individuals of French ethnicity left their marks on the Philadelphia region early in the twenty-first century. Their presence was felt in nearly every aspect of modern urban life, from sports to electoral politics, and from the performing arts to religion.

In 2018, the Philadelphia 76ers basketball team had two highly regarded players of French African heritage. One of these, Joel Imbiid, a native of Cameroon, was named a starter in the NBA All-Star Game that year. Because professional ice hockey in North America has long been dominated by French Canadians, the Philadelphia Flyers have often fielded Quebecois and other players of French Canadian heritage. Among dozens of such skaters over the past forty years, the name of Bernie Parent stands out for his effort in winning the Stanley Cup for the Flyers in 1974 and 1975. He was inducted into the Hockey Hall of Fame in 1984. Some half dozen players of French descent have captained the Flyers over the years. In 1976, a Californian of French descent, Dick Vermeil, was hired as head coach of the Philadelphia Eagles. During the next six years, he brought that professional football team from mediocre rankings to the 1980 Super Bowl XV. Starting several years later, Vermeil became a prominent sports announcer for CBS and ABC. A 2006 film, the sports drama *Invincible*, depicted the true story of his coaching of the wide receiver, Vince Papale, during his time with the Eagles.

Nearly forty years after Vermeil helped make them a competitive team, the Eagles for the first time won Super Bowl LII in 2018. That greatest football championship has always evoked intense interest across the United States; with its outcome in 2018, delirium reigned in Philadelphia. A surprising reference to France became a part of the postvictory celebration when a limited-edition commemorative wine was created in a combination of French and American oak barrels. The concoctions, named "Championship Red" and "Championship Bubbly," were reportedly available online or in Philadelphia-area state stores.[40]

Yet, French sporting influences today are by no means restricted to Philadelphia's professional clubs. One result of our era's ever-increasing cultural connections is the establishment in recent years of a popular game originating a century or more ago in France's southern region of Provence. Pétanque, the French version of boccie or bowls, is now played by Francophone and Francophile residents in West Philadelphia's Clark Park on Sundays. A young Philadelphia architect, Bill Craig, first witnessed the game being played when on a cycling tour of Brittany. He sought out other would-be players in his home city, with the dual goal of enjoying the low-key recreational activity while conversing in French with other players. The group is now an official club hosting two competitive tournaments annually.[41] (See Figure 13.6.)

The du Pont name has been prominent in northern Delaware, which is part of the greater Philadelphia region, since Pierre Samuel and his sons first arrived there in January 1800.[42] Having soon become one of the richest families in America, a number of du Ponts have contributed to the economic, social, and cultural life of the nation.

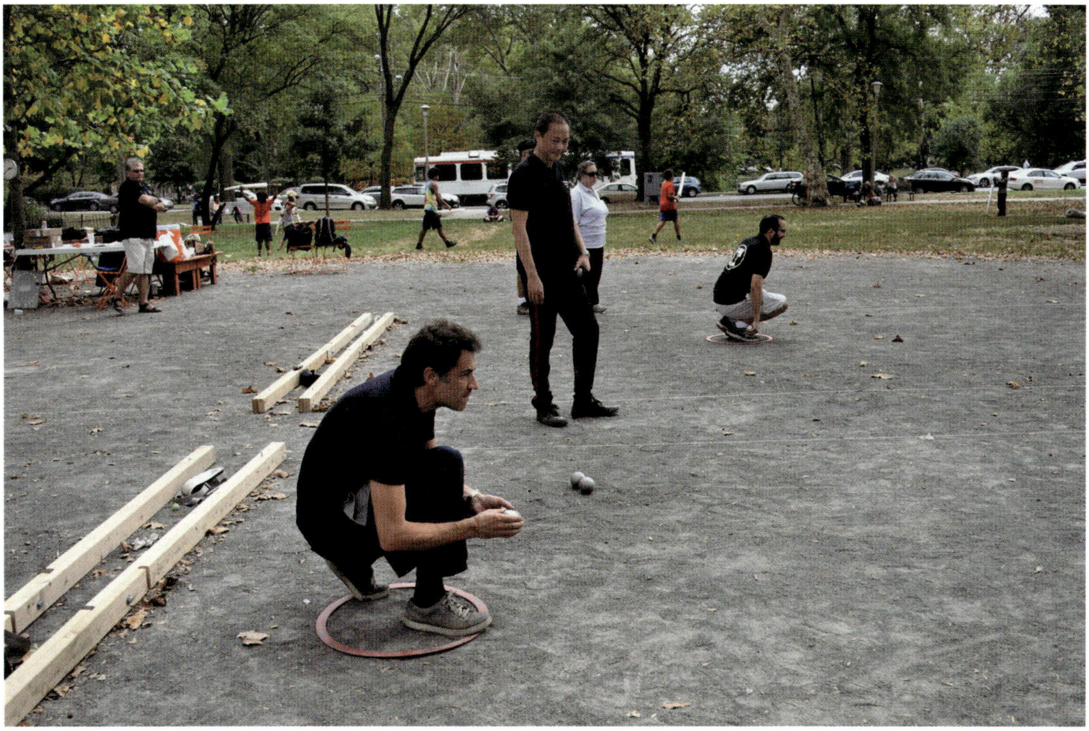

Figure 13.6 Pétanque in Philadelphia. Pétanque players in Philadelphia differ from the usual participants in France—who are typically older working-class men—by including young and old of all races, male and female, professionals as well as students. "West Philly residents, amoureux de pétanque," *Philadelphia City Paper*, posted Wednesday, August 21, 2013 (Lalita Clozel). Available at www.philadelphiapetanque.com. A game of bowls that originated in the south of France has been transplanted to Philadelphia. The local club is now associated with the Federation of Pétanque USA. (Courtesy of Mirai Yasuyama)

Meanwhile, Delaware's economy was heavily reliant on jobs provided by the family's chemical operations there. A late twentieth-century figure of political prominence was Pierre "Pete" du Pont IV (1935–), a Republican who held Delaware's sole congressional seat from 1971 to 1977. He was then elected governor, serving two terms, from 1977 to 1985. In that office, he led the effort to pass Delaware's Financial Center Development Act, which drew more than thirty banks to establish their headquarters in the state and to make it a center of the credit card industry. In 1988, he launched a bid for the Republican nomination for the presidency. When that proved unsuccessful, he largely retired from an active political career.[43] In the 1990s, another du Pont, John Eleuthère (1938–2010), made notorious headlines when he was arrested then convicted of the January 1996 murder at his home of the Olympic champion freestyle wrestler Dave Schultz. That made him the only member of the Forbes 400 richest Americans ever to be convicted of murder.[44]

Several current and recent leaders in the arts in Philadelphia are of French heritage. From 1982 until her unexpected death in 2008, Anne d'Harnoncourt (1943–

2008) was the director and chief executive officer of the Philadelphia Museum of Art. She was partially of French heritage, the only child of an early director of New York's Museum of Modern Art, René d'Harnoncourt. During the decade before she was named director, she was curator of twentieth-century art and a specialist in the work of Marcel Duchamp.[45] After her death, the approach to the museum's west entrance from Kelly Drive to Fairmount's summit was renamed in her memory.

Christopher d'Amboise (1960–) led the Pennsylvania Ballet as its artistic director and president from 1990–1994. A choreographer and teacher of dance, he is the son of the noted ballet dancer Jacques d'Amboise. For many years, the French Swiss conductor, Charles Dutoit (1936–), held important posts with the Philadelphia Orchestra after he had made a name for himself as conductor of the Orchestre Symphonique de Montréal and other leading orchestras. From 1990–2019, he directed the Philadelphians in their summer series in Saratoga, New York. In 2007, he was named the orchestra's chief conductor and artistic director and became conductor laureate in 2012. But, in 2017, his very distinguished career ended in disgrace. Accusations of sexual misconduct from a number of women caused the orchestra to sever its ties with him, as did other orchestras with which he was associated.[46]

Meanwhile, a younger Quebecois and native of Montreal, Yannick Nézet-Séguin (1975–), was named the orchestra's music director in 2010. His skills as a musician and appeal to audiences quickly placed him in the front rank of classical music conductors. His Philadelphia Orchestra contract was soon extended to 2025–2026. The orchestra's Gallic connections were spread further when the French maestro, Stéphane Denève (1971–) was appointed as principal guest conductor in 2014. In addition to his responsibilities in Philadelphia, Denève became music director of the St. Louis Symphony in 2019–2020 while continuing to direct the Brussels Philharmonic and the Centre for Future Orchestral Repertoire. Meanwhile, in 2018, Nézet-Séguin began his tenure as music director of the Metropolitan Opera in New York while continuing to lead the Philadelphians.

A Roman Catholic cleric whose ancestry was both French Canadian and Native American became the archbishop of Philadelphia when named to that post by Pope Clement XVI in 2011. Charles J. Chaput (1944–) is a member of the Order of Capuchin Friars, a branch of the Franciscans, who served as bishop of Rapid City, South Dakota, and archbishop of Denver before being named to head the Philadelphia Archdiocese, the ninth such prelate to serve in that post. He is regarded as a conservative on matters of doctrine, and an advocate for Catholics to participate actively in the nation's political life. He was the subject of controversy in 2004 for his alleged view that the faithful should not support the Democratic nominee for president, John Kerry, a Roman Catholic, because of the candidate's pro-choice positions regarding abortion.[47] He retired as archbishop in 2020.

From the time the United States won the Revolutionary War, achieving its independence, in 1781, American political figures have typically invoked the Franco-American alliance on such occasions as France's Bastille Day celebrations on July 14, or at other times when French governmental officials are present.[48] That invocation

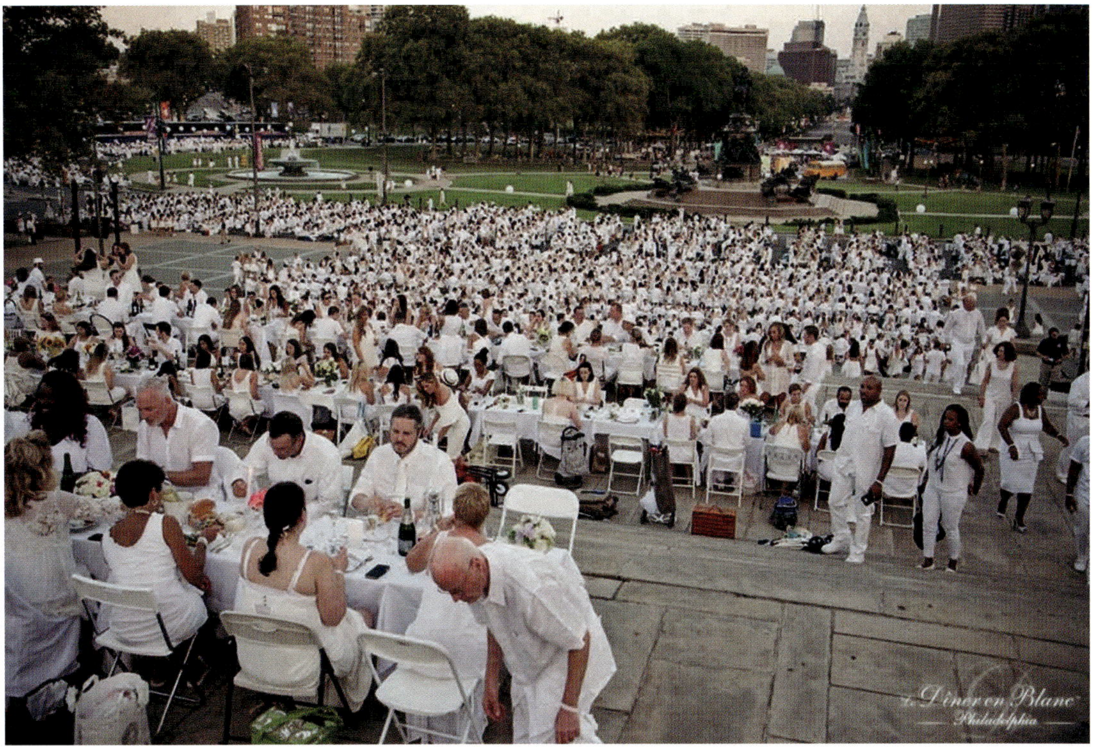

Figure 13.7 Philadelphia's "Dîner en Blanc" has become the largest such event in the United States. These festive summer picnics are held in more than seventy cities around the world. (Photo courtesy of Georgi Anastasov)

has largely become a sentimental token for celebratory occasions rather than a sincere reminder of special ties. True, there have been occasions when the old alliance has been refreshed—perhaps most notably when General Pershing proclaimed "Lafayette, we are here!" while American troops landed to join the French and allied cause in World War I. But, at other times, even if nothing like the Quasi-War has again divided the two nations as it did in the 1790s, a sense of pique, if not hostility, comes to the fore. When the government of France refused to join the American invasion of Iraq in 2003, a few indignant members of Congress demanded that their cafeteria should replace "French fries" with "freedom fries." In the following year's presidential campaign, one candidate was mocked by supporters of his opponent for the fact that he spoke French fluently and so might take orders from Paris. At about the same time, the Alliance Française de Philadelphie noticed a decline in those wanting to take French language instruction in its school, as did other such institutions across the nation.

Yet, if there are occasional bumps in the long road of French American amity, the enormous appeal of French culture repeatedly smooths the way forward. Food and the French etiquette connected with it are an enduring example. In 1988, a French gentleman invited a group of friends to join him in an elegant bring-your-own picnic in a public park in Paris with the proviso that all should dress in white so that they could find each other in a crowd. Thus was born the "Dîner en Blanc," which has now become a chic summer event in more than seventy cities around the world every summer. Philadelphia launched its first such dinner in 2012, which had grown to draw some six thousand guests by 2019, making it the largest such Dîner en Blanc in the United States. Each year, the organizers choose an iconic location, which remains a secret until the day of the event. Food, wine, tables, chairs, and tableware all are carried onto the site by the guests, who clear away the remains of their party at the end.[49] (See Figure 13.7.)

The year 2018 brought to a close an annual Bastille Day celebration that was unique to Philadelphia. At Eastern State Penitentiary—that long-disused prison where the practice of solitary confinement was criticized by Alexis de Tocqueville in the 1830s—a playful reenactment of the storming of the Bastille was presented every July 14 starting in 1994. That trigger of the French Revolution was by then so distant from contemporary life that it could be safely parodied by Philadelphians. For many of the occasions at the penitentiary, entertainment was provided by the Bearded Ladies, a cabaret troupe featuring mostly drag portrayals of such notables as Edith Piaf, Joan of Arc, Benjamin Franklin, Vladimir Putin, and a six-foot-tall Baguette. A bearded Marie Antoinette cried "Let them eat cake!" before tossing great quantities of Tastykakes—dessert snacks produced by a Philadelphia baking institution—to the thousands in attendance. Following this early evening free performance both inside and outside the prison walls, restaurants in the surrounding Fairmount neighborhood offered French-themed food and drink specials. This tradition came to an end with the decision of the Eastern State Penitentiary Historic Site, which manages the enormous structure, to increase its focus on criminal justice reform at the same time it was working to preserve the historic facility to serve its ever-growing number of visitors, which had increased fourfold over the previous ten years.[50]

We can confidently conclude that, with the end of the penitentiary's Bastille Day event, other manifestations of French culture will continue to arise and thrive in Philadelphia. There, at least as much as is the case in other large American cities, the French legacy and the French presence are ineradicably a part of its history and its future, crucial ingredients in the melting pot that has made the United States of America a distinctive society almost from its very beginning.

[Conclusion]

The French and Philadelphia

For some three hundred years, one feature of the French presence in Philadelphia has made it historically unique: the contributions of comparatively few individuals have very much outweighed the somewhat small numbers of French and Francophone people who have immigrated to the Philadelphia region. Perhaps some of this may have been foreordained by the influence of French intellectuals from the Enlightenment who so powerfully informed the nation's founders, contributing the fundamental ideas that have shaped the United States, including, of course, Philadelphia, from its birth down to the present day. But that disproportionate influence of the few upon the many has recurred several times since Penn created his "greene Countrie Towne" in the 1680s. It is evident in the way French immigrants became part of the region's business and professional elite from late in the eighteenth century. It accounts for the Parisian cast to Philadelphia's most iconic boulevard and for the Beaux-Arts style of many of its important buildings and public spaces. It is evident in how Philadelphia came to house some of the world's most impressive collections of French art. It also helps explain the late twentieth-century development of Philadelphia as a culinary destination, with French restaurants and restaurateurs leading the way.

Because this influence of a comparative few is in general that of a cultural and social elite, it means that the contributions have more often been made to the city's high culture than to its mass culture. We see French influence in the prominence of its fine arts holdings, impressive public structures, elegant boulevard, and fine restaurants, rather than in what is peculiar to its popular music, public celebrations, or sports.[1] All in all, the presence of the French and the heritage of France have contributed greatly to Philadelphia's character as a cultural and educational center. In the process, the interplay of Philadelphians and their compatriots with France as well as French individuals within the Philadelphia region have left distinctive marks on one of America's greatest and most distinctive cities.

The Founding Fathers perceptively realized the value of the visual arts to create an image of the new nation and promote its aspirations and achievements to the world. John Adams traced the progression of his needs to a time when the arts could take their place: "I must study politics and war that my sons may have liberty to study mathematics and philosophy. My sons study mathematics and philosophy, geography, natural history, naval architecture, navigation, commerce and agriculture in order to give their children a right to study paintings, poetry, music, architecture, statuary, tapestry and porcelain."[2] Thomas Jefferson's residency in Paris from 1784 to 1789 inspired him to write to a friend: "Were I to tell you how much I enjoy [French] architecture, sculpture, painting, music, I should want words."[3] He avidly acquired more than sixty paintings during his residency in Paris, importing them to America with hundreds of books, eager to share the aesthetic and intellectual riches of France's cultural heritage in order to foster America's emerging identity. His recommendation in 1785 of Jean-Antoine Houdon to execute a sculpture of George Washington demonstrated the sophistication of his eye and mind. Houdon crossed the Atlantic with Benjamin Franklin, whose features he commemorated in marble, creating an indelibly lifelike image in stone. Well before the invention of photography, sculpture busts and portraits preserved the identity of presidents, patriots, and citizens to commemorate their achievements and express appreciation for their service to the country or cause. Houdon created several of the iconic images of prominent figures of the early republic and was so esteemed that he was made an honorary member of the American Academy after its founding in 1808.

Charles Willson Peale patriotically applied his prodigious talent to documenting the likenesses of many individuals who played key roles in the cause of independence and nation building. In his museum, he created the first national portrait gallery to memorialize the statesmen, legislators, and military heroes at home and from abroad so that his paintings could educate the public and promote the political and social ideals he believed these figures incarnated. His contribution to the founding of the Pennsylvania Academy of the Fine Arts in 1805, the first museum and art school in the nation, made Philadelphia a central destination for art training.

Peale had traveled to England to study with Benjamin West when he was an aspiring painter, but, when his son Rembrandt decided to embrace the profession, the younger Peale opted for Paris rather than London. France's investment in its artists through financial support of its official art schools and exhibitions, its awards and honors, along with the art treasures of the royal collection that was opened to the public after the Revolution, offered a wealth of artistic experience that could not be had in the United States. Opportunities to apprentice to an established master and compete to have works accepted at the Salon drew American artists to Paris to further their aesthetic education and perfect their technical skills.

The numbers of American artists traveling to France grew exponentially throughout the nineteenth century as Paris became a cultural magnet for Europe.[4] Thomas Eakins, often considered the most important realist painter of nineteenth-century America, spent four years abroad, from 1866 to 1870, largely in the Parisian studio of the academic painter Jean-Louis Gérôme. His technical training and his exposure to contemporary works of French art profoundly impacted his career on his return to Philadelphia. Many of his most famous paintings resonate with lessons learned and images seen during his time in France where the tradition of the academic nude in art was being challenged by the radical depictions of contemporary female nudity in the art of Gustave Courbet and Édouard Manet. When Eakins taught at the Pennsylvania Academy, he inculcated his students with his conviction that drawing after the nude model taught them more than copying from antique casts, as was customary practice. His career came to be as embattled as that of the French artists who launched modern painting in mid-nineteenth-century Paris. His work proved as instrumental as theirs in turning art away from the conservative norms of the academy toward subject matter that reflected modern life.

From its founding in 1648, the École des Beaux-Arts, the most prestigious art school in France, trained the elite of the aspiring artists—if they were male. Only in 1897 were women finally admitted to its studios. Thus, when Mary Cassatt went to France to study in 1865, she could not expect the same advantages that her fellow male students at the Pennsylvania Academy had experienced. She copied works at the Louvre, studied with Charles Chaplin whose sentimental paintings enjoyed great success especially under the Second Empire, and worked for a while as a private pupil with Gérôme. Sporadic success at showing her work at the Salon impelled Cassatt to exhibit with the renegade impressionist group that had tired of having their work rejected at the Salon and had begun organizing exhibitions in 1874. At Degas's invitation in 1877, Cassatt threw her lot in with the modern artists who embraced subject matter from everyday life, painted with broad brushstrokes and painterly dabs that clearly distinguished their style from the finely detailed and lacquered canvases that crowded the walls of the Salon. Although she spent her professional career in France, the ties she maintained with Philadelphia allowed her work to be shown in forty local exhibitions between 1873 and 1927. In a similar vein, although she is buried in France, her will listed her legal domicile as Philadelphia.

Because of his race, Henry Ossawa Tanner also chose to repatriate to France. When he registered to study at the Pennsylvania Academy in 1879, his admission had to be approved by the antique drawing class because he was African American. After stopping in Paris in 1889 on an overseas tour, he decided to stay and studied at the Académie Julian. As the son of an African Methodist Episcopal Church minister, Tanner capitalized on his upbringing and became famous for his religious paintings. He received support for travel to Palestine and Egypt from Rodman Wanamaker who served as president of the American Art Association of Paris. As had Mary Cassatt, Tanner sent work from France regularly to the Pennsylvania Academy for exhibition; thus both artists maintained their reputations at home and abroad. Both were honored by the French government in their lifetimes with the Légion d'Honneur.

When the French art dealer Paul Durand-Ruel mounted three hundred impressionist works at the American Art Association in New York City in 1886, the exhibition impacted a number of artists who embraced the technique to record aspects of the American landscape on their canvases. Bucks County became a center for a small group of artists who came to be known as the Pennsylvania impressionists. Edward Redfield, Walter Elmer Schofield, and Daniel Garber absorbed the lessons they had learned during their stays in France and applied them to their individual interpretations of the rural landscape around New Hope. The art critic Guy Pène du Bois proclaimed that the realism of Pennsylvania impressionists had its origins in French art but had become authentically American by the vigorous brushwork and adherence to factual detail that characterized their local Pennsylvania scenes.

During the first decades of the twentieth century, New York began to draw artists away from Philadelphia to its galleries, its exhibitions at the National Academy of Design, and its financial support of artists. By the time the work of the Pennsylvania impressionists had reached its peak at the Panama-Pacific International Exposition in 1915, what had seemed innovative in their work now began to look retrograde to a new generation of artists. Scenes of contemporary urban realism, often rendered with dark tonalities, replaced the luminous landscapes of the American impressionists. Artists increasingly chafed under the strictures of the jury system of the National Academy of Design in New York. Robert Henri, who had trained at the Pennsylvania Academy and in France, organized a group exhibition at the Macbeth Gallery of painters who came to be known as The Eight. This inaugurated the momentum for independent exhibitions that led to the International Exhibition of Modern Art, known as the Armory Show, which opened its doors on Lexington Avenue on February 17, 1913. American work dominated in numbers but not in sales or critical notoriety as the European modernists brought their avant-garde stylistic innovations to American eyes. The fractured forms of cubism and strident clashing colors of fauvism made American art, in the words of William Glackens, one if its exhibitors, seem arid and bloodless. As Milton Brown concluded, after the Armory Show, American art was never the same again.[5] Many artists began to shed the shackles of realism and traditional perspective while the artistic capital slowly shifted away from France to America due to the world wars that tore apart the European dominance in the arts and made America a refuge and New York the new center of art.

From its founding to the present, the physical map of Philadelphia reveals much about French influence here. As is true for any human settlement, the profile of the city is unique in its built structures and their arrangement and relationship to the city's geographic location. The configuration that arose in the 1680s at the southeastern corner of the proprietary colony of Pennsylvania on a nearly rectangular stretch of land between the Delaware and Schuylkill Rivers began, uniquely in North America at the time, as a planned settlement. In the mind of its creator, William Penn, its very form was meant to suggest egalitarianism to its citizens, with streets constructed on a grid marking off blocks of land of regular and nearly identical size. The plan provided space for private enterprise along with robust civic life, while attuning the residents to nature by creating green public spaces in the city's four quadrants and, at the center, a square for municipal government. Penn's plan was modest in what it imagined for the city's life and future growth but ambitious in its assumption that a harmonious community could arise there.

More than two centuries later, after Penn's green country town had grown into one of the nation's industrial powerhouses and spread far beyond the founder's imagined settlement, city planners from France transformed the city with a bold initiative completely out of character for Philadelphia at the time. Their plan nonetheless respected, even reinforced, Penn's model of an urban settlement that placed civic virtue at its center, brought green landscapes to its heart, and prepared the city, serendipitously if unintentionally, for its postindustrial future. The resulting Benjamin Franklin Parkway was, in the view of one critic, the greatest achievement of its kind in America.[6]

Thus, the settlement created by a radical English dissident was partially transformed centuries later by French architects nurtured in a very different aesthetic tradition. Yet, as we have seen, the influence of France and the French on Philadelphia had been present from Penn's day onward (Penn himself employed winemakers from Languedoc and Poitou to tend his vineyards at Pennsbury Manor), so connecting threads are visible throughout the intervening centuries. Consider Pierre L'Enfant in the eighteenth century. He was something of an enfant terrible during his lifetime, but his American legacy reflects the design influences he partook of while growing up in Paris and Versailles. The formal gardens laid out by André Le Nôtre for Louis XIV must have been deeply implanted in L'Enfant's vision of planned landscapes. It was Le Nôtre who extended the westward vista from the Tuileries Palace in the heart of Paris, creating the Grand Promenade, which was lengthened and renamed the Champs-Elysées in 1709. L'Enfant's debt to the master is apparent in his plan for the federal capital. Had his goals for Robert Morris's great mansion in Philadelphia not proved ill-fated, we might today have glimpsed a hint of Versailles in Philadelphia's center city.

Baron Haussmann's wholesale remaking of Paris during the reign of Napoleon III made the map of the French capital a variant of L'Enfant's plan for the District of Columbia. A public administrator rather than an architect, Haussmann was also inspired by the formal landscapes and broad boulevards created by Le Nôtre and, like his seventeenth-century predecessor, had the command of a royal purse to bring his vision to life on a grand scale. The rise to world prominence of the architectural teachings of the École des Beaux-Arts coincided with Haussmann's ascendancy in Paris, its teachings reflecting in many respects the precepts of his reconfigured city.

Paul P. Cret absorbed those same teachings. When he arrived in Philadelphia as a young architect early in the twentieth century, he carried with him a view he shared, whether knowingly or not, with Philadelphia's founder: both he and Penn believed that the public realm was more important than the private. As a way of demonstrating that idea, Penn had suggested placing civic government at the town's center—a unique idea in America at the time. Cret was instrumental, half a century after that dream was finally realized with the construction of City Hall, in making that most important civic building the endpoint of his elegant new boulevard. The grandeur of the Benjamin Franklin Parkway, like that of City Hall, was meant to elevate the public realm. Penn's plan and the parkway shared an emphasis on civic order.[7]

At about the same time, in Washington, DC, the McMillan Commission was at work refashioning the nation's capital by implementing much of what remained undone from L'Enfant's century-old plan for the city. Aware of the source of L'Enfant's inspiration, the commission chair, Senator John McMillan of Michigan, traveled to Versailles to view Le Nôtre's work firsthand. Meanwhile, its members turned to Haussmann's Paris for a guide.[8] Just as Haussmann had borrowed from L'Enfant, the commission now made many references to the Parisian boulevards and squares of Haussmann. At the heart of their project was the creation of a National Mall, a variation on L'Enfant's design for a grand boulevard stretching from Capitol Hill. One of the first ornaments to be constructed on the new mall was the Pan-American Union, built to the design of Paul Cret and Albert Kelsey, an older, prominent Philadelphia architect who had long supported the parkway project in his hometown. The Pan-American Union would cement Cret's reputation nationally.

Meanwhile, the French influences on the built environment of Philadelphia's parkway district radically transformed Penn's city, emphasizing not its intimacy but its grand scale and high ambitions. It seems clear from our perspective today that the Cret-Gréber plan for the parkway was *too* ambitious for its time. Gréber turned its upper reach into parkland less out of deference to Penn's priority for green space than because civic institutions originally planned to be headquartered there refused to move. The boulevard had been designed to connect Philadelphia's civic heart to its great public park—a matter it succeeded at almost too well when it became a kind of highway for motor traffic. (That nineteenth-century park itself was largely an homage to the Schuylkill River and its tributary, the Wissahickon, returning those waterways in their passage through the city to their natural state in Penn's day.)[9]

But even in its semifinished state, the parkway accomplished much, and, by early in the twenty-first century, the parkway district was at last maturing as a cultural and recreational destination for both citizens and visitors. In that sense, it was finally approaching completion. Today this quarter houses the greatest collections of French art in Philadelphia, if not the nation. Inside the Barnes Foundation's new home, Paul Cret's design for the galleries in their original Merion location has been exactly replicated. Next door, the Cret-Gréber-designed Rodin Museum displays more of that sculptor's work than can be seen anyplace else outside of France. The Philadelphia Museum of Art at the parkway's Fairmount terminus holds a number of great collections of French art as well as many other works from the hands of those whose inspiration and training came from France. However serendipitous the conditions that placed so much French art along the boulevard designed by Frenchmen, the result is a wonderfully holistic amalgam of French-inspired art and architecture.

Also, in the current century, the city has expanded the parkway district as an attractive public space. The creation of Dilworth Park at Fifteenth and Market Streets brings the parkway visually to City Hall's portal while creating a place for rest and recreation at the city's very center. The subsequent remodeling of John F. Kennedy Plaza (a.k.a. LOVE Park) in the next block to the northwest opened the vista fully from City Hall to the Philadelphia Museum of Art, making the connective purpose even clearer.

Both Cret and Jacques Gréber continued as important city planners in Philadelphia. Cret assisted Mayor John Reyburn at the pathbreaking city planning conference of 1911, and in that same year became a leading member of the Art Jury as well as the designer of important structures in and around Philadelphia. By the time of his death, he may have trained and inspired more architects than anyone of his generation in America.[10] During the 1930s, Gréber acted as a consultant to the City Planning Commission. He addressed issues of the Schuylkill River embankments, approaches to the Delaware River Bridge (now named for Benjamin Franklin) and Franklin Square, and the development of traffic routes through the city and around Rittenhouse Square and the West and East River Drives through Fairmount Park. He also advised in the development of the central Post Office and Thirtieth Street Station as well as the further development of the Parkway and Pennsylvania Avenues.[11]

Cret, meanwhile, planted a number of memorials in his native land to the dead of World War I. In honoring Americans who had fallen on the battlefields of France, he left a legacy there that revealed both his French roots in the Beaux-Arts tradition and his growth and development as a Philadelphia architect. The result was a visual reminder of deep Franco-American connections, renewed as they had been in the terrible war so recently concluded.[12] Cret himself had nearly died during that war, surviving at least three gas attacks while serving the French army in which he had enlisted. His wife, Marguerite, volunteered as an army nurse. Once the United States entered the war, Cret naturally was made a translator. And when his Château-Thierry Memorial was completed in 1930, the two allegorical figures he placed in front depicted America and France, of course.[13]

Philadelphia's French legacy continues, not just in the bricks and mortar such as are still supplied abundantly in the housing and commercial stock of the Girard Trust but in the less tangible work of French-derived civic organizations. (See Chapter 13 for a review of the work of the Alliance Française de Philadelphie and others in the Philadelphia region.)

In the field of education, a response to the presence of large numbers of French and French-speaking residents in the region was the establishment in 1991 of the French International School of Philadelphia in the suburb of Bala Cynwyd. EFIP (its French acronym) provides bilingual education in French and English to children from preschool through the eighth grade. Attracting American and French students as well as children from elsewhere, the creation of a multicultural environment for learning is a feature of the school's pedagogy.[14] In addition, the French Heritage Society, which maintains a Philadelphia chapter, has for many years provided financial support to maintain and restore architecturally important sites to French culture in France and the United States. The society also sponsors educational and cultural exchanges between the two countries.[15]

The strong presence of French and Francophone residents here prompted this comment by the consul-general of France in Washington, DC, on a visit to Philadelphia in 2006: "Philadelphia is the U.S. city that has attracted the greatest concentration of direct French investments abroad. More than the economic presence, that has facilitated the excellent integration of a vast community of French people living in Philadelphia into American society, as is easily demonstrated in the dynamism of the French quarter situated in center city."[16]

In 2014, Philadelphia became a World Heritage City, the first to receive that designation in the United States. In making the case for membership, the team representing the mayor's office asserted that "Philadelphia is the largest and most complete fulfillment of the kind of model city envisioned by Enlightenment architects." Their summary of that view put it very succinctly: "Philadelphia embodies a continuing notion of idea as place."[17] That characterization is a reminder of the importance of Enlightenment ideas, especially those of French philosophes, in the birth and growth of this city, ideas that eventually became the bedrock principles of the American republic. Those ideas were translated into place in many of the physical monuments of the city, from Independence Hall and several of its Greek Revival neighbors to the Second Empire City Hall and the French-inspired boulevard sweeping outward to Fairmount Park. Apostles of the École des Beaux-Arts and the City Beautiful movement it inspired in America placed an emphasis on social order and the public good at the center of their aesthetic. Like the philosophes before them, they viewed the pursuit of the rational as the pursuit of the ideal. Paul Cret in Philadelphia viewed the neoclassical architecture of the early nineteenth century in America as a visual reminder of democratic norms.[18] That, too, explains how a sleek and modernized version of that architecture became his signature style.

Yet, Philadelphia's embodiment of idea as place did not, in fact, begin only with its adoption of Enlightenment ideals in the eighteenth century nor has it ended in our time. William Penn's grand idea became his vision for a new, harmonious city in the wilderness, which grew to exemplify that dream more fully than in any other European settlement on the North American continent. The clearest example in the recent past may be the transformation of the dense commercial neighborhood around Independence Hall, beginning in the 1960s, into a landscaped open space meant to showcase the place and the ideas that gave birth to a new nation. The long Independence Mall created in the heart of the historic district now somewhat resembles the parkway district northwest of City Hall. It stretches from the northeast corner of Washington Square past Independence Hall to the southeast corner of Franklin Square, thus tangentially connecting two of Penn's original green spaces. The greenway continues at a right angle to the east between Walnut and Chestnut Streets, leading walkers past a number of monuments to the nation's early history—the American Philosophical Society, Second Bank of the United States, and Carpenters' Hall among them. That walkway ends at City Tavern, across from which Welcome Park, the city's tribute to William Penn, greets visitors on Second Street.

One of the great products of the ideas that sprang from Independence Hall in the eighteenth century was the Constitution of the United States. In 2003, the newly created National Constitution Center opened facing Independence Hall from the northern end of the mall, a place where the public can explore those ideas. A number of other sites in and around Independence National Historical Park invite further exploration of the history of the United States and the ideas that have inspired the nation. A new Museum of the American Revolution beckons from Third Street at Walnut. Almost across the street, a refurbished First Bank of the United States will become a museum to tell the story of the nation's financial history. French influence is visible in all these sites.

Throughout the Society Hill neighborhood just to the south, small parks and greenways allow visitors to appreciate the city's renewed respect for one of its oldest and most serenely beautiful residential quarters, even while they are being led to the public buildings and places of worship that continue to make it a vital community. To the north of Society Hill, the revived commercial and residential quarter known as Old City provides many reminders of the centrality of this neighborhood to Philadelphia in its early days. Here are historic houses of worship, a number of museums, Benjamin Franklin's residence and burial place, the Betsy Ross House, and Elfreth's Alley, America's oldest, continually inhabited residential street. These neighborhoods, too, share a French presence.

French ideas about cuisine and hospitality have also been expressed in a specific place since Philadelphia's French Quarter was so designated at the end of the twentieth century. That designation acknowledges the fact that those several blocks just to the north of Rittenhouse Square contain French hostelries and restaurants. It is also a reminder that these marks of French culture, and French cuisine in particular, are scattered throughout the city for the enjoyment of a wide swath of Philadelphians.

In the spirit of Ernest Hemingway's claim that Paris is a movable feast, our book has attempted to focus on a selection of the relay of influences and interactions that have resulted from the contacts between Philadelphia and French culture. Social, political, economic, and aesthetic ties have linked Philadelphia and France from its earliest days and continue to do so to the present moment. Without doubt, further chapters of this continuing relationship will reveal themselves as the feast moves into the future.

[Notes]

Introduction

1. Brian G. Armstrong, *Calvin and the Amyraut Heresy* (Madison: University of Wisconsin Press, 1969).

2. His admiration was partially expressed in his well-known comment about one of Penn's presumed acts after arriving in Pennsylvania: "The first step he took was to enter into an alliance with his American neighbors, and this is the only treaty between these people and the Christians that was not ratified by an oath and was never infringed," as quoted in Charles F. Howlett and Robbie Lieberman, *A History of the American Peace Movement* (Lewiston, NY: Edwin Mellen Press, 2008), p. 33.

3. François Furstenberg, *When the United States Spoke French* (New York: Penguin, 2014), p. 183.

4. Penny Balkin Bach, *Public Art in Philadelphia* (Philadelphia: Temple University Press, 1992).

5. With the exception that the city's major league hockey team, the Philadelphia Flyers, has always included star players of Quebecois or French heritage.

Chapter 1

1. Jason Laughlin, "320-Year-Old Bridge Readied for Next 100," *Philadelphia Inquirer*, March 19, 2018, p. A2.

2. A century later, two descendants of Huguenots who fled to America, John Jay and Henry Laurens, would play important roles in the American Revolution and its aftermath. George Washington, too, had a Huguenot ancestor among his otherwise English forebears. The first of his ancestors to arrive in Virginia was a young Huguenot from Ile de Ré, France, who first immigrated to England, then to America in 1620. This Nicolas Martiau was Washington's great-great-great-grandfather.

3. George Struble, "The French Element among the Pennsylvania Germans," available at journals.psu.edu/phj/article/download/22432/22201/0.

4. Frank McLynn, *1759: The Year Britain Became Master of the World* (New York: Grove, 2004), pp. 35–36.

5. Geoffrey Plank, *An Unsettled Conquest: The British Campaign against the Peoples of Acadia* (Philadelphia: University of Pennsylvania Press, 2003), p. 149. See also Christopher Hodson, *The Acadian Diaspora: An Eighteenth-Century History* (Oxford: Oxford University Press, 2012).

6. Available at http://www.acadian-cajun.com/expa.htm. Acadian-Cajun Genealogy and History—Exile Destination: Pennsylvania.

7. Quoted in Wilton Paul Ledet, "Acadian Exiles in Pennsylvania," Pennsylvania Historical Association, *Pennsylvania History* (April 1942), p. 119.

8. Like a number of other low-lying islands where the Delaware widened south of the city, Province Island became attached to the Pennsylvania shoreline as the result of landfill in the late nineteenth and early twentieth centuries. That land is now the site of Philadelphia International Airport.

9. William W. Cutler III, "Philadelphia, Pittsburgh, and the Historiography of Urban Public Education in Pennsylvania," *Pennsylvania Magazine of History and Biography* 141, no. 3 (October 2017), p. 221.

10. Maurice Jackson, *Let This Voice Be Heard: Anthony Benezet, Father of American Abolitionism* (Philadelphia: University of Pennsylvania Press, 2009); Roger A. Bruns, "Anthony Benezet and the Natural Rights of the Negro," *Pennsylvania Magazine of History and Biography* (Philadelphia: Historical Society of Pennsylvania, January 1972).

11. David L. Crosby, ed., *The Complete Anti-Slavery Writings of Anthony Benezet, 1754–1782: An Annotated Critical Edition* (Baton Rouge: Louisiana State University Press, 2013).

12. Ledet, "Acadian Exiles in Pennsylvania," p. 125.

13. Ibid., pp. 118–128. An interesting nineteenth-century account of these events is William B. Reed, "The Acadian Exiles, or French Neutrals, in Pennsylvania, to which is appended a Relation of Their Misfortunes by John Baptiste Galerm," *Contributions to American History*, Historical Society of Pennsylvania (Philadelphia: J. B. Lippincott, 1858). Reed's account begins by citing Henry W. Longfellow in the 1853 London edition of his "Evangeline."

14. In 1895, a writer sought to clarify that Holy Trinity was the burial place of the (imaginary) lovers in her own verse:

Up yonder square, dear reader
If wandering thoughtfully,
You'll find the little graveyard
Of HOLY TRINITY;
And there, amid their brethren,
'Tis said, they slumber sweet,
Evangeline, the faithful,
With Gabriel at her feet.

Eleanor C. Donnelly, "The Acadians in Philadelphia," *Records of the American Catholic Historical Society of Philadelphia* 6 (1895), pp. 1–2.

15. François Furstenberg, *When the United States Spoke French* (New York: Penguin, 2014), p. 28.

CHAPTER 2

1. John Locke, *Second Treatise of Government*, ed. C. B. Macpherson (Indianapolis: Hackett, 1988).

2. Locke spent five years in exile in the Netherlands during the reign of James II. When James was overthrown, Parliament invited the Dutch monarch, William of Orange, and his wife, Mary,

the daughter of James II, to ascend the British throne. Locke returned to England in the same ship that brought Queen Mary back to her native land.

3. The works of these writers and interpretations of them through succeeding centuries are voluminous. For a sampling of modern editions and commentary on each, see Charles de Montesquieu, *Montesquieu, The Spirit of the Laws*, ed. Anne M. Cohler, Basia C. Miller, and Harold S. Stone (Cambridge: Cambridge University Press, 1989); A. Owen Aldridge, *Voltaire and the Century of Light* (Princeton, NJ: Princeton University Press, 1989); Christopher D. Wraight, *Rousseau's* The Social Contract*: A Reader's Guide* (London: Continuum Books, 2008); Marie Jean Antoine Nicolas Caritat, marquis de Condorcet, *Condorcet's Political Writing*, Cambridge Texts in the History of Political Thought, ed. Steven Lukes and Nadia Uribinati (Cambridge: Cambridge University Press, 2012).

4. François-Marie Arouet de Voltaire, *Letters on the English*, "Letter IV—on the Quakers," in *The Harvard Classics*, ed. Charles W. Eliot, vol. 34, pt. 2 (New York: P. F. Collier and Son, 1909–1914).

5. Donald S. Lutz, "The Relative Influence of European Writers on Late Eighteenth-Century American Political Thought," *American Political Science Review* 78, no. 1 (1984), pp. 189–197; Susan Gordon, *Montesquieu: The French Philosopher Who Shaped Modern Government* (New York: Rosen, 2006).

6. Will Durant and Ariel Durant, *The Story of Civilization*, vol. 10, *Rousseau and Revolution* (New York: Simon and Schuster, 1967), p. 708.

7. Matthew P. Bergman, "Montesquieu's Theory of Government and the Framing of the American Constitution," *Pepperdine Law Review* 18, 1 (December 15, 1990), p. 20. The author cites William Bradford, a member of the Continental Congress, for his claim that the delegates chose Carpenters' Hall so that they might have access to its library during their deliberations.

8. *The Spirit of Laws by Montesquieu: A Compendium of the First English Text*, ed. with an introduction by David Wallace Carrithers (Berkeley: University of California Press, 1977).

9. Joseph Hammon, *Le chevalier de Bonvouloir* (Paris: Jouve et cie., 1953); Tom Shachtman, *How the French Saved America: Soldiers, Sailors, Diplomats, Louis XVI, and the Success of a Revolution* (New York: St. Martin's, 2017), pp. 4–9.

10. Alexis de Tocqueville, *L'ancien régime* (Oxford: Oxford University Press, 1927), p. 155.

11. Stacy Schiff, *A Great Improvisation: Franklin, France, and the Birth of America* (New York: Henry Holt, 2005), p. 3.

12. Schiff, *Great Improvisation*, pp. 38–39; Durant and Durant, *Story of Civilization*, p. 905.

13. William E. Leckey, *History of England in the Eighteenth Century*, 8 vols. (London, 1887), vol. 3, p. 268.

14. For a fuller account of Beaumarchais's role, see Shachtman, *How the French Saved America*, pp. 30–35.

15. Washington to Hancock, February 11, 1777, available at www.founders.archives.gov.

16. Yet, initially, some members of Congress were ready to rebuff Lafayette, whom they evidently saw as just another in a line of incompetent French adventurers unable to serve the American cause effectively. Insulted by that initial reaction, Lafayette considered returning home. But Baron de Kalb persuaded him that he would merely look foolish if he returned so soon, given how fervently his voyage had been opposed in France. Shachtman, *How the French Saved America*, pp. 84–85.

17. City Tavern was directly across Second Street from the Slate Roof House, which had been William Penn's city residence. That house was demolished in the mid-nineteenth century and has been the site, since 1976, of Welcome Park, which features displays depicting Penn's life. In that same year, the long-vanished City Tavern was reconstructed and today replicates the kind of fare served there in the eighteenth century.

18. Olivier Bernier, *Lafayette: Hero of Two Worlds* (New York: E. P. Dutton, 1983), pp. 51–52.

19. Bernier, *Lafayette*, p. 56.

20. Ibid., p. 60.

21. Shachtman, *How the French Saved America*, pp. 101–104.

22. Ibid., pp. 118–121.

23. Schiff, *Great Improvisation*, p. 160. For a full account of Adams's criticism of Franklin in Paris, see H. W. Brands, *The First American: The Life and Times of Benjamin Franklin* (New York: Doubleday, 2000), pp. 547–549.

24. Schiff, *Great Improvisation*, p. 159.

25. The Philadelphia Museum of Art has several of the mislabeled bisque figures in its collection.

26. Schiff, *Great Improvisation*, p. 192.

27. Ibid., p. 80.

28. Harlow Giles Unger, *Lafayette* (New York: John Wiley and Son, 2002), pp. 110ff.

29. Bernier, *Lafayette*, p. 105.

30. Unger, *Lafayette*, pp. 134–142.

31. Abbé Robin, *Nouveau voyage en Amérique septentrionale, en l'année 1781: Et campagne de l'armée de M. le comte de Rochambeau*, trans. Annette H. Emgarth (Philadelphie et se trouve à Paris: Chez Moutard, 1782). The encampment is commemorated in a bronze tablet in the courtyard near the west portal of Philadelphia's City Hall.

32. Rachel Jirka, commenting on the account of Louis-François-Bertrand Dupont d'Aubevoye de Lauberdière, *Journal de l'armée de Rochambeau*, in Valérie Bajou, *Versailles and the American Revolution*, catalog for the exhibition (Château de Versailles: Gourcuff Gradenigo, 2016), p. 120.

33. Robin, *Nouveau voyage en Amérique*.

34. Unger, *Lafayette*, pp. 150–159.

35. As quoted by Schiff, *Great Improvisation*, footnote, p. 289.

36. Bernier, *Lafayette*, p. 135.

37. Schiff, *Great Improvisation*, pp. 293–295; Unger, *Lafayette*, pp. 160–161.

38. Jonathan R. Dull, *A Diplomatic History of the American Revolution* (New Haven, CT: Yale University Press, 1987), pp. 144–151.

39. Schiff, *Great Improvisation*, pp. 321–323.

40. Rochambeau's aide acclaimed the pavilion in his diary: "One cannot imagine a building in better taste; simplicity is there united with an air of dignity," as quoted in Jean Jules Jusserand, France's longtime ambassador to the United States early in the twentieth century, *With Americans of Past and Present Days* (New York: Charles Scribner's Sons, 1916), p. 217. L'Enfant would gain fame a few years later as the principal designer of the new federal capital in the District of Columbia.

41. Agnès Repplier's paraphrase of Rush's description in *Philadelphia: The Place and the People* (New York: Macmillan, 1899), pp. 261–263. She places the date of the Fete du Dauphin in July 1781, however, some three months before the child was born.

42. As quoted by H. W. Brands, *First American*, p. 638.

43. Ibid., p. 647.

44. David McCullough, *John Adams* (New York: Simon and Schuster, 2001), p. 330. We paraphrase Jefferson as quoted by McCullough.

45. Schiff, *Great Improvisation*, p. 399.

46. Paul Claudel, in a speech to the Society of the Cincinnati, quoted by René de la Croix, duc de Castries, La France et l'Indépendence américaine (Paris, Perrin, 1975), as cited by Valérie Bajou, *Versailles and the American Revolution*, p. 15.

47. Valérie Bajou, "The American Representatives at Versailles," ibid., p. 64. See also Pierre Eugène du Simetière [*sic*], *Collection des portraits des généraux, ministres et magistrats qui se sont rendus célèbres dans la Révolution des Treize États-Unis de l'Amérique septentrionale* (Paris, 1781, London, 1783).

48. Simitière made his ambition clear in the broadside advertising his museum: "He takes this public opportunity to return his grateful thanks to all those persons who for several years past have from various parts of this Continent contributed to increase his Collection, and hopes he will continue to be favored with such articles as may fall in their possession, more particularly as he intends his Cabinet to be hereafter the foundation of the first American Museum." (Courtesy of the Library Company of Philadelphia.)

49. Paul G. Sifton, *Historiographer to the United States: The Revolutionary Letterbook of Pierre Eugène Du Simitière* (New York: Vantage, 1987); see also John C. Van Horne, *Pierre Eugène Du Simitière: His American Museum 200 Years After* (Philadelphia: Library Company of Philadelphia, 1985).

Chapter 3

1. As cited in Paul Staiti, *Of Arms and Artists: The American Revolution through Painter's Eyes* (New York: Bloomsbury, 2016), p. 1.

2. As cited by David Jayne Hill, "A Missing Chapter of Franco-American History," *American Historical Review* 21, no. 4 (July 1916), p. 713.

3. As cited by Charles Henry Hart and Edward Biddle, *Memoirs of the Life and Works of Jean-Antoine Houdon* (Philadelphia: printed for the authors, 1991), p. 101.

4. ". . . son large front peint les fortes pensées et son col robuste la fermeté de son caractère." P. S. du Pont de Nemours, "Lettre sur la Salon de 1779," *Archives de l'Art Français* (1908), pp. 106–107.

5. On Franklin's bust versions, see Jack Hinton, Melissa Meighan, and Andrew Lins, *Encountering Genius: Houdon's Portraits of Benjamin Franklin* (Philadelphia Museum of Art in association with Yale University Press, 2011). See also Anne L. Poulet, *Jean-Antoine Houdon: Sculptor of the Enlightenment* (Washington, DC: National Gallery of Art with the University of Chicago Press, 2003).

6. Letter to Sarah Bache, Passy, June 3, 1779. Available at franklinpapers.org.

7. Letter from Thomas Jefferson to George Washington, July 10, 1785, as cited in Francis Henry Taylor, "Jean-Antoine Houdon: 1828–1928." *Bulletin of the Pennsylvania Museum* 24, no. 122 (October 1, 1928), p. 17.

8. Cited in ibid., p. 7

9. Ibid., p. 10

10. Hart and Biddle, *Memoirs*, p. 186.

11. The Marquis de Lafayette as cited in *Proceedings of the Board of Aldermen of the City of New York* 68 (New York: Charles W. Baker, Printer, 1860), p. 87.

12. Poulet, *Jean-Antoine Houdon*, p. 263.

13. The original intent was to create a Washington monument for Washington Square, which never happened. But the Washington monument now at Eakins Oval was the long-delayed memorial to George Washington that was proposed many years earlier. It was not unveiled until 1897 and was first installed at the Green Street entrance to Fairmount Park, then moved to its current location in 1928.

14. Houdon as cited by Guilhelm Scherf, "Houdon, 'Above All Modern Artists,'" in Poulet, *Jean-Antoine Houdon*, p. 17.

15. See Lillian B. Miller, "Charles Willson Peale as History Painter," in *New Perspectives on Charles Willson Peale*, ed. Lillian B. Miller and David C. Ward (Pittsburgh, PA: Published for the Smithsonian Institution by the University of Pittsburgh Press, 1991), pp. 145–165.

16. David C. Ward, *Charles Willson Peale: Art and Selfhood in the Early Republic* (Berkeley: University of California Press, 2004), p. 30.

17. Charles Coleman Sellers, *Charles Willson Peale* (New York: Scribner, 1969), p. 157.

18. As cited in Sellers, *Charles Willson Peale*, p. 22.

19. In addition to Gérard, Peale painted the portraits of the Marquis de Lafayette; Anne César, Chevalier de la Luzerne who succeeded Gérard in Philadelphia in 1779; Louis Le Bègue de Presle Duportail, who was appointed the Continental Army's chief of engineers in 1777, seeing the battle at Monmouth and Yorktown; Jean Baptiste, Chevalier de Ternant, who served as deputy quartermaster on Baron von Steuben's staff with Washington at Valley Forge in 1778 and became France's minister to the United States in 1791; Jean-Baptiste-Donatien de Vimeur, the comte de Rochambeau, whose command of a large French force greatly aided the victory at Yorktown in 1781; François Jean de Beauvoir, marquis de Chastellux, who became one of the three major generals with Rochambeau when the French expeditionary forces were assigned to the Revolutionary Continental Army in 1779; Constantin François Chasseboeuf, comte de Volney, author of the 1803 *Tableau du climat et du sol des États-Unis*, who was elected to the American Philosophical Society; Joseph Bonaparte, brother of Napoleon, who arrived in America in 1815 and lived near Philadelphia until 1832; and Pierre François, comte de Réal, who migrated to America in 1818 and remained until 1827; Louis-Antoine-Jean-Baptiste, Chevalier de Cambray-Digné, who was part of the corps of engineers commanded by Duportail. See Doris Devine Fanelli, *History of the Portrait Collection, Independence National Park* (Philadelphia: American Philosophical Society), 2001.

20. Karie Diethorn, "'good and faithful paintings': Charles Willson Peale's Philadelphia Museum Portraits," in Fanelli, *History of the Portrait Collection*, p. 69.

21. Brandon Brame Fortune, "Charles Willson Peale's Portrait Gallery: Persuasion and Plain Style," *Word and Image* 6, no. 4 (October–December 1990), pp. 308.

22. Brandon Brame Fortune, *Portraits of Virtue and Genius: Pantheons of Worthies and Public Portraiture in the Early American Republic, 1780–1820.* Ph.D. diss, University of North Carolina, Chapel Hill, 1986, pp. 199–200.

23. Charles Coleman Sellers and Charles Willson Peale, "Charles Willson Peale with Patron and Populace—A Supplement to 'Portraits and Miniatures by Charles Willson Peale': With a Survey of His Work in Other Genres," *Transactions of the American Philosophical Society*, New Series, 59, no. 3 (1969), p. 18.

24. As cited by Frank Whitney, *Jean Ternant and the Age of Revolutions* (Jefferson, NC: McFarland, 2015), p. 84.

25. On Lavater's influence on Peale's portraiture, see chapter 5 of Fortune, *Portraits of Virtue.*

26. On the fascinating role these portraits played in diplomatic relations, see Todd Lawrence Larkin, "A 'Gift' Strategically Solicited and Magnanimously Conferred: The American Congress, the French Monarchy, and the State Portraits of Louis XVI and Marie-Antoinette." *Winterthur Portfolio* 44, no. 1 (Spring 2010), pp. 31–76.

27. Larkin, "A 'Gift,'" 70.

28. I am very grateful to Karie Diethorn, chief curator of the Independence National Historical Park Service, who communicated this image to me.

29. Karie Diethorn provided the history of these images.

30. Sellers, *Charles Willson Peale*, p. 188.

31. Charles Coleman Sellers, *Portraits and Miniatures by Charles Willson Peale*, vol. 42, pt. 1 (Philadelphia: Transactions of the American Philosophical Society, 1952), p. 184.

32. As cited in Laura Auricchio, *The Marquis: Lafayette Reconsidered* (New York: Alfred A. Knopf, 2014), p. 83.

33. Lloyd Kramer, "America's Lafayette and Lafayette's America: A European and American Revolution," *William and Mary Quarterly* (1981), p. 228.

34. David R. Brigham, *Public Culture in the Early Republic: Peale's Museum and Its Audience* (Washington, DC: Smithsonian Institution Press, 1995), p. 59.

35. John C. Milley, "Introduction" to Fanelli, *History of the Portrait Collection*, p. 17.

36. Rembrandt Peale, in an autobiographical sketch he sent to Charles E. Lester, recalled as a youth poring over a box of engravings that his father collected. Charles E. Lester, *The Artists of America: A series of Biographical Sketches of American Artists; with Portraits and Designs on Steel* (New York: Baker and Scribner, 1846), p. 201.

37. David R. Brigham, "'Ask the Beasts, and They Shall Teach Thee': The Human Lessons of Charles Willson Peale's Natural History Displays," *Huntington Library Quarterly* 59, nos. 2–3 (1996), p. 190.

38. Ibid., p. 183.

39. As cited in François Furstenberg, *When the United States Spoke French* (New York: Penguin, 2014), p. 109.

40. See William Howard Adams. The Paris Years of Thomas Jefferson (New Haven, CT: Yale University Press, 1997).

41. David C. Ward, "Creating a National Culture: Charles Willson Peale's 'George Washington at the Battle of Princeton' in History and Memory," *Record of the Art Museum, Princeton University* 70 (2011), p. 5.

42. Benjamin Franklin to Charles Willson Peale, July 4, 1771, in *The Selected Papers of Charles Willson Peale and His Family*, vol. 1, eds. Lillian B. Miller, Sidney Hart, and David C. Ward, (New Haven: Yale University Press, 1983), pp. 99–100.

CHAPTER 4

1. Joseph J. Ellis, *The Quartet: Orchestrating the Second American Revolution, 1783–1789* (New York: Alfred A. Knopf, 2015).

2. Garry Wills, *James Madison* (New York: Henry Holt, 2002), pp. 26–27.

3. Keith Michael Baker, "On Condorcet's 'Sketch,'" *Daedalus* 133, no. 3 (Summer 2004), pp. 56–64. The work mentioned is the *Esquisse d'un tableau historique des progrès de l'esprit humain* [Sketch for a historical picture of the progress of the human mind], 1794. Condorcet wrote the work during the months he was in hiding, from October 1793 to March 1794, after the revolutionary government declared him a traitor. In March 1794, he was arrested and imprisoned. Two days later, he was found dead in his cell, either as the result of suicide by poison given to him by a friend or of murder. He was fifty years old at the time of his death.

4. H. W. Brands, *The First American: The Life and Times of Benjamin Franklin* (New York: Doubleday, 2000), pp. 557–561.

5. Brands, *First American*, p. 673.

6. Norman Schofield, "The Intellectual Contribution of Condorcet to the Founding of the US Republic 1785–1800," *Social Choice Welfare* 25 (2005), pp. 303–318; Iain McLean and Arnold B. Urken, "Did Jefferson or Madison Understand Condorcet's Theory of Social Choice?" *Public Choice* 73 (1992), pp. 445–457.

7. A recent study of that aspect of Jefferson's life has re-created the likely menu for that event. Charles A. Cerami, *Dinner at Mr. Jefferson's: Three Men, Five Great Wines, and the Dinner That Changed America* (Hoboken, NJ: Wiley, 2008), p. 1. See also Thomas J. Craughwell, *Thomas Jeffer-*

son's Crème Brulée: How a Founding Father and His Slave James Hemings Introduced French Cuisine to America (Philadelphia: Quirk Books, 2012), pp. 146–147. Hemings was also the half-brother of Jefferson's deceased wife, Martha, the son of her father, John Wayles, and his enslaved concubine.

8. Joseph E. Cooke, "The Compromise of 1790," *William and Mary Quarterly: A Magazine of Early American History and Culture*, vol. 27 (1970), pp. 524–545; Joseph J. Ellis, *Founding Brothers: The Revolutionary Generation* (New York: Alfred A. Knopf, 2000), p. 51.

9. Many have argued that the cost of France's assistance to the rebel cause during the American Revolution was a factor in prompting the French Revolution. A contrary view is that of one recent writer, who concluded "this was not the case. Britain dealt better with its expenditure, even though this was far higher, by making considerable savings in the 1780s, and by negotiating better peace terms and trade deals with its former colonies." Valérie Bajou, *Versailles and the American Revolution*, catalog of the exhibition (Château de Versailles: Gourcuff Gradenigo, 2016), p. 17.

10. Marc Leepson, *Lafayette: Lessons in Leadership from the Idealist General* (New York: Palgrave Macmillan, 2011), pp. 136–140; Noel B. Gerson, *Statue in Search of a Pedestal: A Biography of the Marquis de La Fayette* (New York: Dodd, Mead, 1976), pp. 81–83.

11. Jefferson's wording in the Declaration of Independence, "all men are created equal," became in the French declaration, "Men are born and live free and equal in rights" [*Les hommes naissent et demeurent libres et égaux en droits.*] (Article 1)

12. Georges LeFebvre, *The Coming of the French Revolution* (Princeton, NJ: Princeton University Press, 2005), pp. 212–213. Given the slowness of communication across the Atlantic in 1789, it is doubtful whether the authors of the French declaration had read the American Bill of Rights. In fact, they did not need to do so because they shared so many of the same views.

13. James R. Gaines, *For Liberty and Glory: Washington, Lafayette and Their Revolutions* (New York: W. W. Norton, 2007), pp. 345–346

14. Leepson, *Lafayette*, pp. 151–153; Paul S. Spalding, *Lafayette: Prisoner of State* (Columbia: University of South Carolina, 2010), pp. 1–15.

15. Dennis K. Johnson, "Milestones: First Flight in America," AOPA Pilot, July 1, 2017, available at www.aopa.org/news-and-media/all-news/2017/july/pilot/first-flight-in-America.

16. Conor Cruise O'Brien, *The Long Affair: Thomas Jefferson and the French Revolution, 1785–1800* (Chicago: University of Chicago Press, 1996), p. 152.

17. François Furstenberg, *When the United States Spoke French: Five Refugees Who Shaped a Nation* (New York: Penguin, 2014), pp. 23–24. Among other Frenchmen witnessing the balloon flight was Pierre L'Enfant, who would soon leave a lasting mark on the nation's new capital and a far less lasting one on Philadelphia, where he labored through much of the 1790s.

18. *Federal Gazette* (Philadelphia), January 9, 1793.

19. Furstenberg, *When the United States Spoke French*, pp. 62–67.

20. George Wilson, *Stephen Girard: America's First Tycoon* (Conshohocken, PA: Combined Books, 1995), pp. 51–63, 113–133.

21. Richard G. Miller, "The Federal City, 1783–1800," *Philadelphia: A 300-Year History* (New York: W. W. Norton, 1982), p. 185.

22. O'Brien, *Long Affair*, pp. 152–153.

23. As quoted by Furstenberg, *When the United States Spoke French*, p. 49.

24. As quoted by O'Brien, *Long Affair*, p. 163.

25. Ibid., chapter 5, pp. 178–190.

26. Ibid.; also Harry Ammon, *The Genet Mission* (New York: W. W. Norton, 1971).

27. Henry Savage, *Discovering America: 1700–1875* (New York: Harper and Row, 1959), pp. 70–73.

28. James McClelland and Lynn Miller, *City in a Park: A History of Philadelphia's Fairmount Park System* (Philadelphia: Temple University Press, 2016), p. 54. See also Henry Savage and

Elizabeth Savage, *André and François André Michaux* (Charlottesville: University of Virginia Press, 1986).

29. McClelland and Miller, *City in a Park*, pp. 54, 166. In the late nineteenth century, the Pennsylvania legislature began the creation of the commonwealth's forest system on public lands. More than eighty-five thousand acres in south central Pennsylvania were named the Michaux State Forest in the botanists' honor.

30. Lafayette had already noted that he was proud to be an American citizen before there was such a thing as a French citizen. Actually, not until passage of the Constitution's Fourteenth Amendment in 1868 did American citizenship, rather than that conferred by states, clearly exist. The U.S. Congress did not formalize Lafayette's status as an American until 2002, when it made him an honorary citizen.

31. David Clary, *Adopted Son: Washington, Lafayette, and the Friendship That Saved the Revolution* (New York: Bantam Books, 2007), p. 413.

32. As cited by Furstenberg, *When the United States Spoke French*, p. 97, who also provides evidence from other writers that tend to support such a figure. See also Gary B. Nash, "Reverberations of Haiti in the American North: Black Saint Dominguans in Philadelphia," *Pennsylvania History* 65 (1998), pp. 43–73.

33. French Benevolent Society records are now housed at the Historical Society of Pennsylvania, where they are cataloged as Collection MSS141, available at www2.hsp.org/collections/manuscripts/f/FrenchBenSocMSS141.html.

34. Arnold Whitridge, "French Emigrés in Philadelphia," *Virginia Quarterly Review* 44, no. 2 (1968), pp. 285–301.

35. Furstenberg, *When the United States Spoke French*, pp. 6–7, 59–62.

36. Ibid., pp. 1–6, 67–75.

37. Ibid., introduction, chapters 1–2, pp. 1–137; Frances Sergeant Childs, *French Refugee Life in the United States, 1790–1800: An American Chapter of the French Revolution* (Baltimore, MD: Johns Hopkins University Press, 1940).

38. Michel Poniatowski, *Talleyrand-Perigord, 1789–1799* (Paris: Délégation a l'Action Artistique de la Ville de Paris, n.d.), p. 105.

[En quête d'aventures dans cette ville pudibonde, dominée par une population de prudes quakers, il offrit le spectacle d'un éveque catholique, se promenant superbe de désinvolture, en plein jour dans la rue principale, tenant tendrement par le bras une belle mulatresse . . .] Authors' translation.

39. Furstenberg, *When the United States Spoke French*, p. 95, reproduces the last page of the *General Advertiser*, November 27, 1794.

40. *Le chirurgien dentist*. The English translation, *The Surgeon Dentist or Treatise on the Teeth*, was not published until 1946. See also A. I. Spielman, "The Birth of the Most Important 18th-Century Dental Text: Pierre Fauchard's *Le Chirurgien Dentist*," *Journal of Dental Research* 86, no. 10 (2007), pp. 922–926.

41. Emile B. Gardette, *Biographical Notice of (the Late) James Gardette: Surgeon Dentist of Philadelphia* (Philadelphia, 1850). This tribute by Gardette's son states that his father was also the first to use gold foil instead of lead or tin for fillings and that he was an early advocate for removing diseased teeth before they could spread decay to others.

42. La Rochefoucauld-Liancourt, François-Alexandre-Frédéric, duc de, *Des prisons de Philadelphie: Par un Européen*, 4th ed. (Paris: Chez Madame Huzard, librairie, rue de l'Éperon, no. 7, Janvier 1819).

43. Richard G. Miller, "Federal City," pp. 177–178. Anne Bingham commissioned the full-length portrait of Washington by Gilbert Stuart that became known as the "Lansdowne portrait" after she presented the finished work to Lord Lansdowne.

44. Furstenberg, *When the United States Spoke French*, lists these residents, their names, their occupations, and street number of their residences in an appendix, pp. 426–428. See also Billy G. Smith and Paul Sivitz, "Identifying and Mapping Ethnicity in Philadelphia in the Early Republic," *Pennsylvania Magazine of History and Biography* 140, no. 3 (October 2016), pp. 393–411.

45. In addition to the eagle carved from mahogany, LeGrand also created Corinthian capitals from the same material for the bank's interior. These were removed early in the twentieth century when the interior was remodeled by architect James Windrim, who replaced the original barrel-vaulted ceiling with a glass-paneled rotunda dome. At least one LeGrand capital is now in the collection of the Philadelphia Museum of Art. Construction of the First Bank was "under the direction" of Samuel Blodgett, although the architect was likely James Hoban, who in 1792 had been named the winner in the design for the new president's mansion in the new federal capital on the Potomac. Matthew Baigell, "James Hoban and the First Bank of the United States," *Journal of the Society of Architectural Historians* 28, no. 2 (May 1969), pp. 135–136.

46. Gary B. Nash, *Forging Freedom: The Formation of Philadelphia's Black Community, 1720–1840* (Cambridge, MA: Harvard University Press, 1988), pp. 141–142.

47. Diana Forbes-Robertson, "Asylum in Azilum," *American Heritage* 27, no. 3 (1976), pp. 195–203.

48. Furstenberg, *When the United States Spoke French*, pp. 238–245.

49. Ibid., pp. 4, 196.

50. Richard G. Miller, "Federal City," pp. 193–198.

51. Samuel F. Bemis, *Jay's Treaty: A Study in Commerce and Diplomacy* (New Haven, CT: Yale University Press, 1962); John Jay, *On the Peace Negotiations of 1782–83, as Illustrated by the Secret Correspondence of France and England* (New York: American Historical Association, 1888).

52. Philadelphia had been a Federalist stronghold at the time Washington was first elected president. But, in 1791, the nation underwent its first financial panic as the result of speculation and a sudden collapse in the prices of scrip issued for the infant (First) Bank of the United States. Even though Hamilton moved quickly to bail out financial markets, the panic "resulted in profound political and cultural shifts in Philadelphia," converting the city from a Federalist bastion into a center of Jeffersonian Republicanism. Scott C. Miller, "'Never Did I See So Universal a Frenzy': The Panic of 1791 and the Republicanization of Philadelphia," *Pennsylvania Magazine of History and Biography* 142, no. 1 (January 2018), pp. 7–48.

53. Stuart Leibiger, "Historical Meddling: The French Connection," *Philadelphia Inquirer*, December 25, 2016, pp. C1, C3.

54. Page Smith, *John Adams*, vol. 2 (Garden City, NY: Doubleday, 1962), p. 983.

55. Richard G. Miller, "Federal City," p. 194.

56. Quoted by Furstenberg, *When the United States Spoke French*, pp. 114–115.

57. David McCullough, *John Adams* (New York: Simon and Schuster, 2001), pp. 552, 556, 560; Smith, *John Adams*, pp. 268–269, 283, 952–965.

58. McCullough, *John Adams*, pp. 495–498; William Stinchcombe, "The Diplomacy of the XYZ Affair," *William and Mary Quarterly*, vol. 34 (1977), pp. 590–617.

59. McCullough, *John Adams*, p. 500.

60. Ibid., p. 567.

CHAPTER 5

1. Edgar P. Richardson, "The Athens of America, 1800–1825," *Philadelphia: A 300-Year History*, ed. Russell F. Weigley (A Barra Foundation Book, New York: W. W. Norton, 1982), pp.

208–257; James McClelland and Lynn Miller, *City in a Park: A History of Philadelphia's Fairmount Park System* (Philadelphia: Temple University Press, 2016), chapter 1.

2. Ryan K. Smith, "The 'Mad' Engineer: L'Enfant in Early National Philadelphia," *Pennsylvania Magazine of History and Biography* 138, no. 3 (July 2014), p. 273.

3. Smith, "'Mad' Engineer," p. 278.

4. Ibid., p. 294.

5. Ryan K. Smith, *Robert Morris's Folly: The Architectural and Financial Failures of an American Founder* (New Haven, CT: Yale University Press, 2014).

6. Smith, "'Mad' Engineer," pp. 284–286; Jeffery M. Dorwart, *Fort Mifflin of Philadelphia: An Illustrated History* (Philadelphia: University of Pennsylvania Press, 1998).

7. Smith, "'Mad' Engineer," p. 282.

8. Scott W. Berg, *Grand Avenues: The Story of the French Visionary Who Designed Washington, D.C.* (New York: Pantheon Books, 2007); Kenneth R. Bowling, *Creating the Federal City, 1774–1800* (Washington, DC: American Institute of Architects Press, 1988); Elizabeth Sarah Kite, *L'Enfant and Washington* (Baltimore, MD: Johns Hopkins University Press, 1929). In 1901–1902, the U.S. Senate's McMillan Commission produced a report recommending a partial redesign of the capital to bring it more nearly into accord with L'Enfant's original plan. His "grand avenue," for example, became the National Mall. Then, thanks to the efforts of the French ambassador to the United States, Jean Jules Jusserand, L'Enfant's importance began to be more fully recognized. In 1909, the body of the man generally known as Pierre L'Enfant was exhumed and reburied in a place of honor high on a hill in Arlington National Cemetery.

9. Soon after he arrived in North America, Duportail wrote a letter to a friend in France revealing his disillusionment over the revolutionary cause he had joined: "People here, though at war with the English, hate the French more than they do the English . . . and in spite of all that France has done and will do for them, they would prefer to become reconciled with their former brothers." Duportail to Saint-Germain, November 12, 1777, in Arthur P. Watts, "A Newly Discovered Letter of Brigadier-General Duportail," *Pennsylvania History*, 1 (1934), pp. 101–106.

10. Paul K. Walker, *Engineers of Independence: A Documentary History of the Army Engineers in the American Revolution, 1775–1783* (Washington, DC: Office of Administrative Services, Office of the Chief of Engineers, 1981).

11. "To George Washington from Louis Le Bègne de Presle Duportail, 10 February 1790," *Founders Online*, National Archives, accessed September 29, 2013, https://founders.archives/gov/documents/Washington/05-05-02-0067. (Original source: *The Papers of George Washington*, Presidential Series, vol. 5, *16 January 1790–30 June 1790*, ed. Dorothy Twohig, Mark A. Mastromarino, and Jack D. Warren. [Charlottesville: University Press of Virginia, 1996], pp. 126–128.)

12. Duportail's letter to Washington. See also Theodore Thomas Belote, "The Scioto Speculation and the French Settlement at Gallipolis: A Study in Ohio Valley History," *University [of Cincinnati] Studies,* 2nd ser., vol. 3, no. 3 (September–October 1907), pp. 1–82.

13. *Regulations for the order and discipline of the troops of the United States: to which is added an appendix containing the United States Militia Act, together with the law organizing the militia of the state of New-York, as now amended by United States Army*; Friedrich Wilhelm Ludolf Gerhard Augustin Steuben, Baron von, 1720–1794, John Davis Batchelder Collection (Library of Congress) DLC; United States. Militia Act, New York (State), Act to Organize the Militia of This State (Albany: Printed for Daniel and Samuel Whiting, 1803).

14. Robert H. Robins, "Du Ponceau and General and Amerindian Linguistics," in *Early Nineteenth-Century Contributions to General and Amerindian Linguistics: Du Ponceau and Rafinesque*, the Prix Volney series, vol. 2, ser. ed. Joan Leopold (Dordrecht, Netherlands: Kluwer Academic, 2000), pp. 1–36.

15. Pierre S. du Pont, *Physiocratie, Ou constitution naturelle du gouvernement le plus avantageux au genre humain* (Paris : A. Leyde, chez Merlin, 1767).

16. Richard Haggard, "The Politics of Friendship: Du Pont, Jefferson, Madison, and the Physiocratic Dream for the New World," *Proceedings of the American Philosophical Society* 153, no. 4 (December 2009), pp. 419–440.

17. "Voilà notre La Fayette dans la Patrie. J'en suis bien aise et de ce ques plusieurs de ses amis et des miens cessent d'etre maltraité, de ce qu'on parait aimer les consulter. Mais je souhaiterais que le tout fut fait pas des formes moins arbitraires et moins *romaines*.

"L'evangile dit que dieu a donné le Royaume des Cieux Rapientibus. Il en fait autant de ceux de la terre. C'est pour cela que je prefère les veritables Républiques." *The Papers of Thomas Jefferson*, vol. 31, *1 February 1799–31 May 1800*, ed. Barbara B. Oberg (Princeton, NJ: Princeton University Press, 2004), pp. 385–386.

18. Marc Duke, *The du Ponts, Portrait of a Dynasty* (New York: Doubleday, 1979).

19. Marc Duvoisin, "Family's Reach Influenced Business, Politics and Arts," *Philadelphia Inquirer*, January 28, 1996, p. A14ff.

20. Thomas J. Fleming, *The Louisiana Purchase* (New York: John Wiley and Sons, 2003).

21. James E. Lewis Jr., *The Louisiana Purchase: Jefferson's Noble Bargain?* (Chapel Hill: University of North Carolina Press, 2003).

22. George Wilson, *Stephen Girard: The Life and Times of America's First Tycoon* (Conshohocken, PA: Combined Books, 1995), pp. 261–263.

23. Wilson, *Stephen Girard*, pp. 247–253.

24. Donald R. Adams Jr., *Finance and Enterprise in Early America: A Study of Stephen Girard's Bank, 1812–1831* (Philadelphia: University of Pennsylvania Press, 1975), p. 30.

25. Wilson, *Stephen Girard*, p. 272.

26. Christopher P. George, *Terror on the Chesapeake: The War of 1812 on the Bay* (Stroudsburg, PA: White Mane Books, 2000), pp. 87–104.

27. George, *Terror on the Chesapeake*, pp. 105–113.

28. The day after witnessing the attack on the fort, Francis Scott Key wrote a poem he titled "The Defense of Fort McHenry." Soon his verse would be set to the tune of an English drinking song and become known across the nation as "The Star-Spangled Banner." Scott S. Sheads, *The Rockets' Red Glare: The Maritime Defense of Baltimore in 1814* (Centreville, MD: Tidewater, 1986), pp. 108–109.

29. News that a peace had been achieved did not reach America until February 1815. In the interim, the most decisive battle of the war had been won at New Orleans by the United States under the command of General Andrew Jackson in January.

30. Both the First and Second Bank buildings still stand and are now part of Independence National Historical Park. The Second Bank building, by William Strickland, is one of the nation's first and finest examples of Greek Revival architecture; it houses a national portrait gallery honoring many important figures from the period of the American Revolution, mostly done by Charles Willson Peale. Some nine leading Frenchmen are among them. As of this writing, plans are underway to restore the First Bank building as well. That would permit Independence National Historical Park officials to increase their emphasis on Philadelphia's role in the nation's financial history.

Chapter 6

1. On Rembrandt Peale in France see Lois M. Fink, "Rembrandt Peale in Paris," *Pennsylvania Magazine of History and Biography* 110, no. 1 (January 1986), pp. 71–90; William T. Oedel, "After Paris: Rembrandt Peale's Apollodorian Gallery," *Winterthur Portfolio* 27 (Spring 1992), pp. 1–27;

Lillian B. Miller, *In Pursuit of Fame: Rembrandt Peale 1778–1860* (Washington, DC: National Portrait Gallery, Smithsonian Institution in association with the University of Washington Press, Seattle, 1992), esp. pp. 87–100; Carol Eaton Hevner, "The Portraiture of Rembrandt Peale: Artistic Aspirations and Stylistic Changes," in *Rembrandt Peale 1778–1860: A Life in the Arts* (Philadelphia: Historical Society of Pennsylvania, 1985).

2. As cited in Oedel, "After Paris," p. 3.

3. As cited by Lillian B. Miller, "Rembrandt Peale: The Career of an American Master," in *Rembrandt Peale 1778–1860: A Life in the Arts*, exhibit catalog (Philadelphia: Historical Society of Pennsylvania, 1985), p. 14.

4. For Peale's first stay in Paris in 1806, see William L. Chew III, "The Easel and the Eagle: Rembrandt Peale Views Napoleonic France," available at www.napoleonicsociety.com/english/pdf/j5chew.

5. Fink, "Rembrandt Peale in Paris," p. 74.

6. "From Thomas Jefferson to Charles Willson Peale, 13 March 1808," *Founders Online*, National Archives, last modified March 30, 2017, available at http://founders.archives.gov/documents/Jefferson/99-01-02-7612.

7. Given the hucksterism of the Peales, it comes as no surprise that the circus showman P. T. Barnum purchased Peale's Museum in 1842.

8. Peale as cited in G. G. Simpson, "The Beginnings of Vertebrae Paleontology in North America," *Proceedings of the American Philosophical Society* 86 (1942), p. 15.

9. Fink, "Rembrandt Peale in Paris," p. 72.

10. "When I was preparing to return to America, [Denon] pressed me to remain, saying that as Gerard had commenced history, and could paint no more portraits, he would give me all the Imperial portraits to paint; candidly adding, 'I prefer Gerard to you, but I prefer your portraits to any other here.'" Rembrandt Peale in a letter to Charles E. Lester, *The Artists of America: A Series of Biographical Sketches of American Artists—with Portraits and Designs on Steel* (New York: Baker and Scribner, 1846), p. 207.

11. Quoted by Charles Willson Peale in a letter of October 6, 1808, in *The Selected Papers of Charles Willson Peale and His Family*, vol. 2, *Charles Willson Peale: The Artist in His Museum, 1791–1810*, ed. Lillian B. Miller, Sidney Hart, and David C. Ward (New Haven, CT: Yale University Press, 1988), p. 1145.

12. "Original Letters from Paris, Addressed by Rembrandt Peale to C. W. Peale, and Rubens Peale," *Port folio*, 4, no. 3 (September 1810), pp. 278–279.

13. Rembrandt Peale, "Reminiscences," *The Crayon* 1, no. 2 (January 10, 1855), p. 23.

14. As cited in Oedel, "After Paris," p. 8.

15. Jefferson to Mme de Bréhan, March 19, 1789, in *The Papers of Thomas Jefferson*, vol. 14, ed. Julian Boyd et al. (Princeton, NJ: Princeton University Press, 1958), p. 656.

16. Susan Stein, *The Worlds of Thomas Jefferson at Monticello* (New York: H. N. Abrams in association with the Thomas Jefferson Memorial Foundation, 1993), p. 29.

17. Lillian B. Miller, "The Peales and Their Legacy, 1735–1885," in *The Peale Family: Creation of a Legacy 1770–1870* (New York: Abbeville Press in association with the Trust for Museum Exhibitions, and the National Portrait Gallery, Smithsonian Institution, 1996), p. 56.

18. "To Thomas Jefferson from Charles Willson Peale, 21 February 1808," *Founders Online*, National Archives, last modified March 30, 2017, available at http://founders.archives.gov/documents/Jefferson/99-01-02-7468.

19. Rembrandt Peale, "Travels in France—for the Port folio," *Port folio* 3 (February 1810), p. 87.

20. Peale, "Travels in France," p. 88.

21. As cited by Chew III, p. 1.

22. "Benjamin Henry Latrobe to Thomas Jefferson, 19 May 1811," *Founders Online*, National Archives, last modified March 30, 2017, available at http://founders.archives.gov/documents/Jefferson/03-03-02-0505.

23. As cited in Miller, *In Pursuit of Fame*, p. 106.

24. As cited by Oedel, "After Paris," p. 12.

25. As cited by Fink, "Rembrandt Peale in Paris," p. 77.

26. "I hope he will, when surrounded by the great examples which are now in Paris, of Grecian and Italian art, direct his mind to what are their real excellencies, and reflect upon the dignity which they give to man, and to the countries where they were produced.

Although I am friendly to portraying eminent men, I am not friendly to the indiscriminate waste of genius in portrait painting; and so I hope that your son will ever bear this in mind, that the art of painting has powers to dignify man, by transmitting to posterity his noble actions, and his mental powers, to be viewed in those invaluable lessons of religion love of country, and morality: such subjects are worthy of being placed in view of the most instructive records to a rising generation." Benjamin West to C. W. Peale, September 19, 1809, quoted in *The Port folio*, 3 (1809), p. 8.

27. Latrobe to Jefferson.

28. Lester, *Artists of America*, p. 208.

29. As cited in Miller, *In Pursuit of Fame*, p. 111.

30. See Wayne Craven, "The Grand Manner in Early Nineteenth-Century American Painting: Borrowings from Antiquity, the Renaissance, and the Baroque," *American Art Journal* 11 (April 1979), p. 41.

31. Helen Berkley, "A Sketch of Joseph Buonaparte," *Godey's Magazine and Lady's Book* (April 1845), p. 187.

32. As cited in Charles Coleman Sellers, *Charles Willson Peale* (New York: Scribner, 1969), p. 481n70.

33. As cited in Doris Devine Fanelli, *History of the Portrait Collection, Independence National Park* (Philadelphia: American Philosophical Society, 2001), p. 19.

34. James Fenimore Cooper, *Notions of the Americans: Picked Up by a Traveling Bachelor*, vol. 1, "Introduction" by Robert E. Spiller (New York: Frederick Ungar, 1963), p. 61.

35. Cooper, *Notions of the Americans*, p. 145.

36. As cited in Sellers, *Charles Willson Peale*, p. 472n45.

CHAPTER 7

1. *Blackwood's Edinburgh Magazine* (Edinburgh, U.K.), vol. 11 (January–June 1822), p. 685.

2. Patricia Tyson Stroud, *The Man Who Had Been King: The American Exile of Napoleon's Brother Joseph* (Philadelphia: University of Pennsylvania Press, 2005), p. 22.

3. Stroud, *Man Who Had Been King*, pp. 14–15. A Philadelphia lawyer who would become a good friend of Joseph, Charles J. Ingersoll, viewed Bonaparte's interception in Maryland as directed by Monroe. See his *History of the Second War between the United States of America and Great Britain*, vol 1. (Philadelphia: Lea and Blanchard, 1853), p. 380.

4. Stroud, *Man Who Had Been King*, p. 15. The Philadelphia house, at 260 South Ninth Street, remains a private residence, the core of a late twentieth-century enclave named Bonaparte Court.

5. Lansdowne declined after Joseph Bonaparte's residence and burned down on July 4, 1854, when the empty structure was set afire by boys playing with fireworks. The property was purchased for Fairmount Park in 1858 and the ruins of the house were demolished. The site of the estate is marked today in the name of the park's Lansdowne Drive.

6. Charles J. Ingersoll to Alexander J. Dallas, Philadelphia, April 27, 1816, Ingersoll Papers, Historical Society of Pennsylvania.

7. From the inscription accompanying the photograph of Breck in the Philadelphia Athenaeum's Bonaparte collection.

8. That city residence, Dunlop House, occupied the entire block between Market and Chestnut Streets and Twelfth and Thirteenth Streets. Although the mansion is long gone, the block abuts that just to the west, long known as Girard Square, which remains the property of the Girard Trust today. Stroud, *Man Who Had Been King*, pp. 49–50. An 1807 watercolor painting of Dunlop House is in the Stephen Girard Collection at Girard College.

9. Bonaparte's letter ends with this encomium, "I cannot omit . . . what I have said so often, that the Americans are, without contradiction, the most happy people I have known; still more happy if they understand well their own happiness." From the Public Broadcasting System program, "Bonaparte's Retreat," available at http://www.pbs.org/video/state-of-the-arts-bonapartes-retreat/.

10. Gayle Keck, "The Other Bonaparte," *American Archaeology*, winter 2018–2019, pp. 27–32. She quotes Richard Veit, an archaeologist whose team worked on the site in 2006–2008 and uncovered thousands of items from the mansion: "The mirror pieces bring to mind Versailles."

11. He sometimes referred to that woman, Anna Savage, as his American wife.

12. In its collection of art and memorabilia relating to Joseph and Napoleon Bonaparte, the Philadelphia Athenaeum exhibits a small watercolor portrait of Emilie Lacoste from 1823. It notes that years later in France, she had an affair with the writer Prosper Mérimée that led him to duel with her husband. The Athenaeum's Bonaparte Collection also includes several pieces of furniture attributed to Michel Bouvier for the Point Breeze residence.

13. Stroud, *Man Who Had Been King*, pp. 115–116. Charlotte's husband, Napoleon Louis (1804–1831) was the son of Napoleon's brother, Louis (1778–1846). Two years younger than Charlotte, Napoleon Louis was the older brother of Charles Louis Napoleon (1808–1873), who would eventually bring about the creation of the Second Empire as Napoleon III.

14. Stroud, *Man Who Had Been King*, pp. 27–29.

15. J. Rickard (February 24, 2016) *Emmanuel, Marquis de Grouchy, 1766–1847*, available at http://www.historyofwar.org/articles/people_grouchy.html.

16. Philip J. Haythornthwaite, *Who Was Who in the Napoleonic Wars* (London: Arms and Armour, 1998), p. 224.

17. For a fuller account of the Point Breeze house and collection, see Patricia Tyson Stroud, "Point Breeze: Joseph Bonaparte's American Retreat," *Antiques* (October 2002), pp. 130–139.

18. Napoleon III, *The Political and Historical Works of Louis Napoleon Bonaparte*, vol. 2 (London: 1852), p. 143.

19. Stroud, *Man Who Had Been King*, p. 188. For their family relationship, see p. 188n8.

20. "Bonaparte's Retreat."

21. Robert C. Smith, "Philadelphia Empire Furniture by Antoine Gabriel Quervelle," *Magazine Antiques* (September 1, 1964).

22. Smith, "Philadelphia Empire Furniture." A pier table almost identical to those Quervelle made for the East Room is in the collection of the Philadelphia Athenaeum. A large conference table by him, with later extensions, still serves in the Athenaeum's board room. The Philadelphia Museum of Art owns his bookcase and secretary desk, which won a silver medal at the Franklin Institute in 1827.

23. See Chapter 4.

24. A house Bouvier built for his family in 1850 remains a handsome residence in the 200 block of South Third Street.

25. Shirley Streshinsky, *Audubon: Life and Art in the American Wilderness* (New York: Villard Books, 1993), p. 39.

26. Richard Rhodes, *John James Audubon: The Making of an American* (New York: Alfred A. Knopf, 2004), p. 5.

27. Rhodes, *John James Audubon*, p. 222.

28. Robert McCracken Peck and Patricia Tyson Stroud, *A Glorious Enterprise: The Academy of Natural Sciences of Philadelphia and the Making of American Science* (Philadelphia: University of Pennsylvania Press, 2012), pp. 74–80.

29. Peck and Stroud, *Glorious Enterprise*, p. 80.

30. The Syme portrait is now in the collection of the White House.

31. For his own account of his early years, see Chateaubriand's *Memoires from Beyond the Grave: 1768–1800*, translated from the French by Alex Andriesse, with an introduction by Anka Muhlstein (New York: New York Review Books, 2018).

32. T. J. Ellinson, *The Myth of the Noble Savage* (Berkeley: University of California Press, 2001).

33. Peck and Stroud, *Glorious Enterprise*, p. 80.

34. Charlene Mires, *Independence Hall in American History* (Philadelphia: University of Pennsylvania Press, 2015), pp. 48–50; David Clary, *Adopted Son: Washington, Lafayette, and the Friendship that Saved the Revolution* (New York: Bantam Books, 2007), pp. 443–444, chapter 6.

35. Auguste Levasseur, *Lafayette in America in 1824 and 1825*, trans. John D. Godman, vol. 1 (Philadelphia: Carey and Lea, 1829), p. 143. Or see Levasseur, *Lafayette in America in 1824 and 1825*, trans. Alan R. Hoffman (Homestead, FL: Lafayette, 2006).

36. Lafayette was made an honorary citizen of the United States by an act of Congress in 2002.

37. Joseph Epstein, *Alexis de Tocqueville: Democracy's Guide* (New York: Harper Collins, 2006), pp. 25–33.

38. Their study, Du système pénitentiare aux États-Unis, et de son application en France, was published in two volumes in 1833. Beaumont published a novel as a social critique of slavery in America, *Marie, ou l'esclavage aux États-Unis* in 1835, also in two volumes.

39. Alexis de Tocqueville, *Democracy in America*, trans. and ed., Harvey C. Mansfield and Delba Winthrop (Chicago: University of Chicago Press, 2000). The original two-volume work is *La démocratie en Amérique* (1835/1840).

40. Commentators on Tocqueville include, in addition to Epstein, *Alexis de Tocqueville*; Jean-Claude Lamberti, *Tocqueville and the Two Democracies*, trans. Arthur Goldhammer (Cambridge, MA: Harvard University Press, 1909); Harvey C. Mansfield, *Tocqueville: A Very Short Introduction* (Oxford: Oxford University Press, 2010); J. P. Mayer, *Alexis de Tocqueville: A Biographical Essay in Political Science*, trans. by M. M. Bozman and C. Hahn (New York: Viking, 1940). Mayer's work is a publication with commentary on Tocqueville's notebooks while traveling in America.

41. Mayer, *Alexis de Tocqueville*, epigraph, p. vi.

42. As quoted by Martin Garbus, "America's Invisible Inferno," *New York Review* 63, no. 19 (December 8, 2016), p. 24. See also, Edward T. Gargan, *De Toqueville* (London: Bowes and Bowes, 1965), p. 42.

43. Alexis de Tocqueville, *Journey to America*, 2 vols., ed. J. P. Mayer (New Haven, CT: Yale University Press, 1960), pp. 214–215.

44. Tocqueville, *Journey to America*, pp. 224–225. In the same period, Samuel Breck, the prominent Philadelphian and Francophile, noted in his diary the irony of enfranchised blacks who dared not exercise their franchise at the polls. *Diary of Samuel Breck* (Philadelphia: Historical Society of Pennsylvania, 1978), p. 505.

45. Andrew Diemer, "'The Same Power Which Protects the White Man Should Protect the Black': Pennsylvania, Black Citizenship Rights, and Slavery in the 19th Century," Philadelphia, Historical Society of Pennsylvania, *Legacies* 16, no. 2 (Fall 2016), pp. 112–119.

46. Julie Winch, *A Gentleman of Color: The Life of James Forten* (Oxford: Oxford University Press, 2002).

47. Tocqueville, *Democracy in America*, vol. 1 (New York: Vintage Books, 1945), pp. 31–32.

48. *Vidal et al. v. Girard's Executors*, 43 U.S. 127 (1844). Girard had specified that no clergyman should be admitted to the grounds of his college, presumably to forestall religious battles for young minds. Plaintiffs argued that the order was an affront to Christianity, but a unanimous court in effect established as constitutional a freedom from religious indoctrination in private schools.

49. George Wilson, *Stephen Girard: The Life and Times of America's First Tycoon* (Conshohocken, PA: Combined Books, 1995).

50. Athenaeum exhibit: *Bastille to Broad Street*, Michel De Chaumer text note.

51. Michael Lewis as quoted in Athenaeum exhibit: *Bastille to Broad Street*, "Thomas Ustick Walter."

52. That church was demolished and replaced with a new structure in 1910.

53. The hall was built by the Musical Fund Society, which continues to the present day to support music and musicians in the city. After orchestral concerts moved to the Academy of Music, the Musical Fund Hall remained to present lectures and other public events through the rest of the nineteenth century. The first national convention of the fledgling Republican Party was held there in 1856. Several times in the twentieth century, ownership of the building changed hands and the building's interior deteriorated to the point that it could no longer serve as an auditorium. In the 1980s, all but the exterior walls were demolished and the building was reconstructed to house apartments. See Louis C. Madeira, *Annals of Music in Philadelphia and History of the Musical Fund Society from Its Organization in 1820 to the Year 1858* (Philadelphia: Lippincott, 1896), pp. 148–149.

54. John Andrew Gallery, *Philadelphia Architecture: A Guide to the City*, 3rd ed. (Philadelphia: Paul Dry Books, for the Center for Architecture, 2009), pp. 53, 68. LeBrun's design for the Academy of Music was in partnership with Gustavus Runge.

55. James McClelland and Lynn Miller, *City in a Park: A History of Philadelphia's Fairmount Park System* (Philadelphia: Temple University Press, 2016), pp. 24–25, and chapter 4, p. 2. The authors are grateful to Elizabeth Browne for calling their attention to the participation of Emile Geyelin in the design of the Jonval prototype.

56. As quoted in "Thomas W. Evans," Pierre Fauchard Academy, available at www.Fauchard.org/publications/23-thomas-w-evans.

57. As noted in the text above, Napoleon I had proclaimed his son as his heir at the time of his final abdication. Known in exile as the Duke of Reichstadt, the boy had died at age twenty-one in July 1822, never to reign as Napoleon II.

58. Samuel Hughes, "Crowns and Confidences," *Pennsylvania Gazette* (University of Pennsylvania), available at www.upenn.edu/gazette/1199/hughes.html.

59. Susan Snyder, "Penn Link to Napoleon III Returns from France," *Philadelphia Inquirer*, May 31, 2015, p. D5, available at www.dental.upenn.edu/friendsofevans.

60. *Croquis d'Architecture*, 1867–1869. John Maass, *The Glorious Enterprise: The Centennial Exhibition of 1876 and H. J. Schwarzmann, Architect-in-Chief* (Watkins Glenn, NY: American Life Foundation, 1973), p. 50 and figs. 14–15 following p. 96, for two views of the Escalier plan and its resemblance to Schwarzmann's Memorial Hall.

61. Joseph L. Borkson, *Philadelphia: An American Paris* (Philadelphia: Camino Books, 2002), pp. 93–113. See Chapter 9.

CHAPTER 8

1. Vanderlyn as cited in William T. Oedel, "John Vanderlyn: French Neoclassicism and the Search for an American Art" (Ph.D. diss., University of Delaware, 1981), p. 88.

2. Walter Benjamin, *Selected Writings, Volume 3, 1935–1938*, trans. Edmund Jephcott, Howard Eiland, and others, ed. Howard Eiland and Michael W. Jennings (Cambridge, MA: Belknap Press of Harvard University, 2002), p. 25.

3. E[arl] S[hinn], "Art-Study Abroad," *Nation* 3, no. 62 (September 6, 1866), p. 195.

4. A painter and mezzotint engraver, John Sartain emigrated from England to Philadelphia in 1830, where he became a highly influential person on the art scene of the city. He had eight children, four of whom became artists. His family was closely connected with Eakins. His daughter Emily studied art at the Pennsylvania Academy, where she met Eakins. They became romantically involved, but he terminated the relationship while he was in Paris. John Sartain's letter of introduction helped Eakins gain admission to the École des Beaux-Arts in 1866. His son William was in Paris with Eakins in 1868, and they remained lifelong friends. William remained in Paris until 1877 and studied with Léon Bonnat. His father used to call him and Eakins "the two young firebrands from Paris." See Lloyd Goodrich, *Thomas Eakins*, vol. 1 (Cambridge, MA: Harvard University Press, 1982), p. 134. On the Sartain family, see Katharine Martinez, Page Talbott, and Elizabeth Johns, *Philadelphia's Cultural Landscape: The Sartain Family Legacy* (Philadelphia: Temple University Press, 2000).

5. Earl Shinn as cited by Kathleen A. Foster, *Thomas Eakins Rediscovered: Charles Bregler's Thomas Eakins Collection at the Pennsylvania Academy of the Fine Arts* (New Haven, CT: Yale University Press, 1997), p. 27n19.

6. The influence of France on Eakins during his European sojourn from 1866 to 1870 was first discussed at length by Gerard Ackerman, "Thomas Eakins and His Parisian Masters Gérôme and Bonnat," *Gazette des Beaux-Arts* 73 (April 1969), pp. 235–256. Thorough investigations of his Paris experience can be found in the many writings by Kathleen A. Foster, Barbara H. Weinberg, Elizabeth Milroy, and Alan Braddock, all of them cited in this chapter and to whom I owe an intellectual debt. Due to the limited scope of this book, not every aspect of the impact of French culture on Eakins's sculpture and photography could be included.

7. H. Barbara Weinberg, "Studies in Paris and Spain," in *Thomas Eakins*, ed. Darrell Sewell (Philadelphia: Philadelphia Museum of Art in association with Yale University Press, 2001), p. 15.

8. On Eakins and the Universal Exhibition, see Carol Troyen, "Innocents Abroad: American Painters at the 1867 Exposition Universelle," *American Art Journal* 16, no. 4 (Fall 1984), p. 19.

9. Letter to Benjamin Eakins, September 8, 1869, as cited in *The Paris Letters of Thomas Eakins*, ed. William Innes Homer (Princeton, NJ: Princeton University Press, 2009), p. 279.

10. Letter to Benjamin Eakins, September 8, 1869, p. 248. Eakins's slovenliness evidently never improved. When William Clark reviewed Eakins's *Crucifixion* in 1882, he remarked that Eakins was "a man whom one would not be likely to ask to dinner, in spite of the respect one has for his work!" As cited in Goodrich, *Thomas Eakins*, vol. 1, p. 197. Benjamin and Frances Eakins visited Thomas in Paris in July 1868. Frances wrote in her diary: "He's just the same old Tom he used to be, and just as careless looking . . . but he's the finest looking fellow I've seen since I left Philadelphia." As cited in Sidney D. Kirkpatrick, *The Revenge of Thomas Eakins* (New Haven, CT: Yale University Press, 2006), p. 106.

11. Letter to Benjamin Eakins, October 29, 1868, in *Paris Letters*, p. 230.

12. Letter to Benjamin Eakins, Fall 1869, in *Paris Letters*, p. 296.

13. Very little of Eakins's work from his student years has survived, either destroyed by him or his family or not brought home when he returned. His oil sketches *Carmelita Requeña* and *Street Scene in Seville* from his Spanish visit demonstrate the influence of Bonnat, Couture, and Velázquez in the free brushwork and bright colors. William Innes Homer perceives the disciplined drawing in *Carmelita Requeña* as evidence of Eakins's studies with Gérôme. William Innes Homer, *Thomas Eakins: His Life and Art* (New York: Abbeville, 2002), p. 44.

14. Foster, *Thomas Eakins Rediscovered*, p. 37.

15. Letter to Benjamin Eakins, Fall 1869, in *Paris Letters*, p. 284.

16. Trevor Fairbrother, "Thomas Eakins, Philadelphia, Paris and New York," *Burlington Magazine* 144, no. 1188 (March 2002), p. 193. Fairbrother is referring to the first edition of Lloyd Goodrich, *Thomas Eakins, His Life and Work* (New York: Whitney Museum of American Art, 1933).

17. This painting is the first in a series of nineteen oils, watercolors, and drawings on the subject of rowing. Extensive studies of the rowing-pictures painting can be found in Elizabeth Johns, *Thomas Eakins: The Heroism of Modern Life* (Princeton, NJ: Princeton University Press, 1983), pp. 19–45; Helen A. Cooper, Martin A. Berger, Christina Currie, Amy Beth Werbel, *Thomas Eakins: The Rowing Pictures* (New Haven, CT: Yale University Press, 1996).

18. *Philadelphia Evening Bulletin*, April 27, 1871, as cited in Gordon Hendricks, *The Life and Work of Thomas Eakins* (New York: Grossman, 1974), pp. 70–71.

19. As cited in Hendricks, *The Life and Work of Thomas Eakins*, pp. 70–71.

20. As cited in Goodrich, *Thomas Eakins*, vol. 1, pp. 185–186.

21. As cited in Marc Simpson, "The 1870s," in Sewell, *Thomas Eakins*, p. 44.

22. See Joel Isaacson, "Impressionism and Journalistic Illustration," *Arts* 56 (June 1982), pp. 95–115.

23. Letter to Benjamin Eakins, March 6, 1868, in *Paris Letters*, p. 199.

24. Goodrich, *Thomas Eakins*, vol. 1, p. 47.

25. Alan Braddock, *Thomas Eakins and the Cultures of Modernity* (Berkeley: University of California Press, 2009), p. 96.

26. Letter to his mother Caroline Cowperthwait Eakins, October 1, 1866, in *Paris Letters*, p. 20.

27. Letter to Fanny Eakins, November 13, 1867, in *Paris Letters*, p. 160.

28. Letter to Fanny Eakins, November 13, 1867, in *Paris Letters*, p. 161.

29. Fragment of a letter, November 26, 1866, in *Paris Letters*, p. 73.

30. Letter to Fanny Eakins, June 21, 1867, in *Paris Letters*, p. 130. Johnson had alienated the Radical Republicans in Congress and the barb reflects the polarization of the nation in the aftermath of the Civil War.

31. Letter to Benjamin Eakins, April 23, 1869, in *Paris Letters*, p. 254.

32. Letter to Fanny Eakins, July 8, 1869, in *Paris Letters*, p. 268.

33. Letter to Benjamin Eakins, March 6, 1868, in *Paris Letters*, p. 198.

34. Letter to Benjamin Eakins, March 14, 1870, in *Paris Letters*, p. 198.

35. As translated and cited by Goodrich, *Thomas Eakins*, vol. 1, p. 116.

36. Goodrich, *Thomas Eakins*, vol. 1, p. 118. Kathleen Foster provides a full analysis of how Eakins incorporated Gérôme's teachings in this watercolor to please the master. Foster, *Thomas Eakins Rediscovered*, pp. 83–86.

37. As translated and cited by Lois Marie Fink, *American Art at the Nineteenth-Century Paris Salons* (Cambridge: Cambridge University Press, 1990), p. 216.

38. Earl Shinn, "The Water-Color Society's Exhibition," *The Nation* 20 (February 18, 1875), p. 120.

39. *Philadelphia Press* (March 5, 1875).

40. As cited in Hendricks, *The Life and Work of Thomas Eakins*, p. 87. Johns, *Thomas Eakins*, p. 55.

41. Johns gives an accounting of the history of surgery and Eakins's anatomical studies in her chapter on *Gross Clinic*, pp. 46–81.

42. Samuel D. Gross, M.D., *Autobiography*, vol. 2 (Philadelphia: George Barrie, 1887), p. 302.

43. Samuel D. Gross, MD., *A Sketch of the Life, Character, and Services of Ambrose Paré* (Philadelphia: J. B. Lippincott, 1861).

44. As cited in Goodrich, *Thomas Eakins*, vol. 1, p. 128.

45. Gross, *Autobiography*, vol. 1, p. 176.

46. "My anatomy studies & sculptures, especially the anatomy[,] comes to bear on my work & I construct my men more solid & springy & strong." Letter to Benjamin Eakins, September 8, 1867 [or 1868], in *Paris Letters*, p. 149.

47. In his psychoanalytic interpretation of this painting, Michael Fried makes the analogy between the scalpel and the writing tool held by Eakins. Gross was a highly productive author, and Eakins's father was a writing master. Michael Fried, *Realism, Writing, Disfiguration* (Chicago: University of Chicago Press, 1987), p. 230.

48. William J. Clark, "The Fine Arts: Eakins' Portrait of Dr. Gross," *Philadelphia Daily Evening Telegraph* (April 28, 1876), p. 4, as cited in *An Eakins Masterpiece Restored: Seeing* The Gross Clinic *Anew*, ed. Kathleen A. Foster and Mark S. Tucker (New Haven, CT: Philadelphia Museum of Art in association with Yale University Press, 2012), p. 138.

49. Clark, "Fine Arts," p. 139.

50. "Some Recent Art," clipping from an unidentified newspaper, ca. April 1876—Bregler Collection PAFA, as cited in Foster and Tucker, *Eakins Masterpiece Restored*, p. 139.

51. As cited in Hendricks, *The Life and Work of Thomas Eakins*, p. 97.

52. As cited in Foster and Tucker, *Eakins Masterpiece Restored*, p. 144.

53. [Earl Shinn], "Fine Arts: Exhibition by the Society of American Artists," *The Nation* 28, no. 716 (March 20, 1879), p. 207, as cited in ibid., p. 144.

54. Kathleen A. Foster, "A Portrait of Ambition: Eakins, *The Gross Clinic*, and the American Centennial," in Foster and Tucker, *Eakins Masterpiece Restored*, p. 40.

55. Letter to Emily Sartain, November 16, 1866, in *Paris Letters*, p. 71.

56. Johns, *Thomas Eakins*, p. 102.

57. As cited in Goodrich, *Thomas Eakins*, vol. 1, p. 146.

58. Manet's 1863 *Luncheon on the Grass* became the *succès de scandale* of the Salon des Refusés, and his *Olympia* caused such an uproar at the Salon of 1865 that it had to be moved higher on the exhibition wall to avoid vandalization.

59. Scholars such as Homer have recognized the influence of French realism on Eakins but have not commented at length. "Eakins may have learned something, too, from the realists in France and from the French Barbizon school and its American exponents." Homer, *Thomas Eakins*, p. 85.

60. Gerald M. Ackerman discusses the relationship of the two men and their art in "Gérôme and Manet," *Gazette des Beaux-Arts* 70 (1967), pp. 163–176.

61. Gerald M. Ackerman, *The Life and Work of Jean-Louis Gérôme* (London: Sotheby's, 1986), p. 160.

62. Tillet in *Le Siècle* as cited by Klaus Herding, *Courbet: To Venture Independence*, trans. John William Gabriel (New Haven, CT: Yale University Press, 1991), p. 22.

63. As cited in Steven Z. Levine, "Courbet, Bronzino, and Blasphemy," *New Literary History* 22 (1991), p. 696.

64. As cited in Goodrich, *Thomas Eakins*, vol. 1, p. 157.

65. As cited in Hendricks, *Life and Work of Thomas Eakins*, p. 114.

66. Letter to Benjamin Eakins, May 9, 1868, in *Paris Letters*, p. 210.

67. "What ruins the picture is much less the want of beauty in the model (as has been suggested in the public prints) than the presence in the foreground of the clothes of the young woman, cast carelessly over a chair. This gives a shock which makes one think about the nudity—and at once the picture becomes improper!" As cited in Goodrich, *Thomas Eakins*, vol. 1, p. 157.

68. Pierre Bourdieu, *Manet: Une Révolution symbolique* (Paris: Seuil, 2013), p. 31.

69. A good overview of the critical reception of Manet's painting can be found in Alan Krell, "Manet's *Déjeuner sur l'herbe* in the *Salon des Refusés*: A Reappraisal," *Art Bulletin* 65 (June 1983), pp. 316–320.

70. As cited in George Heard Hamilton, *Manet and His Critics* (New Haven, CT: Yale University Press, 1954), p. 54.

71. Eakins enjoyed the satirical journal *Le Charivari* and sent copies of it home to his family. Reason, *Thomas Eakins and the Uses of History* (Philadelphia: University of Pennsylvania Press, 2010), p. 130. Richard Brettell has assumed Eakins's familiarity with *Le Journal amusant* in "Thomas Eakins and the Male Nude in French Vanguard Painting, 1850–1890," in Doreen Bolger and Sarah Cash, *Thomas Eakins and the Swimming Picture* (Fort Worth, TX: Amon Carter Museum, 1996), pp. 80–97.

72. On the issue of clothing in Manet's *Déjeuner*, see Marcia Pointon, *Naked Authority: The Body in Western Painting, 1830–1908* (Cambridge: Cambridge University Press, 1990), pp. 113–120.

73. Henry Adams, *Eakins Revealed: The Secret Life of an American Artist* (New York: Oxford University Press, 2005), p. 251.

74. As cited in Homer, *Thomas Eakins*, p. 97.

75. As cited in Marc Simpson, "Eakins's Vision of the Past," in Sewell, *Thomas Eakins*, p. 215.

76. As cited in "Thomas Eakins and American Art," in Sewell, *Thomas Eakins*, p. xix.

77. As cited in Simpson, "The 1870s," 32.

78. The most thorough discussions of the work can be found in Elizabeth Milroy, "'*Consummatum est*': A Reassessment of Thomas Eakins's *Crucifixion* of 1880," *Art Bulletin* 71, no. 2 (June 1989), pp. 269–284; Reason, *Thomas Eakins*, pp. 119–146.

79. "Cependant, la première impression que cette toile nous laisse, c'est qu'elle représente, elle aussi, un supplicié, le juste supplicié, comme le dit la noble et calme expression de sa tête résolument tournée vers le ciel, du geste d'une victime qui en appelle au souverain juge,—mais qu'enfin elle ne représente pas un Dieu." Ernest Duvergier de Hauranne, "Salon de 1874," *Revue des Deux Mondes* 3 (1874), p. 664.

80. Octave Mirbeau, "Le Salon V," *L'Ordre de Paris* (May 12, 1874).

81. G. R. R. "French Fine Art at the Late Paris International Exhibition," *Magazine of Art*, vol. 2 (1878–1879), p. 15.

82. As cited in Goodrich, *Thomas Eakins*, vol. 1, p. 193.

83. "Revolting beyond expression is Thomas Eakins's 'Crucified Christ,' a bold piece of realism, in which there is some good painting and much bad color. Mr. Eakins finds in this picture the worst possible excuse for making a study of the nude figure. His Christ is the subject of the dissecting room table—sickening, repulsive to the last degree." As cited in Marc Simpson, "The 1880's," in Sewell, *Thomas Eakins*, p. 108.

84. Kathleen A. Foster, "Eakins and the Academy," in Sewell, *Thomas Eakins*, p. 99.

85. Letter to Benjamin Eakins, May 9, 1868, in *Paris Letters*, p. 210.

86. Doreen Bolger and Sarah Cash have focused on this painting in *Thomas Eakins and the Swimming Picture.*

87. For an astute discussion on the eclipse of the male nude for the depiction of the female, see Abigail Solomon-Godeau, *Male Trouble: A Crisis in Representation* (New York: Thames and Hudson, 1997).

88. Bazille as cited in Dianne W. Pitman, *Bazille: Purity, Pose, and Painting in the 1860s* (University Park: Pennsylvania State University Press, 1998), p. 14.

89. As cited in Goodrich, *Thomas Eakins*, vol. 1, p. 174.

90. A full account of the controversy surrounding Eakins's removal from the academy can be found in Kathleen A. Foster and Cheryl Liebold, *Writing about Eakins: The Manuscripts in Charles Bregler's Thomas Eakins Collection* (Philadelphia: published for the Pennsylvania Academy of the Fine Arts by the University of Pennsylvania Press, 1989).

91. "The End of Eakins," *Philadelphia Evening Item* (February 15, 1886), p. 1.

92. Foster, "Eakins and the Academy," p. 106.

93. As cited in Foster, *Thomas Eakins Rediscovered*, p. 145.

94. Darrell Sewell, *Thomas Eakins: Artist of Philadelphia* (Philadelphia: Philadelphia Museum of Art, 1982).

95. Thomas Eakins, letter to Benjamin Eakins, May 9, 1868, in *Paris Letters*, p. 208.

96. Émile Zola, "Nos Peintres au Champ-de-Mars," *La Situation*, 1 juillet, 1867.

97. Maxime du Camp, "Le Salon de 1863," *La Revue des Deux Mondes*, 15 juin 1863, pp. 892–893, as cited by Elizabeth Anne McCauley, "Sex and the Salon: Defining Art and Immorality in 1863," in *Manet's 'Le Déjeuner sur l'herbe,'* ed. Paul Hayes Tucker (New York: Cambridge University Press, 1998), p. 38.

98. Earl Shinn, "Fine Arts: The Lessons of a Late Exhibition," *The Nation* 26 (April 1878), p. 251, as cited in Foster, *Thomas Eakins Rediscovered*, p. 144.

99. Foster and Liebold, *Writing about Eakins*, p. 23.

100. "Eakins Chats on Art of America," *Philadelphia Press* (February 22, 1914), as cited in Braddock, *Thomas Eakins and the Cultures of Modernity*, p. 2.

CHAPTER 9

1. *Articles of Association*, December 26, 1805, of the Pennsylvania Academy of the Fine Arts.

2. As cited in Anne d'Harnoncourt, "Preface" to Suzanne G. Lindsay, *Mary Cassatt and Philadelphia* (Philadelphia: Philadelphia Museum of Art, 1985), p. 7.

3. Nancy Mowll Mathews, *Mary Cassatt: A Life* (New Haven, CT: Yale University Press, 1994), p. 15.

4. Letter of Eliza Haldeman to Mrs. Samuel Haldeman, May 15, 1876, in Nancy Mowll Mathews, *Cassatt and Her Circle: Selected Letters* (New York: Abbeville, 1984), p. 46.

5. As cited in Andrew J. Walker, "Mary Cassatt's Modern Education: The United States, France, Italy, and Spain, 1860–73," in *Mary Cassatt: Modern Woman*, Organized by Judith A. Barter with contributions by Erica E. Hirshler, George T. M. Shackelford, Kevin Sharp, Harriet K. Stratis, and Andrew J. Walker (New York: Art Institute of Chicago in association with Harry N. Abrams, 1998), p. 22. Eliza Haldeman explained Cassatt's use of the surname Stevenson in a letter to her parents: "It is much pleasanter when one is a girl as it avoids publicity." Letter of Eliza Haldeman to Mr. and Mrs. Samuel Haldeman, May 8, 1868, as cited in Mathews, *Cassatt and Her Circle: Selected Letters*, p. 54.

6. Eliza Haldeman reported on the popularity of the Salon of 1868: "The place is crowded with visitors and on last Sunday, which is a free day, there were 30,000 people in the Palace and some

six thousand turned away from the doors, the Rooms being too full to admit them." Letter of Eliza Haldeman to Alice [?] Haldeman, May 13, 1868, in Mathews, *Cassatt and Her Circle: Selected Letters*, p. 56.

7. As cited in Lindsay, *Mary Cassatt*, p. 37.

8. Jules Claretie, *L'Indépendance belge*, juin 15, 1867, as cited in Carol Armstrong, *Manet Manette* (New Haven, CT: Yale University Press, 2002), p. 97.

9. Letter of Emily Sartain to John Sartain, May 8, 1873, in Mathews, *Cassatt and Her Circle: Selected Letters*, p. 118.

10. "Voilà quelqu'un qui sent comme moi," Degas, as cited in Achille Segard, *Mary Cassatt: Un Peintre des enfants et des mères* (Paris: Librairie Paul Ollendorff, 1913), p. 35.

11. Louis Leroy, "L'Exposition des impressionistes," *Le Charivari* (April 25, 1874), p. 2.

12. Leroy, "Exposition des impressionistes," p. 3.

13. " . . . Degas m'engagea à ne plus envoyer au Salon et à exposer avec ses amis clans le groupe des Impressionnistes. J'acceptai avec joie. Enfin je pouvais travailler avec une indépendance absolue sans m'occuper de l'opinion éventuelle d'un jury! Déjà j'avais reconnu quels étaient mes véritables maîtres. J'admirais Manet, Courbet et Degas. Je haïssais l'art conventionnel. Je commençais à vivre." Segard, *Mary Cassatt*, pp. 7–8.

14. Letter of Mary Cassatt to Louisine Havemeyer, as cited in Nancy Mowll Mathews, *Mary Cassatt* (New York: Harry N. Abrams, publishers in association with the National Museum of American Art, Smithsonian Institution, 1987), p. 33.

15. The sitter had been misidentified for many years as Cassatt's sister Lydia. However, Suzanne Lindsay clarified this issue, which has since been accepted. Lindsay, *Mary Cassatt*, p. 41.

16. K. Baedeker, *Paris and Its Environs* (London: Dulau, 1878), p. 79.

17. Much has been written from the feminist point of view on women in opera boxes, most notably by Griselda Pollock, "The Gaze and the Look: Women with Binoculars—A Question of Difference," in *Dealing with Degas: Representations of Women and the Politics of Vision*, ed. Richard Kendall and Griselda Pollock (London: Pandora, 1992), pp. 106–130; Tamar Garb, "Gender and Representation," in *Modern Art and Modernism: A Critical Anthology*, ed. Francis Frascina et al. (New Haven, CT: Yale University Press in association with the Open University, 1993), pp. 219–289; Carol Armstrong, *Odd Man Out: Readings of the Work and Reputation of Edgar Degas* (Chicago: University of Chicago Press, 1991); Temma Balducci, *Gender, Space, and the Gaze in post-Haussmann Visual Culture: Beyond the Flâneur* (London: Routledge, 2017).

18. F.-C. de Syène [Arsène Houssaye], "Salon de 1879," *L'Artiste* (May 1879), p. 292.

19. Diego Martelli, "Gli impressionisti, mostra del 1879," *Roma Artistica*, June 27 and July 5, 1879, as cited in *The New Painting, Impressionism, 1874–1886: An Exhibition*. Directed and coordinated by Charles S. Moffett with the assistance of Ruth Berson, Barbara Lee Williams, and Fronia E. Wissman (San Francisco: Fine Arts Museum, 1986), p. 276.

20. George Lafenestre, "Les Expositions d'art," *Revue des Deux Mondes* (May–June 1879), p. 481.

21. Letter of Robert Cassatt to Alexander Cassatt, May 21, 1879, in Mathews, *Cassatt and Her Circle: Selected Letters*, p. 144.

22. Charles Baudelaire, *The Painter of Modern Life and Other Essays*, trans. and ed. Jonathan Mayne (New York: Da Capo, 1964), p. 34.

23. Henry Havard, "La Peinture indépendante: Huitième Exposition des Impressionnistes," as cited in Barter, *Mary Cassatt: Modern Woman*, p. 111.

24. As cited by Laura Gascoigne, "A School of Her Own." *Apollo* 187 (May 2018), p. 100.

25. Philippe Burty, "Exposition des œuvres des artistes indépendants," *La République Française*, April 10, 1880, p. 2.

26. Joris-Karl Huysmans, *L'Art moderne*, 1883, as cited in Charles S. Moffett, *The New Painting, Impressionism, 1874–1886* (Seattle: University of Washington Press, 1986), p. 359.

27. Gustave Geffroy, *La Justice*, April 19, 1881, as cited in ibid., p. 359.

28. As cited in Gary Tinterow, "The 1880s: Synthesis and Change," in Jean Sutherland Boggs, Douglas W. Druick, Henri Loyrette, Michael Pantazzi and Gary Tinterow. *Degas*. New York: Metropolitan Museum of Art, 1988. et al. *Degas* (New York: Metropolitan Museum of Art, 1988), p. 396.

29. As cited in Mathews, *Mary Cassatt: A Life*, p. 307.

30. Letter of Mary Cassatt to Louisine Havemeyer, March 12, 1915, in Mathews, *Cassatt and Her Circle: Selected Letters*, p. 254.

31. On the Degas-Cassatt relationship, see George T. M. Shackelford, "*Pas de deux*: Mary Cassatt and Edgar Degas," in Barter, *Mary Cassatt: Modern Woman*, pp. 109–143.

32. Jean-Louis Vaudoyer, "Petites Expositions," *La Chronique des arts et de la curiosité: Supplément à la Gazette des beaux-arts*, November 21, 1908, p. 371. This painting was not exhibited in public until 1927.

33. Judith A. Barter, "Mary Cassatt: Themes," "Mary Cassatt: Themes, Sources, and the Modern Woman," in Barter, *Mary Cassatt: Modern Woman*, p. 66.

34. "Without bias, one is obligated to state that feminine works . . . have an artificial allure that shows their author to be incapable of making an idea profound, or of feeling a form; one always divines in them a horror of truth, and a searching for the pretty, which are at the heart of all feminine temperaments. In Mlle. Cassatt there is nothing of all this; she possesses a style of drawing that is precise and supple, and a frankness of execution worthy of a man, and a man of great talent." Jules Antoine, "Beaux-Arts, Galerie Durand-Ruel—Deuxième exposition des peintres-graveurs," *Art et critique* 2 (March 5, 1890), p. 172, as cited and trans. Pamela A. Ivinski, "'So Firm and Powerful a Hand': Mary Cassatt's Techniques and Questions of Gender," in *Women Impressionists*, ed. Ingrid Pfeiffer and Max Hollein (Ostfilder: Hatje Cantz, 2008), pp. 183–184.

35. As cited in Lindsay, *Mary Cassatt*, p. 23.

36. As reported by Cassatt in a letter to Homer Saint-Gaudens (director of fine arts at the Carnegie Institute, Pittsburgh), 1922, in Mathews, *Cassatt and Her Circle: Selected Letters*, p. 335.

37. As cited in John Hutton, "Picking Fruit: Mary Cassatt's 'Modern Woman' and the Woman's Building of 1893," *Feminist Studies* 20 (Summer 1994), p. 334.

38. As cited in Hutton, "Picking Fruit," p. 335.

39. Cassatt as cited in a letter from Sara Hallowell to Bartha Palmer, February 6, 1894, in Mathews, *Cassatt and Her Circle: Selected Letters*, p. 254.

40. As cited in Griselda Pollock, *Mary Cassatt* (New York: Harper and Row, 1980), p. 8.

41. As cited in Lindsay, *Mary Cassatt*, p. 9.

42. Ibid.

43. As cited in Kevin Sharp, "How Mary Cassatt Became an American Artist," in Barter, *Mary Cassatt: Modern Woman*, p. 160.

44. Segard, *Mary Cassatt*, p. 188. Translation mine.

45. Suzanne G. Lindsay's excellent catalog *Mary Cassatt and Philadelphia* remains the central source of information on the artist and her connections with the city.

46. *Inquirer*, February 3, 1905, as cited in ibid., p. 24.

47. André Mellerio, "Mary Cassatt," *L'Art et Les Artistes* 12 (November 1910), p. 71, as cited by Adelyn D. Breeskin, "Introduction" to *Mary Cassatt: 1844–1926* (Washington, DC: National Gallery of Art, 1970), p. 12.

48. In addition to Sharp's essay, see Hadrien Viraben, "Constructing a Reputation: Achille Segard's 1913 Biography of Mary Cassatt," *American Art* 31, no. 1 (Spring 2017), pp. 98–113.

49. See Erica Hirshler, "Helping 'Fine Things Across the Atlantic': Mary Cassatt and Art Collecting in the United States," in Barter, *Mary Cassatt: Modern Woman*, pp. 177–211.

50. The American artist and writer Joseph Pennell recounted his memory of this: "There was every kind of man and boy, from sixty to twenty, in that class, except black men, and one day the Chairman of the School Committee appeared with a solemn announcement that he was coming. But this time the chairman came in state, accompanied by the secretary, other members of the committee, and the professor. And he said something like this. A drawing has been sent in and passed. The person who made it has been notified that he is admitted to the school. He has come and the secretary has seen him. He is a colored man. Now there is no rule in the Pennsylvania Academy of Fine Arts excluding people of color from the schools. But, knowing the feeling on the subject, I have placed the matter before the antique class; and I wish the life class to meet and decide whether he should be admitted. We met, and we decided that we had no objection. I do not remember a dissenting voice." Pennell as cited in Naurice Woods, *Henry Ossawa Tanner: Art, Faith, Race, and Legacy* (New York: Routledge, 2018), p. 26.

51. Tanner as cited in Woods, *Henry Ossawa Tanner*, p. 52.

52. Robert Henri and his circle are discussed in Chapter 11.

53. Woods, *Henry Ossawa Tanner*, p. 65.

54. Tanner as cited in William R. Lester, "Henry O. Tanner: Exile for Art's Sake," *Alexander's Magazine* 7 (December 15, 1908), p. 73.

55. Tanner explained his rationale for painting these images: "Since his return from Europe he has painted many Negro subjects. He feels drawn to such subjects on account of the newness of the field and because of a desire to represent the serious and pathetic side of life among them, and it is his thought that other things being equal, he who has the most sympathy with the subject will obtain the best results. To his mind, many of the artists who have represented Negro life have only seen the comic, the ludicrous side of it and have lacked sympathy with and affection for the big heart that dwells within such a rough exterior." Tanner as cited in Woods, *Henry Ossawa Tanner*, p. 75.

56. Darrell Sewell has also suggested that Tanner may have been influenced by a painting by Elizabeth Nourse, *Le Repas en famille*, that won a gold medal at the 1893 Chicago World's Fair. Darrell Sewell, in *Henry Ossawa Tanner*: catalog by Dewey F. Mosby and Darrel Sewell; introductory essay by Dewey F. Mosby; biographical essay by Rae Alexander Minter (Philadelphia: Philadelphia Museum of Art; New York: Rizzoli International, 1991), pp. 123–124.

57. Woods, *Henry Ossawa Tanner*, p. 80.

58. "We visited Earle's Art Gallery on Chestnut Street to see 'The First Lesson' a remarkable life-sized oil painting by Prof. H. O. Tanner, on exhibition there. We found the picture surrounded by a large crowd of spectators and it seemed to be the most admired of all others, and was decided by the best critics to be a very superb picture." *Christian Recorder*, October 5, 1893, as cited in ibid., p. 78.

59. Tanner as cited in Mosby and Sewell, *Henry Ossawa Tanner*, p. 125.

60. Tanner as cited in Dewey F. Mosby, "Paris, Racial Awareness and Success 1891–1897," in Mosby and Sewell, *Henry Ossawa Tanner*, p. 95.

61. Benjamin-Constant as cited in Woods, *Henry Ossawa Tanner*, p. 106.

62. As cited in ibid., p. 110.

63. Thomas Seaton as cited in Marc Simpson, "*The Resurrection of Lazarus* from the *Quartier Latin* to the Musée de Luxembourg," in *Henry Ossawa Tanner: Modern Spirit*, ed. Anna O. Marley (Philadelphia: Pennsylvania Academy of the Fine Arts, 2012), p. 75.

64. As cited in Woods, *Henry Ossawa Tanner*, p. 110.

65. Tanner as cited in ibid., p. 112.

66. Lester, "Henry O. Tanner," p. 73. On issues of race in this painting and others by Tanner, see also Alan Braddock, "Painting the World's Christ: Tanner, Hybridity, and the Blood of the Holy Land," *Nineteenth-Century Art Worldwide*, Fall 2004 (unpaginated).

67. As cited in Woods, *Henry Ossawa Tanner*, p. 119.

68. Morris as cited in ibid., p. 121.

69. Author unknown, "The Academy's Annual Show," *Philadelphia Inquirer*, January 15, 1899, p. 6.

70. Woods, *Henry Ossawa Tanner*, p. 129.

71. Tanner as cited in ibid., p. 246.

Chapter 10

1. The principal architect of Philadelphia's City Hall was John McArthur Jr., a native of Scotland, who was responsible for the design of many public buildings in Philadelphia. In 2007, the American Institute of Architects listed City Hall in twenty-first place among 150 of the organization's favorite structures in America.

2. For commentary on the impact of the French Revival style in Philadelphia, see Joseph L. Borkson, *Philadelphia: An American Paris* (Philadelphia: Camino Books, 2002), pp. 93–113.

3. An informal "gentlemen's agreement" in the 1950s prevented new buildings in center city from rising higher than the 491 feet of City Hall's tower. That height limit was broken by the two towers of Liberty Place, which were completed by 1990, after extensive public debate and approval from the City Council. By 2018, Comcast's two new buildings became the city's tallest, at 974 and 1,121 feet.

4. John Andrew Gallery, *The Planning of Center City Philadelphia from William Penn to the Present* (Philadelphia: Center for Architecture, 2007), p. 20.

5. David B. Brownlee, *Building the City Beautiful: The Benjamin Franklin Parkway and the Philadelphia Museum of Art*, 2nd ed. (Philadelphia: Philadelphia Museum of Art, 2017), pp. 16–17; cited hereafter as *Building*.

6. James Philip Noffsinger, *The Influence of the École des Beaux-Arts on the Architecture of the United States* (Washington, DC: Catholic University of America Press, 1955).

7. "A Boulevard Will Beautify the City," *Philadelphia Inquirer*, April 15, 1894. The author, James M. Beck, was a young lawyer with ties to the city's Republican machine. He would later serve as a stridently anti–New Deal congressman.

8. Brownlee, *Building*, pp. 18–21. See also James McClelland and Lynn Miller, *City in a Park: A History of Philadelphia's Fairmount Park System* (Philadelphia: Temple University Press, 2016), chapter 12: "The Benjamin Franklin Parkway," pp. 180–211.

9. Gallery, *Planning of Center City Philadelphia*, p. 23.

10. Paul P. Cret, Horace Trumbauer, and Zantzinger and Borie, *Parkway Plan as Prepared for the Fairmount Park Art Association*, bird's-eye perspective from east, 1907. Inscribed P.P.C. Horace Trumbauer, C. C. Zantzinger, Paul P. Cret, Philadelphia Museum of Art Archives, No. 90.I. Clarence Zantzinger (1872–1954) may have known Cret in Paris. He earned a diploma from the École des Beaux-Arts in 1901 and had already collaborated with Cret on another project. Brownlee, *Building*, p. 23.

11. It might be argued that the end of the Champs-Elysées at Concorde is the reverse of Cret's scheme for the Philadelphia parkway. The Paris square leads into the heart of old Paris while the proposed plaza at the foot of Fairmount lies just beyond the city's original northwestern edge.

12. That model was created for the May 1911, City Plans Conference, and displayed in the mayor's reception room at City Hall.

13. Brownlee, *Building*, pp. 46–47.

14. Ibid., p. 29.

15. James T. Maher, *The Twilight of Splendor: Chronicles of the Age of American Palaces* (Boston: Little, Brown, 1975), p. 65. See also Brownlee, *Building*, pp. 30ff. Gréber's gardens at Whitemarsh Hall, the Stotesbury estate, included a mile-long allée. After falling into disrepair, the entire property was demolished in 1980.

16. According to David Brownlee, the decision to make the upper half of the parkway more sylvan may also have been prompted by the fact that a number of the cultural institutions invited to relocate there had declined to do so. "Paul Cret and Philadelphia's Modern Classicism," address to symposium presented by the Athenaeum of Philadelphia and the Philadelphia Museum of Art, May 11–12, 2018, Philadelphia. Cited hereafter as Cret symposium.

17. Fairmount Park Art Association, *The Fairmount Parkway: A Pictorial Record of Development from Its First Incorporation in the City Plan in 1904 to the Completion of the Main Drive from City Hall to Fairmount Park in 1919* (Philadelphia: Fairmount Park Art Association, 1919).

18. *Department of the Art Jury, Eighth Annual Report* (Philadelphia: Department of Records, 1918), p. 8.

19. *Professor Cret's Parkway: One Architect's Legacy on Philadelphia's Grandest Thoroughfare*, exhibition at the Athenaeum of Philadelphia, April 30–August 31, 2018; also Jennifer Thompson, "'An Artistic Gem': Paul Cret and the Rodin Museum," Cret symposium, May 12, 2018.

20. See Chapter 12 for more on the Rodin Museum.

21. Thomas H. Keels, *Sesqui! Greed, Graft, and the Forgotten World's Fair of 1926* (Philadelphia: Temple University Press, 2017), pp. 16–34.

22. Jacques Gréber, "Aesthetic and Sociological Aspects of City and Regional Planning," *Proceedings of the American Philosophical Society* 74, no. 1 (1934), pp. 15–19. Gréber's reminder of the economic benefits echoed the argument made forty years earlier by James Beck. See this chapter's note 4 above.

23. That French heritage was explained to the French in an article appearing in a magazine published in Paris in 2017. In a section titled "La touche francophile" containing a double-page spread of photographs of the parkway and a number of its monuments, the writer began by noting, "Au début du xxe siècle, les architects français Paul Cret et Jacques Gréber tracent un boulevard reliant City Hall au musée des Beaux-Arts . . . Inspiré des Champs-Elysées, leur Fairmount Parkway confère à Philadelphie un petit air de Paris. . . ." Xavier Donzelli, "Découverte: Philadelphie, berceau des États-Unis," *Historia* 37 (September–October 2017), pp. 90–105.

24. The Free Library is so closely modeled on the work of Ange-Jacques Gabriel on the Place de la Concorde (1744–1763) that Paul Cret voiced this complaint when its design was approved in 1922: "The Place de la Concorde buildings being a master work, there is no doubt that the Philadelphia Library will be successful on the whole, as far as general proportions and detail are concerned. However, it will be a matter of regret to some that such an important building built by the city will not deserve more than the doubtful praise of being a copy of a good example." Quoted by Brownlee, *Building*, p. 77. Family Court vacated its Logan Square building in 2014 for larger quarters at Fifteenth and Arch Streets. That counterpart to Paris's Ministre Maritime was then slated to be converted into a luxury hotel while retaining its historic features. If that is completed, the Place de la Concorde's twins on Logan Square will even more fully reflect their Parisian counterparts, although in reverse, in which one neoclassical building houses a hotel and the other serves a governmental or civic function. At the time of this writing, the conversion of the

Family Court building into a hotel was expected to begin in 2019. Jacob Adelman, "Hotel Plans Move Forward Again," *Philadelphia Inquirer*, July 10, 2018, pp. A11, A13.

25. The architect of the Free Library (dedicated in 1927) was Horace Trumbauer; that of the Family Court (1941) was John T. Windrim, who also designed the Franklin Institute (1934). Windrim's father, James T. Windrim, had designed the Academy of Natural Sciences (1876) on the south side of the square. The School Administration Building's architect (1932) was Irwin T. Catherine; the Boy Scout headquarters was the work of Charles Z. Klauder (1930).

26. River commerce and navigation are honored in the north fountain in the Place de la Concorde; the southern fountain is a tribute to the Atlantic and the Mediterranean.

27. Margaret Calder Hayes, *Three Alexander Calders* (Middlebury, VT: P. S. Erikkson, 1977), p. 293.

28. As quoted by Seymour I. Toll, "My Way, Calder in Paris," *The State of Letters* (University of the South: Sewanee Review, 2010), p. 590.

29. Toll, "My Way," pp. 599, 601.

30. The quotation is from Hilary Spurling, "High Wire Act," *New York Review of Books* 64, no. 17 (November 9, 2017), p. 22, in her review of Jed Perl, *Calder: The Conquest of Time—The Early Years: 1898–1940* (New York: Alfred A. Knopf, 2017).

31. Jean Lipman, Ruth Wolfe, editorial director, *Calder's Universe* (New York: Viking in cooperation with the Whitney Museum of American Art, 1976), p. 10.

32. Borkson, *Philadelphia*, p. 34.

33. The contract with Frémiet specified no more than three castings of the work: that in Paris; one in Nancy, France; and Philadelphia's. Available at www.associationforpublicart.org/artwork/joan-of-arc. A Philadelphia legend has it that their city's casting is actually the original. See, for example, Lynn H. Miller and Annette H. Emgarth, *French Philadelphia* (Wayne, PA: Beach Lloyd, 2006), pp. xi, 68.

34. Grey Towers Castle and the surrounding Harrison estate were bought by Beaver College in 1929. Since 1962, that land in Glenside, Cheltenham Township, has served as the unified campus of what today is Arcadia University. The castle now serves as an administration building for the university's president and other staff.

35. The Philadelphia Museum of Art was built to the design of the Trumbauer firm, where Howell Lewis Shay was apparently responsible for the basic plan while Julian Abele, the first African American graduate of the University of Pennsylvania's Department of Architecture, most likely prepared the perspective drawings. Abele had earlier worked in France. The firm of Zantzinger, Borie and Medary was a partner. David B. Brownlee, *Making a Modern Classic: The Architecture of the Philadelphia Museum of Art* (Philadelphia: Philadelphia Museum of Art, 1997), pp. 23–24, 60–72. According to Brownlee, *Building*, Abele was primarily responsible for much of the design work as plans for the museum went forward.

36. Brownlee quotes the explanation of Howell Lewis Shay, Trumbauer's assistant, for why several temple forms were connected in the museum plan. Shay begins by acknowledging Trumbauer's desire that it resemble the acropolis. "Then I reminded them, 'Now we have to think about climate. Greece has very little rain and mild temperatures. You can go between the temples on the Acropolis easily. But here we'd have rain and snow and you'd have to put on your galoshes. So why don't we connect these three temples with a series of galleries . . . ?'" *Building*, p. 59.

37. Available at www.philamuseum.org/information/45-227-23.html.

38. Inga Saffron, "Polishing the Masterpiece," *Philadelphia Inquirer*, May 18, 2014, pp. A12–A13, available at www.architectmagazine.com/ . . . /philadelphia-museum-of-art_o.

39. The new Barnes building replaced the Youth Studies Center, a facility to treat troubled

young people. Whatever its social utility, the rather utilitarian study center was not in keeping with the Beaux-Arts ideal of a grand structure to uplift the public.

40. For accounts of the controversy, see John Anderson, *Art Held Hostage: The Battle over the Barnes Collection* (New York: W. W. Norton, 2003); Martin Filler, "Victory!" *New York Review of Books* 59, no. 12 (July 12, 2012), pp. 14–18. Barnes as a collector is discussed in Chapter 11.

41. The new Barnes Foundation headquarters was designed by architects Tod Williams and Billie Tsien. Apart from the arrangement of the galleries, its configuration and outward appearance is very different from that of Cret's building in Lower Merion, although it is very much in the modernist tradition that Cret espoused.

42. Many of these initiatives came from the plan "More Park, Less Way," which was announced at a public meeting on February 4, 2013, by the mayor, deputy mayor, and commissioner of parks and recreation and the nonprofit organization Penn Praxis (available at http://plannphilly.com/praxis-projects/benjamin-franklin-parkway). See also Miriam Hill, "City Planning Leaders Air Parkway Proposal," *Philadelphia Inquirer*, February 5, 2013, p. B5; Harris Steinberg, "Philly's Renewed Urbanity," *Philadelphia Inquirer*, July 11, 2013, p. A16.

43. Philadelphia Parks Alliance, "How Much Value Does the City of Philadelphia Receive from Its Park and Recreation System?" A Report by the Trust for Public Land's Center for City Park Excellence for the Philadelphia Parks Alliance, 2008.

44. In 2011, the 1400 block of Cherry Street became a pedestrian mall, renamed Lenfest Plaza, extending toward the lower parkway. The Pennsylvania Academy of Fine Arts Landmark Building borders the plaza on the south side, its Hamilton Building borders the north. Across Broad Street to the east is the entrance to the enlarged Pennsylvania Convention Center. Two blocks further west, Cherry Street enters the Benjamin Franklin Parkway. The parkway now terminates visually at the west apron of city hall, Dilworth Park, which leads directly to Broad Street through city hall's courtyard.

45. The most recent renovation was completed in 2016.

46. See Chapter 12 for more on Barye.

47. Merson was elected to the Académie des Beaux-Arts in 1892. His work combines the Académie's characteristic neoclassical and romantic traditions in the effort to create what was regarded as the perfect style. Available at www.historyofpaintings.com/merson.htm.

48. They include the Bellau Wood Museum, the Bellicourt Monument, the Château Thierry Memorial, and the Varennes-en-Argonne Monument.

49. Witold Rybczynski, "The Late, Great Paul Cret," *New York Times Magazine*, October 21, 2017, available at www.nytimes.com2014/10/21/t-magazine/the-late-great-paul-cret.html.

50. Rybczynski, "Late, Great Paul Cret." As Rybczynski notes, an unanticipated measure of Cret's reach is his influence on the chief engineer of Hitler's Third Reich, Albert Speer, who studied Cret's work and made the style a grandiose hallmark of that regime. Adopted, too, by Mussolini's Fascists, it came to identify the twentieth century's totalitarian regimes, whereas Cret himself regarded his architectural vision as a celebration of liberal values.

51. Cret was also responsible for the design of three other Philadelphia bridges: the Market Street and the University Avenue Bridges, both of which span the Schuylkill, and the Tacony-Palmyra Bridge over the Delaware.

52. For an account of the Sculpture Internationals, see Penny Balkin Bach, *Public Art in Philadelphia* (Philadelphia: Temple University Press, 1992), pp. 91–100.

53. We are indebted to Pierre Ravaçon for this information about the work of the French Benevolent Society in Cret's time.

54. Philadelphia Athenaeum exhibition, 2011, *Bastille to Broad Street*, text label: "The French Garden: The Versailles of America—Whitemarsh Hall."

55. Maher, *Twilight of Splendor*, p. 65.

56. Meigs, the architect and former U.S. Army officer, was a partner in the firm of Mellor, Meigs, and Howe in Philadelphia. He accounted for the Laverock Farm project in his monograph, *An American Country House* (New York: Architectural book publishing company, 1925).

57. Lewis Mumford, "The Architecture of Escape," *New Republic* 43 (August 12, 1925), p. 23.

58. Borkson, *Philadelphia*, pp. 58–61.

59. See Chapter 5 for more on the du Ponts.

60. Available at www.nemoursmansion.org.

61. Athenaeum exhibit, *Bastille to Broad Street*, text label: "Paul Philippe Cret."

62. Paul Goldberger, "What Does the City Beautiful Mean for the 21st Century?" keynote address, Cret symposium, May 11, 2018.

CHAPTER 11

1. Sylvia Yount, "'In Education, Comradeship, and Common Aims': The Bucks County Painters and the Pennsylvania Academy of the Fine Arts," in *Pennsylvania Impressionism*, ed. Brian H. Peterson (Philadelphia: University of Pennsylvania Press, 2002), pp. 59–61.

2. Guy Pène du Bois, "The Pennsylvania Group of Landscape Painters," *Arts and Decoration* 5, no. 9 (July 1915), pp. 351–354.

3. Thomas C. Folk, *The Pennsylvania School of Landscape Painting: An Original American Impressionism* (Allentown, PA: Allentown Art Museum, 1984), p. x.

4. Brian H. Peterson, ed., *Pennsylvania Impressionism* (Philadelphia: University of Pennsylvania Press, 2002), pp. 7–8.

5. William H. Gerdts, *American Impressionism* (New York: Abbeville, 2001), p. 234.

6. Guy Pène du Bois, "The Boston Group of Painters: An Essay on Nationalism in Art," *Arts and Decoration* (October 15, 1915), p. 457.

7. As cited in Constance Kimmerle, *Edward W. Redfield: Just Values and Fine Seeing* (Philadelphia: University of Pennsylvania Press, 2004), p. 19.

8. As cited in Peterson, *Pennsylvania Impressionism*, p. 6.

9. As cited in Folk, *The Pennsylvania Impressionists* (Madison, NJ: Fairleigh Dickinson University Press, 1997), p. 44.

10. Peterson, *Pennsylvania Impressionism*, p. 31.

11. Ibid., p. 6.

12. Kimmerle, *Edward W. Redfield*, p. 33.

13. As cited in Folk, *Pennsylvania Impressionists*, p. 16.

14. Joachim Pissarro, in *The Impressionist and the City*, ed. Richard R. Brettell and Joachim Pissarro (New Haven, CT: Yale University Press, 1992), p. xlii.

15. Richard R. Brettell, *Pissarro and Pontoise: The Painter in a Landscape* (New Haven, CT: Yale University Press, 1990), p. 104.

16. This holds true for the high years of Pissarro's impressionist and neo-impressionist phases during the 1870s through the mid-1890s when he painted views of Paris and the new boulevards during the last years of his career until his death in 1903.

17. As cited in Gerdts, *American Impressionism*, p. 234.

18. Kimmerle, *Edward W. Redfield*, p. 13.

19. Lloyd Goodrich, "What Is American about American Art?" *Art in America* 51 (August 1963), p. 33.

20. Monet as cited by Katherine Rothkopf in *Impressionists in Winter: Effets de Neige*, ed. Charles S. Moffett, Eliza A. Rathbone, Katherine Rothkopf, and Joel Isaacson (London: Philip Wilson, 1998), p. 84.

21. As cited in Peterson, *Pennsylvania Impressionism*, p. 224.

22. Ibid., p. 50. Gerdts, *American Impressionism*, p. 237.

23. As cited in Kathleen Foster, "Daniel Garber's Trees," *Kresge Art Museum Bulletin* 8 (1999), p. 18.

24. As Lance Humphries has noted, scant information exists regarding Garber's two years in Europe. A letter from Garber to Emily Sartain states that, while in Florence, he and his wife lived in an apartment near the Uffizi and Pitti Palace but does not mention any artworks seen there. Lance Humphries, *Daniel Garber: Romantic Realist* (Philadelphia: Pennsylvania Academy of the Fine Arts, and Doylestown, PA: The James A. Michener Art Museum, 2007), p. 216n71.

25. Kathleen A. Foster, *Daniel Garber, 1880–1958* (Philadelphia: Pennsylvania Academy of the Fine Arts, 1980), p. 18.

26. Humphries, *Daniel Garber*, p. 63.

27. Garber mentioned in his letter to Emily Sartain that when he and his wife traveled through Holland and Belgium, he saw "nearly all of importance." Humphries, *Daniel Garber*, p. 216n71.

28. As cited in Thomas Folk, *Walter Elmer Schofield: Bold Impressionist* (Chadds Ford, PA: Brandywine River Museum, 1983), p. 9.

29. Foster, *Daniel Garber, 1880–1958*, p. 6.

30. Erica E. Hirshler, "At Home in Paris," in *Americans in Paris 1860–1900*, ed. Kathleen Adler, Erica E. Hirshler, H. Barbara Weinberg (London: National Gallery, 2006), p. 111.

31. See H. Barbara Weinberg, Doreen Bolger, and David Park Curry, *American Impressionism and Realism: The Painting of Modern Life, 1885–1915* (New York: Metropolitan Museum of Art, 1994).

32. Henri's diary, January 14, 1927, as cited in William Innes Homer, *Robert Henri and His Circle* (New York: Hacker Art Books, 1988), p. 32.

33. Henri's diary, September 23, 1888, as cited in Bennard B. Perlman, *Robert Henri: His Life and Art* (New York: Dover, 1991), p. 12.

34. Perlman, *Robert Henri*, p. 38.

35. Henri's diary, April 8, 1891, as cited in Rebecca Zurier, *Picturing the City: Urban Vision and the Ashcan School* (Berkeley: University of California Press, 2006), p. 112.

36. Letter by Henri, addressee unknown, January 31, 1892, as cited in ibid., p. 69.

37. Perlman, *Robert Henri*, p. 32.

38. John Sloan as cited in *John Sloan/Robert Henri: Their Philadelphia Years, 1886–1904* (Philadelphia: Moore College of Art, Gallery, 1976), p. 23.

39. Sloan as cited in Helen Farr Sloan, "Robert Henri: An Appreciation," in *Robert Henri: Painter*, ed. Bennard B. Perlman (Wilmington: Delaware Art Museum, 1984), p. xi.

40. Henri's diary, December 1, 1897, as cited in Homer, *Robert Henri and His Circle*, p. 80.

41. Henri's letter to his parents, October 12, 1858, as cited in Perlman, *Robert Henri*, p. 40.

42. For a thorough and highly informative discussion of the Eight and the history of the time, see Elizabeth Milroy, *Painters of a New Century: The Eight and American Art* (Milwaukee: University of Wisconsin Press, 1991).

43. Holger Cahill and Alfred H. Barr Jr. first employed the term in 1934. See Zurier, *Picturing the City*, p.23.

44. W. B. McCormick, "Art Notes of the Week," *New York Press*, February 9, 1908, p. 6.

45. As cited in Milroy, *Painters of a New Century*, p. 37.

46. Ibid.

47. As cited in Valerie Ann Leeds, *My People: The Portraits of Robert Henri* (Orlando, FL: Orlando Museum of Art, 1994), p. 15.

48. Leeds, *My People*, p. 15.

49. Milroy, *Painters of a New Century*, p. 15.

50. Robert Henri, "The New York Exhibition of Independent Artists," *Craftsman* 18 (May 1910), p. 161.

51. *New York American*, June 27, 1912, as cited in Perlman, *Robert Henri*, p. 106.

52. Theodore Roosevelt, "A Layman's View of an Art Exhibition," *The Outlook* 103 (March 29, 1913), p. 719.

53. On Henri and Whitman, see Ruth L. Bohan, "Robert Henri, Walt Whitman, and the American Artist." *Walt Whitman Quarterly Review* 29, no. 4 (Spring 2012), pp. 131–151.

54. Robert Henri, *The Art Spirit* (Philadelphia: J. B. Lippincott, 1960), p. 128.

55. Homer, *Robert Henri and His Circle*, pp. 196–197.

56. Helen Appleton Read, *Robert Henri* (New York: Whitney Museum of American Art, 1931), p. 10.

57. As cited in Sarah Vure, "Henri," in *The Eight and American Modernisms*, ed. Elizabeth Kennedy (New Britain, CT: New Britain Museum of American Art, 2009), p. 57.

58. John Sloan as cited in Perlman, *Robert Henri*, p. xiv.

59. John Sloan as cited in *John Sloan/Robert Henri*, p. 27.

60. As cited by Avis Berman, "Philadelphia Landscape: William Glackens's Early Years," in *William Glackens*, ed. Avis Berman (New York: Skira Rizzoli in association with the Barnes Foundation, 2014), p. 35.

61. As cited in Berman, "Philadelphia Landscape," p. 33.

62. Ibid.

63. As cited in ibid., p. 35.

64. Charles FitzGerald (unsigned), "Art Notes," *New York Evening Sun*, April 11, 1901, p. 4.

65. Milroy, *Painters of a New Century*, p. 37.

66. As cited in Richard J. Wattenmaker, "The Sketchbook Studies of William Glackens," *Archives of American Art Journal* 44, nos. 1–2 (2004), p. 46.

67. See T. J. Clark, "A Bar at the Folies-Bergère," *The Painting of Modern Life: Paris in the Art of Manet and His Followers* (New York: Alfred A. Knopf, 1985), pp. 205–258.

68. James Huneker, "Eight Painters: Second Article," *New York Sun*, February 10, 1908, p. 6.

69. See, for example, Degas's pastel *At the Milliners* in Chapter 9, Figure 9.9.

70. Degas as cited in Ruth E. Iskin, *Modern Women and Parisian Consumer Culture in Impressionist Painting* (Cambridge: Cambridge University Press, 2007), p. 60.

71. Whitman as cited by Zurier, *Picturing the City*, p. 103.

72. Guy Pène du Bois, "The American Section, the National Art: An Interview with the Chairman of the Domestic Committee Wm. J. Glackens," *Arts and Decoration* 3, no. 5 (March 1913), p. 159.

73. The most complete accounting of the reaction to Manet's painting can be found in the chapter "Olympia's Choice," in Clark, "A Bar at the Folies-Bergère," pp. 79–146.

74. Unnamed critic as cited by Judith Dolkart, "William Glackens: 'Intensely Sincere and Intensely Brave'" in *William Glackens*, ed. Avis Berman (New York: Skira Rizzoli in association with the Barnes Foundation, 2014), p. 133.

75. Henri, "The New York Exhibition of Independent Artists," p. 166.

76. Unnamed critic as cited by Dolkart, "William Glackens," p. 110.

77. Forbes Watson, *William Glackens* (New York: Duffield, The Arts, 1923), p. 21.

78. As cited in Nicholas Wadley, *Renoir: A Retrospective* (Sydney: Bay Books, 1987), p. 263.

79. When Barnes published *The Art of Renoir* in 1935, he sent a copy to Glackens, writing "To Butts, who started my interest in Renoir. Albert C. Barnes." As cited by William Gerdts in *William Glackens*. Text by William H. Gerdts. Essay by Jorge S. Santis (New York: Abbeville, 1996), pp. 96–97.

80. Barnes as cited by Colin B. Bailey, "The Origins of the Barnes Collection, 1912–15," in *The World of William Glackens: The C. Richard Hilker Lectures*, ed. Colin B. Bailey (Bonita Springs, FL: Sansom Foundation, 2011), p. 44.

81. Ira Glackens, *William Glackens and the Eight: The Artists Who Freed American Art*, 2nd ed. (New York: Horizon, 1983), pp. 69–70. For a thorough and insightful essay on Glackens and French art, see Martha Lucy, "Glackens, French Art, and the Language of Modernism," in *William Glackens*, ed. Avis Berman (New York: Skira Rizzoli in association with the Barnes Foundation, 2014), pp. 198–206.

Chapter 12

1. See *Inventing Impressionism: Paul Durand-Ruel and the Modern Art Market*, ed. Sylvie Patry (London: National Gallery), 2015.

2. See E. Durand-Gréville, "La Peinture aux États-Unis: Les Galeries privées (premier article)," *Gazette des Beaux-Arts*, ser. 2, 36 (July 1887), pp. 65–75 ; E. Durand-Gréville, "La Peinture aux États-Unis: Les Galeries privées (deuxième et dernier article)," *Gazette des Beaux-Arts*, ser. 2, 36 (September 1887), pp. 250–255.

3. Roger Fry to John G. Johnson, August 21, 1909, John G. Johnson Correspondence Archives, John G. Johnson Papers, Philadelphia Museum of Art, Archives. Roger Fry will be discussed later in this chapter.

4. On patterns of collecting in America, see René Brimo, *The Evolution of Taste in American Collecting*, trans. and ed. (and with an introduction by) Kenneth Haltman (University Park: Pennsylvania State University Press, 2016).

5. See Jennifer A. Thompson, "Collecting Impressionism and Post-Impressionism in Philadelphia," in *Impressionism and Post-Impressionism: Highlights from the Philadelphia Museum of Art*, ed. Jennifer A. Thompson, with contributions by Joseph J. Rishel and Eileen Owens (Philadelphia: Philadelphia Museum of Art in association with Yale University Press, 2019), pp. 9–25.

6. A. H. Shaw, "De Medici in Merion," *New Yorker* (September 1928), p. 29.

7. See Chapter 11.

8. The firm continues today under the name of Saul Ewing Arnstein and Lehr. Johnson also acted as Henry Havemeyer's attorney and was a trustee of the Metropolitan Museum of Art.

9. Johnson had amassed nearly 1,300 works of art, including more than 150 paintings, textiles and other artifacts. He bequeathed them along with his library of nearly 2,500 books, journals, and auction catalogs to the city of Philadelphia. Johnson's paintings for fifty years were exhibited separately at the Philadelphia Museum of Art as the John G. Johnson Collection. In 1989, Judge Charles Klein ruled that the Johnson holdings could be integrated with the rest of the works at the museum to better integrate them with their period and stylistic cognates in the larger collection. See Jennifer A. Thompson, "The John G. Johnson Collection from 1917 to the Present," in Christopher D. M. Atkins, *The John G. Johnson Collection: A History and Selected Works*, available at https://doi.org/10.29075/9780876332764/1.

10. On the relationship between Barnes and Johnson, see Brian Seymour, *Art Collecting and Shaping Publics around the Turn of the Twentieth Century* (Ph.D. diss., Temple University, 2017).

11. On the history of Barnes's acquisitions, see Anne Distel, "Dr. Barnes in Paris," in *Great French Painting from the Barnes Foundation: From Cézanne to Matisse* (New York: Alfred A. Knopf

in association with Lincoln University Press, Philadelphia Museum of Art Edition, 1995), pp. 29–43.

12. Albert C. Barnes, "The Temple," *Opportunity*, May 1924, p. 139, Barnes Foundation Archives. It was also in Guillaume's art gallery in Paris where Barnes became passionate about African art and began to build a premier collection.

13. Robert Ross, *Morning Post*, November 7, 1910, p. 3, as cited in Frances Spalding, *Roger Fry: Art and Life* (London; Granada, 1980), p. 136.

14. Paul Valéry, "The Problem of Museums" (1925), in *The Collected Works of Paul Valéry*, vol. 12, ed. Jackson Mathews, trans. David Paul (New York: Pantheon, 1960), p. 203.

15. Albert C. Barnes to Arthur C. Carles, April 18, 1921, Arthur B. Carles Papers, Archives of the Pennsylvania Academy of the Fine Arts.

16. Dr. William H. Wadsworth, as cited by Edward J. Sozanski, "Barnes at the Pennsylvania Academy: A Scandal in 1923," *Philadelphia Inquirer*, May 4, 2012.

17. Edith Powell, "Peale Portraits—Ultra Modern French Art," *Public Ledger*, April 15, 1923, p. 11.

18. Barnes as cited by Judith F. Dolkart, "To See as the Artist Sees: Albert C. Barnes and the Experiment in Education," in *The Barnes Foundation Masterworks* (New York: Skira Rizzoli, 2012), p. 21.

19. As discussed in Chapter 10.

20. Neil L. Rudenstein, "Albert Barnes and His Foundation: Three Paradoxes," *Proceedings of the American Philosophical Society* 58, no. 2 (June 2014), p. 127.

21. Barnes as cited by Dolkart, "To See as the Artist Sees," p. 14.

22. As cited in Neil L. Rudenstein, *The House of Barnes: The Man, the Collection, the Controversy* (Philadelphia: American Philosophical Society, 2012), p. 127.

23. Mary Ann Meyers, *Albert Barnes and the Science of Philanthropy* (New Brunswick, NJ: Transaction, 2004), p. 220.

24. Ambroise Vollard, *Souvenirs d'un marchand de tableaux* (Paris: Albin Michel, 1934), p. 413.

25. Henri Matisse from a letter to Simon Bussy, May 17, 1933, as cited in Jack Flam, *Matisse: The Dance* (Washington, DC: National Gallery of Art, 1993), p. 63.

26. Distel, "Dr. Barnes in Paris," p. 43.

27. As cited by Jennifer A. Thompson, "For the Study and Enjoyment of My Fellow Citizens," in *Rodin Museum Philadelphia* (Philadelphia: Philadelphia Museum of Art, 2012), p. 17.

28. See Chapter 10.

29. Paul Claudel as cited in the unsigned article, "Philadelphia Opens New Rodin Museum," *New York Times*, November 30, 1929, p. 18.

30. See Wayne Craven, "The Origins of Sculpture in America: Philadelphia, 1785–1830," *American Art Journal* 9 (November 1977), pp. 4–33.

31. Houdon is discussed in Chapter 3.

32. I thank Laura Turner Igoe for calling this image to my attention.

33. Elizabeth Milroy, *The Grid and the River: Philadelphia's Green Places, 1682–1876* (University Park: Pennsylvania State University Press, 2016), p. 159. The original wood statue deteriorated and in 1874 a bronze cast was made that now resides in the Philadelphia Museum of Art.

34. Thomas Eakins had taken up the subject when he painted *William Rush Carving His Allegorical Figure of the Schuylkill River* as discussed in Chapter 8.

35. Craven, "Origins of Sculpture in America," p. 25.

36. "The statue is an allegorical representation of the Schuylkill River. . . . the wavelets of the wind-sheltered stream are shown in the delicate thin drapery, much after the manner of the French

artists of that day whose influence was powerful in America." Rush as cited in Lloyd Goodrich, *Thomas Eakins*, vol. 1 (Cambridge, MA: Harvard University Press, 1982), p. 146.

37. Glenn F. Benge, *Antoine-Louis Barye, Sculptor of Romantic Realism* (University Park: Pennsylvania State University Press, 1984), pp. 35–37.

38. Théophile Gautier, "Nouvelles statues des Tuileries," *La Presse*, no. 91 (October 11, 1836), n.p.

39. Théophile Gautier, "Barye," *L'Illustration* (May 1, 1866), p. 315.

40. Charles Lenormant, *Les Artistes contemporaines*, vol. 2, *Salon de 1833* (Paris: Alexandre Mesnier, 1833), p. 76.

41. Auguste Jal, *Salon de 1833: Les causeries du Louvre* (Paris: Gosselin, 1833), p. 440.

42. Alfred de Musset, "Salon de 1836," *Revue des deux mondes*, ser. 4, vol. 6 (April 15, 1836), p. 172.

43. Anonymous, as cited in Benge, *Antoine-Louis Barye*, p. 35.

44. Rodin as cited by William R. Johnston, "Introduction," in *Untamed: The Art of Antoine-Louis Barye*, ed. William R. Johnston, Simon Kelly, and Ann Boulton (Baltimore, MD: Walters Art Gallery, 2006), p. viii.

45. Russell Thayer as cited by David in "Joan of Arc" in *Sculpture of a City: Philadelphia's Treasures in Bronze and Stone* (New York: Walker, 1974), p. 128.

46. Samuel Gustine Thompson as cited in Sellin, *Sculpture of a City*.

47. Louis Voission as cited in ibid.

CHAPTER 13

1. Thomas J. Craughwell, *Thomas Jefferson's Crème Brulée: How a Founding Father and His Slave James Hemings Introduced French Cuisine to America* (Philadelphia: Quirk Books, 2012), p. 203. Jefferson, his two daughters, and Sally and James Hemings left Paris on September 26, 1789, but bad weather in Le Havre prevented the party from crossing the English Channel for another ten days. They only boarded their ship to sail across the Atlantic from England on October 22. They arrived in Norfolk, Virginia, on November 23.

2. John B. Boles, *Jefferson: Architect of American Liberty* (New York: Basic Books, 2017), pp. 217–218.

3. Charles A. Cerami, *Dinner at Mr. Jefferson's: Three Men, Five Great Wines, and the Evening That Changed America* (Hoboken, NJ: Wiley, 2008), p. 1.

4. *Thomas Jefferson's Farm Book*, ed. Edwin Morris Betts (Chapel Hill: University of North Carolina Press, 1955; repr., Charlottesville, VA: Thomas Jefferson Memorial Foundation, 1999), pp. 15–16.

5. Craughwell, *Thomas Jefferson's Crème Brulée*, pp. 154–158. See also Lucia C. Stanton, *Free Some Day: The African-American Families of Monticello* (Charlottesville, VA: Thomas Jefferson Memorial Foundation, 2000), p. 17.

6. Boles, *Jefferson*, pp. 329–330. See also Annette Gordon-Reed, *The Hemingses of Monticello* (New York: W. W. Norton, 2008), pp. 544–551.

7. *La Physiologie du Goût* has remained in print ever since its publication in 1825. Even so, not everyone with a reputation for fine French cooking has found the work edifying. One recent critic called it "a book far more talked about than read, even among those who care passionately about the history of French gastronomy. Its greatest champions tend to be toastmasters, or else people who have not read it, or else people who have not read much else on the subject." Justin Spring, *The Gourmand's Way: Six Americans in Paris and the Birth of a New Gastronomy* (New York: Farrar, Straus and Giroux, 2017), p. 76. Julia Child viewed *La Physiologie* as a book "whose sole use is

to furnish windbags with stupid quotations." Julia Child and Avis DeVoto, *As Always, Julia: The Letters of Julia Child and Avis DeVoto*, ed. Joan Reardon (Boston: Houghton Mifflin Harcourt, 2010), pp. 73–74.

8. François Furstenberg, *When the United States Spoke French: Five Refugees Who Shaped a Nation*.

9. Furstenberg, *When the United States Spoke French*, pp. 90–91, 105–107.

10. Ibid., pp. 165–168.

11. After Thomas Jefferson was elected president, he hired Lemaire to assume the same position in the Executive Mansion in Washington. Another Frenchman, Honoré Julien, was his chef de cuisine, making the table in the president's house thoroughly French throughout the Jefferson administration. Boles, *Jefferson*, p. 357.

12. In 1786, William Bingham bought a ten-thousand-acre patent for land in southeastern New York, near the Pennsylvania border. The resulting town at the junction of the Chenango and Susquehanna Rivers was named Binghamton and incorporated in 1834.

13. Born in Boston, Breck was the son of a merchant who had been appointed the fiscal agent for the French forces in America. The elder Breck sent his son to Sorèze, an aristocratic French military school, where Samuel lived for four years, learning French fluently. He settled in Philadelphia at age twenty-one in 1792.

14. *Samuel Breck Papers* (Collection 1887), ser. 1. Diaries, 1800–1862, vol. 3 (Historical Society of Pennsylvania).

15. The Athenaeum mounted an exhibit, "Samuel Breck (1771–1862): Books from the Library of a Philadelphia Francophile," December 7, 2013–March 1, 2014, which was accompanied by the Roger W. Moss Symposium, "La France à Philadelphie," December 7–8, 2013.

16. Patrick Glennon, "Hoist a Brew or Two to William Penn," Historical Society of Pennsylvania, *Philadelphia Inquirer*, January 7, 2018, p. C2.

17. Glennon, "Hoist a Brew or Two to William Penn."

18. Lynn H. Miller and Anette H. Emgarth, *French Philadelphia: The French Cultural and Historical Presence in the Delaware Valley* (Wayne, PA: Beach Lloyd, 2006), p. 81.

19. John M. R. Bull, "Blue Laws Won't Fade Away," *Pittsburgh Post-Gazette*, February 18, 2001, p. B2.

20. From 1933, when the Twenty-First Amendment to the U.S. Constitution repealed the Eighteenth, which prohibited the sale and consumption of alcohol within the United States, the sale of package alcohol in Pennsylvania has remained a monopoly of the state. Many have argued that one result of this ostensible effort by the state to control alcoholic consumption has also restricted choice among consumers, including their access to the variety of wines available to Americans living in other states.

21. After World War II, French cuisine increasingly appealed to wealthy Americans, many of whom traveled to France to take part in the revival of gastrotourism, "the uniquely French practice of combining automobile touring with restaurant-going." Spring, *The Gourmand's Way*, p. 34. As early as 1941, New York's Le Pavillon began to set the standard in America for haute cuisine.

22. John Mariani, "The Best French Restaurant in America," *Esquire* 120, no. 3 (September 2003), p. 62.

23. Available at www.starchefs.com/cook/chefs/bio/georges-perrier. The poll was in 1994.

24. Michael Klein, "King Georges: Story of Perrier and Le Bec-Fin Reaches the Screen," *Philadelphia Inquirer*, March 13, 2015, p. D2.

25. Among Windrim's Philadelphia commissions were the Masonic Temple at Broad and Filbert Streets and the Academy of Natural Sciences on Logan Square. Stephen Girard's Trust

continues to this day to control a considerable amount of real estate in Philadelphia, rents from which still support the operation of Girard College.

26. Maison 208 closed late in 2019 after Senat parted ways with his partners. Starr's restaurant is the highly acclaimed Buddakan. Matt Katz, "New Yorkers Answer Philadelphia's Call," *New York Times*, July 22, 2018, p. MB1.

27. Juliana Feliciano Reyes, "French Pastries by Way of Asia," *Philadelphia Inquirer*, January 18, 2018, pp. D1, D4.

28. Reyes, "French Pastries by Way of Asia," p. D3, and Michael Klein, "Talking about His New Creole-Cajun Restaurant with Sean Nevins," *Philadelphia Inquirer*, January 18, 2018, p. D2.

29. The respective companies are Air Liquide: available at www.airliquide.com; Arkema, available at www.arkema.com/en/; Boiron, available at www.boironusa.com; Sodexo, available at www.sodexo.com. Philadelphia-based Sartomer is part of the Arkema Group.

30. Historical Society of Pennsylvania "Memory Stream," "'Les amis' of Phila. French culture," *Philadelphia Inquirer*, February 8, 2015, p. C2; and communication to the authors from Pierre Ravaçon, April 15, 2018.

31. Available at www.fondation-alliancefr.org. Also in the greater Philadelphia region is the Alliance Française de Doylestown, the county seat of Bucks County.

32. Available at www.afphila.org.

33. Miller and Emgarth, *French Philadelphia*, p. 19. For a review, see Murielle Bourlioux, "Si la Philadelphie française m'était contée . . ." *France-Amérique*, May 13–19, 2006, p. 19.

34. Available at www.faccphila.org.

35. Available at www.faccphila.org.

36. These were, respectively, Barry Callebaut USA, available at www.barry-callebaut.com; Boutique Wine Collection, available at www.boutiquewines.info; and Carré d'Artistes, available at www.carredartistesphilly.com.

37. The new headquarters of Saint-Gobain North America meets the federal standard for energy-efficiency in construction: LEED (Leadership in Energy and Environmental Design). For its 350th anniversary, the company published Marie de Laubier, *Saint-Gobain 1665–2015: The History of the Future*, trans. Lisa Davidson (Paris: Albin Michel, 2015), available at www.saint-gobainnorthamerica.com.

38. Available at http://futuresensations.com/the-exhibition. The exhibition also toured Shanghai, Sao Paolo, and Paris.

39. Saint-Gobain also provided specialty glass for such projects as the World Trade Center, Philadelphia's Kimmel Center, and the pyramid outside Paris's Louvre. Allison Steele, "LOVE Park's welcome site to be dining spot," *Philadelphia Inquirer*, March 14, 2019, pp. B1, B8.

40. Available at www.6abc/com/sports/eagles-create-championship-red-wine-to-celebrate-victory/3449785/.

41. Pétanque players in Philadelphia differ from the usual participants in France, who are typically older working-class men, by including young and old of all races, male and female, professionals as well as students. "West Philly residents, amoureux de pétanque," *Philadelphia City Paper*, posted Wednesday, August 21, 2013 (Lalita Clozel). See also available at www.philadelphiapetanque.com.

42. The name has long been rendered either as "DuPont" or "duPont." The former is the choice of the company bearing that name today, while the latter is still preferred by many of the American descendants, who now number more than a thousand, of the first Pierre Samuel. See Chapter 5.

43. During a televised debate among Republican presidential hopefuls, then vice president George H. W. Bush, who eventually won the nomination, pointedly referred to him throughout

as "Pierre," no doubt to suggest that there was something suspect about du Pont's far-off French antecedents. This Pierre S. du Pont IV is the great-great-great-grandson of Eleuthère Irenée, founder of the chemical conglomerate. *New York Times*, National ed., "The Paradox of Pete du Pont: Political Iconoclast with Establishment Roots," December 28, 1987, p. A18.

44. Jeré Longman, "John E. du Pont, Heir Who Killed an Olympian, Dies at 72," *New York Times*, December 9, 2010, p. A33.

45. Karen Heller, "Anne d'Harnoncourt," *Philadelphia Inquirer*, June 2, 2008, p. B8.

46. "Orchestras Cut Ties with Conductor," *New York Times*, December 23, 2017, p. C2.

47. Laurie Goodstein, "For Philadelphia Archdiocese, a Powerful Conservative Voice," *New York Times*, July 20, 2011, p. A17.

48. It is interesting that what in America and much of the rest of the world is known as Bastille Day is not usually called that in France, perhaps because of too-painful associations with the aftermath of the Bastille's fall. In France, the holiday is typically named either le Quatorze Juillet (July Fourteenth) or la Fête Nationale.

49. Victor Fiorillo, "Diner en Blanc Philly Is Now the Biggest Diner en Blanc in the Country," available at www.phillymag.com/Foobooz/2017/08/16/diner-en-blanc-philadelphia-location-2017.

50. Eastern State Penitentiary had a storied history from its opening in 1830 until it closed in 1970. It became the model for hundreds of other prisons worldwide with its wheel-shaped design and cell blocks radiating out from a central watch tower. After its closure, the prison was threatened with demolition by neglect, but by the early twenty-first century, its structures were being stabilized and it increasingly drew visitors interested in prison history and reform. Available at www.easternstate.org.

Conclusion

1. With the exception that the city's major league hockey team, the Philadelphia Flyers, has always included star players of Quebecois or French heritage. Francophone athletes are members of other professional teams. In 2018, the Cameroonian basketball player, Joel Embiid, star player for the Philadelphia 76ers, was named a starter for the NBA All-Star Game.

2. David McCullough, *John Adams* (New York: Simon and Schuster, 2001), pp. 236–237.

3. Harvey Levenstein, *Seductive Journey: American Tourists in France from Jefferson to the Jazz Age* (Chicago: University of Chicago Press, 2000), p. 4.

4. As Lois Fink has remarked: "Whereas only a couple of hundred Americans had exhibited from 1800 to 1870, more than a thousand took part in the Paris exhibitions from 1872 to 1899." Lois M. Fink, *American Art at the Nineteenth-Century Paris Salons* (Cambridge: Cambridge University Press, 1990), p. 113.

5. Milton Brown, *American Painting from the Armory Show to the Depression* (Princeton, NJ: Princeton University Press, 1955), p. 47.

6. The claim, including the out-of-character assertion, is that of Paul Goldberger in his keynote address "What Does the City Beautiful Mean for the 21st Century?" in the symposium presented by the Athenaeum of Philadelphia and the Philadelphia Museum of Art, Paul Cret and Modernism, May 11–12, 2018; cited hereafter as Symposium.

7. These comparisons between the views of Penn and Cret were made by Goldberger, "City Beautiful for the 21st Century."

8. Marc Vincent, "Between Column and I-Beam: The Architectural Theory of Paul Cret," Symposium. The commission's other members were Daniel Burnham, Charles McKim, Augustus Saint-Gaudens, and Frederick Law Olmsted Jr.

9. Except that the Schuylkill, in particular, had become so badly contaminated by industrial waste in the nineteenth century that it took until the end of the twentieth century for it to be restored to the point that such migratory species as shad would return there to spawn.

10. That was the argument advanced in a conversation between two former partners in the firm, H2L2, which grew out of Cret's practice: Robert P. Breading and Barry Eiswerth, "Longtemps après Cret," Symposium.

11. An article in the *Public Ledger* on November 13, 1930, carried this caption below a photograph of Jacques Gréber, Mayor Mackey, Joseph E. Widener (commission chair), E. T. Stotesbury, and Director Walter H. Thomas of the city Department of Architecture: "Experts Offer 50-Year Plan of Beauty and Utility to City Council." We are indebted to Pierre Ravaçon for the photograph.

12. See Chapter 10, fn. 48, for his war memorials in France.

13. Alisa Chiles, "'Nioc! Nioc-Nioc! (Quack, Quack, Quack)': Paul Philippe Cret, Penn's Poilu-Professor, and World War I," Symposium.

14. Available at www.efiponline.com.

15. Available at www.frenchheritagesociety.org.

16. Murielle Bourlioux, "Si la Philadelphie Française m'était contée . . . , France-Amérique," May 13–19, 2006, p. 19, quoting Consul-General Jean-Pierre Alex-Lyondi, as translated by the authors. For more on Philadelphia's French Quarter, see Chapter 13.

17. "The Case for Philadelphia's Becoming a Full Member of the Organization of World Heritage Cities," Mayor's Office of Immigrant and Multicultural Affairs: Global Philadelphia Project World Heritage City, April 28, 2014.

18. Goldberger, "City Beautiful for the 21st Century," and Chiles, "'Nioc! Nioc-Nioc!'" Symposium.

[Bibliography]

Ackerman, Gerald M. "Gérôme and Manet." *Gazette des Beaux-Arts* 70 (September 1967), pp. 163–176.

———. *The Life and Work of Jean-Louis Gérôme*. London: Sotheby's, 1986.

———. "Thomas Eakins and His Parisian Masters Gérôme and Bonnat." *Gazette des Beaux-Arts* (April 1969), pp. 235–256.

Adams, Henry. *Eakins Revealed: The Secret Life of an American Artist.* New York: Oxford University Press, 2005.

Adams, William Howard. *The Paris Years of Thomas Jefferson.* New Haven, CT: Yale University Press, 1997.

Alberts, Robert C. *The Golden Voyage: The Life and Times of William Bingham 1752–1804.* Boston: Houghton-Mifflin, 1969.

Ammon, Harry. *The Genet Mission.* New York: W. W. Norton, 1971.

Anishanslin, Zara. *Portrait of a Woman in Silk: Hidden Histories of the British Atlantic World.* New Haven, CT: Yale University Press, 2016.

Antiques, The Magazine (March–April 2016).

Armstrong, Carol. *Manet Manette.* New Haven, CT: Yale University Press, 2002.

Arthur B. Carles Papers, Archives of the Pennsylvania Academy of the Fine Arts.

Articles of Association of the Pennsylvania Academy of the Fine Arts, December 26, 1805.

Auricchio, Laura. *The Marquis: Lafayette Reconsidered.* New York: Alfred A. Knopf, 2014.

Bach, Penny Balkin. *Public Art in Philadelphia.* Philadelphia: Temple University Press, 1992.

Baedeker, K. *Paris and Its Environs.* London: Dulau, 1878.

Bailey, Colin B. "The Origins of the Barnes Collection, 1912–15." In *The World of William Glackens: The C. Richard Hilker Art Lectures*, edited by Colin B. Bailey. Bonita Springs, FL: Sansom Foundation, 2011, pp. 41–75.

———. *The World of William Glackens: The C. Richard Hilker Art Lectures.* Bonita Springs, FL: Sansom Foundation, 2011.

Baker, Keith Michael, "On Condorcet's 'Sketch.'" *Daedalus* 133, no. 3 (Summer 2004), pp. 56–64.

Baldensperger, Fernand. *Le mouvement des idées dans l'émigration françaises: 1789–1815*. New York: B. Franklin, 1968.

Barnes, Albert C. "The Temple." *Opportunity*, May 1924. Barnes Foundation Archives.

Barter, Judith A. "Introduction." In *Mary Cassatt: Modern Woman*. Organized by Judith A. Barter with contributions by Erica E. Hirshler, George T. M. Shackelford, Kevin Sharp, Harriet K. Stratis, and Andrew J. Walker. New York: Art Institute of Chicago in association with Harry N. Abrams, 1998, pp. 15–19.

Baudelaire, Charles. *The Painter of Modern Life and Other Essays*. Translated and edited by Jonathan Mayne. New York: Da Capo, 1964.

Bell, David A. "The Many Lives of Liberalism." *New York Review of Books* 66, 1 (January 17, 2019), pp. 24–27.

Bemis, Samuel F. *Jay's Treaty: A Study in Commerce and Diplomacy*. New Haven, CT: Yale University Press, 1962.

Benge, Glenn F. *Antoine-Louis Barye, Sculptor of Romantic Realism*. University Park: Pennsylvania State University, 1984.

Benjamin, Walter. *Selected Writings, Vol. 3, 1935–1938*. Translated by Edmund Jephcott, Howard Eiland et al. Edited by Howard Eiland and Michael W. Jennings. Cambridge, MA: Belknap Press of Harvard University, 2002.

Berg, Scott W. *Grand Avenues: The Story of the French Visionary Who Designed Washington, D.C.* New York: Pantheon Books, 2007.

Bergman, Matthew P. "Montesquieu's Theory of Government and the Framing of the American Constitution." *Pepperdine Law Review* 18, no. 1 (1990), pp. 12–15.

Berkley, Helen. "A Sketch of Joseph Buonaparte." *Godey's Magazine and Lady's Book* (April 1845).

Berman, Avis. "Philadelphia Landscape: William Glackens's Early Years." In *William Glackens*, edited by Avis Berman. New York: Skira Rizzoli in association with the Barnes Foundation, 2014, pp. 28–36.

Bernier, Olivier. *Lafayette: Hero of Two Worlds*. New York: E. P. Dutton, 1983.

Bishop, Morris. "Louis-Philippe in America." *American Heritage* 20, no. 3 (April 1969). Available at www.americanheritage.com/content/louis-philippe-america.

Blanchard, Pierre. *Journal of My Forty-Fifth Ascension* (Philadelphia, 1793). Reprint, Philadelphia: Penn Mutual Life Insurance, 1943.

Blumenthal, Henry. *American and French Culture, 1800–1900: Interchanges in Art, Science, Literature, and Society*. Baton Rouge: Louisiana State University Press, 1975.

Boggs, Jean Sutherland, Douglas W. Druick, Henri Loyrette, Michael Pantazzi, and Gary Tinterow. *Degas*. New York: Metropolitan Museum of Art, 1988.

Bohan, Ruth L. "Robert Henri, Walt Whitman, and the American Artist." *Walt Whitman Quarterly Review* 29, no. 4 (Spring 2012), pp. 131–151.

Boles, John B. *American Enigma: Jefferson, Architect of American Liberty*. New York: Basic Books, 2017.

Borkson, Joseph L. *Philadelphia: An American Paris*. Philadelphia: Camino Books, 2001.

Bourdieu, Pierre. *Manet: Une Révolution symbolique*. Paris: Seuil, 2013.

Bowling, Kenneth R. *Creating the Federal City, 1784–1800*. Washington, DC: American Institute of Architects, 1988.

Boyd, Julian et al., eds. *The Papers of Thomas Jefferson*. Princeton, NJ: Princeton University Press, 1958.

Boyer, Abel. *The Royal Dictionary, French and English, and English and French*. London: J. and J. Knapton, 1729.

Braddock, Alan C. *Thomas Eakins and the Cultures of Modernity*. Berkeley: University of California Press, 2009.

Brands, H. W. *The First American: The Life and Times of Benjamin Franklin*. New York: Doubleday, 2000.

Branson, Susan. *These Fiery, Frenchified Dames: Women and Political Culture in Early National Philadelphia*. Philadelphia: University of Pennsylvania Press, 2001.

Breeskin, Adelyn D. "Introduction" to *Mary Cassatt: 1844–1926*. Washington, DC: National Gallery of Art, 1970, pp. 11–18.

Brettell, Richard R. *Pissarro and Pontoise: The Painter in a Landscape*. New Haven, CT: Yale University Press, 1990.

———. "Thomas Eakins and the Male Nude in French Vanguard Painting, 1850–1890." In *Thomas Eakins and the Swimming Picture*, edited by Doreen Bolger and Sarah Cash. Fort Worth, TX: Amon Carter Museum, 1996, pp. 80–97.

Brettell, Richard R., and Joachim Pissarro. *The Impressionist and the City*. New Haven, CT: Yale University Press, 1992.

Brigham, David R. "'Ask the Beasts, and They Shall Teach Thee': The Human Lessons of Charles Willson Peale's Natural History Displays." *Huntington Library Quarterly* 59, nos. 2–3 (1996), pp. 182–206.

———. *Public Culture in the Early Republic: Peale's Museum and Its Audience*. Washington, DC, Smithsonian Institution, 1995.

Bronner, Edwin B. *William Penn's "Holy Experiment": The Founding of Pennsylvania, 1681–1701*. New York: Columbia University Press, 1962.

Brooks, George S. *Friend Anthony Benezet*. Philadelphia: University of Pennsylvania Press, 1937.

Brown, Milton. *American Painting from the Armory Show to the Depression*. Princeton, NJ: Princeton University Press, 1955.

Brownlee, David B. *Building the City Beautiful: The Benjamin Franklin Parkway and the Philadelphia Museum of Art*. 2nd. ed. Philadelphia: Philadelphia Museum of Art, 2017.

———. *Making a Modern Classic*. Philadelphia: Philadelphia Museum of Art, 1997.

Bruns, Roger A. "Anthony Benezet and the Natural Rights of the Negro." *Pennsylvania Magazine of History and Biography*. Philadelphia: Historical Society of Pennsylvania, January 1972.

Burty, Philippe. "Exposition des œuvres des artistes indépendants." *La République Française* (10 Avril, 1880).

Carr, William H. A. *The du Ponts of Delaware*. New York: Dodd, Mead, 1964.

Carson, Gerald. *The Dentist and the Empress: The Adventures of Dr. Tom Evans in Gas-Lit Paris*. Boston: Houghton Mifflin, 1983.

Central Philadelphia Development Corporation. *Completing the Benjamin Franklin Parkway*. Philadelphia, 1999.

Central Philadelphia Development Corporation and the Center City District. "Center City Report: The Benjamin Franklin Parkway, 2001–2005, Recent Accomplishments, New Opportunities." Philadelphia, PA, 2006.

Cerami, Charles A. *Dinner at Mr. Jefferson's: Three Men, Five Great Wines, and the Evening That Changed America*. Hoboken, NJ: Wiley, 2008.

Chastellux, Marquis de. *Travels in North America in the Years 1780, 1781 and 1782*. Revised translation by Howard C. Rice, Jr., 2 vols. Published for the Institute of Early American History and Culture at Williamsburg, VA. Chapel Hill: University of North Carolina Press, 1963.

Chew, William L., III. "The Easel and the Eagle: Rembrandt Peale Views Napoleonic France." Available at www.napoleonicsociety.com/english/pdf/j5chew.

Childs, Frances Sergeant. *French Refugee Life in the United States, 1790–1800: An American Chapter of the French Revolution*. Baltimore: Johns Hopkins Press, 1940.

Clark, T. Wood. *Emigrés in the Wilderness*. New York: Macmillan, 1941.

Clary, David. *Adopted Son: Washington, Lafayette, and the Friendship That Saved the Revolution*. New York: Bantam Books, 2007.

Cooper, Duff. *Talleyrand*. 1932. Reprint, New York: Grove, 2001.

Cooper, Helen A., Martin A. Berger, Christina Currie, Amy Beth Werbel. *Thomas Eakins: The Rowing Pictures*. New Haven, CT: Yale University Press, 1996.

Cooper, James Fenimore. *Notions of the Americans: Picked Up by a Traveling Bachelor*. Introduction by Robert E. Spiller. New York: Frederick Ungar, 1963.

Craughwell, Thomas J. *Thomas Jefferson's Crème Brulée: How a Founding Father and His Slave James Hemings Introduced French Cuisine to America*. Philadelphia: Quirk Books, 2012.

Craven, Wayne. "The Grand Manner in Early Nineteenth Century American Painting: Borrowings from Antiquity, the Renaissance, and the Baroque." *American Art Journal* 11 (April 1979), pp. 4–43.

———. "The Origins of Sculpture in America: Philadelphia, 1785–1830." *American Art Journal* 9 (November 1977), pp. 4–33.

Cret, Paul-Philippe. *Current Biography, 1942*. New York: H. W. Wilson, 1942.

d'Harnoncourt, Anne. "Preface" to Suzanne G. Lindsay, *Mary Cassatt and Philadelphia*. Philadelphia: Philadelphia Museum of Art, 1985, p. 7.

Dickson, Harold Edward, ed. *Observations on American Art: Selections from the Writings of John Neal (1793–1876)*. State College: Pennsylvania State College, 1943.

Diethorn, Karie. "'Good and Faithful Paintings': Charles Willson Peale's Philadelphia Museum Portraits in Doris Devine Fanelli." *History of the Portrait Collection, Independence National Park*. Philadelphia: American Philosophical Society, 2001, pp. 67–70.

Distel, Anne. "Dr. Barnes in Paris." In *Great French Painting from the Barnes Foundation: From Cézanne to Matisse*. New York: Alfred A. Knopf in association with Lincoln University Press, Philadelphia Museum of Art Edition, 1995, pp. 29–43.

Dolkart, Judith F. "To See as the Artist Sees: Albert C. Barnes and the Experiment in Education." In *The Barnes Foundation Masterworks*. New York: Skira Rizzoli, 2012, pp. 9–29.

———. "William Glackens: 'Intensely Sincere and Intensely Brave.'" In *William Glackens*, edited by Avis Berman. New York: Skira Rizzoli in association with the Barnes Foundation, 2014, pp. 128–134.

Donzelli, Xavier. "Philadelphie, Berceau des Etats-Unis." *Historia*, no. 37 (September–October 2017), pp. 90–103.

Duke, Marc. *The du Ponts, Portrait* of *a Dynasty*. New York: Doubleday, 1979.

Dull, Jonathan R. *A Diplomatic History of the American Revolution*. New Haven, CT: Yale University Press, 1987.

du Pont de Nemours, E. I. *Autobiography of an American Enterprise*. Wilmington, DE: du Pont, 1952.

du Pont de Nemours, P. S. "Lettre sur la Salon de 1779." *Archives de l'Art Français*, 1908.

Durand-Gréville, E. "La Peinture aux États-Unis: Les Galeries privées (premier article)." *Gazette des Beaux-Arts*, ser. 2, 36 (July 1887), pp. 65–75.

———. "La Peinture aux États-Unis: Les Galeries privées (deuxième et dernier article)." *Gazette des Beaux-Arts*, ser. 2, 36 (September 1887), pp. 250–255.

Durant, Will, and Ariel Durant. *The Story of Civilization*. New York: Simon and Schuster, vol. 9: *The Age of Voltaire*, 1965; vol. 10: *Rousseau and Revolution*, 1967.

Duvergier de Hauranne, Ernest. "Salon de 1874." *Revue des Deux Mondes* 3 (1874), pp. 651–699.

Earle, John J., III. "Talleyrand in Philadelphia, 1794–96." *Pennsylvania Magazine of History and Biography* (July 1967), pp. 282–298.

Edelstein, Dan. *On the Spirit of Rights*. Chicago: University of Chicago Press, 2018.

Ellis, Joseph J. *Founding Brothers: The Revolutionary Generation.* New York: Alfred A. Knopf, 2000.
———. *The Quartet: Orchestrating the Second American Revolution, 1783–1789.* New York: Alfred A. Knopf, 2015.
Epstein, Joseph. *Alexis de Tocqueville: Democracy's Guide.* New York: Harper Collins, Atlas Books, 2006.
Fairbrother, Trevor. "Thomas Eakins, Philadelphia, Paris and New York." *Burlington Magazine,* 144, no. 1188 (March 2002): 191–193.
Fairmount Park Art Association. *The Fairmount Parkway.* Philadelphia, 1919.
———. *Sculpture of a City: Philadelphia's Treasures in Bronze and Stone.* New York: Walker, 1974.
Fanelli, Doris Devine. *History of the Portrait Collection, Independence National Park.* Philadelphia: American Philosophical Society, 2001.
Fink, Lois Marie. *American Art at the Nineteenth-Century Paris Salons.* Cambridge: Cambridge University Press, 1990.
———. "Rembrandt Peale in Paris." *Pennsylvania Magazine of History and Biography* 110, no. 1 (January 1986), pp. 71–90.
FitzGerald, Charles. "Art Notes." *New York Evening Sun,* April 11, 1901.
Flam, Jack. *Matisse: The Dance.* Washington, DC: National Gallery of Art, 1993.
Fleming, Thomas. *Intimate Lives of the Founding Fathers.* New York: Harper Collins, 2010.
———. *The Louisiana Purchase.* New York: Johns Wiley and Sons, 2003.
Folk, Thomas C. *The Pennsylvania Impressionists.* Madison, NJ: Fairleigh Dickinson University Press, 1997.
———. *The Pennsylvania School of Landscape Painting. An Original American Impressionism.* Allentown, PA: Allentown Art Museum, 1984.
———. *Walter Elmer Schofield: Bold Impressionist.* Chadds Ford, PA: Brandywine River Museum, 1983.
Forbes-Robertson, Diana. "Asylum in Azilum." *American Heritage* 27, no. 3 (1976), pp. 43–49.
Fortune, Brandon Brame. "Charles Willson Peale's Portrait Gallery: Persuasion and Plain Style." *Word and Image* 6, no. 4 (October–December 1990), pp. 308–324.
———. *Portraits of Virtue and Genius: Pantheons of Worthies and Public Portraiture in the Early American Republic, 1780–1820.* Ph.D. diss., University of North Carolina, Chapel Hill, 1986.
Foster, Kathleen A. "The Art of Daniel Garber." In *Daniel Garber: Romantic Realist,* edited by Lance Humphries. Philadelphia: Pennsylvania Academy of the Fine Arts and Doylestown, PA: James A. Michener Art Museum, 2007, pp. 12–21.
———. *Daniel Garber, 1880–1958.* Philadelphia: Pennsylvania Academy of the Fine Arts, 1980.
———. "Daniel Garber's Trees." *Kresge Art Museum Bulletin* 8 (1999), pp. 12–19.
———. "Eakins and the Academy." In Sewell, *Thomas Eakins,* pp. 95–106.
———. "*The Gross Clinic* in Philadelphia and New York, 1875–79." In *An Eakins Masterpiece Restored: Seeing* The Gross Clinic *Anew,* edited by Kathleen A. Foster and Mark S. Tucker. New Haven, CT: Philadelphia Museum of Art in association with Yale University Press, 2012, pp. 71–82.
———. "A Portrait of Ambition: Eakins, *The Gross Clinic,* and the American Centennial." In *An Eakins Masterpiece Restored: Seeing* The Gross Clinic *Anew,* edited by Kathleen A. Foster and Mark S. Tucker. New Haven, CT: Philadelphia Museum of Art in association with Yale University Press, 2012, pp. 35–42.
———. *Thomas Eakins Rediscovered: Charles Bregler's Thomas Eakins Collection at the Pennsylvania Academy of the Fine Arts.* New Haven, CT: Yale University Press, 1997.
Foster, Kathleen, and Cheryl Liebold. *Writing about Eakins: Manuscripts in Charles Bregler's Thomas Eakins Collection.* Philadelphia: University of Pennsylvania Press, 1989.

Founders Online. National Archives. Last modified March 30, 2017. Available at http://founder.archives.gov/documents/Jefferson.

Frey, Carroll. *The First Air Voyage in America*. Philadelphia: Penn Mutual Life Insurance, 1943.

Furstenberg, François. *When the United States Spoke French: Five Refugees Who Shaped a Nation*. New York: Penguin, 2014.

Gaines, James R. *For Liberty and Glory: Washington, Lafayette and Their Revolutions*. New York: W. W. Norton, 2007.

Gallery, John Andrew. *Philadelphia Architecture: A Guide to the City*, 3rd ed. Philadelphia: Paul Dry Books, for the Center for Architecture, 2009.

———. *The Planning of Center City Philadelphia: From William Penn to the Present*. Philadelphia: Center for Architecture, 2007.

Gargan, Edward T. *De Tocqueville*. London: Bowes and Bowes, 1965.

Gascoigne, Laura. "A School of Her Own." *Apollo* 187 (May 2018), 100–101.

Gautier, Théophile. "Barye." *L'Illustration* (May 1, 1866).

———. "Nouvelles statues des Tuileries." *La Presse*, no. 91 (October 11, 1836).

George, Christopher P. *Terror on the Chesapeake: The War of 1812 on the Bay*. Stroudsburg, PA: White Mane Books, 2000.

Gerdts, William H. *American Impressionism*. New York: Abbeville, 2001.

———. *William Glackens*. New York: Abbeville, 1996.

Glackens, Ira. *William Glackens and the Eight. The Artists Who Freed American Art*. 2nd ed. New York: Horizon, 1983.

Goodrich, Lloyd. *Thomas Eakins*, 2 vols. Cambridge: Harvard University Press, 1982.

———. "What Is American about American Art?" *Art in America* 51 (August 1963), pp. 24–39.

Gordon, Susan. *Montesquieu: The French Philosopher Who Shaped Modern Government*. New York: Rosen, 2006.

Gordon-Reed, Annette. *The Hemingses of Monticello: An American Family*. New York: W. W. Norton, 2008.

Gordon-Reed, Annette, and Peter S. Onuf. *Most Blessed of the Patriarchs: Thomas Jefferson and the Empire of the Imagination*. New York: Liveright, 2016.

Gréber, Jacques. *L'architecture aux Etats-Unis*, 2 vols. Paris: Pay, 1920.

Gross, Samuel D., MD. *A Sketch of the Life, Character, and Services of Ambrose Paré*. Philadelphia: J. B. Lippincott, 1861.

———. *Autobiography*, 2 vols. Philadelphia: George Barrie, 1887.

Hamilton, George Heard. *Manet and His Critics*. New Haven, CT: Yale University Press, 1954.

Hamon, Joseph. *Le chevalier de Bonvouloir*. Paris: Jouve, 1953.

Hart, Charles Henry, and Edward Biddle. *Memoirs of the Life and Works of Jean-Antoine Houdon*. Philadelphia: Printed for the Authors, 1991.

Hayes, Margaret Calder. *Three Alexander Calders*. Middlebury, VT: P. S. Erikkson, 1977.

Hendricks, Gordon. *The Life and Work of Thomas Eakins*. New York: Grossman, 1974.

Henri, Robert. *The Art Spirit*. Philadelphia: J. B. Lippincott, 1960.

———. "The New York Exhibition of Independent Artists." *Craftsman* 18 (May 1910), pp. 160–172.

Herding, Klaus. *Courbet: To Venture Independence*. Translated by John William Gabriel. New Haven, CT: Yale University Press, 1991.

Herrick, Cheesman A. *Stephen Girard, Founder, Girard College*. Philadelphia: Set up and printed in the Trade School, 1923.

Hevner, Carol Eaton. "The Portraiture of Rembrandt Peale: Artistic Aspirations and Stylistic Changes." In *Rembrandt Peale 1778–1860: A Life in the Arts*. Philadelphia: Historical Society of Philadelphia, 1985, pp. 20–27.

Hill, David Jayne. "A Missing Chapter of Franco-American History." *American Historical Review* 21, no. 4 (July 1916), p. 713.

Hinton, Jack, Melissa Meighan, and Andrew Lins. *Encountering Genius: Houdon's Portraits of Benjamin Franklin*. Philadelphia Museum of Art in association with Yale University Press, 2011.

Hirshler, Erica E. "At Home in Paris." In *Americans in Paris 1860–1900*, edited by Kathleen Adler, Erica E. Hirshler, and H. Barbara Weinberg. London: National Gallery, 2006.

———. "Helping 'Fine Things across the Atlantic': Mary Cassatt and Art Collecting in the United States." In Barter, *Mary Cassatt: Modern Woman*, pp. 177–211.

Homer, William Innes, ed. *The Paris Letters of Thomas Eakins*. Princeton, NJ: Princeton University Press, 2009.

———. *Robert Henri and His Circle*. New York: Hacker Art Books, 1988.

———. *Thomas Eakins: His Life and Art*. New York: Abbeville, 2002.

Humphries, Lance. *Daniel Garber: Romantic Realist*. Philadelphia: Pennsylvania Academy of the Fine Arts and Doylestown, PA: James A. Michener Art Museum, 2007.

Huneker, James. "Eight Painters. Second Article." *New York Sun*, February 10, 1908, p. 6.

Hutton, John. "Picking Fruit: Mary Cassatt's 'Modern Woman' and the Woman's Building of 1893." *Feminist Studies* 20 (Summer 1994), pp. 318–348.

Iskin, Ruth E. *Modern Women and Parisian Consumer Culture in Impressionist Painting*. Cambridge: Cambridge University Press, 2007.

Ivinski, Pamela A. "'So Firm and Powerful a Hand': Mary Cassatt's Techniques and Questions of Gender." In *Women Impressionists*, edited by Ingrid Pfeiffer and Max Hollein. Ostfilder: Hatje Cantz, 2008, pp. 178–187.

Jackson, Maurice. *Let This Voice Be Heard: Anthony Benezet, Father of American Abolitionism*. Philadelphia: University of Pennsylvania Press, 2009.

Jal, Auguste. *Salon de 1833: Les causeries du Louvre*. Paris: Gosselin, 1833.

John G. Johnson Correspondence Archives, John G. Johnson Papers, Philadelphia Museum of Art, Archives.

Johns, Elizabeth. *Thomas Eakins: The Heroism of Modern Life*. Princeton, NJ: Princeton University Press, 1983.

John Sloan/Robert Henri: Their Philadelphia Years, 1886–1904. Philadelphia: Moore College of Art Gallery, 1976.

Johnston, William R. "Introduction." In William R. Johnston, Simon Kelly, and Ann Boulton. *Untamed: The Art of Antoine-Louis Barye*. Baltimore: Walters Art Gallery, 2006, pp. viii–xiii.

Jones, Howard Mumford. *America and French Culture*. Chapel Hill: University of North Carolina Press, 1927.

Katz, Ron. *French America*. French Heritage Society, EDM, 2001.

Keck, Gayle. "The Other Bonaparte." *American Archaeology* (Winter 2018–2019), pp. 27–32.

Kennedy, Roger G. *Orders from France: The Americans and the French in a Revolutionary World, 1780–1820*. New York: Alfred A. Knopf, 1989.

Kimmerle, Constance. *Edward W. Redfield: Just Values and Fine Seeing*. Philadelphia: University of Pennsylvania Press, 2004.

Kirkpatrick, Sidney D. *The Revenge of Thomas Eakins*. New Haven, CT: Yale University Press, 2006.

Klamkin, Marian. *The Return of Lafayette, 1824–1825*. New York: Charles Scribner's Sons, 1975.

Klein, William M., Jr. *Gardens of Philadelphia and the Delaware Valley*. Philadelphia: Temple University Press, 1975.

Kramer, Lloyd. "America's Lafayette and Lafayette's America: A European and American Revolution." *William and Mary Quarterly* (1981), pp. 228–241.

———. *Lafayette in Two Worlds: Public Cultures and Personal Identities in an Age of Revolutions.* Chapel Hill: University of North Carolina Press, 1996.

Lafenestre, Georges. "Les Expositions d'art." *Revue des Deux Mondes* (May–June 1879).

Lamberti, Jean-Claude. *Tocqueville and the Two Democracies,* translated by Arthur Goldhammer. Cambridge, MA: Harvard University Press, 1989.

Larkin, Todd Lawrence. "A 'Gift' Strategically Solicited and Magnanimously Conferred: The American Congress, the French Monarchy, and the State Portraits of Louis XVI and Marie-Antoinette." *Winterthur Portfolio* 44, no. 1 (Spring 2010), pp. 31–76.

Laverty, Bruce, Michael J. Lewis, and Michelle Taillon Taylor. *Monument to Philanthropy: The Design and Building of Girard College, 1832–1848.* Philadelphia: Girard College, 1998.

Leeds, Valerie Ann. *My People: The Portraits of Robert Henri.* Orlando, FL: Orlando Museum of Art, 1994.

Leepson, Marc. *Lafayette: Lessons in Leadership from the Idealist General.* New York: Palgrave Macmillan, 2011.

LeFêvre, Georges. *The Coming of the French Revolution.* Princeton, NJ: Princeton University Press, 2005.

Lenormant, Charles. *Les Artistes contemporaines, 2. Salon de 1833.* Paris: Alexandre Mesnier, 1833.

Leroy, Louis. "L'Exposition des impressionnistes." *Le Charivari* (April 25, 1874).

Lester, Charles E. *The Artists of America: A Series of Biographical Sketches of American Artists; with Portraits and Designs on Steel.* New York: Baker and Scribner, 1846.

Lester, William R. "Henry O. Tanner: Exile for Art's Sake." *Alexander's Magazine* 7 (December 15, 1908).

Levasseur, Auguste. *Lafayette in America, 1824–1825: Journal of a Voyage to the United States,* translated by Alan R. Hoffmann. Manchester, NH: Lafayette, 2007.

Levenstein, Harvey. *Seductive Journey: American Tourists in France from Jefferson to the Jazz Age.* Chicago: University of Chicago Press, 2000.

Levine, Steven Z. "Courbet, Bronzino, and Blasphemy." *New Literary History* 22 (1991), pp. 677–714.

Lewis, James E., Jr. *The Louisiana Purchase: Jefferson's Noble Bargain?* Chapel Hill: University of North Carolina Press, 2003.

Lindsay, Suzanne G. *Mary Cassatt and Philadelphia.* Philadelphia: Philadelphia Museum of Art, 1985.

Lopez, Claude-Anne. *Mon Cher Papa: Franklin and the Ladies of Paris.* New Haven, CT: Yale University Press, 1966.

Lucy, Martha. "Glackens, French Art, and the Language of Modernism." In *William Glackens,* edited by Avis Berman. New York: Skira Rizzoli in association with the Barnes Foundation, 2014, pp. 198–206.

Lutz, Donald S. "Franklin, Lafayette, and *The Lafayette.*" *Proceedings of the American Philosophical Society* 108, no. 3 (1964), pp. 181–223.

———. "The Relative Influence of European Writers on Late Eighteenth-Century American Political Thought." *American Political Science Review* 78, no. 1 (1984), pp. 189–197.

Martinez, Katharine, Page Talbott, and Elizabeth Johns. *Philadelphia's Cultural Landscape: The Sartain Family Legacy.* Philadelphia: Temple University Press, 2000.

Mathews, Nancy Mowll. *Cassatt and Her Circle: Selected Letters.* New York; Abbeville, 1984.

———. *Mary Cassatt.* New York: Harry N. Abrams, in association with the National Museum of American Art, Smithsonian Institution, 1987.

———. *Mary Cassatt: A Life.* New Haven, CT: Yale University Press, 1994.

Mayer, J. P. *Alexis de Tocqueville: A Biographical Essay in Political Science*, translated by M. M. Bozman and C. Hahn. New York: Viking, 1940.

———, ed. *Alexis de Tocqueville: Journey to America*. New Haven, CT: Yale University Press, 1960.

McCartney, Clarence Edward, and Gordon Dorrance. *The Bonapartes in America*. Philadelphia: Dorrance, 1939.

McCauley, Elizabeth Ann. "Sex and the Salon: Defining Art and Immorality in 1863." In *Manet's 'Le Déjeuner sur l'herbe,'* edited by Paul Hayes Tucker. New York: Cambridge University Press, 1998, pp. 38–74.

McClelland, James, and Lynn Miller. *City in a Park: A History of Philadelphia's Fairmount Park System*. Philadelphia: Temple University Press, 2016.

McCormick, W. B. "Art Notes of the Week." *New York Press*, February 9, 1908.

McCullough, David. *John Adams*. New York: Simon and Schuster, 2001.

McMaster, John Bach. *The Life and Times of Stephen Girard: Mariner and Merchant*, 2 vols. Philadelphia: J. B. Lippincott, 1918.

Meyers, Mary Ann. *Art, Education, and African-American Culture: Albert Barnes and the Science of Philanthropy*. New Brunswick, NJ: Transaction, 2004.

Miller, James. *Can Democracy Work? A Short History of a Radical Idea, from Ancient Athens to Our World*. New York: Farrar, Straus and Giroux, 2018.

Miller, Lillian B. "Charles Willson Peale as History Painter." In *New Perspectives on Charles Willson Peale*, edited by Lillian B. Miller and David C. Ward. Published for the Smithsonian Institution by the University of Pittsburgh Press, 1991, pp. 145–165.

———. *In Pursuit of Fame: Rembrandt Peale 1778–1860*. Washington, DC: National Portrait Gallery, Smithsonian Institution in association with the University of Washington Press, Seattle, 1992.

———. "Rembrandt Peale: The Career of an American Master." In *Rembrandt Peale 1778–1860: A Life in the Arts*. Philadelphia: Historical Society of Philadelphia, 1985, pp. 12–19.

Miller, Lillian B., Sidney Hart, and David C. Ward, eds. *The Selected Papers of Charles Willson Peale and His Family*, vol. 2. *Charles Willson Peale: The Artist in His Museum, 1791–1810*. New Haven, CT: Yale University Press, 1988.

Milley, John C. "Introduction" to Doris Devine Fanelli, *History of the Portrait Collection, Independence National Park*. Philadelphia: American Philosophical Society, 2001, pp. 3–12.

Milroy, Elizabeth. "'*Consummatum est*. . .': A Reassessment of Thomas Eakins's *Crucifixion* of 1880." *Art Bulletin* 71, no. 2 (June 1989), pp. 269–284.

———. *The Grid and the River: Philadelphia's Green Places, 1682–1876*. University Park: Pennsylvania State University Press, 2016.

———. *Painters of a New Century: The Eight and American Art*. Milwaukee: University of Wisconsin Press, 1991.

———. *Thomas Eakins' Artistic Training 1860–1870*. Ph.D. diss., University of Pennsylvania, 1986.

Mirbeau, Octave. "Le Salon V." *L'Ordre de Paris* (May 12, 1874).

Mires, Charlene. *Independence Hall in American History*. Philadelphia: University of Pennsylvania Press, 2015.

Moffett, Charles S., Eliza A. Rathbone, Katherine Rothkopf, and Joel Isaacson. *The New Painting, Impressionism, 1874–1886*. Seattle: University of Washington Press, 1986.

Moreau de Saint-Méry, Médéric-Louis-Elie. *Moreau de St-Méry's American Journey 1793–1798*. Translated and edited by Kenneth Roberts and Anna M. Roberts. Garden City, NY: Doubleday, 1947. French-language version, *Voyage aux Etats-Unis d'Amérique 1792–1798*. New Haven, CT: Yale University Press, 1913.

Mosby, Dewey F. “Paris, Racial Awareness and Success 1891–1897.” In *Henry Ossawa Tanner*, catalog by Dewey F. Mosby and Darrel Sewell; introductory essay by Dewey F. Mosby; biographical essay by Rae Alexander Minter. Philadelphia: Philadelphia Museum of Art; New York: Rizzoli International, 1991, pp. 86–97.

Musset, Alfred de. “Salon de 1836,” *Revue des deux mondes*, ser. 4, 6 (April 15, 1836), pp. 144–176.

Nash, Gary B. *First City: Philadelphia and the Forging of Historical Memory*. Philadelphia: University of Pennsylvania Press, 2001.

———. *Forging Freedom: The Formation of Philadelphia's Black Community, 1720–1840*. Cambridge: Harvard University Press, 1988.

Neal, John. *Observations on America Art: Selections from the Writings of John Neal (1793–1876)*. Edited by Harold Edward Dickson. State College: Pennsylvania State College, 1943.

Newbold, David M. *Talleyrand in Philadelphia*. Philadelphia: Philadelphia Forum, 1947.

New Painting, Impressionism, 1874–1886: An Exhibition, The. Directed and coordinated by Charles S. Moffett with the assistance of Ruth Berson, Barbara Lee Williams, and Fronia E. Wissman. San Francisco: Fine Arts Museum, 1986.

O'Brien, Conor Cruise. *The Long Affair: Thomas Jefferson and the French Revolution, 1785–1800*. Chicago: University of Chicago Press, 1996.

Oedel, William T. “After Paris: Rembrandt Peale's Apollodorian Gallery.” *Winterthur Portfolio* 27, no. 1 (Spring 1992): 1–27.

———. “John Vanderlyn: French Neoclassicism and the Search for an American Art.” Ph.D. diss., University of Delaware, 1981.

“Original Letters from Paris, Addressed by Rembrandt Peale to C. W. Peale, and Rubens Peale,” *Port Folio*, n.s. 4, no. 3 (September 1810), pp. 278–279.

Peale, Rembrandt. “Reminiscences.” *The Crayon* 1, no. 2 (January 10, 1855), pp. 22–23.

———. “Travels in France—for the Port Folio.” *Port Folio* 3 (February 1810), pp. 86–101.

Peck, Robert McCracken, and Patricia Stroud. *A Glorious Enterprise: The Academy of Natural Sciences of Philadelphia and the Making of American Science*. Philadelphia: University of Pennsylvania Press, 2012.

Pène du Bois, Guy. “The American Section, The National Art: An interview with the Chairman of the Domestic Committee Wm. J. Glackens.” *Arts and Decoration* 3, no. 5 (March 1913).

———. “The Pennsylvania Group of Landscape Painters.” *Arts and Decoration* 5, no. 9 (July 1915), pp. 351–354.

Perl, Jed. *Calder: The Conquest of Time—The Early Years, 1898–1940*. New York: Alfred A. Knopf, 2017.

Perlman, Bennard B. *Robert Henri: His Life and Art*. New York: Dover, 1991.

Plank, Geoffrey. *An Unsettled Conquest: The British Campaign against the Peoples of Acadia*. Philadelphia: University of Pennsylvania Press, 2003.

Pollock, Griselda. *Mary Cassatt*. New York: Harper and Row, 1980.

Poniatowski, Michel. *Talleyrand-Périgord, 1789–1799*. Paris: Délégation a l'Action Artistique de la Ville de Paris, n.d.

Poulet, Anne L. *Jean-Antoine Houdon. Sculptor of the Enlightenment*. Washington, DC: National Gallery of Art with the University of Chicago Press, 2003.

Powell, Edith. “Peale Portraits—Ultra Modern French Art.” *Public Ledger*, April 15, 1923.

Proceedings of the Board of Aldermen of the City of New York 68. New York: Charles W. Baker, Printer, 1860.

R., G. R. “French Fine Art at the Late Paris International Exhibition.” *Magazine of Art* 2 (1878–1879), p. 15.

Read, Helen Appleton. *Robert Henri*. New York: Whitney Museum of American Art, 1931.

Reason, Akela. *Thomas Eakins and the Uses of History*. Philadelphia: University of Pennsylvania Press, 2010.

Repplier, Agnès. *Philadelphia: The Place and the People*. New York: Macmillan, 1899.

Roosevelt, Theodore. "A Layman's View of an Art Exhibition." *The Outlook* 103 (March 29, 1913).

Rosenblatt, Helena. *The Lost History of Liberalism: From Ancient Rome to the Twenty-First Century*. Princeton, NJ: Princeton University Press, 2018.

Rothkopf, Katherine. *Impressionists in Winter: Effets de Neige*. London: Philip Wilson, 1998.

Rudenstine, Neil L. "Albert Barnes and His Foundation: Three Paradoxes." *Proceedings of the American Philosophical Society* 58, no. 2 (June 2014), pp. 120–127.

———. *The House of Barnes: The Man, the Collection, the Controversy*. Philadelphia, PA: American Philosophical Society, 2012.

Savage, Henry, Jr. *Discovering America, 1785–1875*. New York: Harper and Row, 1959.

Savage, Henry, Jr., and Elizabeth J. Savage. *André and François André Michaux*. Charlottesville: University Press of Virginia, 1986.

Scherf, Guilhelm. "Houdon, 'Above All Modern Artists.'" In *Jean-Antoine Houdon: Sculptor of the Enlightenment*, edited by Anne L. Poulet. Washington: National Gallery of Art with the University of Chicago Press, 2003, pp. 17–26.

Schiff, Stacy. *A Great Improvisation: Franklin, France, and the Birth of America*. New York: Henry Holt, 2005.

Schofield, Norman, "The Intellectual Contribution of Condorcet to the Founding of the US Republic, 1785–1800." *Social Choice Welfare* 25 (2005), pp. 303–318.

Segard, Achille. *Mary Cassatt: Un Peintre des enfants et des mères*. Paris: Librairie Paul Ollendorff, 1913.

Selected Papers of Charles Willson Peale and His Family, The. 4 vols., edited by Lillian B. Miller. New Haven, CT: Yale University Press, 1992, 1983.

Sellers, Charles Coleman. *Charles Willson Peale*. New York: Scribner, 1969.

———. *Portraits and Miniatures by Charles Willson Peale*. Philadelphia, PA: Transactions of the American Philosophical Society, 42, pt 1. Philadelphia, PA: 1952.

Sellers, Charles Coleman, and Charles Willson Peale. "Charles Willson Peale with Patron and Populace: A Supplement to 'Portraits and Miniatures by Charles Willson Peale.' With a Survey of His Work in Other Genres." *Transactions of the American Philosophical Society*, n.s., 59, no. 3 (1969).

Sellin, David. "Joan of Arc." In Fairmount Park Association, *Sculpture of a City: Philadelphia's Treasures in Bronze and Stone*. New York: Walker, 1974, pp. 124–131.

Sewell, Darrel, ed. *Thomas Eakins*. Philadelphia: Philadelphia Museum of Art in Association with Yale University Press, 2001.

———. *Thomas Eakins: Artist of Philadelphia*. Philadelphia: Philadelphia Museum of Art, 1982.

Shachtman, Tom. *How the French Saved America: Soldiers, Sailors, Diplomats, Louis XVI, and the Success of a Revolution*. New York: St. Martin's, 2017.

Shackelford, George T. M. "*Pas de deux*: Mary Cassatt and Edgar Degas." In Barter, *Mary Cassatt: Modern Woman*, pp. 109–143.

Sharp, Kevin. "How Mary Cassatt Became an American Artist." In Barter, *Mary Cassatt: Modern Woman*, pp. 145–175.

Shaw, A. H. "De Medici in Merion." *New Yorker* (September 1928), p. 29.

Shinn, Earl. "Art-Study Abroad." *The Nation* 3, no. 62 (September 6, 1866).

———. "The Water-Color Society's Exhibition." *The Nation*, 20 (February 18, 1875).

Simpson, G. G. "The Beginnings of Vertebrae Paleontology in North America." *Proceedings of the American Philosophical Society* 86 (1942), pp. 130–188.

Simpson, Marc. "The 1870s." In Sewell, *Thomas Eakins*, pp. 27–40.

———. "The 1880s." In Sewell, *Thomas Eakins*, pp. 107–120.

Sloan, Helen Farr. "Robert Henri: An Appreciation." In *Robert Henri: Painter*. Wilmington, DE: Delaware Art Museum, 1984.

Smith, Bill G., and Paul Sivitz. "Identifying and Mapping Ethnicity in Philadelphia in the Early Republic." *Pennsylvania Magazine of History and Biography* 140, no. 3 (October 2016), pp. 393–411.

Sozanski, Edward J. "Barnes at the Pennsylvania Academy: A Scandal in 1923." *Philadelphia Inquirer*, May 4, 2012.

Spalding, Frances. *Roger Fry: Art and Life*. London: Granada, 1980.

Spalding, Paul S. *Lafayette: Prisoner of State*. University of South Carolina Press, 2010.

Stacton, David. *The Bonapartes*. New York: Simon and Schuster, 1966.

Staiti, Paul. *Of Arms and Artists. The American Revolution through Painter's Eyes*. New York: Bloomsbury, 2016.

Stanton, W. S. *Outline History of the Fairmount Parkway, 1871–1935*. Philadelphia: Philadelphia City Planning Commission, 1935.

Streshinsky, Shirley. *Audubon: Life and Art in the American Wilderness*. New York: Villard Books, 1989.

Stroud, Patricia Tyson. *The Emperor of Nature: Charles-Lucien Bonaparte and His World.* Philadelphia: University of Pennsylvania Press, 2000.

———. *The Man Who Had Been King: The American Exile of Napoleon's Brother Joseph*. Philadelphia: University of Pennsylvania Press, 2005.

———. "Point Breeze: Bonaparte's American Retreat." *Antiques* (October 2002), pp. 130–139.

Struble, George G. "The French Element among the Pennsylvania Germans." Available at https://journals.psu.edu/phj/article/viewFile/22432/22201.

Sweeney, John J., ed. *The Painter's Eye: Notes and Essays on the Pictorial Arts by Henry James*. London: Rupert Hart-Davis, 1956, p. 216.

Syène, F. C. [Arsène Houssaye]. "Salon de 1879," *L'Artiste* (May 1879).

Taylor, Francis Henry. "Jean-Antoine Houdon: 1828–1928." *Bulletin of the Pennsylvania Museum* 24, no. 122 (October 1, 1928), pp. 13–21.

Thompson, Jennifer A. "Collecting Impressionism and Post-Impressionism in Philadelphia." In *Impressionism and Post-Impressionism: Highlights from the Philadelphia Museum of Art*, edited by Jennifer A. Thompson, with contributions by Joseph J. Rishel and Eileen Owens. Philadelphia: Philadelphia Museum of Art in association with Yale University Press, New Haven, CT, 2019, pp. 9–25.

———. "For the Study and Enjoyment of My Fellow Citizens." In *Rodin Museum Philadelphia*. Philadelphia: Philadelphia Museum of Art, 2012.

Tocquevillle, Alexis de. *Democracy in America*, translated and edited by Harvey C. Mansfield and Delba Winthrop. Chicago: University of Chicago Press, 2000.

———. *Journey to America*. New Haven, CT: Yale University Press, 1959.

Troyen, Carol. "Innocents Abroad: American Painters at the 1867 Exposition Universelle." *American Art Journal* 16, no. 4 (Autumn 1984), pp. 2–29.

Unger, Harlow Giles. *Lafayette*. New York: John Wiley and Sons, 2002.

Valéry, Paul. "The Problem of Museums" (1925) in *The Collected Works of Paul Valéry*, edited by Jackson Mathews, translated by David Paul (New York: Pantheon, 1960).

Vaudoyer, Jean-Louis. “Petites Expositions.” La Chronique des arts et de la curiosité:supplément à la Gazette des beaux-arts (November 21, 1908).

Versailles and the American Revolution. Valérie Bajou, general editor. Catalog for the exhibition. Château de Versailles: Gourcuff Gradenigo, 2016.

Vollard, Amboise. *Souvenirs d'un marchand de tableaux.* Paris: Albin Michel, 1934.

Vure, Sarah. “Henri.” In *The Eight and American Modernisms*, edited by Elizabeth Kennedy. New Britain, CT: New Britain Museum of American Art, 2009, pp. 57–75.

Wadley, Nicheolas. *Renoir: A Retrospective.* Sydney: Bay Books, 1987.

Walker, Andrew J. “Mary Cassatt's Modern Education: The United States, France, Italy, and Spain, 1860–73.” In Barter, *Mary Cassatt: Modern Woman*, pp. 21–43.

Ward, David C. *Charles Willson Peale: Art and Selfhood in the Early Republic.* Berkeley: University of California Press, 2004.

———. “Creating a National Culture: Charles Willson Peale's ‘George Washington at the Battle of Princeton’ in History and Memory.” *Record of the Art Museum, Princeton University* 70 (2011), pp. 4–17.

Watson, Forbes. *William Glackens.* New York: Duffield, the Arts, 1923.

Wattenmaker, Richard J. “The Sketchbook Studies of William Glackens.” *Archives of American Art Journal* 44, nos. 1–2 (2004), pp. 2–47.

Weinberg, H. Barbara. *The Lure of Paris: Nineteenth-Century American Painters and Their French Teachers.* New York: Abbeville, 1991.

———. “Studies in Paris and Spain,” In Sewell, *Thomas Eakins*, pp. 13–26.

Wheaton, Barbara Ketcham. *Savoring the Past: The French Kitchen and Table from 1300 to 1789.* Philadelphia: University of Pennsylvania Press, 1983.

Whitney, Frank. *Jean Ternant and the Age of Revolutions.* North Carolina: McFarland, 2015.

Whitridge, Arnold. “French Emigrés in Philadelphia.” *Virginia Quarterly Review* 44, no. 2 (1968), pp. 285–301.

Wills, Garry, *Cincinnatus: George Washington and the Enlightenment—Images of Power in Early America.* New York: Doubleday, 1984.

———. *James Madison.* New York: Henry Holt, 2002.

Wilson, George. *Stephen Girard: The Life and Times of America's First Tycoon.* Conshohocken, PA: Combined Books, 1995.

Winch, Julie. *A Gentleman of Color: The Life of James Forten.* Oxford: Oxford University Press, 2002.

Woods, Naurice Frank, Jr. *Henry Ossawa Tanner: Art, Faith, Race, and Legacy.* New York: Routledge, 2018.

Yount, Sylvia. “‘In Education, Comradeship, and Common Aims’: The Bucks County Painters and the Pennsylvania Academy of the Fine Arts.” In *Pennsylvania Impressionism*, edited by Brian H. Peterson. Philadelphia: University of Pennsylvania Press, 2002, pp. 59–61.

Zurier, Rebecca. *Picturing the City: Urban Vision and the Ashcan School.* Berkeley: University of California Press, 2006.

[Index]

Page numbers in italics refer to figures.

Lynn Miller is Professor Emeritus of Political Science at Temple University. He is the author of, among other works, *Global Order: Values and Power in International Politics*, *Crossing the Line* (a novel), and *Postcards from Delphi* (a memoir). He is the coauthor (with James McClelland) of *City in a Park: A History of Philadelphia's Fairmount Park System* (Temple).

Therese Dolan is Professor Emerita of Art History at Temple University's Tyler School of Art and Architecture. She is the author of *Manet, Wagner, and the Musical Culture of Their Time* and *Inventing Reality: The Paintings of John Moore*, and the editor of *Perspectives on Manet.*